THE
OF

Independence Edition

VOLUME VI

THE PAGEANT OF AMERICA

A PICTORIAL HISTORY OF THE UNITED STATES

RALPH HENRY GABRIEL

EDITOR

PETER GUILDAY   HARRY MORGAN AYRES

ASSOCIATE EDITORS

OLIVER McKEE

ASSISTANT EDITOR

CHARLES M. ANDREWS	ALLEN JOHNSON
HERBERT E. BOLTON	WILLIAM BENNETT MUNRO
IRVING N. COUNTRYMAN	VICTOR H. PALTSITS
WILLIAM E. DODD	ARTHUR M. SCHLESINGER
DIXON RYAN FOX	NATHANIEL WRIGHT STEPHENSON

ADVISORY EDITORS

DAVID M. MATTESON

INDEXER

From the life portrait, 1784, by C. W. Peale (1741–1827) in the Faculty Room, Nassau Hall, Princeton University

GENERAL WASHINGTON AT THE BATTLE OF PRINCETON

THE PAGEANT OF AMERICA

THE WINNING OF FREEDOM

BY

WILLIAM WOOD

RALPH HENRY GABRIEL

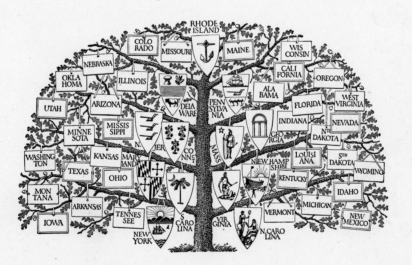

NEW HAVEN · YALE UNIVERSITY PRESS

TORONTO · GLASGOW, BROOK & CO.

LONDON · HUMPHREY MILFORD

OXFORD UNIVERSITY PRESS

1927

TABLE OF CONTENTS

Edwin Mims, Jr., has done the major part of the work in preparing Chapter I.

Stanley McC. Pargellis has given material assistance in the preparation of Chapters II, III and IV.

MILITARY FOLKWAYS OF EARLY AMERICA

ETWEEN 1914 and 1918 the common people of the Occident learned by experience more of the realities and potentialities of war than their predecessors of any
previous generation had known. They saw a fiery dragon cross and recross the
fields of Europe, a devouring monster, threatening the existence of civilization. Since
1918 they have been repeating with a haunting fear, "It must not be again." War at
last stands before the world in its true guise, a crude and ineffectual attempt to solve
the problems that arise in the intercourse of peoples. It has ceased to be respectable;
no nation arrogates glory to itself for initiating an armed conflict. Yet the boom of
batteries and the rattle of machine guns still break the quiet of once peaceful communities. The smoke of battle sometimes seems to fade out above one field of conflict only to
cast a shadow across another. War, almost as ancient as man himself, still persists. Its
roots lie deep in human life. From the beginning of social organizations larger than the
family group all men, save those living like the Esquimaux in extreme isolation, have
been compelled to adjust themselves to the fact of human conflict. The military aspects
of the folkways of a people are, at times, as fundamental to their well being as the getting
of food and raiment or the maintaining of government. Few people ever learned this fact
with greater cost to themselves than the folk of ancient Britain.

Their power collapsed first before the legions of Rome and then in the face of the
invasions of the Angles and Saxons. In course of time these latter conquerors were confronted with the menace of the Viking raiders from across the North Sea. The quiet of
an Anglo-Saxon coast village would suddenly be broken as the Northmen beached their
boats and, clad in mail and armed with spears and swords, ran toward the houses. Not
long did such raids find the villages defenseless. The freemen of the shires organized in
defense of their homes. The sheriff had authority to call them out for training. The
"fyrd," as the levy was named, was, in reality, a national militia, intended, except in
times of great emergency, for service in its own county. But the kings of Anglo-Saxon
England, beginning with Canute, felt the need of a more permanent force and maintained
small bodies of paid troops, "huscarles," at their own cost. Out of antiquity, therefore,
have come two of the fundamental adjustments of the English people to the ever present
possibility of war, a militia and a standing army. In later years Englishmen developed
their defense policy by the addition of a third element, a navy. The century following
the birth of this new arm saw some of the descendants of the Anglo-Saxons crossing
the Atlantic to build their homes on the wild shores of North America.

In 1588 the folk who lived along the southern shore of England had hurried in terror
from their homes to watch from the chalk cliffs the largest fleet the world had ever seen
standing up the Channel laden with a Spanish army of invasion. The English navy had
parried the blow. As a result the servants of the London Company who built their

habitations in Virginia less than a quarter of a century later were confident, even though once a Spanish ship looked in at the mouth of the James, that the English sea dogs would keep the Spaniard in his place and protect their tiny enterprise. Seventeenth-century New England had little fear from France so long as English warships were powerful in European waters. England's empire was the outgrowth of sea power as well as of commercial expansion and religious development.

In the forest region of what is now the eastern part of the United States the English pioneer came in contact with the Indian living by hunting and garden-farming in a neolithic culture. After centuries of evolution the red man had adjusted himself to the continent of North America. The smoke arising from the fires of an Indian village drifted over an area recognized by neighboring peoples as being the hunting ground of a particular tribe. Tribal wars occurred. The Iroquois, like the Romans of old, were conquerors, extending their domains with tomahawk and arrow. Every able-bodied Indian man was trained after the red man's fashion to be a warrior. When conflicts occurred, the war chief led the braves in loose formation or no formation at all. The tactics were those of the panther, a stealthy approach followed by a sudden stroke. The painted warrior utilized the cover of the forest which he knew so well. A battle was little more than a loosely coördinated series of personal encounters. The victors brought home the scalps of the vanquished as the modern soldier brings his decorations. The English, building their habitations not far from the pounding surf, soon found that war with all its primitive and terrible ferocity was the price which they must pay for their new homes.

At first, the puzzled and fearful Indian was inclined to be friendly. But, as the white men overran the tribal hunting grounds and pushed their clearings farther into the forest, tribe after tribe danced the wild war dance about the camp fires. The English colonist had brought with him to the New World weapons and a little knowledge of the military practices of seventeenth-century Europe. John Smith and Miles Standish were professional soldiers. The tactics of the time were founded on the pike, the matchlock, primitive artillery, and a variety of hand weapons used by soldiers both mounted and on foot. European armies, composed of closely packed masses, maneuvered in open fields and depended chiefly upon shock action for success. Such armies could neither be raised in the sparsely settled colonies nor maneuvered effectively in the forest. As well go fox-hunting with a cannon as attempt to run down a hostile tribe with a regiment organized after the European model. The white men, when they fought their darker neighbors, soon found themselves using Indian methods: an open formation, the utilization of cover, and dependence upon swift movement and surprise. They learned, strangely enough, from the American Indian many of the fundamentals of that open-order fighting which has come to be characteristic of modern wars. Moreover, the interlopers from across the Atlantic borrowed the stockade from their enemies. Unlike the red man, however, they built log forts, and, in course of time, developed these into the blockhouse, that practically impregnable forest fortification.

Only to a small extent did the white man use the bow and arrow, in spite of the fact that part of his English heritage was the tradition of the long bow with which his ancestors had overthrown the armies of medieval France. Yet the bow and arrow were in many ways superior for American use to the European matchlock which the colonists had brought. The Indian weapon was light and practically silent; it enjoyed the immense advantage of rapid fire and could be used under most weather conditions. The Brobdingnagian firearm upon which Miles Standish depended, with its rest for firing, its short range and inaccuracy, its burning fuse which a rain extinguished and which betrayed its possessor with smoke by day and fire by night, was unsuited to Indian war. Perhaps the English colonists might have returned to the long bow had it not been for the appearance in America in the latter half of the seventeenth century of the more efficient flintlock. This gun, when developed in the eighteenth century on the Pennsylvania frontier by German-Swiss immigrants into the American rifle, became a highly useful and formidable weapon. In the hands of both Indians and whites it helped to increase the slaughter of the wars between the races.

These conflicts arose out of a desperate struggle for the control of territory from which to gain subsistence. Here was war stripped of all the glamour that has sometimes been thrown about it, a naked, primitive, conflict of life. The Indian was the child of a race vigorous, able, and peculiarly proud. The unfortunate absence of domesticable animals from his habitat had been the chief factor in preventing his achievement of a much higher culture. In the seventeenth century he found himself pitted against the descendants of those ancient barbarian tribes who had brought down the Roman Empire. Like Attila in Europe the white man was the invader. He looked upon the redskin as a treacherous, ruthless, and murderous savage, yet he borrowed the practice of scalping and at the same time used his own methods of mutilation. The early sons of Massachusetts quartered the body of the defeated King Philip and carried the head from village to village. The descendants of these fighting pioneers have recounted many times the suffering of the frontier folk when Indian war broke suddenly upon them. But scant heed is taken of anguish like that of the Pequot tribesman returning to the charred fort where by a sudden night stroke the military power of his people had been destroyed. He found the bodies of women and children mingled with those of the fallen braves; from the surrounding forest their spirits called to him for vengeance and he was impotent. The stronger race took full advantage of its power to drive a weaker people forever from their ancestral homes. War sometimes has the awful finality of death. One should not assume, however, that the seventeenth-century conflicts with the redskins turned colonial America into a race of Indian fighters.

These wars were intermittent, and they rarely extended to the community behind the actual frontier. Never, after the earliest settlements, did the Indians jeopardize the existence of a colony. As the whites increased rapidly in numbers, there appeared along the coast a settled community busy with the tasks of peace and forgetful of the rigorous tasks of the pioneers. To such communities, engrossed with farming, fishing, or the enterprises of a developing merchant marine, came four times in less than a hundred years news of war with the French who lived to the eastward in Nova Scotia and to the northward in the valley of the St. Lawrence. Allies of these hated enemies were many tribes of northern Indians. Three successive generations of English colonists participated with varying effectiveness in the conflicts that were to determine the fate of the larger part of the North American continent. During these formative years were fixed in the customs of the English colonists military habits and points of view whose influence has not even in the twentieth century wholly disappeared from American life.

Early in the history of colonial America the militia system of England had been transferred to the New World, and, perhaps as a result of the natural tendency of a frontier community to go backward for a time along the path of evolution, the transplanted institution resembled much the ancient Anglo-Saxon fyrd. The fyrd was intended primarily for the defense of the shire and was under the control of the local sheriff; in North America the militia was an affair of the individual colony whose government laid down regulations under which it operated and commissioned the officers who took command. Sentiment against the use of militia outside the boundaries of the colony was strong. Said the North Carolina militiaman: "Let the New Yorkers defend themselves. Why should I fight Indians for them?" In spite of the Indian wars of the seventeenth century and the French and Indian conflicts of the eighteenth, a striking characteristic of the colonial militia was its ineffectiveness. On the relatively infrequent training days rustics and artisans gathered at the rendezvous to wheel through a few drills under the command of officers who knew scarcely more than their men. The short exercises over, the would-be defenders of their communities turned to the more pleasant business of merrymaking. The militia learned but little either of European tactics or the methods of Indian warfare. Drill books were scarce and, had they been available, would doubtless have changed the situation but little. The average colonial American was too preoccupied with peace-time labors to give much heed to military affairs. Except perhaps in the last French and Indian War only people living on the frontier were in danger of attack. A broad and mountainous "no man's land" separated the French settlements from the English colonists. To make an effective stroke across the wilderness required a mighty military effort. The English navy prevented the French from ravaging the American coast. The lack of effective military development was, therefore, in part the result of a sense of security.

All but the last of the French and Indian wars originated in Europe and the principal engagements were fought in the Old World. The colonial militiaman expected to be called out only if his immediate locality were threatened. In the event of an expedition outside the colony — against Louisbourg or Quebec — he might, if it served his interest or inclination, volunteer for the enterprise. On such occasions bounties were frequently offered and emphasis was laid on the prospect of plunder. In the same way bounties were offered for Indian scalps, male scalps bringing more than female. When the expedition ended, the enlistment expired. In North America the French and Indian wars were on both sides essentially predatory conflicts unrelieved by any motive of idealism. As a consequence the average eighteenth-century colonist felt little or no responsibility for aiding personally in prosecuting any of them to a successful conclusion. No militaristic tradition like that of ancient Rome or early twentieth-century Germany was established among those descendants of the English long bowmen who settled in the New World. Osgood has left a picture of their feeble fighting organization: "In the colonial wars only small bodies of troops were employed and they for the most part militia drawn from the farms and shops and almost destitute of military training. Their leaders were little better than the rank and file and terms of service were very short. Discipline was weak and ineffective. Military authority was often at the lowest ebb. The administrative arrangements also, under which the forces were called out, trained, armed, fed, clothed, and transported. were of the simplest and crudest nature, and whole departments of activity as they had been developed in European armies, even at that time, were nearly or wholly lacking."

Twelve years after the veterans of the last French and Indian War returned to their villages to resume the work of peace New England again heard the bark of the militiaman's musket and felt the stir and excitement of the assembling of armies. This time the British redcoat was the enemy, the hated tool of an imperial government that was passionately charged with attempting to undermine American liberties. April and May, 1775, saw the highways about Boston full of dusty men tramping to the camps sometimes as organized bodies, sometimes as individuals, armed and unarmed. Never have men better expressed the genius and the limitations of their generation. They were inspired by the noblest of causes. They were fighting mad. But they had only the vaguest conception of the realities which faced them if they were to succeed in imposing their will on the government of the most powerful empire of the day.

The Revolution began and remained a people's war. Inevitably the men who rushed to arms fell back upon the customary military organization of the past, the militia and the short term enlistment. Inevitably also they carried into war the customs and points of view of peace. The specialist was still a rarity in the typical eighteenth-century colonial community and, with a *naïveté* born of their generation, these rebellious Americans failed to comprehend that the fighting of battles and the management and maneuvering of troops is a complicated art to be undertaken only by men of special training. Instinctively they looked to the leader in peace to become the leader in war. In the southern colonies and in New York the officer was likely to be of the aristocracy. In parts of New England the one who could recruit a company of fifty-nine men was commissioned a captain and he who could raise ten companies became a colonel. The democracy that was making itself felt in American life was frequently reflected in the election of company officers. The transfer of the customs of peace to the military service found an extreme expression in the staff officer whom the commander in chief discovered shaving one of his privates in the presence of visitors. As of old bounties were offered. A few months after he assumed command at Cambridge Washington wrote: "Never were soldiers whose pay and provisions have been so ample. . . . There is some reason to dread that the enemies of New England may hereafter say that it was not principle that saved them but that they were bribed into the preservation of their liberties." The Patriot Americans put the faith of ignorance in the fighting powers of the untrained soldier. Fortunate for them that the last struggle with the French had given them a handful of experienced men who could direct affairs in the early phases of the war while the conflict was training and tempering the officers and men who were to see it through to the end.

One of the most striking features of the Revolution is the tenacity with which the American people, as represented by their state governments and the Continental Congress, clung to the Englishman's traditional dislike of a standing army. Such a force was deemed the weapon of tyranny. Congress feared a standing army, even of its own creation, scarcely less than the enemy. Was it not fighting such an army aided by mercenary Hessians? Moreover, it feared to put the control of the army in the hands of one man and hence long refused to create an office like that of the Secretary of War. The year 1776 saw Washington's militia force melt away at an appalling rate before a victorious enemy. In spite of this Congress adopted the one year enlistment period for the Continental or regular army. Events, however, finally drove the Revolutionary government to call for volunteers for the duration of the war. In 1779 Congress offered two hundred dollars to such recruits, a bounty which one state raised to seven hundred and fifty dollars, a suit of clothes a year, and one hundred acres of land. By the appeal to patriotism and to cupidity a continental force was raised which became the mainstay of the Revolution. These were the men who passed through the Gethsemane of Valley Forge and stood fast. They were the ones to whom Von Steuben brought the discipline, training and morale which made success against the enemy regulars possible. Their numbers were never adequate and an ineffective service of supply drove them more than once to desperation and to the verge of mutiny. Summer after summer they embarked upon campaigns only to find themselves serving side by side with raw levies of untrained and frequently better paid militia whose discipline was lax and who, after a few short weeks of service, would return to the warm hearth and the quiet tasks of peace. Few things are more significant of the mettle of this Continental army and the spirit of sacrifice which was the foundation of its power than the fact that its members had chosen the harder service instead of becoming militiamen.

Von Steuben brought to this army the tactics of eighteenth-century Europe, and with genius adapted them to the peculiarities of the American soldier and American conditions. He did not, however, deviate much from the accepted canons of military practice. His troops marched and fought in close-order formation as did their British and German enemies. They learned to fire by companies or platoons and to execute a bayonet charge. But they fought two ranks deep instead of three. By their side, however, appeared more than one organization which expressed in both training and equipment the genius of the New World. Of these Morgan's Riflemen are the most famous. Morgan's men were clad in the frontiersman's buckskin garb and were schooled in the Indian's methods of forest fighting. They carried in their hands the frontiersman's rifle. Its long range and deadly accuracy made it, when handled by men trained from boyhood to shoot, a weapon without peer in its day. Such troops had appeared in the last French and Indian War where they had been known as rangers. They reached their apogee in the forest battles which stopped Burgoyne's advance and brought about his momentous surrender. Through the rangers the military methods of the red man made their way into the white man's army.

One of the first acts of the independent United States was to reaffirm the military tradition which found its origin in Anglo-Saxon England. In April, 1783, peace was proclaimed. In June of the following year the Congress of the Confederation passed the following resolution: "And whereas, standing armies in time of peace are inconsistent with the principles of republican governments, dangerous to the liberties of a free people, and generally converted into destructive engines for establishing despotism; it is there-fore resolved . . . that the commanding officer be and he is hereby directed to discharge the troops now in the service of the United States, except twenty-five privates to guard the stores at Fort Pitt and fifty-five to guard the stores at West Point and other maga-zines, with a proportionable number of officers, no officers to remain in the service above the rank of captain." The new government, practically without a navy to supply the protection once enjoyed as a result of British sea power, entrusted the defense of its territory and its citizens to the militiaman. Well into the nineteenth century the policy was continued with little change in spite of the fact that the ship of state was navigating in very troubled seas. This retention of the traditional policy of defense is evidence, not only that it was deeply rooted in American life, but that it was in harmony with the temper of the American people of the times.

The isolation of the eighteenth century persisted. Three thousand miles of ocean separated the American coast from England and France. No powerful and menacing neighbor lived in North America who might, at any moment, launch the thunderbolts of war against the peaceful communities of the United States. Under such circumstances Americans were content with a tiny navy built just at the end of the eighteenth century at the time of the war with France, and with a small standing army scarcely sufficient to man the frontier posts. The character of the people themselves also had much to do with the decision.

A typical American of the early nineteenth century was the sea captain, schooled to courage and self-reliance on many a dangerous voyage on merchant ship or whaler. Another was the farmer-pioneer who, west of the Appalachian mountains, cleared and tilled for a space his self-sufficient farm and then sold out to push on to new lands and new opportunities. The former was capable of being turned, with a little training, into a capable naval officer, but the latter, though ever a fighter, did not easily make a good soldier. Son of the frontier, he was reared in the sturdy individualism which was the outstanding characteristic of his kind, and was imbued with the democracy of the West. Boy and man, he used his fists in sport and sometimes in deadly earnest. The duel with pistols persisted in his communities long after it had disappeared in the East. He feared no man or nation. Child of a people who with the enthusiasm of youth were conquering a wilderness, he was at heart a braggart — Andrew Jackson told him that he could lick his weight in wild cats. In 1812 he expected to walk into Canada and, with a few swift blows, make it his own. But his untutored independence prevented his submission to the inevitable discipline of a military force and his leveling democracy made him rebel against the necessary distinction between officer and enlisted man. He tended to be unruly and insubordinate. The complicated military art was quite beyond his ken. He would personally have none of soldiering in time of peace and saw scant need for a professional standing army. His concept of what was required in time of war was to have every able-bodied man take a gun and fight. These are some of the reasons why the Americans of the early nineteenth century displayed the paradox of being at the same time a belligerent and a non-militaristic people. In the War of 1812, in part forced by the same Westerners, the citizens of the United States learned some cruel lessons.

A majority of the American people entered with light hearts upon the second war with England; Canada would soon be theirs. Only in New England was there sullen opposition. Twenty-nine years had passed since the close of the Revolution. The people were not so fortunate, as at the outbreak of the War of Independence, in possessing experienced officers fit for the field. The National Government had done nothing to conserve and pass on the great body of military knowledge which the Revolution had called into being. West Point had been established but had languished for lack of support. As a result the American people suffered the humiliation of seeing general after general blunder through campaigns that violated practically every principle of military strategy. The militia, a "broken reed" in Washington's opinion, marched to the border of New York and refused to go further not even to succor comrades in the direst straits across the Niagara River. At Bladensburg on the Potomac other militia who had assembled to protect the national capital fled like sheep before the determined British force. The supreme tragedy, however, was that unnecessary and hence inexcusable waste of human life which was the inevitable result of a system which made it necessary for officers to get their training on the field of battle rather than in classroom and training camp. Never were those bitter words spoken by "Light Horse Harry" Lee during the Revolution more apt: ". . . a government is a murderer of its citizens which sends them to the field uninformed and untaught, where they are to meet men of the same age and strength, mechanized by education and discipline for battle. . . ." Again and again, when properly prepared for war, Americans demonstrated a fighting ability of the highest quality. MacDonough's exhibition at Plattsburg of sheer fighting will coupled with brilliant planning and maneuvering is unsurpassed in the annals of war. The American people were both inspired and chastened by this conflict with England. Not without significance was the rapid development of West Point in the two decades following the war.

If the War of 1812 gave to the United States an efficient academy for the professional soldier, it gave but little else. The sickness and death which dogged the steps of the untrained militia armies were forgotten. The inability of these citizen troops to stand before disciplined regulars unless behind breastworks was also forgotten. Nevertheless, the Americans were still the same high spirited, sanguine people as before their heads were bowed in mourning and defeat. For their chief defense they still depended, like the ancient Anglo-Saxons, upon the militia, that is, upon themselves. They were the militiamen who had fled at Bladensburg; they the backwoods warriors who at New Orleans had slaughtered the hosts of Pakenham. They had at last begun dimly to perceive that the complicated art of war requires specialists for effective leadership. But, as before the war, they looked to their isolation for their protection. Still individualists and democrats, they disliked as of old the military service. They elected their popular generals president but would not pay the taxes necessary to support a permanent military establishment adequate to their needs. Nor did the belligerency of previous decades disappear. They brusquely pushed the Indian westward; they despoiled a demoralized Mexico of priceless territory. They were still the same aggressive people who, refusing to learn by experience, waited until after a conflict had begun before they prepared to fight. And they faced the future chance of war with the incorrigible optimism of youth.

RALPH H. GABRIEL

CHAPTER I

THE CHANGING MILITARY ART

THE world has probably never seen more belligerent people than those who for the past two thousand years have inhabited the continent of Europe. The virtually world-wide extension of the present culture is, in part, the result of their fighting will and ability. In fact, not the least important part of that culture has from the beginning been the military art. Repellent as the resort to force may be, the historian cannot blink the fact that war is one of the important factors which has shaped the development of civilization as well as the destinies of peoples. Not always have the peoples of Europe led the world in the military art. At various times they have learned much from invaders who have sought to drive them from their lands.

The military art is composed of two essential phases, quite distinct, yet extremely difficult to define. Military men from time immemorial have struggled with the problem of definition of the two words "tactics" and "strategy." The former refers to weapons, or, more precisely, the manner in which weapons are used in actual combat to make them most effective. In the eighteenth century infantry advanced into battle in close formation, that is, shoulder to shoulder and two or three ranks deep; in the twentieth they rush forward in thin waves for a short distance, lie down, and then rush forward again. The different method is primarily due to the development of weapons. The solid eighteenth-century masses would melt away before the withering fire of the modern machine gun or be blasted out of existence by artillery fire. Tactics, therefore, depend upon weapons and change as weapons change. Strategy is quite a different matter. It consists in the placing of armed forces at the proper time at the particular point where they can damage the enemy most and in keeping the adversary as ignorant as possible of the movement. The principles of strategy are eternal and may be studied as well in Caesar's *Commentaries* as in the modern textbook. The surprise of an enemy, maneuvering to get between his army and its base, striking him in the flank or rear are all practices known to antiquity. They will continue to be used as long as war persists.

The development of the military art since the fall of Rome has, therefore, been principally the evolution of weapons and of tactics. The invention of gunpowder was of epoch-making importance. It marks the beginning of modern warfare, for on explosives used in some form modern armies and navies depend almost entirely. Even the cavalryman charging with his ancient saber has also his automatic pistol. Other inventions, although subordinate to this in importance have, from the early bayonet to the twentieth-century aeroplane, played their part in causing the military art to be a changing one. It must continue to be modified so long as the material aspects of civilization remain in process of evolution. In the eighteenth century, with which this volume is principally concerned, Europeans had no equals on the earth in the art of conducting war.

9

1 Early Sixteenth-Century Knights and Pikemen, from Louis-Napoleon Bonaparte, *Études sur le Passé et l'Aventr de l'Artillerie*, Vol. I, Paris, 1851, after bas-relief on tomb of Francis I

THE PASSING OF THE MEDIÆVAL KNIGHT

By 1500 the plumed knight of the days of chivalry had passed, and with him had gone the long lance and the armored horse of the joust. Survivals of the ancient fighting type still persisted at such exhibitions as that of The Field of the Cloth of Gold in the days of Henry VIII. Colorful as were these knights of a later day, their trappings were overdeveloped and ornate, and their skill directed to public entertainment rather than to sustained campaigning. War had lost some of the picturesqueness of former times. On many a field of battle appeared half-armored foot soldiers, mercenaries from Switzerland, men who had never known feudalism in their mountain home. They came to assist kings to retain their thrones or to make war upon a royal rival. They advanced into battle in solid phalanx with row on row of fourteen-foot pikes gleaming in the sun. Many a gallant knight drove his steed straight against such a mass of infantrymen only to be unhorsed by their long pikes and slain with the heavy halberds. With the pikeman in the field the feudal cavalier, sheathed in heavy mail, ceased to be the symbol of military power. The age of chivalry had passed.

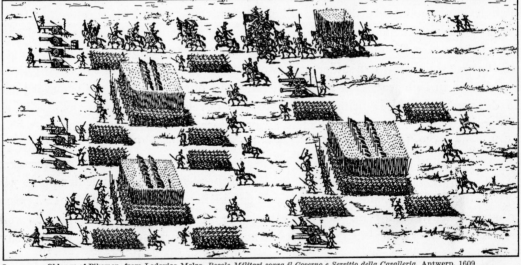

2.   Oblongs of Pikemen, from Lodovico Melzo, *Regole Militari sopra il Governo e Servitio della Cavalleria*, Antwerp, 1609

NEW TACTICS IN THE SPANISH ARMY

Fifteenth-century Spain, still engrossed after centuries of warfare in the heavy task of expelling the Moors from within her borders, knew little of the new military art that during the Renaissance had been developing in the countries north and east of the Pyrenees. The dense oblongs of pikemen, massed together row upon row, with a few ranks of halberdiers at the corners, were not to be found in the armies of Aragon or Castile. Not until three years after Columbus had made his first momentous voyage to America, and Gonsalvo of Cordova, the tactician of the Spanish army, had been defeated at Seminara, did Spain learn that Spanish shortswords and Spanish bucklers could not stand against Swiss pikes. Moreover, the Spaniards, in their attempts to pierce the solidity of the opposing forces, had discovered that their crossbows were of little value, and that neither terrain nor entrenchments could obstruct the ponderous, concentrated advance of so many pikemen. Gonsalvo promptly proceeded to assimilate into his own army the methods of the mercenaries who had defeated him, but he was wise enough not to discard entirely the swords and bows with which his men had become very skillful. Spain had started on the road toward military ascendency.

3 Fifteenth-Century Fieldpieces, from Louis-Napoleon Bonaparte, *Études sur le Passé et l'Avenir de l'Artillerie*, Vol. I, Paris, 1851

THE ADVENT OF ARTILLERY

COLUMBUS' discovery marked the beginning of Spain's great period of colonial and military supremacy. As Spanish adventurers skirted the American coasts, and here and there ventured inland, their imagination began to glow with visions of power and limitless riches. Meanwhile on the plains of Lombardy and Tuscany Spanish armies were fighting on fields where Charles VIII of France had assembled the most highly perfected artillery of Europe. John Zizka, the famous blind general of the Hussite wars, had less than a century before introduced artillery in the form of exceedingly small guns mounted on carriages which could be drawn over the country to form a "wagenburg" or traveling fortress. The Bureau brothers, Masters of Artillery in France under Charles VI and Charles VII, had disencumbered the guns of their superfluous wooden structure. At the same time they had begun to enlarge certain types in which mobility should be sacrificed to range and power. Artillery had proved itself to be of enormous value against the dense masses of pikemen or charging horsemen. From Italy artillery made its way to Spain and from Spain to America. So that cannon as well as savage bloodhounds aided the governors of Santo Domingo in maintaining their tyranny over the conquered native population. Cortés, sailing in 1519 from Santiago for Mexico, had, in addition to his crossbows, swords, and pikes, ten bronze, breech-loading guns and four smaller falconets.

4 Fifteenth-Century Fieldpieces, from Louis-Napoleon Bonaparte, *Études sur le Passé et l'Avenir de l'Artillerie*, Vol. I, Paris, 1851

THE ARQUEBUS

PROBABLY the transition from small artillery to hand guns that the soldier himself could carry and shoot without a support was made shortly before the opening of the sixteenth century by the "landschnekts," mercenaries from Swabia, rivals of the Swiss. As early as 1496 some of their number had been hired to aid in the instruction of the Spanish army. In the first quarter of the next century the Spaniards pushed forward the development of the hand gun and achieved a perfection of firing that placed them beyond the reach of any military rival. The gutterals of "hackenbusch," the name of the new weapon, were replaced by the softer "arquebus" and under that name the piece was carried to America.

5 Spanish Infantrymen (with arquebus) in Central America, 1524, from Theodore de Bry, *Americae Pars Sexta*, Frankfort-am-Mainz, 1596

6   Sixteenth-Century Cavalry Weapons and Armor, from Jacobi of
Wallhausen, *L'Instruction et Gouvernment de la Cavallerie* (n. d.)

CAVALRY

AT the beginning of the sixteenth century cavalry, having lost its hegemony in the domain of war, was undergoing modification. The traditional cavalryman was the heavily armored knight carrying a lance. The Venetians, imitating the Turks, had taught Europe the efficacy for shock action of virtually unarmored horsemen. The deep column formations were fast being abandoned and troops galloped into action in line. Cavalry showed signs of regaining its lost prestige. But the Spanish use of the arquebus checked the development. The deadly fire of the Spanish infantry compelled a return to heavier armor and to deeper columns. In the rapid military changes of the following centuries cavalry tactics and organization were the most unstable of any unit. Various types of mounted warriors developed in different parts of Europe, as new weapons were perfected.

SPANISH MILITARY SUPREMACY

THE Indians of America were amazed enough at the flash of the Spanish cannon and arquebus. But their superstitious awe was excited even more by the sight of rows of galloping horses and glistening horsemen, charging upon them. At the battle of Tabasco Cortés led his own excellent horsemen to a decisive victory, and Pizarro in Peru relied on the cavalry, which had with such difficulty followed him across the Andes into the valley stronghold of the Incas. In the very year of the downfall of Inca power, 1525, Spain by a brilliant victory at Pavia in Italy had definitely won a position as the dominant military power of Europe, which she held undisputed during the first century of America's history. Nobles and young lords flocked to join the ranks of the Spanish infantry, and when, as sometimes happened, they could not follow the great Gonsalvo, they sailed in all their costumed splendor, with their glittering arquebuses and bucklers, for military adventure on the new mainland to the west. The massed formation of Indians and the buildings in the background of the picture show that the artist had never been in America.

7   Capture of the Inca Sovereign, 1525, from Theodore de Bry, *Americae Pars Sexta*, Frankfort, 1596

8 Cortés and Alvarado attacked by Aztecs, from Palacio, *Mexico a Traves de los Siglos*, Mexico City, 1889, based on contemporary canvas in Tlaxcala

9 Aztec Spearmen, carrying shields and wearing cotton armor, attacking the Arquebusiers and Crossbowmen of Alvarado, from Palacio, *Mexico*, based on contemporary codex, *Jeroglifico di Duran*

THE SPANIARD AND THE AZTEC

IN the Aztecs the Spaniards met warriors worthy of their prowess. These fighting Indians armed with spears and arrows tipped with razor-edged obsidan. About their chests the Aztec fighting men wore a tough armor made of heavy cotton fabric. Trained to war as few peoples have been, and worshipping a bloody war-god, the soldiers of Montezuma were dangerous foemen. But Cortés, equipped with roaring artillery, was able to injure not only the bodies of his opponents but assail their morale as well. The Aztec empire collapsed. In the desert region of Arizona and New Mexico the Spanish conquistadores found a specialized form of Indian defense, great pueblos whose outer walls of adobe, solid near the earth, had entrances only at a considerable elevation. (See Vol. I, No. 285.) The pueblo was an apartment house and fortress combined, admirably adapted to desert fighting where an attacker rarely had the food and water necessary for a protracted siege. But against the field artillery which the Spaniard dragged into the desert country the crude walls of the pueblo were of no avail.

10 Encounter between Spaniards and Aztecs, contemporary native painting in the Convent of Cuanhtlantzinco, Mexico, from Publications of the Department of Anthropology, Chicago University, *Bulletin 3*, Pl. 7, Chicago, 1898

SIEGE CANNON

THE significant improvements in material that had been made during the fifteenth century by French masters of artillery included not only the smaller pieces evolved from the "wagenburg," but also cannon of huge caliber and dimensions adapted from the siege engines, in use by the armies of Europe during the Middle Ages and even earlier, to hurl great missiles against the walls of beleaguered citadels. They were moved with extreme difficulty but were of most excellent use in the sieges of fortified castles and of towns. The besiegers of Constantinople in 1453 made most advantageous use of great siege cannon supplied by the French.

11 Typical Sixteenth-Century Siege, from Louis-Napoleon Bonaparte, *Études sur le Passé et l'Avenir de l'Artillerie*, Vol. II, Paris, 1851, after a contemporary sketch in the MS. of Vasselieu [Nicolay Lionnais]

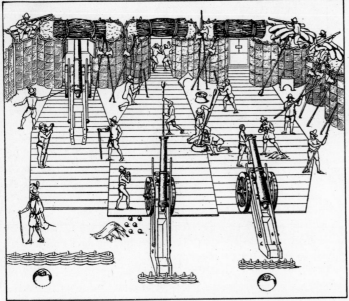

12 Interior of Sixteenth-Century Fort, from Louis-Napoleon Bonaparte, *Études sur le Passé et l'Avenir de l'Artillerie*, Vol. II, Paris, 1851, after a contemporary sketch in the MS. of Vasselieu [Nicolay Lionnais]

THE FORT

FROM remote antiquity European peoples had known siege warfare. Many a primitive village had been compelled to stand off an enemy. In the Middle Ages great castles of stone with towers and battlements and encircling moats had arisen, powerful strongholds where the baron could retire and defy his enemies. Many times the castle was forced to undergo a siege but there was no standard plan of attack, the tactics of the aggressor depending upon the whim of the commander, and those of the defender upon the particular conditions of the temporary emergency. Such siege-craft began to change during the sixteenth century, when Spain was establishing a solid foothold in the Americas. Military men of Europe began to experiment with and to write on the strategy and tactics both of siege and defense. Manesson, Errard-de-Bar-le-Duc, Alain de Ville, and many others evolved systems of laying out fortified towns and of the best methods of besieging them. The commercial city was beside the feudal manor and its population required protection. The fort, therefore, began to be a distinct and technical unit. In the picture the cannon, from right to left, are being loaded with powder, with ball, and being fired. Note that the doors of the embrasure are closed on the right and are being opened in the center.

THE FORT IN AMERICA

As the Spanish empire in America grew more permanent, the number of its forts in the New World steadily increased. They were significant of the fact that life west of the Atlantic was becoming stabilized. There were trade routes and seaports to be protected; there was wealth which must be guarded at all hazards. Forts were built first in the cities from which the gold and silver were shipped, and at Nombre de Dios, the great port where the overland caravans unloaded on to the ships bound for Spain. The fort in America meant that the process of transferring the contemporary military practices of the mother country to the colony had been completed. New Spain was armed and organized to meet its enemies in precisely the same manner as the kingdom of Philip II. In all the world there was no empire like that of Spain. The picture shows defensive works and the positions of cannon on the ramparts.

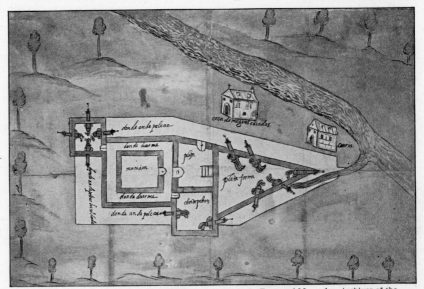

13   Spanish Fort at Santa Elena, built 1566, from a sketch in the Papers of Menendez, Archives of the Indies, Seville, Spain

THE FIRST FRENCH CHALLENGE TO SPAIN

FRANCE during the sixteenth century, impotent from religious civil war, had done little to weaken the military supremacy of Spain in Europe or her colonial supremacy in the New World. Verrazano had explored the coast line of the new continent, claiming it for Francis I. Each year fishing vessels sailed from the harbors of Britanny and Normandy, bound for the Newfoundland fishing banks. Cartier had claimed in the name of France a stretch of land that lay far to the north. But no French outpost had been transplanted until Ribaut in 1562 settled with his little band of Huguenots in

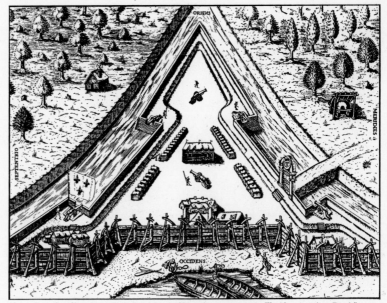

14   Fort Caroline, from T. de Bry, *Brevia Narratio eorum quae in Floridae Americae Provicia Gallis acciderunt*, Frankfort, after a sketch by Jacques Le Moyne, 1591

northern Florida. The flag, flying from the parapet of Fort Caroline and the crest over the gate, both emblazoned with the "fleur-de-lys," were the first European challenge which the Spanish conquistadores had received. The French fort was destroyed, and the military power of Spain continued to expand.

15   Detail of Champlain's Attack on the Iroquois Village, from Champlain, *Voyages*, Paris, 1619, after his own sketch

THE FRENCHMAN AND THE INDIAN

HENRY IV at last brought unity and stability to the administrative machinery of his kingdom. Then under him and his successor, Louis XIII, France began to build an empire in the forests of America. Champlain was the first and perhaps the greatest of its founders. His enterprise brought him into armed conflict with the greatest fighting people among the northeastern Indians, the Iroquois. He observed their methods of fighting in the woods; he learned, to his cost, their skill with bow and arrow; he studied the palisades with which they fortified their villages. Champlain confronted such a village deep in the forest and with neither cavalry nor artillery advanced against it. Again, as in New Spain, the methods and weapons of Europe overcame the barbarian brave. The Frenchman resorted to the time-honored device of constructing a "Cavallier with certain woods, which commanded them from above their palisades: on which Cavallier four or five of our arquebusiers would be placed who should fire down upon their palisades and galleries, which were well provided with stones, and by this means the enemy would be dislodged, who were annoying us from their galleries above, and in the meantime we gave the order to get some boards to make a kind of mantlet to protect and guard our troops from the blows of stones and arrows which they ordinarily used. Their village was enclosed with four good palisades of large pieces of wood, interlaced the one with the other, where there was not more than a half foot between them, thirty feet high, and the galleries as in the manner of a parapet that they had covered with double pieces of wood."

16 Detail of Henry VIII's Attack on Boulogne, 1543, from *Journal of the Society of Army Historical Research*, Vol. I, No. 5, from an engraving after the coeval painting at Cowdray in Sussex, the seat of Lord Viscount Montague, published in 1788

ENGLISH MILITARY CONSERVATISM

FRANCE, trailing far behind Spain in the art of war, had nevertheless been progressive if England be taken as the normal. Only five years after Columbus, Cabot had claimed the shores of North America for his adopted sovereign, Henry VII. But the advantage was ignored during a century of Tudor self-centeredness. While the two Henrys ruled in England, the art of war, as all other arts on the continent, was revolutionized. During the supremacy of the Swiss pikemen, of the "landschnekts," of the Spanish infantry of Gonsalvo and Pescayra, England, with her inherent conservatism, had in the face of every argument clung with veneration to the long bow and the bill, a cross between the halberd and the ax.

Henry VIII, the greatest archer of his kingdom, had lent the prestige of his patronage to the long bow. He was also a dilettante in the realms of artillery, administering pet names to the pieces of his favorite battery. Moreover, by 1543, as is evident from this illuminating contemporary picture, pikes and the arquebus had been introduced into the English army.

ENGLAND'S ARMY

ALMOST to the end of the sixteenth century the courts of Europe were familiar with the repeated gossip that England was antiquated in her military equipment and that her tactics were beneath contempt. Daniel Barbaro, Venetian ambassador at the court of Mary, wrote, in 1551, an estimate of the fighting forces of the Tudor kingdom. "The infantry . . . is divided into four sorts. The first is of archers, who abound in England and are very excellent, both by nature and from practice, so that the archers alone have been seen to rout armies of 30,000 men. The second is of bill-men, their weapon being a short thick staff with an iron like a peasant's hedging bill . . . With this they strike so violently as to unhorse the cavalry. The third are the harquebusiers, who are good for little as only a few of them have had practice south of the channel," and finally, "the pikemen, more recently added to the ancient militia of England." The nations "south of the channel," confident of their all-powerful arquebus and of the matchlock musket which was being perfected in Spain, looked with scorn upon the armies of England, still depending upon the weapons of the Middle Ages. But their judgment was, in one respect, faulty. They were one day to discover that English genius followed the paths of the sea and that all the forts which Spain had built with such skill in the New World were powerless to protect Spanish commerce from the menace of the Elizabethan sea dog.

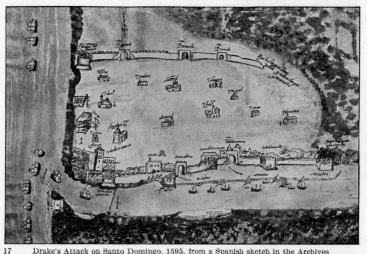

17   Drake's Attack on Santo Domingo, 1595, from a Spanish sketch in the Archives of the Indies, Seville, Spain

MODERNIZATION OF ENGLAND'S ARMY

THAT he might crush rebellion in the Low Countries, the Duke of Alva developed the Spanish army into the most efficient engine of war the world had yet seen. English troops, sympathizing with the Dutch cause, crossed the channel to fight the haughty Spaniard. Sir Humphrey Gilbert, Sir Philip Sidney, Leicester, Essex, and John Morris all served under the Dutch commander, Maurice of Nassau. The Dutch had learned well the organization and tactics of the enemy. The English volunteers brought back to their own army the practices of the Dutch. As a result, England, for the first time, began to modernize her military forces. About 1565 the Spaniards had enlarged the arquebus into a much heavier gun, the matchlock, which, when fired, had to be supported on a rod extending to the ground. When the first colonists embarked for Jamestown, this ponderous musket was replacing the primitive arquebus as the English weapon of fire.

18 Seventeenth-Century Musket and Musketeer, from Jacques de Gheyn, *Maniement d'Armes, d'Arquebuses, Mousquetz, et Piques, en conformité de l'Ordre de Monseigneur le Prince Maurice de Nassau*, Amsterdam, 1618

19 Detail of Smith's Capture of King of the Pamaunkeys, from John Smith, *Generall Historie*, London, 1616

THE ENGLISHMAN AND THE INDIAN

DESPITE the development of the musket the earliest colonists relied largely on the arquebus, the explosion of which alone was sufficient at first to rout the native warriors. But the Englishman, like the Frenchman and the Spaniard, had to learn slowly the strategy of Indian warfare, with its tactics of small scattered war parties firing from ambush, and experienced, even more than his colonial rivals, its hardships and terrors. The picture, obviously not drawn in America, illustrates the contemporary European tendency to think of Indians fighting in the massed formations familiar to the Old World.

THE ADOPTION OF INDIAN TACTICS

WHEN the Indian brave let fly an arrow his missile did not have behind it the force of the arrow of an English infantryman. The Indian bow was not the equal of the long bow and Indian arrows could not pierce the armor of the early colonists in Virginia and Massachusetts. But the Indian by trading secured European firearms, the one great advantage hitherto of the white man. From the edge of the clearing now came, instead of the flint-tipped shaft, the roar of arquebus and musket. The average white man in America had to learn to fight, for war in Europe had been a professional game between mercenaries. Such colonists as had served in the army had learned that troops should advance into battle in great masses and in close formation. In America the forest closed in, cloaking unseen enemies. No frontiersman in America knew when he might be transformed suddenly from a hunter-farmer into a soldier and, without the numbers or knowledge necessary for massed attacks after the European mode, give battle to an elusive foe. Moreover, European masses were unsuitable for fighting among trees. Under such circumstances the frontiersman slowly made the Indian's tactics his own.

20 From the painting *On the War Path*, by Howard Pyle (1861–1909) for Woodrow Wilson, *A History of the American People*, New York, 1901. © Harper & Bros.

21   Seventeenth-Century Matchlock, original in the Massachusetts Historical Society

THE MATCHLOCK IN AMERICAN CONDITIONS

IN a sense the English were unfortunate in beginning their colonies in America just as the long bow was falling into disuse, for the bow and arrow was in many respects a superior weapon for forest fighting. Its lightness made it easy to carry and its silence was an important element in surprise. Moreover, it had the inestimable advantage of rapid fire. Beside this invention of the stone age the unwieldy matchlock seemed clumsy indeed. To fire the piece the soldier must cant or tip it until the lock was

22   Butt and Trigger of a Seventeenth-Century Matchlock, original in the Massachusetts Historical Society

uppermost and the barrel on one side. This was necessary in order that gravity should help make the connection between the powder in the pan, ignited by the burning fuse, and that in the barrel. Though the canting prevented a true aim, this was of little consequence for the guns were not accurate and could be fired effectively only at close range. Ordinarily the matchlock had no sights. The white man took grave risks, when with such a weapon he ventured into conflict with the lurking redskin darting silently from cover to cover, shooting arrows now from one tree and now from another, and finally closing with the war club and the tomahawk. After many a successful native ambush the invader's scalped corpse was left for carrion birds. The matchlock made a surprise attack difficult — the glow of the burning fuses lighted the night and their smoke, carried on the breeze, gave warning by day. If rain fell, the gun was useless, for the matches must be kept dry. Yet this was the weapon which enabled the first generation of English adventurers to maintain their precarious foothold on the edge of the continent.

23   The Palisade at Wethersfield, Conn., from Henry R. Stiles, *Ancient Wethersfield*, Vol. II, New York, 1904

THE PALISADE

GRADUALLY the English colonist learned from experience with his Indian enemy the types of warfare best suited to the new continent. The strategy and tactics of defense that he finally evolved in crude and unprofessional outline were made up of a blend of the pioneer himself. The Indian palisade, if well constructed and vigilantly guarded, was a sufficient protection against most attacks. The brave did not have the artillery of Europe but he sometimes used a crude battering ram not unlike those of the Romans.

THE BLOCKHOUSE

To the palisade the frontiersman added the blockhouse, an almost perfect fortification for warfare. Blockhouses at the corners of palisades enabled the defenders to enfilade the entire front of the defensive works. The overhanging second story made it possible to shoot down upon attackers below. The one weakness of the building was that it could be fired with burning arrows dropped on its roof. In spite of this defect, however, the blockhouse remained the standard fortification until the frontier, advancing westward, left the forest regions of the east and spread out on the grasslands of the continental interior.

24   Block House, Fort Halifax, Winslow, Me.
© The Halliday Historic Photograph Co., Boston

SEVENTEENTH-CENTURY MILITARY EVOLUTION

ENGLISH settlers in seventeenth-century America, closing at nightfall the gates of the palisades which surrounded their tiny villages, were quite ignorant of the military changes that were affecting contemporary Europe. Gustavus Adolphus, the Swedish military genius of the Thirty Years' War, was making innovations tending toward greater mobility. The armor of the infantry and cavalry was being gradually abandoned; the pike was being greatly shortened and its use curtailed until by 1700 it was practically superseded by the bayonet; the

25   French Battery of Mortars, Seventeenth-Century, from *Mémoires d'Artillerie recueillis par le Sr. Surirey de Saint-Rémy* . . ., Paris, 1697

A. "Fascinage" or "Epaulement" to keep the battery covered from the fire of the enemy. *B.* Filling mortar with "fourrage" or earth, with a piece of wood called "dame" or "demoiselle." *C.* Putting bomb into mortar. *D.* Putting mortar in battery while officer places quadrant on mouth of mortar to give proper angle of elevation. *E.* Firing the fuse of the bomb and then the train of the mortar. *F.* Pickets which serve as aiming points for the directing of the mortars, all these mortars being on their platforms. *G.* Barrel filled with earth for the service of the mortars. *H.* Small magazine covered with fascines and with earth where powder for mortars is taken.

matchlock was being lightened and the rest supporting it abolished. Both the artillery and the cavalry had been separated into light and heavy divisions. In the infantry the ranks of musket fire had been reduced to three. These changes had made their way into France and England. After the death of the great Gustavus, France made rapid strides toward the military leadership of Europe. Louis XIV needed an efficient army for his ambitious schemes of empire. His officers developed organization and specialization to a point hitherto unknown. Vauban revolutionized the strategy of siege warfare. In 1690 Louis established the first artillery schools.

THE SPREAD OF THE FRENCH EMPIRE

As France perfected her military organization at home, her colonial empire spread from the original settlement at Quebec along the lakes to the west, down the valleys of the Ohio and Mississippi, whose waters flowed into the crippled Spanish Main, and to the frozen bay which Hudson had discovered and where the English had already established forts and factories. The expansion was the work of the explorer, the fur trader, and the missionary, but behind these pioneers was military power holding the territory which they claimed for France. French imperial dreams inevitably brought on conflict with the rival English. From 1689 till 1763 France and England clashed continually in the Old World and the New. Meanwhile less gold and silver was reaching Spain from the colonies in tropical and sub-tropical America. With the defeat of the Armada in 1588 the day of Spanish greatness had passed.

26   Attack on Fort Nelson by D'Ibérville, 1697, from Bacqueville de la Potherie, *Histoire de l'Amerique Septentrionale*, Paris, 1751

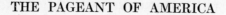

27   Eighteenth-Century Flint-Lock Musket, from the collection of the New York Sons of the American Revolution,
                                    Fraunces Tavern, New York City

THE FLINTLOCK

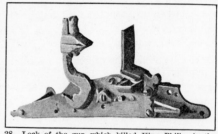

In the seventeenth century, there occurred in weapons a development of great importance. Before King Philip's War (1675-76) turned the frontier of Massachusetts into a smoking ruin, the English colonists had armed themselves with a new gun, the flintlock or, as it was officially called, the firelock. The awkward burning fuse of the matchlock gave way to a flint and steel which struck sparks into the priming pan. Though still retaining the smoothbore, it was superior to its predecessor in range and accuracy. King Philip's braves, armed with the matchlock, were unable to fight successfully against their white antagonists equipped with the new weapon. When the great war chief of the

28   Lock of the gun which killed King Philip, in the
     cabinet of the Massachusetts Historical Society,
     Boston

Wampanoags had been killed and his uprising put down, the New Englanders and New Yorkers were able to concentrate their attention on the danger from the French settlements to the north. In the impending conflicts the English had no advantage in armament. France had adopted the flintlock in 1630, full sixty years before the official action of England. Before the end of the seventeenth century French factories at Maubeuge and Charleville were supplying the French troops in America with the new gun. As the century ended rival factories in London and Birmingham began turning out great quantities of firelocks for the use of the army at home and for sale in the growing market of America. Many gunsmiths in the colonies also added to the supply. With flintlocks in their hands sentries in many a frontier village stood guard against a French or Indian raid.

ENGLISH ARTILLERY

In spite of the personal interest that Henry VIII had taken in the development of English artillery, it reached no state of effective organization until after the fighting in the Low Countries, where England had gone to school to Spain in the art of war. The Spanish explorers had, a hundred years before, made excellent use of their cannon against the Central and South American Indian, but in the early stages of the English colonies, English artillery was of a crude sort and insignificant in the Indian wars. Not until 1672 was the English Artillery Laboratory established at Woolwich, while the reorganization of English artillery took place in 1682 under Master-General Lord Dartmouth. The cannon at Plymouth, presented by the British Government in honor of the tercentenary of the landing of the Pilgrims, and typical of the seventeenth century, show the backward state of artillery in the mother country.

29   Seventeenth-Century British Cannon, now at Plymouth, Mass., from a photograph
                of the original. © A. S. Burbank, Plymouth, Mass.

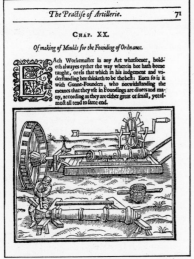

30 Making Moulds for the Founding of English Ordnance, from Robert Norton, *The Gunner, Shewing the Whole Practise of Artillery . . .*, London, 1628

31 French Furnace for Founding Cannon, from *Mémoires d'Artillerie, recueillis par le Sr. Surirey de Saint-Rémy*, Paris, 1697

THE CASTING OF CANNON

THE casting of cannon in the seventeenth century was a most elaborate process, requiring a well-equipped establishment and a great amount of technical knowledge and experience. Robert Norton in *The Gunner*, etc., London, 1628, explains the difficulties of the Master of Ordnance. "For the foundings of great ordnance there are special sorts of earthes, whereof the moulds and modells are compounded either to cast in brasse or iron, whereof it behooveth to seek the best, namely, that are able to withstand the fire and receive the melted mettals, so that they may render them to be cast and founded neatly without being subject either to be diminished, crackt or peeled, when they shall be nealed, which is such a matter as without experience can not be done well. . . ." Naturally during the colonial period, both in the English and French colonies, the artillery came always from the mother country, and this habit of dependence rendered it difficult for the American military leaders to secure a sufficient supply of cannon during the first years of the Revolution.

MILITARY ORGANIZATIONS IN THE COLONIES

OCCASIONALLY military organizations in the English colonies grew out of older ones in England. The Honorable Artillery Company of London was chartered by Henry VIII in 1537. In the following century, certain of its members having migrated to the Massachusetts Bay Colony, and, desiring to organize a similar company, petitioned Governor Winthrop for a charter. The charter was refused at first on the ground that it was "dangerous to erect a standing authority of military men," but was finally granted in 1638. The legislature gave the company some land and it became a permanent organization.

During the years when the Indian crisis was most serious there had been an attempt in Massachusetts at compulsory service, and training with half pikes and bows and arrows, but it soon became the custom in the English colonies to trust to a temporary levy for each particular emergency. Each colony was careful to keep control of its own troops, and was jealous of any attempted interference on the part of another. This spirit of isolated obedience was the cause of much disciplinary trouble at the beginning of the Revolution.

32 Charter of the Ancient and Honorable Artillery Company, from the original court record, Massachusetts Bay Colony, in the State Archives, Boston

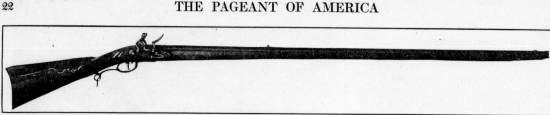

33   Rifle of Christopher Gist, in the collections of the Historical Society of Western Pennsylvania, Pittsburgh

THE RIFLE

OUT of the American wilderness came the first great improvement in firearms subsequent to the development of the firelock. Not for formal war but for hunting and for Indian fighting was the rifle perfected. Guns with rifled bore were in use in Europe as early as 1500; but two centuries passed with little progress made in the short, heavy, clumsy rifle piece with a bore an inch or so in diameter and a terrible recoil. After shooting, the user spent a quarter of an hour hammering a lead ball down the barrel with a mallet and an iron ramrod. Such was the gun known to some German and Palatine Swiss gunmakers who were part of the German immigration into Pennsylvania in the early eighteenth century. "The immigrant gunsmiths began in America an immediate output of their wares for use upon the abundant game of the new country. . . . But in America the pioneer travelled the immense wilderness, dependent upon his weapon for food and life. The weapon must be accurate, and must waste none of the powder of the charge, hence a long barrel was necessary. Ammunition sufficient for a long period must be carried on the person, hence a small bore weapon that many charges might weigh little. It was important that the sound of the shot should be the least possible, that it might not reach the ears of distant savages; therefore the barrel needed to contain the greatest possible amount of metal to absorb sound vibrations and still be manageable. Speedy repetition of fire was absolutely necessary if the rifle was to be a competitor of the murderous Indian's bow; hence there must be an improvement in seating the ball." — C. W. SAWYER, *Firearms in American History.*

34   Interior of Rifle-Boring Mill on Tulpehocken River, Penn., from the Pennsylvania German Society *Proceedings*, Vol. X, 1899

MANUFACTURE OF RIFLES IN THE COLONIES

"ALL these changes did not occur at once. Pioneers and gunsmiths consulted and experimented and changed and improved a little at a time here and there until, perhaps as early as 1750, a new form of weapon had come into general use. This was the long, slender, graceful, heavy, small-bore rifle, using a ball of an ounce in weight — which could be fired in rapid sequence because the ball was lubricated. . . . No heavy iron ramrod, deforming both the ball and the grooves, was now needed. No great amount of time was used in loading the pioneer's rifle. In the stock of the gun there was a little box with a hinged cover. In it was kept a lot of circular pieces of greased linen or leather all the same size and cast with a die. The powder being poured into the rifle barrel and the rifle held perpendicular with the butt on the ground, one of the greased patches was laid on the muzzle, concentrically, the ball placed on it and pressed into the bore with the thumb. Then the light wooden ramrod was drawn from the thimbles, the head put to the ball, and with one long sweep of the arm the lubricated ball slid down the barrel until it stopped upon the powder. A few whangs with the ramrod expanded the ball by flattening it so that it held its position. The powder was fine of grain and quick of ignition; therefore when the rifle was fired the impact of the explosion acting upon the inertia of the lead, caused the ball to expand circumferentially and, with its cover fill the grooves, preventing the escape of gas and receiving rotation. Upon exit from the muzzle the unfastened patch became detached from the ball, which flew towards the mark. And so patiently and ingeniously had the pioneers and the gun-smiths experimented, some little idea of the relation of the velocity of the bullet to its caliber, mass and velocity of flight had dawned upon the new American riflemakers, and, allowing that the distance was under one hundred yards, the area of the mark ten inches square or more, a ball directed by an experienced marksman was almost sure to find the mark." — C. W. SAWYER, *Firearms in American History.*

A FRENCH FORT IN ACTION

THE English army has produced no genius in the art of fortification and siegecraft comparable to Vauban, who, under Louis XIV, had, by the creation of his *Corps du Génie*, established his theories so firmly that they became standard practice for the French troops in Europe and in America. During the period of the four colonial wars between France and England, the superiority in artillery fire lay for the most part on the side of the former nation. There were few changes in details until Gribeauval, in

35   Drill of French Gun Squad, from *Mémoires d'Artillerie, recueillis par le Surirey de Saint-Rémy* . . ., Paris, 1697

A. Charging the piece. *B.* Pushed into battery position. *C.* Aiming the piece. *D.* Firing. *E. F.* Going for powder to the small magazine. *G.* Soldiers rolling powder from the large to the small magazine. *H.* Large powder magazine. *I.* Sentinels.

1765, became the new head of French artillery. The illustration shows the interior of a typical French fort.

SIEGE TACTICS AFTER VAUBAN

THE objective of the besieger was to make a breach in the works of his enemy through which an assaulting party could enter the fort. Artillery was the weapon chiefly used to batter down the hostile ramparts, though sometimes they were undermined and blown up. The first phase of a siege was the artillery duel in which the attacker sought to silence the enemy batteries. Since the effective range for cannon was some six or seven hundred yards, the first battery positions were about that distance from the fort. Just behind the guns was run a parallel trench from twelve to fifteen feet wide and three feet deep, with a parapet toward the enemy four feet high. The trench contained the infantry which protected the batteries against sorties from the fort. Approach trenches were then run forward in zigzags toward the ramparts and a second parallel trench was run some three hundred yards nearer the fort. This also was to defend the batteries. Again, approach trenches made it possible to build the third parallel very close to the fort. The artillery advanced with the trenches and, when the enemy fire power was greatly reduced, the cannon could be turned to their second task of breaching the hostile walls.

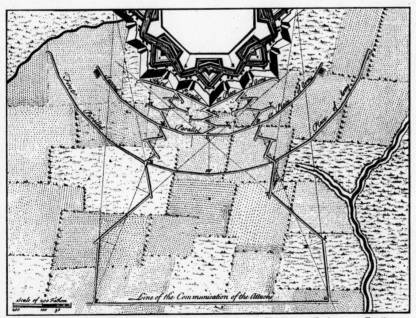

36   Diagram Showing Vauban's System of Parallels, from Le Blond, *The Military Engineer or a Treatise on the Attack and Defense of all Kinds of Fortified Places* . . ., London, 1759

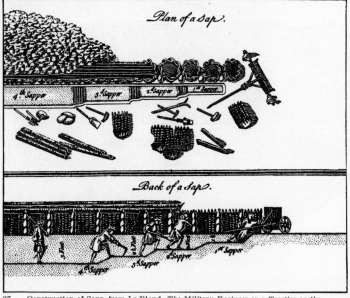

Plan of a Sap.

Back of a Sap.

37   Construction of Saps, from Le Blond, *The Military Engineer or a Treatise on the
      Attack and Defense of all Kinds of Fortified Places*, London, 1759

LATTER PHASES OF SIEGE

THE last stage of the siege saw flying saps extended beyond the third parallel skirting the very base of the ramparts, making it possible for the attacker to defend his batteries now banging away from positions very close to the hostile redoubts. These are but the barest essentials of Vauban's solution of the problem of taking a fort.

FORTS IN AMERICA

EXPERT as some of them were in handling the rifle, the English colonists could not be the main military reliance of Britain in meeting the French challenge for the control of the valleys of North America. Troops trained, armed, and disciplined after the European manner, must be sent across the Atlantic before campaigns could be decisive and the tough structure of the French empire battered down. In a country like North America, characterized by great distances, the fort, though it served a slightly different purpose, became as important a military unit as in Europe. In the Old World its chief use was to defend cities and frontiers; in America it performed the same two functions but, in addition, when placed at a point of strategic importance, it maintained imperial control over a great area of unoccupied land. Vauban's tactics of siegecraft had been devised for warfare on the level plains of Europe, where the strokes and counter-strokes could be executed with a precision approximating that of a game of chess. On the other hand, in America the engineer frequently encountered, as at Lake George, New York, great difficulties arising from the hilly nature of the terrain. It was often discovered, in constructing defenses at a point of strategic importance, that it was impossible to locate the fort without enabling an enemy to command it by mounting cannon on a nearby hill. So Sugar Hill, long deemed impossible of scaling with artillery, dominated Ticonderoga, while the position of Fort Oswego on Lake Ontario, commanded in like manner, had to be changed a number of times. At Lake George measures were taken to prevent attack from no less than three hills about the fort.

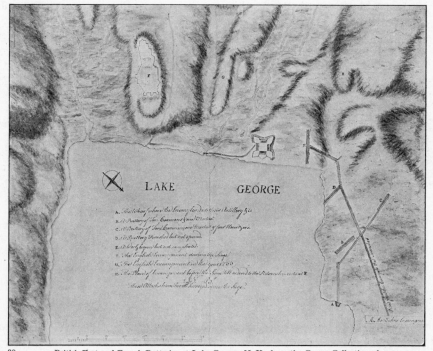

LAKE   GEORGE

38   British Fort and French Batteries at Lake George, N. Y., from the Crown Collection of
           American Maps, British Museum, London

IMPORTANCE OF BACK COUNTRY FORTS IN AMERICA

GUARDING the strategic headwaters of the Ohio was the primary task of Fort Pitt, a fortification perfected, as far as man could make it, against the weapons of the time, and located at the junction of waterways draining important valleys of unoccupied territory. The outer defenses were cleverly devised to take advantage of the protection offered by the rivers; since it was impossible for an attacking party to approach across the water barrier, the fort could be assailed from but one side.

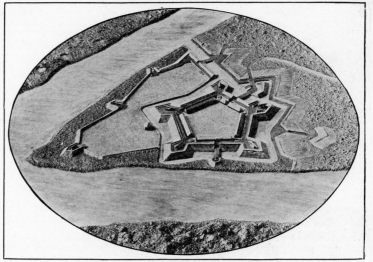

39   Model of Fort Pitt in the Collections of the Historical Society of Pennsylvania

Cannon were found in both the outer and inner works. Bastions were skillfully placed to enfilade every outer and inner wall with both cannon and musket-shot. The walls themselves did not rise vertically from the ground but sloped backward at a relatively sharp angle so as to make the task of battering them down exceedingly difficult. On the landward side, the works were cut with three apertures through which sorties could be made when it was necessary to counter-attack a hostile force. Each aperture was skillfully planned to keep the defending troops passing through it under cover until actually on the flat land outside the fort and ready to charge the enemy. The barracks and magazines were properly within the inner defenses. Such a fort, if properly manned and supplied, could only be taken by an exhausting siege.

40   Interior of the Bastille Armory, Paris, from *Mémoires d'Artillerie, recueillis par le Sr. Surirey de Saint-Remy* . . ., Paris, 1697

THE SECOND HUNDRED YEARS' WAR

FRANCE, with her highly organized and specialized administrative system; with her magnificently equipped arsenals at Mont Royal, at Nozon, at Maubeuge and Charleville; with row upon row of standardized flint-locks safely stored in the "impregnable" recesses of the Bastille; with her well-drilled regulars, whether of the regiment of Carignan or of less famous units, marching with perfect cadence and bearing through the streets of Quebec and Montreal, all commanded by a single centralized power, embarked upon a series of wars in the seventeenth and eighteenth centuries with an enemy conservative in military matters but brilliant on the sea, and with that enemy's colonies — thirteen isolated units, jealous of one another and of any attempts of the mother country to systematize activities. Yet on the Plains of Abraham, in 1759, France's enemy, aided by her thirteen individualistic colonies, was the victor.

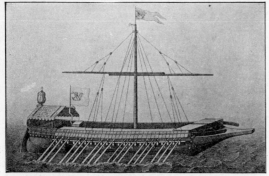

41   Venetian Galley, from Charnock, *History of Marine Architecture*, London, 1801

THE MEDIÆVAL FIGHTING SHIP

IN naval as in military evolution strategy and tactics have depended upon the development of weapons and materials. The early battleships were boats propelled by oars like those of the Greeks, the Romans, or the Vikings. Through the Middle Ages the galley persisted, while many improvements, particularly with respect to the arrangement and handling of the oars, made it an increasingly efficient craft. Such a fighting ship often proved itself a formidable weapon when used as a ram. It also relied on the swords of the crew and missiles such as bolts from heavy crossbows fastened to the bulwarks, bows and arrows, weights dropped by various devices onto the enemy deck, and various means of setting the hostile vessel on fire. Until the perfection of artillery the naval commander had no means of penetrating the walls of an enemy ship. When the sail replaced the banks of oars, the effort to get above an enemy in order to hurl projectiles down upon him led to the building of high ship-walls and the creation of veritable floating castles. Such ships varied in displacement from thirty up to two hundred and fifty tons, and carried from twenty or so to some hundred and thirty seamen. Beside the sailors were large numbers of land soldiers in heavy armor, equipped with mediæval infantry weapons and brought on board to grapple with the land force quartered on the enemy ship.

THE *HARRY GRACE DE DIEU*, 1512

HENRY VIII was the first great modern reformer of the English navy. By his confiscation of the monasteries he had accumulated into his own hands great resources with which to finance the desired naval improvements. Skilled Italian workmen were imported to construct new ships equipped with cannon. The art of naval warfare was revolutionized by the adaptation of cannon to ships. The new weapon could shatter the walls of enemy ships by a direct horizontal blow. The *Harry Grace de Dieu* (called

42   The *Harry Grace de Dieu*, from Charnock, *History of Marine Architecture*, London, 1801, after contemporary drawing in Pepysian Collection, Cambridge, Eng.

also more familiarly "The Great Harry"), built in 1512, represents an interesting intermediate stage. The towers and castles, the very high decks and parapet masts are still in evidence. But combined with them are rows of the newly introduced cannon. With a preponderance of weight on the upper decks, and the resulting top-heaviness, there was the constant danger of overturning in case of a sudden veering or shifting position. The habits of centuries were difficult to break. In this transitional period of the early sixteenth century it was the custom to fire one salvo of the new cannon, and then resort again to the older and more familiar tactics.

43   Embarcation of Henry VIII from Dover, 1520, from the painting by Hans Holbein, 1460–1524, in the Royal Apartments, Windsor Castle; photograph by courtesy of *Country Life*, New York

THE STUART NAVY

THE remainder of the century witnessed a steady improvement in the size and capacity of England's ships, in the length of voyages, in the science of navigation and in seamanship. Likewise a great change was taking place in the personnel of the fighting force. The ratio of land soldiers to seamen in naval battles decreased rapidly. Under the old conditions it was considered desirable to crowd together onto the floating fortresses as many soldiers as space would allow. The regular complement on a ship of the size of the *Harry Grace de Dieu* was seven hundred,

44 An English Ship of War of 1602, from *The Mariner's Mirror*, London, 1913, after painting said to have been done by Adam Willaerts in 1619, in possession of W. J. F. Backer

and, when an attack was expected, even more. In 1512 out of the three thousand men in the English navy, seventeen hundred and fifty were soldiers. By 1603 the number of men had increased to eight thousand three hundred and forty-six, of whom only two thousand and eight were soldiers.

THE *SOVEREIGN OF THE SEAS*, 1637

WHEN the *Sovereign of the Seas* was completed in 1637, over a century had passed since the introduction of brass cannon, which had proved so superior to the iron for naval uses. During that century the use of the former had become universal, changing completely the conception of what constituted a fine ship of war. The forecastle was done away with entirely, and the aftertower and the height of the sides greatly reduced. The arrangement of ordnance was the reverse of the earlier practice. The greatest number of guns was on the lowest deck. In all there were one hundred and thirty-two: thirty cannon (60 pounders) and demi-cannon (32 pounders) in the lower tiers; thirty culverins (18 pounders) and demi-culverins (10 pounders) in the third tier; twelve light guns in the forecastle; fourteen "murthering" guns on the two half decks; ten chase guns forward, ten chase guns aft beside "many loopholes in the cabin for musket shots."

45 From contemporary engraving, 1640, by John Payne in the Dominion Archives, Ottawa

THE RISE OF THE FRENCH NAVY

UNTIL 1620 and the abortive reforms of Cardinal Richelieu, France had made no sustained attempt to develop a well organized sea force. She had watched from a distance the early struggle for naval supremacy between Portugal and Spain replaced by the later rivalry of England and Holland. She had seen the English navy grow from an indirected levy of forty-two ships in 1641 to a national fleet of one hundred and fifty-four at the Stuart restoration, before Louis XIV and his efficient colonial minister Colbert determined to protect with a

46   *L'Hercule*, from Paul LaCroix, *XVIIIme Siècle*, Paris, 1882, after an original drawing by Ozanne

modernized sea force their own growing empire in America. In the next forty years a new type of ship, the frigate, began to be built in increasingly large numbers, both by the English and the French. Practically all traces of the mediæval sea fort had disappeared. The frigate was built close to the water, and the masts, formerly of a single stick, were divided into two and often times three separate spars. On the older ships such as the *Sovereign of the Seas*, the calibers of the guns ranged from sixty pounds down to one pound. On the new frigate there were usually only two calibers, 18 pound and 12 pound.

47   "A First Rate Ship of War," from The Encyclopedia Britannica, 2nd Edition, London, 1783

NAVAL CONTRIBUTION OF THE COLONISTS

THE frigate was the typical battleship to the end of the American Revolution. No other innovations of importance were made during the colonial period. To the art of naval warfare the American colonists made no contribution so significant as was their perfecting of the rifle to the tactics on land. It was, rather, a period in which the foundations of the later American navy were being laid. The colonists, especially those of New England, turned in ever greater numbers to commerce and to fishing, so that by the time of the Revolution, a large school of hardy, practical, well drilled American seamen had been created. With Massachusetts as their leader, the northern colonies had organized naval expeditions against the French in Port Royal, in Quebec, and in Louisburg. (See Nos. 67, 72, 88, 120.) But the enduring

48   The Harbor of Halifax, "drawn on the spot" by R. Short, published 1764, in the New York Public Library

contribution of the colonies lay along quite different lines. From the great uncleared forests of New England, giant trees were marked with the king's arrow and later felled to make masts for British frigates. The middle colonies were a market for hemp from which the rigging and ropes for British frigates were manufactured; while from the pine forests of the Carolinas came quantities of tar, indispensable in the building of British frigates.

CHAPTER II

INDIAN, FRENCH, AND SPANISH WARS, 1636–1748

RED men and white inevitably clashed when the red were naturally set upon holding, and the white equally set upon obtaining, an independent homeland within the selfsame area. There resulted such purely Indian fighting as the earlier settlers experienced in the three wars called after the Pequots, King Philip, and Râle. But just as inevitably the whites clashed when both the French and British were determined to expand their settlements, extend their trade routes, and establish their spheres of influence over as much ground and as many strategic points as they could possibly hold or even claim. Time and again these French and British whites crossed swords, sometimes in purely colonial expeditions, such as Frontenac's French and Indian raids and Phips' retaliatory expedition in 1690, or sometimes as colonial contingents in imperial expeditions, such as those against New France in Queen Anne's War (1702–13) or the one against Louisbourg in 1745, when, except for the squadron from the royal navy, every soldier, sailor, and vessel was American. The Indians were an ever-dwindling factor in the growing conflict between the rival European colonizers. Most sided with the French, who treated them better and dispossessed them less. But the formidable Iroquois, being enemies of the French, always sided with the British, on whom they were dependent for their trade.

The Pequot War gave the whites a much stronger foothold in New England, but it was not until they had won King Philip's War forty years later (1676) that they could safely extend their settlements up the Connecticut valley; nor was it till after Râle's (or Lovewell's) War, which ended fifty years later still, that the Maine and New Hampshire coast settlements shook off the prowling Abnakis. The Indian raids were sudden tiger-springs out of the wilds, a quick kill of every white who could be instantly struck down, and an equally quick elusive retreat with plunder and prisoners. The better armed and much better organized whites struck back more systematically, turned tribal feuds to their own advantage by using convenient Indian allies, and followed up their victories by pushing the frontier still farther into the Indian country.

King William's (1689–97), Queen Anne's (1702–13), and King George's (1739–48) were imperial wars, in which the great central forces fought out the decisive issues in Europe. But as the French and British were always on opposing sides their American possessions were of course involved, sometimes in minor Indian fighting, sometimes in French and Indian raids, sometimes in British colonial counterstrokes, and sometimes in joint naval and military expeditions which included both imperial and colonial forces, with sundry Indian allies on both sides. During King William's War, Frontenac, the Lion of New France, triumphed over the American colonial expedition (which Phips led up by sea against Quebec) as well as over all the Iroquois; while Iberville, his French-Canadian naval counterpart, took Newfoundland and Hudson's Bay. But Queen Anne's War excluded the French from both these places and deprived them of Acadia as well; while King George's, though indecisive by itself, proved but the prelude to the final conquest of New France.

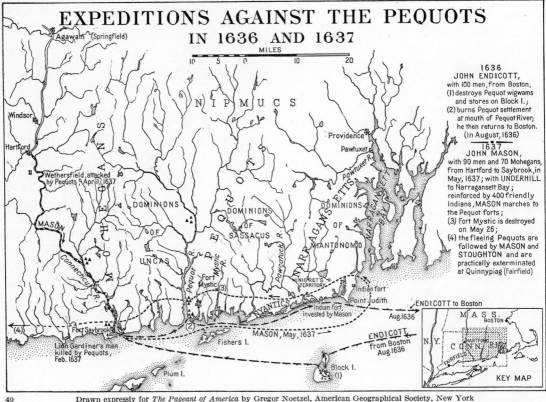

EXPEDITIONS AGAINST THE PEQUOTS
IN 1636 AND 1637

1636
JOHN ENDICOTT,
with 100 men, from Boston,
(1) destroys Pequot wigwams
and stores on Block I.;
(2) burns Pequot settlement
at mouth of Pequot River;
he then returns to Boston.
(In August, 1636)

1637
JOHN MASON,
with 90 men and 70 Mohegans,
from Hartford to Saybrook, in
May, 1637; with UNDERHILL
to Narragansett Bay;
reinforced by 400 friendly
Indians, MASON marches to
the Pequot forts;
(3) Fort Mystic is destroyed
on May 26;
(4) the fleeing Pequots are
followed by MASON and
STOUGHTON and are
practically exterminated
at Quinnypiag (Fairfield)

49   Drawn expressly for *The Pageant of America* by Gregor Noetzel, American Geographical Society, New York

THE PEQUOT WAR

THIS first Indian war to plague the New England settlements has been described in another volume (Vol. I, page 220). One day in 1636, near Block Island, John Gallop, seeing Indians aboard a drifting vessel, boarded her, found John Oldham's corpse, and killed or drove away the Indians. Then Governor Vane of Massachusetts sent out John Endicott to punish the Block Island red men.

50   Statue of Mayor John Mason at Mystic, Conn.

But these Indians were insignificant compared with the warlike Pequots, who, living in eastern Connecticut, menaced the peaceful growth of the Connecticut river towns. The Pequots were said to have committed many outrages. So Endicott made for the Pequot River, now the Thames, defeated a band of Pequots, devastated some Pequot territory and returned home. The following year, John Mason, with some ninety men and nearly fourscore friendly Mohegans, set out from the tiny settlement at Hartford. He was heavily reinforced by Indians at Saybrook, where he embarked and sailed east toward Narragansett Bay. This maneuver threw the Pequots off their guard. When Mason marched back into their country he was able to take Fort Mystic by surprise and destroy it. Probably six hundred men, women, and children perished in the flames of the burning Indian fort or were shot down while trying to escape. Such a massacre so crippled the Pequots that they decided to separate into small parties and abandon their country. A few went to Long Island and others to the interior. A larger party fled toward the country of the Mohawks. The whites relentlessly pursued this latter group, caught up with them near the present Fairfield, Connecticut, and practically wiped them out. A handful, eluding their enemies in the Fairfield battle, continued on their way to the Mohawks, who put them to death. Such was the tragic end of the Pequot nation.

FIRST INLAND MEETING OF THE FRENCH AND BRITISH, 1666

IN 1663 New France (see Vol. I) became a royal province. In 1665 Louis XIV's own viceroy came out with the first whole regiment of French regulars ever seen in North America. Even three of the famous Iroquois tribes, Senecas, Oneidas, and Onondagas, were so impressed that they sent embassies to sign peace at Quebec. But the other two, the Mohawks and the Cayugas, stood aloof. So in January, 1666, the French marched off to force peace on the Mohawks. But, mistaking the trail, they suddenly found a British outpost near Schenectady. Both sides were astounded: the French to find the British instead of Iroquois or Dutch; the British to find the French in force so far south, having marched through the Iroquois country, along the line of Lake Champlain, in the very middle of the winter. Well might the *Relation of the March of the Governor of Canada* into New York exclaim: "Surelie so bold and hardie an attempt hath not happened in any age." For the moment there was a real and universal peace between the French and the British; so the

51   Drawn expressly for *The Pageant of America*
by C. W. Jefferys (1869–)

astonished forces parted with many compliments on both sides. But both were full of foreboding, more especially the French, who at once saw the difference between the rather stagnant Dutch and the ever-expanding British.

ON THE EVE OF KING PHILIP'S WAR

IN spite of the destruction of the Pequots, the powerful tribes of southern New England, especially the Narragansets, continued by their very presence to threaten the peace of the New England frontier, which lay in the region of the modern Worcester county, along with a few scattered towns, such as Hatfield and Deerfield, along the Connecticut River. Upon the death of the friendly Massasoit, Philip became the chief sachem of the Wampanoag tribe and ruler of its principal possession, the Mount Hope peninsula, which lay within the territory claimed by Plymouth colony. Philip regarded with apprehension the slow encroachment of the whites upon his lands. The treaties his predecessors had signed, and which he too had signed, were of no avail to protect permanently his hunting range. For nine years after his elevation to the chieftainship, though charged with secret plotting, Philip of Pokanoket watched and prepared. Philip plotted secretly until the alarmed whites forced him to promise at Taunton, in 1671, to surrender all his English arms to the government of Plymouth. A little later he agreed to acknowledge himself a subject of the British king, to pay a yearly tribute, and to permit disputes to be adjudicated by the Plymouth Governor. But such a promise, if kept, would have meant the subjection of his people; and proud Philip did not mean to keep it long.

52   Treaty with King Philip, 1671, at the Old Church, Taunton, Mass., from the painting, 1901, by
W. S. Savory in the collection of the Ancient and Honorable Artillery Company, Faneuil Hall, Boston

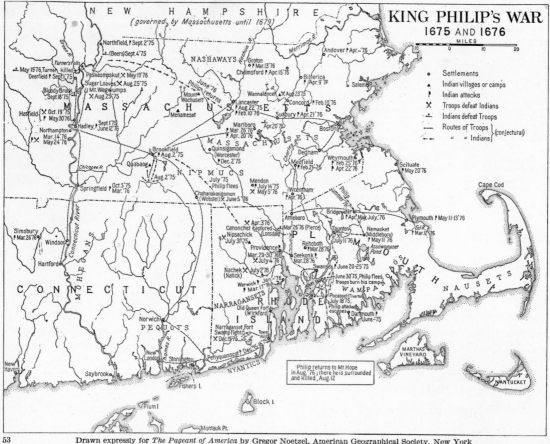

KING PHILIP'S WAR
1675 AND 1676

Drawn expressly for *The Pageant of America* by Gregor Noetzel, American Geographical Society, New York

53

OUTBREAK AND EXTENSION OF KING PHILIP'S WAR

THREE years later, by an attack on the settlement at Swansea, June, 1675, Philip struck his first blow, rousing both the Plymouth and Massachusetts authorities to action. Their troops drove Philip into hiding at Pocasset (Tiverton). But the desirability of impressing the Narragansets, who lived across the bay, caused Massachusetts to make a useless demonstration in that region, and permitted Philip, after a raid on Dartmouth, to escape to the north. Thus far the theater of war had been confined to a single colony, with but one tribe participating. But now it was to extend along the whole frontier.

Massachusetts was suspicious of the fidelity of the Nipmucs, who seemed to be undoubtedly preparing for war. After a war party had attacked Mendon, a detachment of twenty men was sent to find out the truth of the rumors concerning their disaffection, and the exact damages of the Mendon assault. This detachment, having agreed to meet the Nipmucs not far from Brookfield, was set upon by the very Indians with whom they had expected to parley. Eight were killed, and the survivors fled to Brookfield. There they and the inhabitants took refuge in the fortified house of John Ayres, where, on August 2, 1675, they maintained a brave defense against the fire-arrows and burning wagons of their enemies. Timely word of their plight reached Lancaster, and Major Simon Willard, with forty-seven troopers, hastened the thirty miles to their relief. He found the garrison holding out heroically, after a siege of three days. As a consequence of this attack Brookfield was abandoned.

54 The Attack on Brookfield, from an engraving after a drawing by A. R. Waud, in E. S. Ellis, *Indian Wars of the United States*, New York, 1892

BLOODY BROOK, 1675

THE Brookfield disaster caused Salem and Connecticut to send troops to Hadley to relieve the terror-stricken inhabitants of the Connecticut valley. One force was ambushed and slain, but another succeeded in reaching Northfield and in removing the settlers to Hadley. Near the neighboring town of Deerfield the corn was stacked, and on September 18 Captain Lathrop of Salem, with some seventy men and teamsters, was sent to gather it. On the way home his men marched carelessly, no scouts being thrown out to give warning of attack.

55   From a wood engraving in possession of the publishers, after the drawing by F. O. C. Darley (1822–88)

Six miles south of Deerfield the Indians from various tribes had massed near the spot where the road dipped to cross a tiny brook. As the heavy wagons were struggling through this marshy ground the volley burst from the forest. Dazed with fear, Lathrop's men were shot down; though some fled for brief moments of safety to the shelter of the wagons. One man clubbed his way through with his musket; another hid in the bushes by the brook and escaped. But the rest were wiped out; and though reinforcements forced the Indians to retire, the death of these seventy young men was the severest blow New England had yet suffered. Deerfield, the third frontier town, was abandoned.

THE GREAT SWAMP FIGHT AT KINGSTON, RHODE ISLAND, 1675

WHILE the war still raged in the Connecticut valley, Massachusetts decided upon a test of strength with the Narragansets. Strongly fortified in the center of the great swamp at North Kingston, this tribe harbored enemy refugees and defied attack. Massachusetts, Plymouth, and Connecticut raised in November, 1675, a thousand men, who, with some friendly Mohegans, made the difficult passage to the Indian stockade over the ice and snow. It stood on a raised plot of ground, protected by a rude abattis of trees and by rough blockhouses. But there was an opening on one side. Through this the New Englanders made their attack on December 19. The Indians, some thirty-five hundred in number, gave back a deadly fire. Only a part of them had firearms, and but little ammunition. When that was exhausted, the whites attacked the palisaded enclosure within the stockade and set fire to the wigwams, as the Indians fled in terror. Yet even this success did not break the power of the tribe, which was forced north into alliance with the Nipmucs. Fiercer than ever flamed the war between the races. To the Indian's deep resentment at the deliberate encroachments of the whites was added the bitter memory of the hundreds of slain, women and children as well as the braves, whom he was compelled to leave unburied at the fort, which had failed to give him protection.

56   From the painting by W. S. Savory in the collection of the Ancient and Honorable Artillery Company, Faneuil Hall, Boston

57 Death of King Philip, from an engraving by Childs after the drawing by F. O. C. Darley in Washington Irving, *The Sketchbook of Geoffrey Crayon, Gent.*, New York, 1852

THE END OF KING PHILIP'S WAR

THE United Colonies raised another thousand men and made arrangements to supply them with provisions, by sea and by land. During the spring and summer of 1676 the combined Indian tribes again made swift attacks upon a score of villages along the frontier, from Groton and Chelmsford to Providence and Warwick (see map, No. 53). In the Connecticut valley, Northampton, Hadley, and Hatfield were attacked, and the terror-stricken frontier settlers often refused to leave their homes for any task whatsoever. But the New Englanders likewise gained victories. Captain Turner won a success at the Falls; a party of Connecticut volunteers captured and executed Canochet, the Narraganset chief, while Major John Talcott, with Connecticut troops, led a notable raid through the Narraganset country, capturing or slaying over two hundred, and gradually clearing the country of Indians. At last, their power broken, their cornfields destroyed, and their provisions exhausted, the Indians either surrendered or fled disheartened to more distant regions. Philip himself was slain in August; but his death did little else than mark the close of the war, for he appears, after the early fighting, to have played little active part in it. In New Hampshire and Maine, the Saco Indians, aggrieved at their treatment by the frontiersmen, continued to desolate the defenseless settlements along the shore that they had attacked as early as 1675. The inhabitants could get little help, and the small bodies of troops were as bewildered by the darting blows of the forest warriors as were the panic-stricken families. Not till the treaty of Casco in 1678 was there an end to the dreary story. The peace was to last only eight years, till another set of raids in the first French and Indian War repeated the tale of bloodshed. But hereafter southern New England was free from Indian wars at home.

THE FRENCH AND THE IROQUOIS

THE Iroquois, or Five Nations, the ablest and most powerful group of red men in the northern colonies, held the country from the Hudson to the Great Lakes, and claimed to exercise jurisdiction over the lakes themselves and as far as the lands of the Illinois (see Vol. II, Chapter III). Inevitably these ambitions, coupled with the fur-trading interests which were the great source of French wealth in Canada, brought the Indians and whites into conflict. The Iroquois resented the construction of French forts in the Ohio region, and retaliated by destroying occasional French fur canoes. Moreover, the English sought to exercise control over the Iroquois, with whom indeed they carried on a rather extensive trade. Governor De la Barre of Canada was far too weak to cope with the Five Nations. At his invitation certain of their chiefs met him in conference at Montreal in 1683; but the discussion bore no fruit. The fears of the Iroquois would not be quieted by anything short of the removal of the French forts that were beginning to dot the shores of the lakes and the Mississippi; and De la Barre failed to intimidate the fierce ambassadors by bluster or a show of force. But he made preparation for war in the following year.

58 Conference between Governor De la Barre and Representatives of the Five Nations, from the mural painting by G. W. Breck (1863–1920) in the Flower Memorial Hospital, Watertown, N. Y.

DE LA BARRE'S FRUITLESS EXPEDITION, 1684

DE LA BARRE was no leader for an expedition into the Indian country. Yet he determined to chastise the Senecas, who guarded the western door of the Iroquois' Long House. His movements should have been vigorous and brisk, but, instead, he was dilatory. He left Quebec on July 9, wasted ten days at Montreal, and fifteen at Fort Frontenac on Lake Ontario. His provisions, collected with difficulty, ran low, and his troops caught a deadly fever. He felt it impossible to advance farther than La Famine (Salmon) River; there he concluded an inglorious peace, which made him the butt of Iroquois orators, and was keenly felt throughout all Canada. News of the disgrace reached France, and De la Barre was recalled. Le Sieur de Denonville was sent out as his successor.

DENONVILLE DEFEATS THE SENECAS, 1687

DENONVILLE, a more spirited man than his predecessor, took steps to ensure the success of his expedition. Fort Frontenac was strengthened. His lieutenant at that post invited the neighboring Iroquois to a feast at the fort, seized them as they came in answer to the bait, chained them in pillories, and later sent them to the galleys in France. This act of perfidy, designed to prevent the Senecas from gaining information, was to be richly repaid by the infuriated braves two years later. In spite of all Denonville's precautions, the Senecas learned of the advance of his forces and of his intentions. In July he landed his sixteen hundred royal troops and militia on the southern shore of Ontario, and commenced his march. The Senecas prepared an ambush, as La Hontan's curious map shows; but, ignorant of the number of men in the French forces, they attacked the advance guard under the impression that it was the main body and fled from the field when they discovered the mistake. Denonville destroyed four villages, laid waste as much as he could not carry with him, and commenced the construction of Fort Niagara. He had attained a partial victory; but in warfare of this nature, the only definite success could come from the continuance of the raids and destruction until the Senecas were forced to sue for peace. Denonville returned to Montreal with his task unfinished. Throughout the next winter and spring the Iroquois hovered about the French settlements, burning and pillaging. In the councils of the Long House were spoken speeches filled with hatred for the French.

59   Camp of De la Barre on Lake Erie, from La Hontan, *Nouveaux Voyages dans L'Amérique Septentrionale*, La Haye, 1703

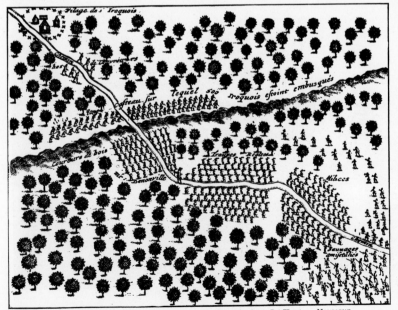

60   Governor Denonville's Expedition against the Iroquois, from La Hontan, *Nouveaux Voyages dans L'Amérique Septentrionale*, La Haye, 1703

61   From the painting by C. W. Jefferys in possession of the publishers

THE MASSACRE AT LACHINE, AUGUST, 1689

THE memory of the treachery at Fort Frontenac (now Kingston, Ontario) kept alive in the Indian heart the determination for revenge. On the stormy night of August 5, 1689, some fifteen hundred Iroquois cautiously landed above the little village of Lachine on the St. Lawrence, and silently distributed themselves about the houses. At the signal the war whoop rang out, and the massacre of inhabitants, men, women, and children, began. The French treachery to the Iroquois braves was repaid in blood. No English settlement ever experienced such a terrible blow as the Indians delivered here. The devastation extended over seven and a half miles; two hundred victims fell; and ninety were carried away prisoners. The troops at Montreal, a short distance down the river, hindered by Denonville's express commands, made little effort to check the bloody work, and the Iroquois escaped. New France had never been so badly in need of a strong arm and courageous heart.

FRONTENAC RETURNS TO CANADA, 1689

COUNT FRONTENAC had been Governor of Canada from 1672 to 1682 and had ruled it with an iron hand, though likewise with a sympathetic heart. His quarrels with the Bishop and Intendant had caused his recall. But now that Canada was in such peril from both Iroquois and whites (for King William's War was just beginning) Louis XIV sent him back. Few figures in the New World are so striking as that of this seventeenth-century nobleman, who had devoted his whole life to the service of the French court and took his keenest delight in the appreciation his guests expressed for his horses, his estates, his wine, and himself. None the less, under the habiliments of the courtier, there beat the heart of an implacable and relentless soldier, whose imperious mien and quick temper was admirably suited to dealing with North American Indians. Frontenac, though now in his seventieth year, could seize the tomahawk with as wild a yell as any Iroquois ever uttered, and lead a war dance with complete abandon. Quebec hailed his return with rapture.

62   From the painting by C. W. Jefferys in possession of the publishers

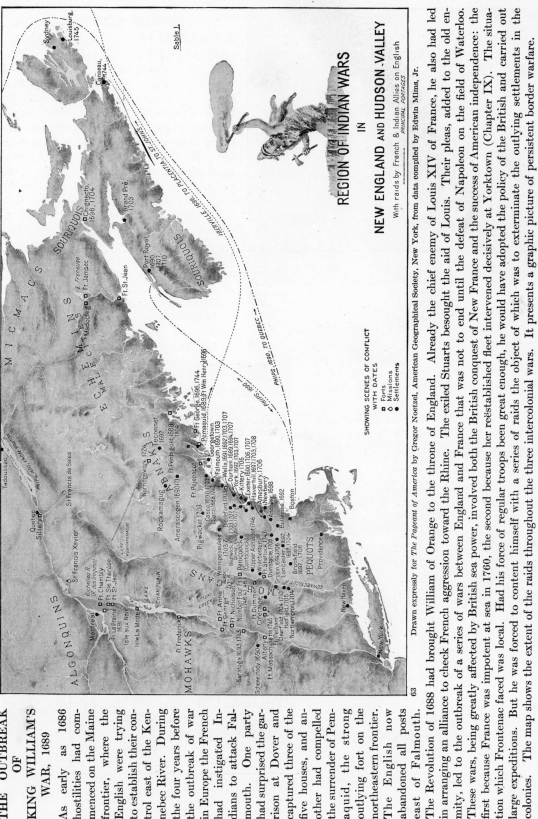

REGION OF INDIAN WARS

IN

NEW ENGLAND AND HUDSON VALLEY

With raids by French & Indian Allies on English

PRINCIPAL PORTAGES

SHOWING SCENES OF CONFLICT
WITH DATES
□ Forts
◇ Missions
● Settlements

Drawn expressly for *The Pageant of America* by Gregor Noetzel, American Geographical Society, New York, from data compiled by Edwin Mims, Jr.

THE OUTBREAK OF KING WILLIAM'S WAR, 1689

As early as 1686 hostilities had commenced on the Maine frontier, where the English were trying to establish their control east of the Kennebec River. During the four years before the outbreak of war in Europe the French had instigated Indians to attack Falmouth. One party had surprised the garrison at Dover and captured three of the five houses, and another had compelled the surrender of Pemaquid, the strong outlying fort on the northeastern frontier. The English now abandoned all posts east of Falmouth.

The Revolution of 1688 had brought William of Orange to the throne of England. Already the chief enemy of Louis XIV of France, he also had led in arranging an alliance to check French aggression toward the Rhine. The exiled Stuarts besought the aid of Louis. Their pleas, added to the old enmity, led to the outbreak of a series of wars between England and France that was not to end until the defeat of Napoleon on the field of Waterloo. These wars, being greatly affected by British sea power, involved both the British conquest of New France and the success of American independence: the first because France was impotent at sea in 1760, the second because her reëstablished fleet intervened decisively at Yorktown (Chapter IX). The situation which Frontenac faced was local. Had his force of regular troops been great enough, he would have adopted the policy of the British and carried out large expeditions. But he was forced to content himself with a series of raids the object of which was to exterminate the outlying settlements in the colonies. The map shows the extent of the raids throughout the three intercolonial wars. It presents a graphic picture of persistent border warfare.

64   Drawn expressly for *The Pageant of America* by C. W. Jefferys

THE SCHENECTADY RAID, 1690

EARLY in 1690 Frontenac organized three war parties of French and Indians. One, starting from Montreal, was to strike at the frontier of New York; a second, from Three Rivers, at that of New Hampshire; a third, from Quebec, was to ravage again the settlements of Maine. The story of one raid is that of all. They mark the definite adoption by the French of the Indian mode of warfare. Setting out from Montreal toward the end of January, a war party of some two hundred men, after a desperately hard march through the snow, found Schenectady completely unguarded against surprise. No sentinels peered from the blockhouse; the western gate was wide open. Bitter cold and falling snow seemed to afford ample protection. Silently the attackers entered the gate, and burst upon the blockhouse and the private dwellings. For two hours the slaughter lasted, most of the victims being women and children who were tomahawked by the Indians as they rushed in terror out of doors. John Glen, a settler who had been kind to some Frenchmen captured by the Mohawks, was spared with his family, and fifty old men, women, and children escaped death. But the number killed was sixty, and Schenectady was burnt to the ground. A month later the second party took Salmon Falls, and then, uniting with the third party, laid siege to Fort Loyal (Falmouth). Captain Davis surrendered on the promise that the lives of the inhabitants should be spared. The agreement was not kept; some were killed by the Indians, some carried away captive.

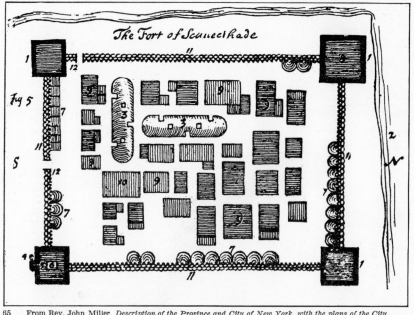

65   From Rev. John Miller, *Description of the Province and City of New York, with the plans of the City and several forts, . . . in the year 1695*, London, 1842, in the New York Public Library

1. The Blockhouses. 2. River running beside the fort. 3. Indian wigwams. 4. The flagstaff. 5. A sentry box. 6. The spy-loft. 7. Sties for hogs. 8. The blockhouse, designed for Church. 9. Those and others like them are houses. 10. A great barn. 11. The Treble stockado. 12. The fort gates.

THE COLONIES PLAN THE "GLORIOUS ENTERPRISE," 1690

GOADED to action by Frontenac's raids, the colonies, answering the summons of Leisler, Governor of New York, met in conference. Delegates from Massachusetts, Plymouth, Connecticut, and New York assembled at New York and determined upon the "Glorious Enterprise" which Pieter Schuyler, the stalwart mayor of Albany, was instrumental in proposing. One force was to attack Montreal by way of Lake Champlain; the second was to go by sea against Quebec. Fitz-John Winthrop of Connecticut, chosen as leader of the land troops, found at the outset difficulty and discouragement. Smallpox broke out at Albany, and the food was insufficient and bad. Not till the first of August did the army march northward, only to learn that canoes could not be built to transport them, and that their pork had become "scarce eatable." Most of the army returned on August 20 to Albany, weary and sick. A detachment of one hundred and forty English and Indians, however, under Pieter Schuyler's brother John, had descended upon the French settlement of La Prairie, killed or captured some twenty-five Canadian farmers, destroyed their barns, and returned in safety to Albany.

66 Pieter Schuyler, Mayor, Albany, N. Y., 1686–94, painted by order of Queen Anne in 1710 during his visit to London, original in the Mayor's Office, Albany

SIR WILLIAM PHIPS TAKES PORT ROYAL, 1690

BEFORE the conference at New York, Massachusetts merchants had sunk capital in a buccaneering enterprise against Port Royal (in Nova Scotia) the plunder from which would pay rich interest on their investment. The Massachusetts General Court furnished the armed sloops necessary to transport the troops, and Sir William Phips was chosen as leader. In May, 1690, Phips dropped anchor in the harbor of Port Royal. The little garrison, taken by surprise, surrendered without resistance. When Phips came back in triumph "with the Governor of

67 Sir William Phips, from an unauthenticated portrait in the Maine Historical Society, Portland, Me.

Port Royall, two Priests, and about sixty Souldiers, with their guns and stores of Warr and Plunder," enthusiasm rose to fever-pitch and Phips became the hero of the day. With confidence Massachusetts now threw herself into the forwarding of the "Glorious Enterprise." This poster was magnificently answered. Boston hummed with warlike preparations; and Phips sailed in August, 1690, with four little men-of-war, forty other vessels, all more or less armed, and twenty-three hundred soldiers. The flagship, *Six Friends*, Captain Sugars, forty-four guns and two hundred men, led the long line out to sea from the tiny fishing settlement of Hull, bearing the united good will of all New England. But Phips was no fit commander for a sea and land enterprise.

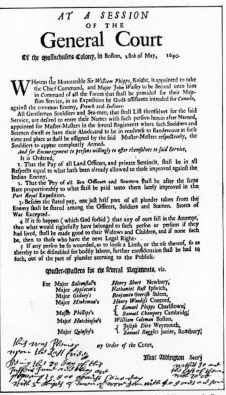

68 Recruiting Poster for "Gentlemen Souldiers and Seamen" to join the New England Expedition against Quebec, 1690, in the Massachusetts Historical Society

69   From the painting *Frontenac Answering Phips' Emtssary* by
C. W. Jefferys, in possession of the publishers

PHIPS SUMMONS FRONTENAC
AT QUEBEC, 1690

PHIPS' ill-timed delays permitted the construction of defenses for the western exposed side of Quebec; but the town was still dangerously weak when, on October 15, the watchers on the city heights saw the English fleet approach up the river. Frontenac had been at Montreal, where the main body of the troops were stationed, but had hurried back to Quebec on learning of Phips' approach, leaving all the French forces straining every nerve to follow him. Phips must have expected to find Quebec an easy prey when he sent his messenger, Captain Savage, with a demand for the surrender of the city. Savage was led blindfolded into one of the grand rooms of the Chateau St. Louis. When the bandage was removed he found himself surrounded by a glittering array, prepared for battle. From Frontenac's lips came the fiery answer to the summons he delivered: "Tell your General I'll send him his answer by the mouth of my cannon."

LE RÉGIMENT DE
CARIGNAN

FATUOUS councils of war aboard the fleet wasted three valuable days during which the magnificent regulars of Carignan were marching from Montreal, gathering, as they passed, every man of the local militia. Then, on the third wasted day, the sound of martial music came floating down on the evening breeze to Quebec and Phips' fleet. The officer of the watch

70   Arrival of the Carignan Regiment at Quebec, 1690, drawn expressly for
The Pageant of America by C. W. Jefferys

aboard the flagship called his seniors up on deck. Then they summoned a prisoner, De Grandville, and asked him what this music meant. He recognized the shrill, sweet treble of the fifes, the stirring roll of side-drums, and the throbbing rhythmic regularity of the big deep bass. He likewise knew the very air they played — "Yes, that's our regimental march." And there, on the historic Heights of Abraham, marched the eager, rescuing brigade, fifteen hundred strong, led by the regulars of Carignan.

MAJOR WALLEY ATTACKS QUEBEC, 1690

THE only course left to Phips was to land troops on the Beaufort shore, and attempt to struggle through the rough country, to the assault of the city itself. The heights of Quebec were well defended by cannon, and in the city was a number equal to all that Phips could muster against them. The American commander foolishly cannonaded the sheer face of the Quebec cliffs, whence his ships were answered by three tiers of cannon. Phips' artillery attack took place before that civilian soldier, Major Walley, could get into position to assault the town. While the commander was shooting away the larger part of his ammunition, Walley lay in camp, his men wet, shivering with cold and sickening with smallpox. Food and other necessary supplies which were to have been brought him by small vessels did not come, the commanders proving insubordinate.

71   Major John Walley, from doubtful portrait in the *Yearbook*, Society of Colonial Wars of Massachusetts, Boston, 1898

THE STRONGHOLD OF QUEBEC

FRONTENAC hoped that Walley would cross the St. Charles, but the American sensed the danger of disaster in such a move. The day after Phips' bombardment Walley went aboard ship to explain the necessity of withdrawing the troops. In his absence they became involved in an inconclusive skirmish with the Canadians. On the third night after the bombardment the soldiers returned to the ships. La Hontan's curious picture diagrams roughly the position of the main fleet, of the bombarding squadron, of Walley's camp, and the location of the fighting on shore.

72   Plan of Quebec, 1690, from La Hontan, *Nouveaux Voyages dans l'Amérique Septentrionale*, La Haye, 1703

A. City of Quebec.   B. Fort or castle or home of Governor.   C. Battery of cannons. D. Island of Orleans.   E. Pointe de leui.   F. Seignory of Beauport or Marquiseship(?). G. Village under Beauport Manor.   H. English fleet.   I. The English shallop, which awaits return of commander.   L. English vessels cannonading the city.   M. English shallops landing troops.   N. Location of landing of English troops.   O. Grove where troops were repulsed.   P. Coureurs de bois, officers and savages rushing to the grove. Q. Mission of the Recollect Fathers.

WEARY YEARS OF BORDER WAR, 1690–97

AFTER the failure of Phips in his artillery duel and the withdrawal of Walley's troops from their position on shore there was nothing to do but abandon the expedition. The fleet started on its long journey homeward. Some vessels did not arrive in Boston till February. Discouraged and disheartened by the failure of the Quebec expedition, her credit exhausted, and her citizens weary of war, Massachusetts planned no more Glorious Enterprises. Occasionally an operation, very much like those of King Philip's War, brought a brief gleam of relief. Captain Convers ably and heroically defended the garrison at Wells, Maine, against a superior force of Indians. Proclamations of the kind here represented show the intense bitterness and ferocity of the border warfare. Benjamin Church, a noted Indian fighter, though somewhat doubtful of the promises of the General Court to recompense him and his men, conducted two raids, one an extended journey as far as St. John's. The fort at Pemaquid was rebuilt.

Church's proclamation (No. 74), characteristic of the man and his times, reads: "For the better encouragement of such as shall voluntarily list themselves (as private sentinels) and

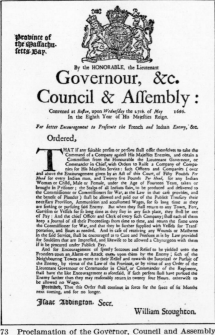

73   Proclamation of the Governor, Council and Assembly of Massachusetts Bay, 1696, for better encouragement to prosecute the French and Indian Enemy, from broadside in the Public Library, Boston

aprove themselves good souldiers under my comands: Those may certifie that if it shall please god to faviour us so far that we get any advantage by the act of the Generall Court: as to scalp money, prisoners or plunder. Every private centenell attending order and behaving themselves well and souldier like in fight; shall have equal share with the officers: the officers being considered in their wages by the country: And as a testimony of the truth and reallity of my Intentions for the performance hereof I have hereunto subscribed my hand."

74   Manuscript proclamation of Benjamin Church, 1696, encouraging enlistment against French and Indians, original in the Newberry Library, Chicago

CONTINUING INDIAN RAIDS FROM THE NORTH, 1697

HANNAH DUSTIN saw her home burnt and her new-born babe dashed to death when the Indians raided Haverhill, Massachusetts. She, Mary Neff, and a boy from Worcester, were carried off to an Abnaki village by a group composed of two braves, three squaws, and seven children. One night, when all the Indians were asleep, the three captives killed ten and wounded an old squaw, who escaped with a small boy. Then the three avengers found their perilous way home, bearing the ten scalps with them. Hannah Dustin, a mother herself, who struck down and scalped the children of her captors, epitomizes the savageness of this war between the races.

THE FAR–FLUNG BATTLE LINE

RADISSON, fur-trader and explorer, had given the French their first claim to Hudson's Bay; though, to their disgust, he had afterward traded with the British. In 1670 the famous Hudson's Bay Company was formed. Next year the sale pictured here was held at its London headquarters. Another year later, a Frenchman, Father Albanel, was the first white man to reach the Bay by the overland route from the St. Lawrence. There, to his intense disappointment, he saw boats fly the British flag. He realized that the French settlement in the valley of the St. Lawrence now lay between English holdings both south and north. The strategy of

75 Statue by Calvin H. Weeks on the Hannah Dustin monument, Haverhill, Mass. © The Halliday Historic Photograph Co., Boston

Frontenac and his superiors at Versailles must be directed not only toward defeating the English of New England and New York, but toward driving the hated rival out of the inaccessible Hudson Bay's region as well. The latter task was one of tremendous difficulty. Many miles of primeval forest lay between Quebec and James Bay and the voyage around Labrador into enemy waters was long and dangerous, only to be undertaken by a skillful seaman and daring captain.

76 *The First Hudson's Bay Company's Fur Sale in London*, 1671, from Sir William Schooling, *The Hudson's Bay Co.*, 1670–1920, after original painting in the office of the Hudson's Bay Company, London

77 Le Moyne d'Iberville, from Pierre Margry, *Découvertes et établissements des Français dans l'ouest et dans le sud de l'Amérique septentrionale, 1614–1754*, Paris, 1879–88

IBERVILLE'S RAIDS IN HUDSON'S BAY, 1696–97, 1699

IN the same year as Hannah Dustin's exploit the French turned suddenly on their English opponents in Newfoundland and Hudson's Bay. Young Iberville was the third of the ten magnificently fit sons born to Charles Le Moyne, Sieur de Longueuil, and to the belle of Montreal. Five were killed in action. Four became Governors: one, Bienville, being the first to rule Louisiana. Two were in the regular navy of France; and one of these, Iberville, became a great French hero. Iberville had already twice struck the British in the north, once in an overland expedition to Moose Factory and to Forts Albany and Rupert. Again in 1689 he had captured the *Hampshire* with a heavy load of furs. In 1694 he had taken Fort Nelson. Now, in 1697, he performed the greatest exploits of all.

IBERVILLE'S NEWFOUNDLAND RAID, 1696–97

No English colonist of his day was a match for the intrepid Iberville. For his like one must look forward to George Rogers Clark who in the Revolution broke the British power in the Northwest. From a raid at Pemaquid Iberville dashed at Newfoundland in 1696. English fishermen had established winter settlements all along the best harbors of the whole southeastern coast. He struck and ravaged Placentia. He followed this with a midwinter march so full of incredible hardships that no one believed it had been made until the results appeared. When Iberville left the island only two trifling English hamlets remained; while the fear of the French commander spread southward to New England and even to the far-off Virginian coast.

Drawn expressly for *The Pageant of America* by Gregor Noetzel, American Geographical Society, New York

IBERVILLE CONQUERS HUDSON'S BAY

EARLY in July Iberville, in command of *Le Pélican*, sailed from Placentia. In his squadron were four fighting ships and a vessel for carrying stores. Before the end of the month they entered Hudson's Bay where they were soon caught among masses of floating ice. The store ship was lost and the rest were in grave danger. *Le Pélican* at last made the open sea alone and Iberville turned her prow toward Fort Nelson. He came to grips with an English flotilla of twice his own strength. Wisely deciding not to become the center of a circle of fire, he made straight for the *Hampshire*. As he closed with her, his well-known handsome face, superbly stalwart figure, and floating long fair hair told the British who he was. "You shan't escape this time," they shouted. "Prepare to board!" he thundered in reply. But the *Hampshire* sheered off. He then cut in between the other two with terrific port and starboard broadsides, crippling both. Then, cleverly keeping to windward of the *Hampshire*, he fought her intensively, closed at precisely the right moment, fired every double-shotted gun right into her hull, and sank her with all hands.

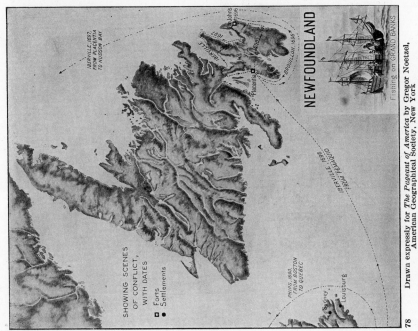

Drawn expressly for *The Pageant of America* by Gregor Noetzel, American Geographical Society, New York

80   The Wreck of *Le Pélican*, from Bacqueville de la Potherie, *Histoire de l'Amérique Septentrionale*, Paris, 1751

IBERVILLE TAKES FORT NELSON ON HUDSON'S BAY

A STORM now broke, driving the crippled *Pélican* helpless down the Bay, her decks covered with the dead and dying. In the darkness of the night the ship ran aground not six miles from Fort Nelson. The men struggled through the icy water to the snow banks on the shore. At this desperate moment Iberville's other ships arrived. In spite of the relief they brought it was still a question of capturing Fort Nelson and the supplies there or spending the winter in the woods. Finally the stern old Governor, Bailey, capitulated, and was permitted to return to England. Iberville was master of the Bay.

The Treaty of Ryswick, marking the end of the war, was signed the same year. In the colonies conditions remained exactly as they were before it opened. No possession had permanently changed hands, for the French reoccupied Acadia, and the English regained a footing on Hudson's Bay. The English frontier had slightly contracted, but could quickly be extended again.

BRIEF YEARS OF PEACE, 1697–1702

Two events occurred during this short interval that had an important bearing upon the future. The new French Governor, De Callières, carrying out the plans of Frontenac, signed a treaty of peace with his powerful foes, the Iroquois. As a direct consequence, in the war that was soon to follow, the New York frontier was comparatively free from attack. Secondly, the great struggle for control of the fur trade, which carried with it the control of the continent, turned men's eyes westward. Years before, Denonville had attempted to found a fort at the strategic strait between Lakes Huron and Erie, and Englishmen had coveted the increase in trade which such a post would bring them. It remained for La Mothe Cadillac, in spite of some opposition in Canada, to gain the permission of Versailles itself, and

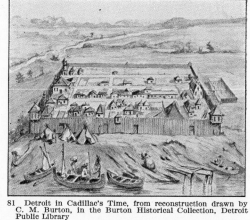

81   Detroit in Cadillac's Time, from reconstruction drawn by C. M. Burton, in the Burton Historical Collection, Detroit Public Library

erect Fort Pontchartrain. Sixty yards square, built of pickets, it stood on the west bank of the strait, a hundred yards from the water, within the present limits of Detroit.

82   Hertel de Rouville, from the Champlain Edition, 1897, of Francis Parkman's works, after the original portrait in the possession of Mrs. H. de Rouville, Montreal. © Little, Brown & Co., Boston

QUEEN ANNE'S WAR, 1702–13

QUEEN ANNE'S WAR, as the War of the Spanish Succession was called in America, found its chief causes in European politics. A French prince had ascended the Spanish throne; and England, Austria, and Holland joined in a struggle to maintain the balance of power. The American phase was the second chapter in the imperial struggle between England and France in North America. The war in the colonies falls into two divisions; the first, 1702–1707, characterized by the renewal of the deadly border raids, the second, 1707–1713, marked by the formation of large expeditions. In August, 1703, the Sieur de Beaubassin, with five hundred French and Indians, swept down upon the border towns of Maine. Scarcely a settlement escaped his furious attacks. In the Connecticut valley the outlying settlements were again exposed to the invader. But the difficulty of finding men to serve in any capacity, and especially on tiresome garrison duty, left practically undefended even remote Deerfield, the most advanced post in the valley.

83   Graves of the Deerfield Victims. © The Misses Allen, Deerfield

THE DEERFIELD RAID

IN February, 1704, Hertel de Rouville, a bold and skillful French soldier, led his band of French and Indians to raid the English settlement at Deerfield, in Massachusetts. The sleepy village sentries had gone to bed. Suddenly the winter silence was rent with appalling war cries. The French and Indians, taking advantage of drifts of snow, clambered over the palisades and began hacking down the doors. Confused fighting followed. At length reinforcements came up from the settlements to the south and drove away the raiders. But forty-eight people had been killed, and over one hundred prisoners led away to New France. There, for the most part, in keeping with the usual French policy, they were well treated.

84   Door of the Sheldon House, Deerfield, Mass., showing holes made by Indian hatchets. © Photograph by the Misses Allen, of the original in the Pocumtuck Valley Memorial Association, Deerfield

CHURCH'S RAID IN ACADIA, 1704

WITH his usual eye for profit, Church submitted to Governor Dudley of Massachusetts a plan for the ravaging of Acadia, which was accepted. At the head of five hundred men Church made his way up the coast, plundering all the settlements he could reach. In Acadia itself the region about Grand Pré suffered from his attacks, but he scarcely felt strong enough to attack Port Royal. He was roundly denounced, upon his return to Boston, for unnecessary cruelty to non-combatants, though his raid was modeled upon those which the French had for so long been making. This was the last and longest expedition which Church ever led.

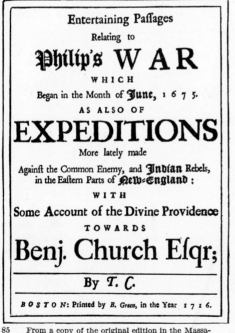

Entertaining Paſſages
Relating to
Philip's WAR
WHICH
Began in the Month of June, 1 6 7 5.
AS ALSO OF
EXPEDITIONS
More lately made
Againſt the Common Enemy, and Indian Rebels,
in the Eaſtern Parts of New-England:
WITH
Some Account of the Divine Providence
TOWARDS
Benj. Church Eſqr;
By T. C.
BOSTON: Printed by B. Green, in the Year 1 7 1 6.

85   From a copy of the original edition in the Massachusetts Historial Society, Boston

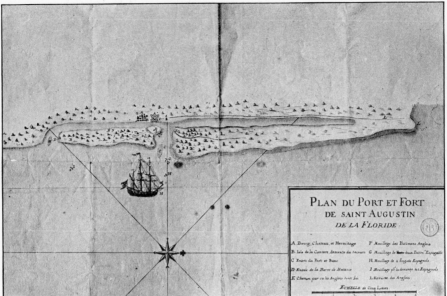

86   Plan of the Harbor and Fort of St. Augustine in Florida, 1703, from the original in the Depôt des Cartes
et Plans de la Marine, Paris

QUEEN ANNE'S WAR IN THE SOUTH, 1702–06

QUEEN ANNE'S WAR gave the South Carolinians an opportunity to strike at the Spanish in Florida, whence constant threats of marauding expeditions had come. Governor Moore, in September, 1702, left Port Royal at the head of twelve hundred militia and Indians, in ten small vessels. Finding soon afterward that no successful siege could be laid against the fort at St. Augustine without a supply of mortars and bombs, he dispatched a sloop to Jamaica to bring them up. But the sloop failed to return; and, when he was waiting for a second vessel sent on the same errand, two Spanish war vessels frightened him away. Two years later, with more success, he led a raid very much like those in the north, and destroyed several Catholic chapels and small fortified towns at the back of St. Augustine. In 1706 a French and Spanish fleet appeared before Charleston. Its delay in negotiating the treacherous entrance to the harbor offered time for the country militia to assemble and for the few vessels that the English owned to be put in readiness. Several brisk skirmishes on land showed that the assailants were no match for the sturdy provincial soldiers; and when finally the tiny English fleet took the initiative, and bore down upon the invaders, they hoisted sail and made off. The episode is noteworthy, not only because of the brave defense of the Carolinians, but because it was the only serious sea expedition conducted by the French against a British continental colony.

THE EXPEDITION AGAINST ACADIA, 1707

THE year 1707 marks the first of the more extensive expeditions against the French. Massachusetts took the lead in raising over a thousand men and providing them with stores and ships. Colonel John March, who had bravely defended Fort Casco from Beaubassin's attacks in 1703, was in command, with Wainwright second. By the end of May the fleet of twenty-five vessels was within the basin, and had landed troops some seven miles from the fort. There all action stopped.

87   Annapolis, Nova Scotia, from a print in Des Barres' *Atlantic Neptune*, 1777

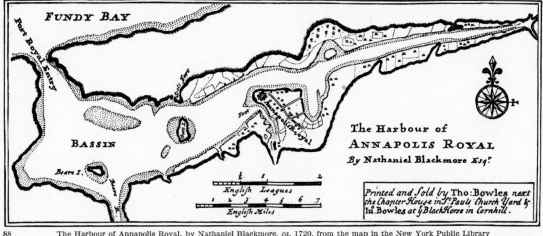

88   The Harbour of Annapolis Royal, by Nathaniel Blackmore, *ca.* 1720, from the map in the New York Public Library

THE FAILURE OF THE MASSACHUSETTS ENTERPRISE

THE French commander, Subercase, was unusually able. Finally, in spite of the fact that the English force outnumbered the French more than three to one, were on the ground early in the year, and had resources enough to win the victory, a council of war decided to return home. Great indignation prevailed at Boston when the news of this fiasco came in; and three civilians were at once sent up to act as a supervising committee over the leaders. In August the colonial fleet was once more in the basin; but Subercase had received reinforcements. Forced to land on the opposite shore from the fort, the New Englanders were repelled whenever they tried to cross the water. In ten days time so many were sick that once more the ill-fated expedition was abandoned.

ANOTHER ABORTIVE EXPEDITION, 1709

THE mother country, persuaded by the arguments of Colonel Samuel Vetch that Canada was fast enclosing the colonies, determined to take a hand. The old plan of a joint expedition against Quebec was again revived. The colonies were asked to contribute men and money; and under the influence of the government in England, not only New York, which hitherto had not participated in this war, but likewise New Jersey and Pennsylvania at last undertook to do their share. Nicholson, late Governor of Virginia, commanded the expedition that was to follow the Lake Champlain route, while an English fleet was to cross to Boston, refit there, and proceed up the St. Lawrence. But England, prevented by European difficulties, failed to do her part. No fleet appeared. Nicholson, with his fifteen hundred men, advanced to the southern end of Lake Champlain, and waited for news that did not come.

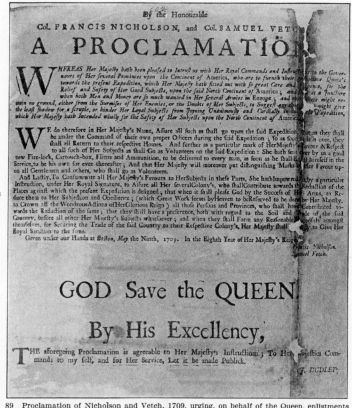

89   Proclamation of Nicholson and Vetch, 1709, urging, on behalf of the Queen, enlistments in the Canadian Expedition, from broadside in the American Antiquarian Society, Worcester, Mass.

THE FALL OF ACADIA, 1710

For six years the great Marlborough had been winning brilliant victories in Flanders, and now England could devote troops and fleets to the projects which men like Vetch had long been drumming into the ears of her leaders. The expedition against Acadia in 1710 is noteworthy, not only because an English fleet arrived in time to be of use, but because, for the first time in colonial history, English regular soldiers landed in the New World as reinforcements in a joint expedition. It marked the beginning of that type of operation which was to prove effective half a century later. Nicholson again commanded the land forces of some two thousand men, a formidable army to lead against a post that was weaker than it had been in 1707. Without opposition he planted his cannon within close range of the fort, and Subercase, to escape useless bloodshed, surrendered. The French marched out with shouldered arms and drums beating. Then the English entered and their officers gave a breakfast to the French ladies in the fort. Acadia became British, and Nicholson, in honor of his queen, changed the name of Port Royal to Annapolis Royal. The fall of Acadia marked the beginning of the conquest of New France by British arms.

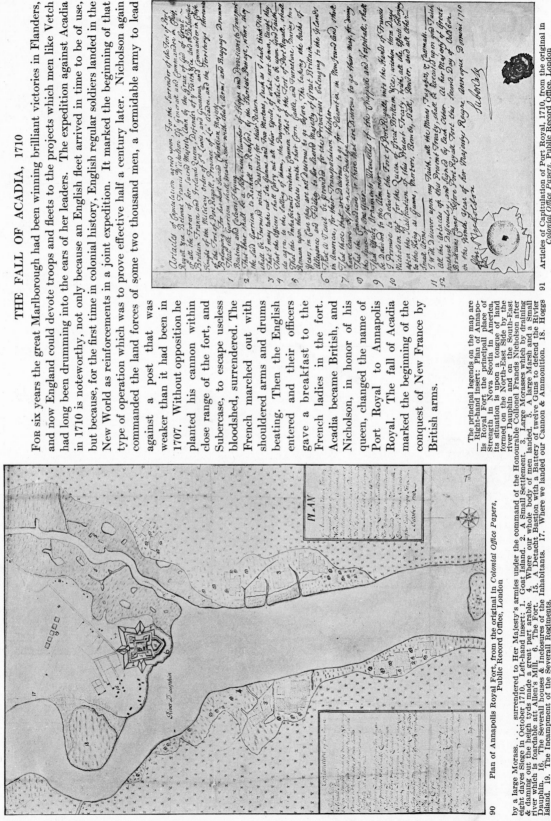

91 Articles of Capitulation of Port Royal, 1710, from the original in *Colonial Office Papers*, Public Record Office, London

The principal legends on the map are
—Right-hand insert: Plan of Annapolis Royal Fort, the principall place of Strength in Nova Scotia in America, its situation is upon a tongue of land formed on the North-East Side by the river Dauphin and on the South-East river which is fourdable att Allen's Mill. 6. The Fort. 16. The Severall houses & Inclosures of the Inhabitants. 17. Where we landed our Cannon & Ammonition. 18. Hoggs

90   Plan of Annapolis Royal Fort, from the original in *Colonial Office Papers*,
Public Record Office, London

by a large Morass. . . . surrendered to Her Majesty's armies under the command of the Honourable Collonel Francis Nicholson after eight dayes Siege in October 1710. Left-hand insert: 1. Goat Island. 2. A Small Settlement. 3. Large Morasses which by draining & damning out the helph tyds made a great part arable. 4. Where our whole body of men landed. 5. A large Marsh and a Small river which is fourdable att Allen's Mill. 6. The Fort. 15. A Detacht Bastion with a Battery of twelve Guns to defend the Rivier Dauphin. 16. The Severall houses & Inclosures of the Inhabitants. 17. Where we landed our Cannon & Ammonition. 18. Hoggs Island. 19. The Incampment of the Severall Regiments.

THE *PROVINCE GALLEY*, 1694–1714

As the New England armada that sailed against Quebec in 1690 formed the first joint naval and military expedition composed of purely American forces, so the *Province Galley* of 1694 may fairly be considered as the first purely professional American man-of-war. This Massachusetts vessel protected the fisheries, convoyed merchantmen, carried the Governors about the seaboard, took troops and munitions to the front, fought French privateers, hunted down pirates, and lent a ready hand against "Skulking partys of the barbarous Bloudie Salvages." In 1705, a new *Province Galley* replaced the original, costing two thousand pounds instead of one thousand, carrying eighteen guns, being seventy-two

92 View of the second *Province Galley*, derived from a vessel in the Burgis View of Boston, 1724, from the *Yearbook*, Society of Colonial Wars of Massachusetts, Boston, 1897

foot on the keel, having a twenty-four foot beam, and measuring one hundred and sixty tons. Her exact rig is apparently unknown. She carried twelve thirty-foot "oarrs." That admirable American seaman, Captain William Pickering, commanded her from 1707; and her full complement varied all the way up to one hundred and ten. Pay also varied, according to the exigencies of recruiting, from a shilling a day upwards, with increase according to rank:— "Voluntiers, not exceeding 12, ffourty shillings apiece p. month: ye Docter ffour pounds p. month." Rations were bounteous, especially when liquid: "1 pound of Bread, 3 Quarts of Beer, half pint peas, to a man p. Day. 2 Messe Pieces of Meat to 5 men p. Day." The "bread" was of course "ship's hard." "Rum here is non" wrote Commissary-General Belcher to Pickering on one occasion, but "there is some at Cape Ann." This gallant little ancestral man-of-war, now carrying twenty-four guns, formed part of the fleet that took Port Royal in 1710. Next year she was to have been the pilot vessel of the whole armada that sailed to disaster under Sir Hovenden Walker, but she reached the Boston rendezvous too late.

93 Muster Roll of the Second *Province Galley*, from the original in possession of the Essex Institute, Salem, Mass.

94 The Iroquois Chief Sa Ga Yeath Qua Pieth Tow, King of the Maquas, from mezzotint in the American Antiquarian Society, after the portrait by William Verelst

IROQUOIS CHIEFS IN ENGLAND

In the same year that Acadia fell, Pieter Schuyler sought to strengthen the friendship of the Iroquois by taking some of their leading braves to England, in order to win the favor of the Crown for further support of the military plans of the colonies against the French. Allies of such great importance must be treated with the consideration demanded by their power. The chiefs were presented to the Queen and were received by the Archbishop of Canterbury. Five sailed, one died. Their portraits were painted in London before they returned to their native woods.

95 The Iroquois Chief Etow Oh Koam, King of the River Nation, from mezzotint in the American Antiquarian Society, Worcester, Mass., after the portrait by Verelst

WALKER'S QUEBEC EXPEDITION, 1711

In 1711 a large fleet carrying a strong army sailed from England for Quebec, stopping at Boston to recruit men and provisions. Admiral Sir Hovenden Walker was the naval commander, while John Hill, brother of the queen's favorite, Mrs. Masham, led the land forces. England has rarely entrusted the lives of her soldiers and sailors and the defense of her honor to such incompetent leaders. An exceptional opportunity to take French Canada was wasted and hundreds of lives were uselessly lost because of criminal blundering. Yet Walker and Hill should not be made to bear the entire blame for the tragedy that followed. They were products of an age when a capricious favoritism raised incompetent adventurers to exalted rank and placed great responsibilities on shoulders quite incapable of carrying them. These two inglorious commanders expressed all too well the political and social code of their times.

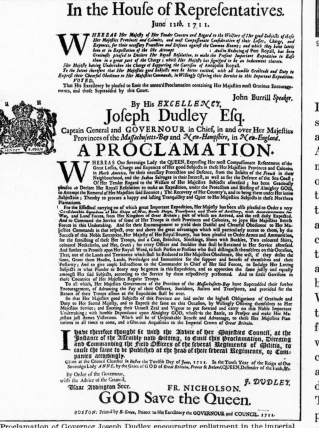

96 Proclamation of Governor Joseph Dudley encouraging enlistment in the imperial expedition against the French, from original in the Public Library, Boston

THE LAST FAILURE OF QUEEN ANNE'S WAR, 1711

SOME twelve thousand men, five thousand of them veterans from England, fifteen ships of the line, and forty-six transports, would, under a courageous and skillful leader, have inevitably taken Quebec. But Walker was not even a seaman of ability. At his feet alone must be laid the blame for the terrible disaster which befell his transports on the night of August 22, a disaster almost without parallel in British naval annals. Any seaman would have kept the southern shore. Walker, disregarding the advice of his pilot, insistently steered north. Too late he saw the white breakers foaming around Egg Island. Eight of his transports ran ashore; over nine hundred men were drowned. Yet still there was ample strength to move against Quebec; nor was the season by any means too far advanced. But Walker, distrusting his pilots, and fearful lest his ships should be crushed in the ice, counseled the abandonment of any further advance. Hill, who might have insisted, as was his place, that the expedition should continue, tamely agreed. Thus ended the last serious operation of the war. Hill was merely stupid while Walker added stubbornness to his folly.

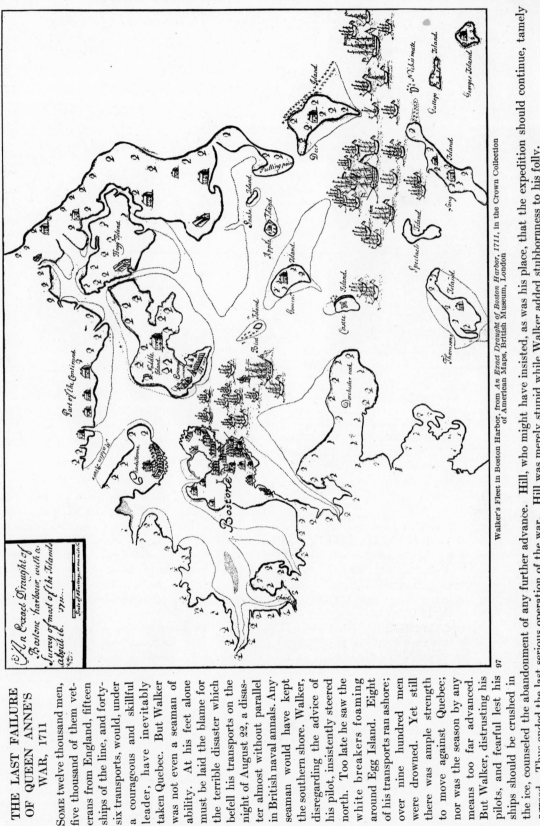

Walker's Fleet in Boston Harbor, from *An Exact Draught of Boston Harbor, 1711*, in the Crown Collection of American Maps, British Museum, London

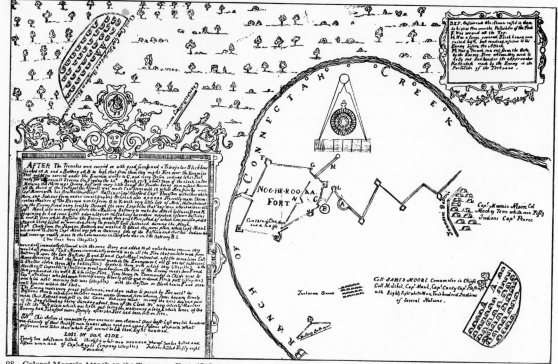

98   Colonel Moore's Attack on the Tuscarora Fort, 1713, from a tracing of the original plan in the South Carolina Historical Society, Charleston

THE TUSCARORA WAR, 1711–13

In North Carolina the white settlers encroached upon lands which the native Tuscaroras claimed. On September 22, 1711, twelve hundred Indians, in detached groups, fell suddenly upon the settlers along the frontier. For three days they pillaged and massacred, along the Roanoke, at Newbern, and at Bath. South Carolina sent aid to her "poor distressed brethren," a force of militia, and Indians from various tribes, under Colonel Barnwell, who drove the Tuscarora braves back to their wooden breastwork some twenty miles above Newbern. One furious fight (January 28, 1712), in which three hundred Indians were killed and one hundred made prisoners, gave the victory to Barnwell; and when peace was concluded, he returned home, much to the annoyance of the still anxious North Carolinians. As feared, the Tuscaroras continued the fight for their hunting grounds.

Governor Thomas Pollock was able, however, in September, 1712, to effect a treaty with Tom Blount, chief among the Tuscaroras, according to which Blount agreed not only to keep his own sections of the tribe neutral but also to capture and bring in Hancock, the most hostile of the chiefs. Again South Carolina sent help, dispatching a force of one hundred and fifty men under Colonel James Moore. About the middle of January, 1713, Moore marched his troops to Fort Reading on the Pamlico River, while the hostile Tuscaroras retired under Chief Hancock to their Fort Nohucke (Nooherooka in plan). On March 20 Moore laid siege. The operations were most skillfully conducted. Blockhouses were built of a height sufficient to enable the whites to fire down into the fort. An attempt was also made to mine beneath the walls, but as the powder was wet, it failed. Eight hundred of Hancock's warriors were taken prisoners, and many more slain. Moore's losses were fifty-eight killed and eighty wounded, of whom the majority were followers of Tom Blount.

99   Treaty signed between Gov. Thomas Pollock and Tom Blount, Sept. 1712, from the original in the Hall of History, Raleigh, N. C.

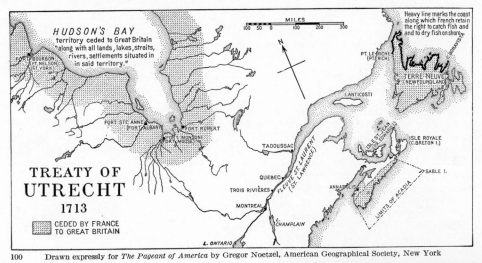

MILES
100 50 0   100   200   300

HUDSON'S BAY
territory ceded to Great Britain
"along with all lands, lakes, straits,
rivers, settlements situated in
in said territory."

Heavy line marks the coast
along which French retain
the right to catch fish and
and to dry fish on shore.

FORT BOURBON
(FT. NELSON)
(FT. YORK)

PT. LE RICHE
(PT. RICH)

TERRE-NEUVE
(NEWFOUNDLAND)

I. ANTICOSTI

ISLE ROYALE
(C. BRETON I.)

FORT STE. ANNE
(FORT ALBANY)
FORT RUPERT
FORT MONSONI
(FORT MOOSE)

TADOUSSAC

ISLE ST. JEAN
(PR. EDWARD I.)

SABLE I.

QUEBEC

ANNAPOLIS

TROIS RIVIÈRES

FLEUVE ST. LAURENT
(ST. LAWRENCE)

LIMITS OF ACADIA

MONTREAL

L. CHAMPLAIN

L. ONTARIO

**TREATY OF
UTRECHT
1713**

[ ] CEDED BY FRANCE
    TO GREAT BRITAIN

100   Drawn expressly for *The Pageant of America* by Gregor Noetzel, American Geographical Society, New York

THE TREATY OF UTRECHT, 1713

THE end of Queen Anne's War brought changes of the
utmost consequences for the future of both Europe and
America. The French prince retained the Spanish throne,
but at a heavy price. Gibraltar went to England, and
Spain signed the Asiento contract, in accordance with the
terms of which England supplied the Spanish colonies with
negro slaves. France gave up Newfoundland (except for
certain fishing rights) and the Hudson's Bay Territory.
Nova Scotia (with most of Acadia), conquered in 1710, was
retained by England. Finally, France recognized the
British protectorate over the Iroquois.

101   Governor Craven's Attack on the Yamasees, from
J. W. Barber, *Elements of General History*, New Haven, 1844

THE YAMASEES IN SOUTH CAROLINA, 1715

THROUGHOUT Queen Anne's War the Yamasees had supported the South Carolinians, had ravaged the
Spanish settlements to the south, and accompanied Barnwell and Moore against the Tuscaroras. But Spanish
intrigues and Spanish gifts, together with the questionable tactics of some English traders, turned them from
their alliance and precipitated
a series of appalling attacks.
Though the vigorous Governor Craven staved off an
impending disaster, in the
summer of 1715 South Carolina's plight was truly desperate. Twelve hundred whites
capable of bearing arms had
some eight thousand foes
with whom to contend. Fortunately, North Carolina and
Virginia sent men and guns.
Craven renewed the attack
so thoroughly that by February of 1716 the province was
practically cleared of Indians.
The tribe, settling upon Spanish territory in Florida,
continued their raids.

102   Contemporary account of the attack on the Yamasees, from the
Boston News Letter, June 13, 1715

A

In the House of Representatives November 17, 1724 ... Read again ... and in answer to his petition. Voted That His Honour the Lieut. Gov. be desired to Commissionate proper and suitable officers that may be agreeable to the Men offering to go out (not exceeding fifty in number) and that they keep exact Journals or accounts of the time they are out in the Woods, and where they go, as well the time they may be at home, or in any Town fitting to go out again, and that they be allowed two shillings and Six pence [p] diem each, the time they were actually out in the service, as to the time fitting out as aforesaid, they subsisting themselves, provided that the time of their being out in this service shall be until the session of this Court in May next: and for their further Encouragement they that be Entitled lover and above the two shillings as is six pence p diem the sum of One hundred pounds for each Male Scalp, and the other premiums established by Law to Volunteers without pay or Subsistence, and that the Commission officers have the loan of a sufficient number of Arms for the use of the Mohques & other Indians who may be willing to Enter & Engage with them in the service, the officers to be accountable for the Arms they receive.

In Council, Nov. 17. 1724. Sent up for Concurrence.
Read & Concur'd with the Clause.   *Wm Dudley Speaker*
Sent Down for Concurrence.

In the House of Representatives Nov. 17th 1724
Read and Concurred   *Wm Dudley Speaker*

103   Order, Nov. 17, 1724, authorizing Payment for Indian Scalps, from the original in the Massachusetts Archives, Boston

RÂLE'S, OR LOVEWELL'S, WAR, 1720–26

FOR a few years after the Treaty of Utrecht the harassed settlements on the Maine coast enjoyed peace. Their activity and growth again aroused the apprehensions of the Indians, who were instigated by the French to recommence the long list of raids. Chief among the Jesuit missionaries was Sebastian Râle, tireless enemy of the English, who was as ready to gird up his cassock for the war he believed necessary as he was to save souls. In the early years the Indians sacked many settlements, and attacked, though without success, an advanced fort at St. George's (see No. 63). The English finally sent out two expeditions which penetrated into the region of the Kennebec and Penobscot Rivers, destroyed the French missions, and completely broke the power of the Abnakis. Râle himself was killed. The exploits of Captain Lovewell, who led three different parties into the north, deserve particular mention.

LOVEWELL'S FIGHT NEAR FRYEBURG, MAINE, 1725

ON the upper part of the river Saco stood an Indian village, long the residence of a formidable tribe. Against this, in the last of his raids, Captain Lovewell directed his little group of forty men. Colonel Tyng transmitted to Governor Dummer the following account of the battle: "On the ninth of this instant, about nine or ten of the o'clock in the Morning, Capt. Lovewell saw an Indian on the opposite side of Sawco pond, & then they immediately left their packs and went about two miles before they came to him; they coming within five or six rods before they saw the Indian, and the Indian made the first shot at them, and wounded Capt. Lovewell, & Sam¹ Whiting, and they Immediately killed the Indian, & returning back to their packs

came within forty or fifty rods of them; the Indians Waylaid them under the banks of a little Brook capt. Lovewell's men being between the brook and the Pond, it being a Pine Plain, the Indians fired upon them both in the front and the rear, shouting & running towards them."

The Indian ambuscade had been successful. Desperate, indeed, was the situation of the party with only one officer remaining unhurt. This man, Ensign Wyman, seems to have directed the retreat of Lovewell's men to the shore of the pond where the water protected their rear. Here occurred, in the words of Parkman, "one of the most obstinate and deadly bush-fights in the annals of New England." The Indians were superior to the whites in the utilization of cover but the latter were better shots. The forest echoed with the firing and the yells of the hostiles. At one stage of the battle the redskins retired for a time to hold an incantation which would procure victory. Seth Wyman, creeping through the bush, shot and killed the chief conjurer. After dark the Indians withdrew without stopping to scalp the fallen. Nine only of the men engaged in the fray remained unhurt. About midnight the men who could, started on their way to the nearest fort. Early the next year the Indians made a lasting peace.

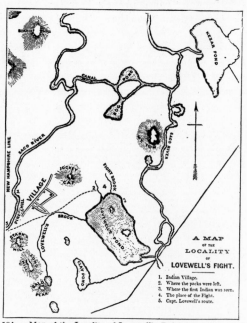

104   Map of the Locality of Lovewell's Fight, from the Bouton Edition of *Lovewell's Great Fight*, Concord, N. H., 1861

KING GEORGE'S WAR

EIGHT years after Lovewell's last fight European diplomacy began to lay the foundations for the next great war. In 1733 France and Spain united in the so-called Family Compact, aimed primarily at England. Six years later the growing tension between English traders and Spanish officials in North America finally snapped and war broke out. The contest soon merged into a larger one, the War of the Austrian Succession, with Prussia and France against Austria and England. The issues were the European balance of power, commerce and colonial possessions. Edward Vernon became the first English hero of the conflict. He was one of those hearty, bluff, devil-may-care sea-dogs who are bound to become popular heroes whenever they get the chance. He had told his fellow politicians that "Porto Bello, the port for the Spanish treasure ships in the Carri-

105   Admiral Edward Vernon, from the portrait by Thomas Gainsborough (1727–88), in the National Portrait Gallery, London

bean, could be taken with six ships." At the outset of the war he led a successful raid against it. But Cartagena, on the north shore of South America and not far east of the Isthmus of Panama, was the key stronghold of the Spaniards. In 1741 Vernon commanded a mighty naval expedition against it.

106   Lawrence Washington, from the portrait, artist unknown, in possession of Mrs. Lawrence Washington, Washington, D. C.

COLONIAL TROOPS FOR CARTAGENA, 1741

A CALL for aid for the army that accompanied Vernon against Cartagena was sent out to the American colonies. "Of the English colonies to the northward, Virginia and Massachusetts furnished five hundred men each to the military force which was engaged. Only about fifty of the Massachusetts men returned." — JUSTIN WINSOR, *Narrative and Critical History*, Vol. 8, p. 292. The able and beloved Governor Gooch of Virginia commanded the colonials, and won grudging praise from his British superiors. Captain Lawrence Washington went in the Virginia contingent and conceived such an admiration for the naval commander that he called his estate on the Potomac, Mount Vernon. An old story, apparently without proof, has it that Lawrence Washington's younger brother George acquired at Cartagena his first taste for the noble profession of arms, obtained a midshipman's warrant, and was only prevented from becoming a regular naval officer by his mother's opposition.

107   From the painting *The Call of the Sea*, by J. L. G. Ferris, in Independence Hall, Philadelphia

108   *A Perspective Draught of the Town, Harbour & Forts of Cartagena, published according to Act of Parliament, 1741,*
from an engraving in the Print Room, British Museum

VERNON'S FLEET LAYS SIEGE TO CARTAGENA

NEVER before had the New World seen so formidable a fleet as that which Vernon commanded: fifty vessels of war, thirty-seven of them ships of the line, carrying eighteen hundred and twenty guns. The accompanying map shows the difficulties which an attack on Cartagena presented. The city was inaccessible from the sea, being protected by rocks and surf. The only entrance to the harbor, so narrow that but one ship could pass at a time, was defended by three strong forts on the side nearest the city, and by one fort and a fascine battery on the Barradera side. The inner harbor was likewise guarded by forts, and between them was a narrow shoal, on either side of which galleons had been sunk. Vernon, early in March, silenced the two small forts, and the army was put ashore. By the end of March the Barradera battery had been taken by assault, and the chief fort opposite taken with the aid of the fleet. The Spaniards sank several ships in the outer harbor, deserted or blew up the forts guarding the inner harbor, and retired to the town. Only one outpost remained uncaptured, Fort St. Lazarre on the hill overlooking the city, and there was little reasonable doubt that Cartagena would fall. Vernon seems to have felt that his work was done, and that the army could finish the task without him. He stubbornly refused to lend the necessary support of the fleet to the attack on Fort St. Lazarre, and Wentworth's assault, early in April, was repulsed with heavy loss. Meanwhile sickness increased at an alarming rate, and the Spanish continued to strengthen their fortifications. A stormy council of war, in which Vernon hinted at the disloyalty of the army, ended in a decision to re-embark the troops and make for Jamaica. It is the story of this siege, with its sharp fighting, its terrible toll of fever victims, which Smollett, a ship's surgeon at the time, tells so effectively in *Roderick Random.*

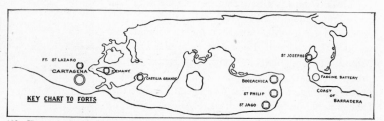

109   Key to the fortifications at Cartagena, detail enlarged from *A Perspective Draught of the Town, Harbour & Forts of Cartagena, published according to Act of Parliament, 1741,* from an engraving in the Print Room, British Museum

SANTIAGO DE CUBA, 1741

BOTH Vernon and Wentworth deserved recall, yet they were allowed to plan another expedition the same year against Cuba. Havana, the central port, was avoided, and Santiago attacked. Again dissension arose between the commanders, and Wentworth lay for three months, not three miles from the town itself, while his army steadily succumbed to the fever. Shirley's optimism had no basis, and most of the colonists who enlisted found foreign graves instead of glory. In late November the attempt was abandoned.

OGLETHORPE'S OPERATIONS IN GEORGIA, 1740–42

KING GEORGE'S WAR brought to a head the trouble that had been fomenting between the Spanish and English over the Florida boundary question. As early as 1738, Oglethorpe had brought troops from England, and upon the declaration of war he made plans for raising colonial forces from both South Carolina and Georgia and attacking the Spaniards. St. Augustine, where about six hundred Spanish troops were stationed, could have been easily reached by the St. John's River and a short march overland.

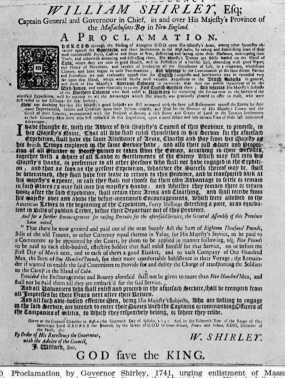

110 Proclamation by Governor Shirley, 1741, urging enlistment of Massachusetts troops for the West Indies, in the Massachusetts Historical Society, Boston

In addition, a small British fleet under Peter Warren was ready to give assistance. But Oglethorpe, with his superior force of two thousand men, wasted much time in useless marches up and down the peninsula between the mouth of St. John's and St. Augustine; and when finally his army was placed before the city, he took no effective measures for success. Some sharp fighting occurred, but nothing was accomplished.

Two years later the positions were reversed, a Spanish fleet and army appearing off the Georgian coast. But it was even worse led than Oglethorpe's expedition had been, and after a few fierce skirmishes, during which Oglethorpe and his men bravely defended Fort Frederica, the Spaniards sailed away.

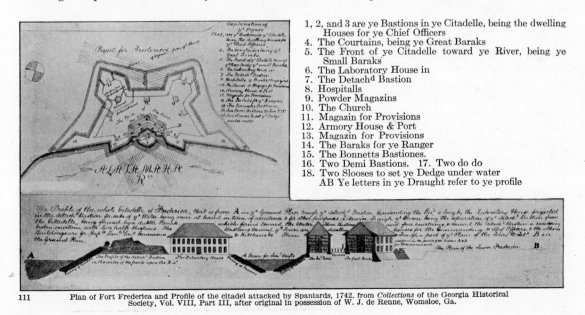

1, 2, and 3 are ye Bastions in ye Citadelle, being the dwelling Houses for ye Chief Officers
4. The Courtains, being ye Great Baraks
5. The Front of ye Citadelle toward ye River, being ye Small Baraks
6. The Laboratory House in
7. The Detach^d Bastion
8. Hospitalls
9. Powder Magazins
10. The Church
11. Magazin for Provisions
12. Armory House & Port
13. Magazin for Provisions
14. The Baraks for ye Ranger
15. The Bonnetts Bastiones.
16. Two Demi Bastions. 17. Two do do
18. Two Slooses to set ye Dedge under water
   AB Ye letters in ye Draught refer to ye profile

111   Plan of Fort Frederica and Profile of the citadel attacked by Spaniards, 1742, from *Collections* of the Georgia Historical Society, Vol. VIII, Part III, after original in possession of W. J. de Renne, Womsloe, Ga.

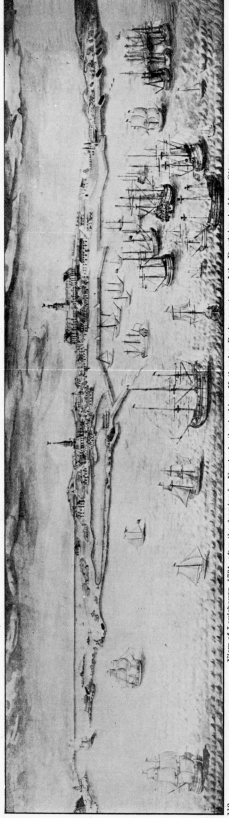

View of Louisbourg, 1731, after the drawing by Verrier in the Archives Nationales, Paris, courtesy of the Dominion Archives, Ottawa

112

LOUISBOURG, 1731, THE CANADIAN GIBRALTAR

IF Cartagena was the stronghold of the Spanish Main, Louisbourg was the Gibraltar of the Gulf of St. Lawrence. France was loth to believe that Acadia was lost forever. Cape Breton Island remained in French possession. On the south shore of this island, toward the eastern end, is a good harbor, ice free, and easy of defense against the type of fighting of the eighteenth century. Here, after the Treaty of Utrecht, France planned a great stronghold which would serve a triple purpose. It would menace the English who ruled the French habitants of Acadia not far to the west. It would provide a base for possible raids upon New England ships and fishing boats passing by it not far off-shore, *en route* to England or to the Grand Banks. And, last of all, it would provide an outer defense for the Gulf of St. Lawrence, its reduction being necessary before any hostile force could appear before Quebec. The fortress of Louisbourg was meant to be, but never really was, like the view above. Dishonest officials stole most of the money and the best materials. Nor was the garrison much better. Of the two thousand men who could be collected for a siege, two-thirds were badly trained militiamen, while half the regulars were "pay-fighting Swiss." Nevertheless, Louisbourg had some strength as a fortress and more importance as the only seaboard link with France.

THE LOUISBOURG EXPEDITION FROM NEW ENGLAND, 1745

WHEN England and France came to grips in King George's War, Massachusetts was led by Governor William Shirley. He shared the common belief that Louisbourg was a menace to New England. New Englanders required little persuasion to aid in an expedition of such obviously vital importance to them. Once the die was cast, war feeling ran high. Massachusetts raised about three thousand men, and Connecticut and New Hampshire added about five hundred each. New York lent some very useful guns. An English naval force, arriving in the Gulf of St. Lawrence, ensured the command of the sea, which was vital to the success of the expedition.

113 William Shirley, 1693–1771, Colonial Governor of Massachusetts, from the portrait, painter unknown, in the State House, Boston

SIR WILLIAM PEPPERELL IN CHIEF COMMAND

THE command of the colonial attacking force was given to William Pepperell (1696-1759). He was an excellent militiaman from Maine, alert, successful in business, one of the richest men in the colonies, honest in politics, cool in a crisis, shrewd in his judgments, and very popular with his fellow-countrymen. All three provinces made him a major-general. He went through with flying colors, and was promoted to lieutenant-general by the king, who also made him the first and only baronet of Massachusetts.

114   From the portrait of Pepperell by George A. Ward in the Essex Institute, Salem, Mass.

115   From the portrait of Warren attributed to John Smibert, about 1645, in the Portsmouth (N. H.) Athenaeum

COMMODORE PETER WARREN, OF THE ROYAL NAVY

WARREN had married an American and was very popular with "my wife's fellow-countrymen." His four British men-of-war, carrying one hundred and eighty guns, and eleven hundred and fifty men, were essential to the success of this great New England expedition; for he alone could have fought off a French flying squadron and maintained a close blockade. He took the fine French frigate *Vigilant* with all her stores bound for Louisbourg, and in addition made a great haul of very rich prizes. No wonder the Provincials were disgusted at the booty found in Louisbourg itself, which was poor when the siege began and ruined when it ended.

YANKEE FIGHTING VESSELS AT LOUISBOURG

THERE were thirteen Provincial armed vessels, carrying over one thousand men. The *Massachusetts* was commandeered on the stocks at Portsmouth, put in charge of Captain Edward Tyng, armed with forty guns, and given one hundred and fifty men. The *Molineux* and *Fame* were full-rigged ships of the same kind. There were also three snows, one of which, the *Shirley*, was taken into the Royal navy, together with her Yankee skipper, John Rous, who became a regular post captain, R.N. The New Englanders were exceedingly able sailors, for that age. When about one hundred transports are added, it will be seen

116   Frigate *Massachusetts*, enlargement from a chart in James Gibson, *A Journal of the Late Siege by the Troops from North America . . .*, London, 1745

what a very large fleet and convoy New England sent to Louisbourg. As a matter of fact, it was more natural, at that time, for New England to send seamen than landsmen on any distant enterprise, because her people depended mostly on the sea for both the necessities and the luxuries of life.

117   Hauling the Yankee Guns at Louisbourg, drawn expressly for *The Pageant of America* by C. W. Jefferys

THE NEW ENGLANDERS LAND IN FORCE

THE American attackers on shore were double the number of the whole French garrison; and the American and British sailors added together brought the grand total odds up to four against one. Yet this detracts nothing from the magnificent work done in getting up the guns. So bad was the surf that a boat was lost for every gun landed; and so terribly obstructive were the rocks and bushes and, far worse still, the slimy, bottomless bogs, that two hundred men had to tow each siege gun up on a Meservé sleigh sixteen feet long by five in the beam.

Meservé was a New England shipbuilder who performed sterling services in the final war. The entire army at Louisbourg was purely American and over four thousand strong. Add the one thousand aboard the Yankee fighting vessels, and the two thousand more who worked the Yankee transports, and the greatness of New England's effort will appear in its true light, especially when one considers the smallness of the population and the recent losses in the West Indies. "Pepperell was without engineers; he had a few skilled artillerists, with experience on New England privateers worrying French and Spanish commerce, and Warren lent him several from the fleet; but neither the general nor his men understood the first principles of the arts of siege. Yet his landing, at the head of Gabarus Bay, on April 30 and May 1, was rather skilfully performed; the French outposts were easily driven in, batteries were soon established, and the English securely intrenched." — R. G. THWAITES, *France in America*, 1905. The *Bethel* (belonging to the Quincy family of Boston) was not at Louisbourg.

118   Letter-of-Marque Ship *Bethel*, a pre-Revolutionary ship, from a painting, artist unknown, in the Massachusetts Historical Society, Boston

119   Landing the New England Forces, from an engraving by Brooks, in possession of J. Collins Warren, Boston, after a painting by Stevens

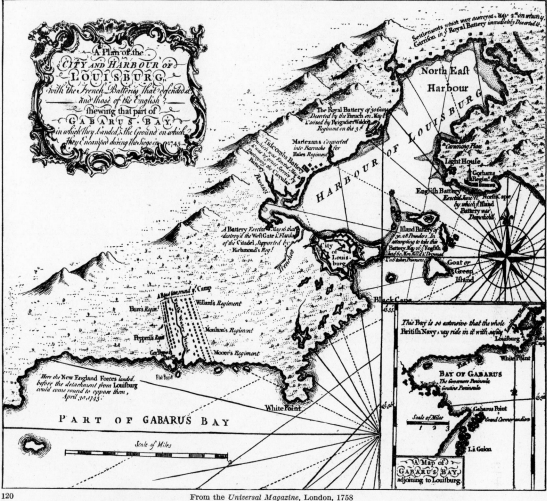

CAPTURE OF THE GRAND BATTERY BY VAUGHAN

FROM the walls of their fort, the French watched anxiously the vigorous preparations of the Americans. The first important event in the capture of Louisbourg was the taking of the Royal Battery, where thirty-five French guns were mounted. "On the 2nd of May Vaughan led four hundred men to the hills near the town (Louisbourg) and saluted it with three cheers, — somewhat to the discomposure of the French, though they describe the unwelcome visitors as a disorderly crowd. Vaughan's next proceeding pleased them less. He marched behind the hills, in rear of the Grand Battery [Royal Battery], to the northeast arm of the harbor, where there were extensive magazines of naval stores. These his men set on fire, and the pitch, tar and other combustibles made a prodigious smoke. He was returning, in the morning, with a small party of followers behind the hills, when coming opposite the Grand Battery, and observing it from the ridge, he saw neither flag on the flagstaff, nor smoke from the barrack chimneys. One of his party was a Cape Cod Indian. Vaughan bribed him with a flask of brandy which he had in his pocket, — though, as the clerical historian takes pains to assure us, he never used it himself, — and the Indian, pretending to be drunk, or, as some say, mad, staggered towards the battery to reconnoitre. All was quiet. He clambered in at an embrasure and found the place empty. The rest of the party followed, and one of them, William Tufts, of Medford, a boy of eighteen, climbed the flagstaff, holding in his teeth his red coat, which he made fast at the top as a substitute for the British flag, — a proceeding which drew upon him a volley of unsuccessful cannon-shot from the town batteries. Vaughan then sent this hasty note to Pepperell: 'May it please your Honour to be informed that by the grace of God and the courage of 13 men, I entered the Royal Battery about 9 o'clock, and am waiting for a reinforcement and a flag.'" — FRANCIS PARKMAN, *A Half-Century of Conflict*, 1892, II, 116–17.

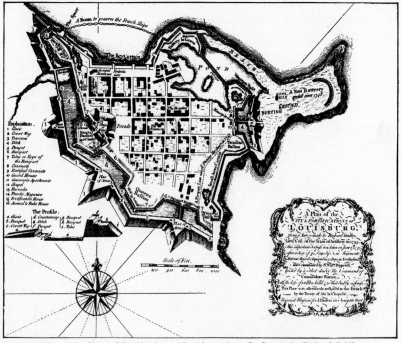

121   Major Seth Pomeroy's Journal, original in the Forbes Library, Northampton, Mass.,
                    courtesy of George E. Pomeroy, Toledo, O.

BOMBARDMENT OF LOUISBOURG

THE Royal Battery was indeed a military prize. "Brigadeer Waldo was sent to occupy the battery with his regiment, and Major Seth Pomeroy, the gun-smith, with twenty soldier-mechanics, was set at drilling out the spiked touch-holes of the cannon. These were twenty-eight forty-two-pounders, and two eighteen-pounders. Several were ready for use the next morning, and immediately opened on the town, — which, writes a soldier in his diary, 'damaged the houses and made the women cry.' 'The enemy,' says the *Habitant de Louisbourg*, 'saluted us with our own cannon, and made a terrific fire, smashing everything within range.' The English occupation of the Grand Battery may be called the decisive event of the siege." — FRANCIS PARKMAN, *A Half Century of Conflict*, II, 117.

THE SURRENDER

THIS was a most eccentric siege; and the attackers would have paid dearly for their rashness, 'prentice gunnery, and absurd councils of war, if the defenders had been better shots and under better discipline. But in zeal, devoted courage, readiness of resource, undauntable endurance against the most trying hardships, as in their invincible will to win, the American Provincials left nothing to be desired. Louisbourg surrendered after a prolonged bombardment just as the Provincials were preparing for an assault. The Americans were disgusted when the anticipated plunder failed to materialize, due apparently to the terms of surrender, but much more to the poverty of Louisbourg.

122   A Plan of the City and Fortifications of Louisbourg from the Survey by Richard Gridley,
                    1745, from the *Universal Magazine*, London, 1758

Explanation of the Plan: 1. Glacis. 2. Covert-Way. 3. Traverses. 4. Ditch. 5. Parapet. 6. Rampart. 7. Talus or Slope of the Rampart. 8. Cazemats. 9. Fortified Cazemats. 10. Guard Houses. 11. Governor's Apartments. 12. Chapel. 13. Barracks. 14. Powder Magazine. 15. Fortification House. 16. Arsenal and Bake House.   The Profile: a. Glacis. b. Banquet. c. Covert Way. d. Counterscarp. e. Ditch. f. Parapet. g. Banquet. h. Rampart. i. Talus.

REJOICING AND THANKSGIVING OVER LOUISBOURG

On July 3, 1745, at one A.M., Captain Bennett arrived in Boston with news of the capitulation of Louisbourg and the reduction of Cape Breton. By daybreak excited crowds filled the streets, and the whole city rejoiced over Pepperell's brilliant achievement. Salutes were fired, bells pealed and the celebrations continued throughout that day and night with fire-works, bonfires and il-luminations in every house. The following Thursday was set as a day of Thanksgiving. New York and Phila-delphia also honored the event, and in England His Majesty and the Lords Justices expressed their approbation by causing salutes to be fired, and by sending Pepperell a gift of five hundred guineas. Shir-ley was modest in writ-ing to the Board of Trade. "I may be permitted to say in jus-tice to His Majesty's New England subjects that their behavior has done no dishonor to his Arms." But sorrow followed hard on the heels of rejoicing. So foul was the state of the fort after the siege that a pestilence broke out which carried off nearly nine hundred of the garrison of twenty-five hundred which Pepperell had left. Massachusetts had spent £183,469 on the expedition. The British Government made good the money which the thrifty Puritans promptly and wisely devoted to the redemption of their wretchedly depreciated paper currency.

123   Governor Shirley's Proclamation for a general Thanksgiving, in the Massachusetts Historical Society, Boston

124   Doggerel verse on the taking of Cape Breton, 1745, in possession of the New York Historical Society

125   Canton of a flag carried at Louisbourg, source unknown,
       in the New York Historical Society

INTER–COLONIAL COÖPERATION

MASSACHUSETTS had furnished the leader of the Louisbourg expedition, and to Pepperell's native colony
has been given the credit for the brilliant victory.
Immediately subordinate to him, however, was Major-
General Wolcott of Connecticut, commanding the
five hundred and sixteen men, constituting his colony's
contribution. New Hampshire issued paper money
to provision its five hundred troops. The Governor
of Rhode Island commissioned a regiment, of which
three companies actually embarked for Louisbourg.
The middle colonies coöperated with money and
supplies, New York with ten eighteen-pound cannon
and £5000, New Jersey with £2000, Pennsylvania
with £4000.

THE PROPOSED SEQUEL TO LOUISBOURG

SHIRLEY was aflame with broad plans of further conquest. The
British Government accepted his revival of the "Glorious Enterprise,"
which embodied a joint land-and-sea expedition against Quebec, along
the lines of Lake Champlain and the St. Lawrence. The colonies
now raised some three thousand men, who gathered at Albany, where
the Iroquois agreed to join the expedition. But the English contingent never came; and for nearly a year the colonials remained uselessly under arms. Then fears of French aggression suddenly replaced
all hopes of an immediate conquest.

THE REAL SEQUEL TO LOUISBOURG, 1746

FRANCE determined to avenge the fall of Louisbourg, and in 1746 dispatched a fleet under D'Anville for the New England coast. This was
to the British Colonies of 1746 even more alarming than the Spanish
Armada had been to England; for no Drake now stopped the way.
Exaggeration and apprehension grew rife. Massachusetts or Virginia
could alone have defeated any force that D'Anville could have landed.

But no one knew
that then. The
Reverend Thomas
Prince's litany, as
rhymed later on, expressed what many another preacher
also felt:

> O Lord! We do not advise;
> But if, in Thy Providence,
> A Tempest should arise,
> To drive the French fleet hence,
> And scatter it far and wide,
> Or sink it in the sea,
> We should be satisfied,
> And Thine the Glory be.

As a matter of fact, this pious request had been answered
before it had been made; for the fleet had already begun
to suffer from storm and disease to such an extent that its
end, without any battle, was as bad as that of the Spanish

A N
ACCOUNT
OF THE
TREATY
Held at the CITY of

Albany, in the Province of *NEW-YORK*,

By HIS EXCELLENCY the

Governor of that PROVINCE,

And the HONOURABLE the

COMMISSIONERS for the Provinces

OF

MASSACHUSETTS, CONNECTICUT,

AND

PENNSYLVANIA,

WITH THE

INDIANS

OF THE

SIX NATIONS,

In *OCTOBER*, 1745.

PHILADELPHIA.
Printed by B. FRANKLIN, at the NEW-PRINTING-OFFICE,
near the Market, M,DCC,XLVI.

126   Title-page of an account of the treaty under
which the Six Nations agreed to join an expedition to Quebec in 1745, copy in the New York
Public Library

127   Duke D'Anville's Fleet, from J. W. Barber, *Interesting
Events in the History of the United States*, New Haven, 1832

Armada. When peace was finally signed at Aix-la-Chapelle in 1748, the conditions were laid down in Europe.
Louisbourg was restored to France, in accordance with the general plan of restoration, and New England
saw her greatest effort come to nothing.

View of Louisbourg, 1745 (following the capture), from a painting, artist unknown, in possession of the family of Everett P. Wheeler, New York

THE TREATY OF AIX-LA-CHAPELLE, 1748

The Treaty of Aix-la-Chapelle which brought to an end the War of the Austrian Succession was little more than a truce. All the mutual conquests in America were returned to their original possessors. With deep dissatisfaction the people of New England saw the French flag again flying above the ramparts of Louisbourg. But England's exigency was great. During the war France had won a position in the Low Countries so menacing to Britain that the return of Louisbourg seemed a fair exchange for French evacuation of the Netherlands. But the Americans looked only at the conditions on their own continent. To them the giving up of Louisbourg was the work of politicians who were blind and stupid as well as corrupt.

128

CHAPTER III

THE CLIMAX OF THE FRENCH AND INDIAN WARS, 1749–63

THE decisive struggle for supremacy in North America differed greatly from the earlier wars. These had consisted mostly of sporadic raids and counterstrokes, with an occasional minor naval and military expedition. Except for Sir Hovenden Walker's fiasco in 1711 (No. 97) no really important force of regulars had ever come out; while the colonies were far too small for any large efforts of their own. But, by the middle of this century, England had become convinced that France, not Holland, was to be her oversea competitor; while in America the westward urge of British settlement, though only just beginning, was surely foreshadowing another inevitable clash with the French, who regarded the Ohio valley as a necessary link with the western fur trade and Louisiana. Both sides eventually sent out really important European fleets and armies, while raising larger local contingents, and employing Indians as before. Regular sieges, pitched battles, and warfare on a comparatively great scale were the direct result.

To Europeans this momentous period became known as that of the Seven Years War (1756–63). For Americans it became more appropriately known as that of the final French and Indian War. But, in the naval and military sense, by far the best of its three historic names is the one its imperial aspect bore in contemporary England, where the immensely pregnant issues of this "Maritime War," fought out to decide the oversea dominion of the world, depended more upon British sea power than upon any other factor in the whole vast problem of empire, trade, and colonies combined. All the great central and finally decisive forces, on both the warring sides, were European, not American; and so the actual forces arrayed against each other in America depended for their fighting lives on keeping in touch with Europe, which of course implied safe Atlantic transportation, which, in its turn, depended on superior sea power, both mercantile and naval. Moreover, America itself was full of inland waterways, many of which were directly, and all of which were indirectly, dependent on sea power; while transportation along these waterways was, at the very least, a hundred times better than transport by land. Thus, wherever we turn, we find sea power the predominant force deciding the fate of French or British in America. The enormously superior English and American-Colonial mercantile marine helped trade and immigration at every turn, while the inferiority of the French marine hindered even alliance with the Indians, who, when free to move about, could get much better and cheaper trade goods from the British.

The final struggle was heralded by the claims the French and British were asserting against each other, especially in the Ohio valley, where George Washington made his first historic appearance in 1753, when asserting the demands of Virginia. Next year the French enforced their counterclaims when he surrendered Fort Necessity. In 1755, Braddock's defeat was a bad start for the British regulars, who thenceforward came out in much greater numbers. Moreover, in the next four years the great Montcalm won four other victories for France. But in 1758 the mighty war minister Pitt, getting all the available resources of the British empire well in hand, won the three successive campaigns of Louisbourg, Quebec, and Montreal, that sealed the fate of New France.

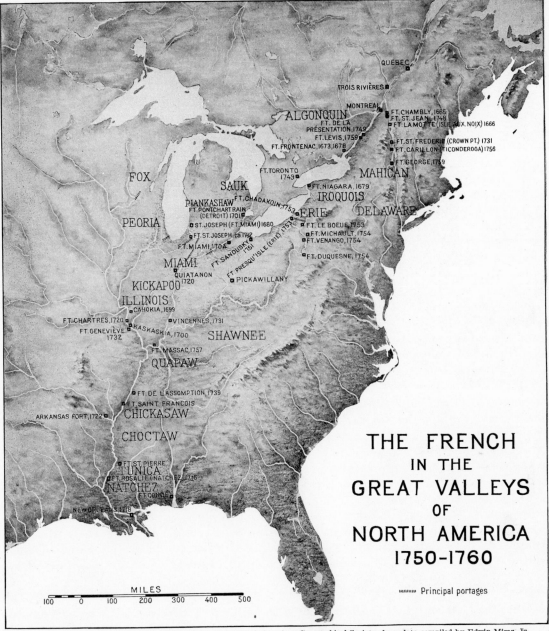

THE FRENCH
IN THE
GREAT VALLEYS
OF
NORTH AMERICA
1750-1760

␣␣␣␣␣␣␣ Principal portages

129 Drawn expressly for *The Pageant of America* by Gregor Noetzel, American Geographical Society, from data compiled by Edwin Mims, Jr.

THE FRENCH DREAM OF AN INLAND EMPIRE

BASED upon prior rights of discovery and exploration, strengthened by the work of missionaries and the erection of forts, the French claim to the great interior valleys of North America challenges our attention and compels our respect (see map, Vol. I, p. 315). To introduce the civilization of France into a region that stretched from the St. Lawrence to New Orleans, and included the Great Lakes, was a magnificent conception, worthy of the great Frenchmen who had labored to execute it. But it also was a scheme of unparalleled audacity, this conquest of a wilderness by a mere handful of missionaries, soldiers, and traders in fur. The French sought to achieve it by using all the arts by which the white man has molded the savage to his purposes. Governors of forts and territories devoted their best efforts to the difficult game of Indian diplomacy. By bribes, threats, and promises they sought to turn the Indian from the English and bind him to themselves.

THE FRENCH AND INDIAN WAR
Showing dates of battles and the forts involved

130   Drawn expressly for *The Pageant of America* by Gregor Noetzel, American Geographical Society, New York

THE BATTLEGROUND OF THE FRENCH AND INDIAN WAR

In 1690 France had aimed at holding the three great gulfs (Hudson's Bay, St. Lawrence, Mexico), the four great rivers (St. Lawrence, Mohawk-Hudson, Ohio, Mississippi) and the five Great Lakes. But now, in 1750, she had lost Hudson's Bay; her Louisbourg outpost on the Gulf of St. Lawrence, like the whole Gulf of Mexico, lay at the mercy of superior sea power; she had lost her Mohawk-Hudson chance; the Ohio and Mississippi could not be held for very long against the vastly outnumbering British Americans; the five Great Lakes would become hopelessly isolated; and so the Lower St. Lawrence alone offered any safe foothold for the time being; and this would in the end belong to whichever side became decisively predominant at sea.

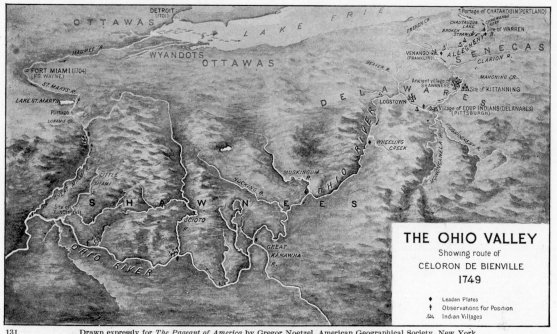

131   Drawn expressly for *The Pageant of America* by Gregor Noetzel, American Geographical Society, New York,
based on contemporary sketch map by Father Bonnechamp

CÉLORON'S LEADEN PLATES

IN 1749, Céloron de Bienville, partly as an enduring token of the French claim to both sides of the Ohio and Allegheny Rivers, partly as a method of impressing the Indians, traveled south along the rivers from Lake Erie, burying leaden plates at various places, near Warren, Pennsylvania, Franklin, Wheeling, West Virginia, Marietta, Ohio, Point Pleasant and Portsmouth, Ohio. One was stolen almost immediately by the Senecas, who brought it to William Johnson; another, represented in the photograph, was found near the mouth of Great Kanawha River. Freely translated, it reads:

"In the year 1749, in the reign of Louis XV, King of France, We, Céloron, commandant of a detachment sent by the Marquis de la Galissonière, Commandant in Chief of New France, to re-establish peace in certain villages of the Indians of these districts, have buried this plate at the mouth of the river Chinodahichetha, the eighteenth of August, near the Ohio, or Beautiful river, as a monument of the renewal of the possession that we have taken of the said river Ohio, of all its tributaries, and of all the lands on both sides to the sources of the said rivers, as the preceding Kings of France have enjoyed or sought to have enjoyed it, and which they have maintained by force of arms and by treaties, especially by those of Ryswick, Utrecht, and Aix-la-Chapelle." This plate vividly recalls France's efforts to establish its power in North America.

132   From the original leaden plate with inscription by Céloron de Bienville, in the Virginia
Historical Society, Richmond

133 First page of the journal of Christopher Gist, from T. Pownall,
A Topographical Description of Such Parts of North America, etc., London, 1776

CHRISTOPHER GIST AND THE OHIO COMPANY

MEANWHILE, the colonies of Pennsylvania, Maryland, and Maryland, whose back settlements stretched
toward the Ohio, were taking steps to gain for themselves some portion of the lucrative Indian trade, and
to protect their settlements.   The Ohio Company,
formed in 1748 by a London merchant and prominent men of Virginia, obtained from the Crown a
grant of two hundred thousand acres on the Ohio.
If they settled a hundred families upon it within
seven years, they were to have three hundred
thousand acres more.   The purpose was fourfold:
trade with the Indians, settlement, protection for the
frontier, and resistance to the French claim of owner-
ship.   The Company erected a storehouse near the
mouth of Wills Creek, a tributary of the Potomac,
commenced to build a road toward the west, and in
1750 sent Christopher Gist, an able woodsman, to
survey the Ohio region for fertile locations for settlement.   In 1752, the French, alarmed by this determined and dangerous intrusion, broke up the English
trading-post at Pickawillany (near the present Piqua,
Ohio) and carried off a few prisoners to Canada.
The whole story affords an excellent illustration of
the method so often adopted of extending the
authority of the British flag, through the activities
of a private company, organized primarily for trade.

YOUNG WASHINGTON'S MISSION TO THE OHIO

IN 1752 the Marquis Duquesne succeeded Jonquière
as Governor-General of Canada.   Energetic and ambitious, he determined to extend southward the sphere
of French occupation and control.   In January, 1753, he dispatched an expedition under Morin, who in June
completed an imposing fort at the strategic point, which was called by the new occupants, Presqu'-Isle (see
map, No. 130).   Only a hundred men, however, were left as guards, the remainder pushing on southward to

the headwaters of Le Boeuf River, or
French Creek, where they built a
second fort.   Because of the lateness of
the season the contemplated third
fort was not begun, and most of the
force returned to Quebec, leaving a
large garrison force at Le Boeuf, and
a small advance post at Venango.
Their movements alarmed Robert
Dinwiddie, the shrewd, capable Scotch
Governor of Virginia, who dispatched
young George Washington, then
twenty-one years of age, with Gist as
guide, to carry a letter to the French
commandant in the region, requesting
him to depart from lands so "noto-
riously" known to belong to the King
of England.   Washington set out in
November, 1753.

134   Washington on the way to Ohio, 1753, from the sculpture by Gutzon Borglum
at the National Sculpture Society Exhibition, New York, 1925

THE MEETING WITH THE FRENCH OFFICERS

WASHINGTON passed by the frontier fort on Wills Creek, Fort Cumberland, by the forks of the Ohio, by Logstown, and came to Venango (see map, No. 130). Here the French commander Joncaire-Chabert, a former lieutenant of Céloron in the expedition of 1749, replied with emphasis, at times profane, that the French meant to keep the Ohio. The Virginian went north to Fort Le Boeuf (on the site of Franklin) to the French commandant, Legardeur de St. Pierre, who politely refused to quit his post until ordered to do so by the Marquis Duquesne, Governor-General of Canada. Washington bore the Frenchman's reply to Dinwiddie,

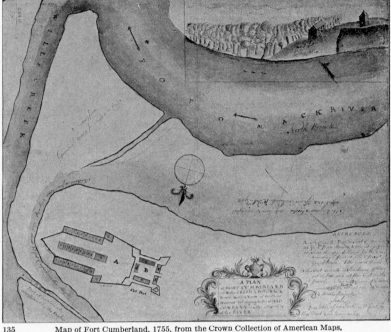

135   Map of Fort Cumberland, 1755, from the Crown Collection of American Maps, British Museum, London

A. The Parade. *B.* The Fort Parade. *a.* Officers' Houses. *b.* The Magazine. *c.* Storehouses. *d.* House for Commanding Officer. *e.* The Officers' Guard Room. *f.* The Guard Room. This Fort is made of Puncheons of Wood cut 12 Feet and set three feet in the ground. There is 10 Pieces of Cannon mounted in the Fort and Bastion. 4 (*sic*) Pounder and 4 small Swivels.

arriving in Virginia in January, 1754, after a long and dangerous journey through the winter wilderness.

AT THE FORKS OF THE OHIO, 1753

"As I got down before the Canoe I spent some time in viewing the Rivers, and the Land in the Fork; which I think extremely well situated for a Fort, as it has the absolute Command of both Rivers. The Land at the Point is 20 or 25 Feet above the common surface of the Water; and a considerable Bottome of flat, well-timbered land all around it, very convenient for Building. The Rivers are each a Quarter of a Mile, or more, across, and run here very near at right angles: *Alighany* bearing N.E. and Monongahela S.E. The former of these two is a very rapid and swift running water, the other deep and still, without any perceptible Fall." — GEORGE WASHINGTON's *Journal.*

136   George Washington at age of twenty-five, from the miniature, artist disputed, in the Metropolitan Museum of Art, New York

137   Washington at the site of Fort Pitt, from the painting by Edwin Willard Deming (1860–) in the National Museum, Washington

THROUGH THE WILDERNESS TO FORT DUQUESNE

This map has been attributed to Washington and was almost certainly sent to the Imperial Government by Dinwiddie when he was reporting in 1754 on the French claims and movements in the Ohio valley. It shows the French in possession of the strategic position at the juncture of the Allegheny and the Monongahela. At the northern edge of the map may be seen Lake Erie. The French were already in control in the region of the Great Lakes. The drawing makes clear the great importance of Fort Duquesne. Its position would enable the French to extend their sphere of influence throughout the Ohio country, which lay downstream from the fort. To wrest this position from the enemy became the great objective of the English. The fort itself was of the type then usual in Europe, where every engineer copied, more or less, what Vauban had standardized. The French, however, like the British colonists, did adapt European works to the American environment, and to the kind of warfare waged in the wild backwoods.

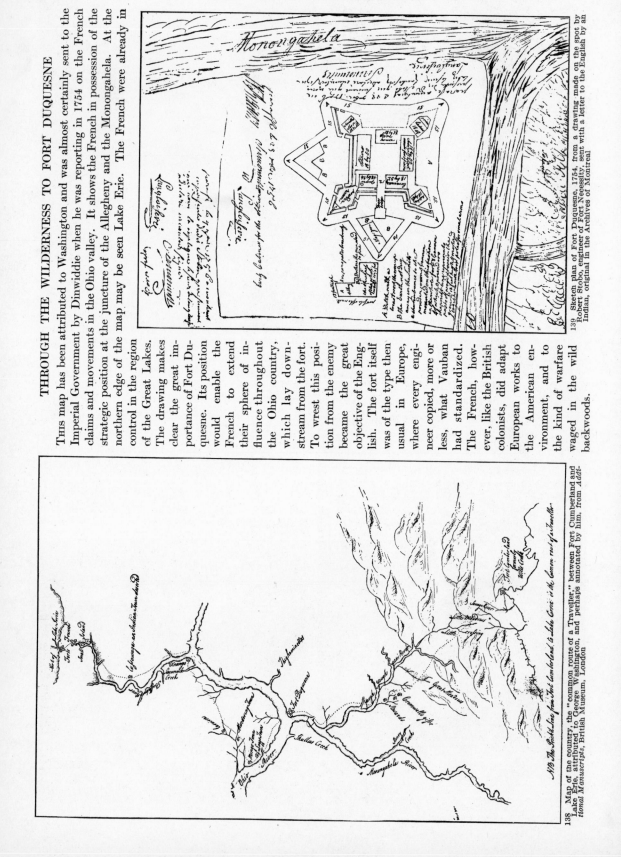

139 Sketch plan of Fort Duquesne, 1754, from a drawing made on the spot by Robert Stobo, engineer of Fort Necessity, sent with a letter to the English by an Indian, original in the Archives of Montreal

138 Map of the country, the "common route of a Traveller," between Fort Cumberland and Lake Erie, attributed to George Washington, and perhaps annotated by him, from *Additional Manuscripts*, British Museum, London

THE OUTBREAK OF HOSTILITIES, MAY, 1754

Convinced by St. Pierre's reply and by the known plans of the French, Dinwiddie sought money from the Virginia burgesses to raise troops for garrisoning a fort at the forks of the Monongahela. In February, 1754, he dispatched a band of backwoodsmen under Captain Trent to construct the fort, and after great difficulties managed to raise a force of three hundred raw recruits, which he sent forward under the command of Fry and Washington, with orders to prevent French advances by force, if necessary. Meanwhile, the French, by intense labor, had moved down a strong force of men and supplies, had driven away Trent's men, and set themselves to the building of Fort Duquesne. To the eastward advanced a small party under Jumonville, bearing much the same orders as Washington, "to repel force with force." The two tiny forces met; the volleys they exchanged opened the war that was to be waged until 1763, on the battle fields of Europe, the plains of India, and around the islands of the sea, as well as in the woods of the New World. Jumonville was killed and his party were taken prisoners. Washington, whom Fry's death had left in command, fell back to a small natural clearing known as the Great Meadows, where he constructed a rude breastwork called Fort Necessity, to dispute the advance of the French.

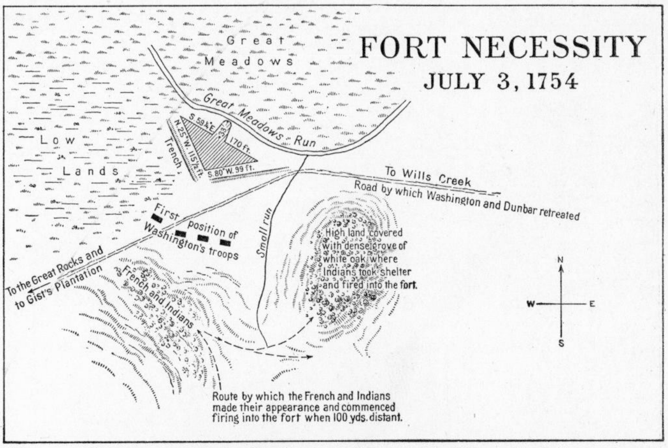

140 Drawn expressly for *The Pageant of America* by Gregor Noetzel, American Geographical Society, New York

THE SURRENDER OF FORT NECESSITY, 1754

On July 3, 1754, Coulon de Villiers, Jumonville's brother, attacked the Virginians in Fort Necessity with a force of some eight or nine hundred French and Indians. From eleven o'clock in the morning Washington's three hundred and fifty troops, weary, half-starved, soaked to the skin by the constant rain, and depleted by the musketry fire from the heights which commanded them, fought off their assailants. In the evening de Villiers offered a parley. Washington, thinking that it was but a pretext to enter the post, refused. The second offer, a few hours later, he was forced to accept. The following day Washington marched out with the honors of war.

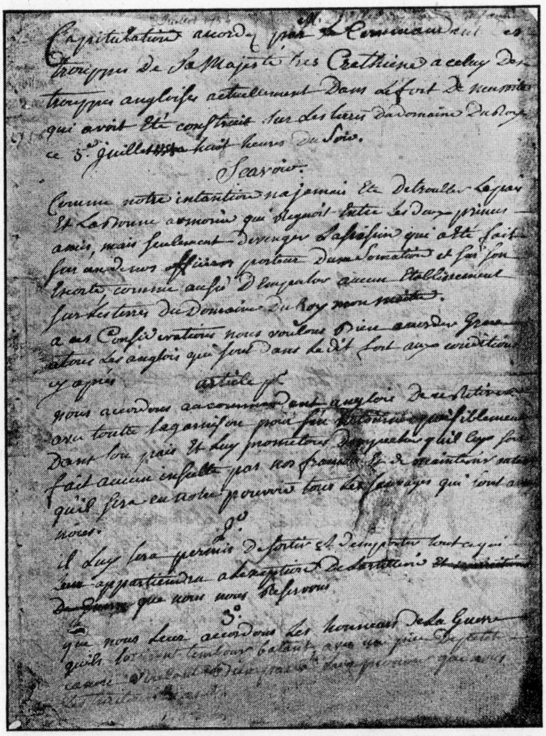

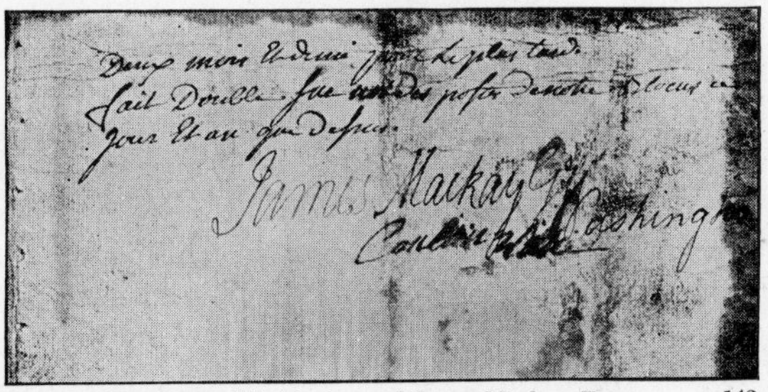

141 First and second pages of Articles of Capitulation of Fort Necessity, signed by George Washington and James Mackay, Esq., from the original in the Archives of Montreal 142

Translation: Capitulation accorded by the commander of the troops of His Very Catholic Majesty to the Commander of the English troops at present in Fort Necessity, which had been built on the lands of the King's domain; this 3rd July at eight in the evening as follows: Since our intention has never been to disturb the peace and the good harmony which reigned between the two prince-friends, but only to avenge the injury inflicted on one of our officers bearer of a *Summons* and on his escort, and to prevent any establishment on the territories of the King my master. Therefore we are anxious to accord grace to the English who are in the said fort on the following conditions: Article I. We accord to the English Commander of this (illegible) with his entire garrison to return peaceably into his country, and we promise him to prevent any interference by our French and to control as far as is in our power all the savages who are our allies. Article II. He will be permitted to march out and to carry with him all that belongs to him with the exception of the artillery which we reserve for ourselves. Article III. We accord them honors of war. They shall march out drums beating, with one of the small cannon, to prove to them that we shall treat them as friends.

143 Washington's Retreat from Great Meadows, after the painting by Howard Pyle (1853–1911) for Woodrow Wilson, *A History of the American People*. © Harper & Brothers

THE RETREAT TO WILLS CREEK

ON the morning of July 4 the young commander began the five days' march back to Wills Creek. There must have remained with Washington, even to his latest days, when the date had become an occasion of national celebration and rejoicing, a certain unpleasant association with the memory of this July 4. For during the early hours of the morning, in a drizzling rain, by the light of a sputtering candle, he had affixed his signature to de Villiers' Articles of Capitulation which van Braam, one of his own soldiers, a Dutchman by birth, had incorrectly translated to him. It was his one surrender. As he rode from the French fort at the head of his dejected men, he little imagined that in twenty four years French soldiers would be officially allied to an independent nation of which he would be the supreme military head.

GENERAL BRADDOCK, 1695–1755

WHEN the news of Washington's defeat reached England, the Newcastle ministry at once made preparations for defense. On the recommendation of the Duke of Cumberland, Edward Braddock, a man of sixty, who had spent forty-five years in military service, was given the chief command and sent, with two regular regiments of seven hundred each, to Virginia. His orders cautioned him particularly to guard against surprise and to bend every effort toward securing an adequate and steady supply of provisions. He was also told, with an amazing ignorance of the country, how he was to take Fort Niagara after Duquesne had fallen. The colonial Governors whom he summoned to meet him at Alexandria found him scornful of colonial methods and ignorant of the difficulties of campaigning in so wild a country. With them he concerted four plans for the summer: he was to move against Duquesne, Shirley against Niagara, Johnson against Crown Point, and Monckton against Beau Séjour in Nova Scotia (see No. 158).

Braddock was a thorough soldier of the Anglo-German school, a capable administrator, conscientious and brave. From the outset difficulties surrounded him, of a sort he had never been called upon to face. He found that the task of procuring wagons and supplies from colonists not greatly interested in his expedition was almost an impossible one; Franklin, who "found them stuck fast for want of horses and Carriage, all their Dependencies for the Articles having failed," procured for him a hundred and fifty wagons and some oats and corn. So slow was the advance, so racking the difficult task of building a road for the baggage, so weakened were the soldiers by the exposure and insufficient food, that two weeks were spent in moving the twenty miles from Cumberland through the primeval forest to Little Meadows.

144   From an unauthenticated lithograph published in London

AMERICAN & BRITISH UNIFORMS · THE FRENCH & INDIAN WAR 1755-1763

NEW ENGLAND MILITIA

NEW YORK PROVINCIALS

ROYAL AMERICANS (60TH FOOT)

NEW ENGLAND RANGERS

FIELD OFFICER VIRGINIA PROVINCIALS

BRITISH GENERAL OFFICER

BRITISH STAFF & AIDES

CAPTAIN 15TH FOOT BRITISH

GRENADIER 35TH FOOT BRITISH

42ND HIGHLANDERS "BLACKWATCH" BRITISH

SERGEANT 28TH FOOT BRITISH

PRIVATE 43RD FOOT BRITISH

OFFICER ROYAL ARTILLERY BRITISH

GUNNER ROYAL ARTILLERY BRITISH

Painted expressly for *The Pageant of America* by H. A. Ogden

BRADDOCK'S MARCH TO THE MONONGAHELA

At Little Meadows Braddock divided his army. The commanding general pushed ahead as rapidly as possible to strike the French at Fort Duquesne. With him were twelve hundred regulars and the Provincials. The remainder of the command, under Dunbar, followed more slowly with the heavy baggage. Braddock's move was the correct one, for he could not afford to fight a battle while encumbered with his trains. By July 8 the advance detachment, making four or five miles a day, had reached the Monongahela River, which Braddock determined to ford twice, and thus avoid the straighter but more dangerous passage along the bank. Though his efforts to retain the Indians proved unavailing, he observed as carefully as possible the cautions against surprise which Cumberland had insisted upon, and which the provincial officers who knew the dangers that attended a forest road recommended. Scouts were thrown out in front; the van under Lieutenant-Colonel Gage (of later prominence in the Revolution) held itself in readiness for any sudden attack. The two fords were safely crossed; the second with some show of triumph, with beat of drums and whistle of fifes, and with colors flying. Re-forming on the farther bank, the army proceeded toward its objective, the lonely French fort, but a few miles beyond.

146 From *Six Plans of the Different Dispensations of the English Army, Braddock Expedition*, printed for T. Jefferys, London, 1758, in the New York Public Library

145 From *Six Plans of the Different Dispensations of the English Army, Braddock Expedition*, printed for T. Jefferys, London, 1758, in the New York Public Library

147 Daniel Hyacinthe Marie Lienard de Beaujeu,
from a photogravure in the Champlain edition,
1897, of Francis Parkman, of the pastel miniature
in the possession of Abbé Verreau, Montreal.
© Little, Brown & Company, Boston

THE FRENCH AND INDIANS BEGIN THE BATTLE

AT Fort Duquesne, Contrecoeur, the commandant, knowing that he could not defend his works against Braddock's guns, had sent out, as a last hope, six hundred and fifty Indians and two hundred Frenchmen and Canadians under Beaujeu and Dumas. They had not time to form an ambush, but posted themselves on the two sides of the path which Braddock was to take, where the rise of ground gave them an advantage and the dense forest protected them. Gordon, an English engineer marking out the twelve-foot road, saw young Beaujeu, in the dress of an Indian, wave his cap. At that signal the Indian war whoop rang out and a sharp musketry fire was poured in on Gage's van. With admirable precision, he wheeled his guns into line and fired into the forest, while his British soldiers replied at first with steadiness. Beaujeu fell dead; the French-Canadians began to falter and give ground, and the Indians, dismayed by the noise of the artillery, showed signs of retreat. But the seventy French regulars stood their ground. Dumas, their leader, effectually rallied the Canadians, and convinced the Indians by standing firm how easy it was to fire with deadly effect at men who could make no effectual reply; for the British were not trained in taking cover to fight a hidden enemy.

148 General Dumas, from a photograph in
Château de Ramezay, Montreal, after a
French original

THE BRITISH COLUMN ROUTED

FOR ten minutes the vanguard received the fire of the enemy. Fifteen out of its eighteen officers, and half the rank and file, fell killed or wounded. Finally, it broke and fled among the ranks of the main body, which was advancing still in column of march. The order to form line of battle had either not been given or had not been heard, and Dumas took advantage of his opportunity to send out a line of flankers along both sides of the enemy column. From the cover of the dense woods the Indians and Canadians poured an intense fire into the huddled red mass, confused by the retreat of the van. Vainly trying to reply to the deadly fire that came from the forest, the British regiments, in close formation, stood for three hours, a splendid target for their foes. Braddock had four horses killed under him. All his staff, except Washington, were killed or disabled by wounds. Sixty-three out of eighty-six British officers were either killed or wounded.

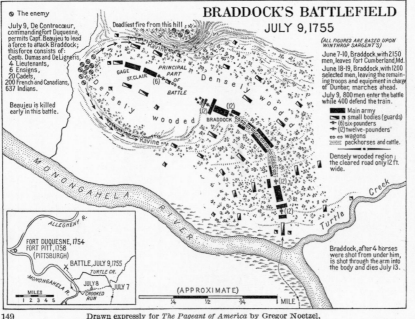

149   Drawn expressly for *The Pageant of America* by Gregor Noetzel,
American Geographical Society, New York

BRADDOCK MORTALLY WOUNDED

SHORTLY after ordering the retreat, Braddock fell mortally wounded and was hurried back the sixty miles to Dunbar's camp, where he died four days later. The army itself, abandoning its guns, baggage, and many of the wounded, retreated in terror along the narrow road. The British arms had received one of the most dramatic and tragic defeats in all their history. Dunbar should have rallied the defeated army, waited for reinforcements from the colo-

150   From the painting *Braddock's Defeat* by Edwin Willard Deming (1860-) in the Wisconsin State Historical Society, Madison

nies, and either advanced again on the fort or held his ground to protect the frontier inhabitants from the raids of the elated Indians, sure to follow their victory. But he retreated in precipitous fashion to Fort Cumberland, hastily destroying cannon, provisions, and wagons. After Dunbar's retreat young Washington undertook the onerous task of doing what he could, with men who were unwilling to serve except on compulsion, to defend a four-hundred mile frontier against the Indian raiders.

SHIRLEY AS COMMANDER-IN-CHIEF

WILLIAM SHIRLEY, to whom passed the chief command after Braddock's death, was, though not a soldier, the only person in the colonies who appreciated the complexities of the military situation, and could be entrusted with great responsibilities. He was acquainted with the nature of the country in which the war was to be fought, and had a sense of the strategic importance of critical points. He saw clearly that the lines of water communication between Canada and the colonies must be defended, from the Kennebec to Oswego. But to his mind Oswego was the point of greatest importance; at all costs it must be kept and used as a starting point for the attack on Niagara which could effectually cut the great line of French communication between Canada and the Ohio valley (see map, No. 129). With two regiments that had been raised in the colonies, though they were on the British establishment, and with the New Jersey provincials, he made the difficult journey to Oswego in the summer of 1755, in the hope that he might attack Niagara. Lack of adequate provision and reinforcement kept him from carrying out his plan. He left his troops behind with orders to strengthen and repair the fortifications at Oswego during the winter, and himself returned to concert measures for the 1756 campaign.

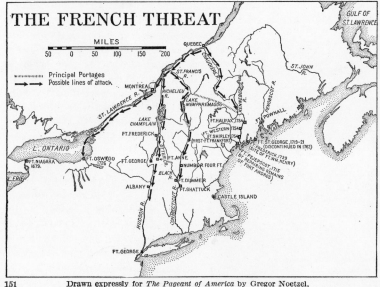

151   Drawn expressly for *The Pageant of America* by Gregor Noetzel, American Geographical Society, New York

SIR WILLIAM JOHNSON'S CAMPAIGN

BEFORE Braddock's arrival in Virginia the northern governments had determined upon an expedition against the French stronghold of Crown Point, guarding the lower end of Lake Champlain, and had selected as leader the Indian trader, William Johnson, whose dealings with the Iroquois had gained for him their confidence and respect. Second in command was Phineas Lyman of Connecticut, a brave and able officer. Collecting his force of thirty-six hundred men and three hundred Indians, Johnson moved north along the Hudson, built Fort Edward at the great carrying place, and Fort William Henry, a stockaded enclosure, at the head of the beautiful Lake St. Sacrament, which he re-christened Lake George. Meanwhile, three thousand French regulars had arrived in Canada from France and moved south from Crown Point to the rocky promontory that was to be Fort Ticonderoga. Thence a picked force of regulars,

152 Sir William Johnson, 1715–74, from a mezzotint by Spooner in the Emmet Collection, New York Public Library

Canadians, and Indians, under Dieskau, advanced by way of Wood Creek to attack Johnson's army. (See map, No. 130.)

153 From a colored print in the Emmet Collection, New York Public Library, after the portrait from life, probably in London

HENDRICK, THE GREAT SACHEM OF THE MOHAWKS

HENDRICK was still the leading Mohawk chief, though grown so old and feeble that he could no longer lead his braves on foot. Johnson provided him with a horse, and, very much against his better judgment, he accompanied the small force of a thousand men which Colonel Ephraim Williams led out to meet the advancing French. "Too few to be successful," said Hendrick," and too many to be killed."

THE FRENCH AMBUSH AT BLOODY POND

DIESKAU's scouts warned him of the advance of the thousand provincials and gave him time to prepare an ambush, which would have been more complete had not some of his Indians fired too soon. But as it was,

the Americans, who had taken no precautions against surprise, were astounded at the fire that burst on them from three sides. The attack was more unexpected and more effectual than that which Braddock had experienced. Both Williams and Hendrick were killed. The remnant of the force hurried back to William Henry and were saved from total extinction solely because they had a larger force to fall back upon. Dieskau wasted precious time before advancing on the rude works at Lake George. His delay enabled Johnson to form a rough breastwork of logs, and to place his cannon in position.

154   Bloody Pond, from a photograph, courtesy of John Arthur Haney

155   Perspective Plan of the Battle near Lake George, 1755, by Samuel Blodget, engraving by Thomas Johnston, from a copy in the New York Public Library

JOHNSON'S COLONIALS AT LAKE GEORGE

IT was almost noon before the French and their Iroquois allies covered the distance to Johnson's camp. The Iroquois remained relatively inactive for the remainder of the engagement. Their devotion to the French was by no means unqualified. On the preceding night they had refused to coöperate with Dieskau in his contemplated attack on Fort Lyman, inasmuch as they had resolved not to disturb the English on territory which they considered as properly belonging to them. Though they had agreed that Johnson's position was an encroachment on French possessions, and had promised to aid Dieskau in driving him out, their coöperation during the vital period of the battle was very slight. It was chiefly a battle between a few French regulars and the three thousand provincials. Both Dieskau and Johnson were wounded. Lyman was in command of the colonials when finally, around four o'clock, the French troops fell back, with the Americans in pursuit. Instead of continuing the attack on Crown Point, Johnson devoted the rest of the campaign to improving and strengthening the two new forts. The whole campaign illustrates the weakness and the strength of the colonial militia. Had they been trained even in the fundamentals of war, they would never have permitted themselves to be surprised at Bloody Pond. But, behind breastworks, they stood their ground and fought effectively. This spirited illustration of the action, made by Samuel Blodget, a sutler in the Massachusetts Rangers, appeared in Boston the same year.

THE CAMPAIGN IN NOVA SCOTIA

THE narrow isthmus in Nova Scotia was the only region in North America where the two frontiers actually touched. As early as 1750 Charles Lawrence, the forceful and energetic Governor of Nova Scotia, had erected Fort Lawrence to stop the further advance of the French from Fort Beau Séjour. But their continued activity, their gradual encroachment upon the trade in the Bay of Fundy, and the fear that they might enter New England itself, led Shirley in 1754 to propose a joint expedition of regulars and provincials. Before Braddock's meeting with the Governors in April, 1755, the plan was well under way. Two thousand New Englanders under Winslow joined the regulars under Lieutenant Colonel Monckton, who was given command of the expedition. By June the English forces had reached the Bay of Fundy.

156   The Honourable Robert Monckton, from a mezzotint by J. Watson after the portrait by Benjamin West

157   Colonel John Winslow, from the portrait attributed to Joseph Blackburn, in Pilgrim Hall, Plymouth, Mass.

THE CAPTURE OF THE FRENCH FORTS

FORT Beau Séjour was a well-planned fort with five bastions, well equipped with cannon. Its commandant, De Vergor, however, a product of the corrupt system which the Intendant Bigot made use of in Canada to increase his own private fortune (see Vol. I), offered but sorry resistance to the forces which Monckton brought against him. Planting their cannon in well-ordered parallels, the British army vigorously pressed the siege, and De Vergor, learning that no help could come from Louisbourg, surrendered. Winslow crossed the narrow isthmus and took Fort Gaspereau on Bay Verte. The possession of Nova Scotia was thus assured to the English; and it was maintained throughout the war by the constant presence of at least three British regiments of the line. Louisbourg alone remained to threaten English control of the northern waters, which meant control of the lucrative fisheries.

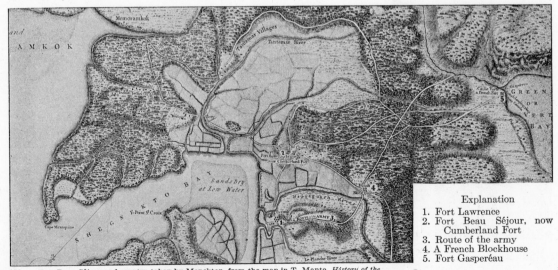

Explanation
1. Fort Lawrence
2. Fort Beau Séjour, now Cumberland Fort
3. Route of the army
4. A French Blockhouse
5. Fort Gaspereau

158   Fort Beau Séjour and country taken by Monckton, from the map in T. Mante, *History of the War in North America*, London, 1772

THE EXPULSION OF THE ACADIANS

GOVERNOR LAWRENCE determined to clinch the control of Nova Scotia by the expulsion of the Acadians, a pastoral group of "Neutral French" who had lived undisturbed for forty years under mild English rule. Opinions will always differ as to the necessity for driving them from their homes. The English believed that the propaganda carried on by the priests, the infamous Le Loutre in particular, constituted a military danger of no mean importance. The French officials undoubtedly hoped to utilize the Acadians to offset the steady English advance toward the Gulf of St. Lawrence. On the other hand, it is extremely doubtful whether an agricultural people, who understood nothing of the part they were expected to play, could ever have been a real menace.

With great secrecy Lawrence distributed among his subordinates the orders for expulsion. All the Acadians who had refused to take the oath of allegiance to King George were assembled at their parish churches, and listened to the reading of the unexpected and harsh orders. Guarded by uniformed, armed soldiers, they were placed on board the ships waiting to take them from their possessions

159   Reading the Order for the Expulsion of the Acadians in the Grand Pré parish church, from the painting by C. W. Jeffreys, in possession of the publishers

and their homes. Five thousand went to the Isle St. Jean (now Prince Edward Island); some to New Orleans, some to the various English colonies along the seaboard, some to Quebec. Those who had the misfortune to meet the avarice of Bigot at Quebec suffered the most, but in no place were they given a kindly welcome. During the next few years, many made the painful journey back to Nova Scotia, where they were permitted to remain.

LOUDOUN SUCCEEDS SHIRLEY IN COMMAND

NOTWITHSTANDING the fourfold campaign of 1755, England and France remained nominally at peace. Finally, in May, 1756, war was officially declared. The English ministry sent to America two new regiments, one of them the famous 42nd Highlanders which became known as the Black Watch, and likewise ordered that there be raised in the colonies four thousand men, who were embodied as the Royal American Regiment. They were mostly Germans from Pennsylvania, officered in part by professional Swiss soldiers from the battle fields of Europe. Shirley was superseded as commander-in-chief by the Earl of Loudoun, one of the Scotch Campbells, a stern disciplinarian, a tireless worker, and an able administrator of army affairs. But Loudoun, like Braddock, was ignorant of American affairs, and impatient with provincial governments whose jealousies prevented, in his opinion, the full assistance which they should have furnished the Crown. Moreover, he had to rely upon the inadequate support which a shifting ministry in England could supply.

160   The Earl of Loudoun, from J. C. Smith, *British Mezzotinto Portraits*, mezzotint by Spooner after a portrait by Allan Ramsay (1713–84)

By the HONOURABLE

SPENCER PHIPS, Esq;

Lieutenant-Governour and Commander in Chief in and over His Majesty's Province of the *Massachusetts-Bay* in *New-England*.

A PROCLAMATION for a publick *FAST*.

WHEREAS Almighty GOD is pleased still to chastize us with the grievous Judgment of War, and to permit the unjust Invasions of the *British* Territories in *North-America*, as well as in other Parts of the World, by the *French*, who have employed the *Indians* in these Parts, as Instruments of their Cruelty in shedding the Blood of Multitudes of Women and Children, as well as Men, upon the Frontiers of these Colonies, with such Circumstances of Barbarity as are most abhorrent, not only to the true Spirit of Christianity, but even to Humanity itself; And whereas the Preparations now made and making against us by our *French* and *Indian* Enemy loudly admonish us of our Danger as also of our Duty, to acknowledge the righteous Hand of God in these Dispensations of his Providence, and to seek a speedy Reconciliation to Him; and the Time of Action of the Forces raised by this and the neighbouring Governments for recovering their just Rights out of the Hands of their Enemies being probably very near, the Voice of Providence doth evidently call upon us to seek to God for his Blessing upon our important Undertakings, without which we have no Ground to hope for Success;

I have therefore thought fit, with the Advice of his Majesty's Council and at the Desire of the Assembly, to appoint Thursday the Twenty-second of this Instant *July* to be observed thro'out this Province as a Day of publick Fasting an' Prayer; Hereby calling upon Ministers and People devoutly to solemnize the same by the deepest Humiliations for our heinous Offences, by which we have highly incensed the Divine Majesty against us, and have caused Him to hide His Face from us, and to punish us with the sore Calamities of War; and also to implore his Commisseration of us, in our present Distresses, and mercifully direct in the Forming and Executing of our military Enterprises, and thereby to deliver us out the Hands of our Enemies, and enable us to recover our Rights and Properties, by them unjustly invaded; that He would keep all Sin out of our Camps, as well as from the whole Community, and make us a penitent and reformed People; that He would inspire our Officers with Conduct and Resolution, and our Soldiers with Faithfulness and Courage; and that, as the Captain of our Salvation, he would lead them on to Success and Victory; That he would graciously preserve the important Life of our Sovereign Lord the KING with all the Branches of His Royal House; and direct His Councils and prosper His just Arms for restor .s and preserving the Peace of *Europe*; and that the Divine Promises and Predictions of the Universal and Spiritual Reign of our Lord and Saviour JESUS CHRIST, the Prince of Peace, may be speedily accomplished. And all servile Labour and Recreations are forbidden on the said Day.

Given at the Council Chamber in Boston, the Tenth Day of July 1756, in the Thirtieth Year of the Reign of our Sovereign Lord GEORGE the Second, by the Grace of GOD of Great-Britain, France and Ireland, KING, Defender of the Faith, &c.

By Order of His Honour the Lieutenant Governour,
with the Advice of the Council.

S. Phips.

J. Willard, Secr'y.

GOD save the KING.

BOSTON: Printed by *John Draper*, Printer to His Honour the Lieutenant-Governour and Council.

161 Governor Phips' Proclamation of a Fast, 1756, invoking blessings on "our important Undertakings," from the Massachusetts Historical Society, *Massachusetts Broadsides*, 1922

MONTCALM, THE LAST GREAT FRENCHMAN OF NEW FRANCE, 1756–59

FRANCE sent out for the new campaigns the Marquis de Montcalm, an exceptionally able general, high-minded, cultured, the descendant of a famous fighting stock. With him came capable assistants, and two fresh regiments. But Montcalm, like Loudoun, found internal troubles awaiting him which were as great a source of anxiety as the enemy itself. The governor-general, Vaudreuil, a narrow-minded though energetic official, had pretensions to military command which he was in no wise fitted to execute. He was, under the autocratic system of government, the supreme authority in military as well as civil matters. Montcalm, who technically commanded only the French regulars, was explicitly required by his instructions to confer with Vaudreuil about all the details of the campaign; for both the French-Canadian regulars and militia were directly responsible to the governor-general. Bigot, the intendant, applied to the financial

THE ABORTIVE CROWN POINT EXPEDITION OF 1756

SHIRLEY, who had visualized more clearly perhaps than any of his fellow colonials the potential danger of continued French activity, again had taken the initiative in formulating a definite campaign of counter-attack. In February he had used all of his influence with the governments of Massachusetts, Connecticut, and Rhode Island to take the lead in raising a minimum of seven thousand men, who, under General Winslow, should attempt again the reduction of Crown Point. They assembled in June at Fort Edward, where difficulties arose with the commander-in-chief sent out from England, who doubted their ability to carry out their intentions successfully. During the entire summer they remained encamped at the head of Lake George, merely repairing Fort William Henry, though preventing, by their presence, any invasion of French forces from Canada. This fruitless experience, coupled with the lack of any real results from the 1755 campaign, discouraged the colonies, and made them regret their useless expenditure of money.

162 From the portrait in possession of the Marquis de Montcalm; Candiac, France

administration of the army the same corrupt methods he practiced in civil affairs. The tiny French naval force was in some measure independent. Far from enjoying the unified command his ability deserved, Montcalm constantly faced this divided authority, suspicion, and corruption. Moreover, he had the aid of a country of scanty resources. The population of New France never reached seventy thousand, as compared with the million and a half inhabitants of the English colonies in 1755.

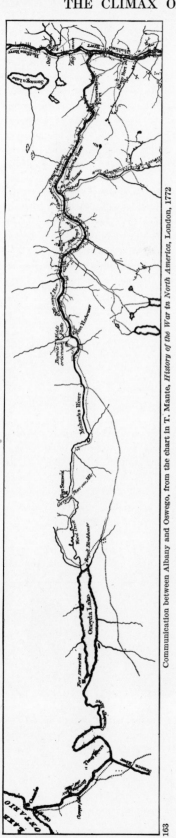

Communication between Albany and Oswego, from the chart in T. Mante, *History of the War in North America*, London, 1772

163

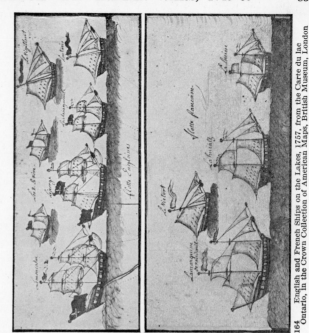

164   English and French Ships on the Lakes, 1757, from the Carre du lac Ontario, in the Crown Collection of American Maps, British Museum, London

THE FRONTIER OUTPOST OF OSWEGO, 1756

OSWEGO had been built some thirty years earlier, partly as a fortress and partly as a trading-post with the Indians; but until Shirley stationed his regiments there in the summer of 1755 it had been defenceless. Shirley had left orders to abandon the old fort and build two new forts on either side of the Oswego River. Had there been any communication between Oswego and Albany, such a task might have been accomplished. But three hundred difficult miles lay between, necessitating transportation by wagon, canoe, and sledge through a wilderness infested with half-friendly Indians. Because it was not even possible to get up supplies for the troops, they passed a frightful winter, on three-quarters rations, in barracks so poorly constructed that the snow drifted in over them as they slept without sufficient clothing. At one time only seventeen men could be found to mount guard, and that only with the aid of supporting sticks. Fully thirty men out of every company perished, and Mercer, the commandant, was on the point of abandoning the fort in March when provisions arrived. In the spring Shirley sent up reinforcements and ample supplies; but the two forts still remained in a wretched and unfit condition to resist attack by cannon.

THE STRUGGLE FOR NAVAL SUPREMACY ON LAKE ONTARIO

SHIRLEY knew the value of gaining naval command of the lake, for upon that depended not only the success of any expedition that might be launched from Oswego but even the safety of the fort itself. In 1755 he built two sloops of ten carriage-guns each, and in 1756 he ordered the construction of two brigantines, an armed sloop, and two hundred and fifty whaleboats capable of holding sixteen men each. But the officer in charge, Captain Broadley, suffered from the same difficulty of transportation in getting his supplies. Lack of experience with the treacherous winds and currents proved disastrous; and the brig, which might have prevented the transport of French cannon, was run ashore and damaged. The tiny French fleet, in control of mariners who understood the tricks of lake navigation, therefore maintained supremacy.

165   The South View of Oswego on Lake Ontario, from the engraving in the *London Magazine*, 1760

THE FALL OF OSWEGO, 1756

MONTCALM spent enough time at Ticonderoga to satisfy himself that De Lévis, his second in command, could maintain the fort against the enemy; then, traveling day and night, he reached Fort Frontenac on Lake Ontario, whence he had determined to attack Oswego. After a week of strenuous activity he embarked his three thousand men, with all supplies and fifty cannon, in two brigades, landed first at Sackett's Harbor, and then at a point within two miles of Oswego. Not until the morning of the tenth of August was Mercer definitely aware of the presence of a hostile force. Fort Ontario was first attacked, and for three days held out against a brisk fire with small arms. On August 13, Mercer, seeing the enemy cannon planted within seventy yards of Fort Ontario, abandoned that rude work to Montcalm, and withdrew across the river to the scarcely more tenable Fort Oswego. Montcalm took possession of the heights on the east side of the river, fixed his cannon to rake the English fort and opened fire at dawn. Mercer was killed at nine. Shortly afterward the English force, unable to use its own few guns because the crumbling walls of the fort could not withstand the recoil, surrendered; though it had only lost five men. The garrison of some twelve hundred were taken to Canada; and Oswego, together with Broadley's ships, was completely destroyed. Montcalm had won a definite and decisive success, had removed the danger to the French line of westward communication, opened a road whereby the Mohawk valley might be attacked, strengthened the alliance of his own Indians, and weakened that of the Iroquois to the English.

MONTCALM'S SIEGE OF FORT WILLIAM HENRY, 1757

IN the spring of 1757 Loudoun sailed north with half his American force to attack Louisbourg, expecting the arrival of a coöperating fleet and army from England. Changes in the English ministry prevented the dispatching of the fleet in time to keep strong French reinforcements from entering Louisbourg, and Loudoun felt it wise to abandon his attempt. Meanwhile Montcalm was preparing his force of eight thousand men for a descent on William Henry. Lieutenant-Colonel Monro commanded there, with General Daniel Webb at Fort Edward. Webb, though he knew in advance of the activity at Ticonderoga, made no attempt to concentrate his forces; and when, on August 4, Montcalm appeared at the head of Lake George, Monro had but two thousand one hundred and forty men.

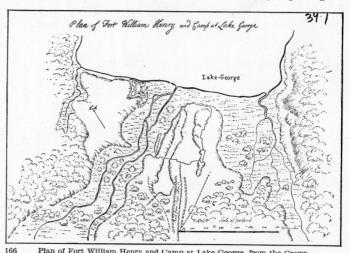

166   Plan of Fort William Henry and Camp at Lake George, from the Crown
Collection of American Maps, British Museum

MONTCALM RECEIVES THE SURRENDER

FOR five days Monro held out gallantly against the superior French force; on August 9, disheartened by Webb's failure to aid him, with half his cannon useless, his garrison weakened by sickness as well as by the fire from Montcalm's twelve- and eighteen-pounders, he surrendered with the honors of war. The map shows admirably Montcalm's steady advance both on the fort and on the entrenched, fortified camp. On the morning of August 9 he had planted his heavy batteries within such close range that further resistance from a fort in which but eight guns were still in working order was hopeless.

THE MASSACRE OF FORT WILLIAM HENRY, AUGUST 9, 1757

UNDER the terms of the capitulation the garrison was to march out with their personal belongings and be escorted to Fort Edward, under promise not to serve again for eighteen months. As they were leaving the fort, with the single six-pounder which Montcalm had allowed them as token of

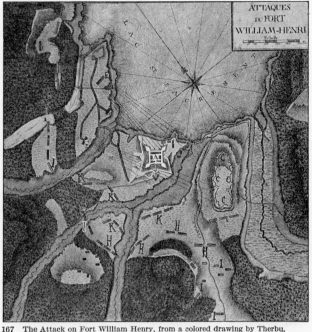

167   The Attack on Fort William Henry, from a colored drawing by Therbu, Lieutenant of Engineers, in the Dominion Archives, Ottawa

A. Ft. William Henry. *C.* Entrenched camp which the English advanced to occupy at the time of the arrival of the French. *E.* Battery of eight cannon and one mortar. *H.* Position of Mr. Lévis during the investment of the Fort. *I.* Position of the troops during the siege. *K.* Their position after the capture during the destruction of the trenches built by the English.

their brave defense, his Indian allies, unable to restrain the appetite for blood which the siege and some abandoned British liquor had aroused, set upon them. In vain Montcalm endeavored to throw himself between the savages and their victims; the utmost that he could do was to protect those at the rear of the column. Most of the English prisoners sought safety in flight, but not before at least fifty, including some of the wounded men who lay in a temporary hospital, had been tomahawked and scalped. This incident was the natural outcome of the policy which the French had always adopted toward the Indians, constantly inciting them to deeds of terror, to raids, to plundering the frontiers. The weakness of New France could be pleaded as excuse. But in the long run the policy contributed its share to the downfall of French power; for massacres such as that at William Henry nerved the colonists to a realization of their common danger, and nerved them to resist strenuously further encroachments from a foe whose Indian allies so often did their worst. The exact apportionment of blame for this massacre is impossible to make, seeing how far back the roots of the trouble ran. But one thing is agreed, that Montcalm and his French regulars were in no way whatever to blame. Indeed, both he and his staff risked their lives to stop the bloody work; and as soon as his own French regulars were summoned, the massacre was stopped.

168   The Surrender of Fort William Henry, from the painting by J. L. G. Ferris (1863–), courtesy of the Glens Falls (N. Y.) Insurance Co.

WEBB AT FORT EDWARD

FOR the next two or three days half-clad, terrified men kept appearing at Fort Edward, on the upper Hudson, a few miles south of Fort William Henry. They found General Daniel Webb cursing the slowness of the colonial militia which he had summoned, and which had begun to appear only by the tenth of August. But the fault was Webb's; he should have sent for the militia a month before, when he first heard from his scouts that the French were making preparations for the attack, and that regiments of French regulars were concentrating at Ticonderoga. The British generals in command of the forts on Lake George had realized fully the unique and valuable aid which a band of rangers, skilled in woodland warfare, able

170   Major Robert Rogers, from a mezzotint portrait (fictitious) published in London, 1776, by Thomas Hart

---

GENERAL ORDERS OF 1757

Supply ye Deficiency of Powder Horns & Bullet Pouches with those Men's Accotrements yt are UnFit for Service.—This To Be Don Emediately & an Account of Such Powder Horns & Bullet Pouches To Be Taken that ye Right Owners Ma Not Loose them.

Fort Edward Augt 10th 1757.
    Parole *Barwick*
    A Return To Be Given in as Soon as Possable of The Number of Privates Belonging To Each Corp That are Come from Fort-Wm. Henry. Specifying those yt Have their Arms. This Return To Be Sign.d By ye Commanding offr of Each Regt.

Fort Edward Augt 11th 1757.
    Parole *Inverness*
    A Return of ye Number of Persons that Hath Return.d from Fort-Wm. Henry Since Yesterday Morning Till To-Day at 12 oClock, Specifying Whether they Brought In any arms or Not. The

65

169   From the privately printed edition of Gen. Phineas Lyman, *General Orders of 1757*, edited by Worthington C. Ford, New York, 1899

---

to traverse great distances on land, over the snow and ice, or through the water, could afford to the more cumbersome regular or provincial troops. Long before the surrender of Fort William Henry, a New Hampshire ranger, Robert Rogers, had reported for service against the Indians. Under his supervision an entire battalion had been organized, consisting of seven companies of forest fighters. In hiding, on neighboring heights, they watched the movements of the French in the forts of Ticonderoga and Crown Point; they also intercepted and destroyed, whenever possible, unsupported bands of reinforcements or foragers. Rogers' pranks, as well as his skill in obtaining prisoners, delighted the British officers. On one occasion,

171   The Battle of Rogers' Rock, Lake George, from the painting of J. L. G. Ferris, courtesy of the Glen Falls (N. Y.) Insurance Co.

he left, tied to the horns of a French bullock he had killed, a note to Hébécourt, the commander at Ticonderoga, expressing his gratitude for the Frenchman's excellent hospitality. In March, 1758, the French commander had his revenge. Having received a reinforcement of two hundred mission Indians and some Canadians, he immediately dispatched them, along with some French regulars, against Rogers' one hundred and eighty rangers, whom Colonel Haviland had sent out from Fort Edward. In the encounter which took place at Rogers' Rock, March 13, Rogers' force, in spite of a heroic defense from three in the afternoon till nightfall, was defeated.

WILLIAM PITT, EARL OF CHATHAM

THE accession to power in England of William Pitt marks a new phase of the French and Indian War. Hitherto the French had been successful against the half-hearted efforts of the colonies, and the badly directed attempts of the British armies and fleets. But now they had to face in Pitt that rare combination of a brilliant mind and a sympathetic spirit. On the five continents and over the seven seas he moved his armies and fleets with uncanny insight and unerring precision. For the first time he used with its full effect the British naval power which had been developing for nearly a century. His thorough grasp of naval power constitutes his first title to fame. At the same time he enjoyed, not only the affection of the English nation that had raised him to power, but the confidence of Scottish Highlanders, colonial Americans, Anglo-Indians, and German allies. "England," said Frederick of Prussia, "has at last brought forth a man." Under Pitt's guidance English money paid Prussians to fight France in Europe and colonials to fight her in North America. While France was draining her resources and men on the battlefields of Germany, Pitt was

172   From the portrait by W. Hoare (1706–92) in the National Portrait Gallery, London

pouring more and more soldiers into the New World. Sheer weight of numbers was to have its effect. For the 1758 campaign Pitt planned three offensives: against Duquesne, Ticonderoga, and Louisbourg. We have met all three plans before, but never under such a leader, nor with such powerful armies. Thus Pitt brought to bear against New France that strength which had been developing in the British colonies. There were jealousies among these colonies and a highly developed local particularism. But they had man power many times greater than the French, then scattered all the way from New Orleans to Louisbourg. Pitt determined to use this to the fullest possible advantage.

THE COLONIES SUPPORT THE CROWN

THE northern colonies had heretofore never put more than seven thousand men into the field at one time. Pitt calmly called upon them for twenty thousand, promising to subsist and arm the forces they raised, and to reimburse them to some extent for the expense of levying and paying their men. The colonies, not unmindful of the massacre at William Henry, responded nobly, and strained their scanty resources to meet the demand. By June they had assembled along the upper Hudson almost the number asked. The southern colonies, though with less zeal, furnished five thousand for the expedition against Fort Duquesne.

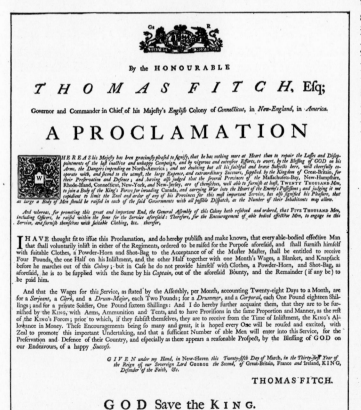

173   Proclamation of Governor Thomas Fitch of Connecticut, 1758, calling for troops to march to Canada, original in the Emmet Collection, New York Public Library

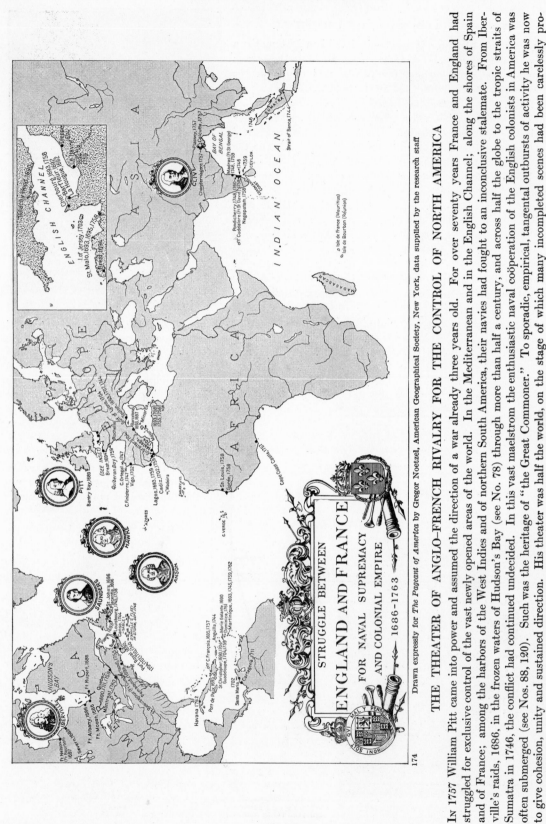

Drawn expressly for *The Pageant of America* by Gregor Noetzel, American Geographical Society, New York, data supplied by the research staff

THE THEATER OF ANGLO-FRENCH RIVALRY FOR THE CONTROL OF NORTH AMERICA

In 1757 William Pitt came into power and assumed the direction of a war already three years old. For over seventy years France and England had struggled for exclusive control of the vast newly opened areas of the world. In the Mediterranean and in the English Channel; along the shores of Spain and of France; among the harbors of the West Indies and of northern South America, their navies had fought to an inconclusive stalemate. From Iberville's raids, 1686, in the frozen waters of Hudson's Bay (see No. 78) through more than half a century, and across half the globe to the tropic straits of Sumatra in 1746, the conflict had continued undecided. In this vast maelstrom the enthusiastic naval coöperation of the English colonists in America was often submerged (see Nos. 88, 120). Such was the heritage of "the Great Commoner." To sporadic, empirical, tangental outbursts of activity he was now to give cohesion, unity and sustained direction. His theater was half the world, on the stage of which many incompleted scenes had been carelessly produced. With full understanding of what had preceded, he prepared for the climax.

NAVAL OPERATIONS
IN EUROPE

PITT's objective was New France. To drive the French out of America would be a crippling blow to the traditional enemy. To drive them out of India would be a great boon to English trade. Pitt pushed both enterprises; but he felt rightly that the fall of New France would mean the end of the war. Quebec was the very center and heart of the French Empire in America. But to get at Quebec by sea Louisbourg must first be taken, and to advance against it by land required the breaking of the French resistance in the region of the southern end of Lake Champlain. Pitt decided to attempt to force both these outlying positions. With the sure sense of strategy that characterized his genius he saw that, if Louis-

175   Model of a 110-Gun Ship, 1760–80, in the Worcester Historical Society, Worcester, Mass.

bourg was to fall, it must be isolated. The naval operations in American waters must be founded upon naval operations in Europe. Lord Anson was in charge of the Admiralty. To Osborne and Saunders, commanding in the Mediterranean, Pitt assigned the mission of preventing the French fleet under La Clue from slipping through the Strait of Gibraltar and crossing the Atlantic to aid Louisbourg. The British commanders faced a difficult problem; for the French fleet was anchored in the neutral Spanish port of Cartagena, while reinforcements were being fitted out at the French naval base at Toulon. The English could not attack Toulon because they must keep their fleet between La Clue and Gibraltar. On the last day of February, 1758, Osborne and Saunders defeated and captured some reinforcements coming from Toulon to La Clue. This engagement, small in itself, ended the campaign in the Mediterranean. A month later La Clue's fleet was being dismantled at Toulon. Meanwhile, Hawke, by a brilliant series of maneuvers in the Bay of Biscay, had succeeded in forcing aground the French fleet preparing in the Basque Roads near LaRochelle. In order to make good its escape it was compelled to throw overboard its stores and guns. There was no hope of refitting the fleet for action in time to be of use in the American campaign.

176   Admiral Edward Boscawen, from the portrait by Sir Joshua Reynolds (1723–92) in the National Portrait Gallery, London

ENGLISH NAVAL SUPREMACY, 1758

A SUCCESSFUL attack on Louisbourg depended upon the full coöperation of the naval and military forces. Pitt chose two commanders who would work well together, Admiral Boscawen, known as "Old Dreadnought," and Jeffrey Amherst (No. 212) whom he took from the battlefields of Germany. Only six French men-of-war were in Louisbourg harbor. Boscawen had forty, of which no less than twenty-three were ships of the line. The same disparity of strength was evident in the two armies. Drucour, the French commandant at Louisbourg, could muster but three thousand regulars, fifteen hundred militiamen, five hundred Indians, and the three thousand sailors from the ships. Amherst, on the other hand, could depend upon twelve thousand picked regulars, as well as upon Boscawen's crews. When the morning mist cleared away on the second of June the doomed French garrison saw the great attacking Armada approach in one vast white-winged crescent.

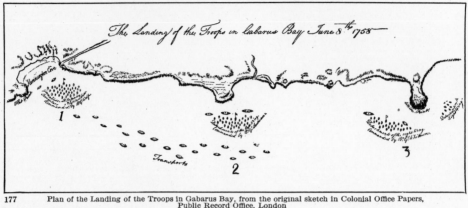

The Landing of the Troops in Gabarus Bay June 8th 1758

177   Plan of the Landing of the Troops in Gabarus Bay, from the original sketch in Colonial Office Papers,
Public Record Office, London

1. Grenadiers, Lt. Infantry, Irregulars, Highlanders, commanded by Brig.-Gen. Wolfe. 2. Detachments of the left
wing, commanded by Brig.-Gen. Lawrence. 3. Detachments of the right wing, commanded by Brig.-Gen. Whitmore

WOLFE EFFECTS A LANDING

Few engagements between the French and English were fought with as much credit to both sides as the second siege of Louisbourg. There were but three landing places on a rocky coast where a wild surf broke incessantly. One after another Boscawen's naval officers advised that getting ashore was impossible; but he determined to make the attempt. The French, strongly intrenched at all three points, awaited the landing parties. Wolfe led the troops at the extreme left where the assault was to be made while menacing feints were made at the center and right. With almost incredible daring and with heavy losses a handful of Wolfe's men got ashore (A) on June 8 (see No. 178). The French defenders were speedily flying for the protecting walls of Louisbourg while the English army (B,B,B) was transferred to shore. The French erected a battery (C) at Black Cape.

THE SIEGE OF LOUISBOURG, 1758

As in the former siege, the Royal Battery was abandoned; but the French destroyed everything of value. Wolfe swept around Northeast Harbor, capturing Light-House Point. Here for days his batteries pounded the French works on Island Battery until its guns were silenced. Meanwhile, Amherst, the commander in chief, established batteries on the hills south and west of the town. From these positions (indicated on the plan) he ran trenches (shown in parallel lines) toward the ramparts of Louisbourg. With terrific bombardments from ships and shore the French contested every foot of the English advance. More than once they sallied forth to engage in hand-to-hand encounters. But they were too few to stem the tide. An English bomb fired one of the ships. When Amherst saw the conflagration he turned the harbor into an inferno of shot and shell to prevent the saving of the ship. She drifted, came into contact with others, and all but two of the French defending fleet were lost. More rapidly, now that there was no bombardment from the fleet, the English pushed their parallels toward Louisbourg. Here, in the end, the terrific fight began to tell. The masonry crumbled and, one by one, the great defense guns were silenced. Drucour fought desperately, but with little hope. Fires broke out in the town behind him, and his wounded reached an appalling number.

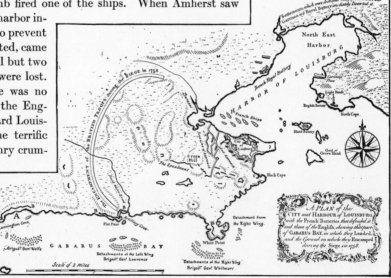

178   Plan of the City and Harbor of Louisbourg, simplified from the chart published by Thomas Jeffreys,
London, 1758, and reprinted by The Champlain Society, 1909

MADAME DRUCOUR

"Various courtesies were exchanged between the two commanders. Drucour, on occasion of a flag of truce, wrote to Amherst that there was a surgeon of uncommon skill in Louisbourg, whose services were at the command of any English officer who might need them. Amherst on his part sent to his enemy letters and messages from wounded Frenchmen in his hands, adding his compliments to Madame Drucour, with an expression of regret for the disquiet to which she was exposed, begging her at the same time to accept a gift of pineapples from the West Indies. She returned his courtesy by sending him a basket of wine; after which amenities the cannon roared again. Madame Drucour was a woman of heroic spirit. Every day she was on the ramparts, where her presence roused the soldiers to enthusiasm; and every day with her own hand she fired three cannon to encourage them." — Francis Parkman, *Montcalm and Wolfe*, II, p. 68, Little, Brown & Co.

179   Drawn expressly for *The Pageant of America* by C. W. Jefferys

180   From the engraving after the painting by R. Paton, published in London, Feb. 1771, by John Boydell, engraver

BURNING THE *PRUDENT*

Two of the French fleet tried at different times to slip past the English blockade, and one, the *Aréthuse*, succeeded, reaching France in safety with messages from Drucour. Two ships escaped the conflagration that destroyed the main body of the fleet. But Captains Balfour and Laforey, with six hundred bluejackets, came in at night by boat with muffled oars; burned the *Prudent* to the water's edge, and towed the *Bienfaisant* off in triumph.

THE SURRENDER OF LOUISBOURG

On June 2 the English fleet had appeared before Louisbourg. On July 26 the last cannon in front of the town was silenced and a breach was made in the redoubts. The time for an assault was at hand. Drucour hoped for favorable terms; but Amherst demanded that the garrison surrender as prisoners of war. Drucour determined to fight on, and supporting him was a council of his officers. But the Prévost, the civil chief of Louisbourg, perhaps remembering the massacre at Fort William Henry, laid before the commandant an urgent memorandum, "the prayer of an intimidated people." Then Drucour surrendered. There was no pillage, for English discipline was stern. The French wounded received the same treatment as the English. Victors and vanquished exchanged courtesies.

Nor did Amherst forget Madame Drucour. A Frenchman who was present recorded that "every favor she asked was granted." Her husband had been compelled to surrender Louisbourg, the invincible, but he had fought so well and so long that the English, because of the lateness of the season, could not proceed, as they had planned, to attack Quebec.

181   A View of Louisbourg in North America in 1758, from the contemporary engraving by P. Canot after the drawing by Captain Ince of the 35th Regiment, in the Emmet Collection, New York Public Library

182   Reconstruction of Fort Ticonderoga, from the drawing, courtesy of A. C. Bossom, New York

THE CAMPAIGN OF 1758 — TICONDEROGA

TICONDEROGA (known to the French as Carillon) was the southern salient of New France along the line of Lake Champlain. Here Montcalm now hoped, like Drucour, to keep the British army long enough at bay to prevent its advance to the St. Lawrence. He hardly dared to think of a decisive victory against so large a force in front, especially when he also had to reckon with the evil machinations of Vaudreuil and Bigot in his rear. The odds in men were four to one against him; over fifteen thousand British regulars and American militia against less than four thousand all told. But more than three thousand of these were excellent French regulars.

183   Lake George from Cook's Mountain, courtesy of the Delaware and Hudson Railroad, Albany, N. Y.

ABERCROMBY'S ARMY EMBARKING FOR TICONDEROGA

ABERCROMBY'S army embarked on a calm cloudless midsummer day in 1758, crowding the lovely waters of Lake George with an array of boats that stretched from shore to shore. America had never seen such pageantry of war. In the center were six thousand brilliant redcoats; on the flanks nine thousand blue provincials. The bands played martial music; the drums roused every rolling echo; while, piercing through, the Highland bagpipes called to their kilted men.

184   From the painting by F. C. Yohn (1875–), courtesy of the
Glen Falls (N. Y.) Insurance Co.

THE DEATH OF LORD HOWE

LANDING early the next morning, Abercromby's troops started through the dense woods toward Ticonderoga. An advance party under the young Lord Howe, the second in command, lost its way in the dark, tangled thickets, and suddenly surprised a French ranging party that was itself trying to grope its way back to the fort. Two hasty volleys were fired, and Lord Howe fell. No other man in the army was so universally admired and respected. Pitt called him "the model of all the military virtues"; Wolfe spoke of him as the best soldier in the army, a man peculiarly fitted for the American war. Young officers strove to be admitted to his regiment; older officers came under the spell of his energy, his clear judgment, his rare military capacity. The only officer in high command willing to discard the traditions of European warfare and adopt the habits of the rangers, he changed the uniforms of his troops, cut their long hair and taught them some of the principles of open-order combat. For himself, he left behind the luxury which too many British generals brought with them into the

185 George Augustus, Lord Howe, 1724–58, from the family portrait in England, photograph by courtesy of S. H. P. Pell, Ticonderoga, N. Y.

field, and lived the same rough life which his troops endured. The provincials recognized in him a sympathetic friend, as the tablet erected to his memory in Westminster Abbey by Massachusetts attests. By his death Abercromby suffered, as he admitted, irreparable loss — how truly irreparable the events of the next few days were to demonstrate.

ABERCROMBY'S MISTAKE

MONTCALM, full of apprehension at the approach of an army so greatly outnumbering his own, finally determined to concentrate his defense on a small hill to the west of the main fort. There he threw up rough breastworks, and on the slopes of the hill he arranged an abattis of logs, with sharpened branches pointing toward the enemy. Abercromby's failure to press on at once gave him time to complete these preparations. On the morning of the eighth, the British army, without its heavy guns, landed two miles below the fortress. Abercromby sent young Clerk, an engineer whose ability was acknowledged by both Wolfe and Howe, to report upon the French defenses. Clerk thought they could be carried by storm; and upon this advice

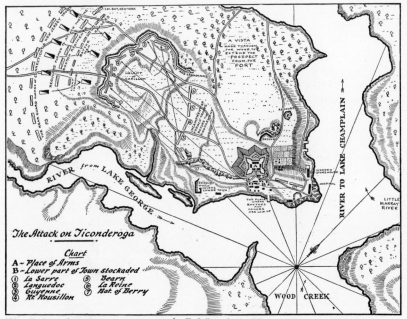

The Attack on Ticonderoga

Chart
A ~ Place of Arms
B ~ Lower part of Town stockaded
① La Sarre   ⑤ Bearn
② Languedoc   ⑥ La Reine
③ Guyenne   ⑦ Bat. of Berry
④ Rt. Rousillon

186   Redrawn from the contemporary map by T. Jefferys in the Library of Congress, Washington

Abercromby, without making further investigation, planned his series of direct frontal attacks upon the French position. Other and wiser courses were open to him: he might have flanked the fortress by marching through to Lake Champlain, cutting off Montcalm's communications, and preparing for a long, effective siege; or he might have brought up the artillery Montcalm feared, and which the French breastwork could not have long withstood. Instead, he threw away the advantage his vastly superior numbers gave him, and arranged his forces to carry the works by storm.

187   The Black Watch at Ticonderoga, from *Harper's Encyclopædia of United States History*,
drawing by Frederic Remington (1861–1909). © Harper & Brothers

THE CHARGE UP THE HEIGHTS

By noon the British forces were in position. The light infantry and rangers drove in the French pickets, and then, in three columns, the massed British redcoats advanced to the assault. Their orders were simple: not to fire until they were within the lines. The three thousand French regulars, from behind the security of their nine-foot embankment, waited till the enemy reached the abattis. Then a sheet of flame burst from their weapons, while the heavy guns from the fort in their rear tore through the British ranks.

In the face of that withering fire the British columns tried vainly, mad and infuriated at their own failure, to struggle through the interlaced branches. As each shattered regiment fell back, fresh ones advanced to take their places. For four hours the slaughter continued. Such a splendid exhibition of useless gallantry is rare in the annals of war. Among the most valiant and reckless were the Scottish Highlanders, some of whom, by superhuman efforts, actually reached the summit of the breastwork. Out of a thousand Scotchmen who entered that bloody field, only three hundred and fifty-three came out unwounded. Sixteen hundred regulars and three hundred and fifty provincials were killed or wounded. Montcalm lost only four hundred. Finally, Abercromby ordered the retreat; and the magnificent army that had landed so proudly two days before returned to its headquarters on the Hudson.

BRADSTREET'S EXPEDITION AGAINST FORT FRONTENAC, 1758

To retrieve as far as possible the disaster at Ticonderoga, Abercromby's council of war, on July 13, recommended the building of a fort at the great carrying-place on the Mohawk, and the dispatching of a force of provincials to attack Fort Frontenac on Lake Ontario. Lieutenant-Colonel Bradstreet, a New Englander who had served with distinction at Louisbourg in 1745 and had proved invaluable in the management of the irregulars engaged in the transportation of supplies, was selected to lead this expedition, which he had long been planning. On August 15, he was at the carrying-place, where Colonel Stanwix was constructing the new fort, with his little army of three thousand men, only a hundred and fifty of them regulars, the remainder provincials from various colonies. By August 22 he launched his men and guns from the harbor of ruined Oswego, in the whaleboats he had built the previous spring for the purpose and headed northward across Lake Ontario toward Fort Frontenac.

188   Bradstreet's Account for Pilots and Interpreters, Nov. 15, 1758,
from the original in the American Antiquarian Society, Worcester, Mass.

189   From the *London Magazine*, 1758

THE CAPTURE OF FORT FRONTENAC

FOUR days later, on August 25, Bradstreet appeared before the French fortress of Frontenac. He found a weak garrison. Of the two hundred and ten persons in the fort fifty-five were either voyageurs or women and children. The troops made little attempt to defend themselves. On the 27th articles of capitulation were signed; and vast quantities of stores, provisions, and furs fell into Bradstreet's hands. Seven of the nine captured vessels were destroyed; two brought back to Oswego the rich booty. In a tactical sense, the chief significance of this expedition is the rapidity with which Bradstreet moved. He proved that men trained in batteaux service could, if properly led, act quickly and well. Strategically, the capture of Frontenac was of great importance. Some of the captured provisions had been destined for Fort Duquesne. Henceforward there was no base of supplies on Lake Ontario from which vessels could safely transport necessities to the southward. The line of French communication with the western forts was cut. The continued occupation of the forts in the Ohio region was rendered hazardous.

JOHN FORBES IN PENNSYLVANIA

THE last part of the 1758 campaign was begun in May by Brigadier-General John Forbes, already suffering from the disease that was to cause his death. His orders were to move against Fort Duquesne. But for the accomplishment of these orders he needed diplomacy more than generalship and patient cajolery more than action. His motley little army of Highlanders, Royal Americans, provincials, and Cherokee Indians required delicate handling, while the inhabitants of the country through which he passed could be persuaded only by the utmost effort to lend their assistance. Inter-colonial jealousies cropped out to distress him.

190   Forbes Directing the Force on the March to Pittsburgh, 1758, drawn expressly for *The Pageant of America* by C. W. Jefferys

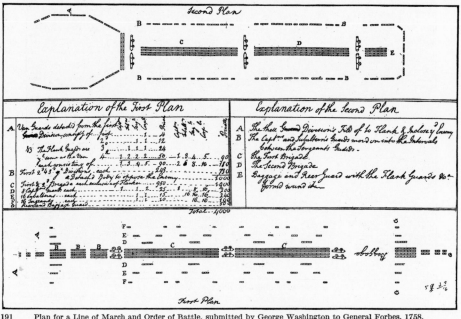

191   Plan for a Line of March and Order of Battle, submitted by George Washington to General Forbes, 1758,
from *Monuments of Washington's Patriotism*, 1843

THE MARCH TO FORT DUQUESNE

THE cutting of a straight road west over the mountains to Duquesne proved to be a slower and more painful labor than Forbes had anticipated; his progress was more snail-like than Braddock's had been, for he undertook to construct forts as he advanced. In the midst of it all, his own strength utterly failed; and, unable to sit on a horse or stand on his feet, he continued, with rare tenacity and determination, to direct operations from a rude cushioned litter, swung between two horses, in which the slightest movement caused intense pain. But he had the aid and support of a few excellent officers, Bouquet of the Royal Americans, Jack Grant of the Highlanders, and Washington and Lewis of the Virginia regiments.

In the middle of September, Grant persuaded Bouquet, who was with the advance party, to let him reconnoitre the French position. Unaccustomed to the region, they became confused in the dark woods, and the French, sallying from the fort with numbers of Indians, inflicted upon them near Loyalhannon a humiliating defeat. Nearly three hundred of Grant's force were killed; many went captive to Montreal. But the defeat did not greatly delay Forbes' steady advance. By November his main body was within striking distance of the objective toward which they had struggled so long.

192 Explanation in Washington's handwriting accompanying the Plan for a Line of March and Order of Battle, from *Monuments of Washington's Patriotism*, 1843

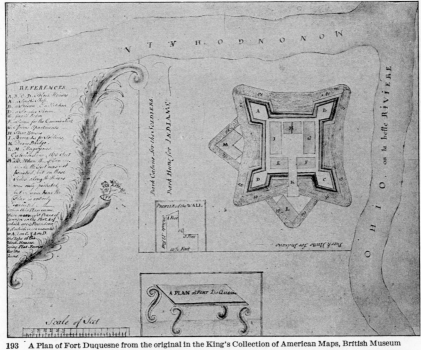

193   A Plan of Fort Duquesne from the original in the King's Collection of American Maps, British Museum

A, B, C, D. Block Houses. *A.* Smith's Shop. *B.* Prison. *C.* Kitchen. *D.* Powder Room. *E.* Guard Room. *F.* Room for the Commandant. *G.* Officers' Apartments. *H.* Store Houses. *I.* Barracks for Soldiers. *K.* Draw Bridge. *L, M.* Magazines. A note on the original states that the Fort had not been finished when the plan was made, but was "picketed on the sides along both rivers." There were eight pieces of cannon in the Fort, the "tops of the blockhouses being platforms for the guns."

FORBES TAKES FORT DUQUESNE, 1758

DE LIGNERIS, the French commandant at Fort Duquesne, short of provisions, deserted by his Indians, sent all but three or four hundred men back to Canada, evidently under the impression that no English force could get through that season. He had no alternative therefore, when the news of Forbes' approach with a picked force reached him, except to abandon the fort, after destroying whatever guns he could. On November 26 the British marched into the great deserted stronghold, and Forbes, dating his letter from "Pittsbourgh," proudly wrote to his great leader: "I do myself the Honour of acquainting you that it has pleased God to crown His Majesty's Arms with Success over all His Enemies upon the Ohio." The severe journey back to Philadelphia laid the last burden on his enfeebled constitution and a few months after his return he died.

CHRISTIAN POST AND THE OHIO INDIANS, 1758

ONE more brilliant exploit, closely connected with the fall of Fort Duquesne, needs to be recorded in this year. To the Ohio Indians, long the allies of the French, their wigwams hung with the scalps of many a murdered English settler, went, unarmed and alone, a simple Moravian missionary, Christian Post. With a quiet courage, as commendable as the mad valor of the Highlanders at Ticonderoga, he fearlessly entered the Indian villages on the Ohio, and, often in the presence of French officers, brought them the message that the English desired peace. That he escaped death is miraculous, that he succeeded beyond the hopes of those who sent him out is more miraculous still. But the Indians were convinced by his pleadings and consented to bury the hatchet, leaving in peace the Ohio valley, which for three years had been a vale of terror to all the middle colonies.

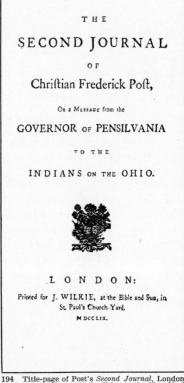

THE

SECOND JOURNAL

OF

Chriſtian Frederick Poſt,

On a MESSAGE from the

GOVERNOR OF PENSILVANIA

TO THE

INDIANS ON THE OHIO.

LONDON:

Printed for J. WILKIE, at the Bible and Sun, in St. Paul's Church-Yard.
M DCC LIX.

194   Title-page of Post's *Second Journal*, London, 1759, from the original edition in the New York Public Library

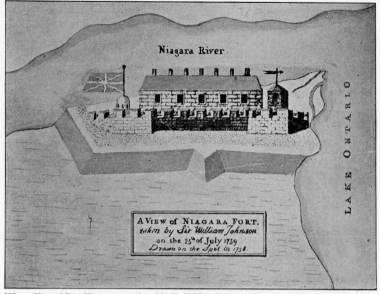

Niagara River

LAKE ONTARIO

A VIEW of NIAGARA FORT.
taken by Sir William Johnson
on the 25th of July 1759
Drawn on the Spot in 1758

195   View of Fort Niagara, reproduced in Sir William Johnson's *Papers*, published by the
University of the State of New York, Albany, 1921

THE CAMPAIGN OF 1759

WITH the capture of Louisbourg, Acadia, Frontenac, and Duquesne, the French outposts on the east and west had been reduced to one, Fort Niagara, which had been largely rebuilt and strengthened by Pouchot, a French engineer. For military purposes, therefore, the frontier had contracted, and the major operations could be levelled at the heart of Canada, Quebec and Montreal. Peculation and corruption continued in the French administration of Canada. The government in Paris, unmindful of the desperate straits to which Montcalm was reduced, steadily refused to send out enough sorely needed men and supplies. Moreover, by this time the British command of the sea was strong enough to have almost certainly intercepted any considerable force. Montcalm had about four thousand French regulars, with perhaps twice as many French Canadians who could be drawn into combatant service outside of harvest time. On the other hand, Pitt sent out more than a quarter of the whole Royal Navy. Amherst, now commander-in-chief, could depend upon thirty-five thousand troops, half of them provincials and rangers. Against so formidable a foe Montcalm could scarcely hope to save Canada for another year. Amherst ordered Stanwix to make "Pittsburgh" safe from any reasonable danger, and sent Prideaux with five thousand men, over half of them New York provincials, and six hundred Indians under Sir William Johnson, to take Niagara. Pouchot, with less than five hundred men, made a gallant defense against the blundering siege tactics of his assailants; but his task was an impossible one. A relief force of Indians and *coureurs de bois*, gathered from the Ohio region, fell into Sir William Johnson's ambuscade, and was cut to pieces. Pouchot surrendered Niagara on July 24; and the whole control of the lakes passed from French hands. There remained only the St. Lawrence River valley, with Montreal and Quebec, besides the precarious French southern outpost of Crown Point.

THE FALL OF TICONDEROGA, JULY 26, 1759

AMHERST advanced up the well-known route toward Lake Champlain with more than eleven thousand men, half of them provincials, an overwhelming force. At Ticonderoga lay Bourlamaque, Montcalm's efficient lieutenant, with twenty-five hundred men, but with orders to retreat slowly before the English. When Amherst arrived before the formidable fortress he found it abandoned. A French deserter told him that a slow match was burning toward the magazine; but before it could be found the calm, dark, summer night was rent by a sheet of flame, against which the last French flag still waved defiance. Dashing through the inferno, a sergeant of Gage's hauled these colors down.

196   Ruins of Fort Ticonderoga.   © Detroit Publishing Co.

AMHERST HALTED AT CROWN POINT

MARCHING toward Crown Point, Amherst found that fortress likewise deserted, for Bourlamaque was making his stand at the Isle-aux-Noix, beyond the north end of Lake Champlain. Here the British were stopped, in spite of their numbers, by four tiny little xebecs, armed with cannon, manned by sailors, an insuperable obstacle (see map, No. 130). Before Amherst's own boats, which should have been built before, were ready, the winter set in, and Amherst himself fell back to restore Crown Point. Had this campaign been planned with an eye to local sea power, and then pushed with energy, Montreal must have fallen into British hands.

197   A French Xebec of twenty guns, from Edmond Paris, *Le Musée de Marine du Louvre*, Paris, 1883

THE QUEBEC CAMPAIGN; SAUNDERS

SIR CHARLES SAUNDERS was one of Pitt's chosen admirals. A man full of zeal, knowledge, experience, and resource, he was entirely fit to lead the greatest fleet that had ever crossed the Atlantic — the greatest war fleet, indeed, that ever was to cross it for hostilities up to the time of the Great World War. In spite of intricate navigation, and of all the French could do to confuse and stop him, Saunders took two hundred and seventy-seven vessels, of which forty-nine were men-of-war, safely up the St. Lawrence. Of the twenty-seven thousand men in the crews a few hundred naval ratings were "prime seamen" from Boston, while a great many hundreds more aboard the transports were first-rate Yankee sailors.

198   General Sir Charles Saunders, from the engraving in the Dominion Archives, Ottawa

GENERAL WOLFE, 1727–59

JAMES WOLFE had been noted by Pitt for high command in spite of his youth — he was only thirty-two. He had been the most promising brigadier at Louisbourg. Now he was to command the little army of under nine thousand men, which really was no more than a landing party from the fleet. Over seven hundred were American rangers, the rest regular troops of the line.

199   From the portrait by Joseph Highmore (1692–1780) in the National Portrait Gallery, London

200   From a contemporary view taken by Captain Hervey Smyth, Aide-de-Camp to General Wolfe, engraving by
                                        Binazech, in the New York Public Library

QUEBEC IN 1759

QUEBEC was not a fortress. But it was a great natural stronghold, particularly in that age of smooth-bore guns; and if the entire resources of New France, poor as they were, had been honestly administered and wholly committed to the incorruptible Montcalm, then even that indefatigable man of talent, Wolfe, could not have won Quebec this year.

201   From a print in possession of the publishers after an original painting, location and artist unknown

FRENCH FIRE SHIPS ATTACKING THE BRITISH FLEET AT QUEBEC

THE French at Quebec sent seven fire ships down on the British fleet with the ebb tide at midnight on June 28–29. All were safely grappled and towed clear by the men-of-war boats. Nearly a month later the French renewed their attempt to burn the main body of the British fleet, this time by sending down no less than seventy-two fire rafts. De Courval, a thoroughly competent and most heroic leader, managed to set a couple of British vessels on fire. But these fires were soon put out, the other rafts were towed clear of the ships, and Courval barely escaped with his life. In the midst of the excitement one British bluejacket was heard hailing another with the pertinent query: "Damn me, Jack; but did you ever take Hell in tow before?"

THE SIEGE OF QUEBEC

IMPEDED at every turn by foolish Vaudreuil and knavish Bigot, Montcalm was forced to put his main body below Quebec. In mere numbers his army was as three against two, compared with Wolfe's nine thousand. But he had only four thousand French regulars, compared with Wolfe's eight thousand British. At first, however, Montcalm succeeded well, for Wolfe

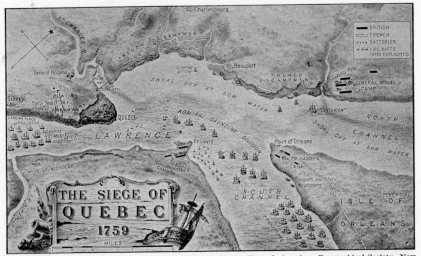

202   Redrawn expressly for *The Pageant of America* by Gregor Noetzel, American Geographical Society, New York, from the plan in Thomas Jefferys, *Natural and Civil History of the French Movement in North and South America*, London, 1761

failed twice: first, to cross the Montmorency fords, a few miles up, and take the French position from the rear, secondly, to rush the Montmorency Heights by a frontal attack.

BOUGAINVILLE

FOR six weeks after his Montmorency defeat Wolfe gradually felt his way into an attack from above, instead of below, Quebec; thanks, of course, to the overwhelming fleet. Montcalm sent a gradually increasing force under Louis Antoine de Bougainville, one of his best officers, to forestall Wolfe. But as Bouganville's underfed men had to scramble across a very rough country, day after day, to keep abreast of the ships, which went up and down with the tide, his whole command was worn out before the final struggle came.

203   From the portrait by Albert Rosenthal in Independence Hall, Philadelphia, after a family portrait

THE TAKING OF QUEBEC

THIS very inaccurate *View of the Taking of Quebec* does, at all events, show how the fleet let Wolfe attack from above. Wolfe's brigadiers had proposed landing more than twenty miles above, where an entrenched British army would have forced Vaudreuil to starve, to fight, or to surrender the whole of New France; for Montcalm could not have got past, as there were

204   From the engraving in the *London Magazine*, 1760

no other roads for an army, and the St. Lawrence was held by the fleet. But Wolfe preferred landing just above Quebec, where an alternative road did exist. It ran west, from the valley of the St. Charles, till it joined the solitary upper road twenty miles west of Quebec. However wrong strategically, Wolfe's landing was a triumph of amphibious tactics, faultlessly carried out by the ships and army on the spot, and admirably supported by the fleet higher up as well as below Quebec.

205   From the painting by C. W. Jefferys in
        possession of the publishers

MONTCALM AT THE BATTLE OF THE PLAINS

THOUGH the British fleet formed an impenetrable screen, and though Wolfe had kept his plan so secret that even his own brigadiers never learned it till eight hours before the landing, yet once more Montcalm had divined what might happen and had twice ordered troops to the spot. Even before Wolfe's brigadiers knew the place of landing Montcalm had ordered a battalion of French regulars to encamp across the very path Wolfe took next morning. But Vaudreuil gave immediate counterorders. Cruel indeed was Montcalm's fate to be yoked with such a partner in command! Even when Wolfe's redcoats appeared on the Plains of Abraham, Vaudreuil still thwarted Montcalm as much as he dared.

THE FRENCH LINE CUT TO PIECES

ON the Plains of Abraham was a comparatively flat and open battlefield, where Indian and French-Canadian tactics were of very little use, and where formed bodies, using collective fire and charging with the bayonet, were on their proper terrain. Montcalm's three little battalions of French-Canadian regulars, untrained and improperly armed for such fighting, streamed off to the flanks, where the militia and Indians kept cover. This left five six-deep French regular battalions face to face with six two-deep British — the first two-deep "thin red line" in the world. Swept in front and on both flanks by withering and well-controlled fire, the French line of battle in the open was smashed to pieces by the charge.

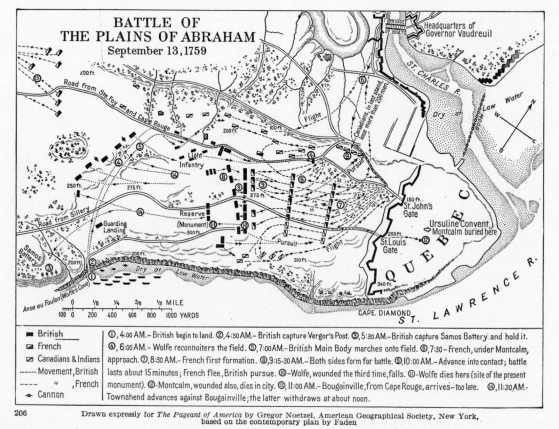

BATTLE OF
THE PLAINS OF ABRAHAM
September 13, 1759

British	①, 4:00 A.M.– British begin to land. ②, 4:30 A.M.– British capture Vergor's Post. ③, 5:30 A.M.– British capture Samos Battery and hold it.
French	④, 6:00 A.M.– Wolfe reconnoiters the field. ⑤, 7:00 A.M.–British Main Body marches onto field. ⑥, 7:30 – French, under Montcalm,
Canadians & Indians	approach. ⑦, 8:30 A.M.– French first formation. ⑧, 9:15-30 A.M.– Both sides form for battle. ⑨, 10:00 A.M.– Advance into contact; battle
······· Movement, British	lasts about 15 minutes; French flee, British pursue. ⑩–Wolfe, wounded the third time, falls. ⑪–Wolfe dies here (site of the present
----- " ,French	monument). ⑫–Montcalm, wounded also, dies in city. ⑬, 11:00 A.M.– Bougainville, from Cape Rouge, arrives–too late. ⑭,11:30 A.M.–
← Cannon	Townshend advances against Bougainville; the latter withdraws at about noon.

207   From the painting, 1771, by Benjamin West (1738–1820), in the War Memorial Collection,
Public Archives, Dominion of Canada, Ottawa

THE DEATH OF GENERAL WOLFE

WOLFE died victorious on the field in the presence of a very few men. This famous picture grouped some important absentees around him for artistic and other effects. Montcalm also lost his life on this bloody field of battle. With Champlain, LaSalle, and Frontenac his name stands in the small list of the great leaders who served France in the New World. His personal fate symbolized the tragedy which had overtaken his country. With him died the dreams of his mighty predecessors.

"GOD BE PRAISED; QUEBECK IS IN ENGLISH HANDS"

IT is impossible for later generations living within the United States to imagine how enthusiastically the northern English colonies welcomed the fall of Quebec. For seventy years Quebec had been the stronghold from which parties of French and Indians had issued from time to time to bring terror to the frontier. Its very name had come almost to symbolize the horrors of border wars. Again and again New Englanders, together with men from New York, had aided expeditions to encompass its downfall. But all had met with failure. It must have seemed to those English-speaking men and women of 1759 too good to be true that Quebec had fallen. For the first time in nearly three quarters of a century their fears of the menace from the north relaxed. No wonder they expressed the deep emotions of the hour in prayers to Almighty God. In England the enthusiasm was unbounded, great bonfires blazed, bells pealed their triumph, while the people exulted one moment in the victory and wept the next for the loss of Wolfe.

208   Newspaper Account published at New London, Conn., Oct. 15, 1759, of the Fall of Quebec, original in the Massachusetts Historical Society, Boston

209 The Chevalier de Lévis, from a photogravure in possession of the publishers after the portrait in the Versailles Gallery

THE FINAL CAMPAIGN OF 1760

Murray, Wolfe's third brigadier, succeeded to the command of the seven thousand men who garrisoned Quebec through the dire winter of 1759–60. Scarcity of food, sickness and suffering reduced that number by the spring to three thousand effective men; but through it all they kept up amazingly cheerful spirits. Lévis, now commanding the French army, passed an even more terrible winter at Montreal. In April, as soon as he could possibly move, he made a

210 Brigadier-General James Murray, from an engraving in the Public Archives, Dominion of Canada, Ottawa

forced march down the St. Lawrence to Quebec where, on the 28th, he sent six thousand men into action against Murray. The latter, instead of remaining within the walls, sallied out to meet his adversary at the Battle of Sainte-Foy (or the second battle of the Plains). After the desperate and bloody fight that followed between these two weakened and weary armies, the British, having lost more than a third of their number, fell back to Quebec. Lévis at once moved up his few guns and commenced a formal siege, the issue of which, as everyone knew, depended on whether it was a French or British fleet that first forced its torturous way up the St. Lawrence channel. Victory on land was useful; but could never be decisive. Whichever side won at sea would inevitably dominate the land as well. But the French West Indian fleet had limped home months before; there was none to replace it; and so the British were bound to win.

VAUQUELIN, FRENCH NAVAL HERO OF QUEBEC

Among both the French and British all eyes turned seaward, and even French hopes ran high. No news had yet come out from Europe, and might not a French fleet arrive to compel the surrender of Quebec just before peace was made at Paris? But there was to be no peace for three more years, and the first fleet up was British. Lévis at once broke camp and retired to Montreal, while Vauquelin, who had fought well at Louisbourg, now fought a rearguard naval action that saved the honor of the flag better than Lévis' victory. Driven ashore at Pointe-aux-Trembles (Aspen Point, twenty miles above Quebec) he kept the *Atalante* in action to the very last against the far stronger *Lowestoff* and *Diana*. When only six officers and six men remained aboard, the British boats rowed in and hailed him to lower his flag. "You must do it yourselves," he answered, "for I will not." The boarding party then hauled his colors down and took the heroic twelve to British headquarters, where they were received with every honor and supplied with every need.

211 The French frigates *Le Pomone* and *L'Atalante* pursued by the British fleet, from Charles de Bonnechose, *Montcalm et le Canada Français*, 1888

FRENCH UNIFORMS · FRENCH AND INDIAN WAR · 1754-1763

LA SARRE
REGIMENT
PRIVATE

COMPAGNIES
FRANCHES DE LA MARINE
PRIVATE

ROYAL ROUSSILLON
REGIMENT
COLONEL

GUIENNE
REGIMENT
PRIVATE

ENGINEER
OFFICER

LIEUTENANT
GENERAL

ARTILLERY
OFFICER

BEARN
REGIMENT
SERGEANT

LANGUEDOC
REGIMENT
CAPTAIN

BOURGOGNE
REGIMENT
PRIVATE

OFFICIER
PORTE DRAPEAUX
(ENSIGN)

CANADIAN
MILITIA

COUREUR
DES BOIS

IROQUOIS
WARRIOR

Painted expressly for *The Pageant of America* by H. A. Ogden

SIR JEFFREY AMHERST

AMHERST closed in on Montreal all through the summer. His own ten thousand troops came down from Lake Ontario. Pouchot, who had been immensely popular with the British officers as a prisoner of war, was now defending Fort Lévis, five miles below Ogdensburg on the St. Lawrence in New York. As the long array of troop-filled boats swept past the little fort, its garrison fired hard, sinking several small craft, though receiving good fire in return. While great guns and small arms were at their very hardest, some British officers, who knew him well, called out: "Good luck to Monsieur Pouchot!" Whereupon the gallant Pouchot climbed the ramparts and stood politely bowing, hat in hand, in the midst of shot and shell.

212 From the portrait by Sir Joshua Reynolds in the National Portrait Gallery, London

213   From a contemporary print in the Public Archives, Dominion of Canada, Ottawa

THE FINAL CAMPAIGN OF 1760 — MONTREAL

EARLY in September the three converging British forces met on the Island of Montreal, Murray having come up from Quebec, strongly reinforced, while Haviland arrived from Lake Champlain. The French-Canadians, seeing New France was lost, went home; and Lévis was left facing an army eight times stronger than his own, to say nothing of Lord Colville's fleet. On September 8 the terms were signed; and France laid down her New World arms forever.

THE TREATY OF PARIS, 1763

THE Treaty of Paris (see Vol. VIII) changed profoundly the military problems of the North American continent. This year saw the fading of the imperial ambitions of France in Canada and the valley of the Mississippi. The line of forts which once stretched from Quebec to New Orleans (see map, No. 129) now served to remind the voyageur in America of the great dream which did not come true. For the English colonists the treaty marked the passing of a great danger. After 1763 the frontiersman in New Hampshire and what was to be Vermont built his cabin and cleared his fields happy in the knowledge that no French raiding party would again lay waste his settlement. Far to the south the people of Georgia saw with satisfaction the Spaniards depart from Florida. West of the Appalachians was a vast area little touched by white settlement and beyond the Mississippi stretched Louisiana, in the possession of Spain.

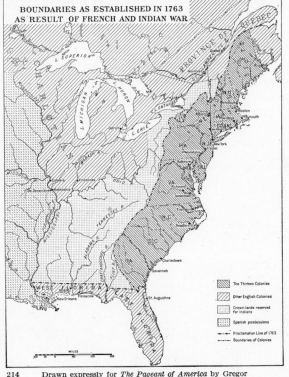

BOUNDARIES AS ESTABLISHED IN 1763 AS RESULT OF FRENCH AND INDIAN WAR

The Thirteen Colonies
Other English Colonies
Crown-lands reserved for Indians
Spanish possessions
Proclamation Line of 1763
Boundaries of Colonies

214   Drawn expressly for *The Pageant of America* by Gregor Noetzel, American Geographical Society, New York

CHAPTER IV

THE AFTERMATH OF THE FRENCH AND INDIAN WAR, 1761–64

WITH the news of the Treaty of Paris, the people of the British Isles rejoiced and the North American colonists who had joined the forces of the king prepared to take up again the tasks of peace. The white tents of the British soldiers, dotting the shores near Montreal, were a token that the French had been decisively driven from Canada. But the task was not yet finished. Pitt had been driven from power before hostilities had ended. His plan for 1761 had been to utilize the troops lying idle in North America after the fall of Quebec and Montreal for an attack upon the French West Indies, those fertile sugar islands whose competition sometimes pressed hard the planters of the British islands. Then had come the news of an alliance between Spain and France. Pitt pressed for an immediate declaration of war upon the new enemy, but fell before he could accomplish his purpose. War was inevitable, however, and, early in 1762, became a fact. To Pitt's plan for the conquest of the French islands was added that of an expedition against that great Spanish stronghold, Havana, the center of the Spanish trade in the New World. This came before the Peace of Paris was signed, and twenty-three hundred provincial troops participated. It was the last oversea expedition in which Americans served under the British flag.

Before the war was over, also, British troops aided by Americans were called upon to protect the frontier of the southern colonies. The Cherokees whose homes were in the southern Appalachians, goaded on by the advance of the white settlers and by indignities they had suffered at the hands of their new neighbors, swept down from their upland strongholds and carried destruction to the border. When British regulars advanced against them, it was clear that the lessons of Braddock's defeat had been well learned. The redcoats knew how to fight in the American wilderness. The Indians could no longer stand against them.

Yet one great Indian leader dared to face them and hoped to throw back the ever advancing frontier. Just after the war was over and English and Americans alike were rejoicing in the calm that followed long years of hostilities, Pontiac rose to give battle anew. One of the most intelligent and statesmanlike leaders that the Indian race has ever produced, so masterful and dominating that his personal power welded discordant tribes who had never acted in unison before, Pontiac brought war to the whole country from the outposts of Pennsylvania to the shores of Lake Michigan. He molded jealous tribes to his will and unified them with a single purpose. He struck suddenly, and with great power. Yet, once more, regular and provincial troops, ably commanded, met and vanquished the undisciplined host. The uprising was not without importance in world politics. It brought home to the British Government the menace that threatened the frontier. The year after it was put down, George Grenville moved in the House of Commons to place a defensive force of ten thousand men in North America and to pay the expense in part from the proceeds of a stamp tax. So began the chain of events which led to the American Revolution.

MARSHALING THE FORCES AGAINST HAVANA, 1762

IN January General Monckton's army of eight thousand men, aided by the fleet under Rodney, conducted a brilliant and difficult siege against the French position at Fort Royal, Martinique, which they finally captured after nearly a month's work. The remnant of Monckton's troops, depleted by sickness, were joined to

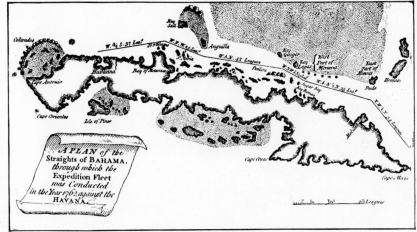

215

From the *London Magazine*, 1763

the army which Lord Albemarle, in command of the expedition against Havana, brought out from England. Amherst was to send additional forces, with some twenty-five hundred provincials, from New York. Albemarle's total strength was to be about fifteen thousand. The fleet was commanded by Admiral Sir George Pocock, who, relying upon Anson's carefully prepared charts, determined to approach Havana, not by the southern route of the galleons, but by the dangerous, little-used Bahama channel. Such a maneuver would not only result in a decided surprise for the Spanish garrison, who never dreamed that a strong force could ever navigate that narrow and intricate channel, it would also cut off any possibilities of French supplies slipping in the back way. Cautiously groping his way by the aid of vessels stationed on the more dangerous shoals, Pocock brought his whole fleet and convoy safely through, a wonderful piece of seamanship and daring.

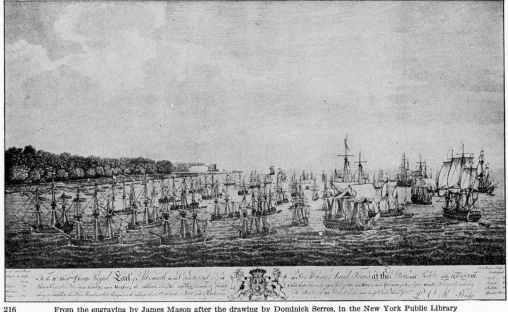

216   From the engraving by James Mason after the drawing by Dominick Serres, in the New York Public Library

THE LANDING OF THE FORCES, JUNE 6

ON June 6, the fleet came in sight of Havana. So secure did the Spaniards feel that when an excited officer burst into headquarters with the astounding news that the British fleet was standing in from the Old Bahama Channel he was severely reprimanded for spreading a false alarm. Pocock dispatched thirteen sail of the line to block up the small Spanish fleet in the harbor, and the next day safely landed the army six miles east of Moro Castle. Brushing aside a force of militia that stood in its path, the army arrived on June 8 beside the principal defenses of Havana.

217   Entering the Breach of Moro Castle by Storm, from the engraving by Canot after the
        drawing by Dominick Serres, in the New York Public Library

MORO CASTLE STORMED, JULY 30

ON a rocky ridge beside the open sea stood Moro Castle, guarding the northern shore of the entrance to Havana Harbor. Albemarle, perhaps unwisely, determined to attack this stronghold rather than the city itself. On June 11 his infantry captured without difficulty a detached redoubt, and set themselves to the planting of batteries. The work was unusually slow and difficult. The rocky ground prevented digging, and both earth and water had to be brought from a distance. Occasional raiding parties from the fortress made unsuccessful forays. On July 1 the batteries opened, aided by broadsides from some of the fleet. But the garrison returned the bombardment from the sea with such telling effect that the English ships withdrew, badly damaged, and thereafter dependence was placed entirely upon shore batteries partly protected behind gabions stuffed with cotton. Then the devastating fever set in. Of the covering party a few miles inland not a man escaped its ravages, while the troops on the ridge suffered also. Throughout the whole weary month of July the siege dragged on, the Spanish garrison defending its walls with great courage and obstinacy.

At length the American contingent arrived, part of its forces having been captured at sea by the French. The effect produced on the tired, fever-ridden besiegers was electric. Three days later, on July 30, the mines under one of the bastions were sprung. Through the narrow breach the storming party entered, and Moro Castle surrendered under its gallant defender, Velasco, who was mortally wounded. In honor of his defense the Spanish navy has never since been without a ship named the *Velasco*.

THE SURRENDER OF HAVANA, AUGUST 14, 1762

FOLLOWING the fall of Moro Castle the siege was pressed home. New batteries were planted along the shore; and after an intense bombardment, in which Fort Puntal, on the southern side of the harbor entrance, was silenced, the Spanish Governor surrendered with the honors of war. Specie and valuables to the amount of three million pounds sterling fell into the hands of the British. Nine of the Spanish ships were captured, the others having been burned on the stocks or sunk in the harbor. Yet the price of victory was heavy. The British lost in the siege less than a thousand killed or wounded; but during the period from June 8 to October 18 they buried five thousand who had died of fever. A third of the Americans died, and many more remained invalids for life. In this last colonial oversea campaign. Rhode Island, Connecticut, Massachusetts, New York, and New Jersey were represented by provincial troops. Phineas Lyman of Connecticut, who had been in service every year since 1755, was in command, and was seconded by Colonel Israel Putnam.

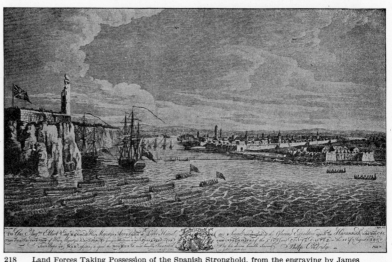

218   Land Forces Taking Possession of the Spanish Stronghold, from the engraving by James
        Mason after the drawing by Dominick Serres, in the New York Public Library

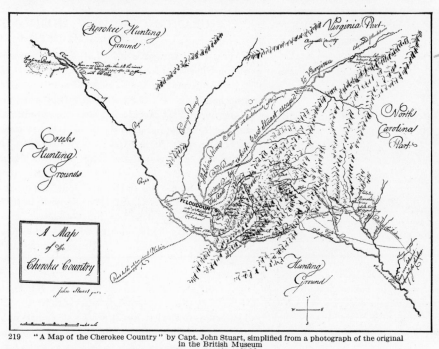

219   "A Map of the Cherokee Country" by Capt. John Stuart, simplified from a photograph of the original
in the British Museum

THE CHEROKEE UPRISING

THE friendship of the powerful Cherokees, who dwelt along the headwaters of the Tennessee, had long been sought by both the French and English. Situated near the back settlements of Virginia and North Carolina, the Cherokees were inclined toward the English. But toward the end of the French and Indian War, the peace, always dubious at best, could no longer be maintained. Some Virginians had killed a group of Cherokees who stole horses; and Governor Lyttleton of South Carolina had treated their chiefs with gross indignity, imprisoning some who came on a peaceful mission. Moreover, at Fort Prince George on the Savannah River the officer in charge, attacked by a small band, murdered the Indian hostages within the fort. The result was disastrous. Up and down the borders the whole tribe rose in fury. Most terrible among the massacres that followed was that of the Calhouns, fifty of whom were killed. In 1760 Sir Jeffery Amherst sent down Colonel Montgomery of the Highland regiment with eleven hundred men. Accompanied by four hundred South Carolinian troops he marched with unusual speed into the Cherokee country. Suddenly the Indians, lying in ambush, burst upon him as they had upon Braddock. Part of his troops plunged into the forest to engage them, while the others hurried to the rear to cut off the retreat. After a sharp contest of an hour, during which Montgomery lost eighty men, the Indians were put to flight. He went on, and reduced to ashes many of the towns and villages on the east side of the mountains. But his orders to return to New York prevented him from relieving famished Fort Loudoun on the Tennessee. Its garrison, under Raymond Demere, capitulated. As they were marching forth, they were attacked, some being killed, others captured. Captain Stuart, the second in command, whose route is shown on the map, was aided by his lifelong friend, the Cherokee chief, and managed to escape to Virginia.

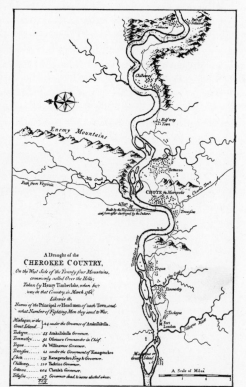

220   "A Draught of the Cherokee Country" (region of Tennessee River), from *The Memoirs of Lieut. Henry Timberlake*, London, 1765

221 "Cunne Shote, the Indian Chief. A Great Warrior of the Cherokee Nation," from a mezzotint engraving by James McArdell after the portrait by F. Parsons, London, 1762(?)

GRANT'S CAMPAIGN AGAINST THE CHEROKEES, 1761

CAPTAIN STUART gave information of the projected plans of the Cherokees for continuing the war, and the following year Lieutenant Colonel James Grant, of the Highlanders, who had been with Forbes at Fort Duquesne, and was now Governor of East Florida, led some twenty-six hundred men, among them the Carolina regiment, into the Indian country. Near the spot where Montgomery had been attacked his force was set upon by a large body of Cherokees, who rushed down the slopes of a hill to meet his advance guard. For three hours the battle continued; but at length the Indians gave way. Grant then marched into the heart of the Cherokee country, burning the cornfields and the villages, killing as many as came within his reach. Those who escaped suffered miserably. Finally, their chiefs sued for peace.

THE FINAL INDIAN WAR CLOUD IN THE WEST, 1760

FRENCH CANADA, at its surrender, included all the country between the Ohio and the Great Lakes, as well as the valley of the St. Lawrence. It was necessary, then, for the British to take possession of the various outposts and forts that still flew the lilies of France. Major Robert Rogers, the famous ranger, was sent on this ominous mission. At a place near the present site of Cleveland, Ohio, he met Pontiac, who, learning the message the white men bore, smoked the pipe of peace, but with growing anger in his heart. For Pontiac, like many other Indians, could not understand why his lands should pass into the possession of an unliked race merely because two white armies had fought a few hundred miles to the eastward. The French, whatever their own motives, had respected the belief of the Indian that he lived and hunted on his own territories. The English, who seldom practiced that kind of diplomacy, showed in all their actions that they regarded the broad forests as the rightful domain of the British Crown. The following spring tiny detachments of the Royal American Regiment were stationed at all the forts which the French had built, at Niagara, Presqu'-Isle, Le Bœuf, and Venango in the East, Sandusky, Miamis, and Detroit by Lake Erie, Ouiatenon on the Wabash, and Michilimackinac, La Haye, and St. Joseph on the far shores of Michigan. For two years this handful of British soldiers passed their dreary time as best they could; while at New York, Amherst, deaf to all warnings that the Indians might prove dangerous, refused to strengthen his garrisons or take steps to conciliate the warriors that frequented them.

222   The Meeting of Major Robert Rogers and Pontiac, from the mural painting by C. Y. Turner (1850-1918) in the County Court House, Cleveland

PONTIAC TAKES UP THE HATCHET, 1763

BRITISH trade goods were far better and far cheaper than French, partly because of the knavish French Intendant Bigot and his whole thieving gang, but mainly because of British sea power, both mercantile and naval. There, however, in most Indian eyes, all Indian advantages stopped, so far as nearly all the English-speaking people were concerned. Indians were no longer humored, but, as a rule, treated with contempt; while over all loomed the dire foreshadowing of dispossession at the hands of English-speaking folk. Resentment grew, spread fast and far, came north from ruined Cherokees, was nursed by French-speaking traders, pro-French Indians, and self-respecting Indians most of all. Pontiac was both medicine man and war chief, and the only Indian having the power of combining many different tribes into a single force. So, when the Delaware Prophet revealed visions of a new Indian life in 1762, and Pontiac himself took up the hatchet in 1763, the Indian frontier was soon aflame with savage war. This war was one of those which inevitably follow all frontier life between two such dissimilar peoples.

223   From the engraving by J. Rogers after the drawing by Chapin

THE INDIAN ATTACK ON FORT DETROIT, MAY, 1763

PONTIAC was a century too late. But he struck hard. His "Conspirators," ignorant of the overwhelming white forces hidden beyond the Indian frontier, were full of hope that they were soon to be revenged. Pontiac's strategic instinct served him well when he attacked Detroit, where Major Gladwin and heroic Captain Campbell commanded the little garrison. Campbell, having attended a conference before the war broke out, was treacherously held prisoner by Pontiac. Then Gladwin sent his schooner for reinforcements. While she lay becalmed at the mouth of the Detroit River, an Indian canoe flotilla darted at her, with Campbell in the bow of the first canoe. "Fire! Fire!! never mind me!" called out Campbell. But a sudden breeze took the schooner into safer waters. The Chippewas afterward killed Campbell and ate his heart, hoping thereby to inherit his transcendent courage. The siege of Fort Detroit was on.

224   From the drawing by Frederic Remington in *Harper's Encyclopaedia of United States History*. © Harper & Bros.

225   An Indian Attack, from the painting by Stanley M. Arthurs
                    (1877–), courtesy of the artist

THE CAPTURE OF THE
OUTLYING FORTS, 1763

DETROIT was reinforced and never taken; though the Indians, with rare persistence, maintained a desultory siege for several months. But most of the other forts fell, and the greater part of their small garrisons were murdered. The Indians, to gain unexpected and sudden entrance, practiced several stratagems. At Sandusky and St. Joseph the officer commanding was called to the gate to speak with a few Indians who came, as was their custom, to loiter about the fort. Suddenly he was seized and overpowered, while other Indians rushed in at the open gate and made short work of the few defenders. At Miamis young Ensign Holmes was betrayed by his Indian mistress, and shot down when he went to her aid. At far Michilimackinac the Chippewas gathered without the fort to play ball, tossed the ball close to the gate, where the British officers were watching, and then rushed in to seize from the hands of their squaws the hatchets which had been hidden under their blankets. Ensign Christie at Presqu'-Isle was warned of the uprising, but could not defend his badly situated fort against the fireballs and blazing arrows of his foes, to whom he surrendered. Two of his thirty men escaped; the rest were killed or taken into captivity. Of the garrison at Venango no survivor remained to tell the story. Fort Pitt was attacked thrice during the summer, but held out successfully, till the approach of Bouquet from the east caused the Indians to raise the siege and go to meet him. Fort Ligonier, in Pennsylvania, though with a garrison of only three men and two boys, likewise managed to stave off the attacks till relief came.

COLONEL HENRY BOUQUET

BOUQUET was a Swiss soldier of fortune who added to an admirable knowledge of the art of war as practiced in Europe the ability to adapt himself to frontier conditions. Together with his friend Haldimand, who later became Governor-General of Canada, he had received one of the earliest commissions in the Royal American Regiment, had been instrumental in raising it, and had devoted himself to training and disciplining his battalion, which was the first and best. The Royal Americans are to-day the King's Royal Rifle Corps, with as splendid a record as any regiment in the British service. Bouquet in 1763–64 established his reputation as one of the greatest Indian fighters to see action in North America. He understood the redskin's fighting methods and had devised plans to defeat his adversaries at their own game. He seemed also to sense the psychology of the forest warrior, for he proved himself as capable in conference as on the field of battle. A dark day dawned for Pontiac when Bouquet started westward with his troops.

226   From a copy of the portrait by Benjamin West, in the Historical Society of Pennsylvania, original owned by George Harrison Fisher of Philadelphia

BOUQUET MARCHES TO THE INDIAN FRONTIER

At New York Amherst took some time to grasp the meaning of Pontiac's "Conspiracy"; and he was late in ordering Bouquet to the front, from Philadelphia to Fort Pitt. The colonial authorities were even slower than Amherst; and when Bouquet reached Carlisle on July 1 nothing was ready. Yet, by his own indefatigable and stimulating work, he succeeded in reaching Fort Bedford on July 25. Eight days later he raised the siege of Fort Ligonier, which contained priceless military stores. Then, remembering Braddock's Defeat, and being himself wilier than the wiliest Indian who ever took the warpath, he pushed on to Bushy Run, from which he intended passing the ambush ground of Turtle Creek the following night.

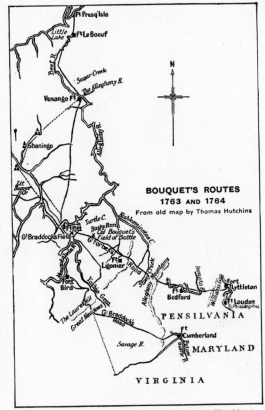

BOUQUET'S ROUTES 1763 AND 1764
From old map by Thomas Hutchins

227 Redrawn from a contemporary map by Thomas Hutchins

228 Bushy Run Battle Field, from Robert Bruce, *The National Road*, 1916

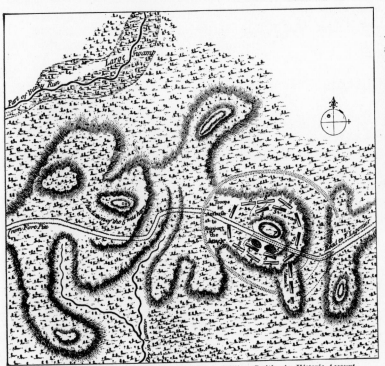

229 From a contemporary map by Thomas Hutchins in William Smith, *An Historic Account of the Expedition Against the Ohio Indians, in the Year MDCCLXIV*, London, 1766

THE BATTLE OF BUSHY RUN, 1763

At the hottest hour of that sweltering fifth of August the woods around Bouquet's advance guard suddenly became alive with yelling braves from Pontiac's hordes of Delawares, Shawnees, Mingoes, Wyandots, Mohicans, Miamis, and Ottawas, who all expected the savage delights of another Braddock's defeat, the field of which was only one short march away. Bouquet hurried reinforcements to the front; whereupon firing broke out in the rear; and it soon became alarmingly certain that his whole force was completely surrounded. Firing steadily, taking proper cover, and quickly charging any Indians that came close enough, Bouquet's little army fought through that anxious afternoon to a still more anxious night.

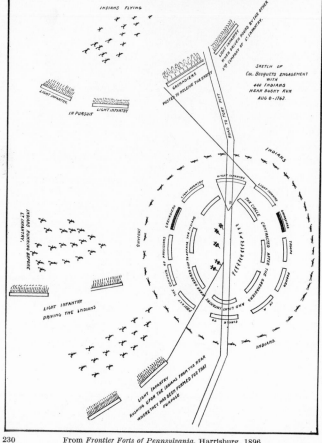

INDIANS FLYING

SKETCH OF
Col. Bouquets Engagement
WITH
400 INDIANS
NEAR BUSHY RUN
AUG 6 -1763.

230   From *Frontier Forts of Pennsylvania*, Harrisburg, 1896

MANEUVERS AT BUSHY RUN, AUGUST 6, 1763

TORTURED by thirst (for the encircling Indians were between them and the water), kept wide awake by exultant war cries, and knowing that Braddock's more numerous force had been slaughtered by a less numerous enemy near by, Bouquet's few hundreds of Royal Americans and Highlanders (drawn up in a circle round the provisions, transport, and stores) now faced a second alarming attack. Then, just when he knew the Indians would be most eager for booty and scalps, Bouquet withdrew some men, as if beaten back, and quietly extended others in ambush on either side of this inviting gap.

THE BLACK WATCH AT BUSHY RUN

SEEING some redcoats retreating and others quickly disappearing, the delighted Indians rushed wildly through the gap, straight for the baggage train. But no sooner had they become a howling, jostling mob than the ambush parties fired intensely into both their open flanks, while the close-formed companies whose retirement had lured them into this death trap suddenly turned and charged them with the bayonet, all ranks cheering like mad. Very few unwounded Indians ran the desperate gauntlet back again. The British victory was complete; and not even the former Indian war cries were any wilder than the yells of exultation with which the gallant Highlanders charged home.

231   From the painting by C. W. Jefferys in possession of the publishers

A MEMORABLE VICTORY

THE prestige of Bushy Run was out of all proportion to the size of the army that won it; for it was, in every sense, a test action between the specially trained Royal Americans and their consummate leader, on one side, and the most expert of Indian warriors, on the other. Moreover, the Highlanders, who had no training whatever in forest warfare, had caught the wily Indians with a deadly close-order charge. Thus, from every Indian point of view, Bouquet and his little army had proved themselves

232　Fort Pitt Blockhouse from the painting, 1832, by Russell Smith in the Historical Society of Pennsylvania

more than a match for the best of Indians on a chosen Indian field.　It now remained for Bouquet to secure the footing he had won.　So he not only relieved but strengthened Fort Pitt, building the blockhouse which still remains in Pittsburg as the only remaining relic of those stirring times.

BOUQUET IN CONFERENCE WITH THE INDIANS, 1764

BOUQUET had become the hero of the frontier; and Pennsylvania raised a thousand men.　He penetrated into the heart of the Indian country.　His savage foes, fearing annihilation, met him in council.　In the presence of his army drawn up in order of battle, their chiefs tendered him an offer of peace.　Bouquet's reply was a master stroke.　He well knew the Indian tendency to interpret concessions and kindness as weakness.　"Sach-

233　After the drawing by Benjamin West in Bouquet, *Voyage Historique et Politique dans L'Amérique,* Paris, 1778

ems, war-chiefs, and warriors, the excuses you have offered are frivolous and unavailing, and your conduct is without defence or apology. . . .　Last summer, in cold blood, and in a time of profound peace, you robbed and murdered the traders, who had come among you at your own express desire. You attacked Fort Pitt, which was built by your consent; and you destroyed our outposts and garrisons, whenever treachery could place them in your power.　You assailed our troops — the same who now stand before you — in the woods at Bushy Run; and, when we had routed and driven you off, you sent your scalping parties to the frontier, and murdered many hundreds of our people. . . .　We shall endure this no longer; and I am now come among you to force you to make atonement for the injuries you have done us.　I have brought with me the relatives of those you have murdered.　They are eager for vengeance, and nothing restrains them from taking it but my assurance that this army shall not leave your country until you have given them ample satisfaction. . . . I give you twelve days from this date to deliver into my hands all the prisoners in your possession, without exception: Englishmen, Frenchmen, women, and children; whether adopted into your tribes, married or living among you under any denomination or pretence whatsoever.　And you are to furnish these prisoners with clothing, provisions, and horses, to carry them to Fort Pitt.　When you have fully complied with these conditions, you shall then know on what terms you may obtain the peace you sue for."

234 English captured by Indians released by Colonel Bouquet, after the drawing by Benjamin West in Bouquet, *Voyage Historique et Politique dans L'Amérique*, Paris, 1778

BOUQUET RELEASING CAPTIVES, 1764

No one better than Francis Parkman can describe the scenes which followed Bouquet's demand for the return of the host of captives that had been taken in the border war. "In the ranks of the Pennsylvania troops, and among the Virginia riflemen, were the fathers, brothers and husbands of those whose rescue from captivity was a chief object of the march. Ignorant what had befallen them, and doubtful whether they were yet among the living, these men had joined the army in the feverish hope of winning them back to home and civilization. Perhaps those whom they sought had perished by the slow torments of the stake; perhaps by the more merciful hatchet; or perhaps they still dragged out a wretched life in the midst of a savage horde. There were instances in which whole families had been carried off at once. The old, the sick, or the despairing, had been tomahawked, as useless encumbrances; while the rest, pitilessly forced asunder, were scattered through every quarter of the wilderness. It was a strange and moving sight, when troop after troop of prisoners arrived in succession, — the meeting of husbands and wives, and fathers with children, the reunion of broken families, long separated in a disastrous captivity; and, on the other hand, the agonies of those who learned tidings of death and horror, or groaned under the torture of protracted suspense. Women, frantic between hope and fear, were rushing hither and thither, in search of those whose tender limbs had, perhaps, long since fattened the cubs of the she-wolf; or were pausing, in an agony of doubt before some sunburnt young savage, who, startled at the haggard apparition, shrank from his forgotten parent, and clung to the tawny breast of his adopted mother. . . . Among the children brought in for surrender, there were some, who, captured several years before, as early, perhaps, as the French war, had lost every recollection of friends and home. Terrified by the novel sights around them, the flash and glitter of arms, and the strange complexion of the pale-faced warriors, they screamed and struggled lustily when consigned to the hands of their relatives. There were young women, too, who had become the partners of Indian husbands; and who now, with all their hybrid offspring, were led reluctantly into the presence of fathers or brothers whose images were almost blotted from their memory. They stood agitated and bewildered; the revival of old affections, and the rush of dormant memories, painfully contending with more recent attachments, and the shame of their real or fancied disgrace; while their Indian lords looked on, scarcely less moved than they, yet hardening themselves with savage stoicism, and standing in the midst of their enemies, imperturbable as statues of bronze. These women were compelled to return with their children to the settlements; yet they all did so with reluctance, and several afterwards made their escape, eagerly hastening back to their warrior husbands, and the toils and vicissitudes of an Indian wigwam." — *Conspiracy of Pontiac*, Little, Brown & Co. Bouquet's work was over and he was back at Fort Pitt. He received the grateful thanks of Pennsylvania, Virginia, and the king. The following year, he died at Pensacola while general commanding the Southern District. Another year, and Pontiac made his absolute submission to Johnson at Oswego. Three years more found Pontiac on the banks of the Mississippi, attending a feast among the friendly French at Cahokia in Illinois. An English trader saw his opportunity, as the famous chief left the festal board and walked toward the forest. The trader spoke to a strolling redskin and offered him a barrel of liquor and other presents if he would kill the chief. The bargain was made; and, as Pontiac entered the forest, the assassin struck him down from behind. So passed a great man.

235 The Death of Pontiac, from Francis Parkman's works, 1897, drawing by De Cost Smith. © Little, Brown & Co., Boston

CHAPTER V

THE OUTBREAK OF REVOLUTION

THE Treaty of Paris in 1763 left Britain with very bitter enemies in France. Moreover, it saved the British colonies from the menace of New France, while training them for warfare on their own account. Again and again they had taken up arms for the overthrow of the French empire in the New World; and many Americans had acquired a certain military knowledge and experience. As a people the Americans did not take kindly to military service in a regular army. They had, indeed, derived from their English ancestry a deep-seated prejudice against standing armies. On the other hand, they had long been in the habit of organizing militia companies which trained at more or less frequent intervals. But such training was of only slight value to the enlisted man; while it left the officer with practically no knowledge of strategy, organization, or the leadership of large bodies. One hesitates to think what might have been the fate of the Revolution had the direction of its military operations devolved upon officers trained solely in the colonial militia. But, as the event proved, Britain, in asking her American colonies to aid in driving the French from the continent, had developed veterans so well trained in the hard school of actual war that, when the time came, they defied her own redcoats.

Of all the Americans the Virginia planter Washington had won the greatest reputation in the final French and Indian War. He had not only studied the military art as a staff officer and a subordinate commander but had had some slight experience in the independent direction of troops. Veterans like Washington were ready to assume control in the critical first years of the Revolution, during which time a group of younger officers could be trained and tested. When to these veterans and aspirants were added foreign officers, like Montgomery of the British, Lafayette of the French, and Steuben of the German armies, the Patriot forces finally enjoyed leadership of a quality which few English statesmen would have thought possible.

Under the command of such officers were troops, who, in the main, were of much higher human quality than those of regular European armies. The "embattled farmer" fighting for liberty and justice, when he was properly trained, made a soldier who was more than a match for the individual European regular. He had intelligence, initiative, and a capacity for sacrifice, which, when tried in the desperate test of Valley Forge, made him a Patriot of unsurpassable devotion to the cause and equally unsurpassable worth upon the field of battle.

It is, however, only fair to acknowledge the three great indispensable foreign aids to victory. First, the British were a divided people, almost as much divided as were the Americans themselves in the War of 1812. Second, the French Alliance helped the Revolution with finance, with soldiers, and with the fleet which ensured the decisive victory of Yorktown. Third, every other foreign navy in the world became the active or passive enemy of the British as the war went on. Such a concentration of hostile power was too great for England to overcome.

(A discussion of the political events which led to the American Revolution will be found in Volume VIII, Chapter II.)

DISTRIBUTION OF BRITISH REGULARS IN 1765

THE Peace of Paris in 1763 gave to England a vast empire. Over India, Canada, and Florida floated the Union Jack. The first two were the fruits of the war with France; the last had been wrested from Spain. But, though humbled for the time, neither Spain nor France was crushed. No one knew when the contest for imperial dominion might break out again. Moreover, Pontiac's war had made clear the extent of the Indian menace on the Western frontier. Inevitably the English Government took up the problem of imperial defense. The chart shows a plan for the disposition of troops admirably conceived to meet every contingency, the location of regiments being indicated by symbols signifying whole regiments, companies, half companies, and detachments. Small detachments should guard Newfoundland, the center of a great fishing industry, from raids by the rival fishermen of

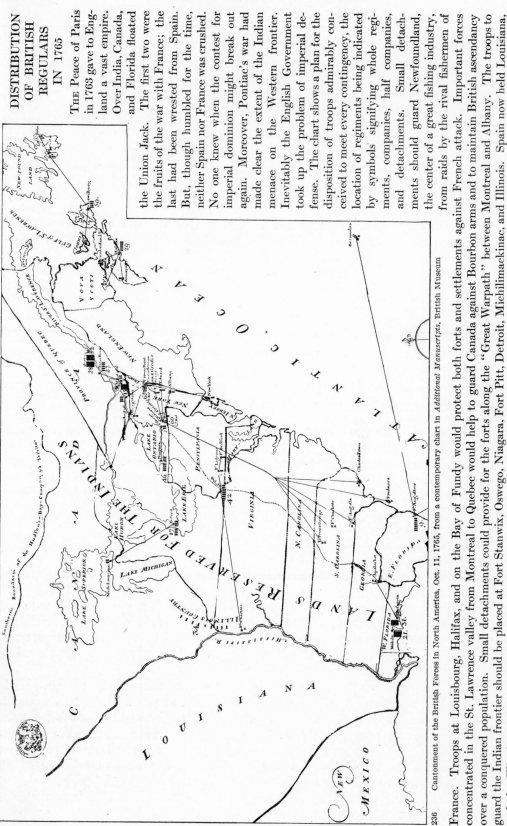

236   Cantonment of the British Forces in North America, Oct. 11, 1765, from a contemporary chart in *Additional Manuscripts*, British Museum

France. Troops at Louisbourg, Halifax, and on the Bay of Fundy would protect both forts and settlements against French attack. Important forces concentrated in the St. Lawrence valley from Montreal to Quebec would help to guard Canada against Bourbon arms and to maintain British ascendancy over a conquered population. Small detachments could provide for the forts along the "Great Warpath" between Montreal and Albany. The troops to guard the Indian frontier should be placed at Fort Stanwix, Oswego, Niagara, Fort Pitt, Detroit, Michillimackinac, and Illinois. Spain now held Louisiana, and the Illinois garrison would stand in the way of a possible Spanish menace from St. Louis. But more threatening were the Spaniards at New Orleans; so British forces would hold Mobile and Pensacola, while other troops would guard the ancient capital, St. Augustine. Grenville, in 1765, thought that the thirteen colonies should share the costs of this defense. So he proposed to levy a stamp tax,

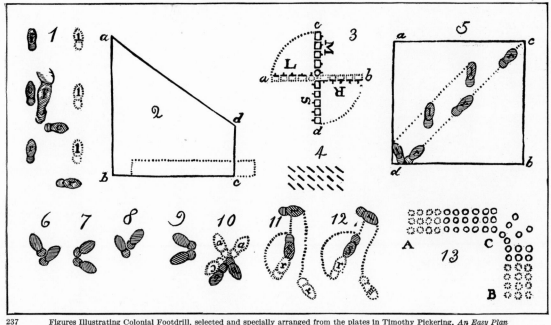

237   Figures Illustrating Colonial Footdrill, selected and specially arranged from the plates in Timothy Pickering, *An Easy Plan of Discipline for a Militia*, Boston, 1775, courtesy of the Massachusetts Historical Society

PICKERING'S DRILL BOOK

TIMOTHY PICKERING of the Salem Militia realized the gravity of the crisis that developed after the Boston Tea Party in 1773. In spite of the activities of the militia the fundamentals of drill and fighting maneuvers were yet to be learned. European drill books, such as the British Manual Exercise, 1764 ("The Sixty-Fourth"), were available for the colonial drillmaster. But, with the exception of Colonel Bland's inadequate treatise, no American had attempted to adapt and codify features especially needed by the colonials. Therefore Pickering's *An Easy Plan of Discipline for a Militia*, 1775, was enthusiastically adopted the following year by the state of Massachusetts for the disciplining of her raw recruits. The most elementary footdrill is carefully covered. The basic motions of right face (Figs. 6–7), left face (8–9), about face (10), to the rear march (11–12), were essential preliminaries to the handling of a mass of men. Oblique march (4) facilitated mobility, but, being a movement difficult for men accustomed to marching alone in the forest, it required special explanation (5). It was likewise necessary that men placed three ranks deep learn to fire without injuring one another. Correct position of the feet, and a proper kneeling posture for the front rank were indispensable (Figure 1. *ff*, left foot and right knee (bent) of front rank; *cc*, left and right foot of center rank, *rr* of rear rank. *lll*, left feet of file to the right). To maintain a steady fire the best method of making cartridges should be known (Fig. 2, soft brown wrapping paper; side *ab* six inches, *bc* five and a half inches, *cd* two inches; dotted lines representing a hollowed piece of wood about six inches long, called a "former," which receives the ball and is covered with paper). Wheeling by line (3) and by column of ranks (13) represent the beginning of more complicated movements which occupy the remainder of Pickering's twelve plates. Several other drill books were called forth by the outbreak of the Revolution, notably in Philadelphia: adaptations of foreign drill books for specialized branches of the service, theoretical treatises on the art of war, military guides for young officers. But in none of them was there such a degree of concentration on the simple fundamentals of mass drill, and none approximated, not even Steuben afterward, to *An Easy Plan* in the number and clarity of diagrammatic illustrations —qualities which created a demand for it even outside Massachusetts.

238   Timothy Pickering, 1745–1829, from the portrait by C. W. Peale in Independence Hall, Philadelphia

GENERAL THOMAS GAGE

GENERAL THOMAS GAGE had been appointed commander in chief of the Royal forces in the colonies when Amherst had been relieved. He was an officer of experience, having seen much active service in the last French and Indian War. In 1774, after a crisis had developed between the home government and Massachusetts, resulting from the passage of the so-called "Intolerable Acts," Gage was made Governor of the colony. The Imperial Government had undertaken to meet violence with coercion, and Gage seemed a fitting man to deal with the rising tide of American resentment. He found the inhabitants busily organizing militia companies and gathering military stores not far from Boston. Events moved with such rapidity that, by the spring of 1775, the military Governor found that his authority extended no farther than the area actually controlled by his small force of soldiers. Gage had to face what many another British commander was called upon to face later on.

239   From the portrait in Murray, *Impartial History of the American War*, London, 1780, engraving by R. Pollard

PREPARATIONS FOR WAR: THE MINUTE MEN

ON February 22, 1775, the London *Packet* published the following dispatch from Boston under the date of January 16: "At a town-meeting at Marblehead the 10th inst. legally convened, they came into several resolutions relative to raising a Militia. The preamble begins with 'Whereas a great part of the inhabitants of this town may soon be called forth, to assist in defending the Charter and Constitution of the Province, as well as the rights and liberties of ALL America, and in order thereto it is necessary that they should be properly disciplined, and instructed in the art of war, RESOLVED, That their pay, per diem, be as follows: private, 2s. — sergeant, clerk, drummer, or fife, 3s. — first lieutenant, 4s. 8d. — second ditt, 4s. — captain, 6s. To attend three days in a week, and four hours in each day. ORDERED, That a Committee of fifteen be appointed to attend to the conduct of ministerial tools and jacobites in this town, that effectual measures may be taken for either silencing them for the future, or expelling them from the community. RESOLVED, That the sum of £800 be immediately raised, and paid into the hands of Captain James Mugford, who is

appointed Receiver and Pay-master for the militia.'" This dispatch shows the situation which Gage confronted. That the Massachusetts people were in deadly earnest was proved by their adoption of an old-time practice of enlisting a part of the militia as "minute men" who would respond to the call of duty at a moment's notice. The minute men were thus the élite of the Patriots at the beginning, as Washington's Continental Regulars were from Independence to the end.

240   From the painting *Arousing the Minute Men*, by John Ward Dunsmore (1856–)
© by the artist

PAUL REVERE'S RIDE

In April, 1775, Gage reached the decision that the time had come to destroy the stores that were being gathered at Concord. It seemed necessary to make a show of force in the face of hostile activities. The story of every hour of that nineteenth of April has been written again and again in the minutest detail — the organization of the detachment in Boston during the night and the stealthy march toward Lexington in the early hours of the morning. In a ringing lyric, written

241   From the painting by John Ward Dunsmore. © by the artist

many decades after the event, Longfellow immortalized one of the two riders who carried to Lexington the tidings of the British movement. The name of Paul Revere has become associated with the rising of the American militiamen which led to the fights at Lexington and Concord. Revere, however, was captured by a party of British officers beyond Lexington, and William Dawes, who had left Boston before Revere, but had followed a longer route, brought the word to Concord.

242 William Dawes, Jr., 1745–99, from the portrait in the Lexington (Mass.) Historical Society, after a family portrait

243 Major John Pitcairn, 1740–75, from the miniature in the Lexington Historical Society, Lexington, Mass.

PITCAIRN MEETS THE MINUTE MEN

Colonel Smith was in command of the detachment that Gage had sent out. He had not marched far from Boston when the ringing of bells and the firing of guns apprised him that the alarm had been given. He sent Major Pitcairn ahead with six companies to secure the bridges beyond Concord. Pitcairn, entering Lexington early on the morning of the nineteenth, found a group of militiamen drawn up on the green.

244   From the painting *The Dawn of Liberty*, by Henry Sandham, in the Town Hall, Lexington, Mass.

THE FIGHT AT LEXINGTON, A CONTEMPORARY ACCOUNT

THE *Essex Gazette*, printed at Salem, Massachusetts, on April 25, contained the following account: "At Lexington, six miles below Concord, a company of militia, of about one hundred men, mustered near the Meeting-house; the troops came in sight of them just before sunrise; and running within a few rods of them, the Commanding Officer accosted the militia in words to this effect: — 'Disperse, you rebels — Damn you, throw down your arms and disperse:' Upon which the troops huzza'd, and immediately one or two officers discharged their pistols, which were instantaneously followed by the firing of four or five of the soldiers, and then there seemed to be a general discharge from the whole body. Eight of our men were killed, and nine wounded. In a few minutes after this action the enemy renewed their march to Concord. . . ." Perhaps the full truth of Lexington will never be known. Some of the details in the account of the Salem paper seem hardly probable in view of the discipline of the British regulars. The affair was a brush but blood was shed, the first blood of a war which rent the British Empire. It fell to the lot of Captain John Parker to command the American troops in this first encounter.

"THE SHOT HEARD ROUND THE WORLD"

COLONEL SMITH, over-taking Pitcairn, reached Concord early in the morning. Establishing a picket at the bridge over the Concord River, he set his troops to work destroying the stores that had not been removed. The local militia were already assembling. They came into conflict with the outpost at the bridge and fired "the shot heard round the world." When Smith had accomplished his mission, he promptly began a rapid march toward Boston.

245   "The Engagement at the North Bridge in Concord," from the engraving by Amos Doolittle after the drawing, Dec. 1775, by Ralph Earl, courtesy of the Lexington Historical Society, Lexington, Mass.
LEGEND: 1. The Detachment of the Regulars who fired first on the Provincials at the Bridge. 2. The Provincials headed by Colonel Robinson & Major Buttrick. 3. The Bridge.

246   "A View of the South Part of Lexington," from the engraving by Amos Doolittle after the drawing. Dec. 1775, by Ralph Earl, courtesy of the Lexington Historical Society, Lexington, Mass.

LEGEND: 1. Colonel Smith's Brigade retreating before the Provincials.   2. Earl Percy's brigade meeting them.   3 & 4. Earl Percy & Col. Smith.   5. Provincials.   6 & 7. The Flanck-guards of Percy's Brigade.   8. A Field-piece pointed at the Lexington Meeting-house.   9. The Burning of the Houses in Lexington.

THE RETREAT TO BOSTON

WHILE the events at Concord were in progress the militia had been coming out everywhere in angry swarms, and Smith soon found his force outnumbered.   The Americans seeking cover in every available tree, stone wall, and building, directed a deadly fire against the column marching in close order.   The British soldiers in their scarlet coats made perfect targets for the enemy snipers and their losses were very heavy.   At Lexington Lord Percy with reinforcements met the harrassed troops and gave them a rest.   But the attack began again as soon as they cleared the town and continued until the British had reached a position of safety at Charlestown under the guns of the men-of-war in the harbor.   The Americans withdrew to Cambridge.   The historic siege of Boston had begun, that was to last until March 17, 1776.

THE ALARM SPREADS THROUGH THE COLONIES

SWIFT couriers carried the news of Lexington and Concord to the distant towns of Massachusetts and on to the neighboring colonies.   The Patriots exulted at the defeat of the British.   But many a man, loyal to the old empire, heard the tidings with grave concern.   War had come, not merely a struggle between England and her colonies but a conflict that was destined in almost every American community to set neighbor against neighbor.   The New England militia tramped to Boston.   But few realized what a desperate business rebellion against the greatest sea power in the world must inevitably be.

In Congrefs, at Watertown, *April* 30, 1775.

Gentlemen,

THE barbarous Murders on our innocent Brethren on Wednefday the 19th Inftant, has made it abfolutely neceffary that we immediately raife an Army to defend our Wives and our Children from the butchering Hands of an inhuman Soldiery, who, incenfed at the Obftacles they met with in their bloody Progrefs, and enraged at being repulfed from the Field of Slaughter; will without the leaft doubt take the firft Opportunity in their Power to ravage this devoted Country with Fire and Sword : We conjure you, therefore, by all that is dear, by all that is facred, that you give all Affiftance poffible in forming an Army : Our all is at Stake, Death and Devaftation are the certain Confequences of Delay, every Moment is infinitely precious, an Hour loft may deluge your Country in Blood, and entail perpetual Slavery upon the few of your Pofterity, who may furvive the Carnage.   We beg and entreat, as you will anfwer it to your Country, to your own Confciences, and above all as you will anfwer to God himfelf, that you will haften and encourage by all poffible Means, the Inliftment of Men to form the Army, and fend them forward to Head-Quarters, at Cambridge, with that Expedition, which the vaft Importance and inftant Urgency of the Affair demands.

JOSEPH WARREN, Prefident, P. T.

247   The Alarm sent out from Watertown, April 30, 1775, from the copy in the Emmet Collection, New York Public Library

248 Israel Putnam, 1718–90, from the original pencil
     drawing by John Trumbull (1756–1843), courtesy of the
     Putnam Phalanx Commandery, Hartford, Conn.

NEW ENGLAND MILITARY LEADERS

To join the American force about Boston came hurrying many of the chief military figures of the New England colonies: Israel Putnam, who had seen service in the West Indies, Seth Pomeroy and Stark, of the French and Indian War, and old Colonel Gridley, who had been military engineer at the first siege of Louisbourg in 1745. Beside the veterans were untried younger men who had become prominent, Benedict Arnold, a New Haven druggist who was a very keen leader in the local militia, and Joseph Warren, president of the Massachusetts Provincial Congress. All set to work busily trying to bring some sort of order among the troops who had assembled in such an impromptu manner. Gridley planned a series of works that would vastly strengthen the American positions about Boston. But he was interrupted by an order to proceed to Bunker Hill on the night of June 16–17 and take charge of the construction of redoubts on high ground overlooking Boston.

PRELIMINARIES OF BUNKER HILL

On May 25, General Gage received reinforcements that brought his army up to six or seven thousand men. With the new troops came three major-generals, all members of Parliament, who were followed across the Atlantic by a bitter jibe from the Whig opposition; for the British parties were irreconcilably divided against each other on the subject of coercing the "rebels."

> Behold the *Cerberus* the Atlantic plough,
> Her precious cargo, Burgoyne, Clinton, Howe!
> Bow, wow, wow!

A British army, trained and equipped, was now in the astonishing position of being held in a state of siege by what was little more than an unorganized mass of armed civilians. Shortly after the arrival of the reinforcements Gage determined to seize the menacing heights at Dorchester and Charlestown. Learning this, the Americans under Prescott forestalled him and on June 16 took up a dangerously advanced position at Breed's Hill somewhat in advance of Bunker Hill. The British army was awakened on the 17th by the guns of the British frigate *Lively* opening fire on the American works already well advanced toward completion. The seizing of Breed's Hill was the rash maneuver of officers as yet little trained in the art of war. By using the ships at his disposal Gage could easily have cut off the retreat of the American detachment across the narrow neck which led to Cambridge, and by landing his army behind Bunker Hill have caught the American force in the rear and destroyed it.

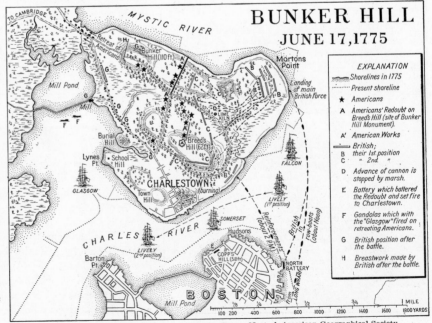

249   Drawn expressly for *The Pageant of America* by Gregor Noetzel, American Geographical Society,
       New York

THE ASSAULT AT BREED'S HILL

THAT a man of Gage's military capacity should have risen to the rank of lieutenant-general was a commentary on the sorry state to which the British army had fallen as a result of political wirepulling and the pernicious system of purchasing commissions. Rejecting all thought of taking advantage of the opportunity which the American position offered, he determined upon an immediate frontal assault, which General Howe was to command. The decision represented not merely the judgment of the commander in chief but was the unanimous

250 "An Exact View of the Late Battle at Charlestown, June 17th, 1775," from the engraving by Bernard Romans (ca. 1720–84), in the Massachusetts Historical Society

1. Boston. 2. Charlestown. 3. Breed's Hill. 4. Provincial Breastwork. 5. Retreating Grounds. 6. Frigate. 7. *Somerset*. 8. Broken Officer. 9. General Putnam.

advice of the council of war he convened to consider the problem presented by the American works. The forenoon was spent in ferrying troops across the Charles River. In the afternoon the British attacked. Since it was the intention to pursue the enemy, the soldiers carried blankets, knapsacks, and food for three days. Encumbered by this heavy equipment the British infantry formed in line of battle and advanced steadily against the redoubts. The Americans were led by a fighting man of high quality, Colonel William Prescott, who, like so many of his officers, had seen service in the French and Indian War. With admirable judgment he ordered his troops to withhold their fire until the advancing infantry was within about fifty yards. Resting their muskets on the works in front of them the militiamen took careful aim. The result was a carnage which threw the British back down the hill. Especially large was the list of officers who fell.

The British regulars reformed and advanced a second time, only to be thrown back again with frightful losses. By this time Clinton had brought reinforcements, and a third assault was made. It met but a feeble opposition; for the American ammunition had run out. With a bayonet charge in which Warren fell the infantry carried the works and drove the Americans, who had no bayonets, across the neck toward Cambridge. During the fight Charlestown was set on fire by the British batteries. Bunker Hill is an example of unnecessary loss of life resulting from an improper battle plan. Unfortunately such murderous frontal assaults were to occur again, not only in the Revolution, but in the War of 1812 and our own Civil War. When the news of the battle reached England, Gage was relieved of command and disgraced. Howe took his place as commander-in-chief of the British armies in His Majesty's rebellious colonies in America.

251   "An original Sketch of the Burning of Charlestown & Battle of Bunker Hill. Taken by a British officer from Beacon Hill, Boston," in the Emmet Collection, New York Public Library

252   The Battle of Bunker Hill, from the painting, 1786, by John Trumbull in the Yale School of the
Fine Arts, New Haven, Conn.

THE RESULTS OF BUNKER HILL

FOR the Americans Bunker Hill was both a defeat and a victory. They had been driven from their position and had lost heavily; but they had demonstrated that American militia behind breastworks could stand against British infantry. The news of the two assaults which had been repulsed roused Americans everywhere to great enthusiasm. Bunker Hill, nevertheless, did some real disservice to the Patriot cause. It created the impression that partly trained militia was all that was needed for the conflict; and so the existing prejudices against regular troops and discipline were strengthened. Not until later were the Americans to learn that discipline and the dull grind of months of training are quite as important as courage if wars are to be won.

THE APPOINTMENT OF A COMMANDER IN CHIEF

THE second Continental Congress, which had begun its sessions in May, 1775, faced an actual state of war. After the battle of Bunker Hill Congress took over the force about Boston in the name of all the colonies and made it the first Continental army. Naturally the proportion of New England men and officers was very great and colonial prejudices against New England were still strong. It was therefore both a politic and a graceful act when John Adams of Massachusetts nominated George Washington of Virginia to be the commander in chief of the Continental armies. From the same motive two other adopted sons of Virginia, Horatio Gates and Charles Lee, both Englishmen who had been officers in the British army, were commissioned major-generals.

253   From the painting *John Adams Proposing Washington for Commander in Chief*, by
John Ward Dunsmore.   © by the artist

AMERICAN UNIFORMS at the BEGINNING of THE WAR OF INDEPENDENCE–1775-1776

"MINUTE MAN" MASS. 1775

GOVERNOR'S FOOT GUARD CONN. 1775

1ST CITY TROOP PHILADELPHIA 1775

LAMB'S ARTILLERY NEW YORK 1775

SMALLWOOD'S MARYLAND REGIMENT 1775-1776

GENERAL OFFICER 1775

MORGAN'S VIRGINIA RIFLEMEN 1775-1776

HASLETT'S DELAWARE REGIMENT 1776

PRIVATE 2ND NEW HAMPSHIRE REGIMENT 1776

CAPTAIN 3RD NEW YORK REGIMENT 1776

PRIVATE PENNSYLVANIA LINE 1776

FIELD OFFICER 2ND CONNECTICUT REGIMENT 1776

SERGEANT 3RD NEW JERSEY REGIMENT 1776

VIRGINIA LIGHT DRAGOONS 1776

Painted expressly for *The Pageant of America* by H. A. Ogden

WASHINGTON, COMMANDER IN CHIEF

WASHINGTON assumed command of the army on July 3, 1775. The first task which confronted him was to teach the officers and men who had been entrusted to his care some of the elementary principles of military organization. The soldiers were, in the main, rough and hearty farmers and mechanics who had come of their own free will to fight, in general, for their liberties, and, in particular, to drive the hated British army out of Boston. From first to last their conduct was marked by the individualism and the personal independence fostered by American frontier and rural life. In most cases they had elected their officers and in some they had rallied to the stirring appeals of a popular local leader. Among New England troops in particular there was practically no distinction between commissioned officer and enlisted man. Washington somewhat

254   General George Washington, 1732–99, from the portrait, 1792, by John Trumbull, in the Metropolitan Museum of Art, New York

bitterly remarked that "they regarded an officer no more than a broomstick." Teamwork is vital to military success; soldiers trained in the school of individualism and having no conception of the conflict upon which they were embarking, though good raw material, could not be welded quickly into an effective fighting force. When Washington attempted to enforce discipline in the most elementary matters many of his officers and men simply went home; and at home there was no public sentiment forcing every able-bodied man of military age into the service. If a man were drafted by the provincial authorities he could send a substitute. In the eighteenth century no western nation had reached such a development that it was generally considered the duty of every citizen of the proper age who was physically fit to share in the defense of his country in the event of war. Such mobilization of the man power of a nation was not to find its full expression until the twentieth century. In the eighteenth war was still looked upon as primarily the business of professional troops. There was, of course, no regular army controlled by the American Patriot party. The Revolutionary movement was compelled to depend for its soldiers upon militia and upon volunteers in an age when volunteering did not have behind it the commanding sanction of public opinion. In American communities, moreover, the division of opinion and of loyalty between the Whigs and Tories was a further handicap to the raising of armies. Quite naturally the familiar bounty system was used practically from the beginning. In all the colonies, however, were men, like young Nathan Hale of Coventry, Connecticut, who volunteered in a spirit of sacrifice to fight for the principles which they held dear.

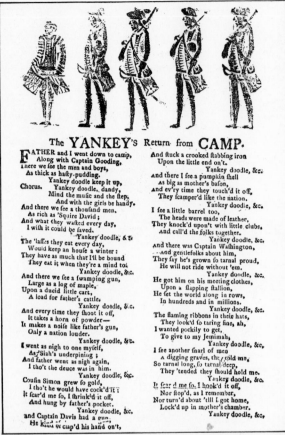

The YANKEY's Return from CAMP.

FATHER and I went down to camp,
  Along with Captain Gooding,
There we fee the men and boys,
As thick as hafty-pudding.
      Yankey doodle keep it up,
Chorus. Yankey doodle, dandy,
      Mind the mufic and the ftep,
      And with the girls be handy.
And there we fee a thoufand men,
  As rich as 'Squire David;
And what they wafted every day,
  I wifh it could be faved.
      Yankey doodle, &c.
The 'laffes they eat every day,
  Would keep an houfe a winter:
They have as much that I'll be bound
  They eat it when they're a mind to.
      Yankey doodle, &c.
And there we fee a fwamping gun,
  Large as a log of maple,
Upon a ducid little cart,
  A load for father's cattle.
      Yankey doodle, &c.
And every time they fhoot it off,
  It takes a horn of powder,—
It makes a noife like father's gun,
  Only a nation louder.
      Yankey doodle, &c.
I went as nigh to one myfelf,
  As 'Siah's underpining;
And father went as nigh again,
  I tho't the deuce was in him.
      Yankey doodle, &c.
Coufin Simon grew fo bold,
  I tho't he would have cock'd it;
It fcar'd me fo, I fhrink'd it off,
  And hung by father's pocket.
      Yankey doodle, &c.
and Captain Davis had a gun,
  He kind of clap'd his hand on't,

And ftuck a crooked ftabbing iron
  Upon the little end on't.
      Yankey doodle, &c.
And there I fee a pumpkin fhell
  As big as mother's bafon,
And ev'ry time they touch'd it off,
  They fcamper'd like the nation.
      Yankey doodle, &c.
I fee a little barrel too,
  The heads were made of leather,
They knock'd upon't with little clubs,
  And call'd the folks together.
      Yankey doodle, &c.
And there was Captain Wafhington,
  And gentlefolks about him,
They fay he's grown fo tarnal proud,
  He will not ride without 'em.
      Yankey doodle, &c.
He got him on his meeting clothes,
  Upon a flapping ftallion,
He fet the world along in rows,
  In hundreds and in millions.
      Yankey doodle, &c.
The flaming ribbons in their hats,
  They look'd fo taring fine, ah,
I wanted pockily to get,
  To give to my Jemimah.
      Yankey doodle, &c.
I fee another fnarl of men
  a digging graves, they told me,
So tarnal long, fo tarnal deep,
  They 'tended they fhould hold me.
      Yankey doodle, &c.
It fcar'd me fo, I hook'd it off,
  Nor ftop'd, as I remember,
Nor turn'd about 'till I got home,
  Lock'd up in mother's chamber.
      Yankey doodle, &c.

255 From the issue, about 1775 (verses attributed to a British
     surgeon), in the Essex Institute, Salem, Mass.

"YANKEE DOODLE KEEP IT UP"

HERE are the humors of the camp, as sung by the facetious Yankee soldier of the day. *Yankee Doodle* is the only one of the war songs of the Revolution that still lives. Its halting rhythm and awkward rhyme may not inappropriately be compared to the drill and the military precision of the early Revolutionary soldier who whiled away the tedium of the camp with its lively verses. The army had no uniform drill regulations. Various manuals, among them the "Sixty-fourth" edition of the *British Manual* and Timothy Pickering's *Easy Plan*, were used by different companies. But the drilling was almost universally bad. As the war lost the impromptu aspect of 1775 the commissioned officers, imitating the British custom, began to lose contact with their men and to leave the work of instruction and drill of recruits to the sergeants and corporals. The next to the last verse of *Yankee Doodle* suggests one of the grimmest aspects of military service in the early years of the war. Lack of discipline meant the absence of the most elementary regulations for camp sanitation. Disease became rife with no adequate hospitals or organized medical personnel to combat it. It is no wonder that Yankee Doodle saw "another snarl of men a digging graves . . . so tarnal long, so tarnal deep."

TICONDEROGA

WHILE the American army was besieging Boston in the winter of 1775–76 its commander was heartened by the arrival of heavy guns from Ticonderoga (No. 273). The hauling of these cannon on sledges over snow and frozen streams was the sequel to a bold adventure of the preceding May. Benedict Arnold had hardly arrived at Boston with his New Haven company after the Battle of Lexington when he asked permission to go to

Ticonderoga and fall upon the place before the garrison was informed of the outbreak of rebellion. Arnold was in the Green Mountain country in May; but the troops which had been placed at his disposal had not yet arrived. Consequently he joined as a volunteer a local expedition under Ethan Allen which had been organized for the same purpose. At the time Ticonderoga and Crown Point were little more than depots for the storage of considerable quantities of cannon and other military supplies, their garrisons being small detachments. Life must have been insufferably dull for the men whose fate it was to be stationed in these fortresses. On north, south, and east settlements were many miles away. The white men who passed by were mainly hunters and Indian traders who stopped to spend the night within the forts, bringing welcome

256 Ethan Allen Gate at Ticonderoga, courtesy of the
     Delaware & Hudson Railroad Co., Albany, N. Y.

news of the distant outside world. In 1775 these British soldiers little dreamed that the fortifications which they guarded were about to become important in war. They heard nothing of Lexington and Concord. On May 10 Allen surprised and captured Ticonderoga with less than a hundred "Green Mountain Boys" and Crown Point fell two days later.

ETHAN ALLEN'S REPORT TO JONATHAN TRUMBULL

PRICELESS military stores thus fell into the hands of the Patriots. With a pardonable display of pride Allen wrote to Governor Trumbull of Connecticut on May 12: "I make you a Present of a Major a Captain and Two Lieuts in the regular Establishment of George the Third I hope they may serve as ransome for some of our Friends at Boston and particularly for Capt Brown of Rhode Island . . . I Conclude Capt [Seth] Warner is by this Time in Possession of Crown Point the Ordinance Stores &c I Conclude Governor Carlton will Exert himself to oppose us & Command the Lake &c . . . I subscribe myself your Honours Ever Faithfull most Obedient and Humble servant

Ethan Allen,
at Present Commander of Ticonderoga."

257   Facsimile of the original in possession of the publishers

258   General Philip Schuyler, 1733–1804, from the miniature, 1792, by John Trumbull in the Yale School of the Fine Arts, New Haven, Conn.

GENERAL SCHUYLER

IN June Congress appointed General Philip Schuyler, a great landlord in the Hudson valley, to command at Ticonderoga, with the mission of leading an invasion of Canada. He found some troops already there and promptly began the construction of boats to aid his advance down Lake Champlain. The end of August found him ready to proceed; but he was stricken with fever, and the leadership of the expedition devolved upon his second in command, Richard Montgomery. Not until two years had passed did Schuyler resume command in the Champlain country.

259   General Richard Montgomery, 1736–75, from the portrait by C. W. Peale in Independence Hall, Philadelphia

MONTGOMERY'S CAMPAIGN IN CANADA

GENERAL RICHARD MONTGOMERY had served with distinction as an officer in the British army during the final French and Indian War. He had married into a strongly Patriot family, the New York Livingstons, had represented Dutchess County in the Provincial Congress, and had been appointed brigadier-general under Philip Schuyler. Young, eager, able, but entirely misinformed as to Canadian conditions, he pressed on against the clogging difficulties of managing his own very heterogeneous force during a most trying winter campaign in unfriendly Canada.

260   Sir Guy Carleton, 1724-1808, from a portrait,
      artist unknown, courtesy of Lady Dorchester, London

SIR GUY CARLETON

MONTGOMERY's opponent was Sir Guy Carleton, Governor of Canada and a general in His Majesty's forces. Carleton had first come out to Canada with Wolfe in 1759, since which time he had served the Crown efficiently in the conquered province. At the outbreak of the Revolution he had but a handful of troops, considering the size and importance of the area for the defense of which he was responsible. Some inkling of the shortage of troops in Canada, and a belief that the French-Canadians would rise to throw off the British yoke, spurred American efforts to strike a swift blow at the famous citadel on the St. Lawrence. Washington gave the plan much thought and heartily approved the enterprise. As finally developed the scheme was to make two attacks, one by way of Lake Champlain under Montgomery and the other overland through the Maine woods to be commanded by Arnold. It was a bold undertaking that almost succeeded in the capture of Quebec. But, of course, as in the French wars, so now, whoever held the command of the sea and could send fleets up the St. Lawrence would hold Quebec permanently, no matter which side won on land.

POSTS ON THE WAY TO QUEBEC

ST. JOHN's, Chambly, and Montreal were the three steps Montgomery had to take on his way to the clinching conquest of Quebec (see map, No. 309). On September 1 he laid siege to St. John's, while Ethan Allen went on to "preach politicks" at Montreal, where one of the New York Livingstons raised four hundred men who joined Montgomery and served right through to Quebec. Allen came to grief, being surrounded, defeated, and taken prisoner at Long Point by the veteran Major Carden, who outnumbered him three to one. But luck returned to the Americans when, on October 18, Major Stopford surrendered Fort Chambly and left all its priceless stores intact for Montgomery to use against St. John's, which, though bravely defended by Major Preston (with seven hundred men) was forced to surrender on the third of November. On the 12th Montgomery took Montreal without a shot, while the other American invaders, under Arnold, suddenly emerged from the wilderness due south of Quebec.

261   St. John's on the Sorel River, from Thomas Anburey, *Travels through the interior parts of America*, London, 1789

THE MARCH OF ARNOLD'S FORCE

ARNOLD left Cambridge on September 13 with a thousand volunteers. He made his way by water to the mouth of the Kennebec River. "Very troublesome indeed," was Arnold's laconic description of the voyage up the Kennebec. The bateaux which Major Colburn had been ordered to have ready for him above Georgetown were at once discovered to be unsatisfactory. It is doubtful if the upper waters of the Kennebec had ever been navigated, except in lightly freighted canoes or pirogues. Arnold realized the difficulties in store. On September 25 he wrote to Washington: "Completed yes; but many of them smaller than the directions given, and badly, very badly, built." And yet in these boats he passed the treacherous headwaters of the Kennebec to the watershed near Lake Chaudière and thence down most of the length of the Chaudière River to the St. Lawrence. His purpose was to surprise the Canadian citadel, Quebec. He met with many unexpected obstacles, suffered appalling hardships; but he overcame them all. Long before he reached his destination his ragged troops were shivering from the approach of the northern winter in the almost impassable wilds. Arnold's advance was a notable feat, rivaling, if not surpassing, George Rogers Clark's winter attack upon Vincennes (No. 447).

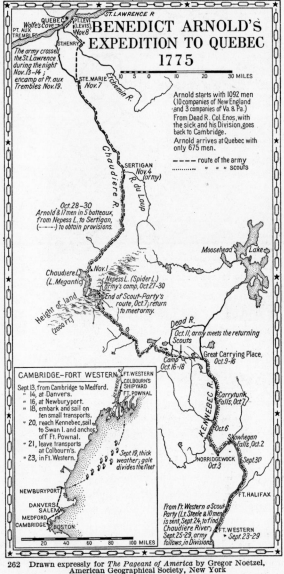

BENEDICT ARNOLD'S EXPEDITION TO QUEBEC 1775

Arnold starts with 1092 men (10 companies of New England and 3 companies of Va. & Pa.)
From Dead R. Col. Enos, with the sick and his Division, goes back to Cambridge.
Arnold arrives at Quebec with only 675 men.

– – – – route of the army
. . . . " " " scouts

262 Drawn expressly for *The Pageant of America* by Gregor Noetzel, American Geographical Society, New York

263 From the painting *New Englanders Marching to Quebec*, by Stanley M. Arthurs, courtesy of the artist

HARDSHIPS OVERCOME

THE boat work was stupendous, with all the broken and obstructed waters, the trying portages, and the impossibility of renewing the scanty supplies. But the boat work was easy compared with the incredibly toilsome trail over rocks, bogs, snow, and ice, and the entangling matted wilds. "And what was it all for? A chance to get killed! The end of the march was Quebec — impregnable!" Food failed. Men began to sicken and die. Over three hundred went back. But the undauntable Arnold pushed on, in a race against starvation, reached the first French-Canadian settlements, and arrived on the St. Lawrence, opposite Quebec, on November 13, two months out from Cambridge. News of his coming spread consternation among the French-Canadians and caused grave anxiety to the regular troops.

264   View of Quebec, 1775, from the engraving in the Public Archives, Dominion of Canada, Ottawa, by Canot, after the painting by Francis Swain based on a drawing by Henry Smith

MONTGOMERY AND CARLETON RACE TO QUEBEC

QUEBEC proved impregnable, for Arnold with his seven hundred men was arrayed against eleven hundred who stood behind the walls. But Montgomery and Carleton were also racing for Quebec; and the chances were that, if Montgomery won, he and Arnold might storm the patchwork wall with success, even if there were no Patriots to open the gates from inside. Carleton, however, slipped through Montgomery's fingers off Sorel, though most of his little force was taken. Having the only armed vessels on the river, he reached Quebec at last and stood at bay.

MONTGOMERY AND ARNOLD ATTACK QUEBEC

MONTGOMERY and Arnold together could barely muster as large a force as Carleton's, and though some reinforcements arrived, the constant wastage was greater among the Americans than among the defenders. The British had better artillery as well as the stronger position; and altogether the taking of Quebec would have seemed hopeless had not the false belief in Patriot help within the walls persisted to the end. The threat

of the New Yorkers to leave as soon as their term of enlistment was up at the end of the year was an additional incentive to immediate action. So, on New Year's Eve, in the dark and stormy morning hours, Montgomery and Arnold made their attacks on the Lower Town barricades, while Livingston made a well-pressed feint against the walls up on the city heights. A, B, C, D, E, and F represent bastions; G the Porte du Palais; H the Governor's house; L the place where Montgomery attacked and was killed; and M the Saut-au-Matelot, where Arnold attacked and was wounded. On the day following this attack there was raised at Boston camp the first common flag of the united colonies. It consisted of the Crosses of St. George and St. Andrew and of thirteen alternate red and white stripes.

265   Detail from "A Plan of the City and Environs of Quebec with its Siege and Blockade by the Americans," engraving by W. Faden in *Atlas of the Battles of the Revolution*, Yale University Library

266   From the painting by John Trumbull in the Yale School of the Fine Arts, New Haven, Conn.

THE DEATH OF GENERAL MONTGOMERY

AFTER carrying in turn the Près-de-Ville and Saut-au-Matelot barricades, Montgomery and Arnold hoped to meet at the foot of Mountain Hill, march up and find the big gate opened by the Patriots inside. Livingston was to come through from the historic Heights of Abraham and join them in receiving Carleton's surrender of the one last British foothold in the whole of Canada. But behind the Près-de-Ville barricade stood fifty men, resolute, well armed, whose sudden gun and musket-fire, at point-blank range, killed Montgomery, together with both his aides and ten more men, besides wounding others farther back. The surprise, the firm resistance, and the extremely narrow front between the cliff and the river, halted the column, convinced the remaining leaders that the barricade could not be flanked, and caused a general retreat.

ARNOLD'S DEFEAT AT QUEBEC

ARNOLD rounded the opposite base of the cliff, hoping to smash the Saut-au-Matelot barricade by shell-fire at close quarters, while most of his men, circling out on the ice of the St. Lawrence, flanked this barricade, which ran a hundred yards from cliff to river. But his gun stuck fast in the snow, and he was severely wounded by a shot from the walls, whence the British sailors' battalion was firing hard on the Americans only a hundred feet below. Morgan then stormed the advanced barricade in his immediate front, took the defenders prisoners, and pressed on to the Saut-au-Matelot barricade itself. But there, after a desperate fight, the British were reinforced; Morgan was also attacked by a sortie from the rear; and more than four hundred Americans were obliged to surrender. The attack on Quebec had failed.

267   Withstanding the Attack of Arnold's Men at the Second Barrier, from *The Century Magazine*, March 1903, drawing by Sydney Adamson. © The Century Co.

268   View of Three Rivers, Canada, from the drawing by James Peachey in the Crown Collection of American Maps, British Museum

THE AMERICANS RETIRE FROM CANADA

STILL suffering from his wounds, Arnold left for Montreal and recuperation. Wooster, bringing reinforcements, took command, but was superseded by the much younger Thomas. On the 6th of May, 1776, up came the British fleet, bringing an army. As there was no American sea power on the St. Lawrence, an immediate retreat became necessary. Thomas died within a month and was succeeded by John Sullivan, who was later to fight against the Iroquois Indians. Cheered by further reinforcements, Sullivan attacked the British at Three Rivers on the 7th of June; but he was defeated by the regulars and men-of-war, whose stronger and better trained forces would also have cut off his retreat had not Carleton purposely kept the route to St. John's open for escape. Thenceforth there was nothing but ever-increasing disaster. Death and disease were everywhere. Jonathan Trumbull wrote: "I did not look into a hut or a tent in which I did not find a dead or dying man."

SCHUYLER TAKES UP QUARTERS AT CROWN POINT

FROM the graveyard of quite half their army, and of all their Patriot hopes, the stricken Americans, after having been joined at St. John's by Arnold, and once more under Schuyler's direct command, retired in July to Crown Point, a few miles north of Ticonderoga, which now became the objective of Carleton, whose forces overwhelmingly outnumbered any army Schuyler could command. But Lake Champlain demanded local sea power and Arnold was desperately turning the lakeside forest into a defensive fleet.

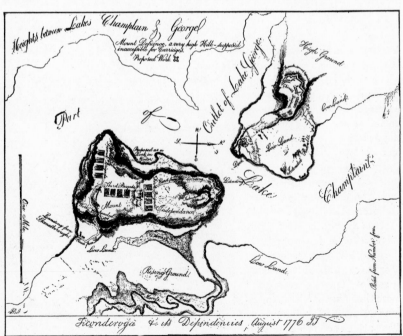

269   Ticonderoga and its dependencies, from the sketch plan in John Trumbull, *Reminiscences of His Own Times*, New Haven, 1841

ARNOLD BUILDS A FLEET ON LAKE CHAMPLAIN

THE schooner *Royal Savage* might be called the flagship of Jacobus Wynkoop, commodore of the tiny American Continental flotilla on Lake Champlain in the early summer of 1776. The illustration, in the Schuyler manuscripts, is said to be the earliest surviving picture of the "Jack and Stripes." Wynkoop was superseded in August by Arnold, who had had a good deal of nautical experience, and who pushed on construction with ceaseless energy. Ship's carpenters were scarce, and so were guns, while skilled naval seamen were scarcer still; but the handy Americans created a little fleet,

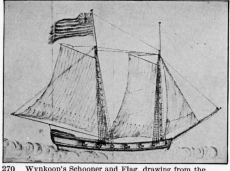

270   Wynkoop's Schooner and Flag, drawing from the Schuyler Papers, New York Public Library

which eventually comprised fifteen vessels, with eighty-six guns throwing six hundred and five pounds, one hundred and fifty-two swivels, and eight hundred and twenty-one men of all ranks and ratings, when the complements were full. Only some seven hundred men served in the Battle of Valcour. The British had no more men; but their own were skilled in naval warfare, while their heavier guns threw over one thousand pounds. The British, under Captain Pringle, were in the naval sense, twice as strong as the Americans.

BRITISH NAVAL VICTORY AT VALCOUR ISLAND, LAKE CHAMPLAIN, OCT. 11, 1776

THE Battle of Valcour Island was the first lake action ever fought by the United States navy. The British, heading south on Lake Champlain, did not discover Arnold till they had passed the island. This

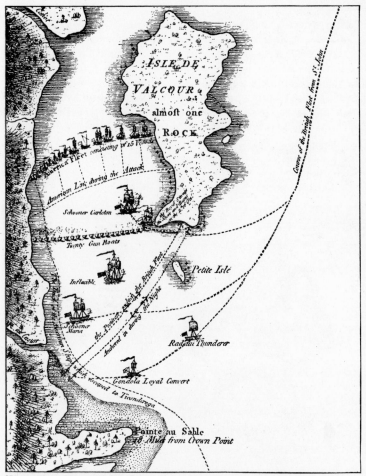

271   The Attack and Defeat of the American Fleet under Benedict Arnold, from a sketch taken by an officer on the spot, in the *North American Atlas*, London, 1777

forced them to beat up from leeward, which disjoined their flotilla, and so prevented what might well have been a crushing attack. Arnold's men fought with splendid resolution, the few skilled gunners did marvelously well, and Pringle hauled off for the night with the intention of annihilating Arnold in the morning by bringing the whole of the British flotilla into action as one concerted force. But Arnold, with consummate secrecy and skill, slipped past by night, ran down the lake and stood at bay on the 13th at Crown Point. Here the fight was at the closest quarters; the Americans offered furious resistance to the British odds until hardly one of their vessels could be kept afloat. Few struck; and then only when resistance was impossible. Most ran ashore and were set afire by their own crews, who left their colors flying. The Battle of Valcour was not merely a gallant action; it was of vast importance to the Patriot cause. For Arnold's flotilla had delayed Carleton till Ticonderoga was able to display such force that he left it in American possession till the following year.

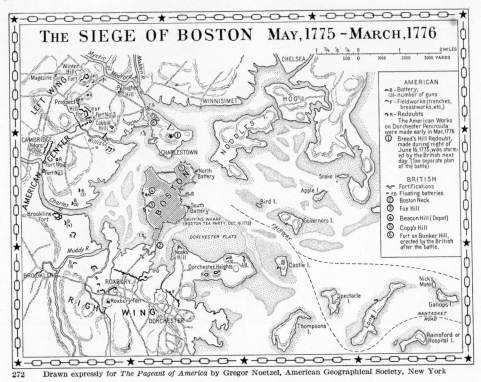

THE SIEGE OF BOSTON MAY, 1775 – MARCH, 1776

AMERICAN
B – Battery,
   (3)=number of guns
F – Fieldworks (trenches,
     breastworks, etc.)
R – Redoubts
   The American Works
on Dorchester Peninsula
were made early in Mar.,1776.
① Breed's Hill Redoubt,
   made during night of
   June 16,1775, was stormed by the British next
   day. (See separate plan
   of the battle).

BRITISH
⌣ Fortifications
FB Floating batteries
② Boston Neck
③ Fox Hill
④ Beacon Hill (Depot)
⑤ Copp's Hill
⑥ Fort on Bunker Hill,
   erected by the British
   after the battle.

272   Drawn expressly for *The Pageant of America* by Gregor Noetzel, American Geographical Society, New York

THE BRITISH ARMY WITHDRAWS FROM BOSTON

TECHNICALLY the American invasion of Canada failed. But its importance on the outcome of the Revolution can scarcely be overestimated. So disturbed was the British Government at the American attempt to win what had once been New France that the British army sent to put down the rebellion was divided in the critical year, 1776. Had Howe added to his own forces the troops which Carleton commanded he must almost inevitably have stamped out American opposition. Meanwhile through a dreary winter Howe remained besieged in Boston. Smallpox broke out among his troops. His supplies ran short and had to be brought from Halifax and England. Washington's position was even worse. There was a time when he could scarcely raise three hundred rounds of ammunition per musket. The timely capture of a British ordnance

vessel greatly cheered the American commander. But his greatest difficulty was in trying to maintain an army at all. Levies were going home as their terms of enlistment ran out. Recruits had to be secured and given at least some training. Early in March Washington seized Dorchester Heights, which Howe had neglected to take. The heavy cannon captured at Ticonderoga which Colonel Henry Knox had brought to Dorchester Heights, made further British occupation of Boston impossible. On March 17 Howe evacuated the town and took his army and a large number of Boston Loyalists to Halifax.

273   Hauling the Guns from Ticonderoga, painting by Gilbert Gaul for *The Army and Navy of the United States*, courtesy of George Barrie's Sons, Philadelphia

CHAPTER VI

THE YEAR OF INDEPENDENCE

THE events of the year 1775, culminating in the siege of Boston and the invasion of Canada, disclosed to the British Government that it must reckon with a serious rebellion extending throughout the Thirteen Colonies. The Congress called to protest against the acts of Parliament had begun to function as a tentative federal government; while a whole army of militia had been called out and, at Bunker Hill, demonstrated an unexpected ability to fight. The crisis found the British unprepared. For some time the navy had been suffering at the hands of successive ministries; and in December, 1774, in spite of the adoption of coercion at Boston, the establishment of seamen was reduced from twenty to sixteen thousand men. Lord Sandwich, then at the head of the Admiralty, was one of the worst of the political group in power. Nor was the army better off. It numbered but thirty-three thousand, a paltry force with which to protect an empire which stretched from India to North America, where alone it extended from Hudson's Bay to Barbados. Not until August, 1775, was it resolved to increase this force by twenty thousand men. The money for augmentation was voted; and Major-General Fraser's regiment of Highlanders was one of the chief results. Englishmen did not take kindly to service in the army; and many of the enlisted men were persons who had been forced into it after being arrested under the Act against Vagabonds. Moreover, the Whig opposition, always opposed to a strong standing army, was particularly resentful of any force that could be used against the American "rebels" whom the Whigs so much admired. Under these circumstances the government naturally fell back upon the general international practice of the times and began to hire mercenaries. But this, in its turn, set both the Whigs in Britain and the Patriots in America more than ever against the government and king.

Actual war was what the British Government wished for every reason to avoid. They preferred to put down the rebellion by political rather than by military means. If ever in her history Britain needed wise leadership it was in the spring of 1776. The plans for that year are in themselves evidence of how far her inefficient ministers had failed her. In November, 1775, Lord George Germain, who had been court martialed and dismissed from the army for cowardice at Minden, was elevated to an office which gave him control of the oversea armies of the Empire. He and the other ministers now planned to confront the Americans with a great naval and military force at the seaport of New York, while at the same time attempting to make peace on the basis of compromise. The British Government completely misjudged the temper of the American subjects of the king when they thought that the men who had been engaged in the fighting of 1775 would be awed by the hiring of Hessian mercenaries. No move was more certain to strengthen the hands of the leaders of the rebellion and inflame the Patriots with hatred against an oppressive government. In the end the government failed to conciliate the Americans with their offers, failed to awe them by a show of force, and failed to destroy the army upon which the success of the rebellion depended. This army, as we shall see again and again, was composed of Washington's Continental regulars, the fathers of the United States army of to-day.

But the American problem was incomparably harder than the British. In 1775 thirteen colonies, more or less united, had embarked upon a struggle for the rights which they felt the British constitution accorded them. Their fight for the "rights of Englishmen" had been met by warlike measures of such a nature as to convince them that there was no hope of securing just and fair treatment from the government to which they owed allegiance. By the spring of 1776 the development of events had brought them face to face with a crisis in which they had to decide whether they were to break forever the ties which bound them to the British Empire and set forth alone upon the unknown course of independence. Naturally there were many people who could not bring themselves to sanction such a step. Nevertheless, it was taken; and war was waged in spite of what would seem almost impossible handicaps for the Patriots in arms. The Congress of the Thirteen Colonies was so engrossed with the political decision which finally took form in the Declaration of Independence that it had little time for military matters. In 1775–76 it depended mostly upon the militia of the different states to fight its battles. When war was definitely a fact, this Congress, with very uncertain powers, was called upon to organize an effective field army, to commission the officers to command it, to organize a commissariat, a service of supply, a medical corps, and other auxiliary branches, and to call into being a central administrative agency that would correspond to the British war office. All this had to be done by men of no training in directing the affairs of a nation of the size and character of the one they had created. Moreover, it had to be accomplished against a large, well supplied, and well officered army of regular troops supported by an overwhelming naval force.

Looking back upon 1776 from the viewpoint of the twentieth century, one cannot but feel that the men who affixed their signatures to the Declaration of Independence set out upon a venture so desperate as to be almost hopeless.

274 From the painting *Reading the Declaration of Independence to Washington and his Officers, July 9, 1776*, by Percy Moran (1862–). © Osborne Company, Newark, N. J.

275 　Town and Harbor of Halifax, Nova Scotia, 1777, engraving by James Mason after the painting by Serres, based on a drawing
by R. Short, original in the Dominion Archives, Ottawa

SIR WILLIAM HOWE AT HALIFAX

IN Halifax Sir William Howe spent the spring of 1776 waiting for reinforcements and Lord Richard Howe's
fleet. The government was slow and ineffective. In spite of some improvement in recruiting and of re-
morseless drafting, the War Office found it necessary to contract in Germany for recruits sufficient to bring
several British regiments up to a respectable strength. So long as the government had decided to use force,
if and when conciliation failed, the swifter the blow the better. Howe was still at Halifax in May when the
movement for independence was gaining momentum in Congress (see Vol. VIII, Chapter III). Not until
June did he get his orders for the new campaign.

THE GERMAN MERCENARIES

GREAT BRITAIN had failed to persuade Russia to supply
mercenaries; Holland had likewise refused. From unofficial
British stations German soldiers were recruited to fill depleted regiments, but the numbers were negligible. Lord
Suffolk opened negotiations for subsidiary troops. A special
agent was sent to the Duke of Brunswick and to the Landgrave of Hesse-Cassel. Speed was essential, price a secon-

276 General Sir William Howe, 1729–1814, from the fictitious portrait, 1777, by Corbutt, in Smith's *British Mezzotint
Portraits*

dary matter. For
each Brunswick sol-
dier the equivalent
of $34.50 levy money
was to be paid. Gen-
eral Riedesel was ap-
pointed commander
of the expedition.
During the war
Brunswick supplied
five thousand seven
hundred and twenty-
three men. Hesse-
Cassel's profits from
the war were the equivalent of five million dollars. Twelve
thousand men were originally contracted for, but a further levy
was arranged of four hundred Hessian Yagers with rifles, three
hundred dismounted dragoons, and three corps of artillery. Lieutenant-General Heister was in command with Lieutenant-General
Knyphausen as subordinate.

277 Baron Wilhelm von Knyphausen, 1730–89,
from an engraving in the Pennsylvania-German
Society *Proceedings*, 1904

278   From the painting *Marinus Willett Preventing the Removal of Arms by the British*, by John Ward
Dunsmore, courtesy of the Title Guarantee and Trust Company, New York

WASHINGTON MOVES TO NEW YORK

As soon as Washington secured possession of Boston he turned his attention to the defense of the middle colonies. On April 13, 1776, Washington himself arrived at New York. The next month found him in Philadelphia asking for more troops to defend the city whose position at the mouth of the Hudson made it strategically the most important point on the Atlantic coast. Congress responded with a call for the local militia. The result was the assembling of the largest army which Washington ever commanded. But an aggregation of untrained and ill-armed men does not make a fighting force that can be depended on for a long campaign of maneuvering and fighting against seasoned regulars. With a motley force, the heart of which were Continentals enlisted until December 31, 1776, and the rest shifting bodies of militia enlisted for a few weeks or a few months, Washington awaited with what composure he could summon the approach of the hostile troops. One small bit of fortune favored him. In June of the preceding year the New York Patriots had seized six hundred muskets in the City Hall. When the Eighteenth Royal Irish had evacuated the town on the sixth of the month a Patriot demonstration had prevented their taking the precious muskets. Washington had sore need of all such supplies to put his army in shape for the impending encounter.

MARYLAND TROOPS JOIN WASHINGTON

COLONEL SMALLWOOD's regiment marched from Annapolis to join Washington in good time for the Battle of Long Island, at which it saw service under General Stirling. Smallwood himself perceived at once where the chief trouble lay with an untrained army. Reporting to the Maryland Council of Safety he said: "Our Commander-in-chief is an excellent man, and it would be happy for the United States if there was as much propriety in every department below him." The great need was for officers who understood the art of war and who could supervise the training of the men. The results of the ignorance of many of Washington's subordinates was soon to become manifest.

279   From the painting *Departure of Smallwood's Command from Annapolis*, by A. Wordsworth Thompson
(1840–96), in the Fine Arts Academy, Buffalo, N. Y.

ADMIRAL HOWE'S DIFFICULT POSITION

ADMIRAL LORD HOWE bore a name most highly honored in America, for his elder brother was the Lord Howe who had so won the hearts of all Americans during the final French and Indian War. Howe was as sincere in his desire for peace as he was skillful and energetic in the handling of his fleet, both before New York and later against the French. In America we see him in the difficult rôle of bearing the olive branch in one hand, the sword in the other. He little realized, however, the determination of the "rebels" whom he sought to placate. While he sought to win them over, valuable time was lost.

280 Admiral Lord Howe, engraving by Dunkerton, 1794, after the portrait by John Singleton Copley (1737–1815)

281 John Murray, 4th Earl of Dunmore, 1732–1809, from an engraving after the portrait by Sir Joshua Reynolds at Dunmore, Scotland

WAR IN VIRGINIA

IN 1776 the British planned to make their major effort at New York; but they were not unmindful of the fact that war had broken out in the South as well as the North. On New Year's Day, 1776, Lord Dunmore, Governor of Virginia, had burned Norfolk, following a defeat at the hands of the local Patriots. This wanton destruction roused the southern Patriots to fury.

THE DEFENSE OF CHARLESTON

THE people of Charleston, chief seaport of the South, were not slow to read the lesson of events to the north of them. On Sullivan's Island at the entrance to the harbor they strengthened Sullivan's Fort with palmetto logs and sand. Their labor was not in vain. Sir Henry Clinton in January had sailed from Boston with

two thousand troops for Cape Fear River. Apparently the British felt that a decisive action in this region would cow the rebellious colonists in the South. It would also impress the powerful Cherokees on the frontier and would aid the British agents in their efforts to incite these Indians against the Americans. In May Sir Peter Parker's fleet from England, with Lord Cornwallis on board, joined Clinton. The British prepared for an attack both by sea and land.

282 From the painting *The Battle of Fort Moultrie* by John Blake White (1781–1859), in the Senate wing of the Capitol, Washington

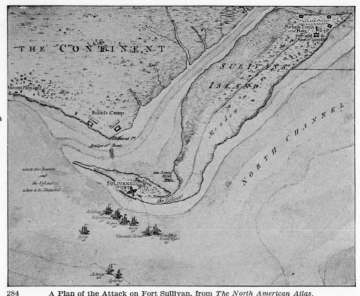

283   General William Moultrie, 1731-1805, from the miniature, 1791, by John Trumbull, in the Yale School of the Fine Arts

284   A Plan of the Attack on Fort Sullivan, from *The North American Atlas*, by William Faden, 1777

BRITISH DEFEAT AT CHARLESTON

On the 28th Parker's squadron poured a hot fire into the fort. "At one time," Moultrie afterward wrote, "three or four of the men-of-war broadsides struck the fort at the same instant, which gave the merlins such a tremble that I was apprehensive that a few more such would tumble them down." Meanwhile Clinton landed a party on Sullivan's Island in the hope of taking the fort from the rear; but was stopped by water too deep to wade. Finally the landing force withdrew and the fleet made off, its decks covered with killed and wounded men. Moultrie, who commanded the fort, had proved himself a good fighter. Charleston was saved, and the Patriot cause in the South was vastly benefited. On July 31 Clinton and Cornwallis sailed and joined Howe at New York, August 1.

285   From an original sketch of Admiral Howe's fleet at anchor in New York harbor, just after the Battle of Long Island, by an English officer on board one of the vessels, in the Emmet Collection, New York Public Library

WASHINGTON FORTIFIES BROOKLYN HEIGHTS

During the spring and early summer Washington's army, aided by civilians from the city, was busy constructing fortifications on both Long Island and Manhattan. With the weapons in use at that day Brooklyn Heights commanded New York; so on the slopes of that low hill was organized a defensive position of great strength. Nathanael Greene of Rhode Island, now a major-general, was in direct charge of the work. "He came to us," later wrote General Knox, "the rawest and most untutored being I ever met with: but in less than twelve months he was equal, in military knowledge, to any general officer in the army, and very superior to most of them." Washington's scheme of defense, however, contained a fatal weakness in that it compelled him to put the East River between the two parts of the army. An aggressive enemy with control of the sea could prevent the transfer of any considerable reinforcements from one wing to the other and therefore could defeat the army in detail.

THE PATRIOT ARMY DIVIDED

WASHINGTON has been severely criticized for putting his force of inexperienced and largely untrained troops in a position which involved such grave risks. Like his officers, he still had much to learn concerning both strategy and tactics. Purely military considerations do not seem to have governed his decision. The morale of his militia army and of the whole Patriot population would have suffered heavily had New York been abandoned without a blow. It is very doubtful if Congress could have been persuaded of the wisdom of such a move.

286   British Ships off Staten Island, 1776, from an original sketch by a British officer, in the Emmet Collection, New York Public Library

Since, under these conditions, dividing the army between Manhattan and Long Island was the only possible way to defend the city, Washington developed the works on Brooklyn Heights and hoped that his adversary would be foolish enough to repeat the fatal assaults of Bunker Hill.

287   The British ships *Phoenix* and *Rose* attacked on the Hudson by American fire boats, Aug. 16, 1776, from *Valentine's Manual*, 1864, after painting by D. Serres from a sketch by Sir James Wallace

PRELIMINARIES OF THE BATTLE OF LONG ISLAND

ON July 3 General Howe's transports, which had sailed from Halifax on June 11, dropped anchor in New York harbor. On July 5 he debarked his army on Staten Island to await the twenty thousand reinforcements which his brother, Admiral Howe, was bringing from England. On August 12 the Admiral arrived and attempted official conciliation with "George Washington, Esq." His letter was handed back to its bearer. On August 27, with an overwhelming force of trained soldiers, and having obtained from the Loyalist population complete knowledge of his enemy's dispositions, Howe prepared to attack. Washington had intended that Nathanael Greene should command on Long Island, but Greene was stricken with fever. The command devolved first upon Sullivan and then, two days before the attack, upon the jovial but incompetent Israel Putnam. Washington's plan was to keep a strong force on a line of hills well in advance of the redoubts at Brooklyn Heights. These troops, under Lord Stirling and Sullivan, were to inflict heavy losses upon an assaulting enemy before retiring to the main position; they were not to be involved in a general engagement in their advance position. Stirling was William Alexander, descendant of a Jacobite refugee who had settled in America in 1715. In 1760 he succeeded in establishing his claim to the earldom of Stirling, and was later to be an ardent advocate of the Patriot cause. The balance of sea power was against Washington, who now was not only liable to be completely cut off from New York, but whose troops in New York were cut off along the Hudson from any Patriot force to the north by the two British men-of-war, *Phoenix* and *Rose*, which had safely run the batteries at Paulus Hook and Greenwich on July 12.

288   General Lord Stirling, d. 1808, from the miniature in Harvard University Library, Cambridge, Mass.

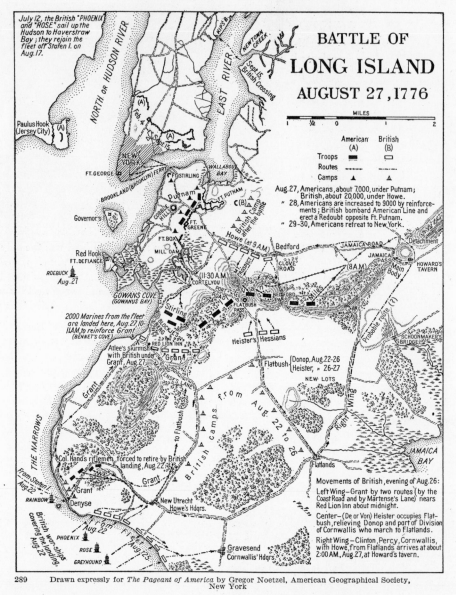

BATTLE OF
LONG ISLAND
AUGUST 27, 1776

July 12, the British "PHOENIX" and "ROSE" sail up the Hudson to Haverstraw Bay; they rejoin the fleet off Staten I. on Aug. 17.

Aug. 27, Americans, about 7,000, under Putnam; British, about 20,000, under Howe.
" 28, Americans are increased to 9000 by reinforcements; British bombard American Line and erect a Redoubt opposite Ft. Putnam.
" 29-30, Americans retreat to New York.

Movements of British, evening of Aug. 26:
Left Wing—Grant by two routes (by the Coast Road and by Martense's Lane) nears Red Lion Inn about midnight.
Center—(De or Von) Heister occupies Flatbush, relieving Donop and part of Division of Cornwallis who march to Flatlands.
Right Wing—Clinton, Percy, Cornwallis, with Howe, from Flatlands arrives at about 2:00 A.M., Aug. 27, at Howard's tavern.

289   Drawn expressly for *The Pageant of America* by Gregor Noetzel, American Geographical Society, New York

THE BATTLE OF LONG ISLAND, AUGUST 27

ON Long Island Howe displayed both his strength and weakness as a commander. His plan of attack was faultless. He proposed to envelop the left flank of Washington's advanced troops. On the night of August 26 he sent Heister's Hessians to deploy in front of Sullivan and hold him in position. At the same time he ordered Grant with a strong force against Stirling on the American right. Grant's orders were to make an ostentatious attack, giving the impression that Howe had chosen this ground for the main battle; but Grant was not to push Stirling back. Meanwhile, Howe with his subordinates, Cornwallis and Clinton, was to encircle the enemy left. A single patrol of five mounted officers guarded Putnam's extreme left. Early on the morning of August 27 this patrol, only one of whom had had any real military experience, was captured near Jamaica Pass by Howe's encircling column. Within six hours Howe's main force was in Sullivan's rear without Putnam having suspected the movement. Meanwhile the American commander, instead of holding his troops in readiness to fall back to Brooklyn Heights, in accordance with Washington's plan, had committed himself to an engagement along Stirling's front. When he discovered his mistake, it was too late. The advanced portion of the American army was either captured or dispersed with heavy losses. Sullivan and Stirling were taken prisoners. Then Howe appeared before the American defenses. He had won a brilliant success.

THE COUNCIL OF WAR, AUGUST 29

THE Battle of Long Island was a heavy blow for the Americans; but the greater part of their army was still intact. Washington, when convinced that Howe had committed himself to a campaign on Long Island, had sent on the day of the battle reinforcements to Brooklyn Heights to fight off a possible assault. Howe wisely declined to sacrifice his men in such an attempt and promptly began siege operations. Here his weakness manifested itself. The larger

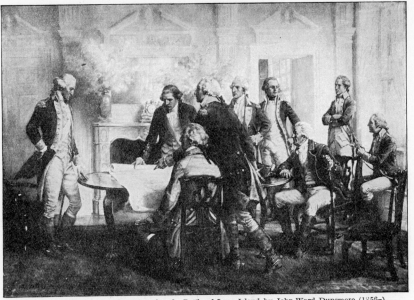

290   From the painting *Council of War after the Battle of Long Island*, by John Ward Dunsmore (1856-), courtesy of the Title Guarantee and Trust Company, New York

part of Washington's army was in his grasp. Had an Allenby been in command of the British the Revolution might have been ended within a short time. As it was, Howe permitted his enemy to escape. The weather certainly was unfavorable for operations by the fleet. But, even so, Howe, with his superior army, could easily have turned into irretrievable disaster any attempt of Washington to cross the East River with his army. Yet that was exactly what that general had determined to do. He recognized that Brooklyn Heights could not hold out and a council of war unanimously supported his decision to evacuate the position. He now demonstrated a military capacity that fully justified his selection as commander in chief.

THE LAST STAND AT NEW YORK

WASHINGTON, keeping his plan well concealed, gathered every available boat. On the night of August 29–30 he transferred his entire army without the loss of a man and with all their military supplies from Long Island to Manhattan. Fortune aided him when a fog came up in the early morning and covered the embarkation

291   The Retreat from Long Island, drawing by H. A. Ogden (1856-), for *The Century Book of The American Revolution*, New York, 1897, courtesy of the artist

of the last troops. The British pickets only arrived in time to fire a few shots at the rear guard. Greene, destined himself to become famous for his Fabian tactics, later remarked: "Considering the difficulties, it was the best effected retreat I ever read or heard of." The latter officer, with sound military judgment, advocated the immediate evacuation of New York and the burning of the city. Washington held the same views, and felt that his army should make a stand at King's Bridge over the Harlem River. But again political considerations prevailed; and Washington's army began to intrench a series of positions reaching from the Harlem River to New York. On September 2, Washington wrote: "The check our detachment sustained on the 27th ultimo has dispirited too great a proportion of our troops and filled their minds with apprehension and despair. The militia instead of calling forth their utmost effort to a brave and manly opposition in order to repair our losses, are dismayed, intractable, and impatient to return."

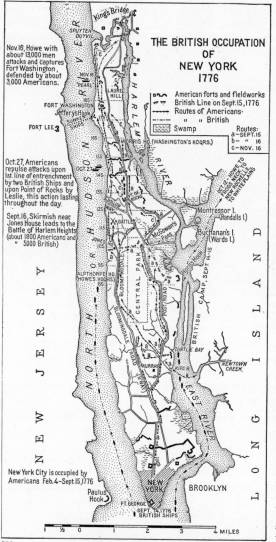

THE BRITISH OCCUPATION
OF
NEW YORK
1776

American forts and fieldworks
British Line on Sept. 15, 1776
Routes of Americans·
  "   "   British
Swamp

Routes:
a—SEPT. 15
b— " 16
c—NOV. 16

Nov. 16, Howe with about 13,000 men attacks and captures Fort Washington, defended by about 3,000 Americans.

Oct. 27, Americans repulse attacks upon 1st. line of entrenchment by two British Ships and upon Point of Rocks by Leslie, this action lasting throughout the day.

Sept. 16, Skirmish near Jones House leads to the Battle of Harlem Heights (about 1800 Americans and " 5000 British)

New York City is occupied by Americans Feb. 4–Sept. 15, 1776

292   Drawn expressly for *The Pageant of America* by Gregor Noetzel,
      American Geographical Society, New York

THE BRITISH OCCUPY NEW YORK

WASHINGTON's disposition of his army on Manhattan Island was fraught with grave danger. His left flank was at Harlem and his right near the city. His main line of communications ran along the north shore of Long Island Sound. The British fleet could sail at will up the Hudson and the East River. The American flanks could, therefore, be easily turned. A detachment from the fleet ascended the Hudson to Bloomingdale and shelled the Americans out of their entrenchments there. This was a warning that the American position was untenable. Then, on September 15, under cover of the fire of another detachment of the British fleet, Howe brought his army across East River at Kip's Bay (East Thirty-fourth Street). The American troops could not stand against the grapeshot from the British artillery, and their retreat became a disorderly rout that threatened Washington's army with destruction. The commander in chief vainly attempted to rally the fugitives and risked his life in the *mêlée*. Again Howe did not push his advantage, and again he allowed his adversary to concentrate his beaten troops at the northern end of the island. Under such circumstances the British army began an occupation of New York that was to last until the end of the war — seven long years. According to an old story, three or four thousand Americans hurrying northward after the landing at Kip's Bay escaped with little loss when they might easily have been cut off by the British, thanks to the ruse of Mrs. Lindley Murray, a clever Patriot lady. Mrs. Murray invited General Howe to stop for refreshments as he passed her door, and detained him long enough for her fellow-countrymen to get away. Washington, gathering his army at Harlem, took up positions too strong for a frontal attack.

293   From a painting *Mrs. Murray's Strategy* by Percy Moran (1862–).   © Gerlach-Barklow Co., Joliet, Ill.

294   From the painting by John Ward Dunsmore (1856–), courtesy of the Title Guarantee and Trust Company, New York

LORD HOWE AND THE COMMITTEE OF CONGRESS, SEPTEMBER 11

FOUR days before the landing at Kip's Bay Lord Howe had at last succeeded in meeting a committee of Congress consisting of Franklin, Adams, and Rutledge. The conference was held at the Billopp house on Staten Island. The Americans made the condition that independence must be recognized before negotiations could begin. Howe unable to meet such terms, regretfully withdrew. There can be no doubt that his disappointment was keen. Service against the Americans who had erected a tablet in Westminster Abbey for their dead brother was distasteful to both the Howes.

295   Tablet by James E. Kelly (1855–) to commemorate the
Battle of Harlem Heights

THE BATTLE OF HARLEM HEIGHTS

HOWE fought a sharp skirmish with the Americans at Harlem Heights on September 16, in which the British attackers were driven off. This brush revived the spirits of Washington's troops and restored confidence. The affair convinced Howe that the wiser plan was to maneuver Washington out of his position at Harlem rather than to attempt to dislodge him by frontal attack. But for almost four weeks after this engagement Howe made no move except to strengthen his position north of New York. When he finally got under way autumn was well advanced. Washington's position was chosen with admirable military skill, both his flanks being well protected. But a threat against his communications with Connecticut, whence he received much of his supplies, would compel him to abandon his works. So on October 21 Howe was in New Rochelle, where he was reinforced by a division of Hessians newly arrived from Europe. Pushing north and west toward Washington's army, the British army encamped on the 25th on the Bronx River four miles from White Plains. Howe hoped to draw his enemy into a general engagement (see map, No. 296).

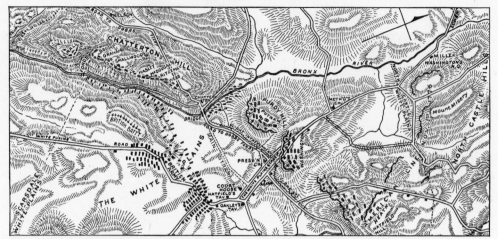

296   From the map compiled by Otto Hüfeland in *Westchester County during the American Revolution*, 1925, courtesy of the Westchester County Historical Society, White Plains, N. Y.

THE BATTLE OF WHITE PLAINS, OCTOBER 28

WASHINGTON moved northward from Harlem to parry the expected blow of Howe; but left a strong detachment at Fort Washington under Greene. Near White Plains the American commander on October 21 posted his troops in strong hill positions north of the village. (See map No. 299.) Washington's right flank lay west of the river, on and near Chatterton Hill. On the 28th Howe attacked vigorously and drove the troops from this position. The British loss was heavy and no real advantage was gained; for the defenders merely fell back to another strong position in the hills. On the 31st the British planned a general assault, which a heavy rain prevented. On the next day Washington withdrew to an impregnable position on North Castle Heights. Since the defeat on Long Island the American force had been dwindling; militia levies were going home, singly or in whole companies. Washington could not hope to win a battle against the whole British army, now twenty thousand strong. Howe had handled the campaign with skill. Forcing Washington so far north separated him from his own troops at Fort Washington on Manhattan and at Fort Lee across the Hudson, thus dangerously dividing the Patriot army. Howe, instead of following Washington, which might have brought on a British defeat, moved his army on November 5 to Dobbs Ferry on the Hudson. Washington, sensing the danger of this situation, took precautions to guard the passes into the Hudson Highlands, whither his army might be forced to flee. Leaving General Lee in command at North Castle, and sending Putnam with three thousand men to take up a position at Hackensack, in New Jersey, he himself rode on the 10th to Peekskill, spending the next day in a reconnoissance of the site of the new defenses at West Point, and then moved down to his new headquarters at Hackensack.

297   General Charles Lee, from the portrait in Thomas Girdlestone, *Facts Tending to Show that General Lee was the author of Junius*, London, 1813

298   *A View of the Attack against Fort Washington*, drawn on the spot by Thomas Davies, Capt., courtesy of Kennedy & Co., New York

THE FALL OF FORT WASHINGTON, NOVEMBER 16

WASHINGTON'S judgment was to abandon the great strongholds at Fort Washington and Fort Lee and to concentrate his army. But Greene had urged holding the fort on Manhattan, and his purpose had been strengthened by an order from Congress. Fort Washington was a work well placed and of very great strength. Most of the American generals regarded it as impregnable. From Fort Lee Washington saw the enemy assault the Manhattan fort on November 16. Howe, with the aid of the fleet which shelled the fort, made a well-planned assault. The Americans fought stubbornly, inflicting heavy losses. The British broke through the outer works and advanced toward the fort itself. There was no alternative but to surrender. The Americans lost some three thousand, killed, wounded, and prisoners, a priceless collection of military stores, and a strategic position of importance. For the Americans the blow was one of the most staggering of the war. Washington early in the morning had crossed the river to see whether the position should be abandoned or not. By this time the enveloping movement by the British had already begun.

THE SURRENDER OF FORT LEE, NOVEMBER 20

HOWE turned at once upon Fort Lee. On the third day after the assault on Fort Washington, General Cornwallis landed on the Jersey shore eight miles above Fort Lee, climbed the steep escarpment, and marched swiftly on the position in the hope of surprising it. The movement was

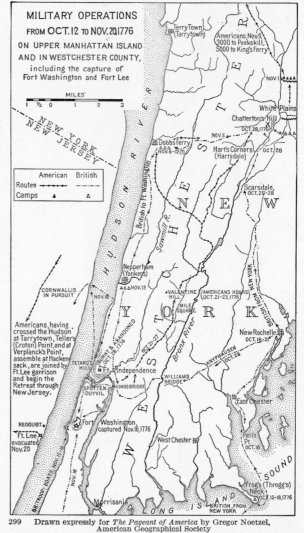

299   Drawn expressly for *The Pageant of America* by Gregor Noetzel, American Geographical Society

disclosed by a deserter, and Greene had just time to get across the Hackensack River, leaving his tents and stores. After the loss of Fort Washington, Washington had ordered Lee at North Castle (No.304) to join him in New Jersey with his troops. After four days he repeated the order. Lee failed to comply with either order. Moreover, the New Jersey militia refused to come out. Washington was in desperate straits. There was nothing to do but to retreat across New Jersey, pursued by Cornwallis with a vastly superior force. The primary responsibility for the loss of Fort Washington must rest upon the Congress. Politicians in urging its retention were trespassing unduly upon the domain of the military commander. This interference embarrassed Washington. Up to this time the campaign of 1776 had been unsuccessful; he was not in the position, therefore, to force his opinions upon the government.

300   The Landing of the British Forces in New Jersey, from a drawing made by a British officer on board the fleet, in the Emmet Collection, New York Public Library

301   From the painting *Hessians on the Road to Trenton* by H. A. Ogden (1856–), courtesy of the American Chemical Agricultural Society, Boston, Mass.

THE RETREAT ACROSS NEW JERSEY, NOVEMBER 20–DECEMBER 8

THROUGH Newark, New Brunswick, Princeton, Trenton retreated the still dwindling American army. The Delaware River was the last desperate American hope. Washington sent men ahead to gather all the boats for miles north and south of Trenton. On December 7–8, the American force escaped into Pennsylvania, and, by confiscating the boats, left Cornwallis no means of immediate pursuit. Five days before, Lee had at last crossed the Hudson at Verplanck's Point north of the Croton River (see map, No. 304) and proceeded toward Pennsylvania in a line roughly parallel with that of Washington. British gold appealed to neutrals more than American paper, and Howe's army lived on the fat of the land. The Patriots were in half despair. Though the Hessians and some of the British roused resentment as they tramped through the country, Howe's victories caused an increase in the Loyalist ranks.

THE CAPTURE OF GENERAL LEE

GENERAL LEE seems to have been both stupid and treacherous. On December 13 a British patrol of the British Sixteenth Light Dragoons captured him in a farmhouse outside his own lines where, in secret, he was writing disloyal communications to another self-advertising commander of American troops, Horatio Gates. His capture, at first regarded as a heavy loss, actually was a blessing, for Sullivan, upon whom the command devolved, pushed rapidly on and with his troops joined Washington beyond the Delaware.

302   From a lithograph by J. S. Templeton in Barnard, *History of England*

303   Handbill of the Committee of Safety announcing General Howe's approach to Philadelphia, from Smith and Watson, *American Historical and Literary Curiosities*, 1852

HOWE ESTABLISHES WINTER QUARTERS

HOWE elected not to attempt to force his way at once across the Delaware, which was a military obstacle of the first importance. He settled down into winter quarters, establishing two outposts on the left bank of the river at Trenton and Bordentown. These posts were the left wing of a series of positions which reached across northern New Jersey to Newark. Howe, with sound military judgment, had originally planned to extend his front only from Newark to New Brunswick; but he had been persuaded to include Trenton and Bordentown in order to protect the New Jersey Loyalists. In accordance with the etiquette of the army, Howe gave the Hessians the position on the left. He ordered Colonel Rall, the commanding officer at Trenton, to throw up redoubts for the protection of his exposed position; but this Hessian failed to comply.

AMERICAN UNIFORMS of THE WAR OF INDEPENDENCE~1775-1783

MAJOR GENERAL 1780

AIDE MAJOR GEN'L. 1780

ENGINEER OFFICER 1780

WASHINGTON'S LIFE GUARD CAPTAIN 1776-'83

4TH REGT. LT. DRAGOONS PRIVATE 1777

ARTILLERY LIEUTENANT 1777-'83

ARTILLERY PRIVATE 1777-'83

INFANTRY N.H.-MASS. R.I.-CONN. 1779

INFANTRY NEW YORK & NEW JERSEY 1779

INFANTRY PENNA.-MD. & VIRGINIA 1779

INFANTRY N.C.-S.C. & GEORGIA 1779

NAVAL CAPTAIN 1776-'83

NAVAL LIEUTENANT 1776-'83

NAVY MARINE CAPTAIN 1776-'83

Painted expressly for *The Pageant of America* by H. A. Ogden

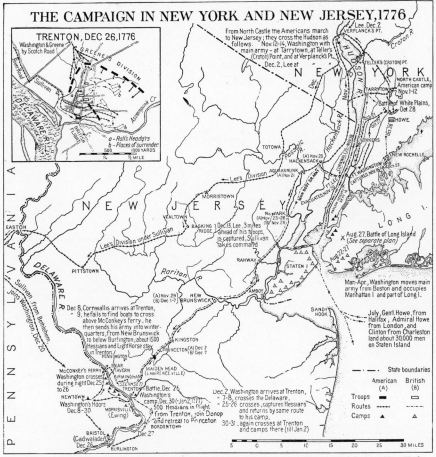

THE CAMPAIGN IN NEW YORK AND NEW JERSEY, 1776

304 Drawn expressly for *The Pageant of America* by Gregor Noetzel, American Geographical Society, New York

THE TRENTON COUNTER–ATTACK, DECEMBER 25–26

LIKE all great generals, Washington had a highly developed political as well as military sense. He was aware that the morale of the Patriots, both in and out of the army, could only be restored by a victory. Moreover, the enlistments of most of his troops ran out at the end of the year. He therefore resolved upon a counter-attack. His plan and its execution was a brilliant solution of a difficult military problem. He made a feint movement against Von Donop, who commanded at Bordentown, and drew that officer south to Burlington. Trenton was consequently uncovered on the south. Knowing the German custom of extensive Christmas revelries, Washington astutely chose this day for his attack. He divided his army into three corps, the first to cross the Delaware near Bordentown and move southward to attack Von Donop, the second to cross at Trenton ferry, and the third, under his own command, to cross nine miles above Trenton and converge with the second upon the village. Weather conditions of the night of the 25th were so bad that only Washington's column got over the river. In the early hours of December 26 the Americans marched through a storm of sleet upon Trenton. Leutze's famous picture obviously depicts only the spirit of the enterprise.

305 From the painting *Washington Crossing the Delaware*, by Emanuel Leutze (1816–68) in the Metropolitan Museum of Art, New York

306   From the painting *Capture of the Hessians at Trenton* by John Trumbull, in the Yale School of the Fine Arts, New Haven, Conn.

THE HESSIANS SURRENDER AT TRENTON, DECEMBER 26

RALL was warned of the attack. He had, however, allowed his men to lose discipline and was unable to assemble his full force quickly enough. Moreover, he had no redoubts behind which his fifteen hundred could fight off Washington's twenty-five hundred. Rall himself was mortally wounded early in the battle. "The hurry, fright, and confusion of the enemy was not unlike that which it will be when the last trump shall sound." Thus wrote General Henry Knox, whose well-placed guns mowed down the front of every formation which the desperate Hessians tried. Sweeping the streets with gunfire and each armed house with musketry, the

Continentals drove the Hessians clear of Trenton, encircled them with fire and steel, broke up their disciplined cohesion, and forced them to surrender. To General Sullivan fell the honor of directing the last phase of the Battle of Trenton. A Hessian regiment sought to escape toward Bordentown by way of the bridge over the Assunpink Creek. But Sullivan had forestalled them and had posted his infantry and cannon in such a manner as to control the bridge. The Germans with a train of wagons and a throng of camp followers found themselves at the bridge swept by effective American fire. They were thrown into confusion. A few escaped but the main body was compelled to surrender, while "the patriot troops tossed their hats in the air." Washington took his prisoners to Newtown, sending them thence to Philadelphia, and returned to Trenton, where he took up a strong position.

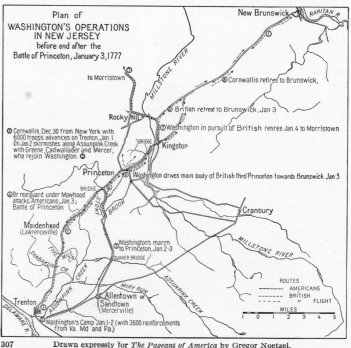

Plan of
WASHINGTON'S OPERATIONS
IN NEW JERSEY
before and after the
Battle of Princeton, January 3, 1777

307   Drawn expressly for *The Pageant of America* by Gregor Noetzel, American Geographical Society, New York

308   From the painting *The Battle of Princeton* by John Ward Dunsmore. © by the artist

THE BATTLE OF PRINCETON AND ITS AFTERMATH, JANUARY 3–4

HOWE was thoroughly disturbed by the reverse at Trenton. He ordered Cornwallis, who was about to depart for England, to hasten against the Americans with a strong force. Cornwallis based his operations on Princeton, leaving a rear guard of three regiments under Colonel Mawhood, and one at Maidenhead under Leslie. Late on the second of January, after retarding skirmishes along Five Mile and Shabakunk Creeks, Cornwallis reached the outskirts of Trenton. Until nightfall there was skirmishing and vigorous artillery duelling along the Assunpink Creek. Meanwhile Cornwallis ordered up his reinforcements. Washington was as much aware as his British opponent that a general engagement between his half-trained troops and the British regulars could have but one outcome. Moreover, the Americans had the Delaware at their backs and could not retreat. During the night the American commander with great secrecy moved his army out of its position and led it by a long circuit through Allentown around Cornwallis' left flank (see map, No. 307). The movement was covered by darkness and by a few men left behind who kept up a feigned activity in the abandoned positions. Cornwallis' outposts and patrols completely failed to secure information of Washington's enterprise. No single important movement in the war was characterized by such audacity as this. For the weaker army to abandon a strong defensive position when in contact with the enemy, to circle his flank and strike his base was a maneuver as surprising as it was brilliant. South of Princeton, Washington came suddenly into collision with two of Mawhood's regiments hurrying toward Trenton. The British commander, concluding that Washington's army was retreating before Cornwallis, gave battle to check it. With well-directed fire, followed by a bayonet charge, he drove back Washington's advance troops in confusion. But there his success ended. Washington himself spurred forward into the fight. He advanced beyond the firing line of his own troops to within thirty paces of the hostile muzzles. The rally was successful; and Mawhood with the remainder of his own regiment fled southward, joining Cornwallis and Leslie, who, crestfallen at being duped by their opponent, were hurrying to the scene. The Americans, greatly superior in numbers, swept the field, driving the remaining British regiment to the village of Princeton, where the third regiment under Mawhood's command had been left. Both regiments fled precipitately to the north, pursued by Washington, who, because of the exhaustion of his men, forsook the tempting bait of New Brunswick and at Kingston diverged northwestwards to winter quarters at Morristown, where, sure of supplies, they might rest. The force of Cornwallis, unable to overtake Washington, retired to their base at New Brunswick, and the New Jersey campaign came to an end.

"In a word, the moral effect of the past campaign was in great measure cancelled, and the whole of the work, excepting the capture of New York, required to be done again." — FORTESCUE, *A History of the British Army*, III, p. 203.

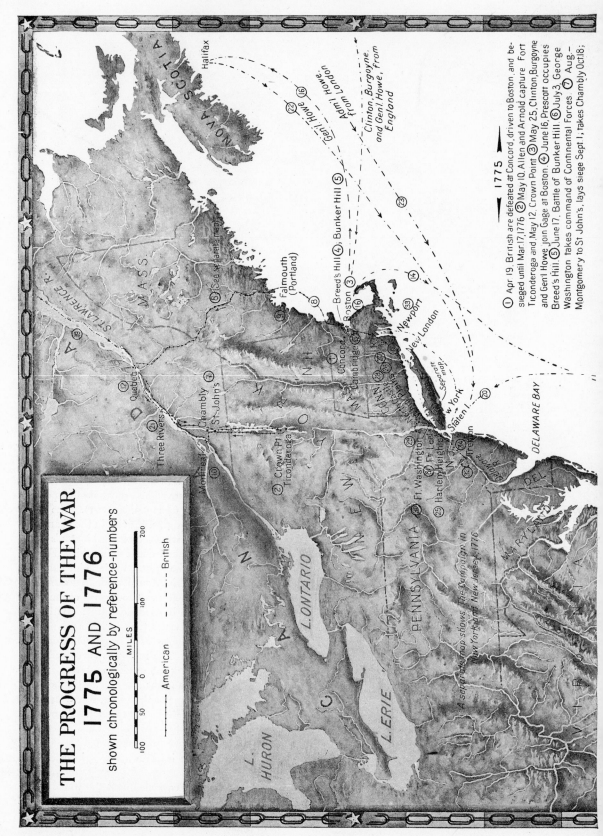

THE PROGRESS OF THE WAR
1775 AND 1776
shown chronologically by reference-numbers

MILES

—————— American
— · — · — British

① Apr.19. British are defeated at Concord, driven to Boston, and besieged until Mar.17,1776 ② May 10. Allen and Arnold capture Fort Ticonderoga and May 12. Crown Point ③ May 25, Clinton, Burgoyne and Gen'l Howe join Gage at Boston. ④ June 16, Prescott occupies Breed's Hill. ⑤ June 17. Battle of Bunker Hill. ⑥ July 3, George Washington takes command of Continental Forces. ⑦ Aug.— Montgomery to St John's, lays siege Sept.1, takes Chambly Oct.18;

A separate map shows the campaign in New York and New Jersey, 1776

reduces St Johns Nov 3. ⑧ Sept 13-Nov.13, Arnold, with Greene, Morgan, Burr, and Dearborn, marches to Quebec ⑨ Oct 18, Falmouth (Portland, Me.) burnt by British ⑩ Nov.12, Montgomery captures Montreal ⑪ Dec 9, Virginia militia defeat Dunmore and take Norfolk. ⑫ Dec 31, Carleton repulses Americans at Quebec; Montgomery killed, siege continues

1776

⑬ Jan 1, Dunmore destroys Norfolk. ⑭ Jan -, Clinton sails from Boston to Cape Fear ⑮ Feb 27, at Moore's Creek, Militia defeat Loyalists. ⑯ Mar 17, Boston evacuated by Howe, occupied by Washington. Howe sails to Halifax ⑰ Washington moves the army, Mar-Apr. to New York ⑱ May 3, Cornwallis in fleet of Sir Peter Parker arrives at Cape Fear ⑲ May 6, Ships from England reach Quebec and lift siege, Thomas retreats to Ft Chambly. ⑳ June 4, Clinton and Cornwallis appear before Charleston; attack on Ft Moultrie, June 28, fails ; July 21 they sail and join Howe, Aug 1. ㉑ June 7, Sullivan attacks Three Rivers, but is routed and retreats to St Johns; July 1. Arnold joins him; they retreat to Crown Point. ㉒ July 3, General Howe with 9000 men from Halifax June 11. lands on Staten Island. ㉓ Aug.12, Admiral Howe with large fleet and 20,000(?)men, from London, arrives at Staten Island. ㉔ Aug.27, Battle of Long Island; Washington withdraws to Manhattan. ㉕ Sept 16, Battle of Harlem Heights. ㉖ Oct 21, Washington withdraws to White Plains. ㉗ Oct. 28, the Battle of White Plains. ㉘ Nov 1, Washington withdraws to North Castle ㉙ Nov. 12-14, Washington moves troops across the Hudson ㉚ Nov. 16, Howe takes Fort Washington ㉛ Nov 20, Howe takes Fort Lee ㉜ Nov.20-Dec. 8, Washington retreats across New Jersey to west bank of the Delaware ㉝ Dec 8, Clinton is sent to Newport ㉞ Dec 25, Washington crosses the Delaware, Dec 26, defeats Hessians at Trenton , returns to west bank, Dec. 30 & 31, he again crosses the Delaware and camps near Trenton

CHESAPEAKE BAY
Norfolk ⑬
GreatBridge
Elizabeth R

Clinton and Cornwallis from Cork

— At end of 1776 —
Washington near Trenton
Howe at New York
Clinton at Newport
Carleton at Quebec

C. Fear
Charlestown (Charleston)
Savannah
St Augustine

NORTH CAROLINA
SOUTH CAROLINA
GEORGIA
FLORIDA (Spanish)

Drawn expressly for *The Pageant of America* by Gregor Noetzel, American Geographical Society, New York

THE PROGRESS OF THE WAR, 1775 AND 1776

THE map emphasizes some important aspects of the Revolution. Most of the population of the revolting colonies lived in a narrow band hugging the coast line from Maine to Georgia. There were practically no important settlements so far from navigable waters as to be removed from the easy possibility of attack. The war was, therefore, a reality to every community. The frontier people had little to fear from British regulars but much from the Indians, the powerful Iroquois in the North and the Cherokee in the South. The Indian menace which the British Government held over the Americans together with the ability of the British to strike at will anywhere along the coast line tended, particularly in the early years of the war, to cause the holding of troops in the individual colonies for local defense and to prevent a great concentration of force at any particular point. Conversely, this imminent and very real danger made for the rapid development throughout all the colonies of an aggressive war spirit. In every community there were active Patriots whose common danger brought about a coöperation between the colonies which few Americans fifteen years before would have dreamed possible

309

310   From the painting *Raising the American Flag at Prospect Hill, Somerville, Mass., Jan. 1, 1776*, by Clyde O. DeLand

THE MEANING OF THE JACK AND STRIPES

AT the beginning of the Revolution all sorts of flags were used afloat and ashore. Some belonged to militia companies or regiments, some to towns or counties, and some to individual states; while others embodied the ideas of liberty, defiance, or armed rebellion which animated the Patriots of the early days. The "Grand Union" Jack and Stripes was used in 1776 not only by Washington on New Year's Day at Somerville but by Virginia at Williamsburg on May 15 and by Arnold that autumn for the Battle of Valcour. The Stars and Stripes have figured in so many Fourth-of-July orations as the banner of liberty under which Independence was achieved that very few American patriots ever stop to think that this now famous and long-established national flag was not adopted as the official standard of the new republic till well on in the third year of the Revolutionary War. It was only "on Saturday, the 14th of June 1777" that the Continental Congress "*Resolved*, That the flag of the thirteen United States be thirteen stripes alternate red and white; that the union be thirteen stars, white in a blue field, representing a new Constellation." (MS. Journal of Congress, Charles Thomson, Secretary No. 2, Vol. VI, p. 1537.)

The Jack and Stripes had not only marked the transition period between the British Union Jack and the American Stars and Stripes, but it had a significant military meaning, as marking the first attempt to create a real Union army. When a state militiaman went home before his term of service had expired, he would find his folks at home agreeing that New Jersey men had no urgent call to obey a Massachusetts officer engaged in fighting Tories somewhere in New York. To counteract the dissipation of force which such local jealousies bred everywhere, the Continental Congress tried to create an all-American army of its own. But the different states practically put recruiting up to auction by offering much higher bounties than the Congress could afford. The states likewise competed among themselves, with the disastrous result that recruits would go from one to another, trying to make a better bargain, and leaving the hopelessly outbidden Continentals in the lurch. Even in 1781, the year of Yorktown, some states were offering a thousand dollars more than Congress; and what made it worse, Congress was trying to get Continentals, who were practically regulars belonging to the nation as a whole, while the states were trying to get the same men to enlist as mere militiamen for short terms of service. Nevertheless, there always were a few Continentals who, under Washington's inspiring leadership, stood fast by the service of the real United States, emerged triumphant from the testing ground of Valley Forge, and laid the foundations for the army of the United States.

CHAPTER VII

BURGOYNE, HOWE, AND VALLEY FORGE, 1777–78

INDEPENDENCE year, 1776, had shown the difficulties of putting down the rebellion by military force. The Revolution had now grown into a formidable war. Distances in America were so great that an invading British army was soon carried too far from its base and compelled to draw back again. The Patriot troops had to fall back before the invader; but they fell back fighting; and Washington was able to prevent a general engagement which might destroy his force. His army at times dwindled dangerously, as his militia went home, often before the expiration of their terms; but Howe found that wherever he sent a force, some fresh local militiamen would soon be swarming round it. Capturing cities was of little consequence. All the important urban centers of the colonies were captured at one time or another during the war; and three, New York, Savannah, and Charleston, were held for considerable periods. The British task was to break the will of a people living in a vast area, most of them on practically self-sufficient farms, and quite enough of them so imbued with the "Spirit of '76" that nothing short of their unconditional surrender could make them yield their independence.

Three ways of waging war against the Revolution with good prospects of success were open to the king's government. The first was a strict naval blockade, accompanied by a few strong garrisons at strategic points, whence sorties could be made against collections of stores or any "rebel" centers. The second, and by far the best, was to combine as much as possible of the first with an unremitting campaign against Washington's army, the complete destruction of which must almost inevitably end the war. The third involved the severance of New England from the rest of the states by winning and holding the line of the Hudson. This last was part of the chosen plan for 1777.

Its success was furthered by the fact that the Revolution had developed into a civil war between Patriots and Loyalists. St. John de Crèvecœur's *Sketches of Eighteenth Century America* describes this terrible aspect of the conflict. "The rage of civil discord hath advanced among us with astonishing rapidity. Every opinion is changed; every prejudice is subverted; every ancient principle is annihilated; every mode of organization, which linked us before as men and citizens, is now altered. . . . This is now the case with us: the son is armed against the father, the brother against the brother, family against family; the nearer the connection, the more bitter the resentment, the more violent the rage of opposition." Howe knew of this fratricidal strife and counted too much upon it to aid him in his operations. He seems to have felt in 1777 that the capture of Philadelphia, the American capital, was all that was necessary to cause the Loyalists to join the king's colors in such numbers as to bring the rebellion to a speedy end. Howe was a good strategist and tactician, but he was not the man to strike unremitting blows against his one important enemy. His superior in England, moreover, was an officer whom he despised. Germain had been court-martialed and dismissed for cowardice at Minden. He had then made his way forward by the backstairs politics typical of his times, until he became the ultimate chief of all the armies operating in America.

311 George III in his coronation robes, painted in 1779 by Sir Joshua Reynolds (1723–92), from the *Works of Sir Joshua Reynolds*

GEORGE III AND SIR WILLIAM HOWE

"GEORGE, be a King!" was the reputed admonition of his German mother, all through his childhood; and his more or less well-intentioned attempts to follow this maternal advice resulted in what all the world knows. Howe, like his brother the admiral and many another British officer, was a Whig, in more or less sympathy, like the great Earl of Chatham and his famous son William Pitt the Younger, with the Patriot cause. The king probably thought that,

failing submission on the part of the "rebels," the shock of arms would turn Howe and other Whiggish officers strongly against these very "rebels." But, as we have seen already, and shall again and again, Howe did not press home any advantage whatever. Whatever his sympathies may have been at the beginning of the war, Howe apparently never let them stand

312 General Howe, 1729–1814, from Andrews' *History of the Late War*, London, 1785

in the way of the performance of his military duty. His failures may be ascribed to inefficiency but never to treachery.

313 Sergeant Jasper replanting the Patriot flag at Fort Moultrie, S. C., June 28, 1776, from the engraving by G. R. Hall, published in 1856, after a painting by J. A. Oertel

THE SPIRIT OF '76

THE British Government and its armies operating in America had to reckon with a spirit in its enemies which had never manifested itself in colonial troops during the French and Indian Wars. There was much that was absurd, or worse, in the American armies of 1777. But they were ennobled by a great cause, and they contained an important nucleus of officers and men, like Sergeant Jasper at Fort Moultrie, who had left home and comfort to risk life itself at the call of duty.

314   From the painting *The Spirit of '76* by A. M. Willard (1836–1918), in Abbot Hall, Marblehead, Mass.

LORD GEORGE GERMAIN, 1716-85

THE chief responsibility for the fiasco of 1777 rests upon Germain. Never has Britain had a worse war minister. The situation which he confronted in the winter of 1776-77 was as follows: Carleton was in Canada with rather more than eleven thousand troops, including some Canadian militia. Howe was at New York with about twenty thousand troops, among whom were included a strong force which had occupied Newport, Rhode Island, in August, 1776. In December Howe had written to Germain proposing a plan requiring another thirty thousand men: ten thousand based on Newport, to operate against New England, and especially Boston; ten thousand in New Jersey, to operate toward Philadelphia with all who could come from New York; and ten thousand to hold the South. Germain wrote that the king approved Howe's plan and suggested in addition a "diversion upon the coasts of Massachusetts Bay and New Hampshire." This was the last letter that Howe received from his chief before he set out in the following summer for Philadelphia. Germain at first promised half the reinforcements that Howe called for; but found he could not obtain even this half from Germany. Because of this failure Germain doubtless listened more attentively to a plan unfolded by Burgoyne, second in command in Canada, and spending the winter, as was his wont, in England. This officer proposed that the greater part of the Canadian force be marched southward via Lake Champlain to unite with Howe in the Hudson valley. This would concentrate the British troops in America into one great force and enable Howe to carry out almost any offensive operation he should deem advisable. Incidentally it would cut New England off from the other states.

315   From a mezzotint by J. McArdell after the portrait by Sir Joshua Reynolds (1723-92)

GENERAL JOHN BURGOYNE, 1722-92

BURGOYNE was a man of society, a politician, and something of a playwright as well. His memorandum, though showing military ability, involved a plan that was fundamentally unsound. At best the scheme of marching one army south from Montreal, another east from Oswego, and a third north from New York, the three to unite near Albany, scattered the British forces widely. Moreover, it drew each of them in its advance far from its base and enabled an active enemy, operating on interior lines, to strike the converging armies separately and perhaps defeat them before they could join. In spite of this obvious defect Burgoyne preferred this plan to the alternative which he discussed, which was to take the Canadian forces by sea to New York. Such a move would have accomplished the concentration of troops desired, and would have put Howe in a position to occupy the Hudson valley almost at his pleasure. In either plan Carleton was to stay in Canada with three or four thousand men. In fairness to Burgoyne, it should be said that he urged Germain to give the commander in the field discretion to move southward to Albany to coöperate with Howe, or eastward into New England to join with the force at Newport, or to take his army by sea if it seemed advisable. The king did not approve the last alternative, fearing an American invasion of Canada. When the orders were issued, Burgoyne, who was selected to lead the army, found that he was given no discretion, but was ordered to proceed to Albany and place himself under the command of Howe. Yet mistaken as the plan was, it might have succeeded had Germain sent definite orders to Howe to coöperate. His failure to do this wrecked the campaign.

316   From the portrait by Thomas Hudson (1701-79), courtesy of the Viscountess Barrington, London

THE DEFEAT OF TRYON IN CONNECTICUT

WHILE these plans were maturing in England, Washington began preparing to defend the Hudson, which he was informed was to be the British objective in the summer campaign. He concentrated stores at Peekskill on the Hudson and at Danbury, Connecticut. But Howe sent a force which destroyed the stores at Peekskill. On April 25 two thousand men under General Tryon landed at Fairfield (Compo on map), and on the next day destroyed the supplies at Danbury and burned the houses of the Patriots. Benedict Arnold, however, turned the Tryon operation into a disaster. Smarting under a recent humiliation inflicted upon him by Congress, when, in spite of his great services, he was not made a major-general, while less conspicuous officers were being promoted, Arnold was on leave in New Haven. Nevertheless he joined the militia that came out to fight Tryon. On April 27 at Ridgefield Arnold managed to handle his untrained levies with the utmost gallantry and skill. Tryon was forced into a retreat like that from Lexington and Concord. Harassed by a deadly sniping fire, the British fell back to the coast, where the marines, landed from the frigates, saved Tryon's exhausted troops. Arnold's success forced Congress to make him a major-general. But his former relative rank was not restored.

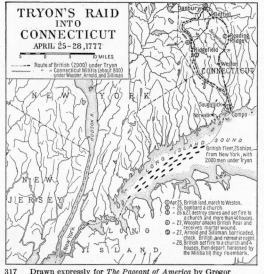

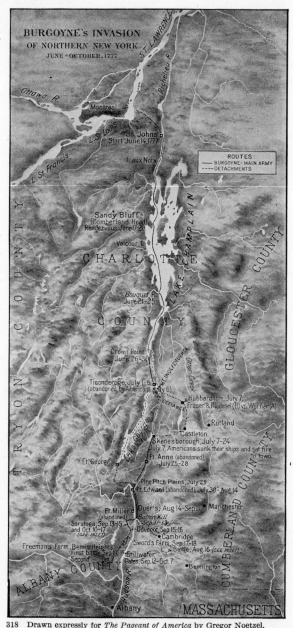

317   Drawn expressly for *The Pageant of America* by Gregor
Noetzel, American Geographical Society, New York

BURGOYNE'S ADVANCE FROM CANADA

ON May 6, Burgoyne landed at Quebec. Carleton aided him loyally in completing his preparations. The Canadians, practically all of whom were French, were not enthusiastic about participating in the war; so the expected levy of two thousand militia dwindled to less than two hundred. Moreover, the French-Canadians were reluctant to accept employment in the transport service which was vital to the success of the whole expedition. In spite of all difficulties, however, Burgoyne assembled his army, which included Hessian troops under Baron Riedesel, with a sufficient number of batteaux on June 20 at Cumberland Head. Eleven days later, he began the investment of Fort Ticonderoga.

318   Drawn expressly for *The Pageant of America* by Gregor Noetzel,
American Geographical Society, New York

TICONDEROGA EVACUATED

THE Americans at Ticonderoga might have made a stand that would have delayed the British. General St. Clair was in command of some three thousand troops who had suffered terrible winter hardships without adequate supplies of clothing or medicines. But blunders had been made in their engineering. Although they had fortified a hill across the lake named Mt. Independence, and with great ingenuity had built a bridge to connect the fort with this eastern position, the American

319   View of Ticonderoga from the middle of the channel in Lake Champlain, from the drawing, 1777, by James Hunter, in the British Museum, London

generals had decided that another hill close to the fort was inaccessible to artillery, and did not fortify it. Burgoyne's commander of engineers reconnoitered this eminence, known as Sugar Hill. Then followed work for a day and a night, at the end of which batteries of twenty-four pounders and eight-inch howitzers were in readiness to deliver a plunging fire into every angle of the fort. On July 6, St. Clair evacuated Ticonderoga, sending such stores as he could get in his boats up the South River to Skenesborough; for the British controlled the passage to Lake George. The army fell back by way of Castleton to the same point. A rear guard action at Hubbardton resulted in an American defeat, Colonel Seth Warner's detachment being separated from the main body and driven eastward into Vermont. The British suffered heavy losses. Burgoyne assembled his army at Skenesborough and prepared to follow his adversaries, who were retreating through a rough, wooded country upon Fort Edward. Between Skenesborough and Fort Edward were no less than forty bridges which the Americans destroyed, and many trees were felled across the road along which the British must advance. Burgoyne, in spite of the difficulties, accomplished the twenty miles to Fort Edward in exactly twenty days. There he found that Schuyler had wisely withdrawn across the Hudson River and had retired southward to Stillwater. From the beginning of the campaign to the occupation of Fort Edward, Burgoyne's accomplishment was a triumph of energy and skill.

ST. LEGER'S EXPEDITION TO FORT STANWIX JUNE–AUGUST, 1777

MILES
0   50   100

St. Leger had about 1700 men; Fort Stanwix – Colonel Gansevoort with 600 men, to be aided by Gen'l. Herkimer with 800 men. Herkimer is defeated at Oriskany, Aug. 6. False rumor disperses St. Leger's army, Aug. 22.

320   Drawn expressly for *The Pageant of America* by Gregor Noetzel, American Geographical Society, New York

ST. LEGER ADVANCES TO FORT STANWIX

WHILE Burgoyne was advancing from Skenesborough to Fort Edward, St. Leger landed at Oswego and prepared for operations against the frontier position, Fort Stanwix. With him were a small nucleus of regulars, some Loyalist volunteers, and a considerable body of Indians. In all, his force numbered something more than fifteen hundred men. With these troops he pushed through the wilderness, arriving before Stanwix on August 3, five days after Burgoyne had occupied Fort Edward.

321   Colonel Barry St. Leger, 1737–89, from a mezzotint by G. Dupont after the painting by Thomas Gainsborough

322   From an engraving by Bartolozzi in the
Orderly Book of Sir John Johnson, Albany, 1882

SIR JOHN JOHNSON, 1742–1830

WITH St. Leger was an interesting frontier figure, Sir John Johnson, son of Sir William Johnson, who had played such a conspicuous part in the French and Indian Wars. No other white man has ever had an influence with the Iroquois Indians equal to Sir William's. He knew the Indian ways and held occasional pow-wows which resulted in carousals at his house. He married, after the Indian fashion, Mary Brant, a sister of the great war chief of the Mohawks (No. 449). He was respected by his forest friends. Sir John Johnson inherited the title, but not the ability of his father. He organized Loyalist companies in the northern counties and commanded them in the St. Leger expedition. Sharing the command with him was Colonel John Butler, a man destined, like Johnson, to become hated for his part in the frontier fighting.

THE BATTLE OF ORISKANY, AUGUST 3–22

FORT STANWIX, renamed Fort Schuyler, was well defended by seven hundred and fifty Americans. St. Leger found it impregnable to attack without artillery, and prepared for siege operations. The militia of the frontier settlements farther down the Mohawk River were called out and led by General Herkimer to the relief of Stanwix. Six miles from the fort, at a place known as Oriskany, Herkimer fell into an ambush cunningly laid by Brant. The Battle of Oriskany was one of the bloodiest small engagements of the war.

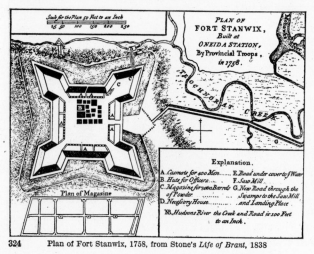

323   The Battle of Oriskany, from a painting, location and artist unknown.
© Rau Studios, Philadelphia

When it was ended, both whites and Indians were content to withdraw from the field. Herkimer's expedition to raise the siege had failed, although his troops had made a gallant fight. Schuyler, who, after an illness, had resumed command of the main American army at Stillwater, called for volunteers among his officers to lead an expedition to the relief of Stanwix. Benedict Arnold presented himself and hurried up the Mohawk valley with a body of volunteers from Schuyler's army. His force was continually augmented as he passed through the frontier settlements along the Mohawk. When near Fort Stanwix Arnold contrived to send messengers into St. Leger's camp with the news that a large force was approaching. The Indians, smarting under their losses at Oriskany, decamped in a semipanic followed by the Loyalists. St. Leger was forced to withdraw his regulars in great haste, leaving behind his camp equipment. His expedition had turned into a fiasco. Within a few days of the raising of the siege of Fort Stanwix, General Howe, who, according to Germain's plan, should have been advancing up the Hudson, landed his army on the shores of Chesapeake Bay.

324   Plan of Fort Stanwix, 1758, from Stone's *Life of Brant*, 1838

THE MURDER OF JANE McCREA

WHILE the St. Leger expedition was still in progress a tragedy near Burgoyne's army had greatly stimulated the opposition to him. Jane McCrea, affianced to David Jones, a Loyalist lieutenant with Burgoyne, was taken prisoner near Fort Edward with her friend Mrs. McNeil, by some of Burgoyne's Indian scouts, who murdered her, though bringing Mrs. McNeil unhurt to Burgoyne's camp. Burgoyne was greatly shocked; and his reproofs offended many Indians, who promptly deserted. But the fact remained that a white girl had been killed by Indians with Burgoyne; and this was circulated with immense success by the Patriots all through New England and New York, where it sowed many a deadly dragon's tooth in Burgoyne's path. Every day saw reinforcements flock singly and in companies into the American camp until the army greatly outnumbered the British.

GENERAL JOHN STARK, 1728–1822

BURGOYNE, having reached Fort Edward on July 30, 1777, was in a difficult position. His orders required him to push on to Albany.

325   From the painting by John Vanderlyn in the Wadsworth Atheneum, Hartford, Conn.

The advance to Fort Edward had been relatively easy, because he could use water transportation for his supplies as far as the southern end of Lake George. But he had been unable to get adequate land transport in Canada; and to march further into enemy country, with numbers against him rapidly increasing, would put a heavy burden upon his inferior baggage train. Moreover, he did not have enough men to enable him to leave behind detachments to protect a lengthening line of communications. He decided to risk a foray against a magazine of stores that the Americans had gathered for the use of Schuyler at Bennington, some thirty miles southeast of Fort Edward. Bennington was on the northern frontier of New England, and the settlers roundabout were frontiersmen, many of whom were experienced in Indian wars. Aroused by Burgoyne's advance, New Hampshire called out its militia, under General Stark, who had seen service in the last French and Indian War, and had distinguished himself at Bunker Hill and Trenton. When Congress failed to promote him according to his due, he had resigned his commission and retired to his frontier farm. Stark now refused to obey orders to join the army at Stillwater and hurried toward Bennington. To this place Burgoyne, with apparently quite inadequate information concerning Stark's force, sent Colonel Baum to capture and bring back supplies. Baum's command, consisting of about six hundred men, was too small for the task in hand. His chief strength was a body of dismounted Brunswick dragoons, who expected to return from the raid with mounts. This German cavalry on foot made a picturesque, if somewhat absurd, picture. "They were equipped with long, heavy riding boots, with big spurs, thick leathern breeches, heavy gauntlets, a hat with a thick feather; at their side a strong sabretasch, and a short heavy carbine, while a big pig-tail was an important part of this extraordinary costume." — CAPTAIN MAX VON ECKLING, *Account of the German Troops in the War of Independence*, Ch. 7.

326   From the painting by U. D. Tenney after the pencil portrait, location unknown, by John Trumbull, in Doric Hall, State House, Concord, N. H.

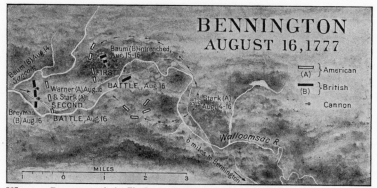

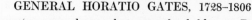

327   Drawn expressly for *The Pageant of America* by Gregor Noetzel, American
Geographical Society, New York

THE BATTLE OF BENNINGTON, AUGUST 16, 1777

Six miles from Bennington, on August 15, Baum, who had learned of Stark's force, encamped, entrenched, and sent back for reinforcements. On the 16th, Stark attacked, after skillfully surrounding the enemy. Superior numbers, vastly superior marksmanship, and an irrepressible will to fight on the part of the frontiersmen, annihilated Baum's detachment in about two hours. Stark, who had seen heavy fighting, later remarked that this "was the hottest I ever saw." From the beginning Stark had committed all his troops to the battle and had kept no reserve. But some time before the engagement he had sent a call for assistance to Seth Warner, then at Manchester, resting and recruiting the troops who had fought at Hubbardton. When Baum was defeated, Stark for a time lost control of his men, who scattered to plunder the German baggage train. He was thus unprepared for action when Lieutenant-Colonel Breymann appeared with a detachment nearly the size of Baum's original force. Battle was promptly joined, but the Americans, unable to form promptly, at first gave way. In the middle of the fight Warner arrived. Then Breymann, with heavy losses, was driven from the field. Far into the night the American riflemen pursued his harassed and confused column shooting point blank from the roadsides into the ranks of the terrified Germans.

328   The Return from Bennington, drawing by James E. Kelly, in the
possession of the artist

GENERAL HORATIO GATES, 1728–1806

Bennington was a heavy, but not a fatal, blow to Burgoyne. Three days after Breymann escaped in the darkness General Gates arrived in the American camp with orders to supersede Schuyler. Gates was an Englishman, the godson of Horace Walpole. He had early chosen a military career and had enjoyed rapid promotion in the British army. He was with Braddock's expedition and was severely wounded in the battle which ended the campaign. Later he saw other active service in the French and Indian Wars. After the conflict he became a Virginia planter. Early in the Revolution Congress commissioned him adjutant-general. Now, partly because of the opposition of New Englanders to the aristocratic Schuyler, and partly because of his own successful intrigue, Gates took command of the northern army. Time was to prove that he was an officer lacking in both courage and ability. But in the contest with Burgoyne he enjoyed much wholly undeserved good luck. Seen from the ranks, he was, in the words of an observant private, "an old granny-looking fellow." But seen from the distant, and most unmilitary, Congress, he was a national hero.

329 From the portrait by Gilbert Stuart (1755–1828),
courtesy of Edward E. Spafford, New York

THE ADVANCE OF BURGOYNE

AFTER Bennington Burgoyne waited almost a month at Duer's while he laboriously assembled the necessary supplies for an advance on Albany. The Americans, meanwhile, under the direction of Colonel Thaddeus Kosciuszko, a Polish nobleman and volunteer, had fortified a table-land known as Bemis Heights, which rose within five hundred yards of the Hudson. Burgoyne, dependent upon the river for his transport, must take this position before he could advance southward. On September 13 Burgoyne crossed to the west bank of the Hudson a little above Saratoga. He had at last begun what he expected was to be the last phase of the march to Albany. For six rainy days his troops crept slowly southward, with little information regarding the American position and strength. Gates' plan seems to have been to hold his army in his fortified camp and to await Burgoyne's attack. This would have been sound enough had the American commander not neglected to fortify a hill just west of his position. Should the enemy gain it and bring up artillery, he could enfilade the American positions and drive Gates out of his fortress. The failure to fortify this hill has never been satisfactorily explained.

330 Thaddeus Kosciuszko, 1746–1817, engraving by Holl from a print engraved in 1829 by A. Oleszezynski, in possession of the publishers

THE BATTLE OF FREEMAN'S FARM, SEPTEMBER 19, 1777

ON September 19 Burgoyne attacked, still with only a hazy knowledge of the strength of his opponent or of the disposition of British troops on the lower Hudson. Dividing his army into three columns he advanced cautiously toward the American position. Riedesel commanded the left column and followed the river bank until he came near to Bemis Heights. Burgoyne led the center and Fraser the right column. A deep and marshy ravine in front of Bemis Heights made an attack on this position impossible. The British general chose to pass the head of the gully and assault the unoccupied hill, though it is not sure that he knew it was undefended. His plan displayed the fatal weakness in Gates' dispositions. That general, however, kept his troops behind their fortifications and allowed the British to develop their positions under cover of the forest. Arnold, commanding the American left, sensed the danger, and, apparently with some difficulty, persuaded Gates to allow him to attack the British on the low ground before they began to mount the hill. He then sent Morgan with his riflemen against Fraser and soon followed with his whole force. A fierce battle between Arnold and the columns of Burgoyne and Fraser developed in a clearing known as Freeman's Farm where Morgan's Rangers fought magnificently. Arnold thought he saw an opportunity to crush Burgoyne, and asked for reinforcements; but Gates, fearing to expose his camp, refused to send them. With heavy losses on both sides the fight continued until, late in the afternoon, Riedesel came up on Arnold's right flank and drove the Americans back. The next day Burgoyne established a fortified camp a mile north of the American position. The British had won a technical victory.

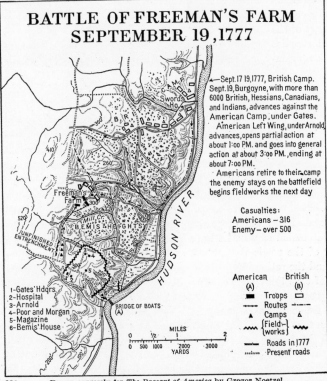

BATTLE OF FREEMAN'S FARM
SEPTEMBER 19, 1777

Sept. 17 19, 1777, British Camp. Sept. 19, Burgoyne, with more than 6000 British, Hessians, Canadians, and Indians, advances against the American Camp, under Gates.

American Left Wing, under Arnold, advances, opens partial action at about 1:00 PM. and goes into general action at about 3:00 PM., ending at about 7:00 PM.

Americans retire to their camp the enemy stays on the battlefield begins fieldworks the next day

Casualties:
Americans – 316
Enemy – over 500

1-Gates' Hdqrs.
2-Hospital
3-Arnold
4-Poor and Morgan
5-Magazine
6-Bemis' House

BRIDGE OF BOATS

MILES
0   ½   1   2
0 500 1000 2000 3000
YARDS

	American (A)	British (B)
Troops	■	□
Routes	———	—·—·—
Camps	▲	▲
Field-works	wwww	wwww
Roads in 1777	———	
Present roads	······	

331   Drawn expressly for *The Pageant of America* by Gregor Noetzel, American Geographical Society, New York

332 Brig. Gen. Daniel Morgan, 1736–1802, from the miniature by John Trumbull in the Yale School of the Fine Arts, New Haven

MORGAN'S RIFLEMEN

BURGOYNE's Indian allies being an object of terror to the militia serving in the Northern Army, Washington had sent Daniel Morgan, now a colonel, with five hundred riflemen. "They are all chosen men," he said, "selected from the army at large, and well acquainted with the use of rifles and with that mode of fighting. I expect the most eminent services from them." After the Saratoga surrender, Burgoyne met Morgan, so the story goes, and seized his hand, exclaiming, "My dear sir, you command the finest regiment in the world."

CLINTON ON THE HUDSON, OCTOBER 3–6

Two days after the fight at Freeman's Farm a messenger from Clinton brought news of the latter's intention to make a British diversion up the Hudson with about two thousand troops. The arrival of reinforcements had at last enabled Clinton to move out of his intrenched positions. On October 6 he captured Forts Clinton and Montgomery near Peekskill. Thereupon a British squadron sailed up the river as far as Kingston, destroying some stores and capturing a few batteries. This was the extent of the operation from New York that Germain had told Burgoyne would place a large army at Albany with which the army from Canada should unite. Meanwhile, Burgoyne, now very short of supplies, had sent back Clinton's messenger with the word that he could hold out only until October 12, and urging his fellow-officer to come to his assistance before that date. Clinton's reply was intercepted and its bearer hanged. It read: "*Nous voici* [Here we are] and nothing now between us and Gates. I sincerely hope that this little success of ours

may facilitate your operations. In answer to your letter of 28th of September by C. C. I shall only say, I cannot presume to order, or even advise, for reasons obvious. I heartily wish you success." There was no hope from the south. In the meantime the Americans under Colonel Brown in Burgoyne's rear had swooped down on Lake George and captured a large part of the flotilla upon which the transport of the British supplies depended. From there they had advanced to Ticonderoga and were holding the place practically in a state of siege.

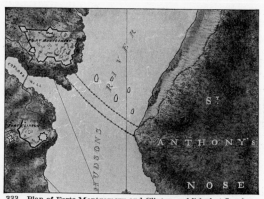

333 Plan of Forts Montgomery and Clinton, published at London, 1779, in the Emmet Collection, New York Public Library

334 Baron Friedrich Adolph Riedesel, 1738–1800, from a portrait, artist unknown, in possession of Baron Albrecht Riedesel, Eisenach, Germany

BURGOYNE'S PERIOD OF UNCERTAINTY

FOR eighteen days Burgoyne lay in his intrenched camp facing his enemy. He attempted to reconnoiter Gate's right flank but obtained no accurate information regarding his works. On August 4, when he called a council of war, he knew practically nothing of his enemy's left or of the roads that might lead around it. Food was running short and the ration had been reduced. On the 5th Riedesel advised his chief that the time had come to strike immediately or retreat at once across the Hudson and await Clinton's moves. Had Burgoyne retired he could undoubtedly have saved his army. Gates was not the man to stop him. But Burgoyne would not go back. Instead, on the 7th, he determined, according to Madame Riedesel, to "make a reconnoissance as near as possible to the enemy's left wing, in order to ascertain whether or not it could be attacked." If he found the enemy works too strong, he would retreat on the eleventh.

THE BATTLE OF OCTOBER 7

On October 7 Burgoyne, making this reconnoissance in force, was heavily attacked, and a desperate battle in the woods developed. Intending only a reconnoitering expedition he had brought on a general engagement. The fight went against him, and he ordered a retirement to his fortified camp. Here, just at nightfall, the Americans stormed and captured a redoubt that gave them control of the works. That night Burgoyne's army turned its face toward Canada. On the British side Colonel Breymann was killed and General Fraser was mortally wounded. Arnold, in leading the charge against the redoubt, was also wounded. One of the dramatic incidents of this confused battle was the sudden appearance of the extremely capable Arnold, in spite of the fact that he had just been deprived of his command by the intrigues of Horatio Gates. Fraser died the following morning. He had asked to be buried on a certain hill in the camp; and Burgoyne determined, though it cost him many precious hours, to carry out his friend's request. At six o'clock the entire

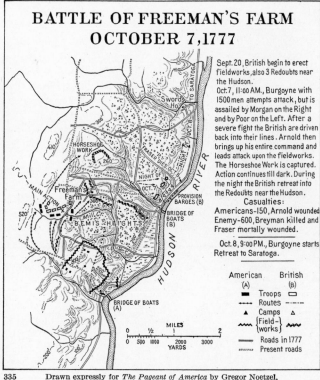

BATTLE OF FREEMAN'S FARM OCTOBER 7, 1777

Sept. 20, British begin to erect fieldworks, also 3 Redoubts near the Hudson.

Oct. 7, 11:00 A.M., Burgoyne with 1500 men attempts attack, but is assailed by Morgan on the Right and by Poor on the Left. After a severe fight the British are driven back into their lines. Arnold then brings up his entire command and leads attack upon the fieldworks. The Horseshoe Work is captured. Action continues till dark. During the night the British retreat into the Redoubts near the Hudson.

Casualties:
Americans-150, Arnold wounded
Enemy-600, Breyman killed and Fraser mortally wounded.

Oct. 8, 9:00 P.M., Burgoyne starts Retreat to Saratoga.

American (A)	British (B)	
■	Troops	□
----	Routes	-----
▲	Camps	△
～～	Field-works	～～
——	Roads in 1777	
•••••	Present roads	

335   Drawn expressly for *The Pageant of America* by Gregor Noetzel, American Geographical Society, New York

body of generals with their staffs were present at the last rites, while the American artillery kept up a brisk cannonade. Gates said afterward that there would have been no firing in that direction had he known that a burial was in progress. When Fraser had been laid to rest, the army moved out. The retreat had begun.

BURGOYNE SURROUNDED

The crisis caused by the defeat of the 7th seemed to overwhelm Burgoyne. His one chance lay in a swift retreat to Fort Edward. With prompt action he might have eluded the victorious Gates, although the latter's army greatly outnumbered his. But Burgoyne vacillated. He sought to retreat, but wasted time. Three days after the battle he sent a strong detachment up the west bank of the Hudson to force a passage to Fort Edward and, when it was within an hour's march of the fort, called it back. During the next three days he

SARATOGA
OCTOBER 10–17, 1777

(A)	American
(B)	British
	Cannon

336   Drawn expressly for *The Pageant of America* by Gregor Noetzel, American Geographical Society, New York

could decide upon no plan of action. On the 13th it was too late; he had been completely surrounded. The Hessian general's (Riedesel's) wife, bitter toward Burgoyne because of the defeat and of his blunders in directing the retreat, has left an unpleasant (and probably exaggerated) picture of him during the days just before he surrendered — days when he was faced with a responsibility too great for him to carry. "He spent half the nights in singing and drinking, and amusing himself with the wife of a commissary, . . . who, as well as he, loved champagne." Of all the major battles fought by Americans the conflicts which led to the fall of Burgoyne remain as to details the most hazy.

THE SURRENDER OF BURGOYNE

337   From the painting *The Surrender of General Burgoyne* by John Trumbull in the Yale School of the Fine Arts, New Haven, Conn.

On October 17, 1777, Burgoyne surrendered with all the honors of war. Present at the field where the British troops deposited their arms there was only a single staff officer of Gates to take possession in the name of the United States. Gates gave a dinner to the chief officers of the royal army; and immediately afterward the five thousand seven hundred prisoners of war began their march to Albany between parallel ranks of the American army. The results of the surrender were immediate, widespread, profound. "Rebellion," wrote a famous contemporary, "which a twelvemonth ago was a contemptible pygmy, is now in appearance become a giant." Saratoga brought on the French alliance, which, changing the balance of sea power, was the sure beginning of the end. (Trumbull's picture is quite inaccurate, so far as actual details are concerned. It simply poses, for pictorial effect, the men in whom most interest centered. See NOTES ON THE PICTURES.)

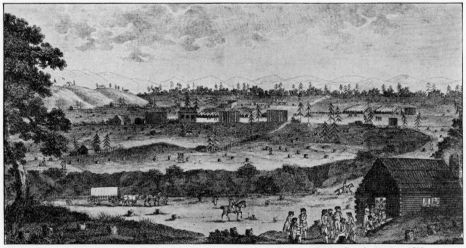

338   Encampment of Burgoyne's Troops at Charlottesville, Va., from Thomas Anburey, *Travels*, London, 1789, print in the Emmet Collection, New York Public Library

BURGOYNE RETURNS TO ENGLAND

It is regrettable to be obliged to add that, after the triumph of Saratoga, Congress broke faith with the British over the Convention, which provided that they were to stack arms, go under guard to Boston, take ship there for England, and not serve in America again during this war. The surrendered army was kept a year in the North, and then sent to Charlottesville, Virginia, and elsewhere. Some died, some escaped, some remained prisoners till the peace of 1783, and some eventually settled in the States. Burgoyne returned to England to face Germain, the man chiefly responsible for his humiliation. He was disgraced. He demanded a trial, where he might have an opportunity to defend himself; but this was refused by the war lord, who saw an opportunity to make the unsupported commander in the field the scapegoat for the whole colossal failure. Yet Burgoyne lived to see Germain humbled and driven from power; while he himself regained his old position in the army.

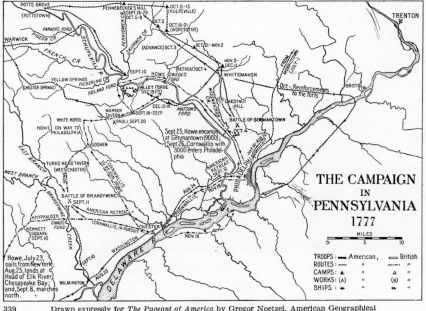

339   Drawn expressly for *The Pageant of America* by Gregor Noetzel, American Geographical
Society, New York

THE OPENING OF THE PHILADELPHIA CAMPAIGN

WHILE Burgoyne was operating in the North, Howe was conducting a campaign in the middle colonies. His objective was Philadelphia, where the Revolutionary central government was located. This campaign affords an opportunity to study the opposing leaders and the qualities of their respective armies. The winter at Morristown had been a hard one for the Continental troops. Washington's army largely melted away and had to be replaced by new levies. In the middle of March he had about three thousand men, of whom two-thirds were militia. In April the American commander wrote: "If Howe does not take advantage of our weak state, he is very unfit for his trust." But Howe left Washington unmolested. In the latter part of May, Howe received reinforcements from England. Washington had meanwhile increased his force to eight thousand. Early in June the campaign began. Washington was busy training his raw troops while the maneuvering was in progress. On May 29, the American commander had moved out of Morristown and taken up a strongly intrenched position at Middlebrook. He had received information of the plan for the converging attack upon Albany, and was preparing to make it as difficult as possible for Howe to coöperate with Burgoyne. Howe and Cornwallis attempted without success to draw their opponent out of Middlebrook and fight a general engagement. They then moved eastward, preparatory to crossing Staten Island to embark the British troops. The actual embarkation of Howe's army on July 23 threw Washington into great perplexity as to the plans of the British commander. He might be going to Boston, Charleston, or Philadelphia, or up the Hudson River toward Albany. To make sure that Howe did not elude him Washington moved his army to the Hudson Highlands and awaited the advance up the river which never came. Washington, in a state of anxiety, was compelled to march and countermarch as his intelligence varied. On July 31 he heard that Howe with his transports was off Delaware Bay.

Howe had intended to advance against Philadelphia by way of Delaware Bay. But when on July 30 it was discovered that the river was fortified and obstructed below the city, the naval commander felt that debarking in the Delaware would be too difficult. So, having proceeded to the Chesapeake on August 16, Howe nine days later began to put his troops ashore at the head of the Elk River. Washington had ample time to bring his army into position at Wilmington for the defense of Philadelphia and from a point twenty miles south of Wilmington saw the British camp. On September 3 Howe moved northward, maneuvering to turn his opponent's right flank. Washington withdrew up Brandywine Creek and on September 10 took up a carefully chosen position at Chad's Ford, where the main road to Philadelphia crossed the creek. Meanwhile Howe concentrated his army at Kennett Square to prepare for the inevitable battle. Washington had selected his position with great skill. His left flank was protected by an impassable gorge. His center could be attacked only by crossing the ford. His right also lay along the creek and could only be attacked by the enemy finding and crossing some ford up-stream, which Washington himself could maneuver to prevent.

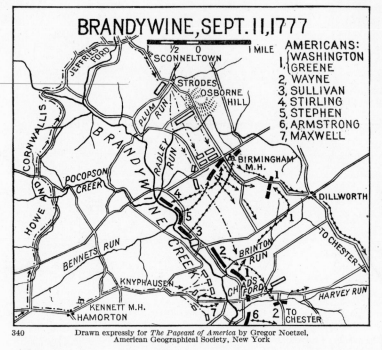

BRANDYWINE, SEPT. 11, 1777

AMERICANS:
1. {WASHINGTON GREENE
2. WAYNE
3. SULLIVAN
4. STIRLING
5. STEPHEN
6. ARMSTRONG
7. MAXWELL

340   Drawn expressly for *The Pageant of America* by Gregor Noetzel,
              American Geographical Society, New York

THE BATTLE OF BRANDYWINE

WASHINGTON apparently hoped that Howe would either make a frontal attack across Chad's Ford or embark upon leisurely maneuvers up the creek. But Howe did neither. His solution of the problem was correct and his execution brilliant. Dividing his army, on the morning of September 11 he sent General Knyphausen to Chad's Ford. Once at the ford Knyphausen unlimbered his guns and opened a heavy bombardment, as if about to force a passage across the creek. But Knyphausen's was merely a holding attack, which would keep Washington's main army in position while the battle was decided elsewhere. Meanwhile, Cornwallis, with ten thousand men, was executing a rapid turning movement which would take him across the stream some twelve miles from Kennett Square and envelop Washington's right flank.

Washington was almost fatally handicapped by lack of an adequate intelligence service. During the forenoon he received confusing reports from American patrols; not until two o'clock did he learn the real character of the turning movement. Lack of good staff-work remained a weakness of the American army. Sullivan finally reported in a brief message that a large force of British had appeared in the rear of his right flank. Washington ordered Sullivan to leave the creek immediately and to take up a position in front of the advancing column. At Birmingham Meeting-house, after executing a maneuver which had been begun too late, Sullivan faced Cornwallis, who was deployed in superior force and ready for action after a surprising march of sixteen miles. Stirling and Stephen took post beside Sullivan. But the British charged in perfect order and drove the Americans in confusion from the field. Washington's foresight had anticipated such an outcome; for he had sent Greene, with a force known as the "Tall Virginians," toward

Dillworth to protect Sullivan in case he had to retreat. Then the American commander in chief galloped to the fight. Knyphausen now admirably played his part. He had observed large bodies of Americans moving northward from Brandywine Creek. Then he heard the firing that announced the opening of the battle at Birmingham Meeting-house. He promptly threw his troops across Chad's Ford and attacked in earnest. The Americans at the ford withdrew. As they fell back some British troops belonging to Cornwallis' column, who had become confused in the wood fighting at Birmingham Meeting-house, and who were making their way toward the sound of battle at the ford, suddenly fell upon the unprotected flank of the Americans and routed it. Had not night intervened, the affair might have proved a disaster. As it was, the Americans reassembled the following day at Chester, the army badly shaken, but still intact and still able to defy Howe.

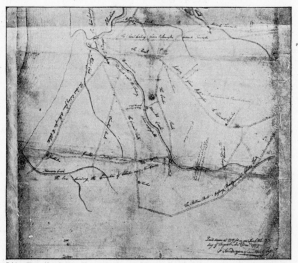

341 Detail of the Topography at Chad's Ford, from an original map annotated by George Washington, in the Historical Society of Pennsylvania, Philadelphia

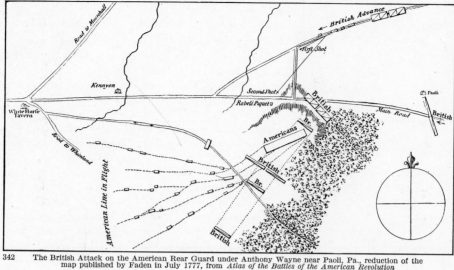

342   The British Attack on the American Rear Guard under Anthony Wayne near Paoli, Pa., reduction of the map published by Faden in July 1777, from *Atlas of the Battles of the American Revolution*

WAYNE'S DEFEAT NEAR WHITE HORSE TAVERN, SEPTEMBER 21

AFTER Brandywine only the Schuylkill River lay between Howe and Philadelphia. On September 16, Washington crossed the river and so distributed his troops as to delay Howe's passage as long as possible. Meanwhile he dreamed of a decisive minor engagement that might seriously injure his antagonist. He sent General Anthony Wayne across the Schuylkill to an excellent position near Paoli, with orders to fall upon Howe's rear guard and capture his baggage train. Howe was then lying in the neighborhood of Valley Forge. Wayne accepted the commission with enthusiasm. Major André has told in his *Journal* the story of what followed. "Intelligence having been received of the situation of General Wayne and his design of attacking our Rear, a plan was concerted for surprising him and the execution entrusted to Major-General Grey. . . . General Grey's Detachment marched at 10 o'clock at night, that under Colonel Musgrave at 11. No soldier of either was suffered to load and those who could not draw their pieces took out the flints. We knew nearly the spot where the Rebel Corps lay, but nothing of the disposition of their Camp. . . . General Grey's Detachment marched by the road leading to White Horse, and took every inhabitant with them as they passed along. About three miles from camp they turned to the left and proceeded to the Admiral Warren, where, having forced intelligence from a blacksmith, they came in upon the out-sentries, piquet and Camp of the Rebels.

343   General Anthony Wayne, 1745-96, from the portrait by C. W. Peale owned by William Wayne

The sentries fired and ran off to the number of four at different intervals. The piquet was surprised and most of them killed in endeavoring to retreat. On approaching the right of the Camp we perceived the line of fires, and the Light Infantry, being ordered to form to the front, rushed along the line putting to the bayonet all they came up with, and, overtaking the main herd of the fugitives, stabbed great numbers and pressed on their rear till it was thought prudent to desist. . . . It was about 1 o'clock in the morning when the attack was made and the Rebels were then assembling to move towards us, with the design of attacking our baggage." Wayne lost a quarter of his fifteen hundred men, but saved his guns and most of his baggage. The subsequent movements were seriously affected by this affair at Paoli. Howe's army, being now quite free from immediate pressure, marched safely on; and, in Washington's own words, "they got so far the start before I received certain intelligence that any considerable number had crossed, that I found it in vain to think of overtaking their rear with troops harassed as ours had been with constant marching since the battle of Brandywine."

344   From the painting *The British Entry into Phila-delphia,* 1777, by H. A. Ogden, courtesy of the artist

CORNWALLIS ENTERS PHILADELPHIA, SEPT. 26

THE surprise of Wayne near White Horse Tavern was one of the most skillful minor operations of the war. It fully justified Grey's reputation for being the best officer in Howe's army next to Cornwallis. Both opposing commanders were fighting men of high quality and both earnest students of the military art. The victory went to the man of the greater experience. Wayne was caught at a disadvantage because he had ordered his men to protect their cartridge boxes from a falling rain by taking off their coats and folding them about the ammunition. His defeat opened the way to Philadelphia. Six days later Cornwallis entered the city, to the great joy of the large number of Loyalists. "The bands struck up the tune of 'God Save the King' amidst the acclamations of several thousand inhabitants. . . . Some of the older spectators, and especially the women, could not avoid comparing that brilliant and martial procession with the destitute and dilapidated army which, trying hard to look its best, had traversed the same line of streets a few weeks before." — TREVELYAN, *The American Revolution,* Vol. IV.

HOWE'S DISPOSITIONS ABOUT PHILADELPHIA

THE capture of Philadelphia did not end Howe's military problems. His base was at Elk River and all his supplies had to be brought overland to Philadelphia. Washington's army was at Shippack Creek. In the past two weeks Howe had defeated it twice. He now took unnecessary risks by dispersing his army in the face of the enemy. The main body of his troops lay at Germantown, but, acting under orders, did not fortify their position. From this force were drawn off three detachments, one to escort supplies from Elk River, one

to hold Philadelphia, and one to feel out the American defenses on the Delaware River below the city. Washington was quick to grasp the opportunity that was offered him. On the night of October 3 Howe learned of exceptional activity in the American camp at Shippack Creek and warned his generals to be on the alert. At seven in the evening Washington's army set out for a night march against Germantown. The American commander was attempting to repeat his success at Trenton. Two columns were to converge upon the British position at Germantown. Sullivan led the American right, Greene the left, and Sterling, in reserve, followed Sullivan's center. The army was to be in position at daybreak. But the dawn of October 4 found Germantown covered with a heavy fog, through which the men could see scarcely forty yards. This circumstance gave a tremendous advantage to the well-disciplined British troops. Sullivan arrived in good time and pushed back the enemy outguards until he arrived at the house of Chief Justice Chew. Greene, having mishaps and a longer road, was late.

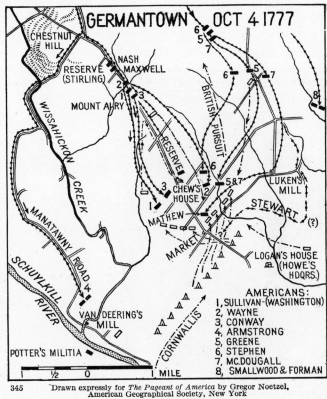

345   Drawn expressly for *The Pageant of America* by Gregor Noetzel, American Geographical Society, New York

THE FIGHT AT THE CHEW HOUSE

COLONEL MUSGRAVE with six companies was posted at the Chew estate a full mile in advance of the British main line. When Sullivan struck him, he got his men into the great stone house of the Chief Justice and turned it into a fortress. The roar of musketry and cannons sounded like a general engagement. Knox, commander of the American artillery, blew in the main entrance; but his fire had little effect on the solid masonry walls. Throughout the long

346   From the painting by E. L. Henry (about 1873), owned by Miss Elizabeth B. Chew, Germantown, Pa.

fight Musgrave, though vastly outnumbered, most gallantly held out. Meanwhile Sullivan had pushed on and attacked the main line. Greene presently came into action; but with another mishap. General Stephen, commanding Greene's right, fired into the troops on Sullivan's left, mistaking them for the enemy. After the battle Stephen was court-martialed, convicted of "unofficer-like conduct" and intoxication, and ignominiously dismissed.

GERMANTOWN AND ITS SIGNIFICANCE

FOR two hours after Greene had gone into action the battle continued. With an irresistible onrush he drove back the doggedly fighting British main line fifteen hundred paces, to the surprise of their own officers. But Sullivan's troops suddenly gave way. The cause for the break in their line still remains something of a mystery. Perhaps their ammunition gave out; perhaps the roar of the fighting at the Chew House in their rear started the rumor that they were being fired on from behind. The retreat of Sullivan left Greene's right uncovered and his flank in danger of being enveloped. With great courage and coolness he extricated his army and fell back, carrying off all his cannon. Washington, meanwhile, was organizing the general retreat. By nightfall the whole force was back at Shippack Creek behind its fortifications. Germantown was a bitter disappointment; but it was in no sense a disaster. The outcome of the battle was of less importance

347   Tablet in Centre Square, York, Pa., commemorating the meeting of the Continental Congress during the British occupation of Philadelphia

than the fact that it had been fought at all. For the general whose troops had been twice defeated in the last few weeks to turn suddenly upon his adversary, assault him in a well-planned attack, fight a stubborn battle, and suffer defeat largely because of ill luck in chancing upon a foggy morning was no bad demonstration that the American army was a military factor of prime importance. Germantown enhanced rather than lowered the morale of the American troops. Yet, for the moment, the army was shaken. Had Howe pressed vigorously after Washington, he might have forced a general engagement, the outcome of which might have been of great significance to the British cause. But, as usual, he let the opportunity pass. His fortune was never to have another. From Bunker Hill to Germantown Howe had demonstrated that he was thoroughly skilled in the soldier's art. He was an able and courageous leader in action. He was skillful in the formulation and execution of a battle-plan. The deficiency which keeps his name from the roll of great generals was much like that of General McClellan in the Civil War. It was his inability to pursue a defeated enemy until he had destroyed him. Had Washington been killed at Germantown, his fame as a great captain would have been secure. Congress, which was holding its meetings in York, voted its thanks to the commander in chief for his efforts at Germantown.

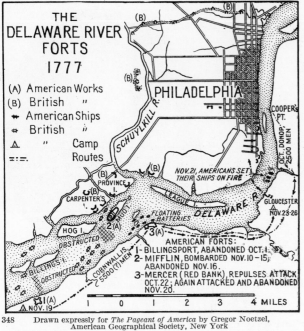

THE
DELAWARE RIVER
FORTS
1777

(A) American Works
(B) British   "
➤ American Ships
⟿ British   "
△   "   Camp
=·=· Routes

PHILADELPHIA

COOPER'S PT.

OCT. DONOP, 2500 MEN

NOV.21, AMERICANS SET THEIR SHIPS ON FIRE

GLOUCESTER NOV.23-26

(B) PROVINCE
(B) CARPENTER'S
MUD I.
FLOATING BATTERIES
HOG I. OBSTRUCTED
2(A)
3(A)
BILLINGS I. OBSTRUCTED
CORNWALLIS, 5500(?) MEN

AMERICAN FORTS:
1 - BILLINGSPORT, ABANDONED OCT.1.
2 - MIFFLIN, BOMBARDED NOV.10-15; ABANDONED NOV.16.
3 - MERCER (RED BANK), REPULSES ATTACK OCT.22; AGAIN ATTACKED AND ABANDONED NOV.20.

1(A)
NOV.19

1   0   1   2   3   4 MILES

348   Drawn expressly for *The Pageant of America* by Gregor Noetzel,
American Geographical Society, New York

THE ATTACK ON FORT MERCER, OCTOBER 22 — NOVEMBER 20

EIGHTEEN days after the battle of Germantown, Howe moved against the American forts commanding the Delaware. To Von Donop, with one regiment of ordinary Hessian infantry and three battalions of Hessian Grenadiers (some twelve hundred men, all told) was given the task of capturing Fort Mercer at Red Bank on the Delaware. Colonel Christopher Greene, a kinsman of General Greene, with about four hundred men held the fort. Greene had decided that his force was too small to defend the outer works of the fortification and had them dismantled. Aided by Chevalier de Plessis, a young Frenchman who had volunteered to serve in Fort Mercer, he fortified the small pentagonal central fort where he planned to make his stand. A dense abattis of fallen trees was placed around the earthworks, which rose ten feet high, and which were faced with planks to make difficult the scaling of their sides. A deep ditch separated the abattis from the walls. On October 22 Greene received Von Donop's summons to surrender. A few minutes later the Hessian battalions, perfectly drilled, were seen clambering over the dismantled outer works and advancing at a run toward the fort itself. As they plunged into the abattis they met the deadly fire of the desperate defenders. Officers and soldiers went down in heaps. A few of the boldest Germans struggled through the abattis and crossed the ditch. Then the American armed galleys from the river sent a cruel, enfilading artillery fire into the enemy's right flank. After forty minutes of fruitless effort, the German columns, sadly thinned, retired toward Philadelphia. Von Donop was found wounded among the dead. Though Washington saw to it that he had every possible attention, he died in a week. He was a brave man fighting a war in which he had no vital interest, a mercenary in the bargain between his Landgrave and the British Government.

DESTRUCTION OF THE *AUGUSTA*

THE attack on Fort Mercer was doubly menacing because Admiral Howe's fleet which had arrived in Delaware Bay, October 4, coöperated with Von Donop and tried to get close enough to shell the fortification. But the obstacles which the Americans had put in the river channel held off the attack. Two ships, in a desperate effort to come to grips with the fort, ran aground, caught fire and were destroyed by the explosion of their own magazines. As events turned out, the gallant defense of Mercer proved to be but a minor engagement, postponing for a few weeks Howe's inevitable conquest of the Delaware. It might well have been, however, the turning point in the Pennsylvania campaign. Such was the hope of Washington as he sent his congratulations to Colonel Greene. Five days before the attack upon Fort Mercer Burgoyne had surrendered at Saratoga (No. 337). The news spread swiftly east and south. For Washington this northern success meant a great opportunity. Howe had captured Philadelphia; but his base was still many miles away at Elk River, and the British army was still weakened by the necessity of defending its long line of communications. If Gates would promptly send Washington heavy reinforcements, then Washington could attack Howe before the Delaware forts fell.

349   From a painting attributed to James Peale (1749–1831), in the
Historical Society of Pennsylvania

HAMILTON'S MISSION TO GATES

WASHINGTON knew well the man he had to deal with in Gates. The officer chosen for the difficult mission to the commander in the north was Washington's aide and the most brilliant man on his staff, Colonel Alexander Hamilton. After waiting two weeks in the hope that Gates would send reinforcements of his own accord, Hamilton was dispatched with a specific request. But, as Gates was not desirous of adding to Washington's glory, Hamilton failed. The handful of troops that finally arrived in Washington's camp at Whitemarsh were too few in number and too late to have any important effect on the campaign.

350 From the miniature by C. W. Peale, identified by C. H. Hart as a portrait of Alexander Hamilton at twenty-one, long supposed to be a portrait of Washington, owned by Miss Mary Burt, Philadelphia

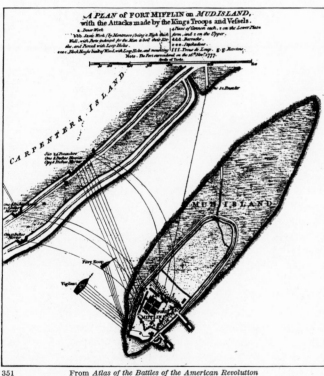

351   From *Atlas of the Battles of the American Revolution*

FORT MIFFLIN, NOV. 10–15

THE small garrisons in the Delaware River forts gave the British a stiff resistance. After the twelve hundred Hessians led by Donop attacking Fort Mercer were completely repulsed with heavy casualties by the Rhode Islanders under Colonel Christopher Greene, Fort Mifflin was reduced, November 10–15, by six ships of Howe's fleet joining with shore batteries in an intense bombardment, the Americans losing heavily. Washington's praise was well deserved. "The defense will always reflect the highest honour upon the officers and men of the garrison. The works were entirely beat down; every piece of cannon was dismounted, and one of the enemy's ships came so near that she threw grenades into the fort. . . ." Howe then sent Cornwallis with fifty-five hundred troops to assault Fort Mercer. The defenders, faced by this overwhelming force, evacuated the fort, November 20. The fall of the Delaware River forts opened the way to Philadelphia for the British fleet. That city now became a British base and the cantonment of the most powerful British army operating in America.

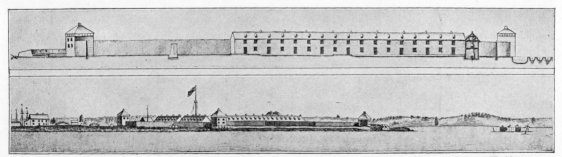

352 Fort Mifflin and works on Mud Island, section from the map by Capt. John Montresor, original in the Library of Congress, Washington

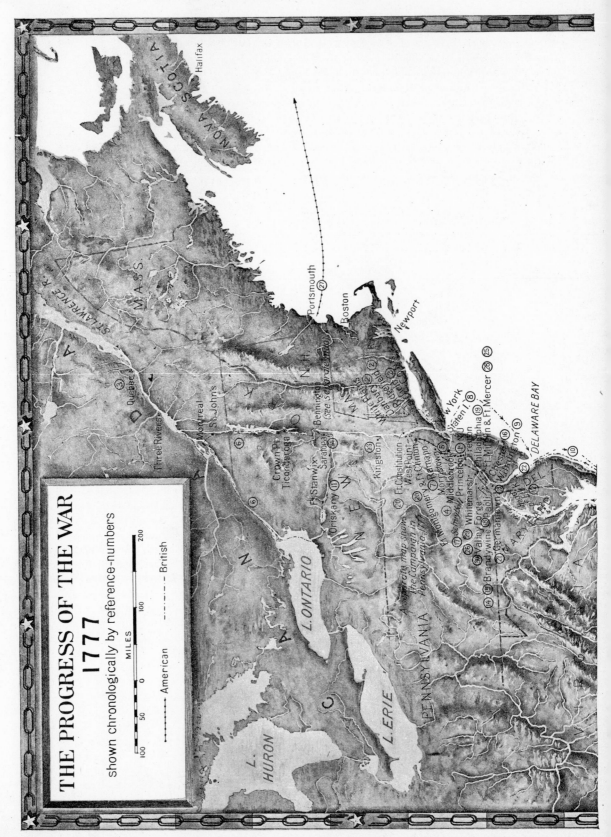

THE PROGRESS OF THE WAR
1777

shown chronologically by reference-numbers

MILES

—•—•— American
—·—·— British

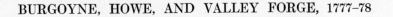

① Jan. 3, Washington defeats British at Princeton, –entrenched at Morristown, Jan. 6 (until May 28) ② Apr. 25, Tryon lands at Fairfield, Apr. 26 burns Danbury; Apr 27, attacked by Arnold at Ridgefield. ③ May 6, Burgoyne arrives at Quebec. ④ May 29, Washington to Middlebrook. ⑤ June –, Gen'l. Howe and Cornwallis manoeuvre in New Jersey against Washington without success and then retire ⑥ June 8 July, British begin operations from Canada under Burgoyne and St. Leger (see separate map). ⑦ July 7, Washington from Middlebrook to Ramapo and The Clove, July 21, to watch British movements ⑧ July 23, Howe sails from Staten 1 with 18,000 men for the Delaware. ⑨ July 24, Washington crosses New Jersey, goes into Pennsylvania, marches through Philadelphia (Aug. 24), halts at Wilmington, Aug. 25. ⑩ July 30, Howe finds Delaware River obstructed and well defended, proceeds to Chesapeake, Aug 16. ⑪ Aug 6, Battle of Oriskany. ⑫ Aug 25, British army begins to land at head of Elk ⑬ Sept 3, Howe moves northward past right flank of Washington. ⑭ Sept.10, Washington takes position in front of Howe at Chad's Ford on the Brandywine. ⑮ Sept. 11, Battle of Brandywine ⑯ Sept 12, Washington's army, reassembled at Chester, stands at Germantown. ⑰ Sept 16, Washington crosses the Schuylkill to meet Howe. ⑱ Sept. 21, Rearguard under Wayne surprised at Paoli ⑲ Sept.26, Cornwallis occupies Philadelphia with 3,000 British , Howe at Germantown. ⑳ Oct. 3, Clinton ascends the Hudson, Oct. 6 he captures Forts Clinton, Montgomery and Constitution. ㉑ Oct 4, Washington attacks British at Germantown. ㉒ Oct. 4, British Fleet, Adm'l. Howe, arrives in Delaware Bay. ㉓ Oct.13, Kingston , on the Hudson, burnt by British. ㉔ Oct 17, Burgoyne surrenders at Saratoga. ㉕ Oct.22, Fort Mercer attacked, held out until Nov 20, when evacuated. ㉖ Oct 29, Washington in strong position at Whitemarsh. ㉗ Nov 1, John Paul Jones sails from Portsmouth in "Ranger" for France. ㉘ Nov.10-15, Fort Mifflin attacked and demolished by Howe ㉙ Dec 4-8, Howe manoeuvres to attack Washington, then retires to Philadelphia ㉚ Dec.15, Washington to Valley Forge

— At end of 1777 —
Washington at Valley Forge
Gen'l Howe at Philadelphia
Clinton at New York
Prevost at St Augustine
Carleton at Montreal and Quebec
Prescott at Newport

CHESAPEAKE BAY
Norfolk

Charlestown
(Charleston)

Savannah

St Augustine

NORTH CAROLINA

SOUTH CAROLINA

GEORGIA

FLORIDA
(Spanish)

353

Drawn expressly for *The Pageant of America* by Gregor Noetzel, American Geographical Society, New York

THE PROGRESS OF THE WAR, 1777

THE first map on the progress of the war (No. 304) left Washington victorious at Trenton on the morning following Christmas Day, 1776. This one finds him victorious at Princeton eight days later. Arnold appears in April as the defender of Connecticut against Governor Tryon. May finds Burgoyne arriving at Quebec to carry out the invasion of the North by combining his own forces, coming south from Canada, with St. Leger's coming east from Lake Ontario, and Howe's or Clinton's coming north from New York. The combination ended in disaster, the New Englanders swarmed round Burgoyne's flank, cut his long and precarious line of communication with his base in Canada, and, combining with the Patriot army under the specious Gates, forced him to surrender in October at Saratoga. Meanwhile Sir William Howe had spent the summer and autumn maneuvering and fighting Washington between New York and Philadelphia, where he finally went into comfortable winter quarters, December 4, while Washington took post several days later at Valley Forge, where, amid almost incredible hardships, the real United States army was eventually born.

TEUCRO DUCE NIL DESPERANDOM.

First Battalion of PENNSYLVANIA LOYALISTS, commanded by His Excellency Sir WILLIAM HOWE, K. B.

ALL INTREPID ABLE-BODIED

HEROES,

WHO are willing to serve His MAJESTY KING GEORGE the Third, in Defence of their Country, Laws and Constitution, against the arbitrary Usurpations of a tyrannical Congress, have now not only an Opportunity of manifesting their Spirit, by assisting in reducing to Obedience their too-long deluded Countrymen, but also of acquiring the polite Accomplishments of a Soldier, by serving only two Years, or during the present Rebellion in America.

Such spirited Fellows, who are willing to engage, will be rewarded at the End of the War, besides their Laurels, with 50 Acres of Land, where every gallant Hero may retire, and enjoy his Bottle and Lass.

Each Volunteer will receive, as a Bounty, FIVE DOLLARS, besides Arms, Cloathing and Accoutrements, and every other Requisite proper to accommodate a Gentleman Soldier, by applying to Lieutenant Colonel ALLEN, or at Captain KEARNY'S Rendezvous, at PATRICK TONRY'S, three Doors above Market-street, in Second-street.

354   From a facsimile of the original issue, 1777, in the Emmet Collection, New York Public Library

THE BRITISH OCCUPATION OF PHILADELPHIA

AFTER the Battle of Brandywine the American Patriots awaited with grave apprehension Howe's occupation of the city of Philadelphia. Already two American seaports had been burned by British raiding parties and Tryon had destroyed the houses of Patriots in Danbury, Connecticut. But Howe was a gentleman of honor. When his army established its quarters in the Quaker City he made the burden as light as possible for his ene-

356   From the painting *Friends and Enemies*, 1778, by H. A. Ogden (1856-). © Goupil & Co., Paris

A LOYALIST RECRUITING POSTER

GENERAL HOWE, in possession of Philadelphia, followed the advice which his prisoner, General Charles Lee, had given him before he had left New York. He issued a call for volunteers from among the Pennsylvania Loyalists. But he was destined to disappointment. The Loyalists did not offer themselves in sufficient numbers to add materially to his military strength. The basis of the appeal of Howe's proclamation should be contrasted with that of the war posters of England, France, or the United States during the World War (Vol. VII). Few Revolutionary documents reflect so vividly the social and patriotic standards of the times.

Philadelphia, December 8, 1777.

REGULATIONS,

Under which the Inhabitants may purchase the enumerated Articles, mentioned in the Proclamation of His Excellency Sir WILLIAM HOWE, K. B. General and Commander in Chief, &c. &c. &c.

1st. NO RUM, or SPIRITS of inferior Quality, are to be sold (except by the Importer) at one Time, or to one Person, in any greater Quantity, than one Hogshead, or in any less than ten Gallons, and not without a Permit first obtained for the Quantity intended to be purchased, from the Inspector of the prohibited Articles.

2d. MOLASSES is not to be sold (except by the Importer) in any Quantity exceeding one Hogshead, at one Time, nor without a Permit as aforesaid.

3d. SALT may not be sold (except by the Importer) in any Quantity, exceeding one Bushel at one Time, for the Use of one Family, nor without Permit as aforesaid.

4th. MEDICINES not to be sold, without a special Permit by Order of the Superintendent General.

By Order of His Excellency Sir WILLIAM HOWE.

JOSEPH GALLOWAY. Superintendent General.

355   From a facsimile of the original issue in the Emmet Collection, New York Public Library

mies who remained within the town; while for the many Loyalists his coming was the occasion of great rejoicing.

THE PENNSYLVANIA FRIENDS

THE Quakers were the chief pacifists of the Revolution. Though they might sympathize with the Patriot cause, they would not fight. Because of their stand a number of the Friends of Philadelphia before the British occupation were forced to go to Winchester, in the Shenandoah valley, where, during most of the winter of 1777–78, they were detained virtually as prisoners. When President of the United States, Washington asked one of the sect why he had been opposed to the Revolution. "Friend Washington," was the reply, "upon the principle that I should be opposed to a change in the present government. All that was ever secured by the Revolution is not an adequate compensation for the poor mangled soldiers, and for the loss of life and limb." "I honour your sentiments," answered the first President, "for there is more in them than mankind has generally considered."

British Barracks, Philadelphia

357   From J. F. Watson, *Annals of Philadelphia*, Philadelphia, 1830

The Press Gang or English Liberty Display'd

358   The Press Gang, from an engraving in the
Oxford Magazine, London, Nov. 1770

BRITISH OFFICERS OF THE EIGHTEENTH CENTURY

THE winter at Philadelphia affords an opportunity to survey some of the characteristics of the king's soldiers fighting to uphold the prerogatives of the Crown in America.   Henry Belcher, a Fellow in King's College and Chaplain to the Forces, published in 1911 a critique of the British army of Revolutionary times.   "The modes of appointment and promotion were full of anomalies. First to be noticed were the infants in arms or toddlers about nurseries. . . . who, being lieutenants or captains, as the case may be, drew public money as pay for services rendered. . . .   The idea apparently was to make some provision for the fatherless children of distinguished or favourite officers. . . .   To pitchfork the knave or fool of the family into a commission in the army was the whole duty of a thoughtful parent. . . .   Parliamentary ideas as to the value of money in promotion of political ends are reflected in the sanction of the anomalous custom of military promotion by purchase in all cavalry and infantry regiments.   This practice or custom was extremely offensive to the royal family of Hanover. . . .   André, Gates, Charles Lee, Montgomery, Amherst, and other Englishmen, whose names are prominent in the American wars of this century, belonged to families of the well-to-do middle class. . . .   On the other hand, Howe, Burgoyne, Gage, Keppel, Clinton, Rawdon, Rodney, Barrington belonged to ancient or ennobled families.   These and others form the class of political admirals and generals and colonels of whom, during this century, we hear so much." — H. BELCHER, *The First American Civil War*, pp. 268, 269, The Macmillan Company.   This unfavorable account, though

true enough in its own way, is not by any means the whole truth. A good many members of the "ancient families" mentioned by Belcher rose, and still rise, to well deserved command; witness their record in the World War. The picture treating of the naval press gang is much more a reflection on the commercial classes who benefited by, but did not fight for, British sea power.

359   British officer and private, 1786, from a lithograph by G. B. Campion in T. W. J. Connolly, *The History of the Corps of Royal Sappers and Miners*, vol. I, London, 1855, in the New York Public Library

360   The Recruiting Sergeant, from the *Oxford Magazine*,
London, Nov. 1770

OFFICERS AND MEN

"To a public so conversant with the care for the British soldier now manifested by men and women of every class and rank . . . it is almost incredible with what neglect the British soldier of the eighteenth century was treated. He was housed in a few barracks scattered about the country; small places, ill-found and ill-adapted for the accomodation of troops. . . . The commissioned officers had no mess, at any rate not on the club model now prevailing. . . . They spent their time, if they were obscure men, either with their mistresses or in drinking, gambling, quarreling and duelling; if ambitious men, they quitted their commands to push their fortunes at court or take their pleasure. Burgoyne left America for the winter of 1775–76 to attend his duties in the House of Commons. Cornwallis was about to leave America for the winter of 1776–77 when he was recalled to the front at Christmas by the disaster to the German troops at Trenton. Howe liked to take his ease at his inn whether in Boston, New York or Philadelphia. Officers saw very little of their men. A formal parade for about an hour comprised all the official duties of the day. Consequently the non-commissioned officers reigned supreme. That they could and frequently did make a man's life more intolerable than a mongrel's is beyond question. . . . Added to these circumstances were the drinking habits of the century. Everywhere the English-speaking races succumbed to a great wave of the drinking custom. Every man in the British Army was familiar with wine-bibbing and pot-tossing. There were senior captains whose capacity for drink was not measurable in bottles. There were men in the ranks who tossed off raw new rum by the tumbler. . . . As every one drank to excess, the Ministers of the Crown, the Pitts, the Graftons, the Foxes, as well as high military officers, the Braddocks, the Howes and the Burgoynes, intoxication in both services, navy and army alike, was too common to attract special reproach." — BELCHER, pp. 272–74.

PHILADELPHIA DURING THE ENGLISH OCCUPATION

GAY indeed was the Quaker City during the winter which Howe and his officers spent within it. Merry making followed hard upon the heels of the summer campaign. A letter of Miss Rebecca Franks, the daughter of a Loyalist, addressed to the wife of a signer of the Declaration of Independence, suggests the brilliance of the social season at Philadelphia when the British army was there. "You can have no idea of the life of continued amusement I live in. I can scarce have a moment to myself. I went Tuesday evening to Sir William Howe's, where we had a concert and dance. I asked his leave to send you a handkerchief to show the fashions. He very politely gave me permission to send anything you wanted, though I told him you were a delegate's lady. Oh, how I wished Mr. Paca would let you come in for a week or two! Tell him I'll answer for your being let to return. You'd have an opportunity of raking as much as you chose, at Plays, Balls, Concerts or Assemblies. I have been but three evenings alone since we moved to town."

361   From the painting *Entertaining the Redcoats, Philadelphia, 1778*,
by H. A. Ogden (1856–), courtesy of the artist

THE RECALL OF HOWE

In the midst of the gaiety of the social whirl the news came to Philadelphia that the resignation of General Howe had been accepted by the British Government, that the general had been recalled, and that Sir Henry Clinton had been appointed commander of His Majesty's forces in North America. The blow marked the end of Howe's career. It dashed, moreover, the hopes of the army, for Clinton was not considered a brilliant commander. With many feelings of regret Howe's officers saw the spring approach, bringing an end to the festivities of the winter and the beginning of a summer campaign under a new leader.

362   From the painting *A Ball at Gen'l Howe's* by J. L. G. Ferris in Independence Hall, Philadelphia

Captain John André took the lead in organizing and preparing for a great fête that should bring to a fitting conclusion the most brilliant season that Philadelphia had ever known.

THE MESCHIANZA

The Meschianza was intended to be the army's unexpressed rebuke to the English Government for recalling Howe and its expression of loyalty and affection to that general. "The ceremonies began with a Grand Regatta. Gaily decked barges, interspersed at intervals with bands of music, moved slowly down a line of war-vessels and transports which, with yards manned and colours flying, extended along the whole river-front of the city. Then the company disembarked on a noble lawn, where a square plot of four acres had been marked out for the Tournament. An English, and an American, Queen of Beauty sat facing each other at either extremity of the ground, attended, both of them, by a bevy of six damsels in Turkish habits and turbans. Six Knights, resplendent in crimson and white silk, and caracoling on grey steeds, rode forth to assert that the ladies of the Blended Rose excelled all others in wit and beauty; and the challenge was accepted by as many Knights of the Burning Mountain, in black and orange raiment, and on coal-black horses. A more impressive sight was the compact hedge of well-drilled infantry, planted stiff and silent around the whole enclosure. The cavaliers ran their tilts, shivered their lances, and then fired pistols at each other until the Marshal proclaimed that the ladies were satisfied with the proofs of love and valour given by their respective champions. When these antics were concluded, the actors and spectators walked in procession to an adjoining mansion, and passed through a hall stained in imitation of Sienna marble, into a ballroom where the walls, picked out in blue

363   The Meschianza at Philadelphia, from J. F. Watson, *Annals of Philadelphia*, 1884 (enlarged edition)

and gold, were reflected in eighty or ninety enormous mirrors. At midnight there was a supper of twelve hundred dishes, lighted by as many wax candles, and served by negroes in oriental trappings, with silver collars and bracelets. The lawn outside blazed with illuminations, and transparencies, and fountains spouting fire; and the proceedings were terminated by the roar and rush of innumerable rockets. That was the last gunpowder which General Howe saw burned in America."
— Trevelyan, *The American Revolution*, IV, pp. 286–87.

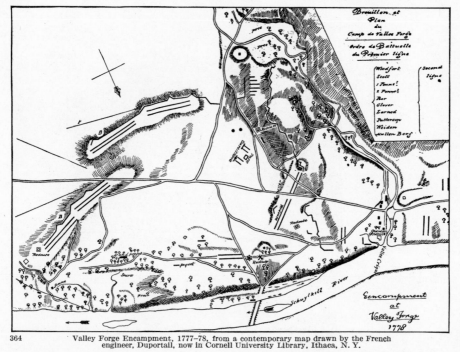

364   Valley Forge Encampment, 1777–78, from a contemporary map drawn by the French
                    engineer, Duportail, now in Cornell University Library, Ithaca, N. Y.

B. Indicates two entrenched positions, beginning at the right, occupied in order by the commands of Woodford,
Scott, Wayne, Poor, Glover, Learned, Patterson, Weedon, and Muhlenberg. Washington's headquarters was at the
unction of the Schuylkill and a creek (at right of chart).

THE VALLEY FORGE ENCAMPMENT, 1777–78

WHEN the campaign of 1777 came to an end Washington established his winter camp at Valley Forge. The soldiers were set to work building rough log huts, chinked with mud and thatched with straw. The enlisted men were told off into parties of twelve, each party to build and occupy a hut. It was an invariable practice of Washington to fortify each place which his army occupied for any length of time. Valley Forge was therefore made practically impregnable. Backed by the Schuylkill River, it was protected in front by steep-sided hills. The camp could only be taken as a result of a protracted siege, obviously impossible in winter. Washington, who could not forget that he had once been a surveyor, himself took an active part in the laying out of the camp. Valley Forge must be made secure because of its nearness to Howe's army. He had chosen this site deliberately in order that he might check the activities of the British foraging parties, and also to launch a swift blow in the spring, if circumstances warranted.

In the rude cantonment on the Schuylkill was enacted one of the saddest, and yet most glorious, dramas in the history of the American people. Owing chiefly to the inefficiency of Congress the organization of the service of supply broke down. At one time food became so scarce that Washington feared the army would break up as a result of the wholesale desertion of famished men. On December 23 two thousand eight hundred and ninety-eight men were unfit for duty from lack of shoes and clothing, and on February 5 the number had been increased by more than a thousand. Lafayette, who had joined Washington's staff, reported of the soldiers that "their feet and legs froze until they grew black, and it was often necessary to amputate them." Woe to the soldier whose fortune it was to go to one of the Valley Forge hospitals, a rough hut like the one he lived in, where he lay without proper medicines, diet, or even covering, side by side with dying and sometimes even dead men. Before the days of scientific medicine there were no adequate means of combating the diseases which inevitably follow the massing of men into armies. Valley Forge has been called the Gethsemane of the American army. Here was a test of the quality of officers and men more searching than the field of battle.

365   Washington at Valley Forge, from the drawing by H. A. Ogden
                  for The Century Book of the American Revolution, 1897

THE PROBLEM OF SUPPLY

VALLEY FORGE demonstrated some outstanding weaknesses of the revolutionary movement. At best the Congress was but a makeshift *de facto* government with uncertain powers. By the end of 1777 the group of able men who had signed the Declaration of Independence had largely disappeared from its ranks, drawn off into foreign or military service or, more commonly, engaged in the reconstruction of the state governments, where officials enjoyed the reality of power. During part of the winter of Valley Forge, Congress was a rump, its sittings at times attended by only nine or ten delegates. Such a body of men, little experienced in the difficult affairs of state, had neither the wisdom nor the power to organize the whole economic power of the people to further the cause of the Revolution. But even more fundamental than such inefficiency was the lack of an adequate system of land transportation. From the beginnings of settlement the colonies had depended upon the sea for the transfer of commodities over long distances. Wheeled vehicles were relatively scarce both in the cities and the country districts. At Valley Forge a congressional investigating committee found

> By HIS EXCELLENCY
> # GEORGE WASHINGTON, ESQUIRE,
> GENERAL and COMMANDER in CHIEF of the Forces of the UNITED STATES of AMERICA.
>
> BY Virtue of the Power and Direction to Me especially given, I hereby enjoin and require all Persons residing within seventy Miles of my Head Quarters to thresh one Half of their Grain by the 1st Day of February, and the other Half by the 1st Day of March next ensuing, on Pain, in Case of Failure, of having all that shall remain in Sheaves after the Period above mentioned, seized by the Commissaries and Quarter-Masters of the Army, and paid for as Straw.
>
> GIVEN *under my Hand, at Head Quarters, near the Valley Forge, in Philadelphia County, this 20th Day of December,* 1777.
> G. *WASHINGTON.*
>
> By His Excellency's Command,
> ROBERT H. HARRISON, Sec'y.
>
> LANCASTER; PRINTED BY JOHN DUNLAP.

366 Washington's Proclamation of Dec. 20, 1777, from the copy in the collections of the Historical Society of Pennsylvania, Philadelphia

the soldiers improvising their own and acting as beasts of burden to drag them. The British navy paralyzed intercolonial communication by sea. Dependent upon undeveloped land transport, the army that remained long in one place tended inevitably to create a local famine. Washington's proclamation is significant of the necessities and the methods of the American commanders. And the farmer reading such a proclamation knew that he would be paid for his grain in depreciated and almost worthless paper money. Many of them hastened to dispose of their crops for the gold which Howe's commissary officers carried in their money-bags.

STEUBEN THE DRILLMASTER

THROUGHOUT the year 1777 Washington was embarrassed by a group of professional soldiers from Europe who sought commissions and glory in the American armies. Most of them were destined to return home disappointed. He chose however from the host of foreign applicants a few officers who were destined to serve well the American cause. He quickly sensed the idealism and the ability of the young nobleman Lafayette (No. 497), and the two became lifelong friends. John Kalb and Chevalier Duportail were others whom America justly honors. But the foreigner whose service counted for the most was a Prussian officer trained on the staff of Frederick the Great whom Washington promptly made Inspector at Valley Forge, Baron Frederick von Steuben. Steuben had arrived December 1, 1777, and had offered his services as a volunteer officer to Congress. In March, 1778, he began the drilling of recruits at Valley Forge. Steuben brought discipline and efficiency to the American army. "He was surprised to find no uniform drill, no similarity of organization and no team work of any kind. . . . Rising at three in the morning, smoking his pipe and drinking his cup of coffee, Steuben proceeded to the parade ground, where he personally taught drill movements. He would illustrate the manual of arms by using the musket in his own hands. Such a democratic demonstration shocked the higher officers, who were still imbued with the British idea of aristocratic aloofness." — W. A. GANOE, *History of the United States Army*, p. 55.

367   From the mural painting in the state capitol, Harrisburg, Pa., by Edwin A. Abbey (1852–1911).
© M. G. Abbey, from a Copley print.   © Curtis & Cameron

368   Major-General Baron von Steuben, 1703–94, from the portrait by C. W. Peale in Independence Hall, Philadelphia

STEUBEN'S PROBLEMS

"STEUBEN's tact and his sensible dealings made even the cavalier see the fruitlessness of trusting everything to the non-commissioned men. Steuben forced the discovery that in a country where caste is obnoxious an officer must gain his results by more direct means. Accordingly, there was established that dignified contact between officer and soldier wherein respect is engendered by fairness and ability. At first the new inspector was particularly struck with the attitude of the officers. 'The captains and colonels,' he said, 'did not consider their companies and regiments as corps confided to them by the United States for the care of the men as well as the preservation of order and discipline. The idea they had of their duties was that the officers had only to mount guard and put themselves at the head of their regiment or company when they were going into action.' He forthwith organized the officers into squads, sections, and companies for drill under his personal direction. In this way was raised up an excellent corps of instructors." — GANOE, p. 55.

THE RESULTS OF DISCIPLINE

THE wisdom of Steuben's employment as instructor in military training was fortified by the fact that he knew his job as an experienced soldier, and knew how to get his ideas executed in daily practice. "Knowing, however, that drill was valueless without the discipline of daily routine, he [Steuben] went minutely into field and company administration. . . . He allowed sinks to be dug no nearer to occupied tents than 300 feet. He charged field officers with seeing that their camps were pitched regularly and properly, especially that kitchens and sinks were put in sanitary places. . . . He established roll-calls of 'troop' and 'retreat' under arms and the 'reveille' and 'noon' without arms. He charged the non-commissioned officers with the making of an accurate check of their men at tattoo to see that the men were in bed. At 'troop beating' he required company officers to 'inspect into the dress of their men,' to 'see that the clothes are whole and put on properly, their [the soldiers] hands and faces washed clean, their hair combed, their accoutrements properly fixed and every article about them in the greatest order.' . . . Due to such painstaking care and labor, the festering camp began to take on the semblance of order and organization in spite of the lack of supplies. Disease was lessened. . . . Officers began to father their organizations. The human touch, zeal, and dignity that have since characterized the best American leaders became noticeable. Troops began to be complimented in orders on their drill. By taking the attitude that the 'indifferent quality of clothing, instead of excusing slovenliness and unsoldierly conduct, ought rather' to excite each man to compensate for those deficiencies by redoubled attention to his personal appearance, Steuben was successful in building morale upon less than nothing. . . . His work could not be ignored. Congress was morally forced to recognize him. Accordingly,

369   From the painting Washington and Steuben at Valley Forge, by Howard Pyle (1853–1911) for Woodrow Wilson, History of the American People. © Harper & Brothers

Washington's orders one day announced to the camp that von Steuben had been made a major-general and inspector-general of the army." — GANOE, pp. 58, 61–2.

AN OFFICER'S FIRST DUTY

Von Steuben's golden rule is contained in the few pregnant words reproduced here, words which he first addresses to the Captain and then repeats, in a slightly different form, when addressing the Lieutenant: "His first object should be to gain the love of his men by treating them with every possible kindness and humanity, inquiring into their complaints, and when well founded, seeing them redressed."

THE CONWAY CABAL

Washington's deliberate retirement to Valley Forge and the resulting months of inactivity

[138]

Instructions for the Captain.

A CAPTAIN cannot be too careful of the company the state has committed to his charge. He must pay the greatest attention to the health of his men, their discipline, arms, accoutrements, ammunition, clothes and necessaries.

His first object should be, to gain the love of his men, by treating them with every possible kindness and humanity, enquiring into their complaints, and when well founded, seeing them redressed. He should know every man of his company by name and character. He should often visit those who are sick, speak tenderly to them, see that the public provision, whether of medicine or diet, is duly administered, and procure them besides such comforts and conveniencies as are in his power. The attachment that arises from this kind of attention to the sick and wounded, is almost inconceivable; it will moreover be the means of preserving the lives of many valuable men.

[141]

being a material object to prevent the soldier loading himself with unnecessary baggage.

Instructions for the Lieutenant.

THE lieutenant, in the absence of the captain, commands the company, and should therefore make himself acquainted with the duties of that station; he must also be perfectly acquainted with the duties of the non-commissioned officers and soldiers, and see them performed with the greatest exactness.

He should endeavour to gain the love of his men, by his attention to every thing which may contribute to their health and convenience. He should often visit them at different hours; inspect into their manner of living; see that their provisions are good and well cooked, and as far as possible oblige them to take their meals at regulated hours. He should pay attention to their complaints, and when well founded, endeavour to get them redressed; but discourage them from complaining on every frivolous occasion.

370 From Steuben's *Regulations for the Order and Discipline of the Troops of the United States,* Philadelphia, 1779

were inexcusable in the eyes of certain political and military leaders. John Adams had epitomized the complaints of many when he criticized Washington's Fabian policy since the outbreak of the war, and General Thomas Mifflin and James Lovell of Massachusetts were outstanding critics of existing strategy. In November, 1777, Congress created a Board of War with Generals Gates and Mifflin as prominent members, and James Wilkinson as Secretary. This board was to direct independently the operations of the Army. One of its special protegés was Brigadier General Thomas Conway, an Irishman by birth, a French soldier by training. Washington and Lafayette considered Conway's claims to a major-generalship presumptuous, while the Board of War advocated the creation of a separate and independent Army of the North with Lafayette as commander and Conway as his immediate junior. When Lafayette refused, the Board of War advanced Conway's candidacy for the office of Inspector-General of the entire army.

The victory of Gates at Saratoga was an arresting contrast to the defeats of Washington. It is difficult to determine the nature and the extent of the factious communications directed to Gates. The first indication was Wilkinson's drunken revelation of a letter which Gates had received from Conway, bemoaning the lack of a capable commander in chief with intelligent assistants. Lord Stirling, the American officer to whom Wilkinson confided the secret, relayed the information to Washington. The result of the exposure was a protracted correspondence beween Gates and Washington, in the course of which Washington's sarcastic logic caused Gates to abandon one position after another; at the end he was glad to retire as honorably as possible by accepting Washington's final offer to close the issue for all time. Conway's career was definitely closed. In the years following, when Washington's prestige was unquestioned, no stigma was more avoided than the suspicion of having participated in the "Conway Cabal."

371 Washington's Letter (last paragraph) to General Gates, February 9, 1778, on the Conway cabal, original in the Gates papers in the New York Historical Society

372   Revolutionary Musket of 1775, used at the Battle of Lexington, from the Lexington Historical Society, Lexington, Mass.

INFANTRYMEN OF THE REVOLUTION

THE Revolution, like all eighteenth-century wars, was primarily an infantryman's war. The chief weapons of the infantryman were the firelock musket, with its attached bayonet, and the hand grenade. The Revolutionary firelock (No. 372) was the most important arm of its time. Its bore was large and it shot a heavy leaden ball often molded by the soldiers themselves. The maximum effective range was little more than a hundred yards. Rapid fire was discouraged and, in fact, in any modern sense, was quite impossible. The gun could be discharged with bayonet attached; though under such circumstances it was not easy to reload. The hand grenade, as in the French and Indian War, was the weapon of a specialized branch, the grenadiers. The powder horn was not used by fully equipped infantry, partly because of the difficulty in the excitement of battle of measuring out the proper amount for the charge. Instead, the powder was put up in paper cartridges which were carried in a cartridge pouch. Twenty-four rounds was a usual amount for a soldier to take into battle. But the smooth-bore musket, though it remained the standard arm in many armies for another eighty years or more, was not the only infantry fire-arm used by Patriots. The rifle had already been used in the final French and Indian War. (See Chapter I.) Now, thanks to the German-American gunsmiths of Pennsylvania, it appeared again in more effective form. It was not hard to load. So comparatively long was its range that it dominated situations in which the very conspicuous redcoats were too far off to fire back with their muskets. So great was the moral effect under such circumstances that Washington liked to camouflage mere musketeers as riflemen, by having their clothes dyed butternut brown, a color which the outranged redcoats had learned to associate with the rifleman from the backwoods. Some officers carried swords; but others were armed like their men. All who could used pistols, which were sometimes rifled too.

373 Contemporary German study of a Revolutionary rifleman and Pennsylvania infantryman, from *Allgemeines Historisches Taschenbuch . . . enhaltend für 1784 die Geschichte der Revolution von Nord-America von C. M. Sprengel*, Berlin, 1784

It should always be remembered that the redcoated British regulars rarely fought alone, that none of them were present at several well-known battles, like Trenton, and that they formed little more than half the total land forces engaged on the king's side. They were in a decided minority during the Canadian campaign. They numbered only eighteen thousand of the whole thirty-three thousand in the British army in 1778, when the Hessians numbered eleven thousand and the Provincials over four thousand. In the winter of 1779–80, when the British garrison in New York exceeded twenty-eight thousand, the redcoat regulars numbered less than fourteen thousand. But still they formed the backbone of the royal army; and so, by way of contrast, this typical redcoat may be set over against the Continental regular who followed the lead of Washington. The redcoat was trained for, and excelled in, close-order line of battle. Hence his victories, and hence his defeats.

374 British Infantryman, uniform of the period of the Revolution, from W. S. Moorsom, *Historical Record of the Oxfordshire Light Infantry*, London, 1863

REGULATION EQUIPMENT

THE American infantry soldier in Massachusetts at this time was required to report with all the articles indicated in the instructions issued to one Shrimpton Hutchinson, of Ward 6, Boston.

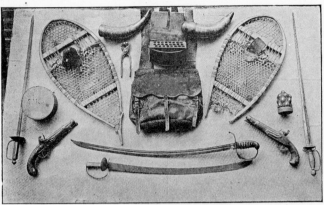

375   Revolutionary relics, from the Essex Institute Collection, Salem, Mass.

BOSTON, Ap 6, 1779

To Shrimpton Hutchinson

SIR,

YOU are hereby ordered and directed, to compleat yourself with ARMS and Accoutrements, by the 12th Inftant, upon failure thereof, you are liable to a FINE of THREE POUNDS: and for every Sixty Days after, a FINE of SIX POUNDS, agreable to Law.

Articles of Equipment,

A good Fire-Arm, with a Steel or Iron Ram-Rod, and a Spring to retain the fame, a Worm, Priming wire and Brufh, and a Bayonet fitted to your GUN, a Scabbard and Belt therefor, and a Cutting Sword, or a Tomahawk or Hatchet, a Pouch containing a Cartridge Box, that will hold fifteen Rounds of Cartridges at leaft, a hundred Buck Shot, a Jack-Knife and Tow for Wadding, fix Flints, one pound Powder, forty Leaden Balls fitted to your GUN, a Knapfack and Blanket a Canteen or Wooden Bottle fufficient to hold one Quart.

376   From an order prescribing the arms and accoutrements of a soldier, dated April 6, 1779, in the Emmet Collection, New York Public Library

THE SOLDIER'S EQUIPMENT

THE picture shows a miscellaneous collection of military equipment. The saddle bags were used at Bunker Hill by Lieutenant John Curtis. One powder horn dates from 1756; the other is decorated with a scrimshaw work map of the Hudson and Mohawk Rivers. The flintlock pistols are English and were used during the War of Independence. The grapeshot was stored in Salem Town House during the Revolution. The cartridge box was in the possession of New Hampshire troops during the war, and the bullet mold has been dated between 1750 and 1800. Of the two rapiers on the outer sides of the group, one was used by an officer at Bunker Hill; at the bottom is the sabre of an artilleryman. The canteen was carried at Lexington, and the snowshoes were worn by Captain Samuel Page of the Revolutionary army.

SALTPETER

DURING the colonial period the powder and practically all of the munitions had been supplied from England. When the declaration of war ended this source of supply the leaders of the new American army turned anxiously to potential resources at home. The Committees of Safety, organized in each state to expedite military preparedness, issued pamphlets of instructions. There was published in Philadelphia in 1775 a pamphlet entitled *Several methods of making salt petre; recommended to the inhabitants of the United Colonies by their representatives in Congress*, and in the following year the New York Committee of Safety issued *Essays upon the making of salt-petre and gunpowder*. Yet throughout the entire war the problem of supplying sufficient powder was a most embarrassing one.

377   From the *Royal American Magazine*, Boston, 1774
A. The flue or chimney below which the furnaces are seen, and of which four are represented.

Fig. 1. A workman ladling the melted Saltpetre out of a furnace into a large copper pan, placed before him for that purpose. This is the last operation, and is what the refiners call roaching the saltpetre. T. A tub, in which that part of the saltpetre is put which has any foulness on it. Near the tub is a basket, for receiving the dross or foulness that rises on the saltpetre, when in a liquid state. The fine particles run through the wicker-work back into the furnace.

Fig. 2. A workman skimming the liquid saltpetre in the furnace, and thowing the scum into a basket, placed on a wooden frame to receive it, X, the tub and basket already (T) described. a. An *axis in peritrochio* (windlass) for drawing up the refined saltpetre into the loft over the refining-house.

378 Gun Factory at Easton, Pa., erected about 1745,
from the *Pennsylvania-German Society Proceedings*, 1906

RIFLE MAKING IN THE REVOLUTION

At the opening of the Revolution, the Germans and Dutch in Pennsylvania had brought the manufacture of rifles to a high degree of perfection. With the suddenly created new demand, every blacksmith was soon forging gun barrels; every cabinet-maker shaping gunstocks; every locksmith making gunlocks, and every gunsmith rifling gun barrels. The Pennsylvania Council of Safety established a gun factory at Philadelphia, employing Golcher to instruct in the art of boring and grinding gun barrels. John Tyler was in charge of rifling at Allentown; Daniel Kleist at Bethlehem, where Daniel Morgan remained several days to have every man's rifle examined and put in order; while John Young, of Easton, received an order from the colony of Virginia for one thousand rifles. The factory shown here visualizes the small scale on which the enterprises were conducted, and the reason for the ever-present dilemma of inadequate weapons and ammunition.

THE COMMISSARIAT

The supply of the fighting forces of the revolting colonies was always a difficult task and, at times, became a matter of critical importance. In general throughout the operations of the first year the army was well fed, though there were many just complaints. Joseph Trumbull as Commissary General proved himself a valuable officer, but he finally found himself working in an impossible system. His deputies were appointed by Congress, and he could not control them when both corruption and inefficiency appeared. Congress, seemingly unwilling to divest itself of any power, permitted him to resign in 1777, while two important campaigns were in progress. His successor, William Buchanan, either from incapacity or from lack of power over his subordinates, proved unequal to the office. Mifflin, the Quartermaster General, who early in the war had faithfully performed his duties, went home in the summer of 1777 on the plea of ill health. There he remained over two months. When he resigned in October, Congress waited a month before accepting his resignation, and three months more before appointing his successor. The terrible breakdown of the system came at Valley Forge.

379 Joseph Trumbull, 1737–78, from the posthumous portrait by John Trumbull in the possession of Louis T. Cheney, Hartford, Conn.

380   From the mural *Winter Encampment at Valley Forge, 1777*, by Harrington FitzGerald in the
State Capitol, Harrisburg, Pa.

381   Jeremiah Wadsworth, 1743–1804, from the portrait by James Sharples (1751–1811) in Independence Hall, Philadelphia

I _Nathanael Greene_ do _swear_. that I will faithfully, truly and impartially execute the office of _Quarter Master General_ to which I am appointed, and render a true account, when thereunto required, of all public monies by me received or expended, and of all stores or other effects to me intrusted, which belong to the UNITED STATES, and will, in all respects, discharge the trust reposed in me with justice and integrity, to the best of my skill and understanding.

Nathanael Greene Q M Gl

Sworn before me the 23 of May 1778

G Washington

382 Nathanael Greene's Oath of Allegiance, Valley Forge, May 23, 1778, from the original in the Archives of Old Records Division, War Department, Washington

JEREMIAH WADSWORTH, COMMISSARY GENERAL

THE conditions at Valley Forge drove Congress to action. The members asked the line officer, General Nathanael Greene, to become Quartermaster General and modified somewhat the management of the system of supply. The new Commissary General was Jeremiah Wadsworth. Washington later wrote to Congress that Greene had brought order out of confusion and had made it possible for the army to leave Valley Forge and promptly pursue Clinton when, in the spring of 1778, he evacuated Philadelphia. But Greene was not always successful, nor was the efficient Wadsworth. The colonies were not a manufacturing country, and the continental currency with which the supplies were purchased went from bad to worse. In December, 1779, the commissaries were without either money or credit, and for nearly six weeks the troops had been on half rations. Other crises followed in the years to come, driving the army at times to the verge of general mutiny. But always they were tided over. Wadsworth resigned in 1779, and Greene in the following year. So great was the indignation of the latter officer at the inefficiency of Congress that he publicly criticized that body. Hot heads declared that he should be dismissed; but his services were indispensable. He was allowed quietly to resume his command in the line. Until the very end of the war soldiers suffered from inadequate supplies of food. Even when the specified ration was available, there were never enough vegetables, nor milk for the sick. When the army was in camp a market was established at which farmers could sell their produce.

"Each Ration to consist of one Pound of Bread made of good Merchantable wheat Flour, one pound of Beef or three quarters of a pound of Pork and one jill of whiskey or Country rum for the Non Commissioned Officers and privates and West Indies rum for the Commissioned and Staff Officers of Merchantable proof Also one quart Salt and two quarts Vinegar to every hundred Rations and eight pounds of Soap and three pound Candles to every seven hundred Rations delivered under this Agreement."

383   Detail from a Provision Contract, 1781, from the original in the Archives of Old Records Division, War Department, Washington

ROBERT MORRIS, SUPERINTENDENT OF FINANCE

IN 1781 Congress, after having tried to manage the finances of the war by means of a Board of Treasury, appointed Robert Morris superintendent of finance. Morris was a wealthy Philadelphia merchant, a man of great ability, experience, and undoubted loyalty to the cause of independence. He not only administered his office faithfully and well but in more than one emergency pledged his private fortune when the credit of the United States failed to secure necessary funds.

384   From the portrait by Gilbert Stuart, courtesy of Mrs. Lucée Morris Tinsley, New York

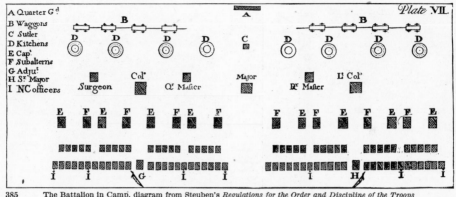

385   The Battalion in Camp, diagram from Steuben's *Regulations for the Order and Discipline of the Troops of the United States*, Philadelphia, 1779

THE CAMP

THE camp of the revolutionary army was much like that of modern times. No. 385 shows an encampment of two battalions with the colors in front of each. No. 386 shows the corner of a camp surrounded by guards, the flags representing battalions and the little squares each marking an individual guard.

Steuben's regulations were simple. "The different guards of the army will consist of 1st. Out post and piquet guards. 2d. Camp and quarter guards. 3d. General and staff officers' guards. The piquet guards are formed by detachments from the line, and are posted at the avenues of the camp, in such numbers as the general commanding thinks necessary for the security of the camp. The camp and quarter guards are for the better security of the camp, as well as for the preserving of good order and discipline. . . . The camp guard of the front line is to be posted three hundred paces in front of it, and that of the second line the same distance in rear of the second line, each opposite the interval of the two battalions who furnish it. Each guard will post nine sentinels. . . . In order to complete the chain of sentinels round the camp, the adjutant general will order two flank guards from the line, to consist of a commissioned officer and as many men as are necessary to form a chain on the flanks. . . ." — *Regulations*, 1779. An example

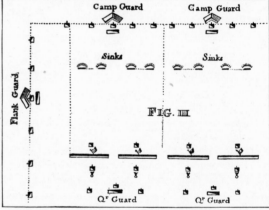

386   The Camp under Guard, diagram from Steuben's *Regulations*

of the placing of a piquet may be found in the map (No. 342).

387   Washington's Camp Bed, courtesy of the United States National Museum, Washington

BRITISH CAMP AT DYCKMAN FARM, NEW YORK

"HERE on the familiar hillside, with the same natural features of rock and forest which then surrounded it, we may see the life of the camp, when in British occupation, faithfully and accurately reproduced." — R. P. BOLTON, *Relics of the Revolution*, New York, 1916.

388   From the painting by John Ward Dunsmore. © by the artist

389 Dr. John Morgan, 1725–89, from the portrait by Angelica Kauffman, courtesy of the University of Pennsylvania, Philadelphia

390 Dr. William Shippen, Jr., 1736–1808, from the portrait by C. W. Peale in Independence Hall, Philadelphia

391 Dr. John Cochran, 1730–1807, from an engraving, courtesy of the Army Medical Library, Washington

THE BIRTH OF THE MEDICAL CORPS

THE history of the medical service is not unlike that of the service of supply. On May 8, 1775, nineteen days after the Battle of Lexington, the Provincial Congress of Massachusetts appointed what seems to have been the first army medical examining board to pass on the qualifications of surgeons for the troops. A few months later Dr. Benjamin Church became the Director General and Chief Physician of the first army hospital, at a salary of four dollars a day. In October, 1775, Church was arrested for "holding a correspondence with the enemy," court-martialed, and sentenced to "be close confined in some secure gaol in the colony of Connecticut." Dr. John Morgan took the place of Church and rose to become Director General and Chief Physician of the general hospitals of the United States, from which position he was removed on January 9, 1777. Two years later a congressional investigating committee reported that "he did conduct himself ably and faithfully in the discharge of the duties of his office." Dr. William Shippen, Jr., had already taken his place. He served with ability until his resignation in January, 1781. Dr. John Cochran was then appointed, retaining the office until the end of the war. These three physicians, Morgan, Shippen, and Cochran, handicapped by a tragic lack of money and by lack of experience in the organization of an army medical corps, played an indispensable part in the War of Independence. Under their direction was a large number of self-sacrificing doctors.

THE MEDICAL OFFICER

THE spirit of the medical officers is reflected in an entry in Thacher's *Military Journal* (1775–83) for January 1, 1781. "We are encouraged to anticipate more favorable circumstances, and more liberal compensation, Congress having at length passed several resolves, entitling all officers who shall continue in service till the end of the war, or shall be reduced before that time as supernumeraries, to receive half pay during life, and a certain number of acres of land, in proportion to their rank. Besides these pecuniary considerations, we are actuated by the purest principles of patriotism; having engaged in the mighty struggle, we are ambitious to persevere to the end. To be instrumental in the achievement of a glorious Independence for our country, and posterity, will be source of infinite satisfaction, and of the most grateful recollection, during the remainder of our days. Notwithstanding the unparalleled sufferings and hardships, which have hitherto attended our military career, scarcely an officer retires without the deepest regret and reluctance." The army surgeon's equipment illustrated here was used by Solomon Drowne, M.D. (1753–1834), in the New York Hospital in 1776.

392 Surgical Instruments, Medicines, etc., used in the Revolution, from the originals in the possession of Henry Russell Drowne, New York

393 A Revolutionary Surgeon's Bill for Services, original in Barnard
College, Columbia University, New York

A REVOLUTIONARY MILITARY HOSPITAL

DR. JAMES TILTON in his *Economical Observations on Military Hospitals*, 1813, pictures and describes a type of hospital used during the Revolution. ". . . the best hospital I ever contrived was upon the plan of an Indian Hut — Fire built in midst of ward, without any chimney and the smoke circulating round about passed off through an opening about 4″ wide in ridge of the roof. The common surface of the earth served for the floor. The patients laid with their heads to the wall round about, and their feet were all turned to the fire. Wards thus completely ventilated. Smoke continued to combat infection without giving least offence to patients . . . more patients could be crowded with impunity in such wards than in any others I have seen tried. This was the expedient I employed in the hard winter of '79–80 when the army was hutted near Morristown."

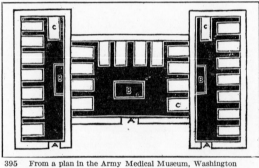

395 From a plan in the Army Medical Museum, Washington
A. Doors. *B.* Fireplaces. *C.* Bunks or bed stalls in which patients were placed.

394   From a sketch in the Army Medical Museum, Washington

RECRUITING AFTER MUTINY IN 1781

BOUNTIES, promises, uniforms, equipment, pay, rations, arms, training, battles and marches, defeat and victory, medical attendance, good or bad camps or billets — all these affected the Revolutionary soldier in different ways at different times. But we must remember how many hardships he had to face, and how many real or seeming injustices he had to stand. On New Year's Day, 1781, the Pennsylvania division under Wayne, having for an entire year received no pay, mutinied. Met by a committee of Congress, mollified, and discharged, they nearly all re-enlisted soon after and did good service. They received the same bounty as new recruits, than whom, of course, they were very much more valuable.

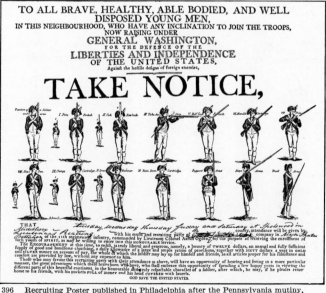

396   Recruiting Poster published in Philadelphia after the Pennsylvania mutiny,
original in the Historical Society of Pennsylvania, Philadelphia

FIFERS AND DRUMMERS

THE fifers and drummers were an indispensable part of the Revolutionary armies. Their shrill but stirring music animated the marching column and inspired the troops advancing into a fight. Of the two the drummer was the more important, for he was nothing less than the bugler of modern times. There was a certain picturesqueness in the assembling of the ragged drummers at Valley Forge for the successive routine beats of the day, carrying out to the best of their ability Steuben's detailed regulations. "The different daily beats shall begin on the right, and be instantly followed by the whole army; to facilitate which, the drummer's call shall be beat by the drums of the police, a quarter of an hour before beating, when the drummers will assemble before the colours of their respective battalions." "*The General* is to beat only when the whole are to march, and is the signal to strike the tents, and prepare for the march. *The Assembly* is the signal to repair to the colours. *The March* for the whole to move. *The Reveillie* is beat at day-break, and is the signal for the soldiers to rise, and the sentries to leave off challenging. *The Troop* assembles the soldiers together, for the purpose of calling the roll and inspecting the men for duty. *The Retreat* is beat at sun-set, for the calling of the roll,

397 From the painting *The Continentals* by Frank B. Mayer (1827–97), 'courtesy ,of Mrs. Francis T. Redwood, Baltimore

warning the men for duty, and reading the orders of the day. *The Tattoo* is for the soldiers to repair to their tents, where they must remain till *reveillie* beating next morning. [There seems to have been no Taps.] *To Arms*, is a signal for getting under arms in case of an alarm. *The Parley* is to desire a conference with the enemy." — STEUBEN, *Regulations*.

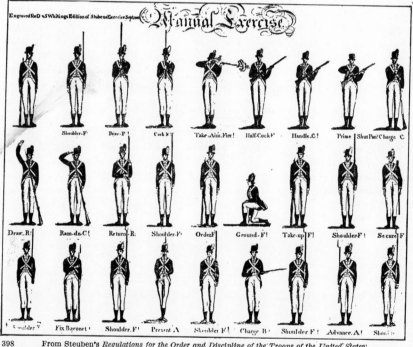

398   From Steuben's *Regulations for the Order and Discipline of the Troops of the United States*; frontispiece from the Albany (N. Y.) Edition, 1803

THE MANUAL OF ARMS

GENERAL VON STEUBEN replaced the older systems used in the war with the perfected manual of arms which greatly enhanced the fighting efficiency of the Continental army. His "Manual Exercise" gives, as nothing else can, an insight into the technique of the infantryman in the handling of his piece. Many useful hours were spent on the snowy ground at Valley Forge in the drill which perfected the soldier in this fundamental aspect of his calling.

Steuben's text of instructions for Manual Exercises covers twenty-seven commands and fifty-eight motions, reading from the first to the ninth command, as follows: "I. *Poise — Firelock!* Two Motions. 1st. With your left hand turn the firelock briskly, bringing the lock to the front, at the same instant seize it with the right hand just below the lock, keeping the piece perpendicular. 2d. With a quick motion bring up the firelock from the shoulder directly before the face, and seize it with the left hand just above the lock. . . . II. *Cock — Firelock!* Two Motions. 1st. Turn the barrel opposite your face, and place your thumb upon the cock, *raising the elbow square at this motion*. 2d. Cock the firelock by drawing down your elbow. . . . III. *Take Aim!* One Motion. Step back about six inches with the right foot, bringing the left toe to the front: at the same time drop the muzzle, and bring up the butt end of the firelock against your right shoulder; place the left hand forward on the swell of the stock, and the fore-finger of the right hand before the trigger; sinking the muzzle a little below a level, and with the right eye looking along the barrell. IV. *Fire!* One Motion. Pull the trigger briskly and immediately after bringing up the right foot come to the priming position. . . . V. *Half-cock — Firelock!* One Motion. Half bend the cock briskly, bringing down the elbow to the butt of the firelock. VI. *Handle — Cartridge!* One Motion. Bring your right hand short around to your pouch, slapping it hard, seize the cartridge, and bring it with a quick motion to your mouth, bite the top off down to the powder, covering it instantly with your thumb. . . . VII. *Prime!* One Motion. Shake the powder into the pan, and covering the cartridge again, place the three last fingers behind the hammer. . . . VIII. *Shut — Pan!* 1st. Shut your pan briskly. . . . 2d. Turn your piece nimbly round before you come to the loading position. . . . IX. *Charge with Cartridge!* 1st. Turn up your hand and put the cartridge into the muzzle, shaking the powder into the barrel. 2d. Turning the stock a little towards you, place your right hand closed with a quick and strong motion, upon the butt of the rammer. . . ." — STEUBEN, *Regulations for the Order and Discipline of the Troops of the United States*.

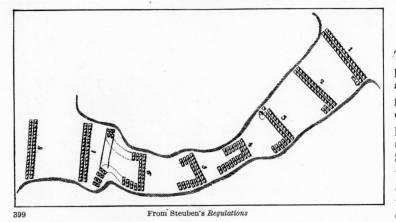

399   From Steuben's *Regulations*

THE ARMY ON THE MARCH

THE army marched as well as paraded in close order after the advent of Steuben. The easygoing march discipline of the early years of the war disappeared and the losses from straggling were greatly reduced. Such a reform was of vital military importance; for it seemed as if the chief task of the Revolutionary armies was marching. Over interminable roads tramped the dusty brigades of Washington and Greene. The British command of the sea made it possible for Howe and Clinton to transfer their troops by water from New York to Philadelphia or to Charleston; but the Continentals must plod overland many weary miles to meet these offensives. The march was made in column of platoons. The Revolutionary soldier knew nothing of a squad of eight men commanded by a corporal. "Squads right — March!" was a command not heard until after the Civil War. In Washington's day the command was addressed to the platoon and was "To the right — Wheel! March!" Steuben's diagram shows seventeen men marching abreast. The column, moving from left to right, is passing a defile which compels the narrowing of the front. When platoon number six reaches the narrow point, the necessary number of files (a file is one front rank man and the rear rank man behind him) drop off the ends of the platoon, face in, and march to the proper position behind their respective flanks. Platoons one, two, and three show the detached files resuming their former positions as the passage widens. Before the American armies learned to perform such movements with precision retreats before the enemy were apt to lead to confusion and disaster.

SECURITY ON THE MARCH

ONE of the oldest problems of students of the military art is that of guarding a marching column against surprise and providing means whereby an attacking enemy may be held off until the troops can assume battle formation. Steuben's rules in his *Regulations* for security on the march do not differ in principle from those in twentieth-century manuals. "The advance guard will march at a distance from the main body proportioned to its strength, having a patrol advanced; and must never enter any defile, wood, &c., without having first examined it, to avoid falling into an ambuscade. The pioneers are to march behind the advanced guard, and must repair the roads, that the column may be obliged to file off as little as possible. The advanced guard, besides its patrols in front, must have a flank guard, composed of a file from each platoon, and commanded by an officer, or non-commissioned officer, to march at a distance of one hundred paces on the flank, and keep up with the head of the advanced guard. If it is necessary to have a flank guard upon each side, a file must be sent from the other flank of each platoon to compose it; and as this service is very fatiguing, the men should be relieved every hour." Ignorance of such rules had been responsible for many a defeat of militia at the hands of Indians in the French and Indian War. After the time of Steuben officers and men were grounded in this basic aspect of the military art.

400   From Ephraim Hoyt, *A Treatise on the Military Art*, Brattleboro, Vt., 1798

A. Advance guard of cavalry. *B.* Advanced corporal with six horsemen, two at *B* and two each at *C*. *D.* Flank guard with two wings of eight or twelve horses each at *E.* *F.* Platoons of Infantry alternating with squadrons of cavalry. *G, H.* Rear guard. "If they meet [the enemy] . . . at the entrance of a hollow way. *I.* opening obliquely upon you . . . infantry forms at *L L L* or on some neighboring heights *M M.*"

A FORMATION AGAINST INDIANS

STEUBEN's battle formations were not mere imitations of those in vogue in Europe. The conventional European infantry formation was in three ranks, to insure greater shock effect in a bayonet assault. Steuben's companies were arranged in two ranks; the English army in America had long experimented with the same device. (The first two-deep "thin red line" in the world was Wolfe's on the Plains of Abraham at Quebec in 1759.) The change was the result of increasing experience with fighting in woods and broken country, that characterized so many of the campaigns of the French and Indian War and of the Revolution. The Indian took cover. Against this elusive enemy the shock troops three ranks deep proved again and again ineffective. Bouquet's Royal Americans, who remained in America until after the Revolution, worked out a definite and very clever system for guarding against and defeating an Indian encircling attack. Out of such adjustments as this came the beginnings of modern tactics with its open order fighting formation.

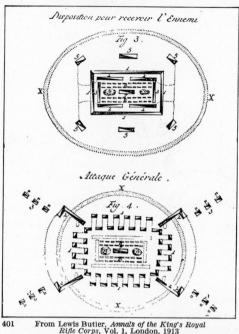

401   From Lewis Butler, *Annals of the King's Royal Rifle Corps*, Vol. 1, London, 1913
Legend: 1. Regular Troops. 2. Chasseurs. 3. Light House. 5. Advanced Guard. 7. Reserve. - 8. Baggage and Provisions. 9. Animals. X. Enemy.

AMERICAN FIGHTING METHOD

ALL through the war, but particularly in the earlier years, the Americans adopted tactics modeled somewhat on those of the Indians. General Burgoyne wrote of his adversaries: "Accustomed to felling of timber and to grubbing up trees, they are very ready at earthworks and palisading, and will cover and intrench themselves wherever they are for a short time left unmolested with surprising alacrity [the modern American army requires but six hours to organize a defensive position and to dig in] . . . Composed as the American army is, together with the strength of the country, full of woods, swamps, stone walls, and other inclosures and hiding places, it may be said of it that every private man will in action be his own general, who will turn every tree and bush into a kind of temporary fortress, from whence, when he hath fired his shot with all deliberation, coolness, and certainty which hidden safety inspires, he will skip as it were to the next, and so on for a long time till dislodged either by cannon or by a resolute attack of light infantry." This type of fighting, which began during the French and Indian War, as the illustration shows, was carefully developed during the Revolution by some units of the American army. Morgan's Riflemen in the Revolution carried forward the traditions of the rangers of the French and Indian War. That such troops could be dangerous enemies Burgoyne learned in his ill-fated campaign. But rangers were, after all, auxiliaries. If the British armies were to be driven out of America, the task must be accomplished by regiments trained in the European methods. Steuben with sound judgment founded his drill regulations on formations well adapted to the arms in use; but with modifications that made for greater efficiency in America.

402   Detail from Samuel Blodget's Plan of the Battle of Lake George, copy in the New York Public Library

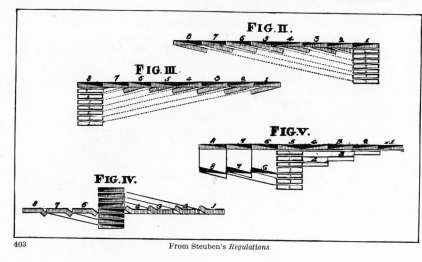

403   From Steuben's *Regulations*

DEPLOYING FOR BATTLE

A Revolutionary column advancing into battle presented a picture vastly different from that of a modern army. Perhaps the enemy had already formed and was awaiting the attack, his musket fire withheld, but his artillery banging away at the advancing column. Suddenly the command would ring out and be repeated down the line: "Take Care to *Display* the Column to the Left! (Figure II) The officers commanding the platoons go to the left in order to conduct them. *To the Left — Face!* The whole face to the left except the front platoon. *March!* The platoons face, step off, and march obliquely to their places in the line; when the second platoon has gained its proper distance, its officer commands *Halt! Front! To the Right — Dress!* dresses his platoon with that already formed, and takes his post on the right; the other platoons form in the same manner." — *Regulations*, 1779. Figure III shows a column forming to the right, Figure IV a column forming a line on the fifth platoon, and Figure V a line forming a column on the first platoon. Such various maneuvers were necessary if the army was to have mobility in passing defiles or obstacles and in the face of an enemy. They are all maneuvers executed in close order and differ but little from the evolutions seen on the twentieth-century parade ground. Precision in their execution was a measure of an army's ability to fight.

THE FIRING LINE

When the firing line was formed, it advanced toward the enemy. As it came within range, the colonel or lieutenant-colonel would give the command: "*Battalion — Halt! Take Care to Fire by Battalion! Battalion! Make ready! Take aim! Fire!* If there be more than one battalion to fire, they are to do it in succession from right to left; but after the first round the odd battalions fire, and soon, as the respective

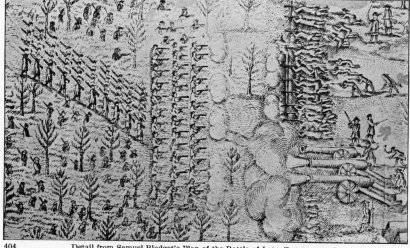

404   Detail from Samuel Blodget's Plan of the Battle of Lake George, copy in the New York Public Library

battalions on their left begin to shoulder; and the even battalions fire when the respective battalions on their right begin to shoulder. . . ." — *Regulations*, 1779. Firing by battalion or platoon was necessary to guard against a bayonet assault. The reloading process was so long and the distance between the hostile lines so small that the enemy might close while the troops were reloading if none had reserved their fire. At times an assaulting force like the Hessians at Fort Mercer would not attempt to fire but would rush forward and try to close at once. In the earlier years of the Revolution the British bayonet charge was greatly feared by the Americans. On their part the Americans, many of whom had long been expert in the handling of their rifles, adopted the practice of taking aim at individual officers instead of merely at the enemy ranks.

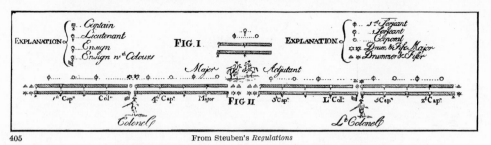

405   From Steuben's *Regulations*

REVOLUTIONARY BATTLE FORMATION

As tactics are always dependent upon the arms used, the character of the firelock determined the nature of the battle formation. Men advanced into conflict in close order, shoulder to shoulder, as though on parade. The fire-fight began at a little more than a hundred yards; the ultimate object being to close with the enemy in bayonet assault. Steuben's diagrams and explanations of the formation of a company and a regiment give a picture of Washington's army after Valley Forge.

"*Of the Formation of a Company.* (Figure I)   A company is to be formed in two ranks, at one pace distance, with the tallest men in the rear, and both ranks sized, with the shortest men of each in the centre. A company thus drawn up is to be divided into two sections or platoons [normally of thirty four men each]; the captain to take post on the right of the platoon, covered by a sergeant; the lieutenant on the right of the second platoon, also covered by a sergeant; the ensign four paces behind the centre of the company; the first sergeant two paces behind the centre of the first platoon, and the eldest corporal two paces behind the second platoon; the other two corporals are to be on the flanks of the front rank." "*Of the Formation of a Regiment.* (Figure II) A regiment is to consist of eight companies, which are to be posted in the following order, from right to left. First captain's. Colonel's. [Each field officer, besides his other duties, commanded a company.] Fourth captain's. Major's. Third captain's. Lieutenant-Colonel's. Fifth captain's. Second captain's. For the greater facility of maneuvering, each regiment consisting of more than one hundred and sixty files, is to be formed into two battalions, . . . with an interval of twenty paces between them, and one colour posted in the centre of each battalion; the colonel fifteen paces before the centre of the first battalion; the lieutenant-colonel fifteen paces before the centre of the second battalion; the major fifteen paces behind the interval of the two battalions; the adjutant two paces from the major; the drum and fife-major two paces behind the centre of the first battalion; their places behind the second battalion being supplied by a drum and fife; and the other drums and fifes equally divided on the wings of each battalion." — *Regulations*, 1779.

THE DUTIES OF LIGHT CAVALRY

THOMAS SIMES in his *Military Guide for Young Officers*, a two-volume treatise published in Philadelphia the first year of the war, gives the following uses for which light cavalry should be employed: — "in reconnoitering the enemy and discovering his motions" [they are also on such expeditions to avoid engaging with the enemy] "to be made use of for distant advanced posts to prevent the army from being falsely alarmed and surprised"; "small patrols to be kept going around the army to prevent desertion. Parties are also to be sent out to distress the enemy by depriving them of forage and provisions, by surprising their convoys, attacking their baggage, harrassing them on the march, cutting off small detachments, and sometimes carrying off

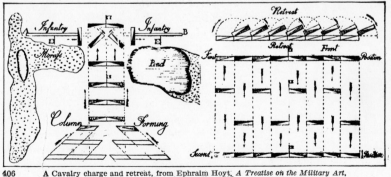

406   A Cavalry charge and retreat, from Ephraim Hoyt, *A Treatise on the Military Art*,
Brattleboro, Vt., 1798

foraging parties. Light cavalry are moreover to be employed in raising contributions, and when the army marches they may compose the advance guard, and when other troops cannot be spared, they may form the rear guard or cover the baggage." Very often, as in the southern campaigns, the cavalry was used in conjunction with infantry detachments.

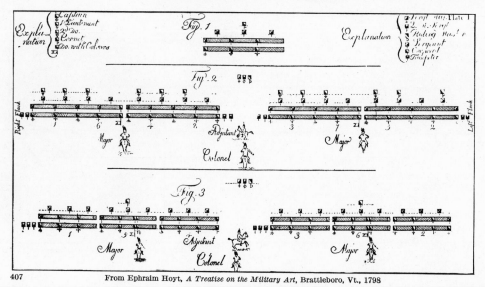

407   From Ephraim Hoyt, *A Treatise on the Military Art*, Brattleboro, Vt., 1798

CAVALRY FORMATIONS

IDEAL formations, such as those pictured in the diagram, were seldom met with in the actual forces that American commanders were compelled to depend on in their strategic maneuvers. Desertion and casualties depleted the ranks of the few American cavalry units. Yet the diagram is valuable in showing the general framework toward which the cavalry commanders were striving. Figure I shows the unit of "the troop" with the captain, the second lieutenant, and the first lieutenant, and behind them, the various non-commissioned officers. It is significant also that the regiment of cavalry could be drawn up in two ways; either as in Figure 2, where, according to Steuben's instructions, it was to consist of eight troops; or, as in Figure 3, when it followed the Prussian Regulations and consisted of six troops.

"Light-Horse Harry," hero of Paulus Hook and of many cavalry encounters in the South, should also be remembered as a soldier who appreciated the need of discipline and training. At the end of the war he wrote this judgment on those who herded armed mobs to the front: "Convinced as I am that a government is the murderer of its citizens which sends them to the field uninformed and untaught, where they are to meet men of the same age and strength, mechanized by education and discipline for battle, I cannot withhold my denunciation of its wickedness and folly."

408   Henry Lee, 1756–1818, from the portrait by C. W. Peale in Independence Hall, Philadelphia

409   A Revolutionary Gun and Carriage, courtesy of the Commandant, Governor's Island, New York

ARTILLERY

THE cannon of the Revolution were small and their range was short. Their chief defect, however, was their lack of mobility. Their most effective use was for the defense or reduction of forts. In the give-and-take of a swiftly moving battle in the open the clumsy cannon were less efficient. In such a conflict they were usually placed between regiments or battalions in the infantry firing line, or sometimes even put into position in front of the line. So placed, they aided in the protection of the flanks and helped in the fire-fight by throwing metal into the ranks of the enemy. But the modern artillery barrage, or the harassing of communications behind a deployed line, was quite unknown to the Revolutionary artilleryman.

HENRY KNOX, 1750–1806

At the Battle of Long Island Knox's artillery regiment counted four hundred and six men. But there were hardly any trained gunners, while the guns were "of various patterns and calibres, second-hand and neglected, or hastily fabricated." Henry Knox was a Boston boy, prominent as an athlete, bookseller, and member of the crack local battery. From Bunker Hill onward he fought all through the Revolution, from which he emerged as the chief of all artillery commanders. "The resources of his genius supplied the defect of means" was Washington's well-earned compliment. We meet Knox again and again, and always among the skillful and the best.

410 Henry Knox, from the portrait by C.W. Peale in Independence Hall, Philadelphia

THE CASTING OF CANNON

The colonists had depended for their supply of cannon on England. From the outbreak of the Revolution to the entry of the French, the Continental troops had to depend for the most part on home supplies, reinforced only by occasional captures of British cannon on the high seas. Again, as in the case of the supply of powder, the Pennsylvania Germans responded to the emergency. The Durham Iron Works, directed by Taylor & Bachouse, manufactured small brass swivel cannon, cannon balls, and gun barrels. The Warwick Furnace of Chester County, Pennsylvania, was in constant operation, casting for the government cannon and cannon balls; and it was here that the American army retreated after the defeat at Brandywine. During 1776 sixty cannon of 12 and 18-pound caliber were cast, and soon afterward the first four-pounders in America. Close by were the Cornwall Furnace, the Elizabeth Furnace of Baron Stiegel, and in Middlesex, Cumberland County, the furnace of William Douing, where the first wrought iron cannon were made.

411 Revolutionary Cannon, cast at Cornwall Furnace, Pa., now on estate of Richard Freeman, Cornwall

THE FRENCH SUPPLY
POWDER

Without a plentiful supply of powder the artillery was doomed to silence in the important crisis of a battle. The crude, hastily constructed factories in the colonies were inadequate. Years of organization were a necessary background to a smoothly running plant. France, naturally, by years of output, had become most proficient in her routine. After the Treaty of Alliance in 1778 she supplied the colonies not only with cannon and muskets but with a more plentiful supply of powder. Factory conditions by 1778 had changed very little from the time of Saint-Rémy, the Master of Artillery under Louis XIV. The illustration shows the various stages in the manufacture of saltpeter.

412   French Powder Factory, from *Mémoires d'Artillerie, recueillis par le Sr. Surirey de St-Rémy*, Paris, 1697

A. Plaster piled up, to be broken to pieces. B. Little wagon which brings the plaster and the earths from the town. C. Workers who break up the plaster and pound the earth. D. Worker who sifts the Plaster & the Earths after they are broken up. E, F. Worker who carries this broken earth to the Tubs. G. Tubs. H. Receptacles. I. Worker who draws water to fill the Tubs. K. Worker who carries the water. L. Worker who pours out the receptacles into a cask.

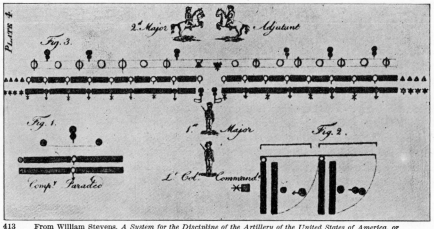

413   From William Stevens, *A System for the Discipline of the Artillery of the United States of America, or the Young Artillerists' Pocket Companion*, New York, 1797

ARTILLERY FORMATIONS

THE formation of the artillery regiment was the same in theory during the Revolution as it was later in 1797, when William Stevens published his *Young Artillerists' Pocket Companion*. Figure 3 shows a typical artillery regiment, as it would have been, had there been no wounded or killed or deserters. "When a regiment is reduced to 160 files, it is to be formed in one battalion with both colors in the center, the Colonel 16 paces before the colors, the Lt. Colonel eight paces behind the Colonel, the Major fifteen paces behind the center of the battalion, having the adjutant at his side. The Drum and Fife Major is stationed two paces behind the center of the battalion, and the drums & fifes equally divided on the wings. Every battalion is in four divisions and eight platoons, no platoon to consist of less than ten files."

414   From Benson J. Lossing, *The Pictorial Field Book of the Revolution*, New York, 1855

AMERICAN FLOATING BATTERY

LOSSING, in his *Field Book of the Revolution* (p. 575), gives the following account of this floating battery. "I am indebted to the kindness of Peter Force, Esq., of Washington city (editor of *The American Archives*), for this drawing of one of the American floating batteries used in the siege of Boston. It is copied from an English manuscript in his possession, and is now published for the first time. I have never met with a description of those batteries, and can judge of their construction only from the drawing. They appear to have been made of strong planks, pierced, near the water-line, for oars; along the sides, higher up, for light and musketry. A heavy gun was placed in each end, and upon the top were four swivels."

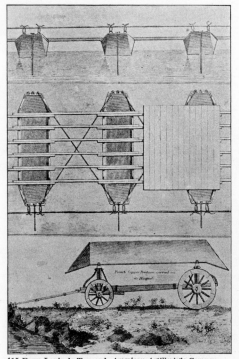

415 From Louis de Tousard, *American Artillerist's Companion, or Elements of Artillery*, Philadelphia, 1809–13

ENGINEERS AID GUNNERS

GUN pontoons bring engineers to the aid of gunners, who often had to ferry their batteries across the many lakes and rivers. These diagrams are from the more elaborate designs of a generation later than the rough-and-ready Revolutionary army, being from Louis de Tousard's *American Artillerist's Companion, or Elements of Artillery*, Philadelphia, 1809–13. But the essentials were the same in both generations.

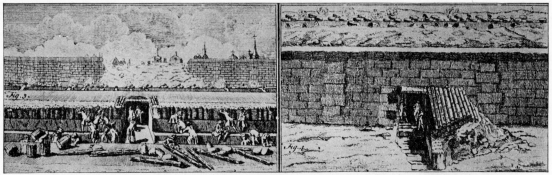

416   From Le Bland, *The Military Engineer or a Treatise on the Attack & Defense of all Kinds of Fortified Places*, composed by M. Le Bland,
Professor of Mathematics for the Use of the French Noblisse (Translated into English — London, 1759)

ENGINEERING CORPS ORGANIZED

UNTIL the entry of the French into the war, trench and siege warfare were conducted either by the artillery or the infantry officer who at the moment happened to be at all versed in the subject. The crudest sorts of trenches and defenses were resorted to; Washington in one of the early battles used a defense of cornstalks, from behind which his men fired. But with the arrival of the French, many of them members of the "Corps du Génie" which Vauban had organized, the American authorities began to attempt a systematization of engineering problems.   On May 27, 1778, Congress authorized that in the Engineering Department three companies be established, "to be instructed in the fabrication of field-works, as far as relates to the manual or mechanical part. Their business shall be to instruct the fatigue parties to do their duties with celerity & exactness, to repair injuries done to the works by the enemies' fire and to prosecute works in the face of it." This corps was organized and conducted primarily by the French, especially Radière, Du Portail, Du Cambray, and by the great Kosciuszko. The headquarters were at West Point.

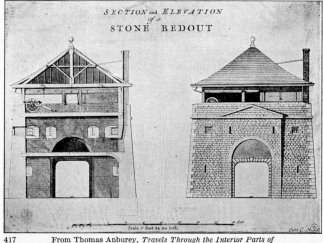

417   From Thomas Anburey, *Travels Through the Interior Parts of
America . . . , 1789*

FORTIFICATIONS

THE forts of the Revolution did not differ in principle from those of the French and Indian War; and in fact many of them dated from the earlier conflict. They varied from solid masonry structures, like that at Crown Point, to the hastily prepared field fortification. The blockhouse, the invention of the American wilderness, served well the purposes of the frontier. For another example of a well developed field fortification see Number 24.

WEST POINT CHAIN BOOM

At West Point is still to be seen a part of the famous chain which was stretched across to Garrison in April, 1778, to prevent the British from sailing up the Hudson. This chain was made by Noble, Townshend, & Co., at the Stirling Ironworks near Sloatsburg, twenty-five miles southwest from West Point. It was carried in pieces to New Windsor in wagons, then unloaded and sent down on floats to West Point, where, under the supervision of the French engineering experts, it was assembled. The links are of two-inch, square, bar-iron and average one hundred and twenty pounds each.

418   From a photograph

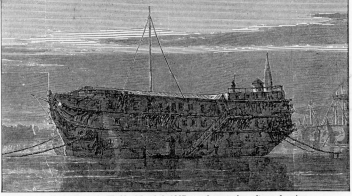

419   From *Harper's Weekly*, March 9, 1867, wood engraving after a drawing
                                    by Charles Parsons

THE BRITISH PRISON SHIP
JERSEY

War inevitably brings with it the capture of prisoners and the problem of caring for these unfortunates. New York city which, after its capture in 1776, was G. H. Q. for the British armies in America throughout the war was the center to which the greater part of those captured in campaigns were brought. The common jails were speedily full. A cheap and practical solution was the fitting up of the hulk of a ship which could be moored off shore. The British used several such vessels anchored off the beach of what is now Brooklyn. Escape from them was extremely difficult on account of the water which had to be traversed. In a day when the private soldier was not treated with the care that characterizes later generations it was too much to expect that the prisons would be healthful, or that the prisoners would be treated with any great consideration. Many tales of horror have come down of those times; of prisoners on hot nights crowded about the grating at the hatchway to get a breath of air, of desperate attempts to escape, which infuriated the Hessian guards and led to brutalities; of the living and the dead lying together in the stifling holds until the latter were buried. Doubtless such stories are true; but they are more significant as evidence of the general prison conditions of the age than of the ferocity of the British captors. One who reads the pleas of the contemporary prison reformer, Howard, will find terrible practices a commonplace in all the jails of the time.

NEWGATE, THE CONNECTICUT PRISON

The British also made their charges of inhumanity against the Americans. Near East Granby in Connecticut is an old colonial copper mine which was used during the Revolution as a place of detention for Loyalists, who would naturally be more harshly treated than other prisoners of war. An anonymous writer in the *Political Magazine* of London for October, 1781, gave the English public an account of the horrors of the place. "The prisoners are let down on a windlass into this dismal cavern, through an hole, which answers the triple purpose of conveying them food, air, and — I was going to say light — but it scarcely reaches them. In a few months the prisoners are released by death, and the colony rejoices in her great humanity and the mildness of her laws. This conclave of imprisoned spirits may be called, with great propriety, 'the catacomb of Connecticut.' . . . The subterranean Vault over which this place is built was wrought about the middle of the 17th Century for the purpose of obtaining Copper Ore, the opening into those Gloomy Caverns is a Desent of 35 feet; from thence Desending in various Serpentine Directions 75 yards, opens to the Well, is in depth 74 feet from the Surface to the Water." The second largest house is the surface section of the guard room. One needs but to go down into the dark passages beneath the crumbling walls of old Newgate prison to sense the horror of captivity there. Britishers and Loyalists would naturally say the worst about this prison, "commonly called Hell," in just the same way as Patriots would say the worst about the *Jersey*.

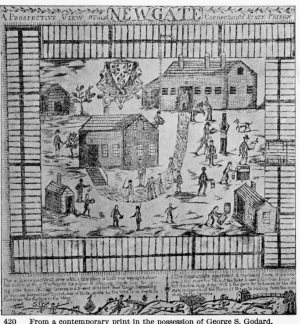

420   From a contemporary print in the possession of George S. Godard,
                      State Librarian, Hartford, Conn.

CHAPTER VIII

THE FINAL CAMPAIGNS IN THE NORTH, 1778–80

ON February 6, 1776, Benjamin Franklin in Paris had the satisfaction of putting his name to the first treaty of alliance negotiated by the United States. He had arrived in the brilliant capital a little more than a year before to take from the clumsy hands of the Connecticut Yankee, Silas Deane, the delicate negotiations with the great Bourbon monarchy, the inveterate enemy of England. Englishmen were not pleased to learn that Dr. Franklin had come on such a mission for they feared him in the diplomat's rôle as they would have no other American. Yet, when he arrived, it seemed as though even the persuasive Franklin must fail to enlist France openly in the cause of the revolting Americans. In the winter of 1776–77 when the Philadelphia philosopher was establishing himself in the society of the gay capital, his fellow countryman, Washington, was working desperately to organize and train the remnant of an army at Morristown in New Jersey. The campaign of 1776 had been a tragedy relieved only by the successful counter-attacks at Trenton and Princeton. The prospect for 1777 was gloomy indeed. When Franklin hinted that France might serve herself by coming to the aid of the Americans, he was informed in effect that his people must demonstrate the possibility of ultimate success. France wisely decided to test the strength and temper of the American rebels before embarking upon the uncertainties of war.

Meanwhile secret French aid to the Americans went on as it had before the arrival of Franklin. Vergennes, the Foreign Minister, was the chief responsible governmental official involved. His efficient agent was none other than the author, Beaumarchais, who screened his activities behind the rather fantastic Spanish name of Roderigue Hortalez & Company. From the Paris warehouse of this alleged firm vast quantities of munitions and clothing, not to speak of cannon, found their way to Marie Antoinette's "dear republicans" across the sea. Franklin watched this aid with satisfaction and bided his time. Finally came the news of Burgoyne's disaster. French enthusiasm waxed as Frenchmen read the details of those battles in which New England farmers had humbled the pride of that "insolent nation" across the Channel. They rejoiced when their government threw off the mask and spoke to England in the old familiar terms of war. The treaty stipulated that neither party should make peace without the consent of the other. The French alliance immediately changed the character of the war. The British navy had now to reckon actively with the French fleet. No longer could the British transfer their armies from port to port on the American coast without fear of communication being cut. Moreover, the other outlying parts of the empire now required even more vigilant guarding, which meant fewer British reinforcements in America.

The consequences of Burgoyne's surrender at Saratoga are evidence of what momentous international consequences sometimes flow from mistakes in the planning and execution of military campaigns. Germain knew, as did every responsible government officer, that, from the outbreak of the rebellion in America, the trading nations of Europe — France, Spain, and Holland — had been covertly hostile to Great Britain. He knew that for many months France had been more or less secretly aiding the revolutionists in America. The danger of foreign intervention had compelled him to hold both naval and military forces in readiness to guard India, the West Indies, and even Britain itself against sudden attack. Under such circumstances the war in America must be conducted with extreme caution, as a defeat would be more than ordinarily important. In spite of such an international situation, however, Germain, together with his fellow ministers, the king, and Burgoyne developed a plan in which an important army under Burgoyne was subjected to grave and quite unnecessary risks, while the coöperating army under Howe was permitted to embark upon an independent enterprise and put itself beyond supporting distance of the northern force. Such was the prelude to the entry of France into the war as the open ally of the Americans. It was England's fortune in this conflict to pay more than once the extreme penalty for the blunders of her leaders.

When the French ambassador at London told the British government with studied insolence of tone that the United States were by their own declaration independent and took his departure, the English people were deeply moved. They roused themselves to combat the ancient enemy. The entry of France did not make a British victory impossible. The British navy, though sadly deteriorated, and unprepared, was superior to the rival fleet. England might still confidently hope to control the sea. Allied armies are notorious for difficulties in effective coöperation. A powerful British force in America, if well supplied and well led, might still destroy the Revolutionary armies, even though they were supported by French troops. Moreover, time was on the side of England. The Revolutionary government was weak; its resources were limited. War is at best a costly business; and the borrowing power of Congress must ultimately be exhausted. Of course France would and did lend money as a means of furthering the conflict; but French resources were themselves limited. The Patriots in America had demonstrated that they could not be bought off with concessions or frightened by force. But they were weakened by the Loyalists living side by side with them; and active and passive Loyalists together probably comprised nearly one-third of the whole population. If one or two British armies could be maintained intact in America for a considerable period, the Revolution might die of inanition. In the event, it nearly did. If British political and military leadership could have avoided disaster, the war might have been brought to at least a partly successful conclusion.

But such hopes were destined not to be realized. The entry of France turned a rebellion into a world war the problems of which were too difficult to be solved by the men who controlled the destiny of Britain. The need of a great man was never more imperative in the history of the British people but no Pitt appeared at Whitehall, no Nelson on the sea, and no Wellington on land. In the end the British Empire was rent asunder, and the English-speaking peoples took their different ways into the future.

THE FRENCH ALLIANCE AND THE TURN
OF THE TIDE, 1778

FROM the very day that peace was signed in 1763 (No. 214) the French were looking for the first signs of weakness in the British Empire overseas. Choiseul, under Louis XV, and then Vergennes, under Louis XVI, were always on the keen alert (see Vol. VIII, page 117). Five years before the Boston Tea Party (see Vol. VIII), the Baron de Kalb came out to see how the American Colonies reacted to the presence of a threatening fleet and other signs of ministerial pressure. Louis XVI and Vergennes took up the reins in 1774. Next year Vergennes submitted an impassioned memorandum in which he urged the new king to seize every possible opportunity to reduce the power and greatness of England. "It is a duty for us to do so . . . now is our opportunity . . .

the Americans are at war with their central government." He then urged an alliance with Spain for the same ends; and suggested secret aid to the Americans immediately, if an open rupture was impolitic just yet or even at all. Sympathy and secret aid would encourage the Americans, who, even if left alone and defeated, would be friendly toward France and embittered toward England. In the same momentous year Benjamin Franklin went to France as the accredited agent of the Continental Congress, with excellent results in furthering French coöperation. Then Beaumarchais stepped in as the master-munitioneer; Vergennes negotiated French and Spanish loans; enthusiasm for the Patriot cause increased in France, and nothing was needed but some spectacular event to bring on the alliance. Finally came Saratoga; and the die was cast. But Saratoga in itself did not reveal the fundamental force on which the Patriotic arms depended. That force was Washington's Continental army, the mere survival of which was fatal to the ministerial cause. France and the continuance of Washington's army were both essential to ultimate victory.

425 Tory Pandemonium, engraving by E. Tisdale, in
     John Trumbull, *M'Fingal*, New York, 1795

THE LOYALISTS

THE French alliance blasted the hopes of the Loyalists. One of the saddest aspects of the Revolution was that civil war which rent communities and even families. Throughout the conflict, as the Patriot cause triumphed in colony after colony, the "Tories" felt the heavy hand of persecution. Frequently they were driven from their homes and reviled by the neighbors who had once been their friends. The great Loyalist landed estates, such as those of the Philipses, the Delanceys, and the Robinsons of New York, which had been acquired during the colonial period, were seized by the revolutionary state governments and held until the end of the war, when, through commissions especially appointed for the purpose, they were divided up and sold to numerous small buyers. Many were the women of gentle breeding who succumbed to the hardships of the refugee's lot or the harshness of the new conditions of life. In Canada the exiles who came to Nova Scotia and the region of the Great Lakes are still known by the title of United Empire Loyalists. Their sufferings left a heritage of bitterness that lasted through several generations; and it was their immediate descendants who formed the backbone of the best Canadian militia in what is now Ontario all through the War of 1812.

THE EVACUATION OF PHILADELPHIA

THE French alliance by bringing the naval power of France into the war made the retention of Philadelphia impossible. The concentration of the British forces at New York was necessary. So on June 18, 1778, Clinton assembled his army south of Philadelphia, crossed the Delaware River, and started on his march to New York. A large number of Loyalist refugees had already been sent by transport under Admiral Lord Howe. Clinton's force was unusually encumbered with baggage, as officers and men wished to take with them many of the things they had accumulated in their long stay in the Quaker city. Clinton traveled on two parallel roads, making for New Brunswick. Washington on the nineteenth moved out of Valley Forge and hastened toward New Brunswick by roads on Clinton's left. The British army moved slowly, partly because of the obstructions placed in its path by militia falling back in front of them, and partly because its baggage train was twelve miles long. For six days the race continued as the two armies marched through a fierce summer heat. The last day found Washington squarely in front of Clinton at Allentown, a few miles east of Trenton. Clinton changed his plan and headed east for Sandy Hook. He now had but one road to use. On this he put his baggage train, under the command of Knyphausen, following himself with the main body. The British commander had fifteen thousand men, his opponent a somewhat smaller number. Washington believed the time ripe for a swift attack while his enemy was embarrassed by his unwieldy train.

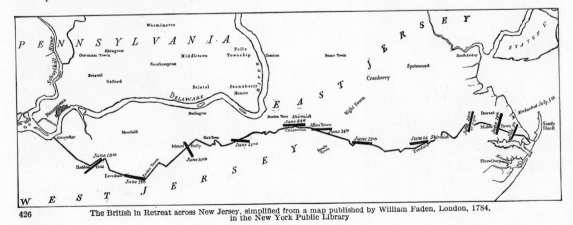

426   The British in Retreat across New Jersey, simplified from a map published by William Faden, London, 1784,
                                in the New York Public Library

BRITISH AND HESSIAN UNIFORMS IN THE WAR OF INDEPENDENCE 1775-1783

PRIVATE
5TH FOOT

LIGHT INFANTRY
10TH FOOT

GRENADIER
40TH FOOT

TROOPER
16TH LT. DRAGOONS

LINE OFFICER
23RD FOOT
(FUSILEERS)

GENERAL
OFFICER

CAPTAIN
17TH FOOT

REGT.
PRINZ FRIEDRICH
OFFICER
(BRUNSWICK)

GRENADIER
REGT. VON RALL
(HESSIAN)

DRAGOON
PRIVATE
(BRUNSWICK)

ERB-PRINZ
FUSILEER REGT.
(HESSIAN)

ADMIRAL
BRITISH NAVY

CAPTAIN
BRITISH NAVY

SEAMAN
BRITISH NAVY

Painted expressly for *The Pageant of America* by H. A. Ogden

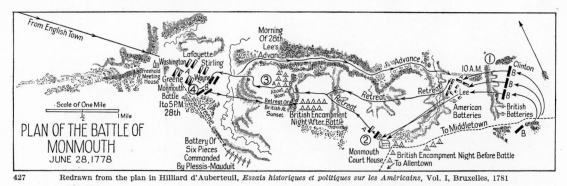

427   Redrawn from the plan in Hilliard d'Auberteuil, *Essais historiques et politiques sur les Américains*, Vol. I, Bruxelles, 1781

LEE AT THE BATTLE OF MONMOUTH, JUNE 28

WASHINGTON estimated that Clinton, because of the necessity of defending his heavy baggage train, could use only about half his troops for a battle. Lafayette commanded the American advance guard. On the evening of June 25 General Charles Lee, who had recently rejoined the army after having been exchanged, requested the command, and Washington complied. On June 26 Lee received orders to move the following morning and to attack the rear of Clinton's column vigorously. The attack would be supported by the main body of the army. At five in the afternoon of June 26, Lee informed his generals that practically nothing was known of the terrain and that orders would be issued by himself on the field in the morning. During the time which intervened between this and the battle he made no personal reconnaissance nor did he have any maps prepared. By seven in the morning Lee's force, which seems to have been a little more than a third of the whole army, was on the road. Not long thereafter an advance detachment which had moved out earlier was in contact with the enemy northeast of Monmouth Court House. A few points stand out among the confused events which followed. Lee advanced to a position marked (1) on the map (No. 427). On the march he was hampered by lack of knowledge of the country and by conflicting information from the front. At, (1) he engaged a strong rear guard of the enemy which he sought to capture by maneuver. As his attack was developing, he sent Washington a report that things were going well at the front. The British were heavily reinforced, though they do not seem to have outnumbered Lee. At this crisis, about ten in the morning, the troop movements which Lee ordered were fatally lacking in coördination. He lost touch with some of his units. The British turned Lee's right flank, which was in the air. A retreat developed due primarily to Lee's mismanagement though some of his subordinates were also culpable. Lee planned to re-form on the west bank of the ravine with his right at Monmouth Court House, thinking the houses of the village were of stone. They were of wood (which a reconnaissance would have brought out) and hence not suitable for the development of a strong point. At this stage (2) the retreat became a general retirement, some units, unknown to Lee, following a more northerly route. Lee did not notify Washington of the changed aspect of the battle. The British under Cornwallis and with the aid of cavalry pressed the Americans hard. For the most part the retirement seems to have been in good order though some units were out of control. Washington's main army was meanwhile on the march, Stirling advancing on the road which Lee had followed in the morning and Greene on a route which would take him to a position south of Monmouth Court House.

428   From the painting *Battle of Monmouth* (*Washington Rebukes Lee*), by John Ward Dunsmore (1856–). © by the artist

A little before noon Washington accidentally heard of the retreat. He hastened toward the front, confronted Lee, and demanded to know the reason for the retreat. The commander in chief was not satisfied by Lee's replies. Washington pushed on and began to organize at (3) a stand that would check the assaulting British while the main army could form for battle. Without at the time formally relieving Lee of command, Washington, in effect, took charge of the troops. His measures were effective; the British advance was held up long enough to enable Washington to get his units into position. Greene was halted on the right on advantageous ground (shown by the battery in the map). Stirling was on the left and Wayne, who had been with Lee, was in the center at (4).

429 Wayne's Stand at Monmouth, bronze tablet by James E. Kelly on
the Monmouth (N. J.) Battle Monument

THE BRITISH DEFEAT AT MONMOUTH

IN late afternoon at the critical phase of the battle Cornwallis delivered a piecemeal attack. Pushing past Washington's delaying force, he struck Stirling, attempted to envelop the American left, and was repulsed with a bayonet charge. Then forming his full force, which had come up, he attacked Wayne and Greene simultaneously. A deadly artillery fire and a determined stand by the American infantry threw back this attack. Two more unsuccessful assaults were made against Wayne, in the last of which Lieutenant-Colonel Monckton was killed, while his troops suffered severely. Followed by fresh American troops, the British then retired and encamped. They moved out at midnight. By dawn they had made a surprising march of thirteen miles. A court-martial suspended Lee for a year for disobedience and "misbehaviour" before the enemy. Later, because of an improper letter, Congress dismissed him from the army.

WASHINGTON'S POSITIONS COVERING NEW YORK

THANKS to Lee's blundering at Monmouth, Clinton reached Sandy Hook without further molestation. From there his army was taken by boat to Manhattan where, on June 30, the fleet under Admiral Howe arrived from Philadelphia. Washington marched leisurely to Haverstraw, crossed the Hudson, and on July 22 established camp at White Plains. By the end of the summer of 1778 Washington and his enemy were in positions which, except for the Yorktown campaign, they were to occupy for five years, that is, till the very end of the war. Washington's army, however, was not the sole factor holding Clinton within his defenses at New York. In fact, he could have taken the offensive at any time had it not been for the French fleet. Unlike Howe, Clinton had to reckon with the chances of a temporary loss of the British command of the sea. This danger had forced the abandonment of Philadelphia. Clinton would have liked to draw in the isolated British detachment at Newport. But his orders from Germain did not permit it. During the winter of 1778–79 Washington, with headquarters again at White Plains, distributed his army in a semicircle of cantonments which reached from Danbury, Connecticut, his extreme left, to Middlebrook in New Jersey, his extreme right. The difficulties in the way of feeding the army were the reason for this dispersal; but the detachments were near enough to be within supporting distance of one another. West Point was fortified and developed as the center of the position. So long as the Americans held this bluff overlooking the Hudson, communication between New England and the middle states could not be interrupted.

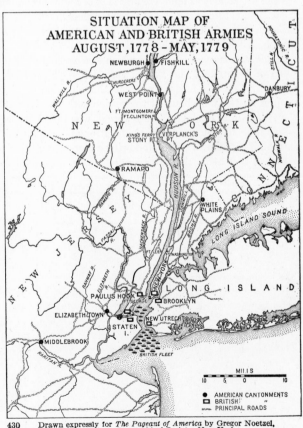

SITUATION MAP OF
AMERICAN AND BRITISH ARMIES
AUGUST, 1778 - MAY, 1779

MILES
10 5 0   10

● AMERICAN CANTONMENTS
□ BRITISH   "
━━━ PRINCIPAL ROADS

430   Drawn expressly for The Pageant of America by Gregor Noetzel,
American Geographical Society, New York

THE BRITISH AT NEWPORT

THE British army had occupied Newport since August, 1776. To this day the reason for its retention still remains something of a mystery. It may have been due to a desire merely to retain a foothold in New England, believed to be the center of the rebellion. Perhaps confused ideas of American geography played a part. At any rate Germain in London, and probably the king, rather than the commanders in America, were responsible for keeping a considerable British force isolated on the Rhode Island coast, in a place of little military significance, and unable to coöperate in active campaigns. The unnecessary risks involved were made clear when D'Estaing with a French fleet arrived in American waters shortly after Clinton had reassembled his entire force at New York.

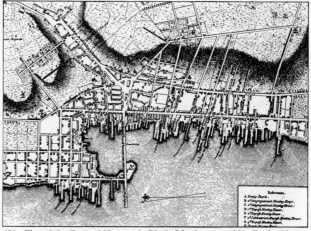

431   Plan of the Town of Newport in Rhode Island, surveyed by Charles Blaskowitz and published by William Faden, London, 1777, in the *Atlas of the Battles of the American Revolution*, in Yale University Library

432   Comte D' (Charles Hector) Estaing, 1729–94, from an engraving after the portrait by F. Sublet

FAILURE OF THE FIRST FRANCO–AMERICAN COMBINATION, 1778

WHILE Clinton was still preparing for the evacuation of Philadelphia, D'Estaing, who, on April 25, had sailed from Toulon with four thousand soldiers, five frigates, and twelve ships of the line, was crossing the Atlantic toward the Delaware capes. Admiral Howe, knowing of his approach, had hastened his own departure and, with his men-of-war and transports, had cleared the capes ten days before the arrival of the French on July 8 (see map, No. 433). D'Estaing then sailed to New York, anchoring off Sandy Hook on the 11th. His fleet was stronger than Howe's; but the French commander had been trained as a soldier rather than a sailor. Mahan has implied that, had a Nelson or a Farragut been in command, the French fleet would have entered the harbor and given battle, which might have resulted in the defeat of Howe and the capture of Clinton's army by a combined French and American force. But such events were not to be. D'Estaing waited eleven days outside of Sandy Hook and sailed away. It is only fair to add that he vainly offered the then enormous sum of a hundred and fifty thousand francs to anyone who would pilot his big ships into New York. He had arranged with Washington for a joint attack on Newport. On August 8 Sullivan arrived before that city with about ten thousand men (see map, No. 433) and with Greene and Lafayette as his chief subordinates. D'Estaing was about to land his troops when Howe's fleet was observed approaching. The French admiral promptly put off for battle; but carried his soldiers with him. For two days the fleets maneuvered. On August 12 both were severely damaged by a heavy storm, and Howe put back to New York. D'Estaing, returning to Newport on August 20, informed the American commanders that he must go to Boston for repairs. In vain Lafayette pleaded with him to land his soldiers, defeat the British, and then proceed to Boston. The Frenchman's action caused bitter feelings in New England. Sullivan, who had closed with his enemy and begun siege operations, at once began to retire. The British, commanded by Pigot, came out from behind their redoubts and on August 29 (Battle of Rhode Island) attacked the Americans without success. Two days later Clinton, who had arrived with reinforcements, took all the British back to New York. On November 4 D'Estaing slipped out of Boston harbor for the West Indies. Admiral Byron, who in June had brought a squadron across the Atlantic to reinforce Howe, had met a storm off Sandy Hook and had put back to Halifax to refit. In late October, his ships repaired, he was off Boston to blockade D'Estaing, when another storm dispersed his fleet, and the Frenchman escaped.

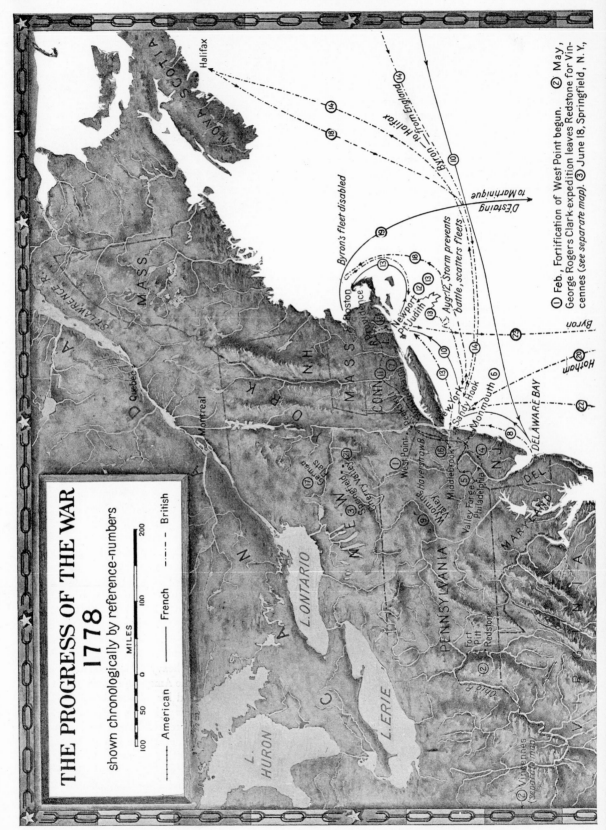

THE PROGRESS OF THE WAR
1778

shown chronologically by reference-numbers

MILES

———— American
+++++ French
-·-·- British

① Feb., Fortification of West Point begun. ② May, George Rogers Clark expedition leaves Redstone for Vincennes (see separate map). ③ June 18, Springfield, N. Y.

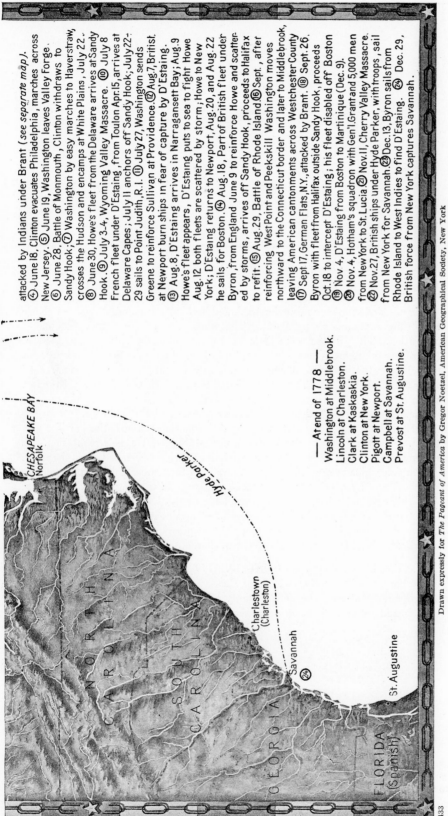

attacked by Indians under Brant (*see separate map*).
④ June 18, Clinton evacuates Philadelphia, marches across New Jersey. ⑤ June 19, Washington leaves Valley Forge. ⑥ June 28, Battle of Monmouth, Clinton withdraws to Sandy Hook; ⑦ Washington by easy marches to Haverstraw, crosses the Hudson and encamps at White Plains, July 22. ⑧ June 30, Howe's fleet from the Delaware arrives at Sandy Hook. ⑨ July 3-4, Wyoming Valley Massacre. ⑩ July 8 French fleet under D'Estaing, from Toulon Apr.15, arrives at Delaware Capes; July 11 anchors off Sandy Hook; July 22-29 sails to Point Judith, R.I. ⑪ July 27, Washington sends Greene to reinforce Sullivan at Providence. ⑫ Aug.7, British at Newport burn ships in fear of capture by D'Estaing. ⑬ Aug.8, D'Estaing arrives in Narragansett Bay; Aug.9 Howe's fleet appears, D'Estaing puts to sea to fight Howe Aug.12 both fleets are scattered by storm; Howe to New York; D'Estaing returns to Newport, Aug.20, and Aug.22 he sails for Boston. ⑭ Aug.18, Part of British fleet under Byron, from England June 9 to reinforce Howe and scattered by storms, arrives off Sandy Hook, proceeds to Halifax to refit. ⑮ Aug.29, Battle of Rhode Island ⑯ Sept., after reinforcing West Point and Peekskill Washington moves northward to the Connecticut border and later to Middlebrook, leaving American cantonments across Westchester County ⑰ Sept.17, German Flats, N.Y., attacked by Brant. ⑱ Sept.26. Byron with fleet from Halifax outside Sandy Hook, proceeds Oct.18 to intercept D'Estaing; his fleet disabled off Boston ⑲ Nov.4, D'Estaing from Boston to Martinique (Dec.9). ⑳ Nov.4, Hotham's squadron with Gen'l.Grant and 5,000 men from New York to St. Lucia ㉑ Nov.11, Cherry Valley Massacre. ㉒ Nov.27, British ships under Hyde Parker, with troops, sail from New York for Savannah. ㉓ Dec.13, Byron sails from Rhode Island to West Indies to find D'Estaing. ㉔ Dec.29, British force from New York captures Savannah.

— At end of 1778 —
Washington at Middlebrook.
Lincoln at Charleston.
Clark at Kaskaskia.
Clinton at New York.
Pigott at Newport.
Campbell at Savannah.
Prevost at St. Augustine.

CHESAPEAKE BAY
Norfolk

N O R T H   C A R O L I N A

S O U T H   C A R O L I N A

G E O R G I A

FLORIDA (Spanish)

Charlestown (Charleston)

Savannah

St. Augustine

Hyde Parker

433

Drawn expressly for *The Pageant of America* by Gregor Noetzel, American Geographical Society, New York

PROGRESS OF THE WAR IN 1778

THOUGH the French Alliance was the greatest feature of 1778, and Monmouth its greatest battle (No. 428), following the British evacuation of Philadelphia, there were many other significant operations, such as the massacres of Wyoming and Cherry valley (No. 447) which resulted in the winning of the West, the operations at Rhode Island, the moves and countermoves in the neighborhood of New York, and the British capture of Savannah (No. 439), George Rogers Clark's expedition to Vincennes (No. 459). The first third of 1778 was one of Howe's most inactive periods. To his Whiggish politico-military mind the occupation of the "rebel capital" would help to make the Revolutionists think better of their own extreme opinions. But the Patriot party was too strong for any reconstruction on his political lines; while the reinforcement of the Patriot army by the naval and military forces of France was also far too strong for any hopes he might still entertain of winning the war by passive or defensive means alone.

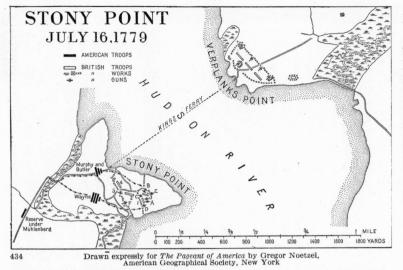

STONY POINT
JULY 16, 1779

▬ AMERICAN TROOPS
▭ BRITISH TROOPS
   " WORKS
   " GUNS

434   Drawn expressly for *The Pageant of America* by Gregor Noetzel,
American Geographical Society, New York

1 and 2. Two companies of the 17th Regiment. 3. Sixty American Loyalists. 4. Two Grenadier companies of the 17th Regiment. 5. Detachment of the Royal Artillery. A and B. One 24 and one 18 pound ship guns. C. One iron 12 pounder. D. One 8 inch howitzer. E, F, and G. One brass 12 pounder each. Two lines of abattis stretched across the point.

RAIDS AND COUNTER-RAIDS, 1779

THE expedition against Stony Point and Verplancks Point, May 31, did not complete Clinton's activity. The raiding expedition in the same month sent by Clinton into the Chesapeake and Tryon's raid on the Connecticut shore in July were valuable in breaking up privateering and impairing civilian morale. They were therefore added reasons for the American counterblow under Wayne at Stony Point on the night of July 15–16. To McDougal was assigned the task of assaulting the works at Verplanck's Point; but orders either miscarried or were misunderstood, and nothing was accomplished. A glance at the map will show the difficulty of taking Stony Point. The whole works were a good example of eighteenth-century field fortification. The garrison was a little more than six hundred. Wayne had twelve hundred. He assaulted shortly after midnight in two columns, with orders, which were literally obeyed, not to fire a shot, but to depend solely on the bayonet. One column, led by Wayne himself, pushed eastward through the abattis straight for the top of the hill. The other followed the north shore and attacked the fort from the rear. When the alarm was given, the Americans were compelled to advance in the face of a tremendous musketry and artillery fire. But they pushed forward steadily and carried the main works with the bayonet. The two columns reached the center of the fort almost at the same time. The entire garrison who had not been killed were taken. It was a brilliant stroke and firmly established Wayne's reputation. It would not have been possible, however, without the training and discipline which Steuben had given the army, or without the arms and ammunition which were coming from France. In September Clinton prepared for the execution of Germain's new plan of conquering the southernmost states and working north. If France forced the conclusion of the war, then some territory would at least be in British hands. But Clinton rightly felt that the enterprise had grave risks; for it required two independent armies in America instead of one. Communication between them and between either and the home base required control of the sea. If this should be lost, disaster might result. Yorktown was to prove the wisdom of Clinton's apprehensions.

PAULUS HOOK, AUGUST 19, 1779

AFTER the affair at Stony Point the Virginia cavalryman, Major Henry Lee, whom we have met already as "Light Horse Harry," raided Paulus Hook on the Jersey shore. Before dawn on August 19 Lee assaulted, and cleared the abattis and ditch without firing a shot. Then the greater part of the garrison surrendered. Lee at once withdrew, carrying off one hundred and fifty-eight prisoners. Both Stony Point and Paulus Hook had been carried by the bayonet alone — two examples of how well the best men had learned their lesson from Von Steuben. Discipline and training had turned the Americans into superior soldiers.

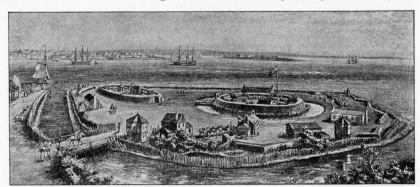

435   From the painting by E. L. Henry.   © New Jersey Title Guarantee & Trust Company, Jersey City

CADRAGQUA LAKE

436   "A Mappe of Colonel Romer's Voyage to ye 5 Indian Nations," from the original, dated 1700, in the King's
Collection of American maps, British Museum, London

THE IROQUOIS COUNTRY

Two weeks before the assault on Paulus Hook Major-General John Sullivan was at Wyoming in Pennsylvania preparing to march into the heart of the Iroquois country. The powerful Six Nations lived in a natural fortress which Romer's map of 1700 does little to suggest. Their villages stretched from beyond the Genesee River on the west through the country of the Finger Lakes to the Mohawk and Susquehanna on the east. On the north the tribal domains were guarded by Lake Ontario and on the west by Lake Erie. On the northeast the Adirondacks lay between them and the lower St. Lawrence, while the Catskills stood guard against the people of the lower Hudson. On the south rose the tumbled Pennsylvania uplands, sloping northward into New York. Within this forest empire lived the greatest of the eastern Indians. For a century they had been allies of Britain. Their friend Sir William Johnson (No. 152) had taught them to respect the Great Father across the water. At first they could not comprehend the Revolution; but, as the conflict developed, they began to

437   Silver medal (eighteenth century) presented by the British to Iroquois as a token of friendship, from W. M. Beauchamp, *Metallic Ornaments of the New York Indians*, State Museum Report, Bulletin 73, Albany, 1905

see on which side their interest lay. In 1768 they had deeded away, by the treaty of Fort Stanwix, a princely domain. Following this, settlers had poured into the Susquehanna valley, bringing the frontier west of the protecting mountains. Scarcely more than three months after the Battle of Lexington the Earl of Dartmouth had sent word to the British agent in the Mohawk valley to "lose no time in taking such steps as may induce them [the Iroquois] to take up the hatchet against his Majesty's rebellious subjects in America." Here was an opportunity to drive back the ever-encroaching white frontier.

FRONTIER RAIDS
BY INDIANS AND TORIES
1778

Americans
American Settlements
Do. raided
Battles

Raiders
Indian Settlements
Do. destroyed
Principal Indian Trails

Drawn expressly for *The Pageant of America* by Gregor Noetzel, American Geographical Society, New York

438

THE IROQUOIS RAIDS OF 1778

PARTISAN war had flamed up along the New York frontier as early as 1776. The first important battle, however, was Oriskany, where St. Leger's troops and the Patriot militia fought to a draw (No. 324). Many an Iroquois brave fell in that fight, and, after St. Leger's expedition had collapsed, the cry for revenge became loud in the councils of the Iroquois. The war spirit of the Six Nations was increased by the activities of a Loyalist, Colonel John Butler, who had been born in Connecticut, but had lived for many years in the Mohawk valley. He had served under Sir William Johnson as Deputy Superintendent of Indian Affairs, and in the campaigns of 1759 and 1760 had commanded Indians under Johnson. In the Revolution he organized a body of irregular troops, known as Butler's Rangers, from the frontier Loyalists who sought refuge at Fort Oswego. Butler's coöperation spurred the Indians to war. In 1778 Butler and Joseph Brant, the Mohawk chief, carried fire and the sword to the quiet settlements in the valleys of the Susquehanna and Wyoming. Never in the history of American border war had destruction been so widespread. On May 30 Brant struck Cobleskill, and on June 18 Springfield. When the year ended, the charred ruins of pioneers' cabins from Wyoming to Cherry Valley were mute evidence that the frontier had been driven back.

THE WYOMING DISASTER, JULY 3–4, 1778

THE Wyoming shaft at Wilkesbarre commemorates an episode in which war assumed one of its ugliest phases. In July Colonel John Butler with some eight hundred whites and Indians, approached the fort at Wyoming, into which the people of the surrounding region had retired. Butler's demand for surrender was refused. The untrained defenders resolved to fight in the open, and five hundred and eighty-two men sallied forth. Underestimating the enemy's number, they crossed the river, where they promptly fell into a trap. The terrible losses suffered in their attempt to regain the fort have come down in history as the "Wyoming Massacre." St. John de Crèvecœur, who got the story from refugees, has described what followed. "They [the Indians] had scarcely finished scalping the numerous victims which lay on the ground when these fierce conquerors demanded the immediate entrance to the fort. It was submissively granted. Above a hundred of them, decorated with all the dreadful ornaments of plumes and colour of war, with fierce and animated eyes, presented themselves and rushed with impetuosity into the middle of the arena. . . . But now a scene of unexpected humanity ensues. . . . Happily these fierce people, satisfied with the death of those who had opposed them in army, treated the defenseless ones, the women and children, with a degree of humanity almost hitherto unparalleled. . . . After this everyone was permitted to go and look for the mangled carcass of his relation and to cover it with earth." — CRÈVECŒUR, *Sketches of Eighteenth-Century America.*

439 Monument at Wilkesbarre, Pa., commemorating the Wyoming Valley Massacre. © Rau Studios, Inc.

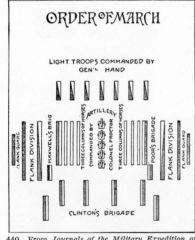

ORDER OF MARCH

LIGHT TROOPS COMMANDED BY GEN'L HAND

FLANK GUARD
FLANK DIVISION
MAXWELL'S BRIG
THREE COLUMNS OF HORSES
ARTILLERY COMMANDED BY COLONEL PROCTOR
THREE COLUMNS OF HORSES
POOR'S BRIGADE
FLANK DIVISION
FLANK GUARD

CLINTON'S BRIGADE

440 From *Journals of the Military Expedition of Major-Gen. John Sullivan against the Six Nations of Indians in 1779*, Albany, 1887, prepared by Frederick Cook, Secretary of State

SULLIVAN INVADES THE INDIAN COUNTRY

ON July 30, 1779, Colonel Hubley, of Sullivan's army, wrote at Wyoming: "I cannot omit taking notice of the poor inhabitants of the town: two-thirds of them are widows and orphans . . . left totally dependent on the public." On the following day Sullivan pushed northward toward the villages of the Iroquois with orders from Washington to accomplish "the total destruction and devastation of their settlements and capture of as many prisoners of every age and sex as possible. It will be essential to ruin their crops now in the ground and prevent their planting more." A line drawn through the last sentence suggests that the commander in chief shrank from inflicting the sufferings of starvation on his forest enemies.

The next month at Tioga Sullivan met General James Clinton, who had brought a force from the Mohawk region through the ruined valley of the Susquehanna. Here a rough fort was built, and the force, numbering about four thousand, pushed on up the Chemung River. Sullivan's order of march and battle represent an interesting solution of the problems which confronted the commander who was required to march an army into the heart of a powerful Indian empire through a rough and forested country in which there were no roads. By Sullivan's command the "order of Battle & the order of March . . . are to be adher'd to at all times when the situation of the Country will possibly admit & where a deviation takes place it must be carried no further than the necessity of that time requires." In both diagrams the troops are disposed in such a way as to meet effectively the Indian ambush and encircling attack.

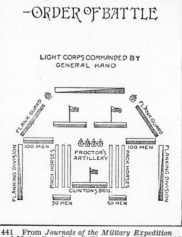

ORDER OF BATTLE

LIGHT CORPS COMMANDED BY GENERAL HAND

FLANK GUARD
FLANK GUARD
FLANKING DIVISION
100 MEN
PACK HORSES
PROCTOR'S ARTILLERY
PACK HORSES
100 MEN
FLANKING DIVISION
CLINTON'S BRIG.
50 MEN
50 MEN

441 From *Journals of the Military Expedition of Major-Gen. John Sullivan, etc.*, Albany, 1887

Head Quarters Smith
Clove June 20th 1779

Sir,

> *I have received your two favours*
> *of the 28th of May and 6th of June —*
> *[¶] I hope before this you will have*
> *received instruction from General Sullivan*
> *respecting the precise line of conduct you are*
> *to observe. Whether your destination shall be*
> *up the Mohock River or to form a junction*
> *in the first instance with the main body at*
> *the head of Susquehannah is a point I have*
> *left to him to decide and to give you directions*
> *accordingly. But as the preparations on the*
> *Susquehannah are completed and the main*
> *body all in motion towards Wyoming; it is*
> *essential you should be ready to move either*
> *way at the shortest notice. Should there be*
> *any delay on your part, when you are*
> *required to commence your operations the*
> *consequences may be very fatal — Therefore*
> *leave it with you to make whatever prepara-*
> *tions you find necessary to enable you to*
> *comply with a sudden call.*

442   Washington's letter to Clinton in the handwriting of Alexander Hamilton,
        from the original in the Library of Congress, Washington

WASHINGTON TO GENERAL JAMES CLINTON

THERE were three Clintons in the Revolution: Sir Henry Clinton, the British commanding general; Governor (and Brigadier-General), George Clinton subsequently Vice-President; and Brigadier-General James Clinton, who served under Greene, was wounded at Fort Clinton, and joined Sullivan against the Indians. In these important instructions to the third Clinton Washington, realizing from his own early military experience the "disagreeable consequences" of surprise Indian attacks, urged him to "make whatever additional preparations you find necessary to enable you to comply with a sudden call." They reveal Washington's anxiety about the old northwestern frontier, which he feared was again becoming a mortal danger not only to the settlers in that neighborhood but to the establishment of a safe frontier for the future United States. There were two dangers: first, the immediate menace of the British and the Indians; second, the future danger of either a British possession, or an "Indian preserve" to exclude American settlers and become a source of endless trouble.

BATTLE OF NEWTOWN, AUGUST 29

ON August 28 a scout brought word of a large number of fires and some Indian scouting parties in the Chemung valley a few miles east of the present site of Elmira. The next day Sullivan advanced toward the position, taking the utmost precaution. As it turned out, the enemy were making their last stand. Some two hundred Loyalists and five hundred Indians were drawn up in a thickly wooded country on the low ground east of the foot of Sullivan Hill (see No. 444, inset). The American force was overwhelming; yet under somewhat similar circumstances, Braddock had suffered a terrible defeat. Sullivan advanced into battle. In correct military style he enveloped the enemy's left and sent his opponents fleeing from the field. Wrote Colonel Hubley in his journal: "In the course of the day we took nine scalps (all savages) and two prisoners." Two days after the battle Lieutenant Barton noted in his journal: "At the request of Major Piatt, I sent out a small party to look for some of the dead Indians — returned without finding them. Toward noon they found them and skinned two of them from their hips down for boot-legs, one pair for the Major, the other pair for myself. On the other side of this mountain was a town said to be of the best buildings we had passed. It was destroyed by Gen'l Poor the evening of the engagement." — *General Sullivan's Indian Expedition*, 1779. Such an entry brings into sharp relief the brutality that war against the Indians developed in the white man.

443   General John Sullivan, 1740–95, from the portrait by V. D. Tenney, after a pencil sketch, 1790, by John Trumbull in the state capitol, Concord, N. H.

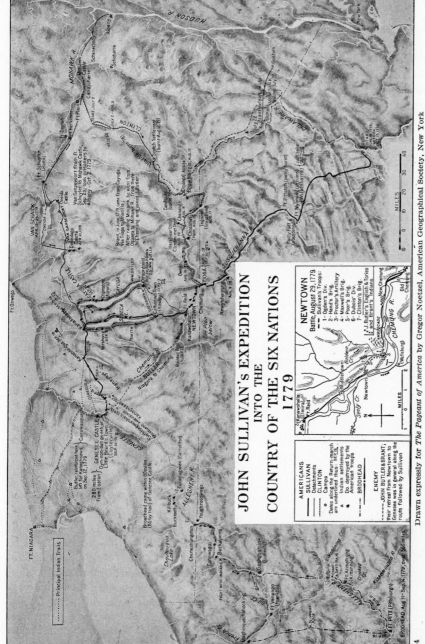

Drawn expressly for *The Pageant of America* by Gregor Noetzel, American Geographical Society, New York

SULLIVAN'S RAID, 1779

Two days later Sullivan's army, having in the meantime sent to the rear all the baggage and heavy guns except four light three-pounders and a small howitzer, continued the devastating march to the Genesee River. Since provisions were short, Sullivan proposed that the commissariat issue half-rations, allowing the men to make up the remainder from the enemy cornfields and orchards. On September 15 in the Genesee country the American general issued the following general order: "The commander-in-chief informs this brave and resolute army that the immediate objects of this expedition are accomplished, viz; total ruin of the Indian settlements,

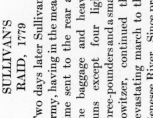

and the destruction of their crops, which were designed for the support of those inhuman barbarians, while they were desolating the American frontiers. . . . The army will this day commence its march for Tioga." No Indian chronicler has left a record of this disaster, as a result of which the Iroquois were ultimately driven from their ancestral home. But a suggestion of what the raid meant to the Indians may be found in Hubley's journal: "Previous to our leaving Jenise [Genesee], a woman with a child came in to us, who had been taken prisoner last year near Wyoming, and fortunately made her escape from the savages. She, with her bantling, was almost starved for want of food; she informs us that the Indians have been in great want all last spring — that they have subsisted entirely on green corn this summer — that their squaws were fretting prodigiously, and continually teasing their warriors to make peace — that by promises by Butler and his minions, they are fed up with great things that should be done for them — that they seem considerably cast down and frightened; and, in short, she says distress and trouble seem painted on their countenances." — O. E. RISING, *A New Hampshire Lawyer in Washington's Army*, p. 85.   The Iroquois never forgot Sullivan, whom they called the "town-destroyer."

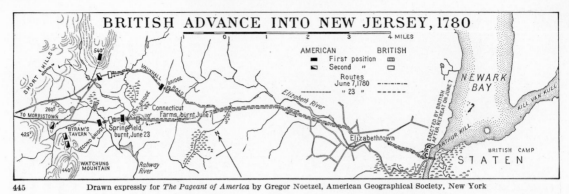

445   Drawn expressly for *The Pageant of America* by Gregor Noetzel, American Geographical Society, New York

KNYPHAUSEN IN NEW JERSEY, JUNE 1780

AFTER Sullivan's return from the Iroquois country, Washington moved his headquarters to Morristown, though keeping his army in a semicircle to the north of New York, as in the previous winter. Clinton, after evacuating Newport on October 25, had already transferred the main scene of war to the South. Knyphausen, left at New York in command of the British forces, remained inactive through the winter and spring of 1779–80. In June the Hessian commander decided on an offensive into New Jersey, where, according to his information, the Loyalist sentiment was strong, and where two Continental regiments had mutinied for want of food or clothing. Crossing from Staten Island on a bridge of boats, with five thousand men, he pushed rapidly toward Morristown on June 7. To his surprise he was met during a large part of the advance by harassing fire from irregular American snipers. To his still greater surprise, when he reached Springfield, east of Morristown, he found a large force of militia, as well as the mutinous regiments, awaiting his attack. He decided not to risk a battle and retreated precipitately, covering his threatened rear by a bridge-head at Elizabeth Town Point. A few days later Clinton returned from the South and promptly determined to redeem this reverse. Sixteen days after his first invasion Knyphausen advanced again toward Morristown with a somewhat stronger force than before. Again his enterprise came to naught, mainly because of the success of Greene in hindering his crossing of the Elizabeth River.

GEORGE ROGERS CLARK AND THE WINNING OF THE WEST, 1778–79

THE story of the expedition of George Rogers Clark is given in further detail in Volume II. Suffice it to say here that Virginia had a charter claim to the territory north of the Ohio River. Governor Patrick Henry, therefore, took an active interest in the proposition of a young Virginian to make a sudden stroke in this region. Clark proposed to surprise the forts at Kaskaskia and Vincennes which he had ascertained were held by small garrisons. He received a commission from the state with authority to raise a force of volunteers. Leaving Redstone Fort in Pennsylvania in May, 1778, with two hundred men he shot the falls of the Ohio during the total eclipse of June 24. Proceeding down the river in his boats he approached his first objective, Kaskaskia. His final advance was by land. On July 4 he crept up on the fortification. That night he surprised his enemy. Kaskaskia fell without the loss of a life. The nearby settlement of Cahokia capitulated. Clark brought with him the news of the French alliance, which made the French people of these wilderness settlements more favorably disposed to him than they might otherwise have been. Father Gibault, the French priest of the region, set off for Vincennes to persuade the flock there to accept the new allegiance. For a time the Americans were in control in that region. Colonel Hamilton of the British army, whose duty it was to govern this wild country from his headquarters at Detroit, could not permit Clark's challenge to go unanswered. Organizing a strong expedition, he advanced to Vincennes and again raised the Union Jack above Fort Sackville. This move, however, was to be but the first step in his campaign against the American intruder.

446   George Rogers Clark, 1752–1818, from the portrait in the Virginia State Library, Richmond

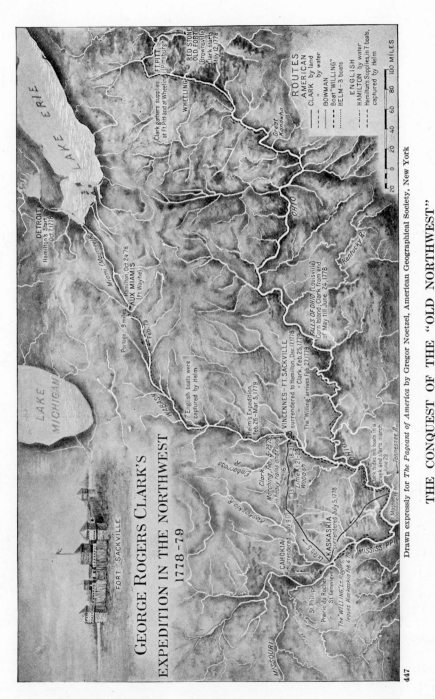

GEORGE ROGERS CLARK'S
EXPEDITION IN THE NORTHWEST
1778-79

FORT SACKVILLE

447

Drawn expressly for *The Pageant of America* by Gregor Noetzel, American Geographical Society, New York

THE CONQUEST OF THE "OLD NORTHWEST"

WINTER covered the wilderness with snow before Hamilton could move against his adversary. Under such circumstances he sent back to Detroit some of his militia and went into winter quarters on the banks of the Wabash. Hamilton did not himself retire to comfortable quarters in the larger post but remained at the front where he planned to be ready at the earliest possible moment in the spring for the final offensive. Meanwhile he faced with what grace he could muster a winter of tedium in a small post in the heart of the wilderness. The winter, however, did not prove to be as uninteresting as he had anticipated. With a sure military sense Clark realized that his only chance of success lay in attacking Hamilton before that commander could assemble his forces in the spring. Although the American force had dwindled greatly as a result of the expiration of enlistments, Clark recruited his numbers from the local French. He then embarked upon that desperate march across a swampy wilderness flooded as a result of thaws until at times his men waded through icy water, carrying their rifles above their heads. The advance and the resulting surprise has become a classic in the annals of forest war. Hamilton was captured and the frontier of British power was driven back to the region of Detroit.

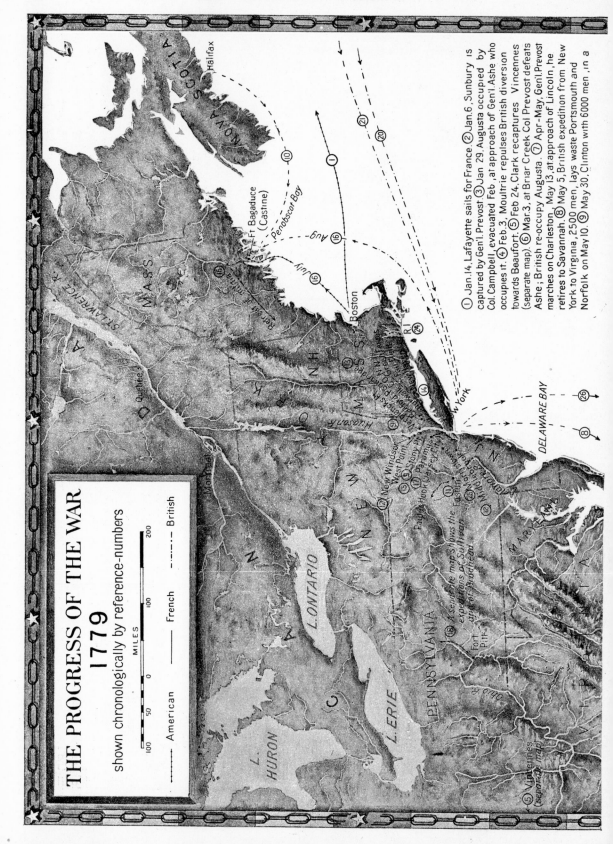

THE PROGRESS OF THE WAR
1779

shown chronologically by reference-numbers

MILES

———— American   ———— French   ------- British

① Jan.14, Lafayette sails for France. ② Jan.6, Sunbury is captured by Gen'l. Prevost ③ Jan. 29, Augusta occupied by Col. Campbell, evacuated Feb., at approach of Gen'l. Ashe who occupies it. ④ Feb.3, Moultrie repulses British diversion towards Beaufort. ⑤ Feb 24, Clark recaptures Vincennes (separate map). ⑥ Mar.3, at Briar Creek Col Prevost defeats Ashe; British re-occupy Augusta. ⑦ Apr–May, Gen'l.Prevost marches on Charleston. May 13, at approach of Lincoln, he retires to Savannah. ⑧ May 5, British expedition from New York to Virginia, 2500 men, lays waste Portsmouth and Norfolk on May 10. ⑨ May 30, Clinton with 6000 men , in a

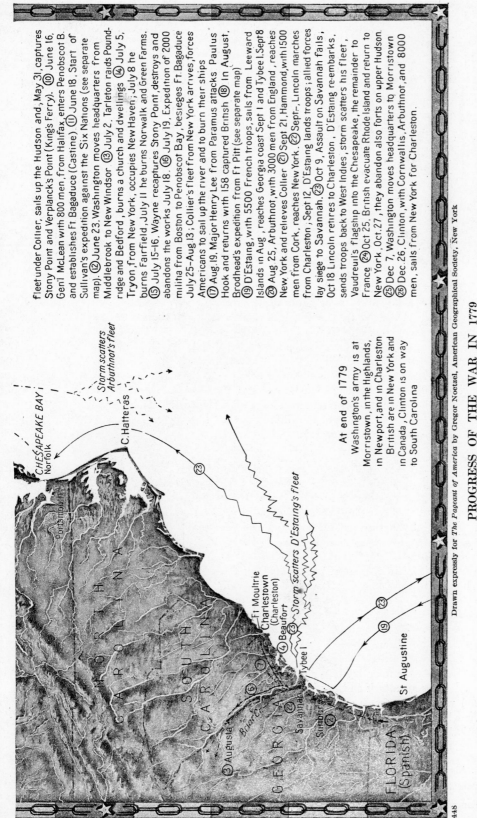

fleet under Collier, sails up the Hudson and, May 31, captures Stony Point and Verplanck's Point (King's Ferry). ⑩ June 16, Gen'l McLean with 800 men, from Halifax, enters Penobscot B. and establishes Ft Bagaduce (Castine) ⑪ June 18. Start of Sullivan's expedition against the Six Nations (see separate map). ⑫ June 23. Washington moves headquarters from Middlebrook to New Windsor. ⑬ July 2. Tarleton raids Poundridge and Bedford, burns a church and dwellings ⑭ July 5, Tryon, from New York, occupies New Haven; July 8 he burns Fairfield, July 11 he burns Norwalk and Green Farms. ⑮ July 15-16. Wayne recaptures Stony Point, destroys and abandons the works July 18. ⑯ July 19. Expedition of 2000 militia from Boston to Penobscot Bay, besieges Ft. Bagaduce July 25-Aug 13; Collier's fleet from New York arrives, forces Americans to sail up the river and to burn their ships ⑰ Aug.19, Major Henry Lee from Paramus attacks Paulus Hook and returns with 158 captured British ⑱ In August. Brodhead's expedition from Ft Pitt (see separate map) ⑲ D'Estang, with 5500 French troops, sails from Leeward Islands in Aug., reaches Georgia coast Sept 1 and Tybee I. Sept 8 ⑳ Aug 25, Arbuthnot, with 3000 men from England, reaches New York and relieves Collier ㉑ Sept 21, Hammond, with 1500 men from Cork, reaches New York. ㉒ Sept-, Lincoln marches from Charleston, Sept 12, D'Estang lands troops; allied forces lay siege to Savannah. ㉓ Oct 9, Assault on Savannah fails, Oct 18 Lincoln retires to Charleston, D'Estang re-embarks, sends troops back to West Indies, storm scatters his fleet, Vaudreuil's flagship into the Chesapeake, the remainder to France ㉔ Oct 25, British evacuate Rhode Island and return to New York, Oct.27, they abandon also forts on upper Hudson. ㉕ Dec 7, Washington moves headquarters to Morristown ㉖ Dec.26, Clinton, with Cornwallis, Arbuthnot, and 8000 men, sails from New York for Charleston.

Storm scatters Arbuthnot's fleet

CHESAPEAKE BAY
Norfolk

C. Hatteras

Portsmouth

At end of 1779
Washington's army is at Morristown, in the Highlands, in Newport, and in Charleston British are in New York and in Canada, Clinton is on way to South Carolina

㉓

NORTH CAROLINA

SOUTH CAROLINA

Storm scatters D'Estang's Fleet

Ft Moultrie
Charlestown (Charleston)
Beaufort
Tybee I

GEORGIA

③ Augusta
Briar Creek
Savannah
Sunbury

FLORIDA (Spanish)
St Augustine

㉓
⑲

448   Drawn expressly for *The Pageant of America* by Gregor Noetzel, American Geographical Society, New York

PROGRESS OF THE WAR IN 1779

THE British under Clinton took Stony Point and a small expedition from Halifax took Castine (10). Wayne struck back victoriously at Stony Point (15) in the summer, as did "Light Horse Harry" Lee at Paulus Hook (17) while the American counterstroke against Castine was a failure (16). In the "Old Northwest," George Rogers Clark made good his hold on the entire country. In the South, to which the British were transferring their main objectives they seemed to be making good their claims to reconquest. The American attack on Savannah with French naval coöperation (23) ended in failure. Various reinforcements, both French and British, crossed the Atlantic; and the year ended with Clinton's departure (26) from New York for Charleston with the largest single transfer of any force, over eight thousand men. On the whole, 1779 was a year of new experiments.

449 Joseph (Thayendanegea) Brant, *ca.* 1742–1807, from a mezzotint by J. R. Smith after the portrait by Romney

THE BORDER WAR OF 1780

WHILE the New Jersey militia were opposing Knyphausen (No. 445), the border war with the Iroquois in New York was blazing forth afresh. The Indians, though they had suffered terrible losses, were not disposed to let Sullivan's raid go unavenged. In April Harpersfield was burned. In May the redskin warriors became active along the upper Mohawk. Three days after Knyphausen's failure at Springfield, German Flats was burned and some prisoners taken. But the war did not break in full fury until midsummer. Sir John Johnson, the son of Sir William, came from Canada with a Loyalist force to reconquer the region about his old home in the Mohawk valley. Coöperating with Johnson was Joseph Brant, the Iroquois chief, known to his Indian followers as Thayendanegea. His devotion to the English had been so increased by the enthusiastic welcome given him during his visit to England in 1775 that he resolved to help them in whatever manner possible against their rebellious colonists. In July, 1780, Brant, with six hundred Indians, accompanied by two hundred Loyalists, made a feint against Fort Schuyler (Stanwix). Then, while the militia of the lower Mohawk was being hurried up the river, he moved swiftly into the Susquehanna valley, turned northward and, on August 2, fell upon Canajoharie. In the fighting fourteen persons were killed and fifty or sixty captured. Then, with more than three hundred head of livestock, Brant disappeared in the forest, leaving the smoking ruins of more than a hundred buildings. Later in the month Brant and Johnson returned to the Mohawk valley and laid it waste. Like the Mohawk valley settlements those in the Schoharie valley (October, 1780) suffered. Finally General Van Rensselaer with a militia force drove out the invaders. Their purely raiding work was done, but they had not been strong enough to compel Washington to weaken his army at West Point in order to deal with them. In October a raid from Lake Champlain resulted in no permanent military advantage. The raids of 1780 are significant of the difficulties that Washington had to deal with in his rear in the same summer that saw Arnold's treason.

THE LAST BORDER RAIDS IN THE NORTH, 1781–83

SULLIVAN'S "total ruin of the Indian settlements," referred to in his dispatch of September 15, did not prevent a recurrence of anxiety on the frontier in later years. It was given to Colonel Marinus Willett to deliver the finishing blow. He had been in Bradstreet's expedition (1758) during the final French and Indian War, and during the Revolution was a capable and devoted officer. In 1781 Governor Clinton of New York appointed Willett to command all state forces, with headquarters at Fort Rensselaer (Canajoharie); a command necessitated by the continued frontier troubles. On July 9 a few Loyalists and some three hundred Indians raided Currytown. Willett, with half as many Patriot militia, went to the rescue from Fort Plain, which was thereafter called Fort M'Kean, in honor of Captain Robert M'Kean, who was killed in the forefront of the fight. On October 24 Willett and Colonel Rowley (of Massachusetts) hurried against Butler's Rangers and Indians, who were destroying Warren Bush. In the following battle of Johnstown the day was saved by Rowley's vigorous attack on the enemy's rear and won by Willett (October 29) when his pursuers overtook and defeated the retreating enemy, whose leader, Major Walter Butler, was killed. The year 1782 was comparatively peaceful, except farther west. Yorktown had been won in October, 1781, and all parties were negotiating terms. But Washington was still anxious to be prepared for a possible renewal of war. So he sent Willett to secure Fort Ontario in February, 1783. Crossing Lake Oneida on the ice, Willett reached Oswego Falls. Lack of men and material however compelled him to retire without a fight.

450 Colonel Marinus Willett, 1740–1830, from the portrait, artist unknown, in the Metropolitan Museum of Art, New York

THE ORIGIN OF ARNOLD'S TREASON

TURNING now from border raids to the centers of Revolutionary power we find the very important "gateway of the North," the fortified stronghold of West Point, in charge of Benedict Arnold, the Revolutionary hero of many a hard-fought field, in Canada, against Burgoyne's invasion, and elsewhere. Arnold had been both a rock of defense and a surpassing leader of attack all through the first three years (1775–78). But, partly owing to inter-state jealousies and partly to other causes, his outstanding services, second only to those of Washington himself, had never been properly recognized by Congress. Hence troubles, doubts, deceit, and treason. While Brant was still in the Mohawk valley Major André, an important British staff officer, was arrested on the banks of the Hudson while returning from a conference invited by Arnold;

451 Benedict Arnold, 1741–1801, from an engraving by Prevost after the portrait by du Simitiére, in the New York Public Library

and American Patriots were shocked with the news of treason that had almost succeeded. In 1779, when Clinton abandoned Philadelphia, Arnold had been placed in command of that city. There is no space here to recount his extravagant living in the Quaker city, nor his courtship and marriage with Peggy Shippen, the beautiful daughter of a prominent Loyalist. Becoming heavily involved in debt, he was charged with peculation by the Council of Pennsylvania. A court-martial found him innocent on all important counts, but guilty of two minor charges, and sentenced him to be reprimanded. Washington, however, in executing the sentence, said: "I reprimand you for having forgotten that in proportion as you have rendered yourself formidable to our enemies, you should have been guarded and temperate in your deportment toward your fellow citizens. Exhibit anew those noble qualities which have placed you on the list of our most valued commanders."

452 Peggy Shippen Arnold (and child), from the portrait by Daniel Gardner (1750–1805) in the Historical Society of Pennsylvania

ARNOLD AND WEST POINT

WEST POINT enabled Washington to retain control of the middle Hudson. The command here was the most important in the northern army next to that of the commander in chief. Arnold sought the post, and Washington placed him in command on August 4, 1779. For over a year (1779–80) Arnold had been in communication with the British General Clinton, vaguely at first, but, as time passed, with a growing definiteness. His motives still remain in part a matter of speculation. Gamaliel Bradford comments: "In a passionate and prejudiced temperament like Arnold's the slights inflicted upon him worked like a maddening poison. 'I daily discover so much baseness and ingratitude among mankind that I almost blush at being of the same species,' he wrote to Miss Shippen, just before his marriage. And the remedy he found was to display on his own part a baseness and ingratitude that no one could surpass." — *Damaged Souls*, pp. 40–41. To Lord George Germain, Arnold wrote: "I was intent to have demonstrated my zeal by an act, which, had it succeeded as intended, must have immediately terminated the unnatural convulsions that have so long distracted the Empire."

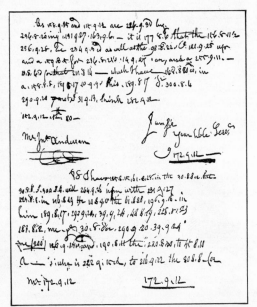

453 Facsimile of part of a cipher letter from "John Moore" (Benedict Arnold) to "John Anderson" (Major André), July 12, 1780, referring to the expected arrival of a French fleet, from the original in the Clinton Papers, William L. Clements Library, Ann Arbor, Mich.

454   André going ashore from the British ship *Vulture*, etching after a pen and ink
sketch drawn by André while in prison

ANDRÉ'S MEETING WITH ARNOLD

MAJOR ANDRÉ, Clinton's adjutant-general, had for some time been carrying on the correspondence with Arnold under the name of John Anderson. Matters had developed to such a point that on September 21 a meeting between André and Arnold seemed necessary. With explicit orders from his chief not to go within the American lines, not to disguise himself, and not to receive any incriminating papers, André sailed up the river in the sloop-of-war *Vulture*, which dropped anchor off Teller's Point, about eighteen miles below West Point. Here Joshua Smith came aboard in a rowboat with the word that he was to take John Anderson on shore to meet General Arnold. That night the two conferred together. About dawn Arnold suggested that the discussion be concluded at Smith's house. André consented, and was disturbed to find it within the American lines. Early in the forenoon the two officers were surprised as a lone American cannon opened on the *Vulture*, Colonel James Livingston having found a four-pounder and started firing on his own responsibility. The *Vulture* dropped down stream. That evening Smith refused to take André to the sloop in his boat; but set him across the river and provided him with a horse. Two days later near Tarrytown, New York, three men apprehended the British officer, wearing a long blue coat instead of his customary garment, searched him, and found incriminating papers in his stocking. Refusing a large offer of money if they would release him, they turned him over to an American outpost.

ARNOLD'S ESCAPE

ON the morning of September 25 Washington was returning from a conference with Rochambeau in Connecticut and was planning to breakfast with Arnold. He had been delayed; and Arnold was at table with Washington's staff when a messenger handed him a paper which contained the news that John Anderson had been apprehended. Without a tremor he excused himself, mounted a horse, fled to a boat, and rowed alone to the *Vulture*. The conspirators had plotted that Clinton should advance up the river, attack West Point, and receive its surrender from Arnold. By a strange combination of fortuitous circumstances it had been defeated. An hour after Arnold's departure Washington arrived, and, suspecting that something was amiss, made dispositions to guard against possible danger. But there was no danger; for Arnold was practically alone in his conspiracy. His reward was a commission as brigadier-general in the British army, and, when he later went to England, six thousand three hundred and fifteen pounds for himself and an annuity of five hundred pounds for his wife and one hundred for each of her children. Such was the sordid end of an episode that was to make the name of Benedict Arnold a synonym for baseness and treachery. Mahan later wrote of him: "It is not the least of the injuries done to his nation in after years, that he should have . . . effaced this glorious record by so black an infamy."

455   Arnold Boarding the British Ship *Vulture*, from the painting by Howard Pyle (1861–1909) for Woodrow Wilson, *A History of the American People*, New York, 1901. © Harper & Bros.

THE TRIAL AND SENTENCE OF ANDRÉ

MAJOR ANDRÉ was brought before a court-martial that contained some of the most distinguished names in the military annals of the Revolution: Greene (as president), Lafayette, Steuben, Stirling, Knox, Stark, and others. Said Steuben: "It was not possible to save him. He put us to no proof, but in open, manly manner confessed everything, but a premeditated design to deceive." The court reported that "Major André ought to be considered as a spy from the enemy, and that agreeably to the law and usage of nations, it is their opinion he ought to suffer death." Reluctantly the court had acted and reluctantly Washington

456   Major John André, 1751–80, from the sketch by himself, done on the day before his execution, original in the Yale University Library, New Haven

approved its findings. The intensity of the feeling of the British officers was expressed by Lieutenant-Colonel Simcoe. "The useless murder of Major André would almost, was it possible, annihilate that wish which . . . has ever operated on the officers of the British army, the wish of a reconciliation and speedy re-union with their revolted fellow subjects in America." — SIMCOE, *Military Journal*, p. 293. Caleb Gibbs wrote the following in his diary under the date of October 2. "At 12 o'clock P.M. Major Andrie Adgt. Genll. to the B. Army was executed persuant to his sentence determined by a board of Genll. Officers. As soon as he got into the cart he said with a firm composure of mind that he was perfectly reconciled to his death but not quite to the mode — he look around and adresed himself to the Officer of the Guard & said with a smile, "it is but for a moment Sir," he seem not in the least agitated in his last moments, not one moment before he was thrown off he was asked if he had any to say as time would be allowed him for that purpose, he said nothing more than he called on all the gentlemen present to bear witness that he died like a brave man — & did —" (From Caleb Gibbs' manuscript diary in Library of Congress.)

NATHAN HALE, 1755–76

457   Statue in memory of Nathan Hale by Bela Pratt, on the Yale University campus, New Haven

THE execution of Nathan Hale was the precedent for that of André Hale was twenty years old when the war broke out. Two years before he had graduated from Yale. Joining as a First Lieutenant in the Seventh Connecticut he had served through the siege of Boston. He was promoted to captain and was with Washington's army when it marched from Boston to New York. About September 1, 1776, Hale became an officer in a small corps of rangers organized to reconnoiter enemy positions. During the anxious days in September, when Washington, round about King's Bridge, was facing Howe, who had thrown his army across Manhattan, the American commander, desiring definite information of his enemy's dispositions, called upon the rangers to secure it. Hale volunteered, posed as a schoolmaster seeking a position, and studied the English positions both on Long Island and Manhattan. Returning to Huntington Bay with his information he was seized as a spy. He was examined before Sir William Howe, was condemned, and executed by hanging on Sunday morning, September 22, 1776. His last words have become classic as an expression of the patriotism of youth: "I regret that I have but one life to give for my country."

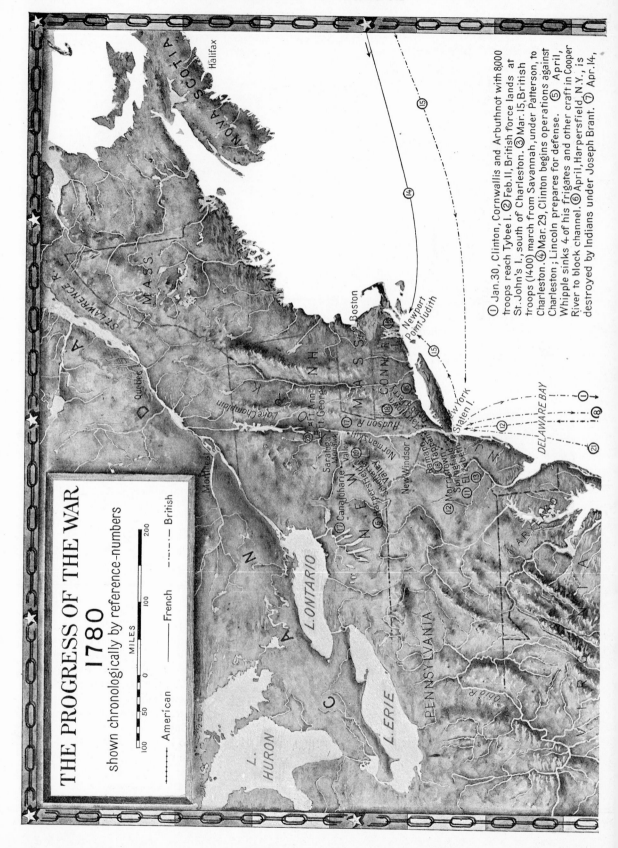

THE PROGRESS OF THE WAR
1780

shown chronologically by reference-numbers

MILES

American ········
French ————
British ─·─·─·

① Jan. 30, Clinton, Cornwallis and Arbuthnot with 8000 troops reach Tybee I. ② Feb. 11, British force lands at St. John's I., south of Charleston. ③ Mar. 15, British troops (1400) march from Savannah, under Patterson, to Charleston. ④ Mar. 29, Clinton begins operations against Charleston; Lincoln prepares for defense. ⑤ April, Whipple sinks 4 of his frigates and other craft in Cooper River to block channel. ⑥ April, Harpersfield, N.Y., is destroyed by Indians under Joseph Brant. ⑦ Apr. 14,

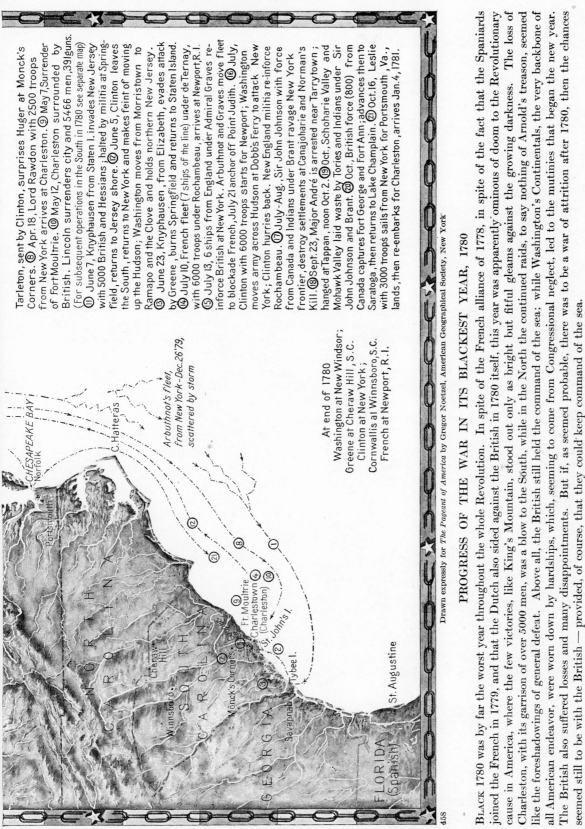

Tarleton, sent by Clinton, surprises Huger at Monck's Corners. ⑧ Apr. 18, Lord Rawdon with 2500 troops from New York arrives at Charleston. ⑨ May 7, Surrender of Fort Moultrie. ⑩ May 12, Charleston surrounded by British. Lincoln surrenders city and 5466 men, 391 guns. (For subsequent operations in the South in 1780 see separate map) ⑪ June 7, Knyphausen from Staten I. invades New Jersey with 5000 British and Hessians; halted by militia at Springfield, returns to Jersey shore. ⑫ June 5, Clinton leaves the South, returns to New York and makes feint of moving up the Hudson; Washington moves from Morristown to Ramapo and the Clove and holds northern New Jersey. ⑬ June 23, Knyphausen, from Elizabeth, evades attack by Greene, burns Springfield and returns to Staten Island. ⑭ July 10, French fleet (7 ships of the line) under de Ternay, with 6000 troops under Rochambeau, arrives at Newport, R.I. ⑮ July 13, 6 ships from England under Admiral Graves reinforce British at New York. Arbuthnot and Graves move fleet to blockade French, July 21 anchor off Point Judith. ⑯ July, Clinton with 6000 troops starts for Newport; Washington moves army across Hudson at Dobb's Ferry to attack New York; Clinton hurries back. New England militia re-inforce Rochambeau. ⑰ July-Aug., Sir John Johnson with force from Canada and Indians under Brant ravage New York frontier, destroy settlements at Canajoharie and Norman's Kill. ⑱ Sept. 23, Major André is arrested near Tarrytown; hanged at Tappan, noon Oct. 2. ⑲ Oct. 2, Schoharie Valley and Mohawk Valley laid waste by Tories and Indians under Sir John Johnson and Brant. ⑳ Oct., British force (800) from Canada captures Fort George and Fort Ann, advances then to Saratoga, then returns to Lake Champlain. ㉑ Oct. 16, Leslie with 3000 troops sails from New York for Portsmouth, Va., lands, then re-embarks for Charleston, arrives Jan. 4, 1781.

At end of 1780
Washington at New Windsor;
Greene at Cheraw Hill, S.C.;
Clinton at New York;
Cornwallis at Winnsboro, S.C.
French at Newport, R.I.

CHESAPEAKE BAY
Norfolk
Portsmouth
C. Hatteras

Arbuthnot's fleet, from New York—Dec. 26 '79, scattered by storm

NORTH CAROLINA
SOUTH CAROLINA
GEORGIA
FLORIDA (Spanish)

Cheraw Hill
Winnsboro
Monck's Corners
Ft. Moultrie
Charlestown (Charleston)
St. John's I.
Tybee I.
Savannah
St. Augustine

458

Drawn expressly for The Pageant of America by Gregor Noetzel, American Geographical Society, New York

PROGRESS OF THE WAR IN ITS BLACKEST YEAR, 1780

BLACK 1780 was by far the worst year throughout the whole Revolution. In spite of the French alliance of 1778, in spite of the fact that the Spaniards joined the French in 1779, and that the Dutch also sided against the British in 1780 itself, this year was apparently ominous of doom to the Revolutionary cause in America, where the few victories, like King's Mountain, stood out only as bright but fitful gleams against the growing darkness. The loss of Charleston, with its garrison of over 5000 men, was a blow to the South, while in the North the continued raids, to say nothing of Arnold's treason, seemed like the foreshadowings of general defeat. Above all, the British still held the command of the sea; while Washington's Continentals, the very backbone of all American endeavor, were worn down by hardships, which, seeming to come from Congressional neglect, led to the mutinies that began the new year. The British also suffered losses and many disappointments. But if, as seemed probable, there was to be a war of attrition after 1780, then the chances seemed still to be with the British — provided, of course, that they could keep command of the sea.

CHAPTER IX

THE CONCLUSIVE CAMPAIGNS IN THE SOUTH, 1778–81

THE War Office in London was responsible for the British plan to conquer the South. Such an enterprise was a virtual admission of partial defeat; for the southern campaign could have little influence toward ending the rebellion in New England, and, more important still, it obviously prevented any effective operations against Washington's army. Yet Washington's army was the very center of the Revolutionary movement; and the commander in chief himself was indispensable to the winning of independence. A good many of his troops were now experienced veterans and as well trained as British regulars; but his service of supply broke down again and again, undermining the morale of his soldiers and impairing their efficiency. To fight this army continuously, to drive it from point to point, to wear it down, and perhaps finally to defeat and destroy it: only by such a course could a British victory be achieved. Such an undertaking would have been hazardous indeed, because of the ability of the American officers and the fighting power of their men. Instead of attempting it the British military authorities, under incompetent Germain, fell back upon the plan of conquering and occupying territory. The South, where Loyalists were many, was chosen as the scene of operations. But the plan of conquest involved grave difficulties. The British army could easily capture places when the troops opposed to it were inferior in numbers or when they were largely untrained militia. Again and again in the southern campaigns Clinton and Cornwallis demonstrated their ability to march where they would. But holding a captured city or village required the detachment of troops from the main army. The larger the area conquered, the greater were the numbers of troops immobilized to defend strategic localities. The British attempted to conquer and garrison Georgia, as well as South and North Carolina, with a force utterly inadequate. To be sure, the Loyalist sentiment in this section was strong. But the Patriot sentiment had been dominant for several years before the campaigns started. In the sparsely settled southern terrain, where woods and swamps were many and villages widely separated, the Patriots developed guerrilla fighting to its highest point in the war. Both the main British army and its detached garrisons were constantly harassed by raids and minor battles. When at last a Franco-American army appeared under able leadership, the problem of retaining their southern conquests became too difficult for the British commanders. The failure of the southern campaigns, with Washington's army still intact, meant the complete defeat of British arms in America. Nothing could have been plainer, except to men like Germain, that if the South could not be permanently conquered when Washington and Rochambeau were absent and British sea power was present, then it would assuredly be lost when Washington and Rochambeau were present and British sea power was absent. This latter contingency was exactly what happened at Yorktown in October, 1781, when Washington and Rochambeau were besieging Cornwallis by land, while De Grasse was holding the seaway with his fleet. By that time, moreover, every other navy in the world was either actively (like the Dutch and Spanish) or passively (like those of the Armed Neutrality of the North) against the completely isolated British.

228

SAVANNAH, 1778

THE three maps on The Progress of the War in 1778, 1779, and 1780 have already shown us that, as 1778 drew to an end, the scene of war shifted mostly to the South. Clinton, carrying out his orders from Germain, sent a force of some three thousand five hundred men under Lieutenant-Colonel Campbell to the mouth of the Savannah River. General Robert Howe had for two years been in command of the American militia in the southern department, where he had been unsuccessful in his war upon the Loyalists, who had retired into Spanish Florida. Congress, upon the dispatching of Campbell, relieved Howe and appointed General Benjamin Lincoln, a soldier of ability and experience. Campbell arrived at the mouth of the Savannah River on December 24, and four days later began disembarking his troops two miles below the city. He had used the intervening days in gaining excellent information concerning his enemy from captured inhabitants. Meanwhile General Prévost with two thousand men was hurrying northward from Florida to unite with Campbell and begin the conquest of the southern states. Howe, learning of the advance of his two assailants at the same time, marched with a small force to the defense of Savannah. On

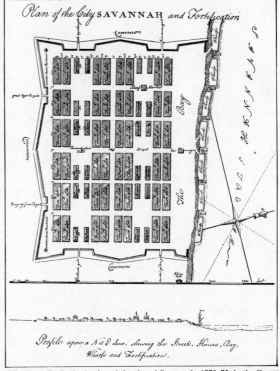

459   From De Brahm's plan of the city of Savannah, 1770–75, in the Crown Collection of Maps, Prints and Drawings, British Museum, London

December 29 Campbell struck him with superior numbers, out-maneuvered him, captured part of his force, and drove the rest headlong from the city. The first blow of the southern campaign was a brilliant success. Campbell promptly began the task of crushing Patriot opposition along the Georgia seaboard, and had largely succeeded when, on January 17, his force and Prévost's were united. Prévost then turned to face General Lincoln, who had appeared on the banks of the Savannah River.

GENERAL BENJAMIN LINCOLN, 1733–1810

LINCOLN had reached Charleston just ten days before the fall of Savannah and had assumed command of the thirty-five hundred miscellaneous men he found there. With what troops he had Lincoln rushed to the defense of Savannah, but arrived too late, and, though inferior to his opponent in numbers and discipline, took up a position on the left bank of the Savannah River. Lincoln was ever a courageous and aggres-

460   From the portrait, 1806, by Henry Sargent in the Massachusetts Historical Society, Boston

sive, if not always a skillful, commander. Meanwhile the militia of Virginia and North Carolina were assembling, while some were already on the march to join him. By February his troops outnumbered his enemy and he took the offensive. He sent a detachment of fifteen hundred men up the river to capture Augusta, the capital of Georgia, which had been occupied on January 29 by Colonel Campbell. The character and patriotism of Brigadier-General John Ashe, commander of this force, could not make up for his lack of training. After occupying Augusta in February, he permitted himself to be surprised at Briar Creek, March 3, his force being annihilated by Prévost's counter-attack. Lincoln, undaunted by the loss of the city, promptly marched on Augusta with his main army, determined to protect the Patriot legislature there, and to cut British communications with the interior. He left General Moultrie with a thousand men on the lower Savannah to guard the roads to Charleston. Lincoln's purpose in seeking to recover Augusta seems to have been to restore the morale of the population, shaken by the continuous successes of the invading British army.

461   "The Harbor of Charleston in South Carolina with a view of the town from the south shore of Ashley River,"
from Des Barres, *Atlantic Neptune*, London, 1780–81

THE ATTACK UPON CHARLESTON

LINCOLN's march against Augusta was a doubtful maneuver. Prévost, as soon as he learned of it, brushed past Moultrie and hurried toward Charleston. Lincoln judged the advance to be a feint, continued to Augusta, and reoccupied the interior strongholds of Georgia. But on May 11 the British army was across the Ashley River and in front of the chief seaport of the South, and Lincoln was hurrying to its defense. The next day Prévost demanded the surrender of the city. But Charleston refused; for aid had come. In February Count Pulaski, the Polish exile, who had been permitted to recruit Pulaski's Legion, which Congress kept under its direct control, had been ordered from New Jersey to South Carolina. For sixty days his Legion had hurried southward, to arrive on the very day that Prévost confronted the city. With Charleston rein-

462 Flag of the Second South Carolina regiment, captured at Savannah, 1779, from Lewis Butler, *Annals of the King's Royal Rifle Corps*, London, 1913

forced and Lincoln coming down on his rear, the British commander was compelled to abandon his enterprise. On the thirteenth he withdrew toward Georgia along the lagoons that line the Carolina shore. In June the hot season came on and for two months both armies were kept inactive.

THE CAMPAIGN AGAINST SAVANNAH, 1779

DURING the sickly summer months of 1779 Governor Rutledge of South Carolina and General Lincoln appealed to Count D'Estaing, the commander of the French fleet in the West Indies, to coöperate in an attack upon Georgia. The Frenchman consented. On September 4 the British in Savannah were amazed at the news of the French fleet at the mouth of the river (see map, No. 448). D'Estaing brought with him six thousand soldiers, in addition to a squadron of thirty-seven ships and over two thousand guns.

THE ARRIVAL OF D'ESTAING

LINCOLN, receiving word from D'Estaing, set off, accompanied by Pulaski, posthaste for Savannah with six hundred Continentals and seven hundred and fifty militia. On September 12 the French commander landed thirty-five hundred men, and, without waiting for Lincoln, on the next day summoned Prévost to surrender. Prévost asked for twenty-four hours in which to consider the demand, in the hope that Colonel Maitland would be able to bring into the city an outlying garrison. That officer, who had already shown unusual ability, succeeded. Prévost thereupon defied D'Estaing, and the siege of Savannah began. On September 16 Lincoln arrived. Meanwhile the French, for lack of horses, had been slow in bringing up their guns. As a result, when the Americans came, they were not ready for an assault. Instead, regular siege operations were decided upon.

463   Count Casimir Pulaski, 1748–79, from the portrait from life attributed to Pulaski's sister Anne, in the possession of Franciszek Pulaski, Warsaw, Poland

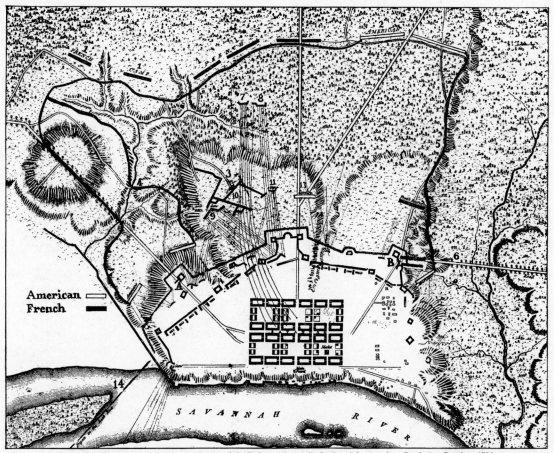

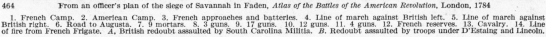

American ☐
French ▅

464   From an officer's plan of the siege of Savannah in Faden, *Atlas of the Battles of the American Revolution*, London, 1784

1. French Camp. 2. American Camp. 3. French approaches and batteries. 4. Line of march against British left. 5. Line of march against British right. 6. Road to Augusta. 7. 9 mortars. 8. 3 guns. 9. 17 guns. 10. 12 guns. 11. 4 guns. 12. French reserves. 13. Cavalry. 14. Line of fire from French Frigate. *A*, British redoubt assaulted by South Carolina Militia. *B*. Redoubt assaulted by troops under D'Estaing and Lincoln.

THE SIEGE OF SAVANNAH, SEPTEMBER–OCTOBER, 1779

TWELVE days had elapsed between the sighting of the French fleet and the arrival of Lincoln, during which time Prévost used gangs of some four thousand negroes, working in reliefs night and day, to throw up redoubts, dig trenches, and build abattis.   Protected on one side by the river and on the other by a swamp, the British army had but a mile of front to organize.   On September 23 the allies began to run their parallels toward the British works.   Ten days later the belated French cannon opened on the defenders.   For five days the bombardment continued without inflicting serious damage.   D'Estaing became worried.   His position was a precarious one.   At any time an enemy fleet might appear, and he feared also the autumnal gales of the southern Atlantic.   He felt that he could lose no more time — he had already been five weeks on the American coast.   At dawn on October 9 the assault was made.   The scheme was well contrived.   The South Carolina militia was to make a demonstration against redoubt *A* on the British left.   A force under Count Dillon was to advance through the swamp and break through the British defenses on their extreme right.   The main blow, led by D'Estaing and Lincoln, was directed against redoubt *B*.   The attack was to be made at daybreak. The militia played their part.   But Dillon became lost in the swamp, was not in position in time, and was driven away by a withering fire as he attempted to maneuver in broad daylight.   Against redoubt *B* the assault was made with the greatest gallantry.   In the face of a terrible fire the French and Americans charged. D'Estaing was twice wounded and Pulaski was killed.   The colors of France and Carolina were planted on the parapet where Captain Taws fought the onslaught.   Taws and many of his men were killed in hand-to-hand encounter.   Then Prévost counter-attacked, caught the assaulting troops in the flank, and drove them back with terrible losses.   Prévost had won, with a total loss of one hundred and fifty-five; while the French and Americans lost eight hundred and thirty-seven.   D'Estaing reëmbarked and sailed away; while Lincoln on the eighteenth retired to Charleston, saddened by the blasting of his hopes.

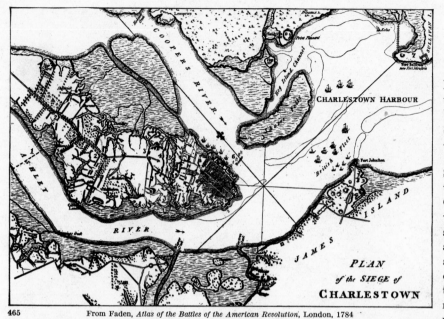

CHARLESTOWN HARBOUR

PLAN
of the SIEGE of
CHARLESTOWN

465   From Faden, *Atlas of the Battles of the American Revolution*, London, 1784

THE BRITISH BESIEGE AND CAPTURE CHARLESTON

News of the raising of the siege of Savannah brought Clinton to the South (see map, No. 448). On February 11, 1780, he landed at St. John's Island about thirty miles south of Charleston. Seven weeks later he began serious operations against this important seaport. Lincoln then commanded only fourteen hundred Continentals and a thousand militia; but Washington was hurrying reinforcements southward. Like Prévost at Savannah, Lincoln protected the landward side of the city with almost impregnable redoubts. Land batteries, obstacles in the harbor, and a small American squadron kept the British fleet from closing in. But the game was hopeless. Clinton began preliminary siege operations on March 29. During the next twenty-eight days he ran three parallels with saps, double saps, and flying saps, after the most approved method of the time. On the twenty-eighth day he reached Lincoln's works. His army now numbered fourteen thousand men. Lincoln was completely surrounded; and surrendered on May 12. Major André checked off the prisoners: seven generals, two hundred and ninety other officers, and five thousand, one hundred and sixty-nine rank and file. Lincoln's surrender is unique in American military annals. Never before or since has an independent army charged with a mission of such importance surrendered to an enemy. Washington was at first inclined to think that Lincoln should have retreated northward before it was too late. But, when he learned all the circumstances, he held Lincoln free of blame. Clinton, victorious at Charleston, determined to make the people of South Carolina feel the power of the conqueror. His proclamations made neutrality impossible and served to embitter further the already terrible partisan war between Patriots and Loyalists. The British commander then sent into the interior several minor expeditions which met with little opposition. Finally, with his main body at Charleston and strong detachments at Savannah and Augusta, he established a chain of posts from Ninety-Six on the west through Camden and Cheraw to Georgetown on the coast (see map, No. 473). Then, in the belief that Georgia and South Carolina were conquered, he sailed for New York, leaving Cornwallis to direct, under his supervision, further operations in the South.

466   From the Ms. Proclamation of General Clinton, dated Charleston, June 1, 1780, urging His Majesty's "deluded subjects" to return to their allegiance, in the Emmet Collection, New York Public Library

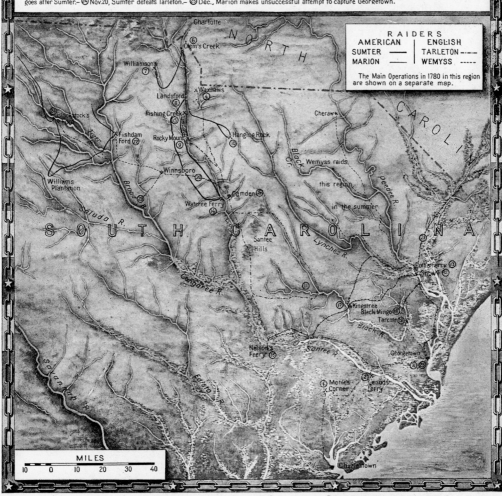

RAIDERS' OPERATIONS IN SOUTH CAROLINA IN 1780

① Apr. 14, Tarleton routs Huger.– ② May 6, Tarleton defeats American cavalry.– ③ May 20, Tarleton establishes English rule in Georgetown. ④ May 29, Tarleton, galloping ahead of main army, routs Buford.– ⑤ May 30, Tarleton rejoins Cornwallis.– ⑥ June 6, Sumter, from Mecklenburg, N.C., encamps. ⑦ July 12, Sumter defeats Huck.– ⑧ July 30, Sumter's rendevous.– ⑨ Aug. 1, Sumter attacks English and retires.– ⑩ Aug. 6, Sumter destroys English post and retires.– ⑪ Aug..., Tarleton raids country; forced back by McCaffrey.– ⑫ Aug. 10, Marion encamps.– ⑬ Aug. 12, Raid by Marion.– ⑭ Aug. 15, Sumter here captures English supply-train.– ⑮ Aug. 18, Tarleton practically annihilates Sumter (who later gathers new force at Clem's Creek).– ⑯ Aug. 21, Marion raids English stores.– ⑰ Aug. 27, Marion defeats Wemyss and retires to N.C.– Marion returns and defeats Loyalists at ⑱ Sep. 14, and at ⑲ shortly after.– ⑳ Oct.– Nov., Tarleton, from Winnsboro, to check Marion.– ㉑ Nov., Marion retires before Tarleton.– ㉒ Nov. 9, Sumter, again in field, defeats Wemyss.– ㉓ Nov., Tarleton, recalled by Cornwallis, goes after Sumter.– ㉔ Nov. 20, Sumter defeats Tarleton.– ㉕ Dec., Marion makes unsuccessful attempt to capture Georgetown.

467   Drawn expressly for *The Pageant of America* by Gregor Noetzel, American Geographical Society, New York

PARTISAN WARFARE IN THE SOUTH

IN 1780 and 1781 South Carolina witnessed civil warfare in its ugliest form. From the successful defense of Charleston early in the war the state had been in the hands of the Patriots. But the people of the region were not of one mind. The back country was settled by a variety of nationalities, who were living more or less separated from one another. Some of these pioneers had but recently come to America. Many village communities were fiercely loyal to the ancient British Government. Others chafed under the political power of the planters on the coast. For practically half a decade the Patriot legislature had held the Loyalists in check with a heavy hand. The fall of Charleston turned the tables. With the British army in control of the state the Loyalists rose to avenge the sufferings which they had been compelled to endure. This drove the Patriots to maddened counter-thrusts. The map shows the operations of one year in the partisan war that resulted. Cornwallis sent Tarleton's cavalry from point to point to destroy the Patriot forces. But Marion, Sumter, and Pickens struck furiously back.

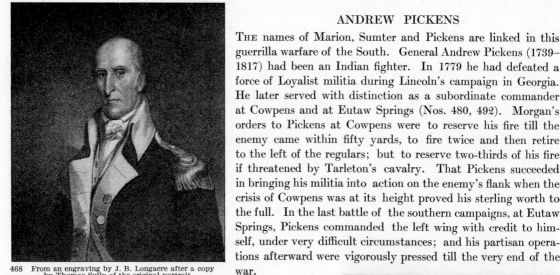

468   From an engraving by J. B. Longacre after a copy
         by Thomas Sully of the original portrait

ANDREW PICKENS

THE names of Marion, Sumter and Pickens are linked in this guerrilla warfare of the South. General Andrew Pickens (1739–1817) had been an Indian fighter. In 1779 he had defeated a force of Loyalist militia during Lincoln's campaign in Georgia. He later served with distinction as a subordinate commander at Cowpens and at Eutaw Springs (Nos. 480, 492). Morgan's orders to Pickens at Cowpens were to reserve his fire till the enemy came within fifty yards, to fire twice and then retire to the left of the regulars; but to reserve two-thirds of his fire if threatened by Tarleton's cavalry. That Pickens succeeded in bringing his militia into action on the enemy's flank when the crisis of Cowpens was at its height proved his sterling worth to the full. In the last battle of the southern campaigns, at Eutaw Springs, Pickens commanded the left wing with credit to himself, under very difficult circumstances; and his partisan operations afterward were vigorously pressed till the very end of the war.

FRANCIS MARION

FRANCIS MARION (1732–95) was a South Carolinian of Huguenot descent who had fought in the last French and Indian War. He became a captain in 1775 under Colonel Moultrie. He rose to fame in 1780, when, as the "damned swamp fox," he inspired Loyalists and isolated British garrisons with dread. Moving swiftly and secretly from point to point, he fell upon his enemies and fought them with a ferocity which only civil war can breed. He served well the Patriot cause; for such continual harrassing aided materially in weakening the army of Lord Cornwallis. Such fighting was a factor in the success or failure of the southern campaign which Germain, in his London office, did not take into consideration.

469   From a portrait now in the South Carolina room
         at Mt. Vernon, painted by H. N. Hyneman and based
         on an early engraving

470   From the portrait by C. W. Peale in
              Independence Hall, Philadelphia

THOMAS SUMTER

THE greatest of the partisan leaders was Thomas Sumter (1734–1832), the "Carolina game cock." Sumter was a Virginian who had been with Braddock, and was an experienced Indian fighter. With a force of less than a thousand irregulars in July and August, 1780, Sumter made two attacks in quick succession upon the British posts at Rocky Mount and at Hanging Rock (see map, No. 467). In both he was beaten off; but in both he inflicted heavy losses on his enemy. His advance raised the whole region between the Santee and the Pedee Rivers to rebellion. With Pickens, Marion, and Sumter on his flanks, Cornwallis' position (see map, No. 473) became embarrassing as the autumn of 1780 approached. His discomfort was increased by news that another American army was assembling in North Carolina. To retire to Charleston would be to give up a conquered state; while to hold passively his present line was to fritter away his army. His mission called for the conquest of North Carolina and even Virginia. So he prepared to strike north as soon as he could count on the Loyalist militia after the harvest was in.

GATES IN THE SOUTH

IN April, 1780, Washington ordered Baron de Kalb, who had come from France with Lafayette, to take two thousand of the Continental line to the aid of Lincoln in South Carolina. It was a long march and there were times when the force was on the verge of starvation. At Petersburg, Virginia, Kalb learned of the fall of Charleston. He pushed steadily on across North Carolina until he entered the theater of operations and encamped in July about fifty miles north of the British post at Cheraw. Here Kalb, experienced soldier that he was, carefully studied the situation and prepared a plan. But on July 25 there arrived in Kalb's camp General Gates, whom Congress, without consulting Washington, had appointed to command the southern army. Kalb submitted his plan to his new superior, who declined to consider it. On the day after his arrival Gates ordered the army to march against Camden, the principal British post, one hundred and twenty miles away. The march was accomplished in two weeks, during which time some twelve hundred untrained militia from North Carolina and Virginia joined the American army. Lord Rawdon, who commanded at Camden, urged Cornwallis to come up with reinforcements; and the British general arrived three days before the battle.

471   General Baron Johann de Kalb, 1721-80, from the portrait by C. W. Peale in Independence Hall, Philadelphia

BATTLE OF CAMDEN, AUGUST 16, 1780

THE Battle of Camden is an example of unnecessary loss of life and military advantage because of the ignorance and folly of the commanding general. Within striking distance of Camden on August 15, Gates, without adequate information either by reconnoissance or otherwise, ordered a night march as a prelude to a surprise attack at dawn. He commanded three thousand and fifty-two men present and fit for duty, a little more than a third of them practically valueless because of lack of training. Cornwallis mustered two thousand one hunded and seventeen, of whom half were well-seasoned regulars. The British commander also ordered a night march. About two in the morning of August 16 the advance guards came in contact some nine miles north of Camden, where the highway lay between two swamps. Both generals deployed, and awaited the day. Gates put his Continentals on his right and his militia on his left, the Virginia troops holding the flank. At dawn Cornwallis attacked his enemy's left and promptly sent the militia flying from the field, carrying Gates with them in the rush. The American reserve of Maryland troops counter-attacked and for a time held up the British advance. Then the American Continentals under Kalb, upon whom the command had devolved, took the offensive. For an hour, until Kalb fell mortally wounded, there was fierce fighting in the woods. As the battle developed Cornwallis discovered that no cavalry opposed him, Gates' mounted troops having fled with the militia. Then the British general sent Tarleton's squadrons to attack the flank and rear of the gallant Continentals. This maneuver destroyed the American army, which abandoned the field in a rout, losing its baggage, artillery, and supplies. Gates covered the sixty miles back to Charlotte on the day of the battle and made Hillsboro, a hundred miles farther, within the next forty-eight hours.

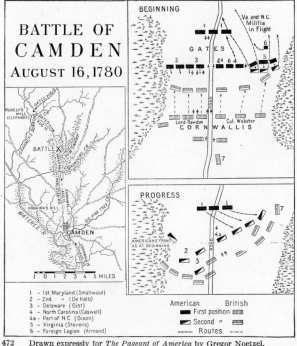

BATTLE OF CAMDEN
AUGUST 16, 1780

1 - 1st Maryland (Smallwood)
2 - 2nd   "   (De Kalb)
3 - Delaware (Gist)
4 - North Carolina (Caswell)
4a - Part of N C (Dixon)
5 - Virginia (Stevens)
6 - Foreign Legion (Armand)

American   British
First position
Second "
Routes

472   Drawn expressly for The Pageant of America by Gregor Noetzel, American Geographical Society, New York

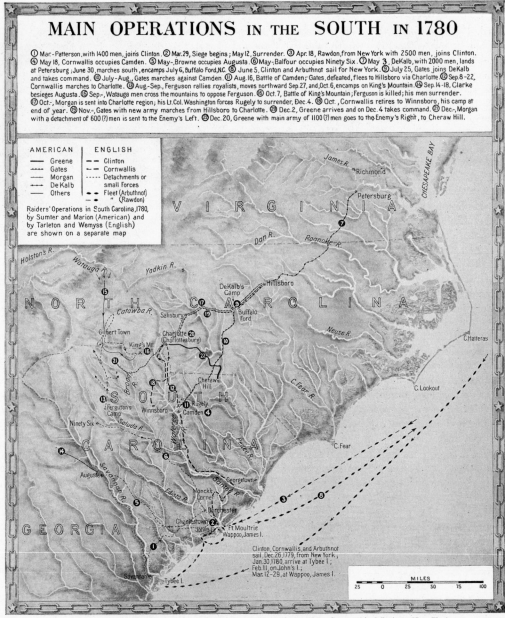

MAIN OPERATIONS in the SOUTH in 1780

① Mac-Patterson,with 1400 men, joins Clinton. ② Mar.29, Siege begins ; May 12, Surrender. ③ Apr. 18, Rawdon, from New York with 2500 men, joins Clinton. ④ May 18, Cornwallis occupies Camden. ⑤ May-, Browne occupies Augusta.⑥ May-, Balfour occupies Ninety Six. ⑦ May 3, DeKalb, with 2000 men, lands at Petersburg ; June 30, marches south , encamps July 6, Buffalo Ford, NC. ⑧ June 5, Clinton and Arbuthnot sail for New York. ⑨ July 25, Gates joins DeKalb and takes command. ⑩ July-Aug., Gates marches against Camden.⑪ Aug.16, Battle of Camden; Gates, defeated, flees to Hillsboro via Charlotte. ⑫ Sep.8-22, Cornwallis marches to Charlotte. ⑬ Aug.-Sep., Ferguson rallies royalists, moves northward Sep.27, and Oct. 6, encamps on King's Mountain. ⑭ Sep.14-18, Clarke besieges Augusta.⑮ Sep-, Watauga men cross the mountains to oppose Ferguson. ⑯ Oct. 7, Battle of King's Mountain ; Ferguson is killed ; his men surrender. ⑰ Oct-, Morgan is sent into Charlotte region ; his Lt.Col. Washington forces Rugely to surrender, Dec. 4. ⑱ Oct. , Cornwallis retires to Winnsboro, his camp at end of year. ⑲ Nov.-, Gates with new army marches from Hillsboro to Charlotte. ⑳ Dec.2, Greene arrives and on Dec. 4 takes command. ㉑ Dec-, Morgan with a detachment of 600 (?) men is sent to the Enemy's Left. ㉒ Dec. 20, Greene with main army of 1100 (?) men goes to the Enemy's Right , to Cheraw Hill.

473   Drawn expressly for *The Pageant of America* by Gregor Noetzel, American Geographical Society, New York

THE INVASION OF NORTH CAROLINA

Two days after the Battle of Camden the brilliant Tarleton, who had been sent against Sumter, succeeded in creeping up on that wily partisan and taking him unawares at Fishing Creek. The surprise was complete and the American losses heavy: one hundred and fifty killed and wounded and three hundred prisoners, against only fifteen killed and wounded on the British side. Cornwallis now had no important force to oppose him. He decided to proceed with the invasion of North Carolina. In September the Carolinians along the way saw two columns of seasoned British troops marching northward toward Charlotte, which point these columns, after two weeks of marching, reached on the twenty-second. A third detachment under Major Ferguson was advancing through the back country at a considerable distance on the left of the main body. Though two American armies had been destroyed in succession, Cornwallis' position was not easy. There was much sickness among his troops; and the partisan leaders, Marion and Sumter, continued their galling attacks upon his detached posts and communications.

474 Bust of Lieut.-Colonel Patrick Ferguson, courtesy of Mrs. G. A. Ferguson, Kirkmundy, Scotland

475 From the painting *Sycamore Shoals; The Departure for King's Mountain* by Lloyd Branson, courtesy of the artist

FERGUSON'S RAID, SEPTEMBER 8—OCTOBER 6, 1780

In Charlotte, the British general found himself in the midst of a bitterly hostile population, who made communication difficult by capturing or shooting down practically every dispatch bearer. In this way Cornwallis was kept in ignorance of Ferguson's plight at King's Mountain until too late to assist him. Ferguson was one of the few British officers in Cornwallis' command who retained any faith in the efficacy of the Loyalist militia of the Carolinas. But Cornwallis, as the commanding general, assumed responsibility for Ferguson's expedition in the back settlements to crush Patriot opposition and recruit further Loyalist levies. While Ferguson was advancing parallel with the main body, a fierce American attack upon Augusta, Georgia (September 14–18, under Clarke) was beaten off by the garrison. The attackers retreated northwestward toward the mountains. The commander at Ninety-Six suggested to Ferguson that he head them off; and Ferguson rashly hastened westward until he had placed no less than seventy miles between himself and Charlotte. An important British force had never before come so near to the southern mountains. News of Ferguson's raid came swiftly to the settlement in the Watauga valley. Promptly the frontiersmen decided upon a counterstroke.

KING'S MOUNTAIN, OCTOBER 7

To his amazement Ferguson suddenly found himself confronted by a force of frontiersmen trained in the hunt and in wars with the Indians. These were mostly borderers (like John Sevier) who had left their farms and come through the mountains directly the alarm had reached them. Ferguson withdrew his force in haste toward Charlotte; but could not reach that place. His adversaries were mounted and brought him to bay on King's Mountain, where, unskilled in the ways of the Indian fighter, he thought he could stand indefinitely. On the afternoon of October 7 the Americans tied their horses at the base of

the mountain and advanced silently up its wooded sides. Their numbers, their unerring aim, and the quiet determination with which they met and checked every bayonet charge brought them victory before nightfall. The affair was as brilliant as it was unexpected, and its importance was out of all proportion to the numbers engaged. Cornwallis had lost a thousand men. Stunned by the reverse, he abandoned his advance and fell back to Winnsboro. Here he contracted a fever and remained incapacitated for several weeks.

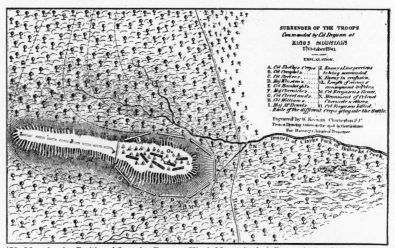

476 Map showing Position of Opposing Forces at King's Mountain, from Ramsay's *Annals of Tennessee*, 1853, engraving by W. Keenan, Charleston, S. C., based on drawing made on the spot by General Graham

477 William Washington, 1752–1810, Colonel of Cavalry, from the portrait by C. W. Peale in Independence Hall, Philadelphia

GREENE TAKES COMMAND IN THE SOUTH, 1780

WHEN Congress received the news of the defeat at Camden of the second commander whom they had appointed over the southern army, they turned to Washington to nominate a third. Without hesitation he chose his ablest subordinate, Nathanael Greene, and sent with him, as second in command, Baron Steuben, who was also charged with the duty of presiding at the court-martial that was to inquire into the conduct of Gates. With these two officers went also Morgan, of Saratoga fame, John Laurens, and "Light Horse Harry" Lee. Taking command in the South on December 4, Greene quickly won the confidence of the cavalryman, William Washington, and of the raiders Marion, Sumter, and Pickens. While the Americans could not muster a large force of troops, they confronted Cornwallis with a group of able, experienced officers, rarely equaled in the Revolution. As for Gates, no inquiry was ever held, but his career was at an end.

GREENE'S PLAN OF ACTION

GREENE in command of the southern army proved himself a leader almost the equal of Washington in military worth. With his few hundred Continentals and a fluctuating body of militia, Greene knew that he could not risk a battle. He therefore decided to carry on and intensify the partisan warfare of the Carolina guerrilla leaders. With this plan he divided his army. Morgan with about six hundred men he sent to coöperate with Sumter on Cornwallis' left flank, and gave him orders to threaten communications and posts all the way to Augusta. At the same time Huger was ordered to advance with the remainder of the army, a little more than a thousand, into the valley of the Pedee, where Marion was active, to threaten Georgetown and Cornwallis' communications with Charleston. Greene went with Huger. Knowing that Cornwallis would attempt to defeat his divided enemy piecemeal, Greene prepared to protect himself by rapid retreat. He sent his chief engineer, Kosciuszko, and his quartermaster, Carrington, to reconnoiter the fords of the various rivers of North Carolina and to gather boats and wagons at strategic points. Meanwhile Cornwallis, encouraged by Germain after the Battle of Camden, became virtually independent of Clinton, the British commander in chief.

478   From the painting *Meeting of Greene and Gates at Charlotte, North Carolina*, by Howard Pyle (1853–1911), for H. C. Lodge, *The Story of the Revolution*, New York, 1898. © Charles Scribner's Sons

TARLETON AGAINST MORGAN

GREENE's audacious maneuver, which was the result of desperation, led his adversary to commit a military blunder. Cornwallis, instead of concentrating his forces and striking swiftly at either of his opponent's forces, scattered his own troops. Remaining with the main body at Winnsboro, he sent one force to guard Camden and on January 1 dispatched Tarleton with his Legion to destroy Morgan. Tarleton, moving rapidly as always, advanced toward Morgan at Grindall, but putting himself to the west of his enemy. He hoped to drive the great ranger eastward, where Cornwallis could destroy him. But Morgan was not to be caught in such a trap. He abandoned his camp on January 14, retreated northwest, and, suddenly halting, offered battle in a most surprising position. When Tarleton reconnoitered it, he found Morgan's little force posted in open woods, with flanks unprotected, and with a river at their backs.

479 Map illustrating Tarleton's pursuit of Morgan, drawn expressly for *The Pageant of America* by Gregor Noetzel, American Geographical Society, New York

But Morgan knew how to handle his untrained militia. "I would not have had a swamp in view of my militia on any consideration; they would have made for it and nothing could have detained them from it. . . . As to retreat, it was the very thing I wished to cut off all hope of. . . . Had I crossed the river, one-half of my militia would immediately have abandoned me." Tarleton, not without justification, anticipated a crushing victory.

THE BATTLE OF COWPENS, JANUARY 17, 1781

ON the morning of January 17, 1781, Morgan prepared for battle. He placed his Continentals and some militia on a low hill in ground half cleared of trees. In front of them were the militia, most of them skilled marksmen, with orders not to retreat until they had fired two volleys "at killing distance." In rear, behind a second hill, Colonel William Washington with a force of cavalry lay concealed. Altogether, Morgan had less than a thousand men, while Tarleton, advancing to the attack, with troops tired after a night march, commanded about eleven hundred. Morgan's militia, using the cover which the ground afforded, inflicted heavy

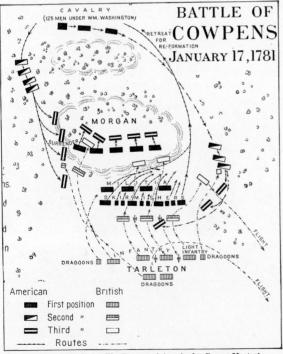

480   Drawn expressly for *The Pageant of America* by Gregor Noetzel, American Geographical Society, New York

losses, particularly in officers, upon the attacking British. Then the state troops retired by the left flank, to re-form behind the hill which had concealed Washington, who came out to cover their retreat and drove off the pursuing cavalry. The British infantry continued its advance upon the Continentals. Tarleton sent out some cavalry to menace his opponent's right, whereupon Morgan wheeled his right battalion to meet the threat. Then came an unpremediated move. Mistaking orders, the whole right wing of Morgan's line, following the flank battalion, fell back with perfect steadiness, as though to change front to the right. Tarleton's troops, already thrown into disorder by the fire of the militia, plunged after the retreating Americans. Then on the British left appeared the militia, ready for action. Just as these troops came in sight, Morgan ordered his retiring lines to halt and fire. The British were taken unawares and Tarleton's force was thrown into inextricable confusion. The commander with a few of his mounted troops made good his escape, but the main body of his force was either killed or captured. Morgan, halting on the field long enough to secure his prisoners, crossed the Broad River the same day, and hurried northeastward to avoid Cornwallis.

481   Lord Charles Cornwallis, 1737–1805, from the portrait by Thomas Gainsborough (1727–1788) in the National Portrait Gallery, London

MORGAN'S ESCAPE TO SALISBURY, JANUARY 18, 1781

LORD CORNWALLIS was himself responsible that the defeat at Cowpens was not quickly neutralized. His plan had been to push on to King's Mountain while Tarleton was coming up on Morgan's right. Such a position would have put him in Morgan's rear when the battle was fought, and would have enabled him to crush the Americans with his superior numbers. But Cornwallis had been slow because of his worries concerning Huger's activities on the Pedee. As a consequence he was some distance south of King's Mountain; and Morgan, although encumbered with his prisoners and his captured supplies, eluded him and hurried northward. Then began the most famous retreat in the annals of the Revolution. The forces, even according to the standards of the day, were small; but both sides were ably led. Cornwallis was easily the best of the British generals who enjoyed independent command in America. As for his adversary, Greene, Tarleton's comment will suffice: "Every measure of the Americans, during their march from the Catawba to Virginia, was judiciously designed and vigorously executed."

482   Col. Banastre Tarleton, 1754–1833, from a mezzotint by S. W. Reynolds after the portrait by Sir Joshua Reynolds, in the Emmet Collection, New York Public Library

THE RACE FOR THE FORDS

WITHIN a week after Cowpens Morgan had marched nearly ninety miles and had put his army across the Catawba (see map, No. 486). Here, on January 30, General Greene, accompanied only by one aide and three orderlies, rode into camp, having come across country from Huger's force. The news of Cowpens determined Greene to unite his army in North Carolina; and he had left Huger with orders to follow up the Yadkin. Meanwhile Cornwallis had made the momentous decision to pursue the American army northward. At

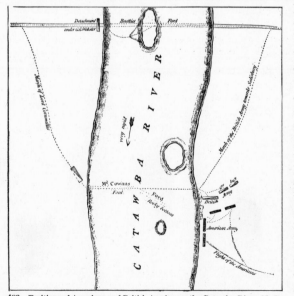

483   Positions of American and British Armies on the Catawba River, N. C., from an engraving in Stedman's *History of the American War*, London, 1794

Ramsour's Mill, some twenty miles southwest of the Catawba, he spent two days in burning all his tents, baggage, extra clothing, and supplies. Most of his wagons went also. The British army was stripping down for a rapid advance. On January 29 Cornwallis reached McCowan's Ford on the Catawba, only to find that the winter rains had swollen the stream. For two days he waited for the water to subside, while Greene hastened for the Yadkin, leaving three hundred North Carolina militia to dispute with Cornwallis the passage of the Catawba. On February 1 the British forced the crossing and dispersed the militia. The next day Greene reached the Yadkin, also swollen with the rains. But there was Carrington with boats. The little force was quickly put across. The last boats were making for the northern shore when Cornwallis' advance guard came hurrying into view. This hurrying forward on the part of Cornwallis was just what Greene himself desired most.

ACROSS THE DAN

By keeping just in front of him Greene was deliberately enticing Cornwallis northward (see map, No. 486), while at the same time bringing his own troops nearer to Steuben, who was assembling reinforcements in Virginia. Cornwallis, having no boats, was forced to seek shallower fords twenty-five miles up the Yadkin. He then hurried toward the upper fords of the Dan in the hope of reaching them before Greene could. But the maneuver was useless. Greene had boats on the lower Dan. Moreover, at Guilford, on February 9, Greene's army was reunited. Still feeling too weak to offer battle, however, he retreated across the Dan. He had won a thrilling race. Both armies were worn by this long mid-winter march. Cornwallis had lost about two hundred and fifty men and now felt keenly the absence of the supplies burned at Ramsour's Mill. Moreover, two hundred and thirty miles lay between him and his base at Charleston. Greene's retreat on his own base had vastly weakened his enemy. The American commander quickly recrossed the Dan, and, as soon as he was reinforced, offered battle at Guilford Court House, on ground he had carefully chosen during his retreat.

484   Major-General Nathanael Greene, 1742–86, from the portrait by C. W. Peale (1741–1827) in Independence Hall, Philadelphia

In these masterly movements Greene showed himself to advantage under the given circumstances, which called for a Fabian defense. Greene's tactics at Guilford were modeled somewhat after those of Morgan at Cowpens. He posted his troops in three lines. The North Carolina militia were in front with expert riflemen on either flank. About three hundred yards in their rear was a line of Virginia militia, with Washington's cavalry on their right, and Lee's on their left, flank. Five hundred and fifty yards in rear of the second line was the third, composed of Continentals. The second line was in the woods; but the first and third were on the edge of clearings, giving in each case a good field of fire. About noon Cornwallis attacked. Greene's first line fired two volleys and fled. The second line stood their ground until the British enveloped the right flank, when they gave way

and retreated past the left of the Continentals. Cornwallis pressed on through the woods to the second clearing and joined battle with the Continentals, the two forces being about equal in number. Here Cornwallis did not sufficiently coördinate his attack. Three somewhat disjointed assaults were launched across the open fields against the four Continental regiments on the rising ground in the woods on the opposite sides. Two were repulsed with heavy loss, one British battalion being driven in confusion from the field and losing nearly half its strength. Greene might have counterattacked at this point; but chose not to risk the possibility of the destruction of his army, which the defeat of such a maneuver might have entailed. He re-formed in his old lines; and when Cornwallis concentrated all his troops for the final assault, Greene withdrew in good order from the field. Cornwallis followed him only a short distance; and before morning the Americans had taken up a good defensive position behind the Haw River.

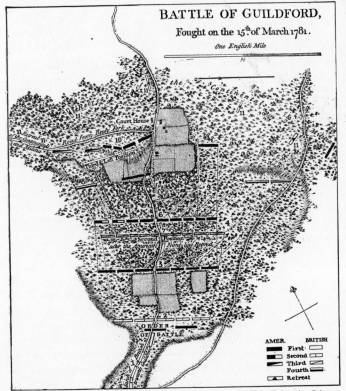

BATTLE OF GUILDFORD,
Fought on the 15th of March 1781.

One English Mile

485   From the *Atlas of the Battles of the American Revolution*, in Yale University Library

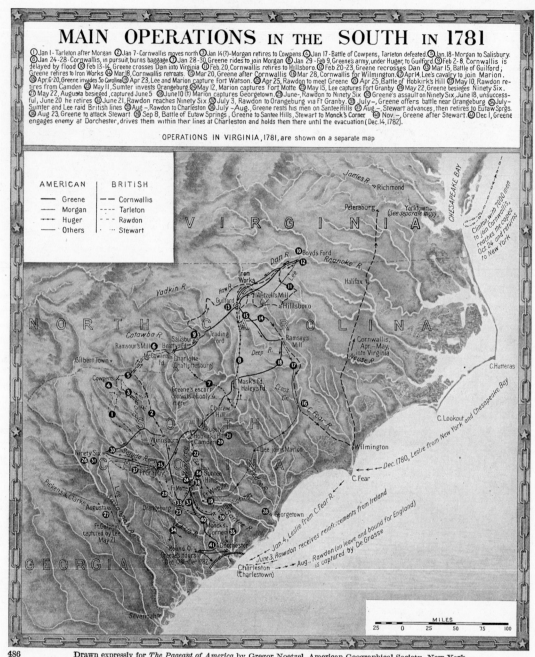

MAIN OPERATIONS IN THE SOUTH IN 1781

①Jan 1 - Tarleton after Morgan ②Jan 7 - Cornwallis moves north ③Jan 14(?)-Morgan retires to Cowpens.④Jan 17-Battle of Cowpens, Tarleton defeated.⑤Jan 18-Morgan to Salisbury. ⑥Jan 24-28-Cornwallis, in pursuit, burns baggage ⑦Jan 28-30, Greene rides to join Morgan ⑧Jan 29-Feb 9, Greene's army, under Huger, to Guilford ⑨Feb 2-8, Cornwallis is delayed by flood ⑩Feb 13-14, Greene crosses Dan into Virginia ⑪Feb.20, Cornwallis retires to Hillsboro.⑫Feb 20-23, Greene recrosses Dan ⑬Mar 15, Battle of Guilford ; Greene retires to Iron Works ⑭Mar.18, Cornwallis retreats. ⑮Mar 20, Greene after Cornwallis ⑯Mar 28, Cornwallis for Wilmington.⑰Apr 14, Lee's cavalry to join Marion. ⑱Apr.6-20,Greene invades So Carolina⑲Apr 23,Lee and Marion capture Fort Watson.⑳Apr 25, Rawdon to meet Greene ㉑Apr 25,Battle of Hobkirk's Hill ㉒May 10, Rawdon re- tires from Camden ㉓May 11, Sumter invests Orangeburg ㉔May 12, Marion captures Fort Motte ㉕May 15, Lee captures Fort Granby ㉖May 22,Greene besieges Ninety Six. ㉗May 22, Augusta besieged , captured June 5 ㉘June 10 (?) Marion captures Georgetown.㉙June-, Rawdon to Ninety Six ㉚Greene's assault on Ninety Six, June 18, unsuccess- ful, June 20 he retires ㉛June 21, Rawdon reaches Ninety Six. ㉜July 3, Rawdon to Orangeburg via Ft Granby. ㉝July-, Greene offers battle near Orangeburg ㉞July- Sumter and Lee raid British lines ㉟Aug -, Rawdon to Charleston ㊱July - Aug., Greene rests his men on Santee Hills ㊲Aug -, Stewart advances, then retires to Eutaw Sprgs. ㊳Aug 23, Greene to attack Stewart ㊴Sep 8, Battle of Eutaw Springs , Greene to Santee Hills, Stewart to Monck's Corner ㊵Nov -, Greene after Stewart ㊶Dec 1, Greene engages enemy at Dorchester, drives them within their lines at Charleston and holds them there until the evacuation (Dec.14,1782).

OPERATIONS IN VIRGINIA, 1781, are shown on a separate map

486   Drawn expressly for *The Pageant of America* by Gregor Noetzel, American Geographical Society, New York

THE BRITISH RETREAT TO WILMINGTON, MARCH 28, 1781

THOUGH technically defeated in battle Greene had made his campaign a great success. Cornwallis had lost a third of his force at Guilford. His enemy was still in the field, with an army intact and aggressive. The British commander had no choice but to abandon his advanced position so far from his base. If he retired to Camden, he admitted the defeat of his whole campaign. If he went to Wilmington, North Carolina, where a base had already been prepared, he could refit his army and perhaps destroy Greene, if Greene should follow him to the coast. In any event, from Wilmington he could strike north into Virginia and attempt to bring the war to a close by a decisive campaign in the Old Dominion. Cornwallis chose the Wilmington alterna- tive. Greene followed him until his objective became certain, then turned quickly southward to drive the British army out of South Carolina.

Cornwallis Retreating!

PHILADELPHIA, April 7, 1781.

Extract of a Letter from Major-General *Greene*, dated CAMP, at *Buffelo Creek*, March 23, 1781.

"ON the 16th Inftant I wrote your Excellency, giving an Account of an Action which happened at Guilford Court-Houfe the Day before. I was then perfuaded that notwithftanding we were obliged to give up the Ground, we had reaped the Advantage of the Action. Circumftances fince confirm me in Opinion that the Enemy were too much gauled to improve their Succefs. We lay at the Iron-Works three Days, preparing ourfelves for another Action, and expecting the Enemy to advance : But of a fudden they took their Departure, leaving behind them evident Marks of Diftrefs. All our wounded at Guilford, which had fallen into their Hands, and 70 of their own, too bad to move, were left at New-Garden. Moft of their Officers fuffered-- Lord Cornwallis had his Horfe fhot under him--- Col. Steward, of the Guards was killed, General O Hara and Cols. Tarlton and Webfter, wounded. Only three Field-Officers efcaped, if Reports, which feem to be authentic, can be relied on.

Our Army are in good Spirits, notwithftanding our Sufferings, and are advancing towards the Enemy; they are retreating to Crofs-Creek.

In South-Carolina, Generals Sumpter and Marian have gained feveral little Advantages. In one the Enemy loft 60 Men, who had under their Care a large Quantity of Stores, which were taken, but by an unfortunate Miftake were afterwards re taken.

Publifhed by Order,

CHARLES THOMSON, Secretary.

§†§ Printed at N. WILLIS's Office.

487 From a Philadelphia broadside outlining Greene's activities in the South, in the Emmet Collection, New York Public Library

488 From an engraving *Marion Crossing the Pedee*, by C. Burt after the painting by W. Ranney in the possession of the publishers

GREENE INVADES SOUTH CAROLINA

GREENE in South Carolina faced a task as difficult as that of dealing with Cornwallis. His militia, their period of enlistment up, had gone home, and his army numbered less than fifteen hundred men, not half the strength of a modern American infantry regiment. He counted on the aid of the irregular forces of Marion, Sumter, and Pickens. Against him was Lord Rawdon, a young officer of twenty-six with more than eight thousand men under his command. But Rawdon with this force was commissioned to garrison and hold two states; and so his troops were inevitably scattered in small detachments. His outer ring of forts lay in a great arc stretching from Augusta on the left through Ninety-Six and Camden to Georgetown on the right. An inner line consisted of Fort Granby, Orangeburg, Fort Motte, and Fort Watson. In each of these posts were from a hundred to a thousand men. Rawdon himself with a small force was at Camden. Toward this point Greene swiftly advanced, hoping to surprise his adversary (see map, No. 486).

FORT WATSON, APRIL 23, 1781

MEANWHILE the American commander kept Lee's cavalry on his left, to watch for a southward move by Cornwallis, and then to join with Marion on the Pedee and attack Fort Watson. Fort Watson was a stockade built on a mound rising forty feet above the plain, and was garrisoned by one hundred and twenty good men. It stood on the Charleston road, beside the Santee River, and straight in the rear of Camden and Hobkirk's Hill. On April 23, after an eight day siege, Fort Watson fell, when the American besiegers, who had been five days preparing the logs, built a tower in one night that commanded the interior of the stockade. The first breach in Rawdon's communications with Charleston had been made. Lee and Marion then hastened to join Greene's force. Greene had found Rawdon informed of his advance and in a good defensive position. The American general thereupon retired to Hobkirk's Hill, about two miles north of Camden, and waited. Greene sent "Light Horse Harry" Lee to join "Old Swamp Fox" Marion in attacking the chain of little posts between Camden and Charleston, which kept the precarious line of communications open to the sea for Lord Rawdon.

489 The Wooden Tower at Fort Watson, from Charles C. Coffin, *The Boys of '76*, after a sketch by Benson J. Lossing

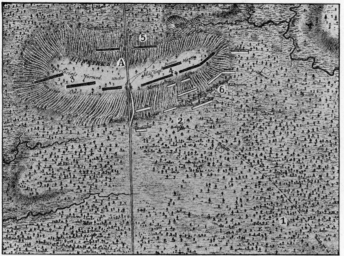

490   From Stedman, *History of the American War*, London, 1794

1. March of British troops in column. 2. Where the British met the American pickets.
3. Virginia Continentals forming the right wing. 4. Maryland Continentals forming the
left wing. 5. Militia in reserve. 6. Battle formation of British under Rawdon. A. Hobkirk's Hill.

HOBKIRK'S HILL, APRIL 25, 1781

LORD RAWDON, British commander in South Carolina, though a large detachment which he had sent in pursuit of Marion had not returned, courageously took the offensive against Greene's outnumbering force. The American commander, reversing the arrangement at Cowpens and Guilford, had deployed his Continentals in the first line, with some militia behind them. Rawdon deployed and attacked Greene's left wing. Greene, thinking he saw an opportunity to destroy his enemy, who had deployed on a narrow front, did not wait to receive him on the high ground, but ordered an assault against the enemy center and the envelopment of both his flanks. This too ambitious maneuver lost Greene the battle. Rawdon threw in his reserves at just the right time, demoralized the 1st Maryland regiment, which comprised Greene's left flank, caused the retreat of the 2nd Maryland, which was next, and thus exposed the flank of the Virginia regiments, which made up Greene's right. The American commander promptly withdrew in good order from the battle and took up a strong defensive position five miles away. Both sides had suffered heavily. The battle had gone to the British. But the fruits of victory went to the Americans. Rawdon did not feel strong enough to maintain his position so far from his base, especially after the fall of Fort Watson. On May 10 he evacuated Camden and retired to Monck's Corner.

THE SIEGE OF NINETY-SIX, MAY 23—JUNE 18, 1781

RAWDON clearly saw that safety for the British troops lay only in their concentration near the base at Charleston. On the day after he had retired from Camden, Orangeburg fell to Sumter, Fort Granby to Lee, and Fort Motte to Marion. The inner line of British forts were all in the hands of the Americans. Only Augusta and Ninety-Six in the outer line remained. Rawdon had ordered Colonel Cruger, commanding at Ninety-Six, to retire to Charleston when he had evacuated Camden; but the message had been intercepted. Greene sent Lee, who moved with astonishing rapidity, to join Pickens and lay siege to Augusta (May 22); while himself marching against Ninety-Six. Augusta was commanded and garrisoned by Georgia Loyalists, who fought with desperation against Pickens' irregulars from their own state. The besiegers repeated the strategy of the wooden tower and forced the surrender of Augusta on June 5. Meanwhile Greene at Ninety-Six was conducting siege operations against a fortification composed of earthen ramparts, a ditch, abattis, and stockade. Cruger had a garrison of five hundred and fifty men, most of whom were New York and New Jersey Loyalists. On May 23 Greene opened his first parallel. Twelve days later three fresh British regiments arrived at Charleston and Rawdon promptly marched to the relief of Ninety-Six. On June 18, with Rawdon close at hand, Greene assaulted the fort, but failed to take it. He then raised the siege; while Rawdon retired with the garrison to Charleston. Here, broken in health, he sailed for home, leaving Lieutenant-Colonel Stewart in command of the British forces in South Carolina.

491   Francis Rawdon, 1st Marquis of Hastings, from *Historical Portraits*, Part II, 1700–1850, Oxford, England, 1919, after the portrait by Samuel Lane

EUTAW SPRINGS, SEPTEMBER 8, 1781

AFTER resting for a few weeks during the hot summer months Greene resumed the offensive. Stewart was new to South Carolina and to independent command. He allowed Greene to march without his knowledge to within striking distance of his army at Eutaw Springs. The American commander advanced into battle in the tried formation of militia in a front line (5, 6) and the Continentals in a second (2, 3, 4). Stewart deployed his force in a single line (11). The militia advanced with steadiness. As the battle was joined, one of the fiercest fights in the southern campaign developed. Stewart did not handle his force skillfully; and Greene, ordering a

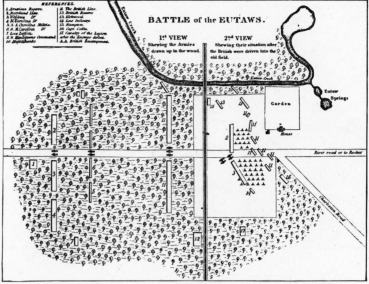

492   From William Johnson, *Sketches of the Life and Correspondence of Nathanael Greene*, Charleston, S. C., 1822

1. American reserve. 2. Maryland line. 3. Virginia line. 4. North Carolina line. 5. South Carolina militia. 6. North Carolina militia. 7. Lee's legion. 8, 9. Henderson's command. 10. Majoribanks. 11. The British line. 12. British reserve. 13. Kirkwood. 14. Lee's Infantry. 15. Hampton. 16. Capt. Coffin. 17. Cavalry of the legion after the enemy's defeat.

general assault, drove him from the field. The British commander had, however, provided against this contingency by ordering the occupation of a brick house and palisaded garden in his rear. Here the British held their ground and re-formed. The American troops meanwhile had entered the abandoned British camp, and, finding rum, became unmanageable. Then the British counter-attacked, and, in their turn, drove the plunderers from the field. Again Greene had lost a battle, this time through the lack of discipline among his troops. Both armies were severely shaken by the encounter and each retired to repair its losses.

THE END OF OPEN WARFARE IN THE SOUTH

NOT long after the battle of Eutaw Springs, Stewart retired into Charleston. The southern campaign had come to an end. Major General Francis V. Greene has summed up the achievements of his namesake. "In the interval [between Greene's assumption of command and Eutaw Springs] Greene's little army had marched nine hundred and fifty miles, fought three battles and a score of minor engagements, conducted five sieges, captured nine posts and taken nearly three thousand prisoners. His army had no organized commissariat or transport system, no tents or camp equipage, and only insufficient clothing. He had no base of supplies, but lived off the country, which, although in the main friendly to him, was filled with a very substantial minority of intensely bitter loyalists. The enemy outnumbered him three to one, and was composed of the best British regulars and Hessians, the well-organized and veteran tory regiments of New York and New Jersey, and a numerous body of local partisans, all well equipped and supplied, and supported by an ample military chest of ready money." — *The Revolutionary War*, p. 253. In looking back at Greene's southern campaign from an age in which the art of war has vastly changed, the American commander still appears one of the greatest leaders of troops that America has produced. His invincible spirit is portrayed in a letter which he wrote in a moment of dejection after Hobkirk's Hill: "We fight, get beat, rise, and fight again."

493   Congressional Medal obverse and reverse, presented by Congress to General Greene, 1781, courtesy of Wayte Raymond, New York

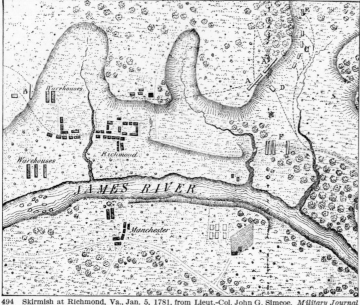

494   Skirmish at Richmond, Va., Jan. 5, 1781, from Lieut.-Col. John G. Simcoe, *Military Journal Operations of . . . The Queen's Rangers During . . . American Revolution*, New York, 1844

CORNWALLIS LEAVES THE CAROLINAS FOR VIRGINIA, 1781

WHEN Cornwallis on April 24, 1781, took the road from Wilmington to Virginia with a little force of about fifteen hundred men, there opened one of the strangest chapters in the history of the Revolution. He had been ordered by his commander in chief to take and hold the Carolinas. But since his victory at Camden he became more and more insubordinate, encouraged in his military attitude by no less an official than the war lord, Germain. At Wilmington, on his own responsibility, and in defiance of his orders, he abandoned the Carolinas and transferred the war to Virginia. One still wonders what military advantage he could hope to win in the Old Dominion that was not more easily obtainable by remaining farther south. Virginia was already the seat of active operations, because it was the base of Greene's army. In November, 1780, Clinton had sent Arnold with sixteen hundred men into the state to interfere with the work of Steuben. Washington had countered by sending Lafayette with twelve hundred. Before the latter's arrival (April 29) Arnold had made a raid on Richmond (January 5). With his usual dash he brought up his troops and drove off the militia, shown at *A A* on the map. He then destroyed a foundry for making cannon, a quantity of military stores and some warehouses and mills. His task accomplished, he hastened back to his boats.

CORNWALLIS IN VIRGINIA, 1781

BENEDICT ARNOLD, after his treason, had served with the British in the North and was now in Virginia in command of a force mostly of Loyalists. In February, Clinton sent Phillips with twenty-six hundred troops to join Arnold and take command in Virginia, and Washington ordered Wayne to follow Lafayette with a thousand men. Clinton later sent more reinforcements. When Cornwallis arrived on May 20 he was in command of more than seven thousand men. So it turned out that the force which was to aid Cornwallis by destroying his adversary's base came under the command of Cornwallis himself, whom Clinton to the very last hoped would return from Wilmington to South Carolina, concentrate his forces, and destroy Greene's army there. When Cornwallis assumed control on the James his enemy was divided: Lafayette being at Richmond with a force perhaps a sixth the size of his own, Wayne not having yet arrived, and Steuben being near Charlottesville, busily recruiting Continental regiments for Greene.

495   A Raid under Arnold, from an engraving in the Grovewood Studio, Summit, N. J., after a painting by Alfred Wordsworth Thompson (1840-96)

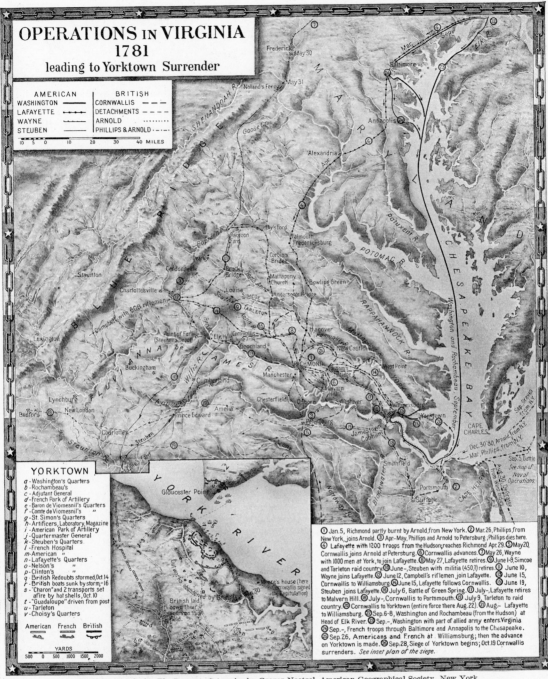

OPERATIONS IN VIRGINIA 1781
leading to Yorktown Surrender

AMERICAN	BRITISH
WASHINGTON ————	CORNWALLIS – – –
LAFAYETTE —•—•—	DETACHMENTS — — —
WAYNE —×—×—	ARNOLD ··········
STEUBEN ————	PHILLIPS & ARNOLD –··–··–

10 5 0   10   20   30   40 MILES

YORKTOWN

a - Washington's Quarters
b - Rochambeau's
c - Adjutant General
d - French Park of Artillery
e - Baron de Viomesnil's Quarters
f - Comte de Viomesnil's "
g - St. Simon's Quarters
h - Artificers, Laboratory, Magazine
i - American Park of Artillery
j - Quartermaster General
k - Steuben's Quarters
l - French Hospital
m - American "
n - Lafayette's Quarters
o - Nelson's "
p - Clinton's "
q - British Redoubts stormed, Oct. 14
r - British boats sunk by storm," 16
s - "Charon" and 2 transports set afire by hot shells, Oct. 10
t - "Guadaloupe" driven from post
u - Tarleton
v - Choisy's Quarters

American   French   British

YARDS
500 0   500 1000 1500 2000

① Jan. 5, Richmond partly burnt by Arnold, from New York. ② Mar. 26, Phillips, from New York, joins Arnold. ③ Apr.–May, Phillips and Arnold to Petersburg; Phillips dies here. ④ Lafayette with 1200 troops from the Hudson; reaches Richmond Apr. 29. ⑤ May 20, Cornwallis joins Arnold at Petersburg. ⑥ Cornwallis advances. ⑦ May 26, Wayne with 1000 men at York, to join Lafayette. ⑧ May 27, Lafayette retires. ⑨ June 1–9, Simcoe and Tarleton raid country. ⑩ June –, Steuben with militia (450,?) retires. ⑪ June 10, Wayne joins Lafayette. ⑫ June 12, Campbell's riflemen join Lafayette. ⑬ June 15, Cornwallis to Williamsburg ⑭ June 15, Lafayette follows Cornwallis. ⑮ June 19, Steuben joins Lafayette. ⑯ July 6, Battle of Green Spring. ⑰ July –, Lafayette retires to Malvern Hill. ⑱ July –, Cornwallis to Portsmouth. ⑲ July 9, Tarleton to raid country. ⑳ Cornwallis to Yorktown (entire force there Aug. 22.) ㉑ Aug.– Lafayette to Williamsburg. ㉒ Sep. 6–8, Washington and Rochambeau (from the Hudson) at Head of Elk River. ㉓ Sep.–, Washington with part of allied army enters Virginia. ㉔ Sep.–, French troops through Baltimore and Annapolis to the Chesapeake. ㉕ Sep. 26, Americans and French at Williamsburg; then the advance on Yorktown is made. ㉖ Sep. 28, Siege of Yorktown begins; Oct. 19 Cornwallis surrenders. *See inset plan of the siege.*

Drawn expressly for *The Pageant of America* by Gregor Noetzel, American Geographical Society, New York

THE CAMPAIGN IN VIRGINIA, 1781, PRELIMINARY TO YORKTOWN

CORNWALLIS in Virginia was singularly ineffective. He drove Lafayette out of Richmond (May 27), but did not follow him more than thirty miles. He then sent Tarleton to make a dash on Charlottesville with his cavalry to disperse the legislature. To Lieutenant-Colonel Simcoe of the Queen's Rangers he gave the mission of taking Steuben's depot at Point of Fork. Steuben retreated westward, and Cornwallis, advancing with his whole army, destroyed the munitions and supplies. On June 10, three days after the British army reached Point of Fork, Wayne joined Lafayette. Cornwallis, without attempting to fight his enemy, returned on June 15 to Williamsburg. Lafayette followed him and was joined by Steuben.

497 Marquis de Lafayette, 1757–1834, from the portrait by C. W. Peale in Independence Hall, Philadelphia

DIVIDED BRITISH COUNCILS

ON July 6 a sharp battle was fought at Green Spring near Williamsburg in which Lafayette was worsted, and forced to withdraw to Malvern Hill (see map, No. 496). Cornwallis did not follow. At this stage the hand of Germain was felt in the operations in Virginia. Cornwallis had retired to the coast to dispatch three thousand troops which Clinton had requested. Just after the battle with Lafayette Cornwallis received a letter ordering him to send the troops and, when he arrived at Portsmouth, whence they were to sail, he found yet other letters from Clinton written in a cordial spirit giving him permission to keep his whole army. The reason for the change was a letter from Germain to Clinton. Clinton had planned a campaign in the Middle States, particularly against Philadelphia. Germain had approved the plan of Clinton's subordinate, Cornwallis. Then Germain, promptly regretting his decision, wrote again to Clinton; but his letter arrived too late. Nor were these larger plans the only cause of confusion. There were more conflicting orders as to whether Portsmouth, Old Point Comfort, or Yorktown should be the British base.

FRENCH TROOPS ARRIVE IN AMERICA

IN July, 1780, about a month before the battle of Camden, a French force of six thousand officers and men under General Rochambeau had landed at Newport, Rhode Island. The army was to operate as a unit and Rochambeau was to place himself under Washington's command.

There is an interesting parallel (which must not, however, be followed up too far) between the French king's instructions to Rochambeau in 1780 and the American President's instructions to Pershing in 1917. The head of each state naturally wished to achieve victory, and since victory depended on coöperation, each commander was duly instructed to coöperate with the allies. But, quite as naturally, each head also wished to preserve the indentity of his own country's forces. Therefore, although Rochambeau wrote to Washington, saying, "We are now, Sir, under your command," he could not forget his king's secret instructions, saying, "that the French troops should not be dispersed, but that they should always act in a body and under French generals, except in the case of temporary detachments, which are to rejoin the principal corps in a few days." How like the problem of the Americans in France during the World War!

Within ten days after its arrival the French fleet that brought the troops was blockaded by a superior British naval force. So long as British naval superiority continued the French army, which would not leave its fleet, was held inactive. Thus for eleven months Rochambeau was prevented from aiding the Revolution.

PLAN DE LA DISPOSITION DES FRANÇAIS DANS RHODE ISLAND

Legende

498 Contemporary Plan of the French Positions at Newport, from the original in the Dépôt des Cartes et Plans de la Marine, Paris

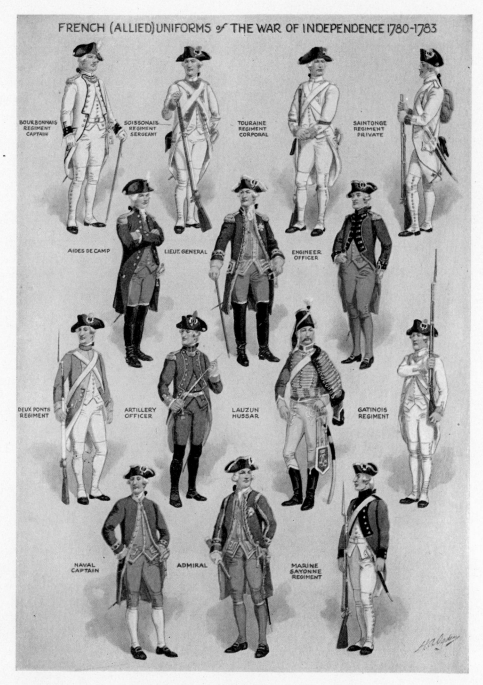

FRENCH (ALLIED) UNIFORMS of THE WAR OF INDEPENDENCE 1780-1783

Painted expressly for *The Pageant of America* by H. A. Ogden

GENERAL ROCHAMBEAU, 1725–1807

ROCHAMBEAU was the best general whom France could have sent to America. His professional standing was of the highest. In 1778 he had led in France the infantry on one side of a great war maneuver undertaken for the purpose of determining whether the system of tactics adopted by the French army should be continued or radically modified. The general opinion was that Rochambeau had demonstrated that the regulations of 1776 were suitable for all needs. Such was the caliber and reputation of the general whom France put under the command of Washington.

NEWS OF DE GRASSE

WITH Rochambeau came two able officers, Chastellux and Lauzun. In the spring of 1781 news arrived that a French fleet under De Grasse was to sail for the West Indies and from thence to the continent to coöperate with Washington and Rochambeau. Washington on May 22 went from his camp at New Windsor to meet the French commander at Wethersfield in Connecticut, where the two planned an attack upon New York, when the arrival of De Grasse's fleet should give naval superiority to the allies. Soon after a small portion of De Grasse's fleet reached

499 Jean Baptiste Donatien de Vimeur, Comte de Rochambeau, from an engraving by T. D. Booth of the portrait by John Trumbull (1756–1843)

Boston with a few reinforcements and the word that the French admiral would arrive on the American coast in July or August. Through Rochambeau Washington sent to De Grasse the suggestion that he might bring troops as well as ships and come to New York, stopping in the Chesapeake on his way.

500   Marquis de Chastellux, from the portrait by C. W. Peale in Independence Hall, Philadelphia

501   Duc de Lauzun, from the portrait by Albert Rosenthal, after Rouget, in Independence Hall, Philadelphia

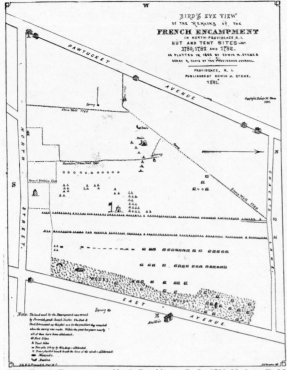

BIRD'S EYE VIEW
OF THE REMAINS OF THE
FRENCH ENCAMPMENT
IN NORTH PROVIDENCE R.I.
HUT AND TENT SITES
1780, 1781 AND 1782.
AS PLATTED IN 1865 BY EDWIN M. STONE.
DERBY & DAVIS OF THE PROVIDENCE JOURNAL.
PROVIDENCE, R. I.
PUBLISHED BY EDWIN M. STONE.
1881.

502   French Encampment, North Providence, R. I., 1780–82, from E. M.
Stone, *Our French Allies in the American Revolution*, Providence, 1881

WASHINGTON AWAITS DE GRASSE

WHILE the French army was still lying in Rhode Island Washington was perfecting his plans. He sent orders to Lafayette and Greene to establish lines of "expresses" which would make possible the forwarding of information with the utmost dispatch. He also directed the two southern commanders to send him detailed information regarding the strength and disposition of the enemy in their respective areas. The American commander in chief was considering three plans: an attack on New York, a campaign in Virginia, or a siege of Charleston. The choice would depend upon circumstances when De Grasse arrived. In June the French, who had left Newport for Providence, were to march westward across Connecticut, joining Washington in the Hudson Highlands. In July the united armies attempted to surprise some British posts at the north end of Manhattan island. A careful estimate of the situation about New York convinced Washington that no general attack could succeed until De Grasse arrived. Clinton had a force of fourteen thousand at his disposal. The Franco-American allied force was slightly smaller. In August came news from De Grasse, in a letter to Rochambeau, definite and precise. He would leave the West Indies on August 13; he would bring twenty-nine vessels, together with three regiments, ten fieldpieces, and some siege cannon and mortars; he would leave the American coast on October 15. At once Washington made the momentous decision to march to the Chesapeake and there join forces with De Grasse. Washington's letter to Lafayette (No. 503) was intended to be captured by the British, and to mislead them into thinking that the great attack was to be made against their position at New York, and not against their hold on the South.

503

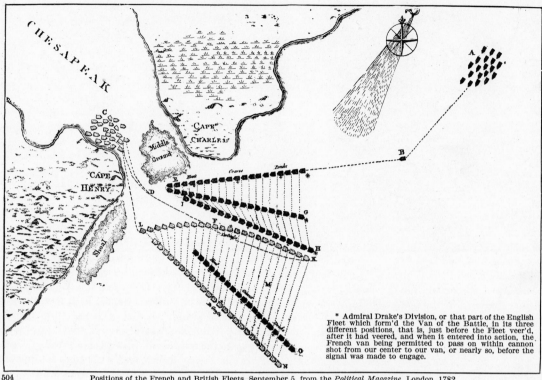

* Admiral Drake's Division, or that part of the English Fleet which form'd the Van of the Battle, in its three different positions, that is, just before the Fleet veer'd, after it had veered, and when it entered into action, the French van being permitted to pass on within cannon shot from our center to our van, or nearly so, before the signal was made to engage.

504   Positions of the French and British Fleets, September 5, from the *Political Magazine*, London, 1782

THE BATTLE OF THE CAPES, SEPTEMBER 5–10

In a sense fortune played into the hands of De Grasse. The British admiral Rodney never anticipated that the French naval commander would take his whole fleet from the West Indies to the American coast. Such a move would jeopardize the French colonies in the West Indies. Rodney, in sending northward his subordinate, Hood, with fourteen ships, and ordering up six more ships from Jamaica (which for some reason never came), thought that he had provided against all dangers. (For the movements of De Grasse's fleet and that of Hood from the West Indies, see No. 540.) Clinton knew of De Grasse's plan to come to the continent; but assumed that Rodney would prevent the French fleet from being dangerous. On August 25, Hood, having arrived in the Chesapeake, sent Clinton a message that he had seen or heard nothing of De Grasse in that region and was sailing for New York to join Admiral Graves, who was commanding there. Three days later he arrived. Then came intelligence that the French fleet, which had lain so long at Newport, had put to sea with a convoy and eight ships of the line under De Barras. Presumably the expedition was bound for the Chesapeake; so Graves with eighteen ships set out to intercept it. To his immense surprise the British admiral found, instead of De Barras, De Grasse with twenty-four ships, anchored behind the Virginia capes. The French fleet immediately put to sea; and on September 5 a severe, but indecisive, battle was fought. For five days following the two fleets maneuvered; at the end of which De Barras appeared and slipped safely within the capes. The French naval force was now overwhelming. Graves promptly put back to New York for repairs.

The naval action off the Virginia capes on September 5 is made clear by the following references, from a contemporary British source, accompanying the above chart: *A*. The English fleet crowding toward Cape Henry, Wind NNE about 11 A.M. *B*. English lookout ship. *C*. The French Fleet first seen at Anchor near Cape Henry about 11 A.M. *D*. Track of the French Van, Standing out at 1–2 past noon. *E*. The English Van Guard just before the Fleet were to form upon the larboard, or same tack with the Enemy. *F*. The French Van Guard at the time the English Fleet veered and came to the larboard tack. *G*. The English after having Veered on account of the Middle Ground ½ past 2 & come to the larboard tack, which put Admiral Drake in the Van & Admiral Hood in the rear, who was at that time 2 miles nearer the Enemy than the center was. *H*. The English partially engaged; the Van and center at Musket Shot, but the rear too distant to engage, being to Windward. *I*. The English rear when the Fleets engaged. *K*. The French Fleet when engaged. *L*. The French rear when the Fleet engaged, *K* being their Van. *M*. The Track of the French declining from the English Van and center. *N*. The track of the French after sunset. *O*. The English forming parallel to the Enemy after the firing had ceased on both sides.

VI—17

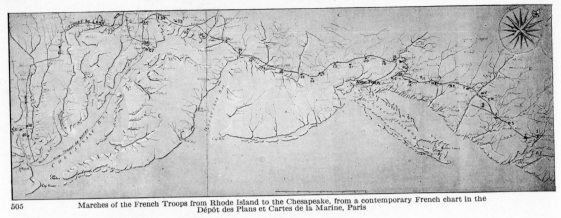

505   Marches of the French Troops from Rhode Island to the Chesapeake, from a contemporary French chart in the
                              Dépôt des Plans et Cartes de la Marine, Paris

THE MARCH TO THE CHESAPEAKE

As soon as the report of De Grasse's plans had been verified by an official dispatch (August 14) Washington had sent an order to Lafayette to prevent Cornwallis from retreating into the Carolinas. A week later the allied army crossed the Hudson at King's Ferry and headed southward. Passing behind the Palisades they struck into northern New Jersey, made a feint at Staten Island, and sped toward Philadelphia. General Heath with twelve small battalions were all the troops that remained to face Clinton, who had been recently reinforced by twenty-five hundred Hessians. When the allied army had been fourteen days on the march and had mostly passed Philadelphia, Clinton wrote to Cornwallis: "By intelligence which I have this day received, it would seem that Mr. Washington is moving an army to the southward, with an appearance of haste, and gives out that he expects the coöperation of a considerable French armament." Clinton's information was correct. On September 14 Washington and his staff arrived at Lafayette's headquarters. Clinton, not as yet realizing the French naval strength in the Chesapeake, had eight days before embarked seven thousand men and written to Cornwallis that he would sail with them as soon as Graves could furnish him a convoy. But Graves, crippled by the battle of September 5, and limping back to New York with the astounding news of De Grasse's force, was not able to furnish the convoy until six weeks had elapsed. Except for a diversion against the Connecticut shore, led by Arnold, Clinton remained inactive, awaiting Graves.

506   The Besieging Force, Yorktown, from an engraving by Skelton in Charles Gavard,
   Supplement aux Galeries Historiques de Versailles, Paris, 1838, after the painting by
   Siméon Fort (1793–1861) in the Versailles Gallery

CORNWALLIS' POSITION

CORNWALLIS, with a little more than five thousand effectives, now faced a combined army of more than sixteen thousand men at the same time that he was blockaded by an overwhelming naval force. He had already prepared the village of Yorktown for defense with additional works at Gloucester Point, directly across the York River. In front of Yorktown, to the west and south, except close to the river, the ground was marshy, with occasional bits of higher level.

To the east the terrain was firm. Cornwallis had thrown up an outer defense, and with great thoroughness had developed the inner defenses. The latter consisted of a stockade and a parapet of earth with redoubts and batteries. The chief difficulty was the smallness of the area, which somewhat cramped the British commander.

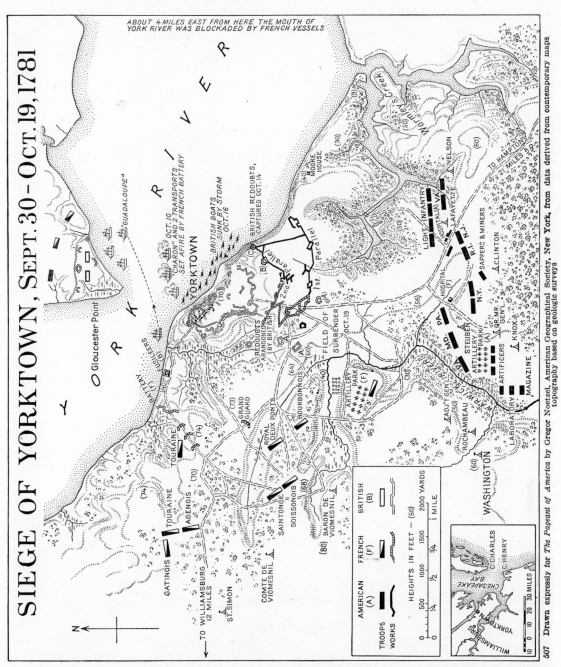

SIEGE OF YORKTOWN, SEPT. 30–OCT. 19, 1781

ABOUT 4 MILES EAST FROM HERE THE MOUTH OF
YORK RIVER WAS BLOCKADED BY FRENCH VESSELS

YORK RIVER

"GUADALOUPE"

O Gloucester Point

OCT. 10.
CHARON AND 2 TRANSPORTS
SET AFIRE BY FRENCH BATTERY

BRITISH BOATS
SUNK BY STORM
OCT. 16

BRITISH REDOUBTS,
CAPTURED OCT. 14

MOORE
HOUSE

YORKTOWN

NELSON

LIGHT INFANTRY

HOSPITAL VA.

LAFAYETTE

R.I.

N.J.

SAPPERS & MINERS

CLINTON

N.Y.

HOSPITAL
(F)

REDOUBTS
ABANDONED
BY BRITISH

FIELD OF
SURRENDER
OCT. 19

PA.

MD.

STEUBEN

KNOX

ARTILLERY
PARK

ADJ'T GEN'L

MR.
GEN'L

BOURBONNOIS

ARTILLERY
PARK
(F)

ARTIFICERS

MAGAZINE

ROYAL
DEUX PONTS

GRAND
GUARD

ROCHAMBEAU

LABORATORY

TOURAINE

AGENOIS

SAINTONGE

SOISSONOIS

BARON DE
VIOMESNIL

WASHINGTON

GATINOIS

TOURAINE

ST. SIMON

COMTE DE
VIOMESNIL

TO WILLIAMSBURG
12 MILES

N

BRITISH
(B)

FRENCH
(F)

AMERICAN
(A)

TROOPS

WORKS

HEIGHTS IN FEET—(50)

0   500   1000   1500   2000 YARDS

¼   ½   ¾   1 MILE

507 Drawn expressly for *The Pageant of America* by Gregor Noetzel, American Geographical Society, New York, from data derived from contemporary maps topography based on geologic surveys

CHESAPEAKE
BAY

C. CHARLES

C. HENRY

YORKTOWN

WILLIAMSBURG

0 10 20 30 MILES

THE YORKTOWN
DEFENSES

FIVE British redoubts *A, A, A,* and *B, C* formed the outer line or first parallel at the outset of the siege. On September 28 Cornwallis abandoned the first three but retained those at *B* and *C,* because the enemy in possession of the latter works could enfilade his entire line. On the left of the first parallel ground was broken on the night of the 30th for five French batteries; and on the same night for three American batteries on the right in this first line. Two French brigades occupied the ground to the left as shown on the map under their regimental names, the three American brigades being stationed on the right. On the night of October 11, four French batteries were begun in the inner or second parallel, and on the same night three American batteries. In the Yorktown defenses the British had erected ten batteries, leaving at their extreme right a detached redoubt which was defended by the Fusiliers. Cornwallis' defensive works were the best possible considering the terrain and the time and means at his disposal.

508   From the painting *Storming the Redoubt*, by Eugene L. Lami in the State capitol, Richmond, Virginia

PROGRESS OF THE SIEGE

On the night of September 30 the French engineers, masters of the art of siege operations, broke ground for the first parallel at six hundred yards from Cornwallis' works. The approaches were carried forward; and on October 11 a second parallel was opened at three hundred yards. De Barras had brought siege guns; and these were now used with telling effect. The second parallel brought the besiegers to the very borders of the inner redoubts; and the next step was the capture of these positions. One was assigned to the French, the other to the Americans. Colonel Alexander Hamilton, now holding a commission in the line, begged Washington to be allowed to lead the American storming party. On the night of October 14, after a fierce encounter, both these redoubts fell. The parallel was promptly extended to include them. The following night the British made a desperate counter-attack; but could not hold the position. The allied guns, enfilading Cornwallis' works, now made his position untenable.

509   From the painting *The Siege of Yorktown*, by Van Blarenberghe, in the Musée de Versailles

CORNWALLIS DECIDES TO SURRENDER

The next night Cornwallis, taking counsel of desperation, tried to ferry his army across to Gloucester Point, in the hope that he might escape by marching toward Philadelphia. But the plan was completely spoiled by a storm which scattered and swamped his boats. With great difficulty he reassembled his forces and opened negotiations for surrender. Clinton, with seven thousand men from New York, was already on the way to his relief. Cornwallis said that he "could not fire a single gun," that his "numbers had been diminished by the enemy's fire, but particularly by sickness," and that "it would have been wanton and inhuman to the last degree to sacrifice the lives" of his troops "by exposing them to an assault, which from the numbers and precautions of the enemy could not fail to succeed."

DECISIVE YORKTOWN

CORNWALLIS the next morning, convinced of the injustice of further demands on his crippled troops, wrote to Washington proposing a day's armistice. With the possibility of the arrival of British reinforcements from New York always imminent, the American commander refused to cede the advantage of time. Cornwallis' proposals must be sent immediately, whereupon two hours' suspension of hostilities would be granted in which to give them proper consideration. The original British concessions proving inadequate, Washington forwarded his own demands, and allowed a prolongation of the armis-

510   Drawn expressly for *The Pageant of America* by Gregor Noetzel, American
Geographical Society, New York

tice, until the morning of the nineteenth when the final signature of surrender was affixed.

Fortescue has said of the blow at Yorktown that it was "the heaviest that has ever fallen on the British army." Cornwallis surrendered, according to Tarleton, seven thousand two hundred and forty-seven men, including noncombatants [five thousand three hundred and sixteen effective]. His defeat meant the virtual end of the war, so far as America was concerned. Cornwallis, upon his return to England, was neither tried nor censured, except in the long controversy which developed between himself and Clinton. He became for many years governor-general and commander in chief in India, where his military successes won a large part of what is now the Indian empire. Fortescue with some bitterness points to Germain, the British war lord, as the man chiefly responsible for the final reverse. "For it is Germain, if to any one man, that the disaster of Yorktown, as of Saratoga, is to be ascribed: to Germain with his blindness to facts, his deafness to wise counsel, his jealousy of commanders in the field, his appalling ignorance of the elements of war, his foolish ambition to direct all operations from Whitehall . . . nothing can excuse the encouragement of disloyalty in a subordinate toward his Commander-in-chief, nor the deliberate insult offered to a Commander-in-chief by ostentatious quotation of a subordinate's opinion against him. . . . There is, in fact, a malignity in the behaviour of Germain towards all the principal commanders in America which bears very strong marks of personal vindictiveness."— *History of the British Army*, III, pp. 397–98.

511   From Washington's diary, Oct. 17, 1781, recording Cornwallis' proposal for a cessation of hostilities and Washington's reply,
original in the Library of Congress

512   From the painting *The Surrender of Lord Cornwallis*, by John Trumbull in the Yale School of the Fine Arts, New Haven, Conn.

AN EYE–WITNESS ACCOUNT OF THE SURRENDER

"AT about 12 o'clock the combined army was drawn up in two lines more than a mile in length, the Americans on the right side of the road, the French on the left. Washington, mounted on a noble steed, and attended by his staff, was in front of the former; the Count de Rochambeau and his suite, of the latter. The French troops, in complete uniform, and well equipped, made a brilliant appearance, and had marched to the ground with a band of music playing, which was a novelty in the American service. The American troops, but part in uniform, and all in garments much the worse for wear, yet had a spirited, soldier-like air, and were not the worse in the eyes of their countrymen for bearing the marks of hard service and great privations. . . .

"About two o'clock the garrison sallied forth, and passed through with shouldered arms, slow and solemn steps, colors cased, and drums beating a British march. They were all well clad, having been furnished with new suits prior to the capitulation. They were led by General O'Hara on horseback, who, riding up to General Washington, took off his hat and apologized for the non-appearance of Lord Cornwallis, on account of indisposition. Washington received him with dignified courtesy, but pointed to Major-general Lincoln as the officer who was to receive the submission of the garrison." — JAMES THACHER, *Military Journal*, 1823. The picture is intended to be little more than a group of portraits.

513
1. Count Deuxponts, Colonel of French Infantry. 2. Duke de Laval Montmorency, Colonel of French Infantry. 3. Count Custine, Colonel of French Infantry. 4. Duke de Lauzun, Colonel of French Cavalry. 5. General Choizy. 6. Viscount Viomenil. 7. Marquis de St. Simon. 8. Count Fersen, Aid de Camp of Count Rochambeau. 9. Count Charles Damas, Aid de Camp of Count Rochambeau. 10. Marquis Chastellux. 11. Baron Viomenil. 12. Count de Barras, Admiral. 13. Count de Grasse, Admiral. 14. Count Rochambeau, General en Chef des Français. 15. General Lincoln. 16. Colonel E. Stevens of American Artillery. 17. General Washington, Commander-in-Chief. 18. Governor Thomas Nelson, Va. 19. Marquis LaFayette. 20. Baron Steuben. 21. Colonel Cobb, Aid de Camp to Washington. 22. Colonel Trumbull, Secretary to Washington. 23. General James Clinton, N. Y. 24. General Gist, Md. 25. Gen. Anthony Wayne, Pa. 26. General Hand, Pa., Adjutant General. 27. General Peter Muhlenberg, Pa. 28. Major Gen. Henry Knox, Commander of Artillery. 29. Lieut.-Col. E. Huntington, Acting Aid de Camp of Gen. Lincoln. 30. Colonel Timothy Pickering, Quartermaster General. 31. Colonel Alex. Hamilton, Commanding Light Infantry. 32. Colonel John Laurens, S. C. 33. Colonel Walter Stuart, Phila. 34. Colonel Nicholas Fish, N. Y.

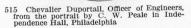

514 Count Axel Fersen, Swedish Officer in French service, from the portrait by C. W. Peale in Independence Hall, Philadelphia

515 Chevalier Duportail, Officer of Engineers, from the portrait by C. W. Peale in Independence Hall, Philadelphia

516 Count François Aboville, Officer of Artillery, from the portrait by Albert Rosenthal, after a family portrait, in Independence Hall, Philadelphia

CORNWALLIS' PRAISE OF THE FRENCH

THE British marched out to their historic surrender with their usual steadiness, to the then popular tune of *The World Turned Upside Down*. The peculiar aptness of the band-master's choice of music has been noted by practically everyone who has written of the surrender.

France reaped the satisfaction of revenge for her downfall overseas twenty-one years before. But she got nothing more; except, indeed, a load of debt which weighed her whole finances down and helped the ruin of her Bourbon kings. Her army in America, however, left an honored name not only among its American allies but among its British enemies. In the report written by Cornwallis the day after the surrender there is a moving passage which well deserves recording: "The treatment, in general, that we have received from the enemy since our surrender, has been perfectly good and proper; but the kindness and attention that has been shown us by the French officers in particular, their delicate sensibility of our situation, their generous and pressing offer of money, has really gone beyond what I can possibly describe, and will, I hope, make an impression on the breast of every British officer, whenever the fortune of war should put any of them into our power."

WASHINGTON AND DE GRASSE

THE day after the great surrender Washington wrote De Grasse a letter of noblest acknowledgment.

"The surrender of York . . . the honor of which belongs to your Excellency, has greatly anticipated our most sanguine anticipations." Washington then boarded the French flagship, exchanged congratulations with De Grasse, and urged immediate operations farther south. But De Grasse felt bound to face the British out at sea. De Grasse, Rochambeau, and Lafayette, all present at Yorktown, are Frenchmen whose names are destined to be held in grateful remembrance by all Americans.

517   From the painting *Washington Visits the French Fleet*, by Percy Moran, courtesy of the artist and Robert Chapman & Co.

518   From the painting *News of Yorktown*, by J. L. G. Ferris in Independence Hall, Philadelphia

CELEBRATION OF VICTORY

THE glorious news of Yorktown sped swiftly up and down the country. Everywhere Patriots joined in celebrations which only the sudden release from years of war can bring. Everywhere Loyalists heard with dejection the news which to them was almost the pronouncement of their doom. But in fact the war was not over. New York, Charleston, and Savannah were still in the hands of the enemy. Washington returned to the task of watching Clinton in New York. And then the tragedy of the American army, which for so many years had fought for national independence, became acutely manifest. There had been times when the troops had mutinied, because of the lack of provisions due to the incompetence and dishonesty of the civilian commissariat. But there was never a time when the Continental regulars were traitors to the cause; and even during their worst mutiny, brought on by exasperating neglect to supply them with their barest needs, they spurned the offer of British gold and hanged the men who made it. Officers were sometimes even worse off than the men. From the beginning of the war their pay had been niggardly and was mostly in arrears. Yet out of it they were expected to clothe themselves and provide for their families. In 1782 a rate of pay was established which is interesting as an ideal that was rarely achieved. A major general, General Greene for example, was to receive thirty-one dollars and sixty cents a month with a fivefold ration of food. A lieutenant was to draw three dollars and fifteen cents and one ration. By way of contrast, it is worth noting that, toward the end of the war, Congress was offering a bounty of one thousand dollars to a private for enlisting. Many an officer was forced to make appeals to friends for aid. While the army lay inactive watching Clinton, a reorganization and combination of regiments squeezed out many old and deserving officers. Many others, officers and men, began going home, as the forces were reduced, to adjust themselves as best they could to civilian life. In these years the word "soldiering" as a synonym for idleness seems to have come into use. When one remembers the hardships and sufferings of the army, many times due to official neglect or peculation, the public stigma which "soldiering" implied seems a bitter return. Moreover, many a discharged soldier finds it very hard indeed to locate in any other employment, when the civilians, who have got the good places while he was defending them, have closed up their ranks. Many of the veterans found their opportunity to begin life afresh. Some of those from New England turned back to the central government the practically worthless paper money which they had received from Congress in return for lands purchased by the Ohio Company. For their share in the founding of Ohio see Volume II.

Illumination.

COLONEL TILGHMAN, Aid de Camp to his Excellency General WASHINGTON, having brought official acounts of the SURRENDER of Lord Cornwallis, and the Garriſons of York and Glouceſter, thoſe Citizens who chuſe to ILLUMINATE on the GLORIOUS OCCASION, will do it this evening at Six, and extinguiſh their lights at Nine o'clock.

Decorum and harmony are earneſtly recommended to every Citizen, and a general difcountenance to the leaſt appearance of riot.

October 24, 1781.

519 Broadside announcing an illumination to celebrate Yorktown, from Smith and Watson, *American Historical and Literary Curiosities*, Philadelphia, 1847.

DEMOBILIZATION

THE laying of the captured flags before Congress was the greatest moment in the history of that body since the passage of the Declaration of Independence. Another moment of intensity came in the spring of 1783, when Washington forwarded to Congress copies of two pamphlets since famous 'as the Newburgh Addresses. Written by an anonymous officer, they called to the minds of their fellows the poverty which they suffered as a result of the neglect of state and national governments alike. They called upon the officers

520   From the painting *Captured Flags from Yorktown Laid Before Congress, Nov. 3, 1781,* by John Ward Dunsmore. © by the artist

to assemble and discuss the redress of their wrongs by force. The temptation was great; for the central government was weak to the point of being practically devoid of authority. To the surprise of many the commander in chief attended the meeting. In perhaps the greatest speech of his life he called upon the men who had worked with and under him to give "one more distinguished proof of unexampled patriotism and patient virtue." The spirit of the United States army was made unmistakably clear in their response to their commander; for the threat contained in the Newburgh Addresses never came to action. Officers and men were soon after demobilized. The "army went home without even a ceremonious 'thank you' from the nation. To this day most of them are unpaid — and will be." — GANOE, p. 88.

THE LAST OF THE CONTINENTALS, 1783

ON November 25, 1783, the steadfast Continental regulars, the backbone of the whole Revolutionary army, paraded through New York in what our own times would have called a Victory March. Next year they were disbanded; and mostly experienced more than the usual troubles in trying to get work. Many, hopelessly unfit through wounds or disease, were forced to beg; as were, indeed, some officers. Even among the highest ranks there was great, and mostly unrelieved, distress. On June 2, 1784, Congress reduced the army down to eighty men, "with officers in proportion"; and even these eighty were kept only to guard the storehouses at Fort Pitt and West Point. The preamble to this masterpiece of mistaken legislation stated that "whereas, standing armies in time of peace are inconsistent with the principles of republican governments," etc., etc. To show that those who really understood the Revolutionary War knew better, we have only to quote the words of Washington himself. "Regular troops alone are equal to the exigencies of modern war, as well for defense as offense, and whenever a substitute is attempted it must prove illusory and ruinous. No militia will ever acquire the habits necessary to resist a regular force. The firmness requisite for the real business of fighting is only to be attained by a constant course of discipline and service."

521   From an engraving by Lande after the drawing *Continental Army Marching Down the Bowery, November 25, 1783,* by Howard Pyle, in J. G. Wilson, *Memorial History of the City of New York,* New York, 1892

522   From the painting by John Trumbull, 1827, in the Yale School of the Fine Arts, New Haven, Conn.

WASHINGTON RESIGNS HIS COMMISSION, DECEMBER 23, 1782

THE actual resignation of George Washington as the commander in chief of all the Union's armies took place on December 23, 1782, in the State House at Annapolis, Maryland, where his farewell to Congress, brief as it was, contained some very moving words. The opening and close of this address contain everything of either national or personal concern:

"MR. PRESIDENT, — The great events on which my resignation depended, having at length taken place, I now have the honor of offering my sincere congratulations to Congress, and of presenting myself before them, to surrender into their hands the trust committed to me, and to claim the indulgence of retiring from the service of my country. Happy in the confirmation of our independence and sovereignty, and pleased with the opportunity afforded the United States of becoming a respectable nation, I resign with satisfaction the appointment I accepted with diffidence; a diffidence in my abilities to accomplish so arduous a task, which however was superseded by a confidence in the rectitude of our cause, the support of the supreme power of the Union, and the patronage of Heaven. . . . Having now finished the work assigned me, I retire from the great theater of action, and bidding an affectionate farewell to this august body, under whose orders I have so long acted, I here offer my commission, and take my leave of all the employments of public life."

Washington's achievements in the Revolution naturally raise all the old questions about the importance of the "great man." Under ordinary circumstances the leader does not "make history" but is the mere expression of his times, while most of his actions are the result of forces over which he has little or no control. There are, however, times of crisis when the great man really does creative work. In the seventeen seventies the Patriots of America put their fortunes to the hazard of a war. At the outset of the struggle they chose Washington, then a Virginia planter of some military experience, to be the commander of their armed forces, not because he was a capable commander, but merely because an acceptable Virginian suited their political exigencies best. For more than seven years he held a post to the responsibilities of which no single one of his Patriot contemporaries was equal. The traitor Arnold might well have been an exception, had his character rung true. But character must ring true in such a conflict; and Washington's indubitably did. His ultimate success was a finely original military achievement; while unshaken devotion to the cause which he espoused, and his ability to hold about him a group of able and loyal officers, with a devoted nucleus of men — the steadfast Continentals — were fundamental to his triumph. A survey of his subordinates, fine officers as many of them were, does not reveal a man who combined the daring and brilliance of the Trenton-Princeton campaign with the character and leadership shown at Valley Forge, and the perfectly conceived and executed plan that led the way to Yorktown. Even under Washington's command the Revolution almost came to naught. It is doubtful whether it could have ever reached complete success without him.

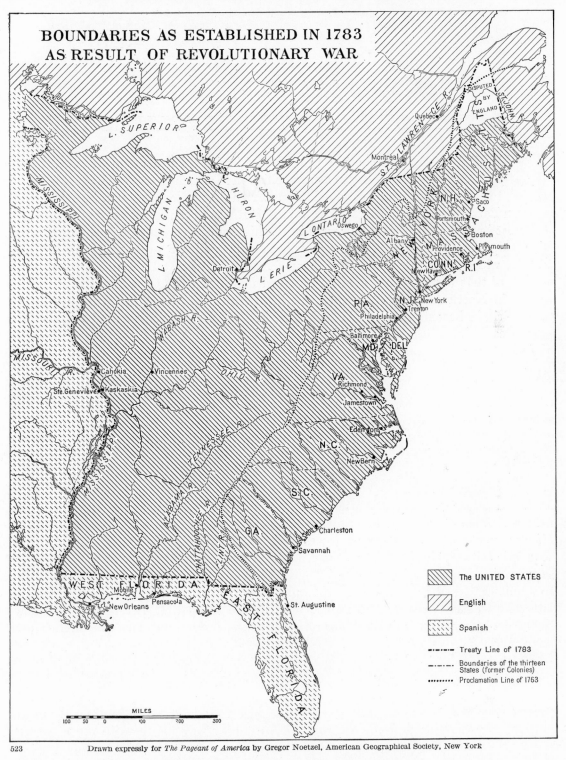

BOUNDARIES AS ESTABLISHED IN 1783
AS RESULT OF REVOLUTIONARY WAR

The UNITED STATES

English

Spanish

Treaty Line of 1783

Boundaries of the thirteen States (former Colonies)

Proclamation Line of 1763

MILES
100 50 0   100   200   300

523   Drawn expressly for *The Pageant of America* by Gregor Noetzel, American Geographical Society, New York

AMERICAN GAINS AT THE PEACE, 1783

THE United States alone, of all the warring countries, gained by the Revolutionary War — and gained enormously. Not only did the original Thirteen Colonies become the Thirteen States of the Union but they acquired the vast hinterland, right out to the Mississippi, up to the Lakes, and almost down to the Gulf.

CHAPTER X

SEA POWER IN THE REVOLUTION

BEFORE peace finally came the War of Independence assumed several quite different aspects. It began as a rebellion in Massachusetts which quickly spread to the thirteen continental colonies. From first to last it was a bitter civil war between Patriots and Loyalists. In New York state it developed into one of the greatest and most important of the Indian wars in the history of the American people. Finally, after Burgoyne's surrender at Saratoga, it became merged in a world war in which Great Britain, without a single ally, found herself in conflict with all the principal maritime nations of that day. Such a conflict involved fighting in the Orient and in Europe as well as in North America. There can be little excuse for the statesmanship which let Great Britain become involved in such a crisis. The Revolution was not an inevitable war; it could have been avoided. Moreover, once begun, it could have been prosecuted to a successful conclusion had the British Government sent proper commanders into the field and exercised proper direction at home.

The worst aspect of this mismanagement in high places was to allow a foreign war to develop with the navy unprepared. For more than a year before France finally entered the conflict the British Government was fully aware of that possibility. Yet during 1777 the fleet was allowed to remain short of numbers and equipment; while it was manned only with the very greatest difficulty. Moreover, suspicion and dissension were rife in the naval establishment, a fact which was largely responsible for Rodney's failure to end the war in the West Indies in his battle with De Guichen on April 17, 1780. More than a hundred years after the conflict the great American naval historian, Admiral A. T. Mahan, in his pregnant study of *The Influence of Sea Power upon History*, wrote of the American Revolution: "The Alliance with France, and subsequently with Spain, brought to the Americans that which they above all needed, — a sea power to counterbalance that of England. Will it be too much for American pride to admit that, had France refused to contest the control of the sea with England, the latter would have been able to reduce the Atlantic seaboard? Let us not kick down the ladder by which we mounted, nor refuse to acknowledge what our fathers felt in their hour of trial."

Fully to understand what sea power meant throughout the Revolution we must remember the extreme dependence of America on Europe for decisive superiority in both the men and material of war. The great populations, great armies, and great navies of those days were European, not American. Their men, munitions, and supplies came much more from Europe than America; and the only way for these to reach America was by crossing the Atlantic. Therefore whichever side could keep the seaways open for its own ships, while closing or even obstructing them for its enemy's ships, would have a decisive advantage. The evolution of a rebellion that broke out in eastern Massachusetts into a world war meant the loss to the British of one of the greatest advantages they had — complete freedom of action on the sea.

THE BEGINNING OF THE NAVY

THE navy of the United States found its humble beginnings in the first year of the Revolution. Two days before the Battle of Bunker Hill, Rhode Island fitted out two sloops, the first American armed vessels commissioned by any public authority. A few weeks later, while the British army lay in Boston, closely besieged by the American army, Colonel Glover, an amphibious soldier of Marblehead, suggested the waylaying of ships that were bringing supplies from Halifax and England to the enemy. Some time later the *Franklin*, *Warren*, *Hancock*, and *Lee* were sent to sea. They were small fishing schooners that had been given armaments. The *Lee* struck a vigorous blow for the Patriot cause when, in November, 1775, she brought into Gloucester the British ordnance brig, *Nancy*, with a priceless cargo of munitions: muskets, ball, powder, fuses, and military tools. The example of Rhode Island was followed by practically all of the other colonies.

524 The Frigate *Warren*, first vessel of the Continental Navy, from a woodcut in *Gleason's Pictorial*, 1852, courtesy of the American Antiquarian Society, Worcester, Mass.

THE NAVY AND THE PRIVATEERS

No precise line can be drawn between privateering and the navy, either in the Revolution or in the War of 1812. A good many men, of all ranks, belonged at different times to both. So did many vessels. Moreover, privateers and men-of-war sometimes cruised together. But still, in their essential natures, privateering and the navy are far apart; for privateering is simply private business done for private gain, though done against a public enemy, while a regular navy is a public service, in the fullest sense of the term, even though prize money may be one of its rewards. The embryonic United States navy evolved, under exceedingly difficult conditions, into a real public service long before the French Alliance came to change the balance of sea power. Continental squadrons worked under Washington at Boston and New York in 1775–76, while Commodore Ezek Hopkins led an expedition against the Bahamas, where he seized many war stores at Fort Nassau. He failed, however, to get recruits, on his return, owing to the far greater attractions of privateering.

525 Congressional broadside signed by John Hancock, ordering registry of American privateers and vessels of war, in the New York Public Library

Paul Jones also appeared, in a small command, in 1776; when, as we have seen already (in Chapter V) Arnold fought the Battle of Valcour. In 1777 the navy operated from the West Indies to western Europe, as well as along its own coast. But the total effect on the balance of sea power was disappointingly small. The navy had only sixty-four vessels altogether; with twelve hundred and forty-two guns and swivels; and its captures were one hundred and six. The privateers were of all kinds: Continental, State, and from friendly foreign ports, with very mixed crews. Altogether they numbered over two thousand, carried over eighteen thousand guns and swivels, had about seventy thousand men in their crews; and either captured or destroyed about six hundred British vessels. In cash values the navy took six million dollars, the privateers eighteen million. In prisoners at sea there were some sixteen thousand taken by the navy and privateers together. The effect on British shipping in 1777 is well shown by Silas Deane's report from France to the Marine Committee of Congress: "It even deterred the English merchants from shipping goods in English vessels at any rate of insurance; so that in a few weeks forty French ships were loaded in London on freight — an instance never known before." Aside from its many other disadvantages, however, privateering was all parts and no whole; and it did not, in spite of its devastations, change the naval situation. Moreover, it ruined some combined expeditions, like the one at Penobscot in 1779; while "the gamble of it" demoralized recruiting when the navy was most in need of men. And yet, with all its faults, privateering was so successful that its resourceful followers well deserve their record among the other annals of the sea.

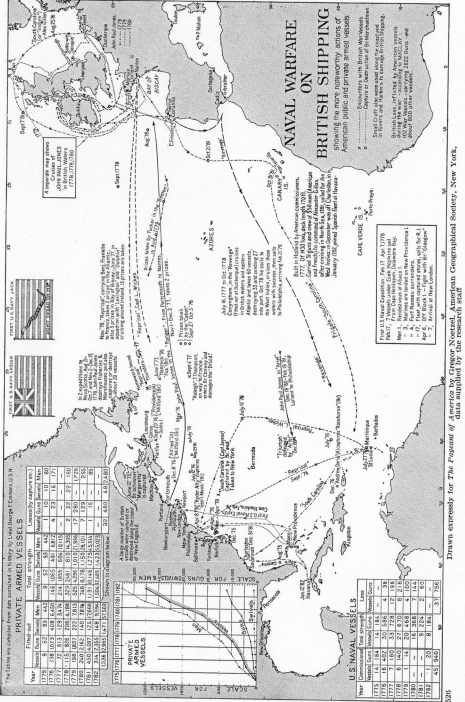

PRIVATEERING DEPREDATIONS

THIS chart is instructive as a partial visualization of the sweep of privateering operations, the complete records of which will probably never be available. The activities of these restless seafarers were ubiquitous. Their ventures being private enterprises, the records of their achievements and failures belonged originally to the families of the persons participating. Many have been lost. "More than two thousand American privateers ranged the seas at one time or another. They swarmed in the West Indies; they cruised along the Atlantic coasts; they sought their prey in the British Channel and the North Sea. They actually cruised off the ports of Spain, in plain sight from the shore, capturing British vessels laden with fish from Newfoundland — selling ships and cargo to the Spaniards at much below their value. In 1781 the Cabots of Beverly received six hundred thousand riales of vellon for their half share in five prizes, the Gardoquis getting the rest. The Derbys of Salem got over sixty thousand dollars on account of prizes that were sold at Bilbao. In one way privateering was an evil, because the privateers and letters of marque attracted men from the decks of regular warships, from the ranks of the army, and from the fields and shops. But they added greatly to the expenditure of the British, interfered with the transport service, and made government and people more willing to acquiesce in American independence." — CHANNING, *History of the United States*, III, 311.

Drawn expressly for *The Pageant of America* by Gregor Noetzel, American Geographical Society, New York, data supplied by the research staff

NAVAL WARFARE ON BRITISH SHIPPING

showing the more noteworthy actions of American public and private armed vessels

- × Encounters with British War-Vessels
- ○ Capture or Destruction of Br. Merchantmen

Small Craft also were used along the coast and in Rivers and Harbors to damage British Shipping.

British Loss inflicted by American vessels:
102 War-Vessels carrying 2622 Guns and about 800 other vessels.

The Tables are compiled from data contained in history by Lieut. George F. Emmons, U.S.N.

PRIVATE ARMED VESSELS

Year	Fitted-out				Total strength				Losses (by capture etc.)			
	Vessels	Guns	Swivels	Men	Vessels	Guns	Swivels	Men	Vessels	Guns	Swivels	Men
1775	9	52	93	442	9	52	93	442		1	10	80
1776	138	1,023	408	6,450	146	1,065	491	6,812	4	23	16	171
1777	72	613	129	3,474	214	1,655	604	10,015	2	22	22	160
1778	115	826	206	4,188	329	2,481	810	14,303	2	22	—	1,729
1779	198	1,837	222	7,813	525	4,296	1,010	21,956	17	280	—	255
1780	240	2,162	140	7,864	748	6,178	1,150	28,101	7	129	—	85
1781	450	4,097	125	12,668	1,191	10,146	1,275	45,514	1	16	—	
1782	314	2,355	148	9,594	1,504	12,485	1,423	55,023	32	480	48	2,480
	1,536	12,965	1,471	57,503					Shown in diagram below			

A large number of British vessels were captured or destroyed along the coast of New England.

U.S. NAVAL VESSELS

Year	Commissioned		Total strength		Loss	
	Vessels	Guns	Vessels	Guns	Vessels	Guns
1775	14	184	14	184		
1776	16	402	30	586	4	38
1777	1	24	33	728	12	198
1778	6	140	27	670	8	216
1779	1	14	20	468	4	100
1780	—	—	16	368	7	144
1781	—	—	9	224	2	60
1782	—	—	1	20	8	184
	45	940			37	756

First U.S. Navy Jack — DON'T TREAD ON ME

First U.S. Navy Ensign

A separate map shows Cruises of JOHN PAUL JONES in British Waters 1778, 1779, 1780

SCALE FOR GUNS, SWIVELS & MEN

SCALE FOR VESSELS

PRIVATE ARMED VESSELS

1775 1776 1777 1778 1779 1780 1781 1782

First U.S. Naval Expedition, Feb.17, Apr.7, 1776
Feb.17, 7 Vessels under Esek Hopkins sail from Cape Henlopen, Delaware Bay.
Mar. 1, Rendezvous at Abaco I.
" 3, Marines are landed on New Providence I.
" 4, Fort Nassau surrenders.
Apr. 6, Fleet with captured stores, sails for R.I.
" 6, Off Block I.—Fight with Br. "Glasgow"
" 7, Arrival at New London.

NAVAL ADMINISTRATION

RHODE ISLAND took the lead in bringing officially before the Continental Congress the question of a continental navy. Finally, after much discussion, the Congress committed itself, on October 30, 1775, to the policy of maintaining a naval armament "for the protection and defence of the United Colonies." Gardner W. Allen has epitomized the history of naval administration from that point on. "The first executive of the service was the Naval Committee which in 1775 began the work of organizing a navy. Next came the Marine Committee which directed naval affairs for four years, ending in December, 1779. Then followed the Board of Admiralty which managed the department a year and a half, when, in the summer of 1781, Robert Morris took charge and as Agent of Marine remained at the head of the navy until after the end of the war." — *A Naval History of the American Revolution*, 1913, I, p. 37. Morris was a most practical Patriot, a good economist, and an excellent administrator of the small means then available.

527   Robert Morris, from the portrait by C. W. Peale
in Independence Hall, Philadelphia

THE NAVY OF THE REVOLUTION

THE type of fighting ship of the Revolution did not differ greatly from those built earlier in the eighteenth century. The warship was a floating battery with wooden sides and driven by sails. During the Revolution the English occasionally used copper to cover the bottoms. The art of handling fleets, like that of using armies, was dependent upon the characteristics of the weapons employed; and the naval officer had to master a technical and highly developed profession. Both England and France had many good commanders. The Americans were dependent primarily upon men who had learned seamanship in the merchant marine and who acquired the technique of naval fighting as the war progressed. The resources of the rebelling colonies were too limited to enable the government to create and put to sea an important fleet. American vessels mostly fought as single ships. Perhaps the most important fleet, measured by the results it achieved, was Arnold's flotilla on Lake Champlain at the Battle of Valcour (No. 271). For the Patriots to defy successfully on the high seas the greatest navy of the century was obviously impossible. The *America* was built at Portsmouth and launched in 1749. She was pierced for forty-four guns. The present *America*, as pictured here, must not be mistaken for the *America* authorized November 20, 1776, but still on the stocks at Portsmouth, N. H., in 1780, and never used in the war. This second *America* was a seventy-four-gun ship-of-the-line. The seventy-four-gun ships-of-the-line-of-battle were luxuries which the infant American navy could not afford at the beginning of the Revolution, and necessities which the French supplied later on. The rating of what would be now called battleships continually rose. Earlier in the eighteenth century a sixty-gun ship-of-the-line was quite common. On the other hand, the flagship that went up to Quebec in 1759 was the ninety-gun *Neptune;* and Sir James Yeo's unused flagship on Lake Ontario in 1814 carried a hundred and two guns.

528   Model of the *America*, a seventy-four-gun ship, courtesy of the Portsmouth Athenaeum,
Portsmouth, N. H.

529 From a fictitious mezzotint portrait published in London in 1776 by Thomas Hart

COMMODORE ESEK HOPKINS, 1718–1802

ON November 5, 1775, Congress appointed an old sea captain of Providence, Rhode Island, Esek Hopkins, to be "commander-in-chief of the fleet." But Congress apparently never intended this high-sounding title to be understood in its two proper senses, either as meaning the supreme command of the whole United States navy, or even that of a certain area or real fleet. The intention seems to have been only to give him a squadron command. Early in 1776 Hopkins, who was at Philadelphia with a small flotilla, was ordered to make a cruise along the southern coast, destroying enemy naval forces in the Chesapeake and in the harbors of North and South Carolina. If successful, he was to return and attack any British vessels in Rhode Island waters. Hopkins disregarded his orders and sailed for Abaco in the Bahamas. In March he landed on the island of New Providence, captured it, and took away the Governor and Lieutenant-Governor prisoners. He then sailed for Block Island, where he engaged the *Glasgow*, a British ship of war of twenty guns. He seriously injured but did not capture his opponent. In April he took his fleet and some prizes into New London. At this time his popularity was great and he was congratulated by the President of Congress. But Hopkins proved inefficient. In March, 1777, he was suspended and was finally dismissed from the service. He was a good seamen, but not equal to the difficult task of naval command. While operating in Rhode Island waters his flagship had been the new frigate, *Warren* (No. 524).

NICHOLAS BIDDLE, 1750–78

YOUNG Nicholas Biddle had been an ensign in the British navy and was one of the few American officers to have had professional training before the war. Biddle was one of Hopkins' captains at the outset of the navy's history. From the beginning he showed promise. Early in 1778 he was in Charleston harbor commanding the frigate *Randolph*. A squadron was organized out of the *Randolph* and four small vessels of the South Carolina navy, with Biddle in command. This flotilla put to sea and headed for the West Indies in search of prizes. On March 7, while east of Barbados, Biddle came in contact with the British sixty-four-gun man-of-war, *Yarmouth*. A hot fight developed in which the British ship was severely handled. Then, when the American commander was maneuvering for a better position, the *Randolph* blew up. So not only a frigate but one of the best of the officers of the young navy was lost to the Revolution.

530 From the portrait by C. W. Peale in Independence Hall, Philadelphia

531 From the portrait by Matthew Pratt (1734–1805), courtesy of the Ehrich Galleries, New York

JOHN BARRY, 1745–1803

BARRY began his naval career in command of the sloop *Lexington* of sixteen guns. Early in 1776 his ship was one of the five vessels engaged in defending the coast of the Middle States after Hopkins had taken his fleet to Providence. On April 7 the *Lexington* fell in with the British sloop *Edward* of eight guns. When his ship was blockaded in Delaware Bay, he fought on land with a body of volunteers at Trenton and Princeton under Washington. In 1794 he became the ranking officer in the United States Navy. Barry served with distinction throughout the war. His last command was the frigate *Alliance*, of thirty-two guns. He saw active duty off the Virginia capes, in the Delaware River assisting the American forts below Philadelphia, off the New England coast, and in the West Indies.

SILAS TALBOT, 1751–1813

SILAS TALBOT's career took him into both the army and navy.
He had been a cabin boy at twelve. At twenty-four he was a
captain in the Rhode Island militia, when he joined the troops
besieging Boston. He was the leader of a fire-ship attack in 1777
against the British *Asia* off New York, was wounded at Fort
Mifflin on the Delaware, and in 1778 captured the schooner
Pigot, guarding Narragansett Bay. He was promoted to
lieutenant-colonel and later made captain in the navy. The last
appointment resulted from an encounter which won him great
applause along the Rhode Island coast. On August 16, 1779,
the *Boston Gazette* published an account of his encounter with a
Loyalist boat. "This moment an express arrived from New
London with an account of the gallant, intrepid Talbot's taking
infamous villain Stanton Hazard, in a Brig of 15 guns out of
Newport, after a short action. Talbot was in a small sloop of
12 guns, and had an inferior number of men on board to the
Tory privateer, which was fitted out on purpose to attack & take
Talbot's sloop." Talbot was one of many captured officers to be

532 From the portrait by Thomas Birch (1779–1851), courtesy of the Ehrich Galleries, New York

confined in Old Mill Prison in England. In 1798 he was squadron-commander against the French in the
West Indies, his flagship being the *Constitution*. The
patriotic artist (No. 533) has combined the events of
two separate actions, fought on different days, into a
single picture; and, having apparently omitted one
of the five vessels, has re-rigged and re-armed the
other four. The picture was painted for Talbot as
a momento. What he wished to illustrate was the
famous capture of the "infamous villain Stanton
Hazard's" Tory privateering brig *King George* in
particular. It was for this capture that Congress
made Talbot a captain of the infant United States
navy, September 17, 1779.

533 Incident in the Life of Commodore Silas Talbot when in command of the *Pigot* and *Argo*, from the painting by Thomas Birch, courtesy of the Ehrich Galleries, New York

JOSHUA BARNEY, 1759–1818,
PRIVATEERSMAN AND NAVAL OFFICER

JOSHUA BARNEY was a fine type of the privateering man turned naval
officer. He was also one of the links between the Revolution and the
War of 1812, when he commanded the little naval force that defended
Washington in 1814. Barney's first cruise was cut very short indeed.
But, being exchanged after capture, he served with credit on the
privateering brig *Pomona* under Isaiah Robinson till he was again
made prisoner and taken to Old Mill Prison, from which he escaped,
disguised as a British officer, and with the connivance of a sentry.
First sheltered by English pro-Americans in Plymouth (England),
then sailing through the British fleet disguised as a fisherman, then
caught by a British privateer, then escaping once more, and making
his way through England, France, and Holland, he was soon afloat

534 From the portrait by C. W. Peale in Independence Hall, Philadelphia

again, this time in Gillon's armed ship, the *South Carolina* (see chart, No. 526). Two years after Barney's final
escape peace was declared and Barney was again in Plymouth, this time as captain of the United States frigate
General Washington, on board of which he gave a splendid dinner attended both by his former English friends
and by admiring British naval officers as well.

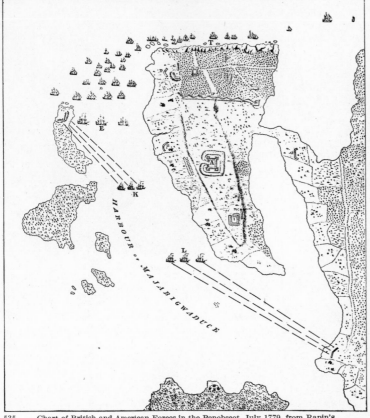

535   Chart of British and American Forces in the Penobscot, July 1779, from Rapin's
                                   History of England, 1785

THE PENOBSCOT EXPEDITION, 1779

In June, 1779, the British from Halifax took Castine, Maine (then called Majabagaduce). Their object was to establish a military outpost on the flank of the American Colonies. Thereupon the General Court of Massachusetts sent out a force of nineteen armed vessels, with the *Warren* bearing the flag of Commodore Dudley Saltonstall, over twenty transports, and one New Hampshire vessel. There were about three thousand men, both naval privateersmen and militia. Saltonstall was quite irresolute. The privateers would never act together as a whole. General Solomon Lovell's landing party (T) was not properly supported. The small British garrison (A) improved its defenses. The three British vessels though attacked and compelled twice to move farther into the harbor (see their three positions, E, K, L) were neither destroyed nor captured. And finally, when a British squadron under Collier came from New York, the American vessels ran up the river and were fired by their own crews. Saltonstall was court-martialed and dismissed. This disaster was very humiliating to Massachusetts but in the next year General Peleg Wadsworth headed a new expedition to Maine which captured several ships, eight cannon and forty prisoners.

JOHN PAUL JONES, 1747–92

Greatest of all the American commanders was a Scotsman, John Paul, known in his adopted country as John Paul Jones. In 1775 he had been appointed "Senior Lieutenant of the Navy." In the following year, in command of the Continental sloop *Providence*, with an armament of twenty-two guns, he made a raid along the coasts of Nova Scotia and Cape Breton Island. He ruined the fishery at Canso and Madame and, twice eluding British warships, took sixteen prizes, of which he brought eight into port. His report of his brush with the frigate *Milford* on this cruise is characteristic of the man. "When he came within cannon shot, I made sail to try his speed. Quartering and finding that I had the advantage, I shortened sail to give him a wild goose chase and tempt him to throw away powder and shot. . . . He excited my contempt so much by his continued firing at more than twice the proper distance, that when he rounded to, to give his broadside, I ordered my marine officer to return the salute with only a single musket."

536   From the engraving by Jean-Michel Moreau le Jeune
      in the Bostonian Society, published in 1781 at Paris

JONES AND THE STARS AND STRIPES

On June 14, 1777, while Burgoyne was still busy in Canada, hastening preparations for his ill-fated march into New York, Congress appointed Jones to the command of the *Ranger*, a new ship of eighteen guns recently completed at Portsmouth. The journal of the same day shows the following resolution: "That the flag of the thirteen United States be thirteen stripes alternate red and white; that the Union be thirteen stars, white in a blue field, representing a new constellation." Jones, in raising this banner over the *Ranger*, seems to have been the first man to raise the stars and stripes over an American warship. The men who embarked on the *Ranger* under the new flag were destined to experience many a thrilling moment before "John Paul Jones, Esq." brought the cruise to an end. On November 1, 1777, with what he called "an orderly and well disciplined crew . . . of one hundred and forty odd," he set sail for France. In February, 1778, in Quiberon Bay, Jones saluted the French flag, and Admiral La Motte Picquet returned the salute. This was the first official recognition of the United States navy by any foreign power.

THE CRUISE OF THE *RANGER*

In April, 1778, Jones left the French coast and made a descent upon Whitehaven. Ill luck attended the venture; so that he was only able to fire one ship of the large number that lay in the harbor. At Carrickfergus Jones found the British warship *Drake* charged

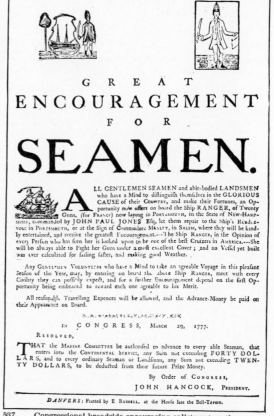

537   Congressional broadside encouraging enlistment on the *Ranger*, 1777, in the Essex Institute, Salem, Mass.

with the special duty of bringing his voyage to an end. The American commander offered battle, and in a little more than an hour forced the *Drake* to strike. Jones was justifiably elated at this taking of an enemy man-of-war in her own waters. When the *Ranger* a few days later brought the *Drake* into Brest harbor an American at that place wrote home: "It was a pleasure to see the English flag flying under the American stars and stripes." But now came a year of troubles for Jones, all ashore. He was in desperate straits to pay his men, sell his prizes, and get a squadron for another and greater cruise. At last an old East Indiaman was bought, renamed the *Bonhomme Richard*, and made the flagship of his squadron of one other American, the

538 From the painting *The Bonhomme Richard and the Serapis*, by Carlton T. Chapman, courtesy of James Barnes and the Naval History Society, New York

Alliance, and three small French vessels. On his famous voyage in the *Bonhomme Richard* in 1779 Jones encircled the British Isles. The *Richard* was rotten, and one of her heaviest guns blew up at the outset of the battle with the *Serapis*, requiring the abandonment of a whole battery. The crew was a mixture of Americans and Europeans. The *Alliance* was commanded by a man already going insane. With such a force Jones alarmed the shipping of the entire east coast and took no less than seventeen prizes. In this cruise, which included the historic conflict with the *Serapis*, Jones began a tradition which has been carried on, but never surpassed, by men like Hull, Farragut, Dewey and the twentieth-century Rogers.

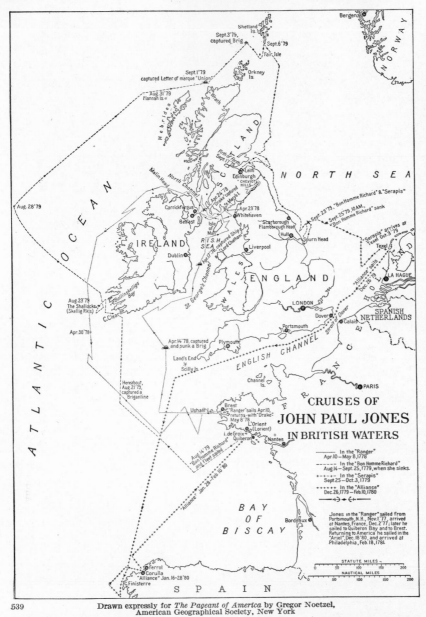

CRUISES OF
JOHN PAUL JONES
IN BRITISH WATERS

———— In the "Ranger"
Apr.10—May 8,1778
- - - - - In the "Bon Homme Richard"
Aug.14—Sept.25,1779, when she sinks.
+·+·+·+· In the "Serapis"
Sept.25—Oct.3, 1779
++++++ In the "Alliance"
Dec.26,1779—Feb.10, 1780
→‖→ ←‖←

Jones in the "Ranger" sailed from
Portsmouth, N.H., Nov.1,'77, arrived
at Nantes, France, Dec.2,'77; later he
sailed to Quiberon Bay and to Brest.
Returning to America he sailed in the
"Ariel", Dec.18 '80, and arrived at
Philadelphia, Feb.18,1781.

STATUTE MILES
NAUTICAL MILES

539   Drawn expressly for *The Pageant of America* by Gregor Noetzel,
              American Geographical Society, New York

PAUL JONES RAIDS THE BRITISH ISLES

On September 23, off Flamborough Head, Jones met the "Baltic trade," a convoy of forty-one vessels escorted by the *Serapis* and *Countess of Scarborough*. The *Pallas*, one of the French ships, engaged the *Countess of Scarborough* and finally forced her to strike. The merchantmen sheered off, stood clear, and escaped. The main battle was between the *Serapis* and the *Bonhomme Richard;* for the *Alliance* disobeyed the signal to join in the action. In the caliber of the crew, the quality of the armament, and in sailing capacity the *Richard* was inferior to the enemy. Jones' only hope lay in closing. He outmaneuvered Pearson, lashed the ships together, and pressed home his attack. Rarely has a commander who won his fight contended with such overwhelming obstacles. The *Richard* was badly holed below the water line and began to settle dangerously. At the height of the battle some under officers either through fear or treachery called to the enemy for quarter. His own ship, the *Alliance*, plunged a broadside into the unengaged side of the *Richard*. Finally the prisoners below were treacherously released; and Jones' quick wit, in setting them to man the pumps to save their lives, only prevented their turning the scale against him. Jones reported that on the decks "the scene was dreadful beyond the reach of language." The crews, with cannon, muskets, and pistols, fought from the ports, the decks, the fighting tops, and rigging. "My situation," said Jones, "was really deplorable. The *Bonhomme Richard* received various shots under the water from the *Alliance*, the leak gained on the pumps, and the fire increased much on board both ships. Some officers persuaded me to strike, of whose courage and good sense I entertain a high opinion, . . . I would not, however, give up the point. The enemy's main-mast began to shake, their firing decreased, ours rather increased, and the British colors were struck at half an hour past ten o'clock." Abandoning the sinking *Richard*, Jones limped with the wounded *Serapis* into Texel on October 3, 1779. Here he was blockaded by a British squadron. The annals of the American navy contain no finer example of skill, courage, and leadership than that found in the duel off Flamborough Head.

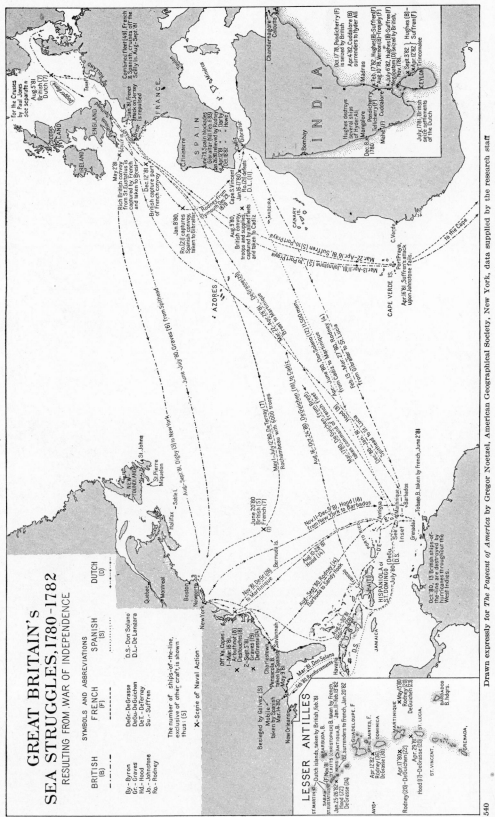

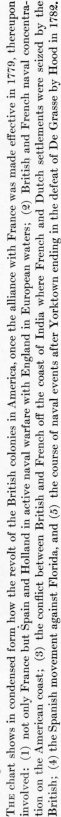

540   Drawn expressly for *The Pageant of America* by Gregor Noetzel, American Geographical Society, New York, data supplied by the research staff

THE chart shows in condensed form how the revolt of the British colonies in America, once the alliance with France was made effective in 1779, thereupon involved: (1) not only France but Spain and Holland in active naval warfare with England in European waters; (2) British and French naval concentration on the American coast; (3) the conflict between British and French off the coast of India where French and Dutch settlements were seized by the British; (4) the Spanish movement against Florida, and (5) the course of naval events after Yorktown ending in the defeat of De Grasse by Hood in 1782.

541   From the painting *The Battle of Ushant*, by Gudin in the
                                Versailles Gallery

THE BATTLE OF USHANT, JULY 27, 1778

FINE as were some of its exploits, the American navy played no appreciable part in determining the outcome of the war. When France, early in 1778, entered the war on the side of the revolting colonies, the French navy counterbalanced that of Britain, and threatened British naval supremacy in American waters. The French collected two fleets, one at Brest under D'Orvilliers and the other at Toulon under D'Estaing, who sailed across the Atlantic to blockade Howe in the Delaware (No. 433). Meanwhile Admiral Keppel succeeded in forcing a fight off Ushant in July; but was unable to win a decisive action (No. 540), and was compelled to put back to England and refit. No one can have followed the fortunes of the war up to this point without having become thoroughly convinced of two things: first, that the backbone of the whole Revolution in America was the Continental army under Washington's command, and secondly, that sea power was the fundamental, preponderant, and universal factor constantly at work throughout the whole vast complex problem. But in 1778 the French navy came in. In 1779 the Spanish navy joined the French. In 1780 the Dutch joined both. And in 1781 the Armed Neutrality of the North added every other fleet in Europe to the list of Britain's enemies. This addition of the Danes, Swedes, Russians, and north Germans meant the closing of the Baltic, whence the British were wont to get most of their shipbuilding supplies. With four actively hostile navies against her, and another four barring her way to the Baltic and its sorely needed naval supplies, Britain faced such a crisis as she had not faced before and has not since. It was this crisis, coupled, of course, with the growing power of the pro-Americans in Britain, that made Yorktown decisive. Then, turning from her civil war against her former colonists, Britain put forth enough sea power to defeat De Grasse in 1782 (No. 550), and save Gibraltar, India, Canada, and the West Indies from the French.

542   View of the Island of St. Lucia, 1778, engraving by P. C. Canot after the painting by D. Serres,
                                in the King's Library, British Museum, London

NAVAL WAR IN THE WEST INDIES

ONE of the motives of France in joining the war against England was to capture British islands in the West Indies. Obviously those of value that were most vulnerable to attack were in the Leeward Islands. Martinique was the chief French base in these waters, while Barbados and Antigua served the British fleet. In September, 1778, an expedition from Martinique surprised the neighboring British island of Dominica and took it. Though of little military importance, the affair indicates that England was not prepared for war in the West Indies when hostilities with France began. At the end of the year D'Estaing left Boston (see No. 433) for Martinique. Meanwhile Admiral Barrington held his fleet at Barbados awaiting orders. By a curious coincidence, the same day, November 4, that D'Estaing put out from Boston harbor, Hotham's British squadron, carrying five thousand soldiers from New York, weighed anchor for Barbados. The two fleets paralleled each other. D'Estaing, when a little south of Bermuda, after a heavy storm which had shaken both fleets, picked up a stray vessel from the English convoy and so learned of his enemy's presence. He promptly sailed for Antigua in the hope that this island was the destination of the British. But on December 10, the British fleet joined Barrington at Barbados.

THE CAPTURE OF ST. LUCIA

BARRINGTON did not permit the soldiers to leave the transports. Three days after the reinforcements had arrived the British troops were in possession of the heights (2) immediately north of Grand Cul de Sac (1). Before evening of the next day the British had taken the commanding ground known as Morne Fortune (3), overlooking the harbor of Carenge (4). The outnumbered French garrison, leaving their guns unspiked and their munitions undestroyed, retired to positions marked (5) on the map. Their retreat left the batteries on the promontory called "The Vigie" (6)

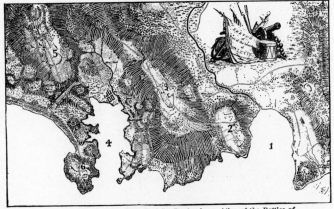

543   Sketch of Part of the Island of St. Lucia, from *Atlas of the Battles of the American Revolution*, in the Yale University Library

in British hands. Barrington had pushed the attack with the utmost swiftness, for he was taking grave risks. His fleet was inferior to D'Estaing's, which also had the advantage of two thousand more troops. If D'Estaing could capture the Vigie, he would be in a position to take the works at Morne Fortune in the rear, destroy the British landing party, and compel Barrington to quit the shore and fight an unequal battle on the open sea, where shore batteries could not help him. But the British held their ground. Then D'Estaing, defeated ashore, frustrated afloat, sailed away. Six months later D'Estaing had his revenge for the capture of St. Lucia by taking the British island of Grenada. Byron meanwhile had relieved Barrington, and now commanded a much larger fleet, though one slightly inferior to the French. On July 6, 1779, Byron attacked the French fleet off the Grenada coast. The British admiral advanced into battle in very irregular order. Though the British were driven off with heavy losses, D'Estaing did not take full advantage of his victory by capturing or destroying vessels that were within his power. While Byron was refitting his fleet, and quite unable to operate effectively, D'Estaing made no move against other British islands. In the West Indian campaign of 1779 two inferior commanders were opposed, and the result was indecisive. (For D'Estaing's operations against Savannah, see page 231.)

A THREATENED FRANCO–SPANISH INVASION OF ENGLAND

IN the very month that Byron and D'Estaing were maneuvering off Grenada, England was facing the greatest naval menace since the Spanish Armada of 1588. In June, 1779, Spain had declared war against Britain, though she had not entered into an alliance with the Americans. In July the French fleet under D'Orvilliers (*AA*), united with the Spanish squadron (*C*) commanded by Cordova. Hardy was in charge of the British Channel fleet (*B*). Moreover, the French had massed some fifty thousand troops (*EE*) at strategic points along the north coast, particularly at Havre and St. Malo. The English counter-concentrations are shown at *DD*. The French plan was to take the Isle of Wight and use Spithead for an anchorage. If things went favorably an invasion was possible. Hardy, whose entire fleet numbered forty, was opposed by sixty-six.

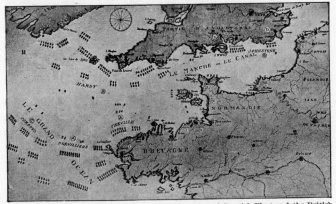

544   Map showing position of the combined French and Spanish Fleet and the British Fleet, July 1779, from the original in the Dépôt des Cartes et Plans de la Marine, Paris

In August the allied squadrons stood up the Channel, while Hardy still remained outside near Scilly with thirty-five vessels. At the crucial stage of the operations the French Government changed its plans and ordered D'Orvilliers to make a landing in Cornwall, near Falmouth. While sailing for the new objective an easterly gale blew the combined fleets out of the Channel. Hardy, avoiding battle, promptly slipped in. The allies then returned to Brest and the danger passed. Well might an officer of the English fleet write before the crisis had ended: "What a humiliating state is our country reduced to!"

545   Admiral Rodney, 1719–92, from the portrait by Sir Joshua
    Reynolds (1723–1792) in the National Portrait Gallery,
    London

RODNEY AND LANGARA

In the autumn of 1779 Spain withdrew her fleet from Brest
and turned her attention more directly to achieving the
chief object for which she had entered the war, the capture
of Gibraltar. Since the declaration of war this great
fortress had been blockaded. By the end of the year the
supplies of the garrison were running low. To the relief of
this indispensable fortification England sent 'Rodney in
December with the Channel fleet. With Rodney were supplies and troops. On January 7 the British admiral captured twenty-two ships: seven ships of war and the
remainder merchant vessels carrying naval stores and
provisions to the Spanish fleet. This fleet was then stationed at Cadiz and was considerably more powerful than
the British force. Nine days later Rodney surprised a
Spanish squadron of thirteen ships under Langara off Cape
St. Vincent. When the Spaniards attempted flight he gave
chase, and fought a running night battle which did not end
until two A.M. When the last shot had been fired six Spanish
ships-of-the-line had been taken and one had blown up.
On the twenty-sixth Rodney dropped anchor at Gibraltar.
"You have taken more line-of-battle ships," wrote the
First Lord of the Admiralty to Rodney, "than have been captured in any one action in either of the two last
preceding wars." The next month Rodney left with a few ships for the West Indies, where he had been appointed to command the Leeward Island station. Here he was in a strategic position of great importance,
both on account of the West Indian trade
and the flanking situation of eastern North
America.   Rodney's relief of Gibraltar was
from the British point of view one of the
most important events of the war. Had
the great fortress at the entrance to the
Mediterranean fallen, the British hold on
India would have been vastly weakened.

546   From a mezzotint, 1786, by Robert Laurie, after the painting by Robert Dodd,
    in *Old Naval Prints, Their Artists and Engravers*, by Charles N. Robinson, London,
    1924

RODNEY AND DE GUICHEN

1780, which saw the British conquest of South Carolina, was
marked in the West Indies by maneuvering and fighting between
Rodney and De Guichen, who now commanded the French
fleet. No less than three battles were fought, all of them indecisive. In the first, April 17, Rodney was not adequately supported by his captains. He always felt that here, because of the
failure of his subordinates, he lost the opportunity to win once
and for all the conflict in the West Indies. His opponent was too
able an officer ever to give him again the opportunity of that day.

547   Comte de Guichen, from an engraving by Hardouin,
    after the portrait by Castelar, in the Bibliothéque
    Nationale, Paris

ST. EUSTATIUS, 1781

HURRICANES in the autumn of 1780 dealt roughly with Rodney's fleet, and he was compelled to put into Barbados with a badly injured and sadly diminished force. Though reinforcements came out in the spring under Hood, Rodney was still inferior to the new French fleet which had appeared in the West Indies under De Grasse. But other tasks than dealing with the French fleet occupied the British admiral during the spring of 1781. On January 27 he received orders to attack the Dutch islands of St. Eustatius and St. Martin. The former had become a great trade center and huge emporium after the war began; and Rodney had already cast longing eyes upon it. On Febru-

548   From the engraving *Surprise de St. Eustache* by N. Ponce, after the drawing by P. C. Marillier in *Receuil d'Estampes*, etc., Paris, 1784

ary 3 he appeared before the island, demanded its surrender, and secured immediate submission. This prize was by far the greatest of the war: more than one hundred and fifty merchant ships and merchandise valued roughly at three million sterling pounds. For three months Rodney stayed on the island. "The amount of money involved," says Mahan, "and the arbitrary methods pursued by him and by Vaughan, gave rise to much scandal, which was not diminished by the King's relinquishing all the booty to the captors, nor by the latters' professed disinterestedness. Men thought they did protest too much." In June De Grasse took the British island of Tobago after an unsuccessful attack upon St. Lucia. Then in August he took his whole fleet to the Chesapeake, where it was the decisive factor in the defeat of Cornwallis and the virtual ending of the American Revolution (No. 510). The illustration shows a French version of the St. Eustatius affair.

THE BATTLE OF THE DOGGER BANK

THE attack upon St. Eustatius followed soon upon a declaration of war by England against Holland. During the year 1780 the Baltic powers were active in trying to compel England to grant certain points that were deemed essential to neutral interests. When Holland joined it England began hostilities against her. In the year of the conquest of South Carolina, therefore, Britain was fighting all the chief trading nations of Europe. The strain which this put upon her navy, at best badly prepared for war, was tremendous. Under such circumstances it seems almost incredible that the British Government should have continued those military operations in the South which were dependent upon the uninterrupted control of the sea along a great stretch of the American coast. Cornwallis' defeat at Yorktown was due primarily to bad strategy on the part of the British ministry. In the same month, August, 1781, that De Grasse arrived off Chesapeake Bay, Admiral Parker, convoying a large merchant fleet from the Baltic to England, fell in

549   From an engraving, 1782, by R. Pollard, after the painting by D. Serres

with a Dutch squadron commanded by Admiral Zoutman and convoying merchant vessels from the Texel to the Baltic. The Dutch merchant ships put back, while the English boats hurried westward across the North Sea to their destination. The escorting squadrons fought the Battle of the Dogger Bank (see map, No. 540). It was a fiercely contested engagement, with great damage and heavy losses on both sides. It did not, however, affect the *status quo* between the nations. "This was," says Mahan, "a most satisfactory exhibition of valour, and a most unsatisfactory battle; magnificent, but not war." Both commanders had shown themselves better fighters than tacticians.

550   From an engraving *Rodney Breaking the Line of the French Fleet*, by D. Lerpinière 1783,
after a painting by Richard Paton

RODNEY'S DEFEAT OF DE GRASSE, APRIL 12, 1782

THE war in the West Indies continued actively into the year 1782. In fact, that spring De Grasse undertook the capture of the British island of Jamaica with a powerful fleet. But Rodney pursued and defeated him off the island of Dominica in an engagement which detracted from, rather than added to, the reputations of both commanding officers. A large part of the French fleet was allowed to escape. But the fight relieved the pressure in the West Indies, and had an effect favorable to England upon the peace negotiations that were already in progress. With Rodney's departure for home a few months later war in the West Indies came to an end.

551   View of the Grand Attack upon Gibraltar, Sept. 13, 1782, from John Drinkwater, *A History of the Late Siege of Gibraltar*, London, 1786

GIBRALTAR

THE Spaniards, assisted by the French, besieged Gibraltar for three years (1779–82); but were defeated by the British, under Eliott, who, of course, owed much to the fleets which helped his sorely harassed garrison. This gallant and able defense distracted a good deal of Franco-Spanish strength from reinforcing the anti-British allies in what might have been more promising directions. On the other hand, like India and several other places, it fully occupied a good deal of the British strength, which, under other circumstances, would have been available for use in America.

JOSHUA BARNEY AGAIN

BARNEY fought the last naval action of the war in the *Hyder Ali* on April 8, 1783, in Delaware Bay, where the British *General Monk* had been causing great loss to Philadelphia shipping. The *Hyder Ali* had long-range guns; the *General Monk* was mostly armed with very short-range carronades. Barney maneuvered well, chose his own range, and forced the *Monk* to strike in half an hour. "Captain Barney with the officers and men of the State ship *Hyder Ali* received the thanks of . . . Pennsylvania" and "an elegant sword" was ordered for Barney. Barney's expert and devoted services by no means ended with the Revolution; for we shall meet him again in the War of 1812, when he was equally distinguished afloat and ashore, especially when making his gallant stand after the "Bladensburg Races."

552   From the painting *Hyder Ali vs. General Monk*, by Louis Phillipe Crépin in the United States Naval Academy, Annapolis

CHATHAM, *April 23.*
HEAD QUARTERS, *April 18, 1783.*

THE Commander in Chief orders the ceffation of hoftilities between the United States of America and the King of Great-Britain to be publicly proclaimed to-morrow at twelve o'clock, at the new building; and that the proclamation which will be communicated herewith be read to morrow evening at the head of every regiment and corps of the army; after which the chaplains, with the feveral brigades will render thanks to Almighty God for all his mercies, particularly for his over ruling the wrath of man to his own glory, and caufing the rage of war to ceafe among the nations.

Although the proclamation before alluded to extends only to the prohibition of hoftilities, and not to the enunciation of a general peace, yet it muft afford the moft rational and fincere fatisfaction to every benevolent mind, as it puts a period to a long and doubtful conteft, ftops the effufion of human blood, opens the profpect to a more fplendid fcene, and, like another morning ftar, promifes the approach of a brighter day than hath hitherto illuminated the Weftern hemifphere.—On fuch a happy day, which is the harbinger of peace, a day which compleats the eighth year of the war, it would be ingratitude not to rejoice: it would be infenfibility not to participate in the general felicity.

The Commander in Chief, far from endeavouring to ftifle the feelings of joy in his own bofom, offers his moft cordial congratulations on the occafion to all the officers of every denomination; to all the troops of the United States in general; and in particular to thofe gallant and perfevering men who had refolved to defend the rights of their invaded country, fo long as the war fhould continue.—For thefe are the men who ought to be confidered as the pride and boaft of the American army; and who, crowned with well earned laurels, may foon withdraw from the field of glory to the more tranquil walks of civil life. While the Commander in Chief recollects the almoft infinite variety of fcenes through which we have paft, with a mixture of pleafure, aftonifhment and gratitude, while he contemplates the profpect before us with rapture, he cannot help wifhing that all the brave men, of whatever condition they may be, who have fhared the toils and dangers of effecting this glorious revolution; of refcuing millions from the hand of oppreffion, and of laying the foundation of a great empire, might be impreffed with a proper idea of the dignified part they have been called to act, under the fmiles of Providence, on the ftage of human affairs; for happy, thrice happy! fhall they be pronounced hereafter who have contributed any thing; who have performed the meaneft office in erecting this ftupenduous FABRIC OF FREEDOM AND EMPIRE on the broad bafis of independency; who have affifted in protecting the rights of human nature; and eftablifhing an afylum for the poor and oppreffed of all nations and religions.——The glorious tafk for which we firft fled to arms being accomplifhed—the liberties of our country being fully acknowledged and firmly fecured by the fmiles of heaven on the purity of our caufe, and the honeft exertions of a feeble people, determined to be free, againft a powerful nation, difpofed to oppress them; and the character of thofe who have perfevered thro' every extremity of hardfhip, suffering, and danger, being immortalized by the illuftrious appellation of the PATRIOT ARMY; nothing now remains but for the actors of this mighty fcene to preferve a perfect unvaried confiftency of character through the very laft act, to clofe the drama with applaufe; and to retire from the military theatre with the fame approbation of angels and men which have crowned all their former virtuous actions. For this purpofe no diforder or licentioufnefs muft be tolerated. Every confiderate and well difpofed foldier muft remember it will be abfolutely neceffary to wait with patience until peace fhall be declared, or Congrefs fhall be enabled to take proper meafures for the fecurity of the public ftores, &c. As foon as thefe arrangements fhall be made, the General is confident there will be no delay in difcharging, with every mark of diftinction and honour, all the men inlifted for the war, who will then have faithfully performed their engagements with the public. The General has already interefted himfelf in their behalf, and he thinks he need not repeat the affurance of his difpofition to be ufeful to them on the prefent, and every other proper occafion. In the mean time he is determined that no military neglect or exceffes fhall go unpunifhed while he retains the command of the army.

The Adjutant General will have fuch working parties detached, to affift in making the preparations for a general rejoicing, as the Chief Engineer with the army fhall call for; and the Quarter Mafter General will, without delay, procure fuch a number of difcharges to be printed as will be fufficient for all the men inlifted for the war; he will pleafe to apply to Head-Quarters for the form.—An extra ration of liquor to be iffued to every man to-morrow to drink, "Perpetual Peace and Happinefs to the United States of America."

553   Washington's Proclamation Announcing General Peace, April 18, 1783, from the *New York Gazette and Weekly Mercury*, May 5, 1783

BRITISH, AMERICAN, AND FOREIGN PEACE, 1783

SPAIN got very little, apart from Minorca; France and Holland nothing at all. The Armed Neutrality dissolved; and the warring world was at peace again in 1783; though staggering under a vast load of debt, and bearing the seeds of future war. What saved the British from further losses was the re-assertion of their sea power. Hood's masterly defense at St. Kitts and Rodney's crowning victory over De Grasse restored the balance lost the year before at Yorktown. Only in the East Indies did the French hold their own at sea, thanks to the consummate work of Suffren, to whom every one of his chief British opponents paid their honoring respects in person when the fleets met after peace.

Patriot America was war-weary, through and through: not, however, that it would no longer fight, when the war came to its doors. The North was still furious with Arnold for his bloody work at Fort Griswold (New London, Connecticut, September 6, 1781). The West still had Tory and Indian troubles, as at Fort Henry (Wheeling, West Virginia, September 11, 1782) where Elizabeth Zane rescued the powder from her brother's house, under a hail of bullets, and carried it safely into the fort, which then kept up so hot a fire that its defender won the day. The South still had the British in its flank at Charleston. But all felt as anxious for peace between the young United States and the old mother country as did the British pro-Americans, who had now turned the king's party completely out of power. At the end of 1783 William Pitt, son of that greatest of all British whigs, the mighty Earl of Chatham, became head of the new government in England; and, with him, there dawned new hopes of mutual understanding and respect.

554   Flag flown from the *Bonhomme Richard* during the engagement with the *Serapis*, in the United States National Museum, Washington

CHAPTER XI

SEA FIGHTS WITH FRANCE AND BARBARY

OLD WORLD wars naturally favored the sea-borne trade of the very efficient seafaring neutral Americans. But Old World claims to exclusive rights at sea made the sudden entry of the independent United States a most disturbing factor. Every sea power conducted as much trade as possible in its own ships, and quite naturally used its navy to enforce its laws. For the new American mercantile marine to enter these lists as a free lance without the use of a navy would have been impossible. In 1793 France and England again took up the sword. In 1795 the British Orders-in-Council against neutral trade with enemy France were raising one kind of war fever in the United States, while the enslavement of American merchant seamen by the Barbary corsairs was raising another. So Congress ordered six frigates "superior to any European frigate of the usual dimension." Jay's Treaty (1794) prevented war with the British, while the blackmail treaty of the next year with Algiers staved off for a few more years the inevitable clash with Barbary. Then the war fever subsided; and only three of the six ordered frigates were built — *United States, Constellation* and *Constitution*.

But Jay's Treaty (see Vol. VIII) angered the French, and Talleyrand tried hard to turn America against the British and make her subservient to France. In 1798 force supplanted Talleyrand's diplomacy; and, as the result of the X, Y, Z episode (Vol. VIII), an informal "Quasi-War" developed quickly. France seized nearly a thousand American vessels. The United States finally abrogated the French Alliance. Meanwhile the new American navy went to the rescue; and, on February 9, 1799, near St. Kitts in the West Indies, fought its first action with a French man-of-war, *L'Insurgente*, of forty guns. From first to last the French lost eighty-four armed craft.

When in 1783 the newly formed states began to seek independent markets and channels of commerce in new quarters of the earth, they were embarrassed for the first time by an enemy which for centuries had hampered the commerce of Great Britain's older rivals. In the Barbary provinces of northern Africa — Algeria, Tripoli, Tunis and Morocco — piracy had long been the officially recognized mainstay of national administration and finance. In Algeria and Tripoli there was a time-honored dynasty of pirate sovereigns. France and Spain and the Italian states were forced each year to pay huge indemnities to these marauding pirates; their coast lines were never safe from destructive raids; their citizens were carried away as captives to suffer, in default of extortionate ransoms, most brutal torture and protracted imprisonments. Special orders of missionaries were organized with the sole aim of bringing aid to the oppressed Christian slaves, perishing slowly in their foul, unlighted dungeons. As early as 1785 two American vessels were captured, and twenty-one American citizens held for ransom until the sum of $59,496 was finally paid for their release. This precedent, so soon established, became for a long time the unquestioned procedure in dealing with the Barbary states. Each year for the rest of the century, money and provisions and ships were sent as indemnity or ransom. The treaty of 1795 with Algiers stipulated a large yearly sum, but the ratio of division among the four claimant powers remained unsettled. In 1801 the Bashaw of Tripoli complained that his own country, by being offered only as much spoils as Tunis, had been insulted sufficiently to justify a declaration of war.

THE FIFTEEN STARS AND FIFTEEN STRIPES

IN 1794 Congress was persuaded to honor the recently admitted states, Vermont and Kentucky, by increasing the stars and stripes to fifteen, the number which formed the national flag from 1795 to 1818. This, therefore, was the flag that flew from American battleships in the war with France, again in the fights with Barbary, and finally in 1812. Old Ironsides and many another famous vessel bore the fifteen stars and stripes. Farragut served under it; and so did Andrew Jackson. To this flag Scott Key wrote his poem. And fifteen was a most artistic number of the stars.

555 From J. Fenimore Cooper, *History of the United States Navy*, extra-illustrated edition by John S. Barnes, in Naval History Society Collections, courtesy of the New York Historical Society

THE FRIGATE *UNITED STATES*

AUTHORIZED by Congress in 1794, as one of the three frigates eventually built, the *United States* (like her more famous sister the *Constitution*, aptly nicknamed "Old Ironsides") was a marked advance on any other frigates in the world. During the War of 1812 she was to win a glory all her own by her consummate defeat of the British *Macedonian* (No. 594).

556 The *United States*, from the *American Universal Magazine*, July 24, 1797

CAPTAIN THOMAS TRUXTON

THE trouble with France, which lasted from 1798 to 1800, saw the testing of the new American navy in the battle between the *Constellation* and *L'Insurgente*. Truxton handled the thirty-eight-gun *Constellation* with a naval seaman's skill, completely outmaneuvered *L'Insurgente*, and poured in broadsides to the best advantage. This first sea fight of the new American navy (on February 9, 1799) was

557 From an engraving by C. Tiebout after the portrait by A. Robertson, in possession of the publishers

fought during Truxton's cruise near Porto Rico. The French fought most gallantly. But Truxton out-pointed them, inflicted seventy casualties to his own four, and compelled them to strike in seventy-seven minutes. Truxton raked *L'Insurgente* twice by crossing her bows, and was just going to rake her again, by crossing her stern, when she struck. The *Constellation* was a practical form of "preparedness" in which Washington took great personal interest.

558 From Edward S. Maclay, *A History of the United States Navy, 1775-1893*, New York, 1894. © D. Appleton & Company

559   Medal voted by Congress to Thomas Truxton, from an engraving in
possession of the publishers

TRUXTON AND
LA VENGEANCE, 1800

On February 1, 1800, west of Guadaloupe, Truxton fought the fifty-gun frigate *La Vengeance*, a far more desperate duel than that against *L'Insurgente*. At last *La Vengeance* lurched off, half-sinking, into the night, with a loss of one hundred and sixty men against the *Constellation's* thirty-nine. Truxton, with mainmast gone, hove to for repairs.

BAINBRIDGE'S
HUMILIATION, 1800

In 1800 Captain William Bainbridge in the *George Washington* was assigned the unwelcome task of carrying the annual tribute to the Dey of Algiers. The Dey seized the *George Washington* and forced Bainbridge to use her as an Algerine transport for the ambassador going to Constantinople with all his harem, servants, horses, cattle, sheep, and treasure. Bainbridge protested against such gross humiliation. But the Dey, pointing to his own encircling batteries, replied:

560   Forms of Torture Practised by Barbary Pirates, from Pietri Dann, *Historie van Barbaryen
Piratijen*, Amsterdam, 1687

"You pay me tribute, by which you become my slaves." Since the only alternative was annihilation, or the more terrible ordeal of slavery and torture, and since the United States really did pay tribute, Bainbridge was constitutionally right to submit. But the iron entered into his soul; and his account of these humiliations, as given to Jefferson in 1801, stirred even that pacifistic President to action of the only kind that could

561   The Slave Market at Algiers, from Pietri Dann, *Historie van Barbaryen
Piratijen*, Amsterdam, 1687

possibly prove effective. Washington (in his address to Congress on December 7, 1796), when smarting under the Congressional neglect of the navy, had put the whole case in a nutshell by pointing out that "to secure respect to a neutral flag requires a naval force, organized and ready to vindicate it from insult or aggression." During 1801–1803 there was an American squadron in the Mediterranean under the successive commands of Richard Dale, Thomas Truxton and Richard Morris.

CAPTAIN EDWARD PREBLE, 1761–1807

IN 1803 Captain Edward Preble superseded Morris. Although on arrival practically unknown to his subordinates, he succeeded, by frequent displays of coolness and bravery, in rapidly winning their confidence. Realizing that a new type of boat was necessary to penetrate the shoals protecting the harbor of Tripoli, Congress had ordered the construction of two brigs and two schooners. The important task of besieging Tripoli was entrusted by Preble to Bainbridge. In spite of the patient skill and daring of Bainbridge, his ship, the *Philadelphia*, grounded during a storm outside the harbor. The Americans, seeing that the pursuing Tripolitans would soon be able to board, made, before their capture, a hurried attempt to scuttle the ship, and throw overboard the cannon.

562   From the family portrait attributed to Rembrandt Peale, privately owned

As the storm subsided, however, the enemy was able to raise the cannon from the shallow water, stop the *Philadelphia's* leaks, float her off, and flaunt her under the eyes of their American prisoners, who were held as invaluable hostages, in the palace-prison of the Bashaw.

THE EXPLOIT OF CAPTAIN DECATUR

WHEN Preble, who had been waiting anxiously at Syracuse, heard the news of the capture of the *Philadelphia*, he realized the necessity of a bold counterstroke to offset the Tripolitan advantage. The ship was too excellent a floating fortress to be allowed to remain unimpaired in the enemy harbor. To Stephen Decatur was assigned the perilous task of destroying it. A Tripolitan ketch, which had recently been captured by the Americans, provided a conveniently disguised method of transportation for Decatur and the five officers and sixty-two men whom he had chosen from his *Enterprise*. In the dark night of February 16, 1804, they approached the unsuspecting *Philadelphia*, which actually threw her ropes to make fast.

563   Stephen Decatur, 1751–1808, from the portrait by Thomas Sully, 1811, in the Comptroller's office, courtesy of the City of New York Art Commission

THE BURNING OF THE *PHILADELPHIA*

IN twenty minutes the *Philadelphia* was fired, and Decatur's men had made good their retreat without loss — and sailed back to Preble in the same small boat, which, in honor of its gallant exploit, was rechristened the *Intrepid*. The Dey, enraged by the burning of the *Philadelphia*, refused all overtures for peace and all suggestions for freeing American prisoners. So nothing but a general attack on Tripoli remained to be done. Here the *Constitution*, foreshadowing her future greatness, led the well-planned advance.

564   From the engraving in the Peabody Museum, Salem, Mass., dedicated to Captain Decatur "by his obedient servant, John B. Guerrazzi," 1803

565   Attack by Commodore Preble's Fleet at Tripoli, August 3, 1804, from a painting by Corné, 1805,
in the Museum of the United States Naval Academy, Annapolis

THE NAVAL ATTACK ON TRIPOLI

IN spite of the overwhelming odds of men and guns against him, Preble inflicted much damage, and during the attack of August 3 Stephen Decatur for the second time proved his heroism by boarding a greatly superior corsair craft.   But in his four attacks he was not able to do more than cause the furious Dey to reduce the ransom of Bainbridge and his men from one thousand to five hundred dollars.   Then on September 4, Captain Richard Somers and twelve other volunteers took the *Intrepid*, now turned into a regular magazine by a hundred barrels of powder, one hundred nine-inch shells, fifty thirteen and a half inch shells, beside a quantity of shot, kentledge, and pieces of iron, and steered her straight into the harbor, with the hazardous hope that they might abandon her in safety before she exploded in the midst of the moored Tripolitan flotilla.   But in some way which will never be known she blew up prematurely, killing her whole

566 ·   Barbary Galleys, from Pietri Dann, *Historie van
Barbaryen Piratÿen*, Amsterdam, 1687

devoted crew.   Further attacks were discouraged for the moment.   The American prisoners remained undelivered.   Preble returned to America, leaving Captain Samuel Barron in charge of an ever increasing squadron.

THE BARBARY MENACE ENDED

SOON after Preble's return home, his services in the Mediterranean were handsomely acknowledged.   A gold medal, accompanied by a vote of thanks, was the first distinction of the kind bestowed by Congress under the new Constitution.   The Truxton medal was purely personal.   This one was a regular war medal given to all ranks and ratings concerned; though not, of course, in gold, except to Preble.

The squadron, which had been left under Barron's command to continue the blockade of Tripoli, remained inactive.   The next move in freeing Bainbridge and his fellow prisoners was a diplomatic-military coup, engineered by William Eaton, United States Consul at Tunis.   Negotiations were opened with the former ruler of Tripoli, who had been deposed by his brother and exiled into Egypt.   Ambitious to be restored to his throne, he agreed to raise an army which Eaton should command, and which should coöperate with the blockading American fleet.   In spite of a six-hundred-mile march across the desert, and a successful joint enterprise with Isaac Hull at Derne, the maneuver was tardy, for Tobias Lear, American Consul General at Algiers, made peace with the Barbary states, who were becoming afraid of the increasing strength of the American fleet.   All tribute for the future was disclaimed, and sixty thousand dollars agreed on as ransom for the prisoners.   For several years the terms of the treaty were carried out.   But later, assured by British agents that the War of 1812 would wipe out the American navy, the pirates were emboldened to renew their attacks.   So that, as soon as the war with Great Britain was ended, two American squadrons were fitted out under Bainbridge and Decatur to end definitely the Barbary menace.   Before Bainbridge reached the Mediterranean, however, Decatur, by a series of brilliant skirmishes, had terrified the rulers of Algeria, Tripoli, Tunis and Morocco into a permanent surrender.

567   Medal voted by Congress to Preble, from
J. Fenimore Cooper, *History of the United
States Navy*, extra-illustrated edition, in the
Naval History Society Collections, courtesy of
the New York Historical Society

CHAPTER XII

WEST POINT EFFICIENCY, 1802–1902

NINETEEN years after the close of the War of Independence, on July 4, 1802, the United States Military Academy at West Point was formally opened. The Superintendent was Major Jonathan Williams of the Engineers. Ten cadets were in attendance. Since the end of the Revolution the people of the United States had been threatened by war with England, happily averted by the Jay Treaty, had been engaged in a conflict with France, and had fought a protracted and finally successful war against the Indians of the Northwest Territory. Henry Knox, as Secretary of War in Washington's cabinet, had urged the founding of a military school. Washington himself, in his last annual message to Congress, had written these emphatic words: ". . . the art of war is both comprehensive and complicated . . . much previous study . . . in its most improved and perfect state, is always of great moment to the security of the nation." In 1800 a proposal of President Adams to found a school for training both military and naval officers together went unheeded. There can be no more striking illustration than this of the non-militaristic temperament of the American people at the outset of their career as an independent nation. Curiously enough the academy was founded in the administration of Thomas Jefferson, who was one of the most pacific of all occupants of the exalted office of President.

West Point began in a day when the educational institutions of the United States were still small and the man who had a college education was a rarity. The curricula of the colleges were founded on the classics and mathematics, with a little "natural philosophy," as science was then called, thrown in. According to modern concepts, the training was not advanced, the standards not high. Boys of high school age were a commonplace in the classrooms of Princeton, Columbia, the University of Virginia, Harvard, and Yale. One need not be surprised, therefore, to find that the entrance examination for admission to West Point was confined to easy arithmetic and that anyone who could pass and who was between the ages of twelve and thirty-four might be admitted as a student. There was no winter term. Even this modest beginning did not guarantee the permanence of an institution in which neither Congress nor the people of the United States had any great interest. Among the many incompetent acts of the Secretary of War, William Eustis, was the near extinction of the Military Academy in 1811, when not one cadet attended. The bitter lessons of the second war with England which broke out the following year were necessary before the American people could be brought to see the necessity of training officers in time of peace who could lead the armed forces of the United States in the event of national emergency.

The first decade and a half of the history of West Point fell in a period when American life was confused by a multitude of tendencies and forces. The frontier was increasing in its importance and influence. The men of the East were busy building or planning turnpikes. Religious revivals were sweeping the country beyond the mountains and a variety of reforms were engaging the attention of the people of the older communities. The ideal and the practice of democracy was becoming a cardinal American principle. And the sentiment of nationalism was making progress against the particularism of the old state loyalties. In the midst of this most interesting *milieu* West Point was born.

568   View of West Point at the close of the Revolution, from the *New York Magazine*, 1791, after a sketch by H. Livingston, engraved by Tiebout

WEST POINT IN 1780

THE original of the map (No. 570) was made by a French engineer, when, at the time of Arnold's treason, West Point was regarded by the Patriot army as the gateway of the north and the center of Washington's positions about New York. Though twenty-two years were still to pass before the Academy was founded, there already was some faint suggestion of its future work in the Engineer School, Library, and Laboratory seen in this contemporary view. Nothing permanent was attempted at this time; and only a very few far-seeing men then contemplated any regular school of war. West Point started as a technical institution of secondary school rank.

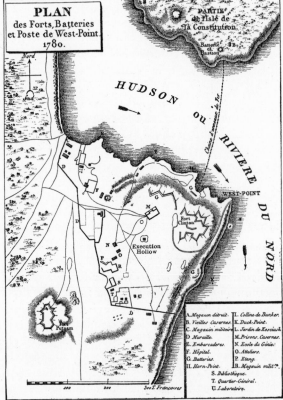

569 Colonel Jonathan Williams, from the portrait by Thomas Sully, 1815, in the United States Military Academy, West Point

570 Plan of the Forts, Batteries, and Post at West Point, 1780, in *The Centennial of the West Point Military Academy*, 1904, after a contemporary French plan

JONATHAN WILLIAMS, 1750–1813

JONATHAN WILLIAMS, first Superintendent of the Military Academy on its establishment in 1802, was the son of a Revolutionary officer and grandnephew of Benjamin Franklin, to whom he became secretary in France, where he studied the art of war. He had an almost impossible task, since there were no tests whatever to weed out the unfit among the nominees admitted. Moreover, the cadets were not amenable to military law, and no class rank existed. Nevertheless, a beginning had been made in founding what still is (with the sole exception of its naval counterpart — Annapolis) the only really national place of education throughout the United States. There and at Annapolis alone exist national schools where the education is not only free, but the pupils are paid by the nation, in return for which they bind themselves to serve a certain time in the army or navy.

THE UNITED STATES MILITARY PHILOSOPHICAL SOCIETY

THE spirit of West Point at the outset of its history is reflected in the establishment of an organization for the promotion of military science in the year of founding. The United States Military Philosophical Society was contemporary with a number of like societies which aimed to promote arts, agriculture and manufacturing. Among the signers of this document in 1802 were five who subsequently rose to distinction in the service. Jared Mansfield (1759–1830) was a native of New Haven and a graduate of Yale, an accomplished mathematician, the surveyor of the Ohio and the Northwest Territory (1803–12), a lieutenant-colonel in the U. S. Engineers, and "professor of natural and experimental philosophy" at West Point till 1828. Macomb, Swift, Armistead, and Totten were all under age, being only twenty, eighteen, seventeen, and fourteen, respectively, at the time they signed this paper. We shall meet Macomb as a victorious general at Plattsburg in 1814. Swift was the first graduate of West Point, where he became Thayer's immediate predecessor (1816–17). He was among the earliest of railway engineers (New Orleans in 1830 and Harlem in 1840). His diary contains a full description of West Point. Totten served all through the War of 1812, was chief engineer at Vera Cruz in 1847 and at Washington in 1861, beside being inspector of West Point until his death in 1884.

COLONEL SYLVANUS THAYER, THE "FATHER OF WEST POINT"

THE man who turned West Point into an institution of national significance was Colonel Sylvanus Thayer, who was appointed superintendent in 1817 when he was thirty-two years old and a captain of engineers. For sixteen years he remained the head of the Military Academy, and during his régime the foundations of the modern school were laid. He

572 Sylvanus Thayer, 1785–1872, from the portrait by Thomas Sully, at Dartmouth College, Hanover, N. H.

MILITARY ACADEMY, WEST-POINT,
12th November, 1802.

AT a Meeting of the Corps of Engineers, called for the purpose of considering the propriety of forming a Society for promoting Military Science, the following preliminary Articles were separately proposed, and unanimously voted.

1. A Society shall be formed for the purpose of promoting Military Science.
2. The place of meeting shall be wherever the Military Academy may be established.
3. The Officers and Cadets of the Corps of Engineers shall be members of right.
4. All other members shall be elected by ballot.
5. Any gentleman, whether a military man or not, may be eligible, under regulations to be made by the constitution.
6. No question shall be permitted in the Society affecting the organization, discipline or internal concerns of any existing Corps belonging to the Army of the United States, the objects of the Society being exclusively confined to the Arts and Sciences.
7. When the Corps of Engineers, or so many of them as may be at West Point, shall sign the Preliminaries, the Society shall be instituted.
8. A President and Secretary pro tempore shall immediately be appointed by ballot, after which a Committee shall be chosen to form a constitution.
9. The next meeting of the Society shall be when the Committee shall give notice to the President pro tempore, that they are ready to report, and he shall call the members together accordingly.

[SIGNED]

Jonathan Williams, Decius Wadsworth, Wm. A. Barron, Jared Mansfield, James Wilson, Alex. Macomb, jun. Jos. G. Swift, Simeon M. Levy, Walter K. Armistead, Joseph G. Totten.

CONSTITUTION.

CHAPTER I.
Of the Society.

1. The Title of the Society shall be the UNITED STATES MILITARY PHILOSOPHICAL SOCIETY.
2. The Society shall have a Seal, the device for which to be hereafter determined by law.
3. The preliminary Articles which have already been assented to, by the Corps of Engineers, shall be considered as a part of the Constitution.

CHAPTER II.
Of Members, and the Manner of their Election.

1. The Officers and Cadets of the Corps of Engineers shall be members of right, but whenever their connexion with the

571 Announcement of Formation of a Society for Promoting Military Science, dated West Point, 1802, in the collections of the New York Historical Society

was the first to take the cadets on practice marches — to Boston, Philadelphia, and Princeton. He put instruction upon an efficient basis by dividing classes into sections small enough to ensure individual attention for every student. He was the first to appoint a Commandant of Cadets, responsible for drill and discipline, an executive officer under the Superintendent with functions similar to those of a dean of students. He used senior cadets as assistant instructors so as to fit them for early command. He was, in fact, the first man who ever made military education a living force in the United States. His pioneering work has led to the development of that group of trained experts upon which the nation has had to depend in time of emergency. His watchwords, "Honor, obedience, efficiency," have been wrought into the very being of West Point.

573   From J. Milbert, *Itinéraire Pittoresque du Fleuve Hudson et des Parties Latérales de l'Amérique du Nord . . .* , Paris, 1826

WEST POINT IN 1826

THAYER'S very success was not without its drawbacks for West Point. The institution had acquired under his guidance such prestige that each congressional nomination of a cadet became an affair of politics. It chanced also that the rise of West Point coincided in part with a decline of the army. Such military policy as the United States has had prior to the Defense Act of 1920 has been of a purely opportunist character. As the War of 1812 receded, its lessons regarding the

necessity of maintaining for the purposes of national security a trained regular force of some size were forgotten. Appropriations for the army were cut, and it was materially reduced. As a result, West Point was

producing more trained graduates than the military establishment could absorb. Because there was no place for them large numbers of graduates had to be commissioned as brevet second lieutenants, a nebulous rank which caused no end of difficulty and ill-will. Moreover, those fortunate enough to get into the service looked forward to almost indefinite continuance in the grades of lieutenant and captain. Under the circumstances, in 1836 alone, one hundred and seven officers resigned, "seeing futures no more lucrative and hopeful than those of uneducated mill hands." That priceless asset, the morale of the army, suffered terribly.

WEST POINT ON THE EVE OF THE MEXICAN WAR

IN the eighteen thirties and forties the roll calls of cadets at West Point contained many names destined to become household words among the people of the United States. In the classrooms of the buildings that looked out over the mighty Hudson and on the drill grounds of the reservation worked able youngsters — Meade, Hooker, McDowell, Hancock, McClellan, Thomas, Reynolds, Sherman, Jefferson Davis, Beauregard, Jackson, Grant and Lee. These men received a training of practically

574   West Point Cadets, 1841, from *The United States Military Magazine*, Philadelphia, 1841, in the Naval History Society Collections, courtesy of the New York Historical Society

collegiate grade. One of the distinctions of West Point is that it is a pioneer among the great technical schools of the United States. Thayer laid its foundations in science at a time when a classical training was popularly considered the chief mark of an educated man.

575   West Point in 1841, from the copy by Lieut. R. S. Smith, after the original drawing by Major L'Enfant, in the West Point Military Academy

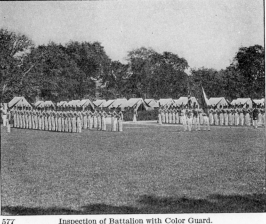

576   Battalion Passing in Review. © Detroit Publishing Co.   577   Inspection of Battalion with Color Guard.
© Detroit Publishing Co.

THE WEST POINT CENTENARY

At the time of its centenary in 1902 West Point could show a record of having produced trained officers for three major wars — the Mexican War, the Civil War, and the Spanish-American War. In addition, American officers had seen service against the Indians on the western plains, in the Philippines, and in the Boxer expedition into China. It had produced in Robert E. Lee and Stonewall Jackson military men of outstanding genius. In addition to purely military service West Point graduates had done important work in exploring and mapping the little known West, and in the planning and carrying through of significant engineering projects. Within a short time after the centennial a West Point engineer undertook the stupendous task of superintending the construction of the Panama Canal. The comment of President Roosevelt in his centennial address was, therefore, no exaggeration: "No other educational institution in the land has contributed as many names as West Point to the honor roll of the nation's greatest citizens . . . taken as a whole, the average graduate of West Point has given a greater sum of service to the country through his life than has the average graduate of any other institution in this broad land."

TWENTIETH–CENTURY WEST POINT

The growth of industrialism has made war increasingly complex. New weapons and new equipment have created a multitude of problems. The twentieth-century regimental commander in order to perform his duties with efficiency must know a vast deal more than was required of Howe, the commanding general of His Majesty's armed forces in America in the early years of the Revolution. The time has long since passed when the West Point training is sufficient for the needs of the higher commanders of the Army of the United States. As a consequence West Point has become the technical school of collegiate rank which gives young men the basic and preliminary training necessary for the profession of arms. Later in life those graduates who have demonstrated their ability by their actual service are sent to the War College for advanced instruction.

Until that happy time when war shall have been forever abolished from the affairs of men, the efficiency of the United States Military Academy must of necessity be of prime concern to American citizens. War forced upon a people who have no trained men to lead armies of defense means inevitably appalling waste of property and life, and may mean national disaster.

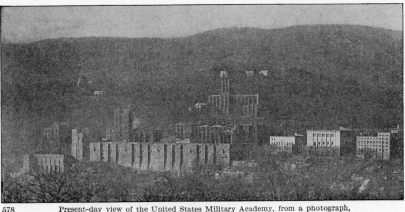

578   Present-day view of the United States Military Academy, from a photograph,
courtesy of Cram, Goodhue and Ferguson, architects of the chapel

CHAPTER XIII

1812 AT SEA

AFTER the War of Independence the United States was but a pigmy among the nations. The chief concern of the people was the establishment of a central government strong enough to maintain the reign of law at home, to guide the national development, and to establish the nation's credit abroad. In the very midst of these great tasks the shadow of European war fell across the land. In 1793 England gave battle to revolutionary France. In spite of the old Treaty of Alliance, which had made possible the independence of the United States, President Washington declared America neutral. He felt that any other course would bring on the destruction of the nation which he was laboring to establish. He made peace with England in the Jay Treaty of 1795, only to find that a resentful France flouted and insulted the American emissaries. During the administration of President Adams came hostilities at sea with the French Republic. As Napoleon rose and waxed in power the wars in Europe assumed a new aspect. England, aided by various allies, fought the conquering Corsican. Sympathy with one side or the other made a deep rift among the American people.

But, during the early years of the nineteenth century, the Napoleonic wars brought prosperity to the Americans, whose neutral merchant marine profited by the exigencies of the times. American shipmasters traded with both sides and even carried goods, either directly or through roundabout channels, from the French West Indies to the mother country. At last the great conflict developed into a stalemate, with England mistress of the sea and Napoleon master on the continent of Europe. Then Americans began to be made aware that European wars might be brought home to them. From the beginning of the conflict England maintained the right of searching American ships for alleged deserters from the Royal navy. Against this the American Government had always protested but without avail. In 1807 the issue was brought to a dramatic climax. A new U. S. frigate, the *Chesapeake*, put out from Chesapeake Bay armed, but quite unprepared for action. The British warship *Leopard* spoke her and demanded the right of searching her crew for certain deserters. The American rightly refused, whereupon the *Leopard* battered her into submission. Only a single gun could be fired from the unready *Chesapeake* before she struck. The incident was a national insult, and the war spirit ran high among the American people. But President Jefferson sought to settle the dispute by peaceful means. In the year 1806 began a struggle between England and Napoleon in which each tried to prevent neutral shipping from aiding the other. The American merchant shippers began to suffer severe losses from both sides. Jefferson determined to fight back with a substitute for war, by declaring an embargo or economic boycott. He sought to tie American shipping at the home wharves and so compel the belligerents to respect American rights. He misjudged, however, the economic power of his country, and the boycott failed. Under his successor, President Madison, the plan was practically abandoned.

Then the new West began to make its voice heard in the councils of the nation. Young men imbued with the frontier spirit, like Calhoun, born in the back country of South Carolina, and Clay, a representative from Kentucky, appeared at Washington. They became "war hawks," driving Madison toward a vigorous policy. Perhaps some of them recognized, what was clear to all thinking men, namely, that Napoleon and England were equal offenders against the United States, so far as their policies were concerned. England, however, in control of the sea had committed more concrete injuries. Moreover, the English fur-trader was the rival of the American on the frontier. The Westerner was convinced that the Englishman was inciting the Indian tribes to rise against him. In 1811 white man and red man clashed at the battle of Tippecanoe. The West demanded war with England to uphold American honor on the sea, to destroy British influence among the Indians, and to free Canada from the British Empire and incorporate it in the United States.

In June, 1812, the year of a presidential election, President Madison sent his famous war message to Congress shortly before the news arrived that the British Government had repealed the obnoxious Orders-in-Council that had caused so much injury to American shipping. New England had deeply resented Jefferson's boycott which had brought much loss and suffering to the maritime towns of that section. New England now resented the war which would destroy their trade with the greatest shipping country in the world. Moreover, conservative New England had little sympathy with the later phases of the French Revolution. The people of this region had largely favored England in her war, first against the radicalism of the day, and later against the conquering dictator, Napoleon. As a result, Congress and President Madison brought about a war which large numbers of the American people were unwilling to support.

The Government, with but a tiny navy at its command, expected to defend its shores by means of land forts against the greatest sea power in the world. Millions had been expended in coast defenses; though the plans for many of them were archaic. As the second war with Great Britain opened, the United States boasted twenty-four forts, thirty-two inclosed batteries, with an armament of seven hundred and fifty guns of various calibers. This war, however, was to demonstrate that a navy rather than coast defenses provides the only real protection for a threatened seaboard.

579 Perry's battle flag at Lake Erie, in the collection of trophy flags, United States Naval Academy, Annapolis, Md.

580   From a painting by Marshall Johnson, Jr. © Detroit Publishing Co.

"OLD IRONSIDES," THE U. S. FRIGATE *CONSTITUTION*

No United States ship no matter what her size has ever had such a war history as the mighty *Constitution*. She was the first vessel authorized by Congress after the Revolution and was one of twelve frigates that were to revolutionize the design of war vessels for half a century thereafter. With more than a century of sea experience, both in peaceful trade and war, maritime Americans were capable of building and handling ships that were the equal of any in the world. Congress, in providing for the fighting ships, had directed that they be made "superior to any European frigate." The great naval architect, Joshua Humphreys of Philadelphia, the builder, Edmund Hart, and the supervising naval officer, Commodore Samuel Nicholson, had all coöperated to make the *Constitution* one of the best warships of the day. Her keel was laid in 1794; her launch was made on October 21, 1797. As she lies to-day moored to her dock in the Boston yard, her length is one hundred and seventy-five feet, her beam forty-three and one-half, and her tonnage eighteen hundred and seventy-six. She mounted batteries varying at different times from thirty-eight to fifty-five guns. She was, of course, a "proper ship," that is, a full-rigged ship. One day in 1809 she logged a speed surpassing fifteen landsman's miles an hour.

Fine as was the *Constitution*, she and her sister frigates were part of but a tiny navy. On the day before he gave up the presidency to Jefferson, John Adams had signed a bill which provided for the reduction of the navy, at the President's discretion, to thirteen vessels, with nine captains, and other officers in proportion. Jefferson had promptly

581   "Old Ironsides," from a photograph by N. L. Stebbins, Boston

begun the task of making the legislation effective. Except for the conflict with the Barbary pirates the navy had languished. On the eve of the War of 1812 it was small indeed to come to grips with the greatest naval power in the world, fresh from victories like that at Trafalgar.

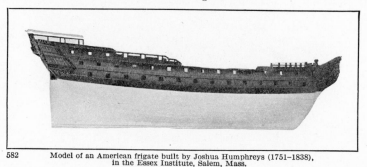

582   Model of an American frigate built by Joshua Humphreys (1751–1838),
                     in the Essex Institute, Salem, Mass.

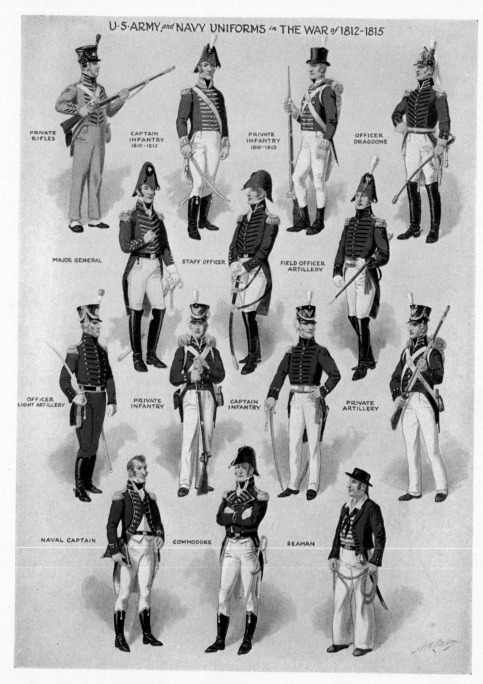

U·S·ARMY and NAVY UNIFORMS in THE WAR of 1812-1815

PRIVATE
RIFLES

CAPTAIN
INFANTRY
1810-1813

PRIVATE
INFANTRY
1810-1813

OFFICER
DRAGOONS

MAJOR GENERAL

STAFF OFFICER

FIELD OFFICER
ARTILLERY

OFFICER
LIGHT ARTILLERY

PRIVATE
INFANTRY

CAPTAIN
INFANTRY

PRIVATE
ARTILLERY

NAVAL CAPTAIN

COMMODORE

SEAMAN

Painted expressly for *The Pageant of America* by H. A. Ogden

THE INDIFFERENCE OF THE DEMOCRATIC REPUBLICANS

President Jefferson and his successor, Madison, had little interest in a navy and but slight conception of its function in defending the commerce vital to the nation's welfare. These men, however, reflected only the general temper of their times. America was still in large part a nation of agriculturists, planters and yeomen farmers. And the farmer's party was in power. Jefferson had planned to defend the coasts with gunboats manned by volunteers in the event of an emergency. But his little "Jeffs," for fear of turning turtle, could not put to sea without stowing their guns in the hold. President Madison, in his annual message of 1811, scarcely seven months before he sent his war message to Congress, devoted twenty-seven lukewarm words to the navy. Watching the trend of events and being a poor man, Captain William Bainbridge applied for leave to accept the command of a merchantman to China. "I have hitherto refused such offers, on the presumption that my country would require my services. That presumption is removed, and even doubts entertained of the permanency of our naval establishment." Admiral Mahan adds that Bainbridge's "case was not singular."

583 Captain William Bainbridge, 1774–1833, from the portrait by J. W. Jarvis in Memorial Hall, United States Naval Academy, Annapolis, Md.

584 A Seaman of 1812, sculpture by Lee Lawrie on the Memorial Tower, Harkness Quadrangle, Yale University, courtesy of the sculptor

NAVAL OFFICERS AND THEIR CREWS

When war came in the summer of 1812, the little navy of the United States was a service with a history and traditions. Nicholas Biddle and Paul Jones had been inspiring pioneers, efficient teachers, by precept and example, of a worthy group of younger officers. Many of these had seen service in the war with France and off the African coast. They came from a people who had developed one of the great merchant marines of the day; and in the early nineteenth century there was less difference between a merchant vessel and a warship than there was a century later. They commanded seamen who were volunteers, men who knew the sea from lifelong experience on fishing boats, merchant craft, and whaling ships. Man for man, their crews were superior to those of the navies of either England or France. Diligently these officers had trained their men in the all-important art of gunnery. When, on the outbreak of war, they put to sea, their ships were excellent, their training good, and their morale high. But their numbers were insignificant; and the government which they served had no well conceived plan of operations. Its own idea, in fact, was to shut up its ships in port. In the summer of 1812 Commodore John Rodgers with a squadron of five ships (two frigates, the *President* and the *United States*, a lighter frigate, the *Congress*, the brig *Argus*, and the sloop *Hornet*) was patroling the coast from Long Island southward to protect American merchantmen from being stopped for search by British warships. Rodgers chanced to be lying in New York harbor when news of the outbreak of war reached him. Within an hour he had put to sea. He thus avoided those government orders which would have scattered the American navy along the coast, inviting piecemeal destruction.

585 Commodore John Rodgers, 1771–1838, from the portrait by C. W. Peale in Independence Hall, Philadelphia

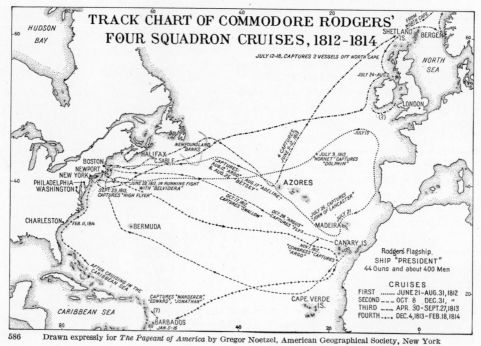

TRACK CHART OF COMMODORE RODGERS' FOUR SQUADRON CRUISES, 1812-1814

586   Drawn expressly for *The Pageant of America* by Gregor Noetzel, American Geographical Society, New York

RODGERS' FOUR CRUISES, 1812–14

RODGERS' plan was to strike boldly at the important sea lanes. Chasing the *Belvidera*, which managed to elude him some distance off the coast, he turned to intercept the plate fleet, as the convoy of British merchant vessels from Jamaica to the home ports was called. Though he sailed as far as the English Channel he found no convoys; and he returned to Boston, having taken only trifling prizes. But he had performed the most useful American naval maneuver of the war. His disappearance eastward into the Atlantic with a powerful squadron had drawn off the British boats along the American coast to protect their own ships on the ocean routes. So American merchantmen, crowding sail to make home and safety after they learned of war, found no enemy ships off Boston and New York. As a result of Rodgers' strategy American waters were virtually

587 From the portrait, 1815, by J. W. Jarvis in the City Hall, New York, courtesy of the City of New York Art Commission

free of hostile vessels during the autumn of 1812. This was the first of four strategic cruises, evidence that the United States navy did effective squadron work in the War of 1812 beside winning the much more famous duels.

CAPTAIN ISAAC HULL, 1775–1843

THE *Belvidera*, after a long-range fight, had managed to give Rodgers the slip and had hurried to Halifax with news of the outbreak of war. At once a strong squadron (*Guerrière*, *Belvidera*, and *Shannon*) made from that port for the American coast. Off Barnegat on the New Jersey shore they sighted an American frigate. This ship was none other than the *Constitution*, which had taken on a crew and stores at Annapolis and was bound for New York. Her commander was Captain Isaac Hull, then in his thirty-eighth year. Hull was typical of the men who officered the American navy. Born in Connecticut he had put to sea as a boy in the merchant service and was in command of a vessel at the age of nineteen. In 1798 he had been commissioned lieutenant in the newly organized navy and had served with distinction in the Barbary wars. Off Barnegat in July, 1812, he suddenly found himself in a situation for which seamanship rather than fighting ability offered the only solution.

588   From the painting by S. S. Tuckerman, in the Knickerbocker Club, New York. © Curtis & Cameron

THE *CONSTITUTION'S* DESPERATE ESCAPE

As Hull saw sails appearing on his flank and in his rear, he assumed that he had come into touch with Rodgers' squadron. Just in time he discovered that he was in imminent danger of capture. The breeze had died down and the sails of the great *Constitution* hung listlessly from their yards. Hull promptly called his boats away and set his men towing the frigate in a race for life against the pursuing British, whose boats were also out. Kedge anchors were also dropped ahead from boats; the deck men walked the capstan round and brought the ship up to the anchor, which was then dropped ahead again. All day this lasted and all night, except for a two hours' rest when the breeze came up. The next day again was hot and calm, and the orders for the day were kedge and tow. The British in the rear gained a little on the American and the quiet of the sea was broken by the booming of cannon. Toward sunset a squall bore down, enabling Hull to play his enemy a trick. He double-reefed all his lower sails, as if the squall were but a prelude of a gale; the pursuing British also double-reefed, supposing Hull to be experiencing a storm. Then, under cover of a driving rain, Hull sped away with all reefs out and made Boston in safety. The escape was partly due to the sailing powers of the *Constitution*.

THE *CONSTITUTION* AND THE *GUERRIÈRE*, AUGUST 19, 1812

The Washington government had decided to supersede Hull; and had sent an officer to relieve him, when he put his fortune to the hazard, in effect defied the government, and stood out to sea. Had he come back empty-handed, his career in the navy would doubtless have been at an end. But, when he sailed again into Boston harbor, he brought with him the crew of the *Guerrière*, having won the first ship duel between the British and American navies. After cruising in the Gulf of St. Lawrence, Hull had come upon the *Guerrière* watching the sea lanes south of the Grand Banks. The *Constitution's* broadside shots were heavier and her crew was larger. But Captain Dacres was not deterred by such odds; for, after a series of tremendous victories in the Napoleonic wars, the British navy was deemed well-nigh invincible.

589   James R. Dacres, Vice Admiral of the Red, from an engraving by Page after the portrait by Bowyer, in possession of the publishers

590   From the engraving *The Capture of the Guerrière by the Constitution*, by D. Kimberly after the
painting by Thomas Birch, in possession of the publishers

THE *GUERRIÈRE* LEFT A BURNING HULK

THE two opponents took their time. The *Guerrière* had a good position; and for an hour appeared at least to be holding her own with ease. Then Hull closed to the very shortest range. The ships ran side by side; and in twenty minutes of magnificent gunnery the *Constitution* doubled the damage she received, brought down a mast of the *Guerrière*, and forced her into a dangerous position from which she could not escape without terrific raking. Then, as the vessels moved again, in such a way as might have let the British rake him from astern, Hull smartly turned. But he fouled the *Guerrière's* bowsprit, which clung to his mizzen-rigging for ten minutes of point-blank musketry, when each side thought the other meant to board. Then the *Guerrière's* foremast and mainmast came crashing down, leaving her wallowing helplessly in the trough of a heavy sea. The ships parted for emergency repairs, the *Guerrière* gallantly trying to get under way with a spritsail. But when the admirably handled, completely masted, and even full-sparred *Constitution* again bore down, Captain Dacres was compelled to strike without another blow. The useless hulk of the British frigate was set on fire. She had been almost literally blown out of the water. The news of Hull's victory preceded him into Boston so that, when he brought the *Constitution* into the harbor, he received from the population crowding the wharves and the house-tops overlooking the bay an ovation such as Boston had never yet accorded to any man. Hull's popular fame rests on this one fight; for he had no further chance of distinction. After peace came, he held a variety of commands at sea and among naval men he had a high reputation for seamanship. The practical significance of his victory was very slight; but its moral effect was tremendous. It was the first bright spot in a very drab year. Moreover, it had demonstrated beyond doubt the qualities of the American frigates, their gunnery, and crews.

591   From the painting by Carlton T. Chapman, in the collection of the Naval History Society,
New York, courtesy of the New York Historical Society

CAPTAIN JACOB JONES

Two months after the defeat of the *Guerrière* came one of the greatest fights of the war. The vessels were only small sloops, five-hundred-tonners. The British *Frolic* was escorting a convoy of merchantmen. The American *Wasp* under Captain Jacob Jones was scouring the western Atlantic in search of prey. Both boats had been roughly handled by heavy gales. They met on October 18, 1812, in a sea that tossed them about like cockle shells, that kept the decks awash, and filled the air with spray. The gunners waited for the muzzles of their cannon to be lifted clear of the water to load and fire. In this wild fray the *Wasp*

592 From the painting by Warren Sheppard in E. S. Ellis, *The Library of American History*. © The Jones Brothers Publishing Co., Cincinnati

managed to shoot straight at deck and hull while the *Frolic's* shots tore away her adversary's upper rigging. The fight lasted a little more than half an hour. Jones, whose top masts were damaged, bore down upon the *Frolic* to board and prevent escape. The boarders found on the enemy decks a terrible carnage. One man unhurt at the wheel and three badly wounded officers, including Captain Whinyates, were the only living men on deck. Captain Jones was preparing to take his prize into Charleston when the British *Poictiers*, a seventy-four-gun ship-of-the-line, bagged both the little sloops and carried them off to Bermuda. But this capture did not dim the fame of the battle with odds exactly even.

593 Jacob Jones, 1768–1850, from the portrait, 1817, by Thomas Sully, in the State House, Dover, Del.

THE *UNITED STATES* AND THE *MACEDONIAN*

TEN days before the fight between the *Wasp* and the *Frolic* Commodore Rodgers had put to sea from Boston for his second cruise. A little way out Captain Decatur (No. 563), commanding the *United States*, a sister frigate to the *Constitution*, was detached for independent cruising in mid-Atlantic, where he fell in with the

594 From the painting by Thomas Birch in the Brooklyn Museum, courtesy of Herbert L. Pratt, New York

Macedonian on October 25, 1812. The odds were roughly three against two in favor of the American. Moreover, Captain Carden was no such tactician as Decatur. In ninety minutes the *Macedonian* had received more than a hundred shots in her hull and had lost a mast. Her casualties were very heavy, while Decatur had but twelve men killed and wounded. The difference was the result in part of Decatur's greater skill in maneuvering and in part of the superior gunnery of the American crew. The *Macedonian* was sailed to Newport and her battle flag was forwarded to Washington, where it was presented to the cabinet, who were then celebrating the capture of the *Guerrière's* flag at a grand official ball.

595   From the painting by Carlton T. Chapman, in the Collection of the Naval History
Society, courtesy of the New York Historical Society

THE *CONSTITUTION* AND THE *JAVA*, DECEMBER 29, 1812

THE fourth sea duel of the year 1812 occurred four days after Christmas off the Brazilian coast. Here the *Constitution*, now commanded by Captain Bainbridge, met the *Java* under Captain Lambert. Both officers were highly skilled in the art of handling ships, and this time the vessels and crews were much more evenly matched, with the odds a little in favor of the American. For an hour the ships maneuvered and fought at long range. Then, as the American gunnery began to tell, Lambert decided to close before being fatally damaged. But his gallant dash failed. The *Constitution's* fire silenced his guns, and, battering his ship beyond repair, set her ablaze. Lambert was mortally wounded. Bainbridge's losses were light; but he was compelled to quit the South Atlantic and go home for repairs. The following lamentation appeared in the British *Pilot*, an authority on naval affairs, when the news about the *Java* came in: "The public will learn, with sentiments which we shall not presume to anticipate, that a third British frigate has struck to an American. This is an occurrence that calls for serious reflection, — this, and the fact stated in our paper yesterday, that Lloyd's list contains notices of upwards of five hundred British vessels captured in seven months by the Americans. . . . Yet down to this moment not a single American frigate has struck her flag. They insult and laugh at our want of enterprise and vigor. They leave their ports when they please and return to them when it suits their convenience; they traverse the Atlantic; they beset the West India Islands; they advance to the very chops of the Channel; they parade along the coasts of South America; nothing chases, nothing intercepts, nothing engages them but to yield them triumph."

THE *HORNET* AND THE *PEACOCK*

CAPTAIN JAMES LAWRENCE, commanding the *Hornet*, had gone south with Bainbridge to patrol the southern American coast. His little sloop was the counterpart of the *Wasp*. On February 24, 1813, he chanced to fall in with the British *Peacock*, a vessel of the same class as his own. Lawrence, however, had a marked advantage in armament. The *Peacock* was sunk with heavy casualties; and Lawrence returned to New York, his sloop crowded with prisoners. His reward was promotion to the command of the frigate *Chesapeake*.

596   From the aquatint by W. Strickland for the *Naval Chronicle*, 1815, in the Collection of
the Naval History Society, courtesy of the New York Historical Society

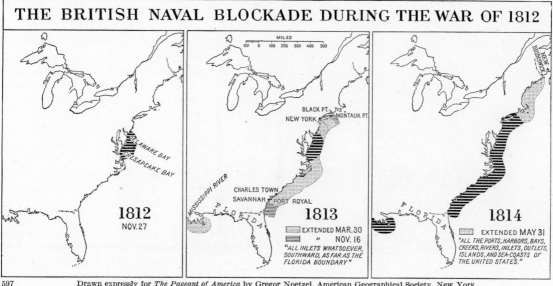

THE BRITISH NAVAL BLOCKADE DURING THE WAR OF 1812

1812 NOV. 27

1813
☰ EXTENDED MAR. 30
☰ " NOV. 16
"ALL INLETS WHATSOEVER, SOUTHWARD, AS FAR AS THE FLORIDA BOUNDARY"

1814
☰ EXTENDED MAY 31
"ALL THE PORTS, HARBORS, BAYS, CREEKS, RIVERS, INLETS, OUTLETS, ISLANDS, AND SEA-COASTS OF THE UNITED STATES."

597   Drawn expressly for *The Pageant of America* by Gregor Noetzel, American Geographical Society, New York

THE BLOCKADES OF THE AMERICAN COAST

THE story of the naval duels, however, is not that of the main naval strategy of the war. The chief reason why the American navy was permitted to put to sea in the early months of the war was the desperate situation in Europe, where, in 1812 and 1813, Napoleon was still a military colossus. His pleasure at the news of American victories on the sea was second only to that of the people of the United States, who were in effect, if not in fact, his allies. To blockade Napoleon's extending domains and to perform other necessary services incidental to a desperate war taxed the British navy almost to the limit of its strength. It had therefore a wholly insufficient force available with which to meet the American assault upon its flank. For this reason the first American blockade was not decreed until November 27, 1812, and then only included Delaware and Chesapeake bays. On March 30 of the following year it was extended to take in New York, Charleston, Port Royal, Savannah, and the Mississippi. A little less than six months later, on November 16, Long Island Sound was blockaded together with every port southwardly to Florida. But Narragansett bay and the rest of New England were still left open. In this region opposition to the war had been strong from the beginning and had increased as the conflict progressed. In 1814 talk of secession was heard in many a New England village and city while "Mr. Madison's War" was decried in the bitterest of terms. Nevertheless, on May 31, 1814, the day after the British peace with France was signed, the whole American coast was declared under blockade. Against these ever extending and ever tightening blockades the little American navy was of no avail, and, as they developed, the ship duels became fewer and fewer.

"THE NEW CARRYING TRADE"

THE blockades drove American shipping from the sea. The people of the little island of Nantucket, dependent almost entirely upon the whale fishery, suffered great hardships. All of maritime New England was plunged into depression relieved only by the prizes that the privateers were fortunate enough to capture. Even the coasting trade was ruined and communication between the states had to be by wagon. "The New Carrying Trade" expressed the bitterness of those who opposed war.

> Ye wagoners of Freedom,
> Whose charges chew the cud,
> Whose wheels have braved a dozen years
> The gravel and the mud;
> Your glorious hawbucks yoke again
> To take another jag,
> And scud through the mud,
> Where the heavy wheels do drag,
> Where the wagon creak is long and low,
> And the jaded oxen lag.

598   From drawing by Stanley M. Arthurs in A. T. Mahan, *Sea Power in Its Relation to the War of 1812*, Boston, 1905. © Little, Brown & Co., Boston

599   The *Chesapeake and Shannon*, from the lithograph by L. Haghe, after the painting by J. C. Schetky, London, 1830, in the New York Public Library

CAPTAIN BROKE

Two days after the declaration of the British blockade of May 30, 1813, occurred the last of the frigate duels. For some weeks Captain Lawrence of the *Chesapeake* had been lying in Boston harbor shipping a crew. The task was more difficult than earlier in the war, partly because of New England dissatisfaction and partly because the profits of privateering were attracting the better seamen into that great gamble. Off Boston Light cruised Captain Philip Broke in the *Shannon*. Mahan has remarked that "his was one of those cases where singular merit as an officer and an attention to duty altogether exceptional had not yet obtained opportunity for distinction. It would probably be safe to say that no more thoroughly efficient ship of her class had been seen in the British navy during the twenty years' war with France." Lawrence had an equally powerful frigate. But her officers and men had not yet learned to know each other as a crew. That Lawrence should seek an action under such circumstances seems incredible; yet, on the first of June, the sails of the *Chesapeake* disappeared below the horizon with those of the *Shannon* not far off.

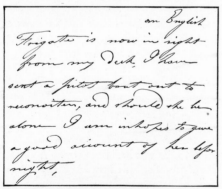

601   Lawrence's dispatch announcing contact with the enemy, original in the Navy Department, Washington

600   Broke's Challenge to Lawrence, from the original dispatch in the Navy Department, Washington

THE CHESAPEAKE AND SHANNON

Lawrence chose to fight at close quarters, distrusting the ability of his crew for emergency maneuvers. But he came on so fast that he overran the mark. Trying for a better position, his headsails were disabled by enemy shot and his ship, suddenly coming up into the wind, got out of hand. Then it was that the *Shannon* swept her with a deadly raking fire, while musket shot increased the carnage. Lawrence and his first lieutenant, Ludlow, fell mortally wounded. A few minutes later Captain Broke himself led a boarding party; and the crew of the *Chesapeake*, not being a coöperative whole, and now practically leaderless, were compelled to surrender. It had been a terrible fifteen-minute fight, with heavy losses on both sides. Lawrence, dying in the cockpit, and knowing that disaster had overtaken him, murmured with his last breath: "Don't give up the ship. Blow her up!" Broke's whole seven years of expert and inspiring work aboard the *Shannon* had at last been brought to the test of battle and found complete at every point. "At last, when the certainty was known," wrote the American, Richard Rush, "I remember the public gloom; funeral orations and badges of mourning bespoke it. 'Don't give up the ship' — the dying words of Lawrence — were on every tongue."

602   Sir Philip Broke, 1776–1841, from an engraving, 1839, by W. Greatbatch, in possession of the publishers

603   Captain James Lawrence, 1781–1813, from the portrait by Gilbert Stuart in the New Jersey Historical Society, Newark

THE BURIAL OF LAWRENCE AND LUDLOW

THE British gave Lawrence and his dead compatriots all the honors of war, and all the homage one side could ever give another. But Captain George Crowninshield sailed to Halifax, under a flag of truce, with a crew of Salem skippers, such a crew as even Salem never saw before and has not seen since, and brought back Lawrence and his first lieutenant Ludlow. Then Hull, Stewart, Bainbridge, Blakeley, Creighton, Parker — six navy captains — bore the pall from the famous India wharf, while the *Rattlesnake* and *Henry* fired their minute guns in turn. Never even in this famous seaman's town has such a seaman's funeral been known.

605 The *Chesapeake* flag taken by the *Shannon*, photographed by permission of the Royal United Service Institution, London

604 Order of Procession in the Lawrence-Ludlow Funeral, Salem, Mass., from *An Account of the Funeral Honors bestowed on the Remains of Captain Lawrence and Lieutenant Ludlow*, Boston, 1813

The *Chesapeake's* battle flag now finds an honored niche in the Royal United Service Institution museum in London; while many a captured British color finds an equally honored home at the United States Naval Academy at Annapolis.

606 Graves of the American and British Captains, Portland, Me., from a photograph by Gay

DIVIDED IN BATTLE; UNITED IN DEATH

OFF the coast of Maine, on September 5, 1813, met two tiny brigs-of-war, the British *Boxer*, Captain Samuel Blyth, and the American *Enterprise*, Captain William Burrows. Though the odds in men were almost two to one against the Englishman, he instantly gave battle. When the desperate fight was over the *Boxer* had been defeated and both captains were dead. Now they rest side by side in the little churchyard overlooking Casco Bay.

607 The Burrows Medal, from facsimile of the original, courtesy of The American Numismatic Society, New York

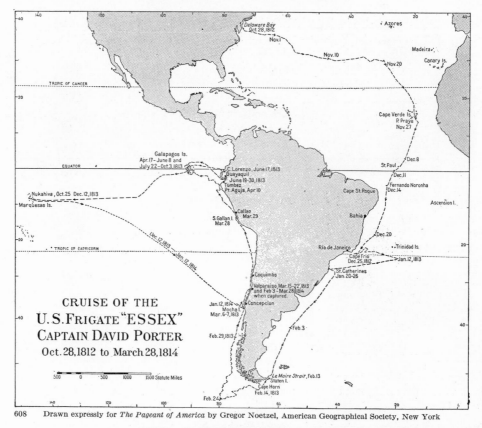

CRUISE OF THE
U.S. FRIGATE "ESSEX"
CAPTAIN DAVID PORTER
Oct. 28, 1812 to March 28, 1814

608   Drawn expressly for *The Pageant of America* by Gregor Noetzel, American Geographical Society, New York

THE CRUISE OF THE *ESSEX*

THE *Essex* is rightly considered one of the most historic vessels in the United States navy; though she was not built by the nation, and though she ended with defeat. In 1798, when resentment ran high against the French Republic, and the United States, preparing to answer force by force, found the national treasury too poor for all the vessels wanted, subscription lists were opened in the great seaport towns which suffered most from French encroachments on neutral rights at sea. Salem at once contributed the *Essex*, whose master-builder began by issuing the following appeal: "To Sons of Freedom! . . . Step forth and give your assistance in building the frigate to oppose French insolence and piracy. Let every man in possession of a white oak tree be ambitious to . . . make the name of America respected among the nations of the world. Your largest and longest trees are wanted, and the arms of them for knees and rising timber. Four trees are wanted for the keel, which, altogether, will measure 146 feet in length, and hew sixteen inches square." From stem to stern and keel to truck the *Essex* was a Salem vessel — woodwork, ironwork, canvas, ropes, and all. Her hempen cables were hove up shoulder high and marched down to the music of the drums and fifes. Six months after her "white oak trees" were growing in the wood lots the *Essex* was "fit to go foreign" and fight any Frenchmen she met. Her cost, then deemed enormous, was seventy-five thousand dollars.

In 1812, Porter, unable to rendezvous with the *Constitution* and the *Hornet* against the British shipping in the South Atlantic, characteristically planned to raid the South Pacific entirely by himself. Not till the *Alabama* raided northern shipping half a century later was there to be such another cruise. Battling her dangerous way around Cape Horn at the worst season of the year, the *Essex* made Valparaiso on March 14, 1813. Then Porter made the Galapagos, where he took three fine British whaling vessels. Next he took two letters-of-marque, which he also manned from the *Essex;* so that he now had a regular flotilla of half-a-dozen sail, with eighty guns, as many prisoners, and three hundred and forty "jackies" of his own. Then Lieutenant Downes cruised off in one of the prizes (rechristened *Essex, Junior*) and presently returned with three new prizes, full, like the others, of whale oil, bone, and priceless naval stores. After wintering in the Marquesas the perfectly refitted *Essexes* returned to Valparaiso in the early spring. There news came in that Porter's old friend, Captain Hillyar of the British navy, was on his way against the *Essex* with the frigate *Phoebe.* Porter, quite calmly confident, prepared for the coming duel.

609 From the painting *The Essex vs. the Phoebe and the Cherub*, in the Peabody Museum, Salem, Mass.

THE *ESSEX* AGAINST THE *PHOEBE* AND THE *CHERUB*, MARCH 28, 1814

HILLYAR, however, brought the powerful armed sloop *Cherub*, besides the frigate *Phoebe*. For six weeks the overmatched American lay at his moorings in the neutral Chilean port of Valparaiso, while the British watched outside. News presently reached Porter that other British vessels were hurrying against him. So he decided on a desperate run for the open sea; but bided his time. On March 28 a violent gale, sweeping across the bay,

610 Captain David Porter, 1780–1843, from the portrait by C. W. Peale in Independence Hall, Philadelphia

parted one of his cables. He therefore decided to cut the other and make his way out. But at the harbor mouth a sudden squall carried away his maintopmast. He knew his ship was doomed; so he turned along the coast and came to anchor about three miles north of Valparaiso. Here, though the *Essex* was well within the three-mile limit, Hillyar chose his position, and, with cannon broadsides which outranged the too many carronades aboard the *Essex*, pounded her to pieces. Porter fought back with all the power at his command; but he could not maneuver for close quarters. Then with a kedge anchor he tried to beach the *Essex* and save his men; but the hawser snapped. At last, when he had but seventy-five of all ranks left, he struck his colors. "We have been unfortunate but not disgraced," he quite correctly wrote, "the defense of the *Essex* has been not less honorable to her officers and crew than the capture of an equal force. . . ."

MINOR NAVAL ENGAGEMENTS

THE defeat of the *Essex* was the American navy's last great fight of the War of 1812. As the British blockade tightened on the American coast, one after another, the frigates were shut up in port. But a few smaller vessels were still at large to worry British shipping and to engage in an occasional battle with an enemy vessel of their own class. On April 29, 1814, Captain Lewis Warrington in the *Peacock*, named after the British sloop that Lawrence had defeated, easily beat the *Épervier* off Cape Canaveral in the West Indies. Two months later (June 28) Commander Johnston Blakeley in a second *Wasp* overpowered the British brig *Reindeer*, which had little more than half the tonnage of the American sloop. The battle occurred on the westerly approaches to the English Channel. On September 1 the *Wasp*, again at sea after having refitted in a French port, picked out one of three British brigs that were chasing a Yankee privateer. Darkness had fallen when Blakeley drove in alongside the *Avon* and for an hour in a black night the two fought racing side by side. Then the *Avon* struck. Not long after the *Wasp* vanished, her fate an unsolved mystery.

611 Medal awarded by Congress to Lewis Warrington, from Joseph Loubat, *Medallic History of the United States of America*, 1879

612 Medal awarded by Congress to Johnston Blakeley, from Joseph Loubat, *Medallic History of the United States of America*, 1879

613   Action off Sandy Hook, January 15, 1815, between H. M. Frigate *Endymion* and the U. S. S. *President*, from an anonymous engraving published in London, May 1, 1815

614   From the painting *The Constitution capturing the Cyane and Levant*, February 20, 1815, by Carlton Chapman in the United States Naval Academy, Annapolis

THE LAST DUELS

THE *President* and *Constitution* were the very last frigates to fight. In December, 1814, "Old Ironsides" managed to get into the open sea under the command of Captain Charles Stewart, a gallant successor to Hull and Bainbridge. Next month Decatur, commanding the *President*, tried to run the blockade of New York. Heavily laden for a long voyage, she was injured when crossing the bar; so, though she damaged in a fight the slightly smaller vessel, the *Endymion*, this well handled British vessel outsailed her and escaped. A little later Decatur was overtaken by two Britishers, the *Pomone* supported by the *Tenedos*, frigates of the class of the *Shannon* and the *Guerrière*. With other Britishers in sight, there was no alternative but surrendering to a quite overwhelming force. Decatur, however, did not strike until he had lost a fifth of his crew and his ship had been disabled.

615   From the portrait by Thomas Sully, 1811, in possession of Mrs. Marie T. Garland, Buzzards Bay, Mass., courtesy of the Pennsylvania Academy of the Fine Arts

CAPTAIN CHARLES STEWART, 1778–1869

STEWART, after having been blockaded at Norfolk in the *Constellation*, had been transferred to the *Constitution* at Boston, whence he twice escaped the blockade. On February 20, 1815, when two hundred miles E.N.E. from Madeira, he met the British *Cyane* and *Levant*, which were no match, both together, for "Old Ironsides," provided that Stewart could keep the range long enough to neutralize their short-range carronades. With

616   The *Constellation*, from a photograph. © by E. Muller, Jr., Inc.

admirable skill he raked them both in quick succession, and forced the *Cyane* to surrender. Then the little *Levant*, having made some emergency repairs, pluckily returned to the fight; but was at last compelled to strike. It was a captain's battle; and Stewart proved his worth.

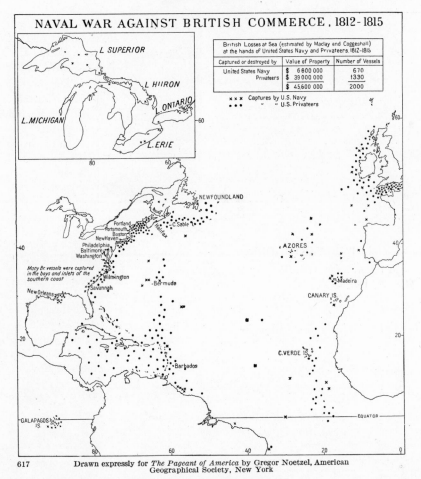

NAVAL WAR AGAINST BRITISH COMMERCE, 1812-1815

British Losses at Sea (estimated by Maclay and Coggeshall) at the hands of United States Navy and Privateers, 1812-1815		
Captured or destroyed by	Value of Property	Number of Vessels
United States Navy	$ 6 600 000	670
Privateers	$ 39 000 000	1330
	$ 45 600 000	2000

x x x Captures by U.S. Navy
• • •   "   "   U.S. Privateers

617   Drawn expressly for *The Pageant of America* by Gregor Noetzel, American
                   Geographical Society, New York

THE PRIVATEERS OF 1812

MORE than five hundred privateers preyed on British commerce, taking more than thirteen hundred prizes, whose total values came close to forty million dollars, a very great sum in those days. Not only were trade routes watched by these privateers, which hung on the flanks and rears of the huge, unwieldy convoys, but the waters of the British Isles were often worse infested still. This was because convoys would persist in scattering, in a mad race for their respective ports, just as soon as they began to near the land. The quick-sailing privateers made many a rich haul in this way, and with comparative impunity; for no escort could possibly defend dozens, and sometimes hundreds, of merchant vessels which were stampeding for home. There could be no doubt at all that American privateering depredations alarmed the whole community connected with the merchant service, and sent not only marine war-risk insurance soaring but helped to raise the price of food and other stock commodities to a height that caused great distress among large numbers of the people. In September, 1814, the great seaport of Glasgow voiced the typical complaints of the time in this formal resolution: — "That the number of privateers with which our channels have been infested . . . have proved injurious to our commerce, humbling to our pride, and discreditable to the directors of the naval power . . . and when we have declared the whole American coast under blockade, it is equally dis-tressing and mortifying that our ships cannot with safety traverse our own channels." And yet, as a means of waging war, privateering was, at its very best, a most inferior and detrimental substitute for the far nobler service of the navy. It was not a national service, but a merely fortuitous mass of individual interests, vessels, and crews, all parts and no whole, and therefore quite unable to exert the well coördinated force by which alone great issues are decided. Moreover, the "gamble of it" attracted many excellent seamen from serv-ice in any proper naval force, beside leading to abuses which caused its abolition in civilized war. Privateering also induced reprisals entailing a very serious counter-account, which is usually forgotten. Finally, privateering was unable to break the Third Blockade, which strangled the sea-borne trade quite effectively in 1814.

No. 23.

SALEM, *September 20* 1814.

This will certify, That Nathan Blood is owner of one Share or fortieth part of the private armed Schooner GENERAL PUTNAM, of Salem, *John Evans*, Commander, and has paid the sum of *three hundred sixty eight Dollars 30 Cents* in full for the same—first cruize:

$368.30

Gamt. M Ward
Job D. Porter } AGENTS.

618   Certificate of shares in the *General Putnam*, original in the Essex Institute, Salem, Mass.

CERTIFICATE OF SHARES IN THE PRIVATEER *GENERAL PUTNAM*

THE *General Putnam* began this cruise too late for very important results. But one of the scrips used to finance her is given here not only because any such scrip is now extremely rare but also because it is thoroughly typical of the vast number once existing.

CROWNINSHIELD'S WHARF AT SALEM, MASSACHUSETTS

THE gold mine of the sea, worked partly, in the earlier stages of the war, by Yankee traders who flourished on the British passes given to those who traded with or for the enemy, but worked at all times by privateering miners too, discharged its choicest ore at Crowninshield's Wharf at Salem all through the War of 1812. Exactly how much real value passed through this famous wharf is probably indiscoverable. Map No. 617 shows the focal centers at which the privateers aimed their shrewdest blows. It also suggests the magnitude of their operations. Some fortunes were made and some were lost in the great gamble. With the end of the war the American privateer disappeared from conflicts in which the United States was involved.

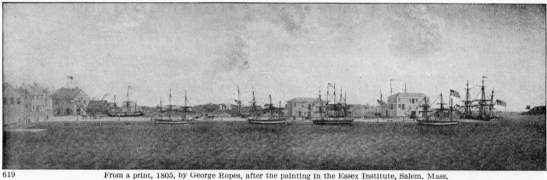

619   From a print, 1805, by George Ropes, after the painting in the Essex Institute, Salem, Mass.

THE PRIVATEER *AMERICA*

THIS, like the *Grand Turk*, was a famous Salem vessel. Built in 1804, of three hundred and fifty tons, with twenty guns and one hundred and fifty men, she was said to be the very fastest craft afloat throughout the War of 1812. Besides, her Captain Ropes believed in all-round training; so he drilled his crew at "great guns and small arms" till they could face a man-of-war. When she reached Crowninshield's Wharf

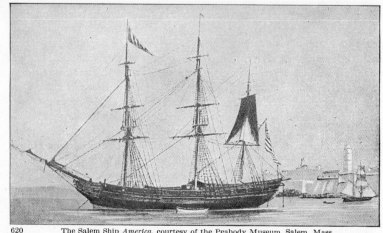

620   The Salem Ship *America*, courtesy of the Peabody Museum, Salem, Mass.

in the spring of 1815 she had made the then enormous total net profit of six hundred thousand dollars.

THE *CHASSEUR*

THE *Chasseur*, mounting sixteen long twelve-pounders, carrying one hundred men, and commanded by that extremely able leader, Captain Boyle, was likewise called the *Pride of Baltimore*, where the papers delighted in singing her praises to the very top of their bent. "She is, perhaps, the most beautiful vessel that ever floated on the ocean . . . you may easily figure to yourself the idea that she is almost about to rise out of the water and fly into the air." Boyle, not to be out-

621 *Chasseur vs. St. Lawrence*, from George Coggeshall, *History of American Privateers*, New York, 1861

done, proclaimed "the United Kingdom of Great Britain and Ireland in a state of strict and rigorous blockade," signed the document as "Given under my hand on board the *Chasseur*," and sent it in to London with the request that it should be posted up at Lloyd's. But the *Chasseur* could strike, and strike hard too, as her many fights and captures prove. Her last battle occurred (in Havana waters) with the British schooner *St. Lawrence*, which was the American privateer *Atlas*, captured in 1813. The *Chasseur* then carried fourteen guns and one hundred and two men against thirteen guns and seventy-six men. But the *St. Lawrence*, cleverly concealing her man-of-war nature, caught the *Chasseur* with a surprise salvo. Yet the *Chasseur* met the situation so well that she took the *St. Lawrence* in fifteen minutes, losing twenty-three men compared with forty.

THE *GENERAL ARMSTRONG*

THIS New York vessel had both a fighting and a profitable career under gallant Captain Guy Champlin, who gave the less resolute among his crew a taste of his determination, when, being badly wounded, and hearing them talk of striking to a bigger British privateer, he told the surgeon to "tell those fellows that if any of them dares to strike the colors I'll fire into the magazine and blow them all to Hell!" Champlin was succeeded by a kindred spirit, Samuel Chester Reid, who anchored in Fayal Roads on December 26, 1814, under what he thought was Portuguese neutrality.

But in came three British men-of-war, on their way to New Orleans, and the boats of one of them — the *Carnation* — rowed alongside the *General Armstrong*. Reid's challenge remaining unanswered, he fired to such effect that the boats hauled off with the loss of over twenty men. By this time the Portuguese were crowding the harbor to enjoy the sight, the Governor and suite having the best view from the castle. Then the boats

622 The *General Armstrong*, from James Barnes, *Naval Actions of the War of 1812*, New York, 1896, drawing by Carlton T. Chapman. © Harper and Bros.

returned to the attack in greater force and boarded with determination; but, after a desperate fight of no less than forty minutes, were again repulsed, this time with a loss of well over a hundred. Next day the *Carnation* stood in and cannonaded till Reid saw the *General Armstrong's* end was near; whereupon he scuttled her and went ashore with all surviving men. Defiant still, he marched into the interior and stood at bay in an old Gothic convent, whose drawbridge he broke down. But the British did not follow; and Reid returned home to be received with all the honors that the South could show him. At warlike Richmond the admiring Virginians toasted him again and again: "Captain Reid — his valor has shed a blaze of renown upon the character of our seamen, and won for himself a laurel of eternal bloom."

CHAPTER XIV

1812 ASHORE

THOUGH the navy won much glory in the war it was far too small to accomplish anything of permanent importance. But in view of the vast preponderance of population and resources on the American side and of British entanglements in Europe, Madison's government thought that the army would conquer Canada and win the war. This government, however, had very slight conception of what was needed for an efficient army. It seems to have thought of a military force in terms of numbers rather than of discipline, training, and expert leadership. From the end of the Revolution to the outbreak of the second war with England the army had fluctuated almost violently in both its paper and its actual size. It had acted as a sort of thermometer to register the extent of the national apprehension in the different crises which had arisen during that period; and such fluctuations had destroyed morale.

At the opening of the year 1812 the army organization was reminiscent of the conditions Steuben found at Valley Forge. There were companies of authorized strength of from sixty-four to one hundred men, while regiments included from ten to twenty companies. The actual number was small (only three thousand) and had received only the training appropriate to service at isolated frontier posts. Congress tried to enlarge suddenly the regular force on the eve of war and then called for volunteers. Both devices failed of the expected results, for men would not enlist. Then the national government suffered the humiliation of appealing to the states and their militia to defend the country. Far from profiting by the experience of the Revolution, President Madison's administration made every mistake that the Continental Congress had committed and one that it had avoided. The government refused to create a unified command under a single general. The war was to be directed by many heads. Such incredible military ineptitude found a fitting climax in the political contractors to whom were entrusted the vital task of furnishing supplies and munitions. General Upton later characterized them as a "swarm of parasites who fattened upon every reverse of our arms."

The offices of the Secretary of War and Secretary of the Navy were held by incompetents whom President Madison did not have the courage to remove. The charter of the First Bank of the United States had been allowed to expire in 1811, so that the government had no serviceable fiscal agency to aid in the difficult task of war finance. West Point had graduated seventy-one cadets. The officers available for high command had had no training suitable to prepare them for their great responsibilities; and the government had no means of measuring their efficiency except the cruel and costly method of actual war. Finally, Madison himself lacked the executive ability necessary for the commander in chief of the armed forces of the United States. Yet Clay pictured a peace dictated at Quebec or Halifax; Calhoun declared that Canada would fall in four weeks; and Jefferson informed Madison that he had never known a war begun under more favorable circumstances.

THE NORTHERN CAMPAIGNS, 1812–13

Though practically unprepared for war, Madison with amazing military ignorance decided upon offensive movements against Canada. The rather vague plan which was worked out was directly dependent upon the character of the northern frontier. Lake Huron, Lake Erie, the Niagara River, Lake Ontario, and a stretch of the St. Lawrence River marked the boundary between the hostile nations. East of the St. Lawrence an imaginary line ran from northern New York around Maine. But in this eastern region the Adirondacks, the Green Mountains and the White Mountains restricted, as of old, military operations against Canada. Montreal and

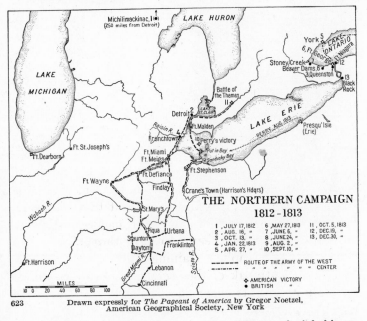

THE NORTHERN CAMPAIGN
1812 - 1813

1 , JULY 17, 1812	6 , MAY 27, 1813	11 , OCT. 5, 1813
2 , AUG. 16, "	7 , JUNE 6, "	12 , DEC. 19, "
3 , OCT. 13. "	8 , JUNE 24, "	13 , DEC. 30, "
4 , JAN. 22, 1813	9 , AUG. 2, "	
5 , APR. 27, "	10 , SEPT. 10, "	

- - - - - ROUTE OF THE ARMY OF THE WEST
" " " " " CENTER

◆ AMERICAN VICTORY
● BRITISH

623   Drawn expressly for *The Pageant of America* by Gregor Noetzel, American Geographical Society, New York

Quebec still remained the most important centers of Canadian population; and in this area the inhabitants were dominantly French. Since the American Revolution, however, English settlements had sprung up along the northern shores of Lake Ontario and Lake Erie as far west as the Detroit River. This thinly-peopled frontier region was known as Upper Canada. Its defense consisted of a fort at Malden at the western end of Lake Erie, Forts Erie and George at the southern and northern ends of the Niagara River, and Kingston at the outlet of Lake Ontario. For the invasion of Canada, therefore, four routes were possible: to strike Upper Canada from the west by a movement based on Detroit, to penetrate its center by crossing the Niagara River, to deliver a blow against its eastern settlements by an operation against Kingston, or to engage the French-Canadians on the old battle grounds at Montreal and Quebec. Canada's strategic weakness lay in the fact that the Canadian settlements formed a very long and narrow strip of land hugging the lake shores and the international boundary. Let an enemy cut this strip anywhere decisively, and he controlled everything to the west of it. The plan adopted by the War Department at Washington under Secretary Eustis was "that a main army should advance by way of Lake Champlain upon Montreal, while three columns, composed chiefly of militia, should enter Canada from Detroit, Niagara, and Sacketts Harbor." On William Hull, Governor of that vast forest area west of Lake Huron known as Michigan territory, was forced the unwelcome task of rolling up what might be called the Canadian right flank. In April and May, 1812, he was in command of a force being assembled in southeastern Ohio. In June he moved northward toward Detroit

624 General William Hull, 1753–1825, from the portrait by Rembrandt Peale, in possession of Miss Julia Hull Smith, Stamford, Conn.

with some sixteen hundred men, three hundred of whom were regulars and the remainder Ohio militia with little military training. Hull had passed Urbana, Ohio, and was toiling toward Detroit when, on June 18, Congress declared war. Eleven days later, not having been informed by his own government that they had declared war, he entrusted some sick men, baggage and his own personal papers to a schooner which sailed from the mouth of the Maumee River for Detroit, while his army marched overland through the wilderness. The inefficiency of Eustis is nowhere more clearly shown than by the fact that the British at Malden, knowing of the declaration several days before Hull, captured the sloop which he had assumed would be protected by a state of peace. It was thus that the American plans came into British hands. On July 12, Hull, having reached Detroit, crossed into Canada and occupied Sandwich. On the following day he proclaimed to the people of Upper Canada that the United States was ready to receive them. Hull then advanced to Malden, which was defended by less than three hundred regulars together with some Indians and militia.

625 From an engraving in the John Ross
Robertson Collection, courtesy of the
Public Library of Toronto, Canada

GENERAL SIR ISAAC BROCK, 1769–1812

THE Detroit campaign was fundamentally unsound. Had Hull held command of the lake, he could have moved his base at will. But now he dared not risk attacking Fort Malden, to whose defenses were added the guns of the British war vessels. Though nothing is so trying to raw troops as lying idle in camp, he remained inactive in front of Malden. His failure to fight undermined whatever confidence in their commander the individualistic frontiersmen who composed the militia had ever really felt. Within a month they were on the eve of mutiny. Hull's inactivity also gave General Brock, Administrator of Upper Canada, time to settle his difficulties with a refractory legislature at the provincial capital, York (now Toronto); hurry to the Niagara front, where he discovered that the American army supposed to coöperate with Hull was still far away; and then go west in person to take command of the defense on the Detroit River.

"MACKINAW," OR MICHILIMACKINAC

GENERAL BROCK, having carefully trained before the outbreak of the war picked companies of militia, was far readier than Hull. He at once sent orders to Captain Charles Roberts, commanding at the Soo (Sault Ste. Marie) to capture the most northerly American frontier fort, Michilimackinac, at the junction of Lakes Huron and Michigan. Roberts acted with wonderful speed and astounded the fort with an overwhelming force. The American commander, who did not know war had been declared, surrendered, and, on August 3, arrived at Detroit with his garrison as prisoners of war on parole, bringing the news that Michilimackinac had been taken by British and Indians and that a horde of redskins from the Northwest were

626 Blockhouse at U. S. Army post, Michilimackinac, built in 1780, courtesy of the Carnegie Institute, Pittsburg, Pa.

on their way to fall upon Detroit. The efficiency of Brock and Roberts had won the wavering Indians of the Great Lakes region to the British cause. A day or two later a party of braves, led by Tecumseh, attacked and routed a force which Hull had sent to guard supplies coming from Ohio. On August 8 the American army abandoned Canada and retired to Detroit. In five more days Brock took command in person at Malden.

BROCK MEETS TECUMSEH

627   From the painting by C. W. Jefferys
in *The Chronicles of Canada*

TECUMSEH did not need to be persuaded to go to war against the Americans. The Indian people whom he led were beginning to feel the relentless pressure of the American frontier. In 1811 Tecumseh's brother, the Prophet, had been defeated by Harrison at Tippecanoe (see Volume II). On August 14, 1812, the great Indian chieftain met Brock, the best British soldier of the War of 1812. The little American army lay within the fort at Detroit, which could be defended so long as supplies held out. But Hull was terrified at the prospect of a siege in such an isolated position, so far from all relief. He considered the abandonment of Detroit and retirement to the right bank of the Maumee, where he would no longer have a broad wilderness between himself and his ultimate base. Colonel Lewis Cass of the militia informed him that the Ohio troops would refuse to obey any order to evacuate Detroit. The Ohio colonels then went so far as to offer to Lieutenant-Colonel Miller of the 4th U. S. Infantry the command of the force in Hull's place, but this subordinate declined to participate in proceedings so subversive of good order and discipline. Brock, therefore, confronted, though he did not know it, an army that was virtually leaderless.

628   United States Fort at Detroit, from the painting by J. S. Holman, owned by Henry A. Wyman, New York

THE SURRENDER OF DETROIT, AUGUST 16, 1812

AUGUST 14 found Hull sending Colonels McArthur and Cass with about three hundred and fifty of their best men to bring up supplies from the Raisin River thirty-five miles south. He still had a thousand men within the fort. Just before dawn of the second day following, Brock crossed the river with three hundred and thirty regulars, about four hundred militia, and five little cannon. During the night Tecumseh with some six hundred braves had put himself between McArthur and the fort. Brock was taking a desperate chance when he planned to storm a powerful frontier fort defended by more men than he commanded. A vigorous enemy should not only have repulsed him but have captured or killed his force, which had a broad stream in its rear. But Brock seems to have read his opponent. As he came up the slope to make his personal reconnaissance, he saw a white flag flying over Detroit. Within an hour Hull had surrendered not only his immediate force but McArthur's as well. No other important campaign undertaken by the army of the United States has ever come to such a humiliating end. Hull was convicted of cowardice by a court-martial and sentenced to be shot. But President Madison intervened with a pardon. His own administration had plunged a nation unprepared into war, and then had embarked upon a campaign that violated every principle of sound strategy. The administration, more than Hull, was responsible for the great disaster at Detroit and for the needless waste of life and property which resulted from lack of preparedness in the campaign to come.

FORT DEARBORN

As the white flag fluttered over Detroit, smoke rose from the log huts within the palisade of Fort Dearborn on the present site of Chicago. On the previous day the garrison evacuating under orders from Hull had

been killed by an overwhelming force of redskins. (See Vol. II.) With the loss of Dearborn, Michilimackinac, and Detroit, the hold of the United States in Michigan territory was broken. This had happened within three months after the declaration of the war that was to bring about the speedy conquest of Canada. Within that area, though unknown at the time, lay rich veins of copper and one of the world's greatest iron deposits. The military policy of the United States which provided for but a tiny army and made impossible the development of highly trained officers had borne fruit. Scarcely more than a thousand armed white men, aided by Indian allies, had taken a prize which, had it been permanently lost, would have seriously affected the development of the American people.

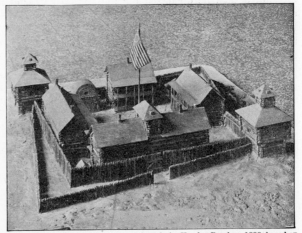

629   Fort Dearborn, from the model made by Vanden Berghen, 1898, based on a sketch by Capt. John Whistler, 1808, in the Chicago Historical Society

630 Maj.-Gen. Henry Dearborn, 1751–1829, from
the portrait by Gilbert Stuart in the Collection of
the Art Institute of Chicago

ORGANIZING THE ARMY IN THE EAST

THE story of the military operations in the East during 1812 was stranger even than that in the West. Henry Dearborn, like Hull a veteran of the Revolution, and a former Secretary of War, was given the highest rank in the army of the United States and ordered to take charge of the offensive movement against Canada. The effort to raise an army for Dearborn demonstrates certain vital weaknesses in the United States of 1812. True national unity had not yet been achieved. A tradition which had its origin in colonial days still persisted that state governments using state troops should look out for their own purely local defense. Moreover, powerful elements in New England and New York were opposed to the war; so that when the government of the United States attempted to requisition militia for the national service, Massachusetts declined, on the ground that no invasion existed, while Connecticut ignored the summons. The New York militia was called out by a Governor who belonged to President Madison's party; but there is some evidence that it had little enthusiasm for its task. Meanwhile the recruiting of a regular army was in progress. Dearborn was lacking in capacity, and the War Department was inefficient. Weeks dragged into months while the main army of the United States was being merely collected. Under the circumstances effective and adequate training of the raw levies was impossible. The Washington Government, on the day before Hull surrendered Detroit, sent orders to Dearborn to make a diversion in his favor on the Niagara front. In September American troops began assembling rapidly on the right bank of the Niagara River. Brock was back from Detroit, organizing the defense along the forty miles between Lakes Erie and Ontario. He had, however, but few troops. England could spare from the struggle with Napoleon only a small contingent for service in North America, and the population of Canada from which militia could be drawn was only half a million. In mere numbers the six thousand eight hundred Americans on the east side of the Niagara River outnumbered their enemies on the western bank by nearly four to one. Major-General Solomon Van Rensselaer, a New York militia officer, was in command. On October 13 Van Rensselaer sent a force of regulars and volunteers against Queenstown which succeeded in getting possession of a bluff overlooking the village and began digging in. Brock swiftly began to concentrate to meet the American offensive. Riding in person to the

631 Maj.-Gen. Winfield Scott, 1786–1866,
engraving by Edwin after the portrait by
Wood, in the *Analectic Magazine*, 1814

scene of action, he organized the units immediately at hand, and assaulted the enemy position. In this action he was killed, an irreparable loss to Canada for whom he had fought so gallantly and so effectively.

632   Queenstown Heights, from an engraving by T. Sutherland after a drawing by
Major Dennis, in the Dominion Archives, Ottawa

British reinforcements, hurrying from Fort George, helped to drive the Americans down to the river bank where they surrendered. Across the river a great force of New York militia watched their comrades go down to defeat while they refused to budge a step outside the limits of their state. The "cowardly dogs," wrote Corporal Stubbs in his diary, "would not come over to assist us when they saw the damned redcoats cutting us up, like slain venson." Brigadier-General Smyth of the United States army commanding a force above Niagara Falls also failed to coöperate.

THE LAST CAMPAIGNS OF 1812

To heap condemnation on the New York militia is easy, but not really fair. They were, in fact, little more than an armed mob, without the discipline and training that alone make it possible even to live at the front — not to mention fight there. After their refusal to go to the assistance of their fellows, however, Van Rensselaer resigned in disgust. Smyth, assuming command, issued several bombastic orders. On the night of November 28 he attempted an attack across the river from Black Rock, a little below Buffalo. His leadership was so bad that not only did he fail to get his main force across the Niagara but he aroused the army to such fury that the militia threatened his life, and he had to pitch his tent among the regulars. The state troops then went home and Smyth took leave of absence. Three months later he was returned to civilian life. So ended the American offensive of 1812 on the Niagara front. All this

633 Alexander Smyth, 1765–1830, commander at Black Rock, from the portrait by Saint Memin in the New York Public Library

time General Dearborn had been in command of the main army at Plattsburg. On November 19 he marched his army to the Canadian border, where his militia refused to leave the state. He then retired to Plattsburg and went into winter quarters. In Wellington's words the American operations were "beneath criticism."

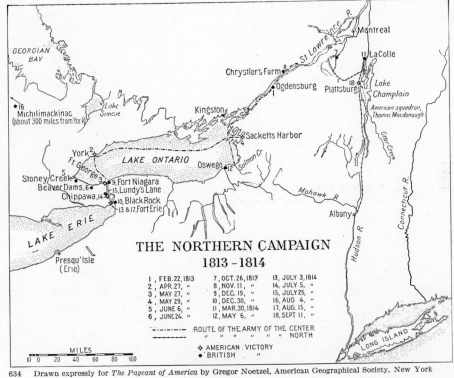

634 Drawn expressly for *The Pageant of America* by Gregor Noetzel, American Geographical Society, New York

THE NORTHERN CAMPAIGN, 1813–14

THE War Department's plan of campaign for the year 1813 was sound enough, as a mere strategic scheme. The actual operations were, however, a very different thing. The capture of Kingston and Fort Prescott, some miles down the St. Lawrence River, was to be the first objective. The accomplishment of this would isolate upper Canada. The army was then to advance along the St. Lawrence against Montreal. For the accomplishment of this a flotilla had been built on Lake Ontario to challenge the British control of the water routes; and seven thousand more or less trained men had been assembled at Sackett's Harbor, the base for naval operations. General Dearborn led the land force, while Commodore Chauncey commanded the ships.

635 Isaac Chauncey, 1772–1840, from the portrait in
the Comptroller's Office, New York, courtesy of the
City of New York Art Commission

636 Sir James L. Yeo, 1782–1819, from an engraving
by H. R. Cook after the portrait by A. Buck, in the
Dominion Archives, Ottawa

CHAUNCEY ON LAKE ONTARIO

CHAUNCEY had been sent to Lake Ontario in the autumn of 1812. With him went many ships' carpenters from the New England coast. In every detail of construction, and especially in the number of skilled hands, the United States enjoyed a great advantage over the British in building flotillas for the inland lakes. Chauncey had established his base at Sackett's Harbor because it was practically the only serviceable harbor on the American shore. In the spring of 1813 he held control of the lake, thereby enabling Dearborn to attack the British positions at York and Fort George at the western end of Ontario. Sir James Yeo finally got the British fleet into condition, with the result that during the remainder of the war the naval situation on Lake Ontario was a stalemate. Both commanders were able officers; but they fought no decisive engagement.

THE SECOND NIAGARA CAMPAIGN, 1813

WITH Chauncey master, for the moment, of Lake Ontario, Dearborn departed from the authorized plan of campaign for the year 1813. On April 27, having crossed Lake Ontario (see map, No. 634), he took York (now Toronto), the capital of Upper Canada. The little victory cost the Americans dear, for General Zebulon Pike, explorer in the Mississippi valley and the Rocky Mountains, was killed when a magazine accidentally exploded. This episode so angered the Americans that they fired the Parliament House. Exactly a month later Dearborn, having abandoned York, captured Fort George at the mouth of the Niagara River after a brisk engagement, in which the little British garrison was driven toward Hamilton at the western end of the lake. Two American generals, with Chandler in command, were sent in pursuit with something more than a thousand men. They reached a point within ten miles of Hamilton, where they encamped without the elementary precaution of placing any outposts. So the active British commander, Vincent, when he attempted a surprise counter-attack, found fortune on his side. With seven hundred men he assailed his opponents at Stoney Creek and took their two generals. After a confused fight both sides withdrew, the Americans retiring on Fort George. Such an episode was a direct result of the negligence of the national government in the matter of training officers.

637   The Attack on Fort George, May 27, from a print in the Dominion Archives, Ottawa

THE CAPTURE OF
FORT NIAGARA

ON June 24, sixteen days after the American troops had retreated into Fort George, Colonel Boerstler was sent out with more than five hundred men and two fieldpieces to destroy a storehouse about seventeen miles away at a place called Beaver Dams. To his horror Boerstler found himself surrounded by Indians. He tried to retreat. But white soldiers blocked the way. Then he surrendered. His opponent was a British lieutenant (FitzGibbon) with a

638   Fort Niagara in 1814, from an engraving by J. L. Pease, in possession of the publishers

handful of soldiers and a party of Indians, the whole force being barely half that of the Americans. Dearborn, abandoning his western campaign, and about to be relieved of command, left General McClure with a force of New York militia to hold Fort George. When the news came later in the year that Colonel Vincent was planning a new attack from Hamilton, the militia refused to serve longer and departed for their homes. Thereupon McClure, burning Queenstown and Newark, near the fort, retired to the east bank of the river. Vincent retaliated by burning Buffalo and other towns. In December he captured Fort Niagara, the British holding this position till the peace.

SACKETT'S HARBOR, MAY 29, 1813

DEARBORN's ill-advised expedition into western Lake Ontario left his base at Sackett's Harbor defended by a dangerously small garrison, commanded, however, by a most excellent militia officer, General Jacob Brown. Prevost at Kingston promptly took advantage of the opportunity his enemy had given him. Two days after Dearborn had attacked Fort George, Prevost mishandled an assault on Sackett's Harbor with a strong force of regulars. Jacob Brown, as Morgan had done at Cowpens, deployed his militia in front, backed by a thin line of regulars. The ill-trained state troops promptly fled. But then the regulars, falling back to the defense of the barracks and blockhouse fought off the British with heavy losses. So General Brown established his reputation as a skillful officer and a fighter who would not accept defeat. The engagement at Sackett's Harbor, however, was the factor which brought Dearborn's expedition to an end; for the British managed to destroy a nearly completed ship, the barracks, and enough stores to reduce Chauncey's hope of predominance throughout the rest of that campaign.

639   Sackett's Harbor, from an engraving by W. Strickland after a drawing by T. Birch in the *Port Folio*, Philadelphia, 1815

JACOB BROWN, 1775–1828

GENERAL JACOB BROWN, though of Quaker descent, was an excellent fighter and admirable leader not only at Ogdensburg and Sackett's Harbor but at Fort Erie, Chippewa, Lundy's Lane, and elsewhere. He received the thanks of Congress, with a gold medal "emblematical of his triumphs"; and in 1821 became the ranking general of the United States army. He was a very fine example of the best type of keen and capable militiaman developed by the war into a first-rate, all-round soldier, and then turned into an equally good regular.

640   From the portrait by J. W. Jarvis, in the City Hall, New York, courtesy of the City of New York Art Commission

641	Colonel Wade Hampton, 1791–1858, from the portrait in possession of Frank Hampton, Sykesland, S. C.

CHÂTEAUGUAY, OCTOBER 26, 1813

IN August, 1813, General James Wilkinson arrived at Sackett's Harbor from New Orleans to take Dearborn's place. He had seen service in the Revolution. Later he had commanded on the western frontier, where he had intrigued with the Spaniards, proving faithless both to them and to his own government. He had had a discreditable part in the episode of the Burr conspiracy (Vol. VIII, page 213). At Sackett's Harbor he proceeded to wrangle for a month with General Armstrong, the new Secretary of War, who had moved his department to the American base. Finally, a plan of operations was evolved. General Wade Hampton, a South Carolina planter and junior to Wilkinson, was to move northwestward from Plattsburg with the army which he commanded at that place. Wilkinson was to push down the St. Lawrence, unite with Hampton, and attack Montreal. Hampton, who despised Wilkinson, and refused to serve under him (all inter-communication being by way of the War Department) made a punctual start. In September he moved his force to Châteauguay in the northern foothills of the Adirondacks. In October he advanced down to Châteauguay River as far as Spears, where his advance guard was decisively checked by De Salaberry (see map, No. 634, 7) commanding a few hundred French-Canadian regulars well supported by other trained men. Hampton, much of whose army was composed of badly trained militia, quite out of supporting touch with Wilkinson, thereupon abandoned his advance and retired to Plattsburg.

642	General James Wilkinson, 1757–1825, from the portrait by C. W. Peale in Independence Hall, Philadelphia

CHRYSTLER'S FARM, NOVEMBER 11, 1813

HAMPTON was already at Châteauguay when Wilkinson, embarking his men in bateaux, sailed down the

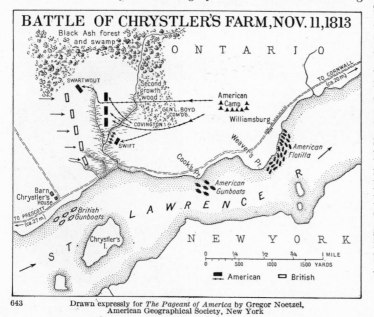

BATTLE OF CHRYSTLER'S FARM, NOV. 11, 1813

643	Drawn expressly for The Pageant of America by Gregor Noetzel, American Geographical Society, New York

St. Lawrence River. A flank guard of some twelve hundred men under General McComb marched along the north bank. On November 11 at Chrystler's Farm a British force from Kingston attacked the American rear. The wholly incompetent General Boyd was landed with three brigades to drive off the enemy. Some two thousand American regulars, commanded by regular officers, fell back before an enemy force of less than a thousand. General Wilkinson at Chrystler's Farm, like General Hampton on the Châteauguay, proved himself a thoroughly incompetent commander. After the battle he retired to French Mills where he went into winter quarters.

THE AFFAIR AT THE RAISIN RIVER

Long before Hull had surrendered in August, 1812, preparations were on foot to reinforce him under the general supervision of William Henry Harrison. But the task of recruiting, supplying, and moving even a few thousand men was so great that Hull's operations had come to an inglorious end before Harrison had begun to move through the forests of northern Ohio and Indiana. In December, 1812, Harrison's force was extended from the Maumee to the Sandusky River (see map, No. 623). General Winchester, commanding the westernmost division, pushed forward in January to Frenchtown on the Raisin River to succor the American inhabitants there. But, having established no outposts, he was promptly surprised by Colonel Procter, Brock's successor as commander in the West. Practically all the American force was killed, wounded, or captured, including Winchester himself, while thirty American wounded were inadvertently left unprotected in Frenchtown, where they were massacred by the Indians. This episode naturally roused the Westerners to fierce resentment.

FORT MEIGS (NOW TOLEDO), MAY 5-9, 1813

During the winter Harrison was forced to remain inactive, because one army melted away and another was being recruited. For several months Procter failed to take advantage of the opportunity thus presented him. Then, in late April, he moved against Fort Meigs, Harrison's chief defensive position on the Maumee. When Procter began his siege Harrison had returned from his recruiting activities. On May 5 Brigadier-General Green Clay arrived with twelve hundred practically untrained Kentucky militia. Eight hundred crossed the river, surprised the British, and drove them temporarily from the field. But these militiamen at once got out of hand and embarked upon a disorganized pursuit, only to be met with a determined counter-attack which resulted in the capture of practically the whole body and the massacre of forty by Indians who were presently stopped by Tecumseh himself. The affair took place in full view of Harrison, who was inside the Fort. A few days later Procter's Indians, tiring of the siege, deserted, thereby compelling the British commander to retire on Malden. In July Procter undertook the last British offensive operation on the western front. He again appeared before Fort Meigs and laid siege to it. Failing to draw its garrison into a fight outside the walls, he left his Indians to cover the fort and moved with his white troops to Fort Stephenson (see map, No. 623) on the lower Sandusky. There Harrison had established his base of supplies. In spite of this, however, when the British threatened this flank, Harrison sent orders to young Major Croghan, who commanded the fort with one hundred and sixty regulars, to burn the base and retreat immediately. But Croghan persuaded Harrison to let him stay and fight it out. Procter foolishly assaulted the stockade and was beaten back with heavy losses. He thereupon abandoned the siege of Fort Meigs and retired across the Detroit River.

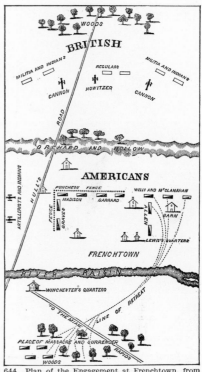

644 Plan of the Engagement at Frenchtown, from Benson J. Lossing, *Pictorial Field Book of the War of 1812*, New York, 1868

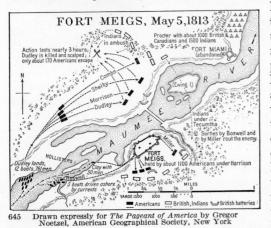

645 Drawn expressly for *The Pageant of America* by Gregor Noetzel, American Geographical Society, New York

646 Lieutenant-Colonel (in 1813 Major) George Croghan, from an engraving by Boyd in possession of the publishers

647 Oliver Hazard Perry, 1785–1819, at the Battle of Lake Erie, from the painting by J. W. Jarvis, in the City Hall, New York, courtesy of the City of New York Art Commission

NAVAL PREPARATIONS ON LAKE ERIE

SINCE the surrender of Hull the American army in the West had been on the defensive. The Washington government had at last become aware of the necessity of controlling Lake Erie if offensive land operations were to be undertaken. Captain Oliver Hazard Perry had been given the responsibility of building and commanding the fleet which was to dispute the naval supremacy of Captain Barclay. By July, 1813, the ship carpenters from the Atlantic coast had completed two brigs and several smaller craft at Presqu'-Isle (now Erie) on the southern shore.

648 Robert H. Barclay, from an engraving in the John Ross Robertson Collection, courtesy of the Public Library of Toronto

Here a sand bar not only protected the Americans but made it impossible for their newly-built ships to get out with their armament aboard. Barclay was therefore compelled to be content with blockading Perry with the ships at his disposal until he had to put back to his base at Fort Malden for supplies. Meanwhile, working under the greatest difficulties, he was trying to complete his new ship the *Detroit*. Before he could return to the blockade, Perry, by a trick known only to experienced seamen, had "cameled" (that is, lifted with broadside floats) his ships over the bar and gone up the lake in search of the enemy. Neither he nor Barclay was fully prepared for the action that followed. Barclay was hurried into action because his supplies were running low. Perry struck before he wished, because the position of General Harrison was becoming increasingly difficult.

THE BATTLE OF LAKE ERIE, SEPTEMBER 10, 1813

THE strength of Captain Barclay was roughly one-third less than that of his opponent. Nevertheless, on September 10, 1813, he willingly accepted the challenge of battle at Put-in-Bay. Perry's flag bearing the motto, "DON'T GIVE UP THE SHIP" flew from the *Lawrence*, a brig of twenty guns (named after Lawrence of the *Chesapeake*). Each opponent had, in addition to his lighter vessels, two heavier ships: Barclay, the *Detroit* and *Queen Charlotte*; Perry, the *Lawrence* and *Niagara*, the latter commanded by Lieutenant

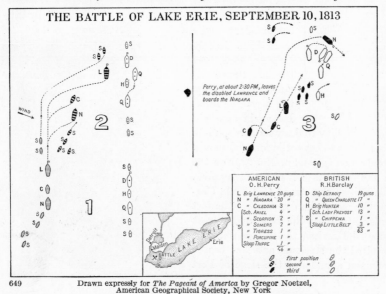

649 Drawn expressly for *The Pageant of America* by Gregor Noetzel, American Geographical Society, New York

Elliott. Perry's orders were to close with the enemy, ship against ship. He led the way by sailing the flagship *Lawrence* straight into action. Barclay's *Detroit* "got the range of him" at first, having more long guns, as opposed to Perry's short-range carronades; so that the *Lawrence* was severely battered before Perry got close enough to let her batteries make an effective reply. Worse still, the *Niagara* lagged behind, quite out of the fight, making it possible for the *Queen Charlotte* to join the *Detroit* in pounding the *Lawrence* into a helpless wreck.

650   The Battle of Lake Erie, from the painting by J. W. Jarvis in the City Hall, New York,
courtesy of the City of New York Art Commission

651   From the painting, 1873, *Perry Transferring His Flag at the Battle of Lake Erie,* by
W. H. Powell, in the Capitol, Washington

PERRY'S NEW FLAGSHIP CHANGES DEFEAT TO VICTORY

BEFORE the *Lawrence* was compelled to strike, however, Perry rowed over, with his flag, to the *Niagara,* which had at last been brought into action. Then, sending Elliott to bring up the rearmost schooners, he again bore down upon his enemy. The *Detroit,* badly wounded, became unmanageable and fouled the *Queen Charlotte,* whereupon the *Niagara's* double-shotted carronades plunged a devastating fire into both. Perry's *Ariel* and *Scorpion* helped to deal the finishing blows to the *Detroit,* while his *Caledonia* assisted in putting the *Queen Charlotte* out of action. Barclay, who had lost an arm at Trafalgar, was twice wounded and had to be carried below; his first lieutenant was mortally hurt, and, in the crisis of the encounter, his second lieutenant was in command. For three hours the battle raged before the last British vessel struck her colors. Perry's kindness to Barclay and the other British prisoners of war completed his practically perfect service on that famous day. His laconic dispatch to Harrison began: "We have met the enemy and they are ours." His victory had changed the whole course of the war on the western front.

652   From the painting *We have met the enemy and they are ours,* by J. L. G. Ferris in
Independence Hall, Philadelphia

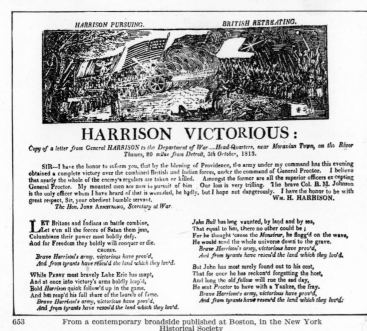

HARRISON VICTORIOUS:

Copy of a letter from General HARRISON to the Department of War....Head-Quarters, near Moravian Town, on the River Thames, 80 miles from Detroit, 5th October, 1813.

SIR---I have the honor to inform you, that by the blessing of Providence, the army under my command has this evening obtained a complete victory over the combined British and Indian forces, under the command of General Procter. I believe that nearly the whole of the enemy's regulars are taken or killed. Amongst the former are all the superior officers excepting General Proctor. My mounted men are now in pursuit of him. Our loss is very trifling. The brave Col. R. M. Johnson is the only officer whom I have heard of that is wounded, he badly, but I hope not dangerously. I have the honor to be with great respect, Sir, your obedient humble servant,
                    WM. H. HARRISON.
The Hon. JOHN ARMSTRONG, Secretary at War.

LET Britons and Indians in battle combine,
  Let e'en all the forces of Satan them join,
Columbians their power most boldly defy.
And for Freedom they boldly will conquer or die.
        CHORUS.
  Brave Harrison's army, victorious have prov'd,
  And from tyrants have rescu'd the land which they lov'd.

While PERRY most bravely Lake Erie has snapt,
And at once into victory's arms boldly leap'd,
Bold Harrison quick follow'd up in the game,
And has reap'd his full share of the laurels of fame.
  Brave Harrison's army, victorious have prov'd,
  And from tyrants have rescu'd the land which they lov'd.

John Bull has long vaunted, by land and by sea,
That equal to him, there no other could be;
For he thought 'cause the Monsieur, he flogg'd on the wave,
He would send the whole universe down to the grave.
  Brave Harrison's army, victorious have prov'd,
  And from tyrants have rescu'd the land which they lov'd.

But John has most surely found out to his cost,
That for once he has reckon'd forgetting the host,
And long the old fellow will rue the sad day,
He sent Procter to have with a Yankee, the fray.
  Brave Harrison's army, victorious have prov'd,
  And from tyrants have rescu'd the land which they lov'd.

653   From a contemporary broadside published at Boston, in the New York
                    Historical Society

THE BATTLE OF THE THAMES, OCTOBER 5, 1813

WHEN Harrison read the message from Perry his army numbered nearly six thousand men, some twenty-five hundred regulars and the rest Kentucky volunteer infantry, together with Colonel Richard M. Johnson's mounted Kentucky regiment. While this latter unit advanced overland to Detroit, Harrison promptly transferred his infantry by water to a point three miles below Fort Malden. Here, to his surprise, he found signs of great demoralization on the part of his enemy, who had decamped fully a week before. "Nothing but infatuation," wrote Harrison, "could have governed General Procter's conduct." The American general thought that his opponent had troops enough to risk a battle on even terms. But Procter, sorely beset with refugee families, a horde of Indians, and all the baggage that he was trying to save, was fleeing up the Thames, his dwindling little army losing daily in morale. In fact, he had no alternative but retreat when Barclay lost control of the lake. On October 5 Harrison caught up with him at Moravian Town. The desperate Procter formed his infantry in lines across the road, the Thames protecting his left and Tecumseh's Indians his right. Then occurred an action "not sanctioned," in the words of Harrison, "by anything that I have ever seen or heard of." A portion of Johnson's mounted troops rode through two lines of infantry while the rest, dismounted, drove the Indians into Harrison's grasp. Procter then fled with a mere handful of weary fugitives. The tragedy of the day was the death of one of the greatest of Indian leaders, Tecumseh. Michigan had been rewon. It is significant, however, that the navy rather than the army fought the decisive action.

654   William Henry Harrison, ca. 1814, engraving by W. R. Jones after the portrait by Wood, in the Analectic Magazine

LA COLLE, MARCH 30, 1814

THE final Canadian campaign of the year 1814 opened at La Colle on the Plattsburg front. Wilkinson, leading a badly trained mixed force against Montreal, where British reinforcements had assembled, came into contact with a fortified stone mill at La Colle on the Richelieu River. It was held by a garrison of some two hundred men and was the most advanced British outpost. These two hundred men did their work well, inflicting heavy losses on Wilkinson's advance guard. That general then retired to Plattsburg. His last important public act had been performed. Rarely in American history has such a rascal held responsible position so long. He stands out, even among the other incompetents, as an almost perfect example of all that a general should not be.

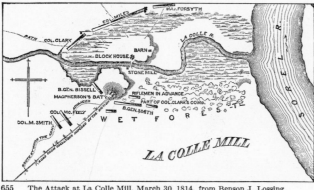

655   The Attack at La Colle Mill, March 30, 1814, from Benson J. Lossing, Pictorial Field Book of the War of 1812, New York, 1868

FORT ERIE (JULY 3), CHIPPEWA (JULY 5), AND LUNDY'S LANE (JULY 25), 1814

IN the preceding February, General Jacob Brown, now a regular, received his first independent command. With more than two thousand men, he was ordered from French Mills to Sackett's Harbor. Here he found the American fleet blockaded and the British in virtual control of the lake. He thereupon decided to carry the war again to the Niagara front. In the early spring and summer about thirty-five hundred men were collected at Buffalo under the command of Brown, ably assisted by two brigadiers, Eleazer W. Ripley and Winfield Scott, and by a force of regulars and Indians under General Peter B. Porter. All these officers owed their present commissions to their proved ability in the battles and campaigns of the previous two years. For once most of the American army was given a period of thorough training before being put into the field. Moreover, experience in campaigning had produced many seasoned veterans. Thus, when, on July 3, Brown threw his army across the Niagara River and took Fort Erie without a fight, he commanded a force of officers and men unlike any that America had hitherto produced during this war. Two days later, after pushing rapidly northward, Brown fought and won a general engagement at Chippewa. "A bold attack, complete response to trained officers, the use of the bayonet, with which the Americans were now completely armed" are the words of that very candid critic, Major Ganoe,

656 Drawn expressly for *The Pageant of America* by Gregor Noetzel, American Geographical Society, New York

in *The History of the United States Army*, p. 138. Some imperfectly trained militia broke at the first shock. But when the British regulars advanced in force the American regulars, though not in much greater numbers, stood fast, maneuvered exceedingly well, fired with precision, and charged home with victorious effect. Chippewa, however, was, in a strategic sense, little more than a preliminary skirmish. Brown's real purpose was to wrest the priceless Niagara peninsula from the enemy. But to do so involved the

taking of Fort George, and that involved coöperation from Chauncey. "For God's sake, let me see you" was Brown's urgent message to Chauncey, who remained at Sackett's Harbor. But Chauncey did not come; so the British were free to move at will by water along the shores of Lake Ontario. Sir Gordon Drummond, their commander, was second in ability to Brock alone on the British side in the War of 1812. He was gallant, resourceful, and the kind of leader whom good soldiers love to follow. He understood the general situation on the Niagara front, and skillfully applied the means at his command to improving the British side of it. The Battle of Lundy's Lane (a little more than a mile from Niagara Falls) was the result of a maneuver forced upon Brown by Chauncey's failure to appear. It was a bloody and stubbornly fought engagement, beginning in the afternoon and carried far on into that stifling midsummer night. It was in truth a drawn battle. Having fought, like the British, to exhaustion, the Americans retired to their camp at Chippewa for water and supplies. Ripley commanded the final phase; for both Brown and Scott were badly wounded. Later on the Americans withdrew to Fort Erie, which Brown had wisely begun to strengthen the very day he took it.

657 Lieut.-Gen. Gordon Drummond, from the portrait by Berthon in the John Ross Robertson Collection, courtesy of the Public Library, Toronto, Canada

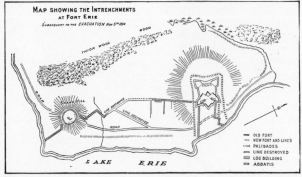

658   Map Showing the Intrenchments at Fort Erie, from Cruikshank, *Documentary History of the Niagara Campaign* (Lundy's Lane Historical Society Publication), 1913

FORT ERIE, AUGUST 15 AND SEPTEMBER 17, 1814

SINCE Fort Erie guarded the junction of Lake Erie with the Niagara River on the Canadian side it was a very desirable point for the Americans to hold. When Drummond attacked it on August 15, there was a desperate fight, but the Americans won the day. Presently Jacob Brown organized a finely coördinated sortie against Drummond, who had now settled down for a siege. On September 17 the Americans burst full upon the besieging British, who, though not driven off at once, retired four days later. All the Americans had done well this time; and Brown at last had the satisfaction of reporting that "the militia of New York have redeemed their character." October passed in maneuvers along the Niagara frontier. The British were on the defensive. But they enjoyed the growing advantage of having their own fleet close by, while Chauncey's remained at Sackett's Harbor. Finally, General Izard, who had come over with reinforcements from Lake Champlain, blew up Fort Erie on November 5 and retired into winter quarters. This ended the war on the whole Niagara frontier.

BRITISH PLANS FOR 1814

IN spite of Brown's campaign on the Niagara front 1814 was a year of grave peril for the United States. Dissention had increased and the nation was virtually bankrupt. The agitated Madison feared at times a general collapse. In April the defeated Napoleon had abdicated and England soon began to send seasoned regulars to North America. Four different thrusts were planned: down the Champlain-Hudson valley, against the coast of Maine, against the national capital, and against New Orleans. The last three were to be from the sea, where the British navy was supreme. Sir Thomas Hardy, Nelson's old flag captain at Trafalgar, took Moose Island on the Maine coast on July 11. After the surrender of Machias, two months later, the Governor of Nova Scotia, Sir John Cope Sherbrooke, proclaimed the annexation of "all the eastern side of the Penobscot River and all the country lying between the same river and the boundary of New Brunswick."

659   Sir John Cope Sherbrooke, Governor of Nova Scotia, from Gilbert Auchinleck, *History of the War between Great Britain and the United States of America*, Toronto, 1855

660   Title-page of a satirical pamphlet in the New York Public Library

THE BRITISH ATTACK ON WASHINGTON, AUGUST 24, 1814

IN July, 1814, news came to the national capital that a British naval force was concentrating off the Potomac with transports carrying an army. Though war had been two years in progress, and though Washington was peculiarly vulnerable from the sea, few measures had been taken for its defense. It rarely falls to the lot of a government to see at such close hand the dire results of its military negligence. Washington was in the midst of an area where the war party was strong. The neighboring states contained more than ninety thousand militiamen on paper. These militiamen belonged to the same virile race as the enemy, and as their sea-faring fellow-countrymen, who had beaten that enemy again and again. Yet, being unprepared for real war they acted as a mere armed mob. On August 24 the British crossed the Potomac at Bladensburg, five miles below the city. The Americans fired hard while the enemy was still on the bridge. But when he had gained the American side and had begun to shoot quite harmless rockets into the air, such a panic seized the untrained American militia that the whole affair acquired the derisive name of the "Bladensburg Races."

BRITISH UNIFORMS in the WAR of 1812–1815

8TH FOOT PRIVATE

3RD FOOT CAPTAIN

FIELD ARTILLERY OFFICER

39TH FOOT PRIVATE

STAFF OFFICER

GENERAL OFFICER

ENGINEER FIELD OFFICER

29TH FOOT GRENADIER CO.

14TH LT. DRAGOONS OFFICER

95TH FOOT RIFLES

9TH FOOT SERGEANT

SEAMAN

VICE ADMIRAL

MARINE

Painted expressly for *The Pageant of America* by H. A. Ogden

WASHINGTON BURNT

CAPTAIN JOSHUA BARNEY, who had destroyed his gunboat flotilla in the Chesapeake to avoid capture, hurried to the scene with four hundred sailors and marines. He stood fast, firing his battery planted squarely across the road to Washington, until, in his own words, "not a vestige of the American army remained,

661   From the contemporary British print published in London, in the New York Historical Society

except a body of five or six hundred [regulars] posted on my right." His little force outflanked and broken up, himself a wounded prisoner, he still had the satisfaction of knowing that he had saved the honor of the flag. He also nobly gave the admiring British officers their due, by reporting that they had treated him "just like a brother."

"The American army had scampered to Washington with a total loss of ten killed and forty wounded among the five thousand militiamen who had been assembled at Bladensburg to protect and save the capital. The British tried to pursue, but the afternoon heat was blistering and the rapid pace set by the American forces was so fatiguing to the invaders that many were bowled over by sunstroke. To permit their men to run themselves to death did not appear sensible to the British commanders, and they therefore sat down to gain their breath before the final promenade to Washington in the cool of the evening. They found a helpless, almost deserted city from which the Government had fled and the army had vanished. The march had been orderly, with a proper regard for the peaceful inhabitants, but now Ross and Cockburn carried out their orders to plunder and burn. At the head of their troops they rode to the Capitol, fired a volley through the windows, and set fire to the building. Two hundred men then sought the President's mansion, ransacked the rooms, and left it in flames. Next day they burned the official buildings and several dwellings." — RALPH D. PAINE, *The Fight for a Free Sea*, pp. 190, 195-96. It is only fair to add that the British thought this a just reprisal for the American destruction of the public buildings at Newark and Toronto (York) as well as a deserved humiliation for the government which had declared war while they were fighting Napoleon, who was at least equally severe on neutral shipping.

662   Facsimile of the original manuscript of the *Star Spangled Banner*, in possession of Henry Walters, Baltimore

THE *STAR-SPANGLED BANNER*

IN September the British made an abortive attempt on Baltimore, their ships being unable to close Fort McHenry, on account of the shoals. All night long, however, the fort and ships kept up a cannonade which might have long since been forgotten had not the sight of the stanch fort's Stars and Stripes next morning fired ardent young Francis Scott Key to write the *Star Spangled Banner* (see Vol. XI, p. 83) as he stood on the deck of the *Minden*, most courteously treated, but under British guard, till he and Dr. Beanes, whose release he had effected, could be safely put ashore. Key had come out to arrange for an exchange of prisoners.

663 From the portrait in the Dominion Archives,
Ottawa, Canada

SIR GEORGE PRÉVOST

THE British invasion by way of Lake Champlain was a most menacing operation. Sir George Prévost had more than ten thousand seasoned redcoats released from European campaigns by the fall of Napoleon. Because of its disciplined experience in campaigning this army was perhaps the most powerful that had ever been assembled on the North American continent. Prévost's first objective was Plattsburg. On September 6 he appeared before Plattsburg with an actual striking force of over seven thousand. Here the gallant General Macomb commanded a very mixed force of less than half as many. On the very eve of Prévost's movement the American Secretary of War, Armstrong, had ordered General Izard with four thousand men from Plattsburg to assist Brown on the Niagara front. This incomprehensible order left the northern frontier open in the very area where the enemy was concentrating. There can be no excuse for the statesmanship which by plunging an almost completely unprepared country into war made possible such a menace to the very existence of the nation as that of Prévost's, and then completed its folly by ordering the army of defense out of the path of the invader.

GENERAL ALEXANDER MACOMB, 1782–1841

MACOMB, an officer of the United States regulars from the age of seventeen, did admirable service all through the War of 1812. His remarkable distinction at Plattsburg consisted in the moral courage he displayed by standing his ground against Prévost's overwhelming forces, which more than doubled his own in numbers and vastly surpassed them in discipline and training. But Prévost decided to await the operations of the navy, and goaded Captain Downie into premature action by a letter hoping that "my reasonable expectations have been frustrated by no other cause" than "the unfortunate change of wind." Downie, smarting under the implication that "another cause" might mean "shyness" to meet the enemy, remarked emphatically to his second-in-command, Captain Pring: "I will convince him that the Navy won't be backward." Prévost assumed a heavy responsibility when he urged the fleet into action without giving it effective coöperation.

664 From a portrait by Thomas Sully, 1829, in the United States Military Academy, West Point, N. Y.

COMMODORE THOMAS MACDONOUGH, 1783–1815

665 From a portrait by J. W. Jarvis, in the City Hall, New York, courtesy of the City of New York Art Commission

THE naval situation on Lake Champlain seemed to favor the British, who had very hastily built a frigate with three hundred men and thirty-seven guns, the *Confiance*. But she was not completely finished, and, as she stood down the lake, workmen were still straining to put her into shape for action. With her were three small vessels, the *Finch*, the *Linnet*, and the *Chub*, together with a flotilla of tiny gunboats. The *Confiance* alone, however, was expected to destroy any American flotilla. Macdonough's fleet consisted of the flagship *Saratoga*, of twenty-six guns, the brig, *Eagle*, of twenty guns, the *Ticonderoga* and the *Preble* of seven guns each, and some trifling gunboats. Macdonough anchored in line inside of Plattsburg bay, his flanks protected by shore batteries. The *Eagle* was ahead and the *Saratoga* next her. The United States navy has never had a finer officer than Macdonough who, facing the British at Plattsburg bay at the age of thirty, was already a veteran of fourteen years' service. He had fought under Bainbridge, Preble, and Decatur in the war with Tripoli. At Plattsburg his consummate skill was no more conspicuous than his devotion to duty or his kindness to his prisoners.

CAPTAIN GEORGE DOWNIE

CAPTAIN DOWNIE was also a brave and able officer. His tragic fate was the result of Prévost's reflection on his courage. Downie wanted to fight his enemy in the open water, where the long-range batteries of the great *Confiance* would give him a vast advantage over his enemy (who was mainly armed with short-range carronades) and practically ensure his winning command of the lake. That he came within a hair's breadth of gaining such control when fighting on Macdonough's own terms is evidence of what he might have done under other circumstances. To compel Macdonough to put out of

666   Grave of Captain Downie at Plattsburg, courtesy of the Delaware and Hudson Railroad Co., Albany, N. Y.

the bay it was necessary for the British to gain possession of the shore batteries which protected the American flotilla. These could only be won by Prévost's throwing his full strength against the Plattsburg fortifications. Had he done this, the capture of the batteries would have been inevitable, and Macdonough would have been driven into the open. Prévost chose, however, to let the navy fight without any real support from the army, apparently on the supposition that Downie's superiority over his opponent at long range would ensure a victory for the British arms at short range, where the Americans had a great advantage. The destruction of Macdonough's fleet would compel the immediate evacuation, if not the surrender, of Plattsburg. Prévost must bear the full responsibility for the failure of a campaign which, if successful, must have profoundly affected the terms of peace. Moreover, had Prévost advanced into the Hudson valley, it is entirely possible, so dire were the straits of the national government and so bitter the opposition of New England, that the "perpetual union" of the United States might have gone to wreck.

THE BATTLE OF PLATTSBURG

ON the morning of September 11 Prévost stood idly by while Captain Downie rounded Cumberland Head and entered Plattsburg bay. With the *Confiance* leading, Downie tried to break the enemy line. But the wind flawed and failed within the bay, so that he could not reach his proper station. A desperate close-range fight began. None of the smaller boats had any real importance in the battle save the *Linnet*, which engaged the *Eagle*. The main battle was between these two, and between the *Confiance* and the *Saratoga*. The first broadside of the British frigate killed or wounded a fifth of the *Saratoga's* complement. But the latter's carronades, full-loaded with massed two-ounce bullets, not only brought carnage to the decks of the larger ship but cut her cables to pieces. In fifteen minutes Downie fell. His flagship began to show the results

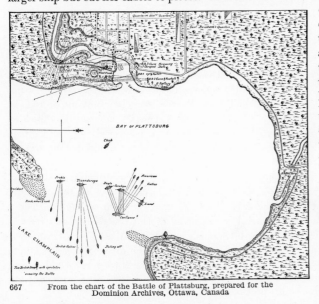

667   From the chart of the Battle of Plattsburg, prepared for the Dominion Archives, Ottawa, Canada

of the devastating rain of shot. But conditions on the *Saratoga* were worse. One after another the guns facing the enemy were put out of action till only a single cannon was left. When this piece leaped from its carriage because of a too heavy recoil and plunged into the main hatchway, the *Saratoga* was silenced. But Macdonough had prepared for such an emergency; and, by cutting the bow cable, and using a stern anchor, he promptly turned his flagship about, so as to bring his unused batteries to bear upon his enemy. The *Confiance* attempted the same maneuver, but was too crippled to execute it. Then the *Saratoga* battered her into submission. Fifteen minutes after the frigate had struck, the *Linnet* gave up to the *Eagle* after a long and gallant fight. The Plattsburg battle was won by expert training controlled by an invincible fighting will and utter devotion to duty.

668   The Battle of Plattsburg, from the painting by Julian O. Davidson, owned by
                    the family of the late Smith M. Weed, Plattsburg, N. Y.

MACDONOUGH'S VICTORY

MACDONOUGH'S victory placed his name above all others on the roll of American naval captains until the Civil War discovered his counterpart in Farragut. With a little flotilla of hastily constructed boats, and fighting against an enemy of superior strength, he had turned back an invasion that threatened the integrity of the nation. Prévost was "down for court-martial"; but died before it was held. His lot has been hard at the hands of posterity. In justice to his memory it should be remembered that he conciliated the French-Canadians, whose racial and religious feelings had been ruffled by his predecessor, Sir James Craig. During this last campaign he must have been a sick man. It was his misfortune to be a mediocre soldier, charged with responsibilities requiring high military as well as political ability. Both he and the Empire paid the penalty of his failure to the full. When the British Government asked Wellington's opinion about respective gains and losses, with regard to urging terms of peace, he rightly pointed out that the complete American command of Lakes Erie and Champlain quite counterbalanced any claims the British could make for their hold across the Niagara River or on the coast of Maine.

669   Macdonough's Victory on Lake Champlain, from an engraving by Benjamin
                    Tanner, 1816, after the painting by H. Reinagle

ANDREW JACKSON, 1767–1845

OUT of the Tennessee frontier there came a man, who, without any professional military training, but with well-learned experience, was to establish his fame as the greatest leader of land forces that America produced during the War of 1812. Andrew Jackson, known for his many personal encounters and as a remarkable

670   From an engraving by A. H. Ritchie of a miniature presented by Jackson to Edward Livingston, in 1815, now owned by John R. Delafield, New York

leader of men, was a major-general of the Tennessee militia. In 1813 the powerful Creeks of the Southwest had gone on the warpath, inspired by Tecumseh, who had visited them as the secret emissary of British agents, to carry out their own desires of driving back the white frontier. They had fallen upon a blockhouse known as Fort Mims (see Volume II) and had carried away from its smoking ruins more than two hundred scalps (August 30, 1813). Savage warfare filled the outlying settlers with terror. Tennessee answered the cry for help by sending Andrew Jackson with twenty-five hundred volunteer infantry and a thousand cavalry into the fastnesses of the Indian country. Surmounting almost overwhelming difficulties, Jackson, in one great battle at Horseshoe Bend (November 9, 1813) utterly broke the Indian power. Jackson, now the hero of the Southwest, became a major-general in the army of the United States. He was ordered to Mobile, in the Spanish territory of West Florida, where he fought off a British naval attack. Later he drove the British from Pensacola, and then returned to New Orleans to parry the heaviest enemy assault of the war.

SIR EDWARD PAKENHAM, 1778–1815

CAPTAIN JOHN DERBY was hurrying home in the Salem ship *Astrea*, under all the sail that she could carry, to say that peace had been made by the Treaty of Ghent on Christmas Eve.   But this news, welcome to both the warring sides, did not arrive in time to stop the Battle of New Orleans, fought a full week after 1815 had begun.   The British had failed at Plattsburg in the first part of their quadruple invasion scheme, but had succeeded in the second and third, in Maine and at Washington.   They now proceeded to the carrying out of the fourth, the attempt to capture that great strategic prize, the mouth of the Mississippi.   Control here meant vast influence over all the hinterland.   The troops who had captured Washington were transferred to Jamaica; other units were added, and placed under the command of a brilliant officer, thoroughly trained and experienced, General Sir Edward Pakenham.   Pakenham was also a rare leader of men. But he was entirely unfamiliar with frontier methods of fighting and with the peculiar conditions of terrain at New Orleans.   Above all, he did not know that dogged, daring incarnation of the frontier spirit under arms, Andrew Jackson.   Welding in a few brief weeks as

671   From a lithograph after an original portrait in England

motly a horde as ever appeared on the American continent into a working, fighting unit, Jackson planned and built defenses for the greatest seaport of the whole Southwest.

THE BATTLE OF NEW ORLEANS

CLOSE to the banks of the Mississippi is dry ground, where plantations can be laid out; a little farther back are swamps and bayous.   Jackson's plan of defense was simplicity itself — merely to prepare on either side of the river ramparts and breastworks stretching from the levees at the river banks to the swamps beyond. Naturally his main position was on the north bank, the same side on which New Orleans stood.   His flanks could not be turned.   He could only be defeated by a frontal assault.   Pakenham, by using an arm of the sea, Lake Borgne, disembarked his troops in late December fairly close to the river and to Jackson's works.   He then pushed a brigade forward by using small boats on the Bayou Mazant to the river itself a little way below the position which Jackson had chosen and which his army was feverishly consolidating.   On the evening of December 24 Jackson surprised this advanced detachment and, aided by the guns of an American warship in the river, fought a stubborn fight.   But he was repulsed and withdrew to his defenses.   A few days later Pakenham had some six thousand men on the river bank ready to attack.   On January 1 the British artillery began preparing for the assault.   It seemed an easy task to batter down the hastily prepared defenses of cotton

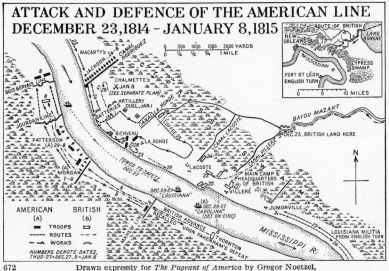

ATTACK AND DEFENCE OF THE AMERICAN LINE
DECEMBER 23, 1814 – JANUARY 8, 1815

672   Drawn expressly for *The Pageant of America* by Gregor Noetzel,
American Geographical Society, New York

bales and cypress logs.   But, to the amazement of the British officers, the American artillery fire was returned to such effect that by noon Pakenham's batteries had been silenced.   Sailors and regulars had served the American guns. The artillery failure, though Pakenham did not realize it, was decisive.   It served, however, to make the British cautious.   For a week Pakenham lay in camp bringing to perfection every possible detail of preparation.   The Americans heard the enemy drums and bugles echo through the cypress woods.

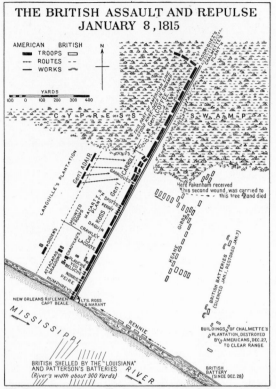

THE BRITISH ASSAULT AND REPULSE JANUARY 8, 1815

673 Drawn expressly for *The Pageant of America* by Gregor Noetzel, American Geographical Society, New York

THE FINAL VICTORY

As Pakenham delayed, the American fortifications grew stronger. Jackson's men knew how to wield the pick and shovel and how to handle the logs that were built into ramparts. Ditches were dug and obstacles prepared. In front of the American works lay a canal. Meanwhile Jackson was maturing his plan of operations when the assault should take place. On January 8, the British commander moved to the fatal attack against enemy works still perfectly intact. He sent a party across the river to engage the American defenses there, but delivered the main blow on Jackson's front. The result was carnage. Jackson bent all his energies toward intensity of fire. He placed all the best shots in front, and kept them supplied with arms ready loaded by the ranks in rear. Twice the magnificent British regulars advanced as though on parade, and as other regulars had advanced at Bunker Hill. Twice the sadly depleted lines went reeling back. Two thousand odd dead and wounded men lay on the field while the Americans had suffered but the slightest loss. The next day was a day of truce; when, to the mournful roll of muffled drums three generals, including the intrepid Pakenham, seven colonels, and seventy-five other officers were buried beside the shallow trenches in which lay the bodies of their men. The war on land had ended.

EFFECTS OF THE WAR

TAKEN as a whole, the War of 1812 is one of the least glorious episodes in the history of the American people. From its operations military students can learn very little, so frequently was the very simplest teaching of strategy and tactics violated. The civilian population can learn more. The complete dependence for the defense of their country upon untrained citizen soldiers had proved a tremendous failure; so great, in fact, that the existence of the nation had been threatened. After the war came the first great days of West Point under Thayer. In spite of this, however, the army was allowed to rust; and the typical citizen of the young United States (wholly misled by the very special conditions that governed New Orleans) con-

tented himself with the belief that Americans could "lick anything under creation" if it came to a fight. The naval operations of the war also had an unfortunate result. The much advertised frigate duels were looked upon, quite justly, as adding much glory and prestige to the American flag at sea. This maritime position had been achieved with a small and even neglected navy. But the people of the day seem not to have recognized that these duels had very little strategic significance and that they played practically no part at all in bringing the war to a victorious conclusion. A popular misconception of the naval needs of a nation with large commercial interests and a growing merchant marine was the result. On the other hand, the sequel to the war has been in the world-wide peace between the English-speaking peoples ever since.

Mercantile Advertiser
EXTRA.

New-York, Saturday Evening, 9 o'clock, Feb. 11.

PEACE.

The great and joyful news of PEACE between the United States and Great Britain reached this city this evening by the British sloop of war Favourite, the hon. J. U. Mowatt, Esq. commander, in 42 days from Plymouth.

Henry Carroll, Esq. Secretary of the American Legation at Ghent, is the welcome bearer of the Treaty, which was signed at Ghent on the 24th December, by the respective Commissioners; and ratified by the British government on the 28th of Dec. Mr. Baker, late Secretary to the British Legation at Washington, has also arrived in the sloop of war, with a copy of the Treaty, ratified by the British government.

Both of these gentlemen proceed immediately for the seat of government.

We understand the Treaty is highly honorable to our country.

The Favourite sailed from Plymouth on the 24 day of January and has brought London papers to the 31st December.

Mr. Hughes, one of our Secretaries sailed in the Transit, from Bordeaux for the U. States on the 30th Dec.

Our Ministers were to remain in Europe until spring.

We learn verbally that the Congress at Vienna had not finished their important business.

We understand that London letters of Dec. 31 represent the affairs of the Continent to be yet unsettled.

From the London Courier of Dec. 31.

PARIS, DEC. 27.

The Duke of Wellington received fast night the important intelligence of the signing of a TREATY OF PEACE between the British and American Commissioners at Ghent, on the 24th of December. The Courier adds, that no comments were made on this important subject in the Paris Moniteur.

674 Announcement of Peace, Feb. 11, 1815, from the original in the New York Historical Society

CHAPTER XV

THE MEXICAN WAR, 1845–48

AFTER the close of the second war with England the people of the United States turned from contemplation of European issues and faced the West. Swiftly and steadily the frontier moved westward until it began to climb the farther slope of the Mississippi valley. Adventurous pioneers crossed the grasslands, where the bison grazed, and then the rugged mountains beyond, to build their cabins in Oregon. Some turned longing eyes southward to the warm and fertile California country, where Spain had once held sway, and which now was ruled from Mexico City. In the decade of the eighteen forties some persons in high office at Washington also looked longingly at California and San Francisco bay opening on the broad Pacific. Here was a priceless domain thinly settled and lightly held.

In Mexico the people faced problems such as come, happily, to but few nations. In 1821 Spanish rule had passed. For three centuries prior to that date Spanish officials had governed the Indians and mixed bloods that made up fourteen-fifteenths of the population. For three centuries a small and essentially feudal aristocracy of whites had exploited and oppressed the masses of the people. But this local aristocracy of whites had not been permitted to share in the high offices of state, which had been open only to the Spanish-born. Independence plunged Mexico into a witches' cauldron. The land of the Aztecs witnessed a confused struggle, in which the aristocracy and churchmen sought to retain their ancient privileges; military adventurers strove to secure power for personal profit; and liberals worked to alleviate the unhappy lot of the common people. Chaos ruled in Mexico, while Americans laid out their plantations in the rich plains of Texas. In 1836 the Texans, under the leadership of Houston and Austin, rose in revolt and established an independent nation. Nine years later Texas became one of the United States. The Mexican Government, with a pride inherited from Spain, had declared that annexation was tantamount to a declaration of war. There were American claims against Mexico, because Americans had lost lives and property in the Mexican confusion. In 1846 President Polk sent John Slidell into the neighboring republic with a proposal to settle the American claims by selling California to the United States, the price being, of course, much larger than the amount of the claims. But no Mexican Government could listen to such humiliating proposals and hope to remain in power. When Slidell failed utterly, Polk and his cabinet decided to settle the dispute between the nations by resorting to war. Just after the cabinet meeting a messenger brought word to the White House that a Mexican force had crossed the Rio Grande, which marked the extreme limit of the Texan territorial claim, and had attacked a reconnoitering party of the American force which had recently been moved to the northern bank. This affair seemed providential to President Polk; and next day the whole country rang with his message that American blood had been shed on American soil. The war for California inevitably followed, an American Texas naturally becoming the halfway house to the Pacific.

675   Pierre Gustave Toutant Beauregard, 1818–93, from the portrait, *ca.* 1846, in the State Museum, New Orleans, La.

676   Ulysses Simpson Grant, 1822–85, from a daguerreotype, 1843, in the possession of Mrs. Louisa Boggs, Macon, Mo.

677   Thomas Jonathan ("Stonewall") Jackson, 1824–63, from a daguerreotype, 1847, made in Mexico City

678   George Brinton McClellan, 1826–85, from W. S. Myers, *The Mexican War Diary of General McClellan*, 1917, courtesy of Princeton University Press

679   Joseph Eccleston Johnston, 1807–91, from a photograph in the Confederate Museum, Richmond

681   George Gordon Meade, 1815–72, from a miniature, *ca.* 1846, courtesy of George Meade, Ambler, Pa.

680   Robert Edward Lee, 1807–70, engraving from a daguerreotype, *ca.* 1846, in the possession of H. P. Cook, Richmond

682   Jefferson Davis, 1808–89, from a miniature, *ca.* 1850, courtesy of Mrs. Gerald B. Webb, Colorado Springs

WEST POINTERS IN THE MEXICAN WAR

It was in the Mexican War that military training at West Point first bore fruit upon any scene of action.   There were about a thousand graduates by now, half with the army, half in civil life, but ready for active service.   Thus, in spite of the indifference of Congress, the country still had, for the very first time, a body of military leaders whose training, devotion, and all-round efficiency made them the equals of those naval leaders who won such honors in the War of 1812.   There were, for instance, no less than fifteen West Pointers who won distinction in the Texan, Californian, and Mexican campaigns, and then rose far higher still in the far greater war of North and South.   The nine leading northerners were Grant, Thomas, Sherman, Reynolds, Hancock, McClellan, McDowell, Hooker, and Meade.   The six leading southerners were Lee, "Stonewall" Jackson, Beauregard, Johnston, Longstreet, and Jefferson Davis.

ZACHARY TAYLOR, 1784-1850

"Old Rough and Ready" was a genial, kindly, unconventional frontier soldier, brave to a fault, the hero of Fort Harrison against a furious attack by Indians at the beginning of the War of 1812, the conqueror of the Seminoles in 1837, and the very type of a "first-class fighting man," so far as minor combats were concerned. But he knew nothing of the greater art of war; and he had no genius whatever for the complex problems of high command. He had no conception of the function and importance of the intelligence service, the "eyes of the army." He neither could nor would maneuver his little army as a whole, though it contained three thousand regulars, the most that had been brought together for many years. Finally, when ordered to confront the Mexicans who were at Matamoros, he built Fort Brown just where an enemy could enfilade it with the greatest ease. But he and his army were singularly fortunate in having his two very able sons-in-law beside him: Horace Bliss, his adjutant, to write his reports and keep headquarters running smoothly; and Jefferson Davis, to turn the scale at

683   From an engraved portrait by Illman in possession of the publishers

Buena Vista. Then, too, the United States army now had many another able junior officer trained and inspired by Thayer, the Father of West Point.

THE SKIRMISH AT FORT BROWN

In April, 1846, Taylor's army lay on the Rio Grande opposite Matamoras, where General Arista commanded a force considerably larger than the three thousand American regulars. After the skirmish which President Polk's government had welcomed as a Mexican declaration of war, active campaigning began. Incredible as it may seem, Taylor never knew that Arista had assumed the offensive and had put himself in a position to threaten the communications with the American base at Point Isabel. Equally queer was the fact that, at the very same time, Taylor, unknown to Arista, was on the road to Point Isabel from the American advanced position on the Rio Grande. When Arista learned of Taylor's march he attacked the fort on the Rio Grande. But the defenders, though badly placed and poorly supplied, fought him off. The gallant commander, Major Jacob Brown, was killed, and the fort thereafter was called by his name.

684   The Camp of the American Army of Occupation, 1845, under Gen. Taylor, from a lithograph after the drawing by Capt. D. P. Whiting, U. S. Infantry, in the New York Historical Society

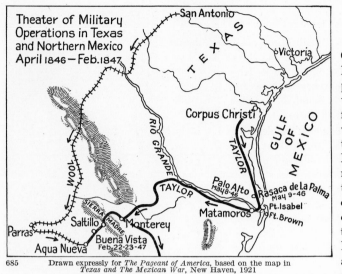

685   Drawn expressly for *The Pageant of America*, based on the map in
                   Texas and The Mexican War, New Haven, 1921

PALO ALTO AND
RESACA DE LA PALMA

ON May 8, Taylor, now returning from Point Isabel, found his enemy barring his path at Palo Alto. A sharp fight developed, confused by the smoke of a grass fire ignited by the conflict. But Taylor's well served artillery cut swaths through the Mexican ranks; and the 5th U. S. Infantry stopped a flanking charge. The next day the Mexican commander, though technically undefeated, retired to Resaca de la Palma. Here, behind an old river channel full of pools and mud, Arista took up what he deemed a strong position. His front was also covered by a ravine and by a dense growth of mesquite and cactus. But the Americans cut their way through and fell upon their adversaries, who did not expect an immediate attack through such country. Discipline and individual initiative, rather than generalship, proved decisive. The routed and demoralized Mexicans not only retreated across the Rio Grande but abandoned Matamoras. In the weeks that followed, the arrival of wholly untrained volunteers increased Taylor's force to some twenty thousand men. Most of the volunteer officers knew nothing practical of war; so these new troops were hard to discipline and still harder to keep well. Thousands fell sick and thousands were sent back. Meade, the future victor of Gettysburg, described these men as one costly mass of ignorance, confusion, and insubordination. In the end three thousand regulars and some three thousand surviving volunteers marched with Taylor into Mexico.

TAYLOR INVADES MEXICO

EARLY in September Taylor started for Monterey. General Wool, starting a raid from San Antonio, and penetrating as far as the town of Parras, whence he turned eastward to join Taylor, encountered no important enemy force. The chief purpose of the advance of the American main army seems to have been to provide the action so loudly demanded by popular clamor. On September 19, still without adequate information of the enemy, Taylor approached Monterey. He divided his army, sending General Worth to capture the road which led to Saltillo. With little real help from Taylor, Worth outflanked and outfought the Mexicans in an action which lasted five days. At the end of these five days, Worth, acting largely on his own initiative, and Quitman, working from the opposite side, had literally hewed their way into Monterey. Taylor was indeed fortunate in his subordinates. But he threw away half their hard-won victory by agreeing to an armistice with his defeated opponent. The Americans secured possession of Monterey and its public property, but allowed the Mexican army to retire intact with their small arms and ammunition. Taylor, with his enemy in his power, had failed to strike a decisive blow. As a result he lost the confidence of the administration at Washington. President Polk was particularly exasperated, because he himself had recently seen his own discreditable game with the exiled Mexican adventurer, Santa Anna, come to naught. Polk had consented to let that wily politician slip into Mexico under American protection in consideration of his securing peace on American terms. But Polk now found Santa Anna at the head of the military party organizing a determined defense against American aggression. So the war must be continued.

686   The Heights of Monterey, from a lithograph after the drawing by Capt. D. P. Whiting,
                          U. S. Infantry, in the New York Historical Society

GENERAL W. J. WORTH, 1794–1849

GENERAL WORTH, twice promoted in the War of 1812, and again for services in Florida, received his fourth battlefield promotion for his work at Monterey. He was later transferred to Scott's army, which was to strike at the heart of Mexico. The administration was belatedly developing a new plan in which Taylor's rôle was merely to maintain a threatening attitude in northeastern Mexico. "Old Rough and Ready," chafing under the slight, obeyed the letter of the instructions of his superiors, but disregarded their advice. The end of the year 1846 found his army dangerously dispersed. A rugged mountain range, the Sierra Madre Oriental, rises above Monterey and, extending from the Rio Grande to the Mexican Plateau, divides the coast plain from the sub-arid interior grasslands. In December Quitman lay at Victoria on the coast plain; Butler was at Monterey; and Worth was stationed at Saltillo in mountain country, with his vanguard at Agua Nueva.

687 From a photograph in the United States Military Academy, West Point

GENERAL J. E. WOOL, 1784–1869

688 From a photograph in the United States Military Academy, West Point

IN January Taylor received orders definitely subordinating him to Scott, who began to requisition his troops for the Vera Cruz campaign. Meanwhile Taylor announced to Senator Crittenden that he was a candidate for the presidency. Drawing together the four thousand seven hundred troops left with him he then advanced to Agua Nueva, south of Saltillo. Wool, having completed his raid through the interior grasslands, had joined him. But during these uncertain winter months Santa Anna had gathered a force of formidable numbers; and was now marching straight against Taylor. Learning of this movement, Taylor retired rapidly to the hacienda known as Buena Vista, and took up a defensive position where the road to Saltillo threaded a narrow mountain pass. In Taylor's opinion Buena Vista was to prove impregnable, free from all danger of any flanking operation.

BUENA VISTA

THE tactics of Buena Vista were dependent upon the peculiarities of the terrain. The bottom of the pass was an old flood plain made by some river of the geologic past. A modern stream had cut a deep channel in this plain, while transient torrents from the mountain sides had gouged out many transverse gullies. Taylor posted his artillery and distributed his infantry to meet an enemy attack down the main road, which ran through the main channel; for he believed that no hostile force could cross the transverse gullies at right angles to this central line. Santa Anna, though no great general, quickly saw through Taylor's mistake. Making a feint against Taylor's main position, he led his troops along the very

outer edge of the plain, under the shadow of the mountains, where the transverse gullies were shallow enough to cross. The first day saw the Mexican commander envelop Taylor's left and seriously menace the rear. A good Mexican army, under a great general, would have annihilated Taylor. But the second day (February 23, 1847) the sheer fighting superiority of the Americans, with the able junior leadership of men like Jefferson Davis, Bragg, and Sherman, won a decisive victory. Nevertheless, Taylor became "the hero of Buena Vista," and in the following year was elected President of the United States.

689   The Battle of Buena Vista, from G. W. Kendall, *The War between the United States and Mexico*, drawings by Carl Nebel, New York, 1851

690   The Flight of the Mexican Army, from a contemporary lithograph by
       N. Currier in the New York Historical Society

THE MEXICAN ARMY

BUENA VISTA, which the Mexicans should have won, brought clearly into view some vital military weaknesses of this Hispanic-American republic. Three centuries of exploitation and oppression had destroyed the initiative of the mass of the people. They were passive, and very ignorant peons. The Indians, many of them sprung from the greatest Indian stock of North America, had lost their pride of race. Such folk who filled the ranks of the army practically as mercenaries had little national consciousness, little patriotism for Mexico. Why should they give their lives that the hated aristocracy should continue to exploit them? They would fight when brought to bay, but, if there was a chance for escape, they would not continue a stubborn and bloody engagement to the end. The Mexican army lacked able leaders; it lacked adequate training; but its chief deficiency was its almost complete absence of morale. Full credit should be given to the efficiency of the American troops, but it was an easy matter to bring down a nation suffering from centuries of inefficient colonial government and which had not yet found itself. The weak collapsed under the blows of the strong. Yet the Mexican did fight and thousands of American homes mourned the loss of those who had died in action or of disease.

KEARNY'S MARCH TO SANTA FÉ

IN May, 1846, when Taylor was beginning his Mexican campaign, Colonel Stephen W. Kearny at Fort Leavenworth in Kansas received orders to march to the conquest of the territory which is now New Mexico and Arizona and thence to advance on California. Kearny, a veteran of regulars from the War of 1812, was the commander of the Second Dragoons. He did not wait to organize all the little bodies of troops under his command but sent them piecemeal toward Santa Fé, the dragoons being in advance. The strategy of the move, from the point of view of the government, was simplicity itself. While Taylor was keeping the Mexicans occupied in the region immediately south of the Rio Grande (No. 685), and Worth was making a raid through the cattle country of northern Mexico, west of the Sierra Madre Oriental, Kearny was to secure possession of the country which Polk had sent Slidell into Mexico to buy (Vol. II). Kearny, however, was but one of several pawns used in the capture of California. For some time one Larkin had been stationed at Monterey, California, as consul, with orders to conciliate the Californians and to "arouse in their bosoms that love of liberty and independence so natural to the American Continent." Commodore John D. Sloat, another

veteran of the War of 1812, commanded a small American squadron in the Pacific, with orders to take California when Mexico declared war. When the conflict began Commodore Robert F. Stockton in the frigate *Congress* was sent round the Horn to reinforce and supersede Sloat. But when he arrived on the California coast in July he found that Sloat had already made a landing at Monterey on the 7th, had run up the American flag, and had proclaimed the possession of California by the United States. (For the full story of the conquest of California, see Vol. II.)

691   General Stephen W. Kearny, 1794–
       1848, from a daguerreotype in the Missouri
       Historical Society, St. Louis

692   Admiral Robert Field Stockton, 1765–
       1866, from the portrait by Thomas Sully, in
       possession of Bayard Stockton, Princeton,
       N. J.

THE CONQUEST OF CALIFORNIA

On August 18, 1846, Kearny had taken Santa Fé without a fight after making a very difficult march. He then turned westward across the arid country of the Southwest. Kearny's march was one long and desperate struggle with hardships brought on by its having to be made through woodless country where cooking was often impossible, where the water was mostly brackish, where gnats and mosquitoes swarmed, where food was as scarce as scurvy was abundant, and where many a man died in his tracks while others went out of their minds. On October 6 a messenger from the West, Kit Carson, brought to the struggling column the glad tidings of the apparent success of the Americans in California. Kearny thereupon left a force to hold New Mexico; and, with only a hundred and fifty men, made a forced march toward San Diego. Some thirty-nine miles east of that place he met and engaged a large body of armed Californians. But his determined little force, though severely handled, held its ground. Then, on January 10, after some sharp fighting, Stockton entered Los Angeles, resistance came to an end, and California became American soil.

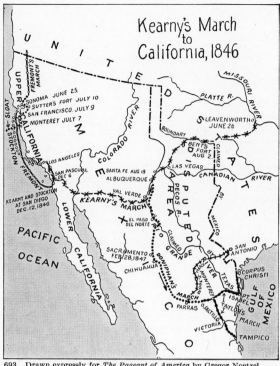

693   Drawn expressly for *The Pageant of America* by Gregor Noetzel, American Geographical Society, New York

WINFIELD SCOTT LEADS THE CAMPAIGN AGAINST MEXICO, 1847

The decisive campaign of the war with Mexico was led by Scott, the greatest military chief the United States produced between the Revolution and the Civil War. To Scott belongs the unique distinction of being the only American who ever served as a general officer in three wars: a brigadier in the last campaign of the War of 1812, the commanding general in Mexico, and the senior whose advice, at the beginning of the Civil War, was infinitely better than the popular cry of "On to Richmond." During the intervals between these wars, Scott was often called on by his country to perform important missions. In 1832, at the end of the Black Hawk War, he negotiated a treaty of peace with the Middle Western Indians, and in 1836 he led an expedition against the Seminoles; in 1838 he supervised the removal of the Cherokees. Scott was known as "Old Fuss and Feathers." He was insistent, perhaps over-insistent, on the niceties of army life, which,

694   From an engraving after a daguerreotype taken at the time of the Mexican War, in the New York Public Library

rightly used, tend to foster discipline. His chief attention, however, was fixed on greater things: on due preparation; on proper organization; on having in time of peace at least a vitalizing nucleus round which an already partly trained reserve could quickly grow into a real army; on the staff study of all probable campaigns before a shot was fired; on the strategy and tactics that such campaigns required; in a word, on all that a later generation has summed up in the term "preparedness." What McClellan wrote in his private diary during the Civil War might well have been written by Scott in Mexico. "I have seen more suffering than I could have imagined to exist — the sufferings of the Volunteers. They literally die like dogs — . . . were it all known in the States . . . all would be willing to have so large a regular army that we could dispense entirely with the Volunteer system." Scott's report about the trained West Pointers who served him so well speaks for itself. "I give it as my fixed opinion that but for our graduated cadets the war . . . might, and probably would, have lasted some four or five years, with, in its first half, more defeats than victories falling to our share."

695   Landing Scott's Army at Vera Cruz, 1847, from a contemporary lithograph
      by N. Currier in the New York Historical Society

THE MILITARY PROBLEM

FULLY to appreciate the really magnificent work done by Winfield Scott and his properly trained troops in this decisive campaign, we must remember not only the Mexican odds against him in mere numbers, and the extreme natural strength of those stupendous terraced mountains, but also the very many drawbacks at the front which were entirely due to want of preparation in time of peace and to bad government administration after war had broken out. The worthless Pillow was a political nominee as a major-general. So demoralizing was his leadership that, at Cerro Gordo, he had to beg for a company of steady regulars to stop his own mishandled men from breaking. Nor were these the only drawbacks. There was a shortage of proper transports afloat, of wagons ashore, and of enough trained men everywhere; while supplies were scarce and money to buy them scarcer still. Finally, all Scott's practical suggestions of 1845 had been set aside for two wasted years. He had proposed mobilizing twenty-four thousand men, welding them into a real army, and striking straight at the heart of the war, from Vera Cruz to Mexico City, in 1846. That he should have succeeded, with only half this total, in 1847, gives his measure as a leader in the field.

Nor must the United States navy be forgotten. The Texan and Californian campaigns were more than half dependent on the sea, while Scott's Mexican campaign was almost entirely based on it. Navy, marines, and merchant seamen, all played their quite indispensable parts. Nor must the militia and the volunteers, however inefficient, be condemned as individuals; for, as men, they at least showed a desire to serve their country and ran the risks of war, while, as units, they did excellent service whenever they got the benefit of discipline and training. The root of all troubles sprang from the ignorance and consequent indifference of the voters and their politicians, not from the forces at the front.

THE NAVY AT VERA CRUZ

THE navy was necessary to get the army to Vera Cruz, which was to be the base for the drive into the heart of Mexico. David Conner, the naval officer commanding the squadron assigned to duty in the campaign, was suffering from ill

696 Matthew C. Perry, drawing
     from an engraving in possession
     of the publishers

health. He performed the preliminary work well, however, and showed skill in putting the troops and siege material ashore. But the fruits of victory were snatched from him at Washington. Conner had the promise of Bancroft, Secretary of the Navy, of an extension of command; but Bancroft was superseded by Slidell, and, in January, 1847, that secretary told the government that Conner had lost the confidence of his men as well as the health required for a tropical campaign. So "Old Bruin" Perry, the younger brother of Oliver H. Perry, who won the Battle of Lake Erie, took command just as Conner had shown his ability to do the work. Perry, if a rather rough sea dog, was an energetic leader and finished with credit the task of coöperating with the army in bringing about the surrender of Vera Cruz. The Mexicans, of course, had no proper naval force with which to oppose the American ships.

697   Landing of Perry's Force at Tabasco, from a lithograph after the painting by Lieut. H. Walke, U.S.N., in the New York Historical Society

U.S. ARMY UNIFORMS *in the* WAR WITH MEXICO, — 1847

ARTILLERY
SERGEANT

INFANTRY
PRIVATE

INFANTRY
MUSICIAN

DRAGOON
PRIVATE

STAFF OFFICER
QUARTERMASTER
DEPT.

MAJOR GENERAL
FULL DRESS

ARTILLERY
FIELD OFFICER

DRAGOON
SERGEANT
(CAMPAIGN)

BRIGADIER
GENERAL
(CAMPAIGN)

ENGINEER
OFFICER
(CAMPAIGN)

INFANTRY
LINE OFFICER
(CAMPAIGN)

INFANTRY
CORPORAL
(CAMPAIGN)

ARTILLERY
PRIVATE
(CAMPAIGN)

RIFLES
PRIVATE
(CAMPAIGN)

Painted expressly for *The Pageant of America* by H. A. Ogden

698   Naval Attack on San Juan de Ulloa, from a contemporary lithograph by N. Currier based on a sketch made during
the action by J. M. Ladd, U.S.N.

BOMBARDMENT OF VERA CRUZ, MARCH 22, 1847

ON March 9, 1847, the landing was made at Vera Cruz without opposition on the part of the Mexicans. General Worth with his regulars were the first on shore. They formed in line of battle and advanced against the sand dunes only to find that no enemy held them. Santa Anna had not yet recovered from his reverse at Buena Vista. At the moment he was desperately busy on the plateau trying to organize an effective resistance capable of halting Scott as he climbed the eastern escarpment. When Scott's batteries were ready he summoned the Mexicans to surrender, and, on their refusal, began his bombardment in conjunction with one from Tatnall's flotilla of gunboats. American preparation for the siege had been rapid and intelligently planned. Vera Cruz faced an overwhelming force. Yet the Mexican defenders stood their ground. On March 27, however, Scott's batteries reduced citizens and garrison to despair, and Vera Cruz surrendered; though the chief citadel, Ulua, on an island off shore, had not been seriously injured. This early surrender made it possible for Scott to proceed with his plans. Scott, with his army from the temperate north, feared the yellow fever more than the enemy. He hurried inland and began to climb toward the cool and healthful plateau before the yellow fever season began. The navy's work of course was never ended all through the war. The last naval action was fought on April 18, 1847, at Tuxpán, the last port held by Mexicans.

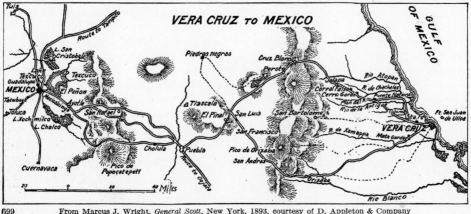

699   From Marcus J. Wright, *General Scott*, New York, 1893, courtesy of D. Appleton & Company

SCOTT'S MARCH TO THE MEXICAN CAPITAL

THE Mexican campaign established for all time Scott's reputation as a military leader of real ability. He faced an unusual variety of obstacles. Behind him was a government which was politically jealous of any popular success he might win, a government which began this campaign a year too late and then failed to give its army either sufficient numbers, training, or supplies. Beside him was a coast on which he dared not linger for fear of yellow fever; though to collect the very minimum of his sorely needed transports and supplies required a certain loss of time. Before him rose the sternly terraced masses of the Mexican upland which barred the way to the capital, and the mountain ranges which guarded the capital on every side, and which had only a few roads through all those hostile passes. Eight thousand feet had to be climbed in face of an enemy who knew every hindering rise or fall, bad turn or commanding position. And yet Scott triumphed over all, over the hindrances from home, over the obstacles of nature, and over the enemy in arms.

700   From G. W. Kendall, *The War between the United States and Mexico* . . .
drawings by Carl Nebel, New York, 1851

CERRO GORDO, APRIL 18, 1847

SCOTT's army began leaving the Tierra Calienta as the flat lowlands are known, on April 8. Ten days later when the Americans had advanced only a part of the way up the escarpment of the plateau, they met Santa Anna in a narrow pass at Cerro Gordo. Scott had between eight and nine thousand men; his enemy he estimated at about twelve thousand. Santa Anna had posted his troops in what he thought was an impregnable position. But Captain Robert E. Lee of the engineers, after a practically perfect reconnaissance, reported to his chief that Santa Anna's left could be turned and his rear attacked by crossing ground which the Mexican commander had assumed was impassable. Scott accepted Lee's judgment and made his plans accordingly. He sent the incompetent General Pillow with a strong volunteer detachment to make a vigorous demonstration against the Mexican right. But the real blow was struck by Worth and Shields on the flank and in the rear of Santa Anna's main position on the heights of Telegrafo, east of the pass. Scott's plan had been thoroughly matured before the engagement and his orders also included directions for the pursuit. With only minor setbacks his whole scheme was carried out. He inflicted heavy losses on his enemy, captured some three thousand men, and drove the remainder in disorganized confusion off the field. The victory at Cerro Gordo opened the way toward the Mexican capital.

PUEBLA

AFTER Cerro Gordo Scott's army marched and climbed through some of the most beautiful country of Mexico. Early in May the plateau was reached and the American troops in high spirits came to rest in Puebla, the second largest Mexican city. For more than a third of the army the campaign was nearing its end. These were the volunteers whose enlistment for one year was about to run out. Lack of adequate training and discipline on the part of both men and officers had caused so much sickness and suffering that very few consented to remain in the army. Scott, with both courage and humanity, though still facing an enemy that outnumbered him, ordered these men to the coast before their terms expired and while they could be moved as an organized body. Then, with wholly inadequate numbers, he remained awaiting reinforcements. Meanwhile his army lived off the country. Provisions were plentiful; for he was now in one of the richest and most thickly settled parts of Mexico. He sought to make his troops as slight a burden as possible to the civilian population. Instead of foraging, he purchased his supplies during his stay at Puebla. In August, when reinforcements had brought his army to nearly eleven thousand men, he prepared for the final advance. This was not undertaken, however, before he and one Nicolas P. Trist (a representative of the State Department, and present with Scott's army since May with orders to negotiate a peace) had apparently been duped by the tricky Santa Anna. On August 7, Scott ordered his advance guard to take the road which led to Mexico City.

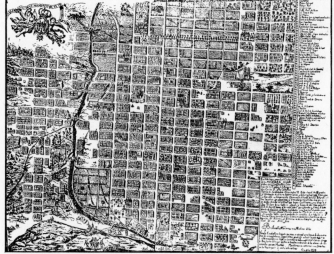

701   Old View of Puebla, from Enrique J. Palacios, *Puebla su territorio y sus habitantes*, Mexico City, 1917, reprint from an eighteenth-century sketch

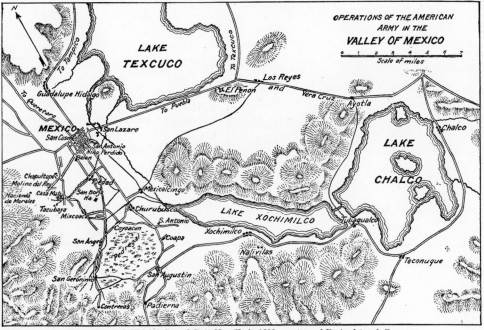

From Marcus J. Wright, *General Scott*, New York, 1893, courtesy of D. Appleton & Company

BATTLES OF CONTRERAS AND CHURUBUSCO

THE Mexican capital lies in a valley ringed by mighty mountains.   Through the passes of these Scott marched unopposed.   As he descended their western slopes he saw below him, as Cortés had seen, the ancient city of the Aztecs with buildings fresh and foliage green after the rainy season.   Between his army and the city lay a chain of broad lakes with narrow arms of land between them.   Across one of these led the road from Puebla to Mexico City; and here on a highland known as El Penon, Santa Anna had established a powerful position.   Scott did not choose to fight his enemy on his own ground.   He turned the Mexican position by advancing south of Lakes Chalco and Xochimilco to a road which connected Mexico City with the south.   Santa Anna promptly moved his army into position to defend his capital against assault from the new direction.   He expected the Americans to attack along the San Augustin-San Antonio-Churubusco road, and prepared to defend the latter two places.   Meanwhile Santa Anna sent a detachment down the Churubusco-San Angel-Contreras road, which lay on the west of a broad and supposedly impassable waste of volcanic rock known as the Pedregal.   This latter force was to slip around the Pedregal on the south and attack the Americans in flank and rear.   Scott reached San Augustin on August 17 and the next day sent Worth north to mask San Antonio.   Meanwhile Scott's engineers, among whom Captain Robert E. Lee again distinguished himself, marked out a road across the Pedregal.   On August 19, while Worth was lying in front of San Antonio, General Smith made his way across the volcanic waste.   During the night Shields followed him with reinforcements.   On the morning of the 20th the Americans surprised and routed the strong Mexican flanking force, which had occupied the heights above San Geronimo.   This surprise attack is the fight known to Americans as the "battle of Contreras."   The Mexicans on both sides of the Pedregal at once withdrew to strong positions at Churubusco.   This fatal 20th of August was a day of confusion and overwhelming defeat for the Mexican defenders of their national capital.   The battle, begun on the heights above San Geronimo, had its second phase in the town of Churubusco, whither Santa Anna's troops hastily retired.   In the thick-walled convent of San Pablo some desperate Mexicans held off the Americans for three hours of bloody fighting.   Another Mexican force made a stand at the bridgehead on the Rio Churubusco.   Scott assaulted and took both positions from the front, and sent Shields and Pierce (later President of the United States) to cut off the enemy retreat.   At a later time, referring to this day Scott wrote: "After so many victories, we might, with but little additional loss, have occupied the capital the same evening."   A Mexican historian added: "Our spirits were worn out; the remnant of our troops demoralized and lost; confusion and disorder had overcome all classes of society."   Three days afterward Scott agreed to an armistice pending peace negotiations.   But these came to naught; and Santa Anna used the time to strengthen his defenses.

703   Enemy Position (left) at Molino del Rey, from a lithograph by N. Currier, New York, 1847, after a sketch by H. Meendey, in the Library of Congress, Washington, D. C.

MOLINO DEL REY

ON September 6 Scott notified the Mexicans of the termination of the armistice, and two days later moved to the attack. Close to the gates of Mexico City stood the Molino del Rey (or King's mill). Near it was a four-sided bastioned fort, the Casa de Mata, where Scott had been informed his enemy had a large supply of powder. On September 8 American artillery opened on these two positions. The artillery fire was soon followed by the assault. In two hours the Mexican defenders who were not killed or captured had been driven out. But the Americans had suffered very severe losses and their victory was useless. They found nothing of value in the arsenal and the affair did not advance their attack upon the city.

CHAPULTEPEC

THE key to Mexico City was Chapultepec. The northern, eastern, and part of the southern sides were precipitous. But on the west the hill sloped gradually to a cypress grove that separated it from Molino del Rey. Chapultepec commanded two of the principal roads leading into Mexico City some two miles away. All day long, on September 12, American artillery battered at the great stone walls of the castle. Next morning the bombardment was resumed.

704   From G. W. Kendall, *The War between the United States and Mexico . . . drawings by Carl Nebel*, New York, 1851

Then two columns attacked, one from the south, the other from the west. The castle was a military academy aud the cadets were formed with the soldiers. Many a patriotic Mexican liberal was fighting that day for the integrity of his country. It was the last stand of a defeated nation. Soon other attacking columns appeared until the fortress was completely surrounded. Then the Americans advanced. But scaling ladders were needed for the steep slopes; and these were slow in coming up. So the troops lay idle, caught in a withering fire until these indispensable ladders were brought to the front. Then came a magnificent assault against a most desperate defense. Before the sun went down Chapultepec had fallen. Mexico, completely beaten, lay at her conqueror's feet.

THE AMERICAN ARMY ENTERS MEXICO CITY, SEPTEMBER 14, 1847

THE Mexican army was shattered past repair. Santa Anna, its commander, fled. And with the formal entry of the now irresistible Americans the climax of the whole campaign was reached. At Guadalupe-Hidalgo in the suburbs of the capital was signed the treaty by which California and much of Arizona, New Mexico, Nevada, Utah, and Colorado became a part of the United States. The Texas boundary was fixed at the Rio Grande. Mexico lost roughly two-fifths of her territory. There were officials in Polk's cabinet who talked of taking the whole of Mexico. When Scott's army had made its way back to the coast it left behind many a gallant fighting man who gave his life that his country might expand. It left behind also a heritage of bitterness which burned deep into Mexican hearts.

705   From G. W. Kendall, *The War between the United States and Mexico . . . drawings by Carl Nebel*, New York, 1851

CHAPTER XVI

EXPERT ANNAPOLIS

THE War of 1812 was the last American war before the advent of steamships on the oceans. The frigate duels of that encounter were a sort of valedictory for the old type of sailing warships. Skill in seamanship, and sheer fighting pluck, were the prime requisites of the officers who trod the decks of boats like the *Constitution*. A technique had been developed for handling squadrons and fleets, knowledge of which was the chief difference between the captain of a warship and of a merchant vessel. The fundamental principles were simple and easy to grasp. In the old navy officers were trained as in the merchant service. The boy in his early 'teens became a midshipman, the "midshipmite" of the old time songs. So the young Farragut shipped with Porter on the famous cruise of the *Essex*. He was in reality an apprentice, growing up in his trade and trained by his masters as they performed their daily tasks. This method produced such brilliant officers as Perry, Macdonough, and Farragut himself. So when forward-looking men began discussing schools for naval officers soon after the War of 1812, they met a conservatism which for many years they could not overcome. The old-fashioned seaman was convinced that "you could no more educate sailors in a shore college than you could teach ducks to swim in a garret."

But before the middle of the nineteenth century two factors brought about a change. One was West Point, where Sylvanus Thayer was giving army officers the technical equipment which played so important a part in bringing the war with Mexico to a speedy conclusion. The other was the appearance of the sea-going steamer. The officers of the old navy could remember the time when there were no "damned steam kettles" aboard any "proper ship." But inexorably they came, and, with them, a multitude of new engineering and other technical problems. The officer who would fit himself for the tasks of the new day must go to school. One of the most important achievements in the long life of George Bancroft, the historian, was the founding of the United States Naval Academy in 1845 while Secretary of the Navy in the cabinet of President Polk. In that year there finally came to fruition a movement that had begun as far back as 1817, when Commander Wadsworth, at the suggestion of Commodore Bainbridge, had taken a crew composed mostly of midshipmen on an instructional cruise along the Atlantic coast in the brig *Prometheus*.

706   Midshipmen embarking for the summer cruise on the old frigate *Constellation*, *ca.* 1890, from a photograph, courtesy of the United States Naval Academy, Annapolis, Md.

707 Professor William Chauvenet, from a
    portrait in the United States Naval Academy,
    Annapolis, Md.

WILLIAM CHAUVENET, 1820–70

THE cruise of the *Prometheus* was not repeated. But, as the years passed, it became more and more clear that the best interests of the navy demanded that something be done for the young midshipmen who corresponded in age to the modern high school boy. These lads were, in too many cases, becoming demoralized as a result of their contacts with "life" in wide-open seaports. When the ship to which they were attached was laid up in a navy yard, the desirability of attending school was too obvious to be ignored. In the 'twenties the national government provided schools at Norfolk and New York. But at these primitive educational institutions attendance was not compulsory. Some commissioned officers, feeling the inadequacy of their training, began attending institutions of higher learning in 1829, when four were in residence at Yale College.

In 1836 a school of more importance than any of its predecessors was established at the Naval Asylum, a home for aged seamen at Philadelphia. Four years later William Chauvenet, a youth of twenty, just graduated from Yale, became a professor in this institution. Chauvenet taught mathematics, and the textbook which he prepared was widely used in the middle of the century. He made the Naval Asylum school a factor of real importance in the training of naval officers; but, even in the best days, it never taught a tenth of the midshipmen in the service. Chauvenet's greatest contribution came in the winter of 1843–44, when he drew up a program for a two-year course of study at the Naval Asylum, and had the satisfaction of seeing it officially adopted by the Secretary of the Navy. A change in secretaries soon after, however, caused the revoking of the order as a result of the representations of older naval officers, who maintained that the midshipmen could not be spared from the ships for two years of schooling on shore. The conservatism of the older men in the service, coupled with the indifference of Congress, made extremely difficult the bringing to pass of vitally needed reforms. The election of Polk in 1844, which brought to an end the uncertain régime of President Tyler, seemed to the forward-looking men in the navy an auspicious time to begin to prepare for the next advance.

GEORGE BANCROFT, 1800–91

IN 1845 Bancroft became Secretary of the Navy and promptly began to move for the establishment of a real naval training school. He confronted, on the one hand, the conservatism of the older officers of the navy, and, on the other, the ignorance of the average congressman regarding the need for expert training in the navy, as well as the inherent congressional opposition to voting adequate funds to either the naval or military service. But, with extraordinary tact and diplomacy, Bancroft aligned in support of his cause both the older and younger elements in the naval service. Two separate boards of naval officers decided that the school should be established at an old army post, Fort Severn, at Annapolis. Then, with the navy behind him, Bancroft astutely avoided Congress. By a judicious use of funds for "instruction" already at his disposal, he actually started the Naval School in the buildings of the old fort which was transferred to his department by the Secretary of War. When the attention of Congress was at last focused on the institution, it was already a *fait accompli*. Such was the backstairs origin of the United States Naval Academy. The episode occurred on the eve of the Mexican War and is significant of the general attitude of Congress toward the army and navy.

708   From the portrait in the United States Naval
         Academy, Annapolis, Md.

ANNAPOLIS IN THE EARLY DAYS

SECRETARY BANCROFT, on August 7, 1845, addressed an inaugural letter to Commander Franklin Buchanan, the first head of the new school: " . . . Thus the means for a good naval school are abundant, though they have not been collected together and applied. One great difficulty remains to be considered. At our colleges and at West Point young men are trained in a series of consecutive years. The laws of the United States do not sanction a preliminary school for the Navy;

709   Commander Franklin Buchanan, 1800–74, from the portrait in the United States Naval Academy, Annapolis, Md.

they only provide for the instruction of officers who already are in the Navy. The pupils of the Naval School being therefore officers in the public service, will be liable at all times to be called from their studies and sent on public duty. Midshipmen, too, on their return from sea at whatever season of the year, will be sent to the school. . . . It will be difficult to arrange a system of studies which will meet this emergency, but with the fixed resolve which you will bring to the work and with perseverance you will succeed. . . . Do not be discouraged by the many inconveniences and difficulties which you will certainly encounter, and rely implicitly on this Department as disposed to second and sustain you under the law in every effort to improve the character of the younger branch of the service." Buchanan was the "father" of Annapolis. Under his régime the best naval teachers of the former period were transferred to the

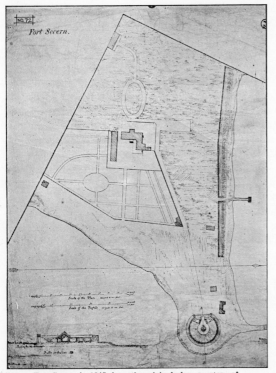

710   Fort Severn in 1845, from the original plan, courtesy of the United States Naval Academy, Annapolis, Md.

new school, among them Lieutenant James H. Ward, who had taught gunnery at the Asylum School; Professor Henry W. Lockwood, for natural philosophy; and Professor William Chauvenet. But the

institution was in no sense of collegiate grade; it was essentially a secondary school, with emphasis on the particular needs of the naval service. In course of time Buchanan became a Confederate admiral, where his record was a long and distinguished one. He not only commanded the *Merrimac* in her epoch-making duel with the *Monitor* but, later, the whole Confederate squadron at Mobile. Yet, long after the Civil War, his name still stuck to Buchanan Row, a line of buildings which, in 1898, was used as quarters for Admiral Cervera and the other senior officers of the Spanish fleet who had surrendered after the Battle of Santiago.

711   Uniforms of 1852, courtesy of the United States Naval Academy, Annapolis, Md.

712   Gun Crew and Mess Squad, U. S. Naval Academy, Newport, Rhode Island, 1864, from a
         photograph, courtesy of the United States Naval Academy, Annapolis, Md.

THE NAVAL ACADEMY IN THE CIVIL WAR

THE fall of Fort Sumter, in April, 1861, brought to the Naval Academy the saddest occasion of its history. On the 24th of the month Superintendent Blake ordered the members of the school aboard the *Constitution;* for troops had taken over the school buildings. The class of 1861 had already met and smoked the pipe of peace, pledging themselves to care for one another however much they might become enemies. Northerners and Southerners alike stood in formation while the band played "The Star-Spangled Banner." Then the boys from the South fell out and said good-bye. The next day the *Constitution* stood down Chesapeake Bay and turned her prow northward. For the duration of the war the school carried on in an old summer hotel at Newport, Rhode Island. But it was a sadly depleted institution. The South had contributed heavily to the personnel of the navy, and great gaps were opened as the southern officers resigned. One after another the three upper classes were sent into active service, but their numbers were far too few even to make good the losses among the regular naval officers, while they could not begin to fill up the new establishments required. The whole navy, including marines, numbered less than ten thousand, of all ranks and ratings, on the outbreak of the Civil War; and less than fifteen hundred of these were officers. No wonder five times as many volunteer officers had to be employed before the war was over.

THE PRACTICE SHIP *CONSTELLATION*

THE greatest of all historic U. S. men-of-war, the *Constitution*, was used at Annapolis until 1871. Then the *Constellation* was used till she went ashore in a fog near Cape Henry lighthouse in 1889. (Admiral Dewey commanded the *Constitution*, *Santee*, and other school vessels just before the *Constitution* left Annapolis.) While the Naval Academy was still at Newport a famous yacht was added to its squadron of practice ships. At Cowes, England, in 1851, the *America* won the first international cup race. She then passed into British hands and, early in the Civil War, was sold to the Confederacy for a blockade runner. Rechristened the *Memphis*, she was captured in the spring of 1862 near the mouth of the St. John's River, Florida. For a brief space she was used as a dispatch boat by the blockading squadron that operated off Charleston. Then after her capture she was hailed before a prize court and bought in by the United States Government. The captors of the *America* gave up their claim to prize money on the condition that she should be turned over permanently to the Naval Academy to be used as a practice ship. In spite of this, however, in 1873 she passed into private hands, and there remained until 1921. Naval men justly resented this breach of faith. Then a group of yachtsmen restored her to Annapolis. So the little yacht which flew the Stars and Stripes so defiantly in 1851 flies them still as a real United States ship. The *America* is a fitting symbol of the friendly rivalry that has replaced the former hostility between the English-speaking peoples.

713   The Frigate *Constellation*, from a photograph, courtesy of
         the United States Naval Academy, Annapolis, Md.

REAR–ADMIRAL DAVID DIXON PORTER, 1813–91

IN 1865 Rear-Admiral David Porter, who had come out of the Civil War with a reputation for bravery and efficiency second only to Farragut's, became Superintendent at Annapolis. His régime was destined to be a remarkable one. Four years of war had sadly disrupted the school, and Porter, with the aid of an able staff, began to build anew. As a result the Academy developed into a technical school of collegiate rank. One of the chief figures in this evolution was the Commandant of Midshipmen, Lieutenant-Commander (later Rear-Admiral) Stephen B. Luce. Luce had come to the Academy in 1859 and had been on service with it during the war. His great contributions to the institution were his teaching and his textbook. Luce's *Seamanship* (first appearing in 1862) became the unrivaled work on its subject. In later years he again contributed to the efficiency of his service by establishing the War College and the Naval Apprentice system.

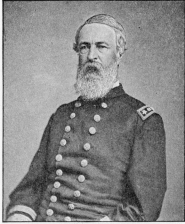

714   From a photograph by F. Gutekunst,
Philadelphia, Pa.

THE U. S. S. *ANTIETAM*

IN spite of the advance of the Naval Academy, the first two decades following the Civil War were years of gloom for the midshipmen and for all the officers in the service. The battle between the *Monitor* and the *Merrimac* had rendered obsolete the wooden ships which comprised the bulk of the American navy. The beautiful *Antietam* was scrapped before launching, as the war demonstrated that the day of the old style fighting ship had passed. Her fifty-foot model serves to remind visitors of the vanished glories of mast and sail. After the war the wooden ships were al-

715   From a photograph of the model in the United States Naval
Academy, Annapolis, Md.

lowed to rot at the wharves while the national government simply marked time. This period was as disheartening to the naval service as it was to the army, for both were starved into utter ineffectiveness. Annapolis was turning out officers as never before, but the posts of the declining navy were filled. There were places for but very few graduates, and promotion was far away. Worst of all, officers who did get to sea served in vessels which they knew they could never take into action.

THE NAVY'S RENAISSANCE

THE Act of March 3, 1883, marks the beginning of the naval renaissance of the United States. Five Secretaries of the Navy led the way in the creation of the new steel navy: William H. Hunt under Garfield; William E. Chandler under Arthur; William C. Whitney under Cleveland; Benjamin F. Tracy under Harrison; and Hilary A. Herbert in Cleveland's second administration. In the early years of the new era a great variety of types denoted that standard forms had not yet been evolved, and that experimentation was the order of the day. Until almost the close of the nineteenth century the discussion lasted as to whether some of the new cruisers should be entirely steam-driven, or should have sails as well. At the Academy the old seamanship drill persisted, but, naturally enough, the rebirth of the American navy had a profound effect upon the morale and instruction at Annapolis. Every year demonstrated more conclusively that the naval officer must be a technical expert. The curriculum was modified to train men to handle new and complex engines of war. Before the end of the century the modern Naval Academy had come into being. In 1898 officers and ships met the supreme test of war.

716 Seamanship Drill in the Old Naval Academy, 1893,
from a photograph, courtesy of the United States Naval
Academy, Annapolis, Md.

717   From a photograph, courtesy of Little, Brown & Co., Boston, Mass.

ALFRED THAYER MAHAN, 1840–1914

It fell to the lot of a midshipman graduated from Annapolis in 1859 to influence modern naval history as few men have. Alfred Thayer Mahan was born at West Point, N. Y., where his father was an instructor at the Military Academy and author of textbooks on civil and military engineering. The son saw plenty of active service during the Civil War, and cruised both the Atlantic and Pacific after that conflict was over. But Mahan was a student as well as a man of action. As early as 1883 he published a little book on naval history. Then, as he began to work through historians' accounts of the past, he became convinced that these writers had failed to grasp a factor of vital importance in the history of modern nations. In 1890 he became a world figure with the publication of his masterly work, *The Influence of Sea Power: 1660–1783.* This was supplemented by later studies of sea power in the French Revolution, in the life of Nelson, and in the American War of 1812. In England, even more than in America, the books made a profound impression, being studied by naval specialists and cabinet ministers, as well as by a large part of the general public. England pondered well the lessons which Mahan taught, and profited thereby. So did Germany, whose Kaiser and other leaders were then beginning the creation of the modern German fleet. To the American navy, therefore, belongs the honor of having trained and numbered among its officers the man who, more than any other, taught the present century the full significance of sea power, when based upon the sure foundation of a navy.

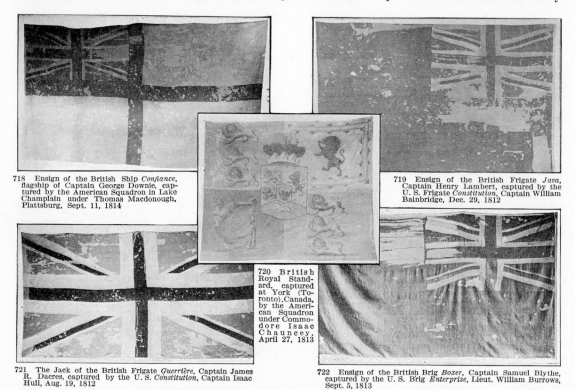

718   Ensign of the British Ship *Confiance,* flagship of Captain George Downie, captured by the American Squadron in Lake Champlain under Thomas Macdonough, Plattsburg, Sept. 11, 1814

719   Ensign of the British Frigate *Java,* Captain Henry Lambert, captured by the U. S. Frigate *Constitution,* Captain William Bainbridge, Dec. 29, 1812

720   British Royal Standard, captured at York (Toronto), Canada, by the American Squadron under Commodore Isaac Chauncey, April 27, 1813

721   The Jack of the British Frigate *Guerrière,* Captain James R. Dacres, captured by the U. S. *Constitution,* Captain Isaac Hull, Aug. 19, 1812

722   Ensign of the British Brig *Boxer,* Captain Samuel Blythe, captured by the U. S. Brig *Enterprise,* Lieut. William Burrows, Sept. 5, 1813

Photographs from originals in the United States Naval Academy, Annapolis, Md.

THE NAVAL ACADEMY'S COLLECTION OF BATTLE TROPHIES

The most conspicuous trophies are those of 1812, which naturally were, and still are, greatly cherished, because they were won from that British navy which was then the "Mistress of the Seas." But France, and Barbary, and Spain are by no means forgotten.

NOTES ON THE PICTURES

5, 7. For De Bry, see Notes on the Pictures, Vol. I.

13. There were two forts Santa Elena, one on the coast of South Carolina; the other in the neighborhood of what is now Columbus, Ga., built by Boyano, 1567, "with" (according to Woodbury Lowery, *Spanish Settlements*) "the consent and assistance of the natives." Boyano, a soldier of Menéndez (see Vol. I) had led a Spanish expedition into the western mountains.

14. For Le Moyne, see Notes on the Pictures, Vol. I.

20. See 143.

23. Reconstruction, essentially accurate.

51. Artist has made a specialty of illustrations on American history. Known for conscientious work based on original study.

52. Reconstruction by a Boston artist of a scene of which few details have been handed down.

54. By an experienced illustrator of American history, architecture of the fortified house open to criticism.

55. Reconstruction, correct in spirit, by a competent artist, prolific illustrator of American history and life. (For a discussion of his work see Vol. XII, chapter on Illustration.)

56. Reconstruction, see 52.

57. See 55.

58. Artist a successful mural painter; details of costume essentially correct.

59, 60. Sketch is by Baron La Hontan, who in 1683 was with De La Barré as a private soldier and was later with Denonville. His sketches, drawn in the distorted perspective of the time, having been made from personal observation, have a certain authority, and appear numerously in his published works.

61, 62, 64. See 51.

65. John Miller was British chaplain at New York. In 1695 he also drew plans of New York, Albany, an Indian fort near Albany, and of Kingston, N. Y., originals of which are in *Add. Mss.* 15490, British Museum.

69, 70. See 51.

72. See 59.

80. De La Potherie was a West Indian Creole who had influential friends at the court of Louis XIV. He was with the French at Hudson's Bay and elsewhere.

87. The *Atlantic Neptune*, a large folio with many authoritative views of ports and harbors, battle plans, etc., is extremely valuable as visualizing American conditions.

92. Later evidence shows the Burgis sketch to be incorrect, the *Province Galley* having had two masts, not one. See H. S. Tapley, *The Province Galley of Massachusetts Bay*, Salem, 1922.

101. Barber, born at New Windsor, Conn., 1798, wrote the text for a large number of popular histories and himself cut on wood hundreds of illustrations, many of them fanciful, some sketched from observation.

107. Artist has painted more than fifty canvases on American history which are rich in color and imbued with deep sentimentality. See also Vols. I, VIII and XI.

112. Ideal view, published probably for its effect as propaganda in France.

113. Portrait was purchased in England and presented in 1926 to the State of Massachusetts.

117. See 51.

119. Picture inaccurate; it represents troops landing from a British man-of-war, whereas the troops were all New Englanders and were landed from Yankee transports.

122. Gridley, born in 1711, was perhaps the earliest military engineer in America. In 1755 he was chief engineer and colonel, serving at Crown Point, and later built the fortifications at Lake George. Gridley planned the works at Breed's Hill and at Dorchester in 1775.

128. Picture gives exaggerated idea of military development of this French stronghold.

134. Miniature has been attributed to J. S. Copley, among others.

137. Artist has painted several other historical pictures, now in the National Museum, also studies of Indian life. (See 150.)

138. Annotations on map strikingly similar to Washington's handwriting, with certain characteristic mistakes in orthography.

139. Stobo, draftsman of this plan, was with Washington at Fort Necessity, where the entrenchments were built under his direction. At the surrender, he was taken by the French to Fort DuQuesne as a hostage to assure faithful observance of the capitulation. He sent this plan of the fort on the back of a letter to Braddock. It was recovered by the French from the general's effects after his defeat and forwarded to Canada.

143. Pyle, a close student of American history and of period costume, prolific illustrator of historical works. See also Vols. I, VI, XII, XIII.

144. No authentic portrait of Braddock is known.

145, 146. Originals in color are in the Ms. journal

of General Braddcok's Expedition in 1755, in the British Museum, with four other plans.

150. See 137.

153. Hendrick in battle wore the uniform of a British officer and sòmetimes a veil. Portrait done in England.

155. Blodget was at Lake George as a sutler to the New Hampshire regiment; plate was engraved on copper by Thomas Johnston at Boston in 1755; next year reprinted in London. Blodget explained that he was "occasionally at the Camp when the Battle was on."

159. See 51.

170. For this and other mezzotint spurious portraits of "rebel officers," published in London 1775 to 1778 and on the Continent, see C. H. Hart, *Frauds in Historical Portraiture*, in ANNUAL REPORT, American Historical Association, Vol. I, Washington, 1915.

171. See 107.

179, 190. See 51.

204. Picture of Wolfe's landing is worthless except as a generalized view of the incident. The landing was begun in the small hours of the morning and troops were out of the transports and on shore by eight o'clock.

207. West's painting, presented by the Duke of Westminster in 1919 to the Dominion of Canada, marked a departure from tradition in that the artist abolished classic costume in robing his characters. This evoked the criticism of Sir Joshua Reynolds, West's master, who would have clothed Wolfe in a Roman toga. West is said to have replied: "The event to be commemorated happened in the year 1756, in a region and time when no warriors who wore such costume existed. . . . The same truth which gives law to the historian should rule the painter. If instead of the facts of action I introduce fiction then shall I be understood by posterity?" The half-naked Iroquois, seated before the dying Wolfe, was a dramatic touch, probably not true to the facts of the scene. It was later pointed out by Henry Laurens that no Indian in battle array would be without moccasins.

219. Map drawn by Captain John Stuart, later British agent and a superintendent of Indian affairs for the southern district.

222. Artist painted murals on American history marked by painstaking study, and attention to details of costume. See Vol. I, 159, 160, 176, 244.

224. Artist a student of Indian life at first hand.

225. By a competent illustrator of American history. See also Vol. I, 177, 234, Vol. III, 86, Vol. XI, 25.

230. Based on the plan in Bouquet, *Voyage Historique et Politique* (see 233).

235. Imaginary reconstruction.

240. Accurate in spirit, by a painter whose many

VI—26

pictures on American history are intelligent reconstructions derived from close study of essential facts and accurate knowledge of details of costume.

244. Essentially accurate.

245, 246. Ralph Earl, artist, and Amos Doolittle, engraver, together went from New Haven to Lexington and Concord immediately after the engagement. Drawings, though crudely engraved, are valuable as contemporary renditions of the scenes. They published four prints in all "neatly engraven on Copper, from original paintings taken on the spot. Price six shillings per set for the plain ones, of eight shillings colored. Dec. 13, 1775." Earl and Doolittle are represented further in Vol. XII.

250. Romans, a Dutch surveyor, draftsman and engineer, served in the Revolutionary Army until June, 1778.

251. Probably by the same hand, that of a British officer, who drew 285, 286 and 300.

252. Picture painted in London at the studio of Benjamin West, finished in 1786. Trumbull in his *Catalogue of Paintings*, explained his project of painting "a series of pictures in commemoration of the principal events in the Revolution, in which should be preserved, as far as possible, faithful portraits of those who had been conspicuous actors in the various scenes, whether civil or military, as well as accurate details of the dress, manners, arms, of the times; with all of which he had been familiarly acquainted." His paintings, therefore, are not, nor were intended to be, reconstructions of the scenes so much as memorials designed for popular subscription. His figures are often of heroic size. Mr. Adams and Mr. Jefferson encouraged him in the prosecution of the plan. Eight pictures were completed, all of small size, painted between 1786 and 1816. The originals were deeded to Yale College in 1831, in addition to fifty-eight miniature portraits, in consideration of an annuity of $1000. (For other military pictures by Trumbull, see 266, 306, 337, 512, 522.)

The Bunker Hill Battle painting (more properly The Death of Warren) depicts the last moments of the action when Warren was killed. The group about him represents him expiring, a soldier on his knee warding off the bayonet of a British grenadier, trying to avenge the death of Colonel Abercrombie, who has just fallen at his feet. Colonel Small tries to save him and seizes the grenadier's musket. Nearby several Americans, their ammunition gone, are seen persisting in "obstinate but fruitless resistance." General Putnam is seen at the side of the painting ordering the retreat, and a party of American troops are making a last stand against the victorious enemy. Colonel Pitcairn, behind Colonel Small, has fallen mortally wounded into the arms of his son. General Howe, British commander, and General Clinton are in the background of the picture. At lower right of the picture, a young American, retiring attended by a negro servant, on seeing Warren fall, hesitates whether to save himself or, wounded as he is, return and offer assistance. In the rear is seen a British column ascending the hill, and in the background the *Somerset*, ship of war. For further discussion of Trumbull's paintings see J. H. Morgan, *Paintings by John Trumbull*, Yale University Press, 1926.

253. The standing figure at the right of the picture is Washington, who, according to the records, on hearing his name proposed as commander in chief, arose and left the room. See 240.

263. See 225.

266. See 252.

270. On the back of this drawing in the Schuyler Papers appears some writing in pencil now very faint. With the aid of a glass, it seems to read: "Wynkoop Schooner Supposed to be the Royal Savage on Lake Champlain Aug. 18, 1776 Continental armed vessel Jacobus Wynkoop Commander 12 guns 4 Prs. — 10 Swivels 50 men. Extract from (not intelligible) of Horatio Gates." Commander Byron McCandless, U.S.N., who has made some study of this vessel's history, writes: "In my opinion this schooner is the *Royal Savage* constructed by the British at St. John's in 1775. The flag was also the artillery flag and the garrison flag, and was the same as that used at Fort Stanwix. Arnold used the *Royal Savage* as his flagship when he commanded the fleet on Lake Champlain."

274. Artist painted many pictures for dealers in historical color prints. See also 293.

275. Serres a prolific painter of naval history, late eighteenth century.

276. So far as is known, there is no authentic portrait of Howe. (See 312.)

278. Artist has painted twenty or more pictures on the Revolution that have merit as intelligent reconstructions, with accurate details of costume. (See also 290, 294, 308, 310, 388, 429.)

279. Artist born in Baltimore, educated at Paris, painted several pictures on colonial history and the Revolution, besides a number of landscapes. See Vol. III.

282. White, a South Carolinian, studied under Benjamin West, painted pictures on the Revolution and southern life, early nineteenth century, many of which were later engraved.

285, 286. See 251.

287. See 275.

290. See 278.

291. Artist an authority on costume and known for many historical paintings and illustrations in textbooks and magazines. See Vol. I.

293. See 274.

294. See 278.

300. See 251.

301. See 291.

305. Picture is a spirited and dramatic attempt to reconstruct a historic moment in American history. It was painted in 1851 at Düsseldorf, Germany, and is perhaps the leading example of the patriotic school of historical painting. Artist used a replica of Washington's uniform which was brought to him by Worthington Whittredge.

306. See 252.

308. See 278.

310. Painting essentially correct, by one of the new school of historical painters.

314. Picture originally conceived of as a humorous study.

325. Vanderlyn's composition gives dramatic expression to a tradition; little is known of the circumstances.

337. In this picture again Trumbull essayed a picture designed as a memorial of the British capitulation rather than as an attempt to reconstruct an actual scene. The British troops had lain down their arms, no American officer being present except Colonel James Wilkinson, who represented Gates. Later Burgoyne and his staff rode to Gates' headquarters and were entertained at a sumptuous dinner. After dinner the British troops, preceded by a company of light dragoons carrying the American flag, marched to the time of *Yankee Doodle* through parallel lines of American troops. Gates and Burgoyne then came out together, the latter in full dress uniform, Gates plainly dressed. Burgoyne offered his sword which Gates took and then returned. They then went back to Gates' headquarters and the British troops were soon on their march to Boston. The five figures in the foreground are: left to right, General Phillips (British), Burgoyne, Gates, Colonel Prescott, Morgan, grouped here to give dramatic effect. The picture contains in addition twenty-two other officer portraits, including Philip Schuyler, who was not at Saratoga, and General Baron von Riedesel.

344. See 291.

362. See 107.

367. By a noted American artist known for his careful studies of costume and period architecture. See also Vol. XII, as mural painter and illustrator.

369. See 143.

380. Based on study of the topography of Valley Forge.

381. Sharples, an Englishman, drew many portraits in crayon between 1781 and 1811, valuable as contemporary likenesses. See Vols. VIII, XI and XII.

388. See 278.

392. Originals part of the medical outfit of Dr. Solomon Drowne, surgeon in the Revolution.

396. Only known copy of this picture.

397. Mayer painted colonial history with intelligence and sympathy. See Vol. III.

402, 403. See 155.

425. Tisdale, designer, engraver, and painter of miniatures, made plates for the *Echo* (see Vol. XI); he also made the designs for the political satire *Gerrymander*, which he himself wrote.

436. Romer's sketch map is valuable as indicating habitat at this date of the elk, wild turkey and beaver in the Iroquois country.

449. Brant was in England in 1786 and sat for this portrait to Romney.

452. Portrait long supposed to be the work of Sir Joshua Reynolds.

455. See 143.

456. Sketch presented to Yale College in 1832 by Ebenezer Baldwin, agent for Jabez L. Tomlinson and Nathan Beers. Tomlinson was officer of the guard where André was a prisoner.

461. See 87.

475. Picture by a southern artist, correct in spirit and atmosphere.

478. See 143.

488. Ranney, born in Connecticut, painter of frontier life in the South and early West.

494. See 279.

505. Maps of the marches of the French troops are also in the Rochambeau Papers, Library of Congress, together with colored drawings of the fifty-four camps on the march from New England to Yorktown.

508. Painting presented to the state of Virginia by W. W. Corcoran at the time of the Yorktown Centennial.

512. Trumbull in his *Catalogue* says: "The painting represents the moment when the principal officers of the British army, conducted by General Lincoln, are passing the two groups of American and French generals, and entering between the two lines of the victors; by this means the principal officers of the three nations are brought near together, so as to admit of distinct portraits." See also 252.

517. See 274.

518. See 107.

520. See 278.

522. According to Washington Irving the members of Congress "were seated and covered as representatives of the sovereignty of the Union."

538. Chapman, a skillful painter of naval history, to which he devoted the study of a lifetime.

548. Fanciful illustration, intended as a souvenir of the action.

553. Proclamation was read April 19, 1783, at the "New Building" (a log cabin for public meetings, levees, religious services, etc.), situated about three miles from the building now known as Washington Headquarters, Newburgh, N. Y.

573. Milbert, French naturalist, painted places of interest in the United States about 1826, also its flora and fauna. See Vols. XII and XIII.

575. Original drawing, about 1780, was by Major L'Enfant, French engineer.

590. Birch, an Englishman who settled in Philadelphia in 1794, did marine pictures and naval battles of the War of 1812. See also Vol. III.

591. See 538.

594. See 590.

595. See 538.

596. Strickland, architect and engineer, also painted portraits and engraved designs and illustrations. See 639, also Vol. XIII.

622. See 538.

627. See 51.

638. Pease, born at Norfolk, Conn., an engraver of many book-illustrations and bank notes.

639. Strickland, born in 1787 at Philadelphia, was eminent as architect and engineer; designed Masonic Hall, Philadelphia, the Bank of the United States, in that city, the United States Naval Asylum, and other public buildings, and he also designed the lid of Washington's coffin.

647. Painting deals with the incident of Perry's transfer to the *Niagara*. (See 651.)

689. Artist was in Mexico at the scene of action.

700. See 689, 702, 703, 705, 708.

INDEX

Titles of books under author are in italics; titles of illustrations under producer are in quotation marks.

Ripley, E. W., Niagara, 319.
Rising, O. E., *New Hampshire Lawyer*, **217.**
Ritchie, A. H., "Andrew Jackson," 324.
Roberts, Charles, Michilimackinac, 308.
Robertson, A., "Truxton," 279.
Robinson, C. N., *Old Naval Prints*, 274.
Robinson, Isaiah, privateersman, 267.
Robinson, John, Concord, 122.
Rochambeau, Comte de, portraits, 205, 249; arrives, 227, 248; as soldier, 249; joint plans, 249, 250; Yorktown, 250, 252–257.
Rockamagug, Me., on map, 37.
Rocky Mount, S. C., action, 233, 234.
Rodgers, John, cruises, 291, 292; portrait, 291.
Rodney, G. B., West Indies, 107, 251, 262, 274–276; cruises, 271; portrait, 274.
Rogers, John, "Pontiac," 111.
Rogers, Robert, rangers, 86; and Pontiac, 110.
Rogers' Rock, fight, 86.
Romans, Bernard, "Bunker Hill," 125.
Romney, George, "Joseph Brant," 222.
Roosevelt, Theodore, on West Point, 287.
Ropes, George, "Crowninshield's Wharf," 304.
Ropes, Joseph, privateer, 304.
Rose, H.M.S., at New York, 143, 144.
Rosenthal, Albert, "Bougainville," 101; "Lauzun," 249; "Aboville," 257.
Ross, Col. ——, New Orleans, 326.
Ross, Robert, Washington, 321, 322.
Rouget, Georges, "Lauzun," 249.
Rous, John, career, 59.
Rouville, Hertel de, portrait, 44; raid, 45.
Rowley, Aaron, Indian expedition, 222.
Royal American Magazine, 187.
Royal American Regiment, 81, 112–115.
Royal Savage, U.S.S., Lake Champlain, 135.
Royal United Service Institution, material from, 299.
Rush, Richard, on *Chesapeake-Shannon* fight, 298.
Rutledge, Edward, reconciliation, 147.
Ryswick, treaty, 44.

Sackett's Harbor, defense, view, 313.
Saco, Me., attacks, 37.
Saco Indians, war, 34.
St. Augustine, plan, 46; expeditions, 46, 57; cantonment, 118.
St. Clair, Arthur, Ticonderoga, 161.
St. Eustatius, capture, 275.
St. John de Crèvecœur, Hector, on civil war, 157; on Wyoming, 215; *Sketches*, 215.
St. John's, Newfoundland, cantonment, 118.
St. John's, Quebec, siege, view, 130.
St. Kitts, defense, 277.
St. Lawrence, H.M.S., *Chasseur* fight, 305.
St. Leger, Barry, expedition, 161, 162; portrait, 161.
St. Lucia, view, 272; attacks, 273, 275.
St. Pierre, L. J. de, and Washington, 71.
St. Simon, Comte de, Yorktown, 247, 253.
Salaberry. *See* De Salaberry.
Salem, Mass., privateering, 264, 304; Lawrence's funeral, 299; and *Essex*, 300.
Salmon Falls, attack, 38.
Saltonstall, Dudley, Penobscot expedition, 268.
Saltpeter, manufacture, 187, 199.
Sandham, Henry, "Dawn of Liberty," 122.
Sandwich, Lord, as head of navy, 137.
Santa Anna, Antonio López de, Polk intrigue, 330; Buena Vista, 331; and Scott, 335–338.

Santa Elena, fort, 14.
Santee, U.S.S., training ship, 342.
Santiago de Cuba, expedition (1741), **57.**
Santo Domingo, Drake's attack, 16.
Saratoga, N. Y., attacks, 37.
Saratoga, U.S.S., Plattsburg, 322, 323.
Saratoga campaign, 165–168.
Sargent, Henry, "Benjamin Lincoln," 229.
Sauk Indians, on map, 67.
Saunders, Sir Charles, naval operations, 89; portrait, 99; Quebec, 99–102.
Savage, Thomas, Quebec, 40.
Savannah, expeditions, plan, 229–231.
Savory, W. S., "King Philip's War," 31, 33.
Sawyer, C. W., on rifle, 22; *Firearms*, 22.
Schenectady, attack, 38.
Schetky, J. C., "*Chesapeake-Shannon*," 298.
Schoharie Valley, raid, 222.
Schooling, William, *Hudson's Bay Co.*, 42.
Schuyler, John, raid, 39.
Schuyler, Philip, in Revolution, 129, 134, 161, 164; portrait, 129.
Schuyler, Pieter, expeditions, portrait, 39; in England, 50.
Scorpion, U.S.S., Lake Erie, 316, 317.
Scott, Charles, Valley Forge, 182.
Scott, Winfield, portraits, 310, 333; Niagara, 319; career and character, 333; Mexican campaign, 334–338.
Sea power. *See* Navy.
Serapis, *Bonhomme Richard* fight, 269, 270.
Serres, Dominick, "Havana Campaign," 107, 108; "Halifax," 139; "Attack by Fire Boats," 143; "St. Lucia," 272; "Dogger Bank," 275.
Seven Years' War, 66.
Sever, John, King's Mountain, 237.
Shannon, H.M.S., *Chesapeake* fight, 279, 298.
Shawnee Indians, on maps, 67, 69.
Shelby, Isaac, Fort Meigs, 315.
Sheppard, Warren, "*Wasp-Frolic*," 295.
Sherbrooke, J. C., Maine, portrait, 320.
Sherman, W. T., Buena Vista, 331.
Shields, James, Mexican campaign, 336, 337.
Shippen, William, Jr., Medical Department, portrait, 191.
Shirley, William, proclamations, 57, 63; portrait, 58; French War, 58, 64, 74, 77, 81–83.
Shirley, Louisbourg expedition, 59.
Short, Richard, "Halifax," 139.
Sidney, Sir Philip, in Netherland, 17.
Siege. *See* Forts.
Silliman, G. S., Tryon's raid, 160.
Simcoe, J. G., on André, 225; *Military Journal*, 225, 246; Virginia, 247.
Simes, Thomas, *Military Guide*, 197.
Six Friends, 39.
Six Nations. *See* Iroquois.
Skelton, Joseph, "Yorktown," 252.
Slave trade, Asiento, 53.
Slidell, John, and Mexico, 327; and Conner, 334.
Sloat, J. D., at California, 332.
Smallwood, William, in Revolution, regiment, 140, **172,** 235; on untrained army, 140.
Smibert, John, "Peter Warren," 59.
Smith, De Cost, "Death of Pontiac," 116.
Smith, Francis, Lexington and Concord, 121.
Smith, Henry, "Quebec," 132.
Smith, J. C., *Mezzotinto Portraits*, 81, 139.
Smith, J. R., "Joseph Brant," 222.
Smith, John, *Generall Historie*, 17.